# Lecture Notes in Computer Science 14424

## Founding Editors

Gerhard Goos

Juris Hartmanis

## Editorial Board Members

The series Lecture Notes in Computer Science (LNCS), including its subseries Lecture Notes in Artificial Intelligence (LNAI) and Lecture Notes in Bioinformatics (LNBI), has established itself as a medium for the publication of new developments in computer science and information technology research, teaching, and education.

LNCS enjoys close cooperation with the computer science R & D community, the series counts many renowned academics among its volume editors and paper authors, and collaborates with prestigious societies. Its mission is to serve this international community by providing an invaluable service, mainly focused on the publication of conference and workshop proceedings and postproceedings. LNCS commenced publication in 1973.

Vallipuram Muthukkumarasamy ·
Sithu D. Sudarsan · Rudrapatna K. Shyamasundar
Editors

# Information Systems Security

19th International Conference, ICISS 2023
Raipur, India, December 16–20, 2023
Proceedings

 Springer

*Editors*
Vallipuram Muthukkumarasamy (iD)
Griffith University
Gold Coast, QLD, Australia

Sithu D. Sudarsan
Centre for Development of Advanced
Computing (C-DAC)
Bangalore, India

Rudrapatna K. Shyamasundar (iD)
Indian Institute of Technology Bombay
Mumbai, India

ISSN 0302-9743               ISSN 1611-3349 (electronic)
Lecture Notes in Computer Science
ISBN 978-3-031-49098-9        ISBN 978-3-031-49099-6 (eBook)
https://doi.org/10.1007/978-3-031-49099-6

This Springer imprint is published by the registered company Springer Nature Switzerland AG
The registered company address is: Gewerbestrasse 11, 6330 Cham, Switzerland

Paper in this product is recyclable.

# Preface

This book comprises the proceedings of the 19th International Conference on Information Systems Security (ICISS 2023), held at the National Institute of Technology (NIT) Raipur, India, between December 16 and 20, 2023. The conference received a total of 129 submissions from authors across the world. This year we followed a double-blind review process. Each submission was reviewed by at least four members from the Program Committee (PC), which consisted of 68 eminent international researchers working in different sub-areas of information security. The PC involved 37 external sub-reviewers in the double-blind review process. The PC Chairs evaluated and discussed the reviews and after a careful consideration of the merits of the papers, accepted 18 full papers and 10 short papers. The net acceptance rate was approximately 22%. A wide range of topics in systems security and privacy are covered, both in theory and in practice. The Program is broadly organized into six technical session tracks: i) Systems Security, ii) Network Security, iii) Privacy, iv) Cryptography, v) Security Using AI/ML, and vi) Blockchains. In addition to the accepted papers, the conference program featured the following Keynotes and Invited Talks by distinguished researchers in the area of information systems security:

1. hinTS: Threshold signatures with silent setup
   by *Sanjam Garg, University of California, Berkeley, USA*
2. How to train & use AI models on sensitive data without compromising privacy?
   by *Nishanth Chandran, Microsoft Research, India*
3. Follow the money
   by *Thomas Silkjær, XRP Ledger Foundation, Denmark*
4. Covert & side stories: Threat evolution in traditional & modern technologies
   by *Mauro Conti, University of Padua, Italy and TU Delft, The Netherlands*

We would like to wholeheartedly thank the experts for delivering their Keynote and Invited talks and our thanks go to Nishant Chandran who also contributed a paper to the proceedings. Further, the conference had the following tutorials:

1. Overview of applications of machine learning in encrypted traffic analysis for cybersecurity
   by *Debapriyay Mukhopadhyay, Vehere Technology, USA*
2. Osquery: A tool for system visibility and threat hunting
   by *Manjesh Kumar Hanawal and Atul Kabra, IIT Bombay, India*
3. Data anonymization techniques
   by *Vishwas Patil, IIT Bombay, India*

In addition to the Tutorials session, ICISS 2023 had a PhD Forum and a Demo session. It is a pleasure to record our thanks to the session chairs for facilitating the conduct of sessions, the participants from industry, the organizers, and the PC members for contributing their invaluable time and expertise in the review process. We are indebted to the tireless efforts put forth by Vishwas Patil towards assisting the PC and in compilation of the proceedings. ICISS 2023 would not have been possible without the contributions of the numerous volunteers who gave their time and energy to ensure the success of the conference and its associated events. Our special thanks go to the local organizing committee headed by Jatoth Chandrashekar, as well as the faculty, staff, and students at the National Institute of Technology Raipur, for all their efforts and support for the smooth running of the conference.

It is our pleasure to express our gratitude to Springer Nature for assisting us in disseminating the proceedings of the conference in the LNCS series. We also extend our sincere thanks to NIT Raipur, IIT Bombay, C-DAC, and NTPC for their generous sponsorship, SERB for sponsoring the travel grants, and IDRBT Hyderabad for sponsoring the best paper award. Last but certainly not least, we would like to thank all the authors who submitted their papers and the attendees. We hope you find the proceedings of ICISS 2023 interesting, stimulating, and inspiring for future research.

December 2023

Vallipuram Muthukkumarasamy
Rudrapatna K. Shyamasundar
Sithu D. Sudarsan

# Organization

## Advisory Steering Committee

| | |
|---|---|
| Venu Govindaraju | University at Buffalo, SUNY, USA |
| Sushil Jajodia | George Mason University, USA |
| Somesh Jha | University of Wisconsin-Madison, USA |
| Atul Prakash | University of Michigan, USA |
| Pierangela Samarati | University of Milan, Italy |
| R. K. Shyamasundar | IIT Bombay, India |

## Patron

| | |
|---|---|
| N. V. Ramana Rao (Director) | NIT Raipur, India |

## General Chair

| | |
|---|---|
| R. K. Shyamasundar | IIT Bombay, India |

## Program Committee Chairs

| | |
|---|---|
| V. Muthukkumarasamy | Griffith University, Australia |
| Sithu D. Sudarsan | CDAC Bangalore, India |

## Organising Executive Committee

| | |
|---|---|
| Venkata Badarla | IIT Tirupati, India |
| Neminath Hubballi | IIT Indore, India |
| Chandrashekar Jatoth | NIT Raipur, India |
| Jayaprakash Kar | LNMIIT, India |
| Vishwas Patil | IIT Bombay, India |
| Somnath Tripathy | IIT Patna, India |

## Tutorial Chairs

Shachee Mishra            IBM Research, India
Vishwas Patil             IIT Bombay, India

## PhD Forum and Posters Chairs

Radhika B. S.                      IIIT Dharwad, India
Shachee Mishra                     IBM Research, India
Vishwas Patil                      IIT Bombay, India
Sangitha Roy                       Thapar University, India
Jeyakumar Samantha Tharani         Griffith University, Australia

## Demo/Industry Track Chairs

Praveen Gauravaram         TCS, Australia
Amrendra Kumar             DRDO, India
Vinod Panicker             Wipro, India
Vishwas Patil              IIT Bombay, India

## Publicity Chairs

Vishwas Patil              IIT Bombay, India
Balaji Rajendran           CDAC Bengaluru, India

## Web Chair

Vishwas Patil              IIT Bombay, India

## Local Organising Committee

N. V. Ramana Rao           NIT Raipur, India
Prabhat Diwan              NIT Raipur, India
Shirish Verma              NIT Raipur, India
Rakesh Tripathi            NIT Raipur, India
Rajesh Doriya              NIT Raipur, India

| | |
|---|---|
| Chandrashekar Jatoth | NIT Raipur, India |
| T. P. Sahu | NIT Raipur, India |
| Sudhkar Pandey | NIT Raipur, India |
| S. P. Sahu | NIT Raipur, India |
| Sanjay Kumar | NIT Raipur, India |
| Suvendu Rup | NIT Raipur, India |
| Pavan Kumar Mishra | NIT Raipur, India |
| Mridu Sahu | NIT Raipur, India |
| R. R. Janghel | NIT Raipur, India |
| Govind P. Gupta | NIT Raipur, India |
| Gyanendra Verma | NIT Raipur, India |

## Program Committee

| | |
|---|---|
| Abhishek Bichhawat | IIT Gandhinagar, India |
| Adwait Nadkarni | William & Mary, USA |
| Alessandro Brighente | University of Padova, Italy |
| Angelo Spognardi | Sapienza Università di Roma, Italy |
| Aniket Kate | Purdue University, USA |
| Anirban Basu | Hitachi R&D, Japan |
| Anish Mathuria | DAIICT Gandhinagar, India |
| Anoop Singhal | NIST, USA |
| Atul Prakash | University of Michigan, USA |
| Ayantika Chatterjee | IIT Kharagpur, India |
| Babu Pillai | Southern Cross University, Australia |
| Balaji Palanisamy | University of Pittsburgh, USA |
| Barsha Mitra | BITS-Pilani Hyderabad, India |
| Bheemarjuna Reddy Tamma | IIT Hyderabad, India |
| Bodhisatwa Mazumdar | IIT Indore, India |
| Claudio Ardagna | University of Milan, Italy |
| Debadatta Mishra | IIT Kanpur, India |
| Dhiman Saha | IIT Bhilai, India |
| Donghoon Chang | IIIT Delhi, India |
| Giovanni Russello | University of Auckland, New Zealand |
| Haibing Lu | Santa Clara University, USA |
| Hyoungshick Kim | Sungkyunkwan University, South Korea |
| Indranil Sen Gupta | IIT Kharagpur, India |
| K. Gopinath | Plaksha University, India |
| Kai Rannenberg | Goethe University Frankfurt, Germany |
| Kamanashis Biswas | Australian Catholic University |
| Kannan Srinathan | IIIT Hyderabad, India |

| | |
|---|---|
| Kapil Vaswani | Microsoft Research, India |
| Laszlo Szekeres | Google, USA |
| Lorenzo DeCarli | University of Calgary, Canada |
| Luigi V. Mancini | Sapienza University of Rome, Italy |
| Mahesh Tripunitara | University of Waterloo, Canada |
| Mainack Mondal | IIT Kharagpur, India |
| Manik Lal Das | DAIICT Gandhinagar, India |
| Maurantonio Caprolu | Hamad Bin Khalifa University, Qatar |
| Murtuza Jadliwala | University of Texas at San Antonio, USA |
| N. Subramanian | SETS Chennai, India |
| Neminath Hubballi | IIT Indore, India |
| Peng Liu | Pennsylvania State University, USA |
| Phu Phung | University of Dayton, USA |
| Puneet Goyal | IIT Ropar, India |
| R. Sekar | Stony Brook University, USA |
| Radhika B. S. | IIIT Dharwad, India |
| Rajat Subhra | IIT Kharagpur, India |
| Ram Krishnan | University of Texas at San Antonio, USA |
| Rinku Dewri | University of Denver, USA |
| Sabrina De Capitani di Vimercati | University of Milan, Italy |
| Salil Kanhere | UNSW Sydney, Australia |
| Sambuddho Chakravarty | IIIT Delhi, India |
| Sandeep Shukla | IIT Kanpur, India |
| Sangita Roy | Thapar University, India |
| Sanjay Rawat | University of Bristol, UK |
| Sanjit Chatterjee | IISc, India |
| Sanjiva Prasad | IIT Delhi, India |
| Sathya Peri | IIT Hyderabad, India |
| Shachee Mishra | IBM Research, India |
| Silvio Ranise | Fondazione Bruno Kessler, Italy |
| Simone Soderi | Scuola IMT Alti Studi Lucca, Italy |
| Somitra Sanadhya | IIT Jodhpur, India |
| S. P. Suresh | Chennai Mathematical Institute, India |
| Srinivas Vivek | IIIT Bangalore, India |
| Srinivasu Bodapati | IIT Mandi, India |
| Subhabrata Samajder | IIIT Delhi, India |
| Subhamoy Maitra | ISI Kolkata, India |
| Subidh Ali | IIT Bhilai, India |
| Sushmita Ruj | UNSW Sydney, Australia |
| Vijay Atluri | Rutgers Business School, USA |
| Vinay Riberio | IIT Bombay, India |

# External Reviewers Invited by the PC

Abdulrahman Alhaidari
Amir Hossein Jafari
Andrea Flamini
Ankit Ravish
Anshu S. Anand
Chinmay Kapkar
Domenico Siracusa
Fabio De Gaspari
Fan Zhang
Frédéric Tronnier
Gurudatta Verma
Jaynarayan T. Tudu
Jingzhe Wang
Joseph Spracklen
Laltu Sardar
Latifur Khan
Lisa Facciolo
Maryam Abbasihafshejani
Morteza Sargolzaeijavan

Munawar Hasan
Nathan Joslin
Nisha Vinayaga-Sureshkanth
Pei-Yu·Tseng
Piduguralla Manaswini
Rahma Mukta
Raveen Wijewickrama
Sabrine Ennaji
Samuel Karumba
Saurabh Sharma
Shyam Murthy
Srinidhi Madabhushi
Stefano Berlato
Sugandh Pargal
Tapas Pandit
Thirasara Ariyarathna
Tikaram Sanyashi
Xiaoyan Sun

# Abstracts of Invited Talks
# and Tutorials

# hinTS: Threshold Signatures with Silent Setup

Sanjam Garg

University of California, Berkeley
https://people.eecs.berkeley.edu/~sanjamg

**Abstract.** In this talk, I will describe hinTS — a new threshold signature scheme built on top of the widely used BLS signatures. This scheme achieves the following desirable features:

- A silent setup process where the joint public key of the parties is computed as a deterministic function of their locally computed public keys.
- Support for dynamic choice of thresholds and signers, after the silent setup, without further interaction.
- Support for general access policies and native support for weighted thresholds with zero additional overhead over standard threshold setting.
- Strong security guarantees, including proactive security and forward security.

This scheme is practical with aggregation time for 1000 signers under 0.5 seconds, while both signing and verification are constant time algorithms, taking 1 ms and 17.5 ms, respectively.

(Based on joint work with Abhishek Jain, Pratyay Mukherjee, Rohit Sinha, Mingyuan Wang, and Yinuo Zhang)

# How to Train and Use AI Models on Sensitive Data without Compromising Privacy?

Nishanth Chandran

Microsoft Research
https://www.microsoft.com/en-us/research/people/nichandr/

**Abstract.** AI models have the potential to revolutionize many domains, but they also pose serious privacy risks. How can we ensure that our data is not exposed or misused when we train or use these models? How can we protect the intellectual property of the model publishers and the privacy of the data owners?

In this talk, I will introduce EzPC, a system developed by Microsoft Research that enables privacy preserving machine learning. I will show how EzPC leverages cryptographic techniques to allow secure and efficient computation on encrypted data, without revealing any information to any party. I will also present some of the recent advances and challenges in this exciting area of research.

How to Incentivize Data Labelers on Sensitive Data without Compromising Privacy?

# Follow the Money

Thomas Silkjær

XRP Ledger Foundation
https://www.linkedin.com/in/silkjaer/

**Abstract.** We will learn how the XRP Ledger Foundation applies *property graph databases* to map blockchain activity to protect users from scams and counter money laundering.

This presentation will unravel the intricate relationship between compliance and the XRPL, showcasing the XRP Forensics initiative that has been integral to the XRPL ecosystem since 2018. Initially focusing on collecting account addresses associated with scams and thefts. The initiative now operates with a robust graph database, compiling comprehensive transaction and account history of the XRPL network. This expansive database includes vital information about VASP (Virtual Asset Service Provider) affiliations and records instances of illicit involvements, thereby empowering real-time monitoring of suspicious accounts and transactions.

Through visual examples, and insightful analysis, this presentation offers a deeper understanding of how property graph databases and proactive monitoring can revolutionize blockchain security. By showcasing the XRP Ledger Foundation's commitment to enhancing transparency, thwarting illicit activities, and collaborating with the broader compliance and blockchain community, this discussion encourages a collective effort towards a safer and more regulated blockchain landscape.

# Covert & Side Stories: Threats Evolution in Traditional and Modern Technologies

Mauro Conti

University of Padua and TU Delft
https://www.math.unipd.it/~conti/

**Abstract.** Alongside traditional Information and Communication Technologies, more recent ones like Smartphones and IoT devices also became pervasive. Furthermore, all technologies manage an increasing amount of confidential data. The concern of protecting these data is not only related to an adversary gaining physical or remote control of a victim device through traditional attacks, but also to what extent an adversary without the above capabilities can infer or steal information through side and covert channels!

In this talk, we survey a corpus of representative research results published in the domain of side and covert channels, ranging from TIFS 2016 to more recent Usenix Security 2022, and including several demonstrations at Black Hat Hacking Conferences. We discuss threats coming from contextual information and to which extent it is feasible to infer very specific information. In particular, we discuss attacks like inferring actions that a user is doing on mobile apps, by eavesdropping their encrypted network traffic, identifying the presence of a specific user within a network through analysis of energy consumption, or inferring information (also key one like passwords and PINs) through timing, acoustic, or video information.

# Overview of Applications of Machine Learning in Encrypted Traffic Analysis for Cyber Security

Debapriyay Mukhopadhyay

Vehere Technology
debapriyaym@gmail.com

**Abstract.** This tutorial is aimed to cover a broad area of Cyber Security called Encrypted Traffic Analysis (ETA). With the growing use of encrypted traffic, the traditional or known approaches to Network Visibility and Network Forensics started to face a tremendous amount of challenges in isolating or detecting suspicious network activities. Fingerprinting of SSL Client Hello and SSL Server Hello messages have gained significant attention in recent years because of its utility in detecting malwares over encrypted channel. But, new techniques like cipher stunting have been devised to defeat this fingerprinting based malware detection. With wide-spread adoption of TLS 1.3 over TLS 1.2, we will miss out getting many information like validity, issuer and subject information of the certificate.

Thus machine learning based approaches have become an important direction for encrypted malicious traffic detection and its containment. Network traffic analysis requires different pieces of information or problems to be solved to satisfy different cyber security use cases. These use cases can be broadly classified into four different types of problems such as – i) Protocol or Application Identification; ii) Network Intrusion and Malware Detection; iii) Device/OS identification and PII leakage detection and iv) VPN tunnel detection, Webpage Fingerprinting, etc. Overall agenda of this tutorial is to discuss on the feature engineering aspects of solving problems from the above use case areas using machine learning. The tutorial will also discuss the ML techniques used and will reveal the interesting results obtained so far.

**Keywords:** SSL/TLS · Cyber Security · Encrypted Traffic Analysis · Network Forensics · Machine Learning.

# Osquery: A Tool for System Visibility and Threat Hunting

Manjesh Kumar Hanawal and Atul Kabra

IIT Bombay
mhanawal@iitb.ac.in, atul.kabra.20@gmail.com

**Abstract.** Continuous monitoring and proactive threat detection help organizations to protect themselves against malicious cyberattacks. As threat detection entirely relies on the available system activity logs (henceforth referred to as simply logs), it is crucial that we have good visibility of the system and high-quality logs are collected. Moreover, collected logs should be made available in a form that is easily accessible, parsable, and co-relatable, for effective processing. In this tutorial, we will discuss Osquery, a tool supported by the Linux Foundations for gathering and processing logs. Osquery allows viewing operating as a database and processing them using OS-independent platforms like SQL, thus making it convenient for use in system monitoring, threat detection, and event correlation.

Osquery supports logs collection from most of the OS like Windows, Linux, and MacOS, which are made available in the form of tables. It provides a set of default tables and allows more tables to be added for logs collected by any other mechanism through Extensions. SQL queries can be scheduled to gather required information from the tables which can be stored locally or sent to a remote server for analysis. Thus Osquery provides a complete telemetry for processing logs.

The tutorial will cover the basics of Osquery and its various features. We will highlight how Osquery is useful in threat-hunting. We will demonstrate a Vajra that is built using Osquery for managing the nodes and threat hunting at scale.

# Data Anonymization Techniques

Vishwas Patil

IIT Bombay
https://sites.google.com/site/ivishwas/

**Abstract.** Data anonymization is a process of transforming a verbatim dataset into a dataset that does not include any direct or indirect reference for a uniquely identifiable entity. The entity can be a person, a computer, an object, or a combination of these. The anonymization process may involve a set of techniques, each adding to the level of anonymization. The anonymized dataset is said to be acceptable when a query ran on it returns an output as close to the output that is obtained on the verbatim data. Data anonymization is challenging because it simultaneously expects two orthogonal properties: anonymity and utility. The utility of the anonymized dataset is inversely proportional to the anonymity guarantees. Therefore, it is crucial to find a balance between these two properties while performing anonymization. Anonymization becomes even more challenging when the dataset transformation is expected to be privacy-preserving; which is a stricter type of data transformation process where the transformed data must not contain record(s) identifying a natural person.

In this tutorial, we will explore numerous data transformation techniques along with their algorithms. Some of these techniques are generic and can be used for any data type, whereas others are data-specific. We will explore application of these techniques to healthcare or network dataset anonymization, depending on the background of the audience.

# Contents

# Systems Security

# A Security Analysis of Password Managers on Android

Abhyudaya Sharma[✉] and Sweta Mishra

Shiv Nadar University, Greater Noida, India
{as388,sweta.mishra}@snu.edu.in
https://snu.edu.in

**Abstract.** Password Managers are software tools designed to help users easily store and access credentials across devices while also reducing, if not eliminating, reuse of passwords across different service providers. Previous research has identified several security vulnerabilities with desktop and browser-based password managers; however, aside from research on possibilities of phishing, the security of password manager applications on mobile devices had never been investigated comprehensively prior to this paper. We present a study of three of the most popular password managers on the Google Play Store including but not limited to their password generators, vault and metadata storage, and autofill capabilities. By building upon past findings, we identify several weaknesses in password managers including generation of weak and statistically non-random passwords, unencrypted storage of metadata and application settings, and possibilities for credential phishing. In addition, we suggest several improvements to mobile password managers, other Android applications, and the Android operating system that can improve the user experience and security of password managers on Android devices. From our observations, we also determine areas for future research that can help improve the security of password managers.

**Keywords:** password manager · android · security · reverse engineering

## 1 Introduction

From ancient Rome to the present day, passwords have been used as a common form of authentication. With the advent of computers and the internet, passwords have become a necessary evil. Despite their popularity and apparent ease of use for both the users as well as the application developers, password-based authentication systems have several known issues. Previous research has shown that reuse of passwords across different websites service providers is commonplace [10,11]. If a user's credentials for one of these websites get leaked through a data breach, an attacker can potentially gain access to the user's other accounts. Moreover, past research has shown that it is difficult for people to remember

V. Muthukkumarasamy et al. (Eds.): ICISS 2023, LNCS 14424, pp. 3–22, 2023.
https://doi.org/10.1007/978-3-031-49099-6_1

passwords that are unlikely to be brute-forced in the foreseeable future [1]. It
has also been observed that most people, including technologically savvy users,
cannot reliably distinguish between strong and weak passwords [30]. In addition, common policies that require users to include digits and special characters
or ones that necessitate a password change after a given period can lead to a
reduction in the overall quality of passwords [17,24,36].

Password managers promise to mitigate these inherent weaknesses of
password-based authentication systems. A password manager is a software tool
that is designed to securely store user credentials and other sensitive information. When using a password manager, a user is only required to remember one
password, the master password. All other credentials are stored in an encrypted
database, referred to as the vault. The database is encrypted using a key that is
derived from the master password. Assuming that the encryption algorithm is
secure and if the master password is strong against current and predicted future
brute-force attacks, it would not be feasible for an attacker with access to an
encrypted vault to retrieve user credentials from it. Moreover, one's cognitive
burden reduces when using a password manager since only one password needs
to be remembered.

Modern password managers are complex pieces of software that include many
features other than just storing user credentials. Browser-based and desktop
password managers have been extensively analysed in the past several security
vulnerabilities have been found. Li et al. [20] found significant vulnerabilities in
popular web-based password managers. Silver et al. [33] found security issues
with autofill implementations. In 2020, Oesch et al. [26] found several security
issues and insecure defaults in many desktop password managers. Although work
has been done on analysing the usability of [32] and possibilities of phishing [5]
on password managers on mobile devices, and concerns have been raised about
mobile password managers using the system clipboard [13,37] in 2013 and 2014,
to the best of our knowledge, no research has been carried out on the complete
password manager life-cycle. Moreover, password managers have considerably
evolved over the past eight years and now use autofill capabilities built into the
operating system that have not been comprehensively investigated earlier. With
more and more people accessing the internet through mobile devices [25], the
security risks of using password managers remain unknown for a large fraction
of the society.

In this paper, we examine in detail three of the most popular password managers on the most popular mobile operating system, Android, including the quality of generated passwords, storage of the encrypted vault and the corresponding
metadata, autofill capabilities, and features specific to each application. In addition to building up on previous work, we make use of reverse engineering as an
effective tool to evaluate password managers. We generate over 35 million passwords and analyse them using established techniques such as the chi-squared and
password strength estimators. We also identify several implementation issues by
observation and manual review of the application source. Furthermore, we discover issues that are unique to password managers on mobile devices and provide
suggestions to improve the security of password manager applications.

Our contributions include:

1. A comprehensive analysis of modern password managers on mobile devices. Our work includes an analysis of password generators, autofill functionality, vault and metadata storage, and unique features of each application. We discover that additional features increase the potential attack surface for security vulnerability and that the evaluation of these features is just as important as the password management interface itself.
2. We generate over 35 million passwords from the three password managers using automation of user interactions and reverse engineering application sources. Using previously used password strength evaluation tools ($\chi^2$ test and password strength meters like zxcvbn), we discover issues in the quality of random passwords. In some configurations, we observe that the strength of generated passwords could be several orders of magnitude lower than what the user expects.
3. We confirm that password generators on Android may still be vulnerable to security issues discovered by past research. We find applications making use of unencrypted metadata which, if obtained by an attacker, can expose personally identifiable information. We find several instances of production of non-random passwords. Our study is the first study on password generation that attributes the cause of this non-randomness to issues in the application source.
4. Our work identifies several areas of improvement for password managers on mobile devices. We suggest better default settings and improvements that can prevent accidental leakage of user credentials. We also discover that password managers on Android are often limited by the APIs offered by the operating system. We also determine potential areas for future research that can help improve the security and usability of password managers on mobile devices.

## 2   Background

This section considers the duties of an ideal password manager and how a password manager can protect its users against data breaches and cyberattacks. We also discuss past research that has been carried out on password managers and how it relates to this work.

### 2.1   Password Managers

Password managers are designed as tools that simplify users' lives by reducing the number of passwords they need to remember. Most password managers are designed around the premise that it is difficult for one person to remember multiple strong passwords, but it is possible to remember one strong password. Password managers refer to this one password that the users must remember as the *master password* [20].

Password managers use symmetric cryptographic primitives to encrypt secrets (for example, login credentials or SSH keys) under a encryption key that can only be derived using the master password. If the encryption algorithm is secure under current and predicted future hardware capabilities, the encrypted contents must be secure. However, such abstractions do not do justice to the flexibility and security provided by modern password managers.

A good password manager can not only help users reduce the number of passwords needed to be remembered, but they can also help in significantly increasing the quality of passwords. The average length of passwords is between 8 and 10 characters [10]. In contrast, most websites allow users to have considerably longer passwords. Since the strength of passwords increases as the length increases, allowing users to store much longer passwords in the encrypted storage when combined with autofill can result in much stronger credentials.

In addition, most password managers now offer built-in random password generators [26], which can further reduce the amount of work required to be done by the user. Password manager applications can start flagging duplicate logins, ensuring that users no longer reuse credentials across the internet. Furthermore, password managers can autofill user credentials using methods that do not make use of the system clipboard. This is necessary since several popular applications have been known to read user clipboards potentially to steal passwords [6].

## 2.2   Related Work

The security and usability of password managers has been analysed several times before.

*Security Analysis of Web-Based Password Managers.* Li et al. [20] analysed five web-based password managers in 2014: LastPass, RoboForm, My1login, PasswordBox, and NeedMyPassword. The authors found critical vulnerabilities in all applications. In four of the five password managers, an attacker could steal arbitrary credentials from the user's encrypted password database. The vulnerabilities ranged anywhere from logical errors, cross-site request forgery (CSRF), cross-site scripting (XSS), and misunderstandings about the browser security model. The authors also found vulnerabilities regarding handling of `<iframe>`s.

*Phishing Attacks on Android Password Managers.* In 2018, Aonzo et al. [5] evaluated the possibility of phishing attacks on four Android password managers as well as the built-in Google smart lock. The authors evaluated the legacy `a11y` framework, OpenYOLO and the then nascent Autofill framework. The authors found out that mobile password managers could not create a secure mapping between application package names and web domain names. The authors discovered that password managers could suggest credentials associated with arbitrary attacker-chosen websites. The authors asserted that the proof-of-concept attacks were made more practical by Android's instant apps.

*Analysis of Autofill Functionality.* Silver et al. [33] examined ten password managers in 2014 regarding their autofill functionality. The authors were able to obtain user credentials from password managers by spoofing authentic websites, highlighting the potential that any attacker in a coffee shop could get hold of users' passwords by simple methods like ARP spoofing. The authors also found that the password managers were vulnerable to clickjacking and the user could authorize autofill to a malicious website without ever realizing it. The authors suggested password managers to not fill credentials without user interaction and to use Content Security Policy headers to prevent JavaScript injection and XSS attacks.

Similar research on XSS attacks has also been carried out by Stock and Johns [35]. Google's Project Zero team also discovered a vulnerability in the LastPass Browser extension where an attacker could create an `<iframe>` that uses the extension's public HTML files as source and gain credentials to the previously visited webpage [27]. The issue was responsibly reported to the LastPass team and was soon fixed.

*Usability of Password Managers.* Pearman et al. [28] analysed the use of password managers in 2019. The authors concluded that the reason for a small percentage of the population actually using password managers correctly was related to a lack of awareness and confusion about the prompts provided by web browsers and third-party password managers. The authors noted that participants were regularly frustrated with the user experience of using password managers and instead went back to memorizing weak passwords.

Seiler-Hwang et al. [32] conducted a survey of 80 users analysing the usability of mobile password managers. The authors concluded that the usability concerns noted on desktop and browser-based password managers are also present on mobile devices. The authors noted that there is poor integration between password managers and other applications and browsers.

*Evaluation of Browser-Based Password Managers.* Oesch et al. [26] evaluated the most popular browser-based password managers in 2019 and discovered several flaws in the implementation. This was the most detailed security study on password managers in over five years and the authors were able to find several security issues with desktop and browser-based password extensions. The authors evaluated five browser extensions and six password managers integrated directly into web browsers. They concluded that compared to previous studies, password managers had considerably improved. However, they found that some of the passwords generated by password managers were so weak that they could pose a security risk for users. They also suggested that password manager applications develop stronger policies for master passwords and not allow users to set weak master passwords.

*Analysis of Storage.* In 2017, Gasti and Rasmussen [16] analysed the database format used by password managers. The authors discovered several vulnerabilities which could lead to attackers gaining sensitive information. This included unencrypted metadata storage as well as leaking information from the encrypted vaults.

*Third-Party Trackers in Android Password Managers.* In March of 2021, Mike Kuketz analysed several popular Android password managers for embedded third-party trackers [19]. The author discovered eight third-party tracking libraries in the Avira password manager, seven in LastPass, four in Dashlane, two each Kaspersky Password Manager and Bitwarden, and one in Enpass. According to the author, it could be possible that decrypted credentials are sent to these trackers.

*Relation to this Work.* Previous analysis of password managers provide us insights into potential vulnerabilities that could be present in mobile password managers. The results of the usability studies help us to determine the security issues that password managers could face if changes are made according to user feedback.

## 3   Analysed Password Managers

In this paper, we analysed three of the most popular password manager applications on the Google Play Store:

- LastPass (version 4.11.1; over 10 million users)
- Dashlane (version 6.2102.0-x86; over 5 million users)
- Bitwarden (version 2.80; over 1 million users)

Although there are over one hundred password manager applications available on the Google Play Store, we chose these password managers for our studies since they represent the broad spectrum of password manager applications available: LastPass is one of the oldest and most popular password managers, Dashlane was released in 2012 and won the People's Voice Webby Award in 2017 for Services & Utilities in Mobile Sites & Apps, and Bitwarden is an open-source application first made available in 2016, currently recommended by CNET, Lifehacker, and U.S. News & World Report as the best password manager [9,18]. All three password managers feature syncing encrypted password databases (commonly referred to as the *vault*) across multiple devices.

The three applications allow us to evaluate password managers created in different technological stacks. LastPass and Dashlane run on the Java virtual machine (JVM) while the Bitwarden app is written in C# using Microsoft's Xamarin. Though LastPass and Dashlane can appear to be similar, the Dashlane Android application is mostly written in Kotlin while the bulk of the LastPass application is written in Java. Since Bitwarden's mobile application, server-side application, web extension, and desktop application are all open-source, it is possible to self-host Bitwarden. This is not possible with the other two applications. Moreover, since Bitwarden is open-source, several other server-side implementations of the Bitwarden protocol have been created by the community, the most notable one being `bitwarden_rs` [15], an open-source server compatible with Bitwarden client software which is written in Rust.

*Vault Encryption.* All three password managers use AES256-CBC for encrypting the vault. For key derivation, Bitwarden and LastPass only support using PBKDF2 to derive the encryption key from the master password [7,21]. In addition to supporting PBKDF2, Dashlane defaults to using Argon2D to derive the encryption key [12]. Table 1 highlights the default key derivation iterations used by the three applications.

**Table 1.** Default key derivation iterations

| Application | PBKDF2 | Argon2D |
|---|---|---|
| Dashlane | 200,000 | 3 (32 MB memory) |
| Bitwarden | 100,001 | Not supported |
| LastPass | 100,100 | Not supported |

# 4 Password Generation

All three applications studied feature a random password generator. LastPass also allows users to generate pronounceable passwords while Bitwarden allows users to generate passphrases (as described in [24]).

## 4.1 Collecting Passwords

To collect passwords from the three applications, we used two different approaches – automating user interactions, and reverse engineering the source code to find the password generation algorithm. We used the official Android Emulator with a virtual Google Pixel 3a (Android 11) running on a Windows 10 Home (Version 20H2, Build 19042.928) laptop with an i7-8705G processor @3.10 GHz and 16 gigabytes of RAM. Alongside the VM, we also used LG V30+ ThinQ running Android 9.0 on Linux Kernel 4.4.153.

*Automating User Interactions.* To interact with the running app, we used Appium, an automation platform created by Sauce Labs which allowed developers to test their applications (Android, iOS, Windows, Web, etc.) via the Selenium WebDriver Protocol.

We initially started with collecting passwords from the Dashlane Android application. We used the recommended `UiAutomator2` driver which internally uses Google's UI Automator. Applications interacting with Appium for Android devices can request the `appWaitActivity` capability and specify an activity to wait for. We gained information about the displayed activities on the screen using `adb shell dumpsys window windows` command while the Dashlane application was running. After automating unlocking the vault and opening the password generator, we could generate passwords reliably from the Dashlane with a program written in TypeScript using WebDriverIO.

However, the process to scrape passwords was quite resource-heavy and slow. The rate of password extraction using this method was a meagre 88 passwords per minute. It would have taken us eight days to generate one million passwords. In addition, reverse engineering was potentially a better choice since if we could successfully reconstruct the password generation algorithm, we could perform a manual review of the source code.

*Adventures in Reverse Engineering.* The first step of our reverse engineering process was to get our hands on the application binaries. Android applications are distributed in Android Package Files (APK) [2]. The bytecode is stored in `classes`$N$`.dex` files at the root of the decompressed APK where $N$ is either an empty string or a number greater than or equal to two. We downloaded the apps from the Play Store on to our emulators. To extract the application's APK, we made use of ADB. We used `adb shell pm path <package.name>` to first find the path to the APK. The APK was then copied to the host using `adb pull`.

We used the open-source tool JADX to decompile the DEX bytecode extracted from the APK to Java source code. During the compilation of Java or Kotlin source code to Dalvik bytecode under release configurations, the androidgradle-plugin transforms the source by inlining methods, obfuscating method names, rearranging methods across classes, etc. Though JADX can perform basic deobfuscation and use Kotlin metadata, we still needed to spend a considerable amount of effort to rename variables, methods, and classes according to their use in the source. Matters were complicated by boilerplate added by Kotlin libraries and coroutines, especially in the decompiled Dashlane source code.

For Dashlane, we were eventually able to find the class containing the source of the password generator, `b.a.a.x0.f`. Using associated Kotlin metadata, we resolved it to be `com.dashlane.ui.util.PasswordGeneratorAndStrength`.

We observed that the LastPass app was slightly less obfuscated than Dashlane. Using the decompiled code, we discovered the class `LPPasswordGenerator` inside the package `com.lastpass.lpandroid.domain`. This class contained the source for both the pronounceable password generator as well as the random password generator.

Both Dashlane and LastPass use `java.security.SecureRandom`, a cryptographically secure pseudorandom number generator, to generate random integers for the password generators. Bitwarden uses `RandomNumberGenerator` through the open-source PCLCrypto library.

We did not need to decompile the Bitwarden application since it is open-source and we could obtain the source of the password generator from GitHub.

After that, we cleaned up the decompiled source to ensure that it could run on any JVM while ensuring that the behaviour remained the same. We created a custom runner that interacted with the obtained source. The passwords were generated on an i7 8705G Windows 10 machine running OpenJDK 11. All generated passwords were stored in an SQLite database for analysis. Over various configurations, we generated over 35 million passwords from the three applications.

## 4.2   Observations

**Fig. 1.** LastPass' Pronounceable Password Generator

Among the password managers, we were able to observe several cases of non-random password generation. If an attacker learns about this information, it becomes possible to guess possible passwords more efficiently, decreasing the strength of the password. To determine if the characters in the passwords were randomly distributed, we used Pearson's chi-squared test for randomness [29] with a 95% confidence interval, as has been done in previous research [26].

*LastPass.* LastPass' pronounceable password generator was, in our opinion, the biggest offender when it comes to producing strong passwords. We discovered that the pronounceable password generator could generate passwords of lengths smaller than what the user specified. This can be seen replicated in Fig. 1; the generator is configured to produce passwords of length 14 but the generated password is of length 6. We observed that approximately one percent of passwords had lengths smaller than expected.

From the produced passwords, we could determine that if the generator is configured to produce passwords of length $x$, the lengths of the generated passwords lie in the range 3 to $x$. To make matters worse, the character distribution of passwords is far from random. The generator also does not follow the English language character frequency distribution (p-value = 0). In addition, out of the $26^3 = 17576$ possible trigrams using the lowercase alphabet, the generator would only produce 5804. Further reducing the strength was the fact that just 500 distinct trigrams make up over half of all produced trigrams. The non-randomness in character and trigram frequency distribution is highlighted in Fig. 2.

The random password generator also did produce non-random character distribution of passwords in some cases; however, we could not identify the cause of this observed non-randomness from the source code.

*Dashlane.* Dashlane's password generator is unique among the three password managers in that it does not allow users to create passwords that are not mixed case. We observed that Dashlane's password generator did produce statistically random passwords when ambiguous characters were included in the character set of the passwords to be produced. However, when ambiguous characters were excluded from the character set, the app did not produce random passwords (p-value = 0). We noticed that the output of the generator was biased towards producing more uppercase characters than lowercase characters (see Fig. 3).

By examining the source code, we determined the cause of this bias. The number of non-ambiguous upper-case characters, according to Dashlane, is 20 while the number of non-ambiguous lowercase characters is 22. The app tries to insert one uppercase and one lowercase character in every password. This has the consequence that uppercase characters are noticeably more frequent.

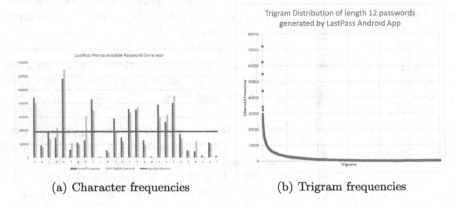

| (a) Character frequencies | (b) Trigram frequencies |
| --- | --- |

**Fig. 2.** Character frequency and trigram distribution for LastPass' pronounceable password generator

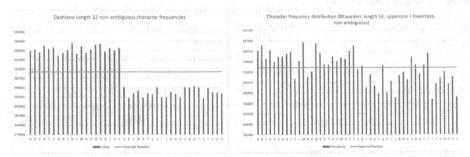

(a) Dashlane (Length 12, non-ambiguous) (b) Bitwarden (Length 14, non-ambiguous)

**Fig. 3.** Character distribution of passwords generated by Dashlane and Bitwarden

*Bitwarden.* Bitwarden's password generator performed slightly better than Last-Pass' password generator and similar to Dashlane's password generator, especially when producing smaller length ambiguous passwords. We found that in our generated password database, the password generator easily produced random passwords according to the chi-squared test whenever the generator was set to produce ambiguous passwords. However, we did see some cases when the computed p-values were below 0.05. This was especially true for passwords of lengths between 12 and 16 characters that were non-ambiguous and contained both uppercase and lowercase letters. One such instance is visualized in Fig. 3. Unlike Dashlane, we were not able to find a distinctive error in the distribution or in the source code.

*Filtering Weak Passwords.* Oesch et al. [26] recommended that password managers should detect and filter out weak passwords. We noticed that none of these password managers has implemented filtering of weak passwords and that it is still possible for generated passwords to be weak against attacks. Instead, Dashlane and LastPass now show the strengths of the produced passwords calculated using zxcvbn [36] on the password generator. In contrast, Bitwarden does not inform users about the strength of the passwords even though it includes the C# port of zxcvbn as a dependency.

## 5   Vault and Metadata Storage

As observed by Gasti and Rasmussen [16] and reiterated by Oesch et al. [26], access to unencrypted metadata can result in leakage of personally identifiable information like usernames, website URLs, account creation times, etc. Hence, encryption of all data produced by the password managers is necessary.

Using the unzipped APKs for Dashlane and LastPass, we were able to find the native libraries that these applications make use of. Applications that run on the Java Virtual Machine can access native code, including any cryptographic primitives provided by the hardware, using Java Native Interface (JNI) [2]. The Android Operating system creates a new user for each application. The OS ensures that the application is only run as that user and that the application data directory is only readable by that user. Although filesystem permissions can, assuming that no vulnerabilities exist in the Linux kernel, prevent other applications from reading data, it is not a replacement for encryption. If an attacker gets access to a device whose storage is not encrypted at rest, the attacker can still read the application data.

Since an ideal password manager should not store any data unencrypted [26], we expect the password managers to not store anything on the disk other than the encrypted vault file.

*LastPass.* We discovered that LastPass depends on three native libraries, `liblastpass.so`, `liblastpass_pbkdf2.so`, and `libtool-checker.so`. We found that the LastPass application also includes a fallback PBKDF2 implementation written in Java in case the implementation typically accessed through JNI is not available. From the reverse engineered source, we were able to conclude that the LastPass application uses a SQLite database for storing the vault, autofill entries, app icons, and the application cache. SQLite is a popular open-source embedded database that has bindings for various languages, including the Android JVM. However, we discovered that `lpcache.db` stores the URLs visited by the user in plaintext. If an attacker is able to gain access to this database, he can figure out the user's visited pages, the title of each visited page, and the time at which the page was last accessed.

*Bitwarden.* Bitwarden is unique among the three password managers in that it does not use a SQL database for storing passwords. We could conclude that the application makes use of LiteDB, an embedded NoSQL database for .NET languages. We also found that the application uses the C# Bouncy Castle APIs for providing cryptographic functions like PBKDF2. Although LiteDB supports AES encryption, Bitwarden does not use that functionality. We suspect that this is because of LiteDB's lack of options to customize the encryption parameters. One security issue we discovered was that Bitwarden uses `Xamarin.Essentials.Preferences` to store application preferences. These preferences are not encrypted by Android and are stored in plain text [23].

*Dashlane.* Dashlane is the only application for which we could not find information about the app being stored in plaintext. This is because the app makes use of SQLCipher, an open-source extension to SQLite that provides transparent AES-256 encryption. When using SQLCipher, applications can unlock the database by providing the encryption key and then run SQL commands like they normally would. By using SQLCipher, the Dashlane app can ensure that the data is encrypted at all times on the disk while also making it easy for developers to interact with the database using standard SQL commands.

### 5.1   Biometric Authentication and root

Biometric authentication is one of the more prominent features of Android password managers and we expect that most users enable it to improve usability. However, it has been discovered that popular forms of biometric authentication like fingerprint sensors are not as secure as generally perceived [31]. Even if we assume that a sensor is 100% accurate, enabling biometric authentication increases the attack surface for all studied password managers. All three password managers make use of the Android keystore system [4] to store encryption keys when biometric authentication is enabled. If an attacker is powerful enough to obtain root access, he will be able to access the encryption key to the vault. Since the attacker can now also access the encrypted vault files, he can obtain all data stored in the vault.

## 6   Autofill

On Android, the autofill capability is provided by the registered `Autofill-Service`. The `AutofillService` is a part of the Autofill Framework [3] and is required to be set by the user in the device settings. No app can set itself as the autofill provider for the device without requiring user interaction with the settings. When an application is showing a login page, the application can request the operating system to pass the current `Views` on screen to the registered `AutofillService`. The autofill service implementation can then parse the contents of the `Views` and then return a response with the user credentials. The credentials returned by the autofill service are displayed on the screen by the operating system. The user can select the ones he wishes to use. These are then filled in the form. All applications discussed have the capabilities to autofill using the Autofill Service.

To test the autofill implementations, we created sample HTML login pages to test the behaviour of the applications when presented with different protocols and application structures. These webpages were served over a local network with differences in protocols (HTTP/HTTPS), validity of the certificates for HTTPS, and browsers. For our investigations, we used the latest versions of Chrome, Firefox, and Edge downloaded from the Play Store.

Autofill failed to work on Firefox reliably. Firefox for Android does provide users with the ability to install the Bitwarden browser extension which is the same as on PC. On PC, for convenience at the risk of an increased attack surface, the extension integrates with the operating system to provide biometric authentication. However, on Firefox on Android, biometric authentication is not supported.

Previous studies on browser extension based password managers have found several clickjacking and XSS vulnerabilities [20,26,33,35]. We could ascertain that these applications are not prone to clickjacking attempts since the autofill menu makes use of Android's accessibility framework and draws over the application window. The application cannot interact with the accessibility menu. Moreover, user interaction is always required before autofilling. XSS attacks are made impossible with the operating system not being written in JavaScript and the application having no way to communicate with the autofill service other than request autofill.

Unfortunately, we found that none of the three password manager applications, except for the LastPass when using the built-in LastPass browser, show a warning when visiting insecure websites (served via HTTP or with an invalid TLS certificate) via a browser. Using techniques like ARP spoofing and in the absence of HTTP Strict Transport Security or when a user is visiting a web page for the first time on a device, an attacker can easily phish credentials without warning from password managers. This is not a limitation of Android's autofill framework; password managers can get information about the scheme that is utilized to visit a web page using `AssistStructure.ViewNode#getWebScheme()`. However, none of the three make use of this method.

We would expect the password managers to at least warn the users that an attacker can see their login information in plaintext. We understand that it is not possible to return warnings from the autofill framework at the time of writing. Therefore, we suggest the Android developers to make it possible for password managers to send a warning in such situations. We also believe that the `AutofillService` should allow the applications requesting autofill using the autofill manager to provide the application either the complete certificate chain or at least the validity of the certificate. These changes would enable password managers to warn users about insecure transport and invalid or changed certificates.

## 7    Other Security Issues

Modern password managers are complex applications that have considerably evolved from simple credential stores. LastPass includes a built-in browser, the LastPass browser, that promises secure browsing; Dashlane includes a VPN in the premium plans that connects to hosts using OpenVPN; Bitwarden includes 'Send', a URL-based file sharing service. These features undoubtedly add to the attack surface of the application and it becomes imperative to evaluate the safety of these features.

*LastPass Browser.* The LastPass Browser is a feature not present in the browser extension. This browser makes use of Android's System WebView. A significant security issue with the browser is that it leaks user searches through DNS requests. On entering any token $x$ into the search bar without a space character, the browser navigates to www.x.com, making a DNS request with the token $x$ in plaintext. Even if the user makes use of an encrypted DNS protocol like DNS over HTTPS or DNS over TLS, the plaintext domain will be visible to the trusted recursive resolver. The plaintext may also be visible on the network through TLS SNI if the queried domain resolves to an IP.

*Master Password Strength.* We found that the master password policies of two of the applications were not up to the mark. Bitwarden had the weakest master password policy, with the only requirement being that its length is more than eight characters. This allows users to set extremely weak passwords, for instance password, as the master password. LastPass is slightly better, requiring one uppercase character, one lowercase character, one digit, and a minimum length of 12. However, we could set an extremely weak password, aaaaaaaaaaA1, without any warning. This password has a zxcvbn [36] strength of just $\frac{1}{4}$ and is estimated to be broken after $10^{4.53148}$ guesses, significantly weaker than the $10^6$ guesses needed to be resistant against an online attack as estimated by Florêncio et al. [14]. This is a cause for concern since passwords created by most users are not secure and that most users cannot adequately distinguish between strong and weak passwords [30].

The only app with an acceptable master password policy is Dashlane. The app measures the strength of the password using zxcvbn and requires that the score is at least $\frac{3}{4}$. Although zxcvbn may not give the true estimation of password strength [22], we believe that this is better than letting users choose passwords themselves and improves overall security.

*Allowing Screenshots.* A user may mistakenly take a screenshot of the application and leak credentials through the saved image. On Android devices, it is possible for application developers to request the operating system to not display the contents of a window in a screenshot or on a non-secure display by setting the FLAG_SECURE flag. LastPass and Dashlane allow users to capture screenshots of the apps. Moreover, this setting is persistent in both apps. If the developers do decide to enable screenshots, in our opinion, the setting should only have effect for the current session. Users may not remember that the setting is active and may end up capturing a screenshot that contains one or more passwords.

*Failing to Detect Duplicate Passwords.* Reused passwords are one of the biggest problems with password-based authentication. The LastPass Android app includes a password health monitoring tool which is supposed to detect reused passwords. In our investigations, we manually created two logins with the same password. Even after several tries, the application failed to detect duplicates. On the other hand, Dashlane reliably and clearly displayed the number of times a password was present in the vault. Bitwarden does not include duplicate password detection in the mobile app.

*JavaScript Injection in Dashlane's Password Strength Check.* Although the Dashlane application is mostly written in Kotlin, we found one potential instance of JavaScript Injection. We discovered from the source code that instead of using a port of zxcvbn for the JVM, Dashlane uses Dropbox's original JavaScript implementation by loading it inside an Android WebView. The WebView loads an HTML file that uses a `<script>` tag to import Dropbox's JavaScript implementation of zxcvbn. When the WebView is ready, JavaScript is enabled. The applications then calls WebView's `evaluateJavascript()` function as follows:

```
webView.evaluateJavascript("zxcvbn('" + password + "')");
```

Since the password is not escaped, this is a potential JavaScript injection vulnerability. Thankfully, the password generator produces neither the single quote character (') nor the backslash (\) character. Therefore, the application is safe from arbitrary random JavaScript code execution from randomly generated passwords. However, the issue still exists when checking strengths of passwords in the vault.

*Automatic Clipboard Clearing.* Prior to the introduction of the Autofill framework, all password managers made use of the system clipboard to fill into applications and browsers. This is dangerous since all applications have access to the clipboard and many applications have been known to scrape the clipboard for passwords [6,13,37]. Dashlane and Bitwarden have taken steps to reduce the likelihood of other apps gaining access to the clipboard contents by offering users to automatically wipe the clipboard (set the clipboard to an empty string) after a specified interval. However, this is not the default setting and must be enabled manually. We recommend that clipboard clearing becomes the default behaviour and that other password managers should implement it as well.

In addition, on Android, several applications and keyboards like the SwiftKey keyboard keep track of the clipboard history. As a result, even after clearing the clipboard, the password is still present in plaintext on the device. Android's clipboard API does not indicate how the clipboard contents should be handled by applications keeping track of the clipboard history. As a result, password manager apps cannot prevent storage by other applications.

## 8    Discussion

In our research, we performed a comprehensive analysis of the complete password manager life-cycle for three of the most popular password managers on the Play

Store. We discovered that password managers on Android suffer from many of the same issues that plague browser-based and desktop password managers [20, 26]. Previously reported issues of copying passwords to clipboard [13, 37] have largely been ameliorated thanks to Android's Autofill framework. Developers of Bitwarden and Dashlane have tried to reduce the likelihood of passwords being read by other applications by setting the clipboard to an empty string after a few seconds. However, because of limitations of the clipboard API, clipboard history apps still store passwords in plaintext.

Storage of unencrypted metadata on the disk has long been a cause for concern [16]. In 2020, Oesch et al. observed that most password managers did store metadata correctly. However, we found that this was not true for LastPass which stores visited URLs unencrypted. Furthermore, attacks first published in 2014 [33] are still possible with all studied password managers on Android devices. We now provide recommendations that can help improve password managers and suggest areas for possible future research.

## 8.1   Recommendations

*Better Clipboard APIs.* Limitations in Android's clipboard API can result in credentials being stored unencrypted on the device. In addition to the suggestions made by previous studies [13, 37], we suggest the Android developers to follow a design similar to the Windows Cloud Clipboard API. If an application sets up a 'sensitive data' flag when setting the clipboard, an operating system window could be drawn over the application on screen, similar to the autofill prompt. An application gets the clipboard data iff the user consents. Otherwise, an empty string is returned. Such a solution would prevent third-party applications from storing credentials in the clipboard history and eliminate the concerns of snooping by malicious applications.

*Differentiate Between HTTP and HTTPS URLs.* As it currently stands, it remains possible for passwords to be phished by spoofing HTTP connections. To rectify this, when autofilling credentials, password managers should not consider HTTP to be the same as HTTPS. If a website is known to use HTTPS through either a public list of HTTPS domains or through prior use of the password manager and if the current webpage uses HTTP, the password managers should ideally not allow autofill. At the very least, users should be clearly warned that the form is insecure. This security feature could even be implemented at the OS level to reduce the responsibilities of password manager developers.

*Filter Weak Passwords.* As recommended by Oesch et al. [26], password managers should filter out weak passwords. In our observations, this has not been implemented by password managers yet. We suggest that password managers take a look into implementing this using existing tools like zxcvbn [36] that they already make use of in other places. Until this can be implemented, we recommend Bitwarden to display the strength of generated passwords to allow users to manually filter out weak passwords.

*Strict Master Password Policies.* In two of the three apps, we discovered that policies for master passwords were not up to the mark. Compared to the observations made by Oesch et al. [26], Dashlane and LastPass now uses a stricter master password policy. However, LastPass' policy does not prevent users from setting weak passwords. Bitwarden, on the other hand, has made no changes and users can still set extremely weak master passwords without warning. Given the low quality of passwords created by users [10] and their inability to distinguish between weak and strong passwords [30], password managers should reevaluate their master password policies.

## 8.2  Scope for Future Work

*iOS Password Managers.* Our studies concentrated solely on Android Password Manager applications. With approximately 72% of all mobiles sold on our planet being Android devices [34], we felt the need to prioritise the study of Android password managers. Since most password managers are native applications with different codebases, password managers on iOS could suffer from completely different security issues. With the rest of the mobile market belonging to iOS devices, we believe it is necessary to have a detailed study on iOS password managers.

*Evaluating Security of Server-Side Software.* Almost all studies on password managers have exclusively been concentrated on the client side of password managers. Since these password managers depend on software running on the developers' servers for password sharing and syncing of the vault across multiple devices, there is a definite need for investigating security of that software.

*Better Password Strength Meters.* As shown in Subsect. 4.2, LastPass' pronounceable password generator produces passwords that are much weaker than expected. Most password strength meters like ZXCVBN [36] and neural network-based strength estimators [36] do not compensate for known character frequency distributions. As a result, the strength displayed in these applications is overestimated. Therefore, there is a need for building efficient password strength meters that can take into account the character and $n$-gram distributions of produced passwords.

*Analysis of Information Collected by Third-Party Libraries.* As discovered by Mike Kuketz [19], password managers include third-party tracking libraries that collect usage statistics and crash reports. During our investigations, we confirmed that all three applications include the tracking libraries detected by Kuketz. In addition, we discovered that the Dashlane application includes sentry-native, an error reporting library. Since these libraries run in the same application sandbox as the password managers, there is a possibility for decrypted credentials in the process memory to be read by these libraries. Thus, it is necessary to investigate whether decrypted credentials can ever be collected and transferred over the network through these libraries.

# 9 Conclusion

Although Android's autofill framework has eliminated the possibility of several issues that have earlier been found in desktop and browser-based password managers [35], passwords managers on Android devices still suffer from issues like storage of unencrypted metadata, generation of non-random passwords, weak master password policies, and leaking credentials through other channels. We observe that users are still responsible for configuring their password managers correctly and that failure to do so may open them up to attacks [26]. With increased media coverage and advertising [8,18], we believe that password managers will continue to increase in popularity. Hence, we encourage future research that helps improve both the security and usability aspects of password managers.

**Disclosure.** All vulnerabilities and issues have been responsibly disclosed to the developers of the password managers. We hope that these issues will be resolved soon and help improve the security of password managers.

# References

1. Adams, A., Sasse, M.A.: Users are not the enemy. Commun. ACM **42**(12), 40–46 (1999)
2. Android Developers: Application fundamentals (2021). https://developer.android.com/guide/components/fundamentals. Accessed 10 Feb 2021
3. Android Developers: Autofill framework (2021). https://developer.android.com/guide/topics/text/autofill. Accessed 18 March 2021
4. Android Developers: Android keystore system (2022). https://developer.android.com/training/articles/keystore. Accessed 14 Jan 2022
5. Aonzo, S., Merlo, A., Tavella, G., Fratantonio, Y.: Phishing attacks on modern android. In: Proceedings of the 2018 ACM SIGSAC Conference on Computer and Communications Security, CCS 2018, pp. 1788–1801. Association for Computing Machinery, New York (2018)
6. Bakry, T.H., Mysk, T.: Popular iPhone and iPad apps snooping on the pasteboard (2020)
7. Bitwarden Inc.: How Bitwarden Works (2021). https://bitwarden.com/products/#how-bitwarden-works. Accessed 13 March 2021
8. Broida, R.: Need a LastPass alternative? This is the best free password manager we've found (2021). https://www.cnet.com/news/need-a-lastpass-alternative-bitwarden-is-the-best-free-password-manager-we-found-2021/. Accessed 2 Apr 2021
9. Business Wire Inc.: Bitwarden Selected as Best Password Manager by US News & World Report (2021). https://www.businesswire.com/news/home/20210113005308/en/. Accessed 2 Apr 2021
10. CSID: Consumer survey: Password habits (2012). https://www.csid.com/wp-content/uploads/2012/09/CS_PasswordSurvey_FullReport_FINAL.pdf. Accessed 10 Mar 2021

11. Das, A., Bonneau, J., Caesar, M., Borisov, N., Wang, X.: The tangled web of password reuse. In: Network and Distributed System Security Symposium (2014)
12. Dashlane Inc.: Dashlane security white paper (2020). https://www.dashlane.com/download/Dashlane_SecurityWhitePaper_November2020.pdf. Accessed 12 Mar 2021
13. Fahl, S., Harbach, M., Oltrogge, M., Muders, T., Smith, M.: Hey, you, get off of my clipboard. In: Sadeghi, A.-R. (ed.) FC 2013. LNCS, vol. 7859, pp. 144–161. Springer, Heidelberg (2013). https://doi.org/10.1007/978-3-642-39884-1_12
14. Florêncio, D., Herley, C., van Oorschot, P.C.: An administrator's guide to internet password research. In: 28th Large Installation System Administration Conference (LISA14), pp. 44–61. USENIX Association, Seattle (2014)
15. García, D.: bitwarden_rs: Unofficial Bitwarden compatible server written in Rust (2021). https://github.com/dani-garcia/bitwarden_rs. Accessed 14 Apr 2021
16. Gasti, P., Rasmussen, K.B.: On the security of password manager database formats. In: Foresti, S., Yung, M., Martinelli, F. (eds.) ESORICS 2012. LNCS, vol. 7459, pp. 770–787. Springer, Heidelberg (2012). https://doi.org/10.1007/978-3-642-33167-1_44
17. Habib, H., et al.: User behaviors and attitudes under password expiration policies. In: Fourteenth Symposium on Usable Privacy and Security (SOUPS 2018), pp. 13–30. USENIX Association, Baltimore (2018)
18. Henry, A., Fitzpatrick, J., Hesse, B.: The Best Password Managers (2019). https://lifehacker.com/the-five-best-password-managers-5529133. Accessed 12 Apr 2021
19. Kuketz, M.: Wie tracking in apps die sicherheit und den datenschutz unnötig gefährdet (2021). https://www.kuketz-blog.de/wie-tracking-in-apps-die-sicherheit-und-den-datenschutz-unnoetig-gefaehrdet. Accessed 10 Mar 2021
20. Li, Z., He, W., Akhawe, D., Song, D.: The emperor's new password manager: security analysis of web-based password managers. In: Proceedings of the 23rd USENIX Conference on Security Symposium, SEC 2014, pp. 465–479. USENIX Association, USA (2014)
21. LogMeIn Inc.: Enterprise Security Model—LastPass (2021). https://www.lastpass.com/enterprise/security. Accessed 17 Feb 2021
22. Melicher, W., et al.: Fast, lean, and accurate: modeling password guessability using neural networks. In: 25th USENIX Security Symposium (USENIX Security 2016), pp. 175–191. USENIX Association, Austin (2016)
23. Microsoft Inc.: Xamarin documentation - Xamarin—Microsoft Docs (2021). https://docs.microsoft.com/en-us/xamarin/. Accessed 4 Apr 2021
24. Munroe, R.: Password strength (2011). https://xkcd.com/936. Accessed 3 Mar 2021
25. Oberlo: What percentage of internet traffic is mobile? (2021). https://www.oberlo.com/statistics/mobile-internet-traffic. Accessed 10 Apr 2021
26. Oesch, S., Ruoti, S.: That was then, this is now: a security evaluation of password generation, storage, and autofill in browser-based password managers. In: 29th USENIX Security Symposium (USENIX Security 2020), pp. 2165–2182. USENIX Association (2020)
27. Ormandy, T.: Issue 1930: lastpass: bypassing do_popupregister() leaks credentials from previous site (2019). https://bugs.chromium.org/p/project-zero/issues/detail?id=1930. Accessed 15 Apr 2021
28. Pearman, S., Zhang, S.A., Bauer, L., Christin, N., Cranor, L.F.: Why people (don't) use password managers effectively. In: Fifteenth Symposium On Usable Privacy and Security (SOUPS 2019), pp. 319–338. USENIX Association, Santa Clara (2019)

29. Pearson, K.: X. on the criterion that a given system of deviations from the probable in the case of a correlated system of variables is such that it can be reasonably supposed to have arisen from random sampling. London Edinburgh Dublin Philos. Mag. J. Sci. **50**(302), 157–175 (1900)
30. Pittman, J.M., Robinson, N.: Shades of perception- user factors in identifying password strength (2020)
31. Roy, A., Memon, N., Ross, A.: MasterPrint: exploring the vulnerability of partial fingerprint-based authentication systems. IEEE Trans. Inf. Forensics Secur. **12**(9), 2013–2025 (2017)
32. Seiler-Hwang, S., Arias-Cabarcos, P., Marín, A., Almenares, F., Díaz-Sánchez, D., Becker, C.: "I don't see why i would ever want to use it": analyzing the usability of popular smartphone password managers. In: Proceedings of the 2019 ACM SIGSAC Conference on Computer and Communications Security, CCS 2019, pp. 1937–1953. Association for Computing Machinery, New York (2019)
33. Silver, D., Jana, S., Boneh, D., Chen, E., Jackson, C.: Password managers: attacks and defenses. In: 23rd USENIX Security Symposium (USENIX Security 2014), pp. 449–464. USENIX Association, San Diego (2014)
34. Statcounter: Mobile Operating System Market Share Worldwide (2022). https://gs.statcounter.com/os-market-share/mobile/worldwide. Accessed 5 Aug 2022
35. Stock, B., Johns, M.: Protecting users against XSS-based password manager abuse. In: Proceedings of the 9th ACM Symposium on Information, Computer and Communications Security, ASIA CCS 2014, pp. 183–194. Association for Computing Machinery, New York (2014)
36. Wheeler, D.L.: zxcvbn: low-budget password strength estimation. In: 25th USENIX Security Symposium (USENIX Security 2016), pp. 157–173. USENIX Association, Austin (2016)
37. Zhang, X., Du, W.: Attacks on android clipboard. In: Dietrich, S. (ed.) DIMVA 2014. LNCS, vol. 8550, pp. 72–91. Springer, Cham (2014). https://doi.org/10.1007/978-3-319-08509-8_5

# The Design and Application of a Unified Ontology for Cyber Security

Khandakar Ashrafi Akbar[1]([☒]), Fariha Ishrat Rahman[1], Anoop Singhal[2],
Latifur Khan[1], and Bhavani Thuraisingham[1]

[1] The University of Texas at Dallas, Richardson, USA
{khandakarashrafi.akbar,farihaishrat.rahman,lkhan,bxt043000}@utdallas.edu
[2] National Institute of Standards and Technology, Gaithersburg, USA
anoop.singhal@nist.gov

**Abstract.** Ontology enables semantic interoperability, making it highly valuable for cyber threat hunting. Community-driven frameworks like MITRE ATT&CK, D3FEND, ENGAGE, CWE and CVE have been developed to combat cyber threats. However, manually navigating these independent data sources is time-consuming and impractical in high-stakes situations. By adopting an ontology-based approach, these cybersecurity resources can be unified, enabling a holistic view of the threat landscape. Additionally, leveraging semantic query languages empowers analysts to make the most of existing data sources. This paper explores how through the application of a semantic query language (SPARQL) on a unified cybersecurity ontology, analysts can effectively exploit the information contained within these resources to strengthen their defense strategies against cyber threats.

**Keywords:** Ontology · OWL · SPARQL · Cybersecurity

## 1 Introduction

In an era of unprecedented network expansion, the ever-growing scale of computer networks has paved the way for malicious entities to orchestrate large-scale attacks, posing a substantial risk to the individuals and organizations that rely on these interconnected systems. Compounding this threat is the relentless ingenuity of attackers, who seek out novel methods to infiltrate and compromise systems, requiring constant vigilance and robust defensive strategies to safeguard against these evolving cyber risks.

Advanced Persistent Threats (APTs) represent a category of highly sophisticated cyber threats carried out by known groups of actors, who have been identified by the tactics, techniques, and procedures (TTPs) they use [20]. While APTs pose significant challenges due to their evolutionary nature [10], the security community remains committed to its ongoing effort to improve defense against these attacks. Information sharing plays a crucial role in this effort; knowledge about

© The Author(s), under exclusive license to Springer Nature Switzerland AG 2023
V. Muthukkumarasamy et al. (Eds.): ICISS 2023, LNCS 14424, pp. 23–41, 2023.
https://doi.org/10.1007/978-3-031-49099-6_2

the perpetrators, their methods, and targets is disclosed through various government and industry channels [20]. The frameworks and data sources, MITRE ATT&CK, D3FEND, ENGAGE, CWE and CVE offer valuable insights into the tactics and techniques employed by threat actors, the weaknesses and vulnerabilities they exploit, and effective countermeasures. However, the information pertaining to APTs is scattered across these different resources, highlighting the need for consolidation to facilitate effective analysis and improve mitigation strategies.

Technical contextualization in cybersecurity is necessary for a prompt, successful cyber threat response. Particularly in post-compromise scenarios, the effectiveness of defending against adversarial behavior significantly improves when analysts can efficiently narrow down their focus, disregarding irrelevant information through analytics [21]. The key challenge faced by analysts is the overwhelming volume of information they need to access in order to effectively analyze incoming attacks. This information gap can significantly impede analysts when responding to time-sensitive threats. In our proposal, we introduce a tool that aims to bridge the information gap by providing analysts with relevant knowledge quickly and efficiently. This is achieved through the creation of an ontology, which streamlines the process of accessing pertinent information in just a few steps.

Ontologies are formal representations of knowledge about a domain, and they provide a structured way to represent the components and relationships of a network. By using ontologies, it is possible to gain a deeper understanding to aid in identifying and preventing the spread of attacks. We developed a knowledge base (KB) in the form of an ontology. This knowledge base (KB) serves to establish connections between various components within the cybersecurity domain. It links ATT&CK tactics and techniques, weaknesses documented in the Common Weakness Enumeration (CWE) database, vulnerabilities listed in the Common Vulnerabilities and Exposures (CVE) database, defensive solutions outlined in MITRE's D3FEND framework, and adversary engagement techniques from MITRE's ENGAGE framework.

By linking these different elements, the KB provides a comprehensive understanding of the relationships between attack techniques, weaknesses, vulnerabilities, defensive solutions, and adversary engagement techniques. This integrated information allows for a more holistic approach to cybersecurity, enabling organizations to identify potential threats, assess their impact, develop effective defensive strategies, and employ adversary engagement techniques to better understand and counteract adversaries.

Without proper inference capabilities provided by an existing KB, security analysts may struggle to extract the necessary information for pre-offensive and defensive tasks. Therefore, our ontology's inferential capability proves valuable in cybersecurity scenarios, such as detecting ongoing attack tactics or techniques and identifying the vulnerabilities that may have contributed to the situation. By utilizing the association information within our ontology, analysts can identify and remove the responsible application from other systems, mitigating potential repercussions.

To demonstrate the utility of our ontology, we can explore the following scenario. The APT kill chain unfolds in stages, and each stage can be linked to one or more tactics from the ATT&CK framework. Once the current stage of an APT campaign is identified, we can leverage SPARQL queries on our ontology to infer the potential tactics and techniques that might be utilized in the subsequent stages. This information enables us to make additional inferences and retrieve all the defensive countermeasures associated with these attack techniques. In the event that a specific attack technique is identified, we can retrieve the corresponding CVE tags, which can further assist in narrowing down the search for suitable countermeasures. Additionally, by retrieving a list of affected products that exhibit these vulnerabilities, we can proactively address and remedy the potential security issues.

Our ontology, coupled with the utilization of SPARQL queries and the integration of multiple data sources, facilitates a faster response to cybersecurity incidents.

Our contribution can be summarised as follows:

1. Construction of a Unified Ontology that serves as a comprehensive Knowledge Base encompassing APT tactics/techniques, weaknesses, vulnerabilities, adversary engagement techniques, and defense countermeasures.
2. Investigation of semantic queries (SPARQL) to extract relevant context and relationships from the Ontology, which can be utilized to draw meaningful inferences and accelerate the response process.

The rest of the paper is structured into six sections. Section 2 provides an introduction to semantic web technologies and the data sources utilized in building the ontology. In Sect. 3, the construction process of our ontology is explained. In Sect. 4, we demonstrate the practical use case of our ontology through example SPARQL queries that extract valuable insights. Section 5 discusses related work in the field, while Sect. 6 outlines potential areas for future research. Finally, Sect. 7 presents the conclusion of the study.

## 2 Background

In this section, we provide an introduction to the semantic web technologies employed for building and exploring our ontology. Subsequently, we present an overview of the data sources utilized in constructing the ontology.

### 2.1 Semantic Web Technologies

RDF [26], or the Resource Description Framework, is a versatile framework designed to represent interconnected data on the web. It provides a simple data model based on subject-predicate-object triples, allowing the description of relationships between resources. RDF's capacity to integrate data from diverse sources makes it a comprehensive proposition language, capable of unifying and consolidating heterogeneous data from multiple origins [23]. OWL [24] is an expressive language for creating ontologies. It extends RDF by providing additional constructs and vocabulary to define classes, properties, and relationships in a more structured and semantically rich manner. OWL allows for the specification of logical constraints, reasoning capabilities, and inference rules to enable automated reasoning and deduction over the ontology. SPARQL [25], a semantic query language for databases, is specifically designed to query and manipulate data stored in the Resource Description Framework (RDF) format. It has been employed to execute queries on the RDF data generated from the ontology.

## 2.2   Data Sources

The ontology is developed using cyber threat intelligence sourced from the following MITRE frameworks and datasources – ATT&CK (Adversarial Tactics, Techniques, and Common Knowledge), D3FEND (Detection, Denial, and Disruption Framework Empowering Network Defense), ENGAGE, CWE(Common Weakness Enumeration), and CVE(Common Vulnerabilities and Exposures).

**ATT&CK** [6] is a comprehensive knowledge base that focuses on adversary behavior and tactics observed in real-world cyber attacks. It categorizes various tactics, techniques, and sub-techniques used by threat actors, providing insights into their strategies and methodologies. The enterprise attack matrix has served as a foundational resource for constructing our ontology. This matrix provides an overview of 14 attack tactics, which are further categorized into 196 techniques and 411 sub-techniques. APT attacks follow a seven-stage kill chain [27], including Initial Compromise, Establish Foothold, Escalate Privileges, Internal Reconnaissance, Move Laterally, Maintain Presence, and Complete Mission. Attackers employ tactics from the MITRE ATT&CK framework throughout these stages. Understanding these stages and tactics helps organizations defend against APT attacks.

**D3FEND** [4] is designed to complement ATT&CK by focusing on defensive techniques and countermeasures. The D3FEND matrix describes 6 defensive tactics, which are further categorized into 22 techniques and 154 sub-techniques. These defensive tactics and techniques are directly linked to Digital Artifact Objects (DAOs), which, in turn, are connected to offensive techniques. The relationship between offensive techniques and defensive countermeasures is established through these DAOs.

**ENGAGE** [7] provides a framework that aligns defenders, vendors, and decision-makers by capturing real-world adversary behavior and guiding strategic cyber outcomes. The ENGAGE Matrix is composed of three main components: Goals, Approaches, and Activities. When adversaries exhibit specific behaviors or techniques from the ATT&CK framework, they inadvertently expose vulnerabilities or weaknesses. By understanding these weaknesses, we can devise engagement activities that exploit these vulnerabilities and enhance our defensive capabilities. Mapping the engagement activities in MITRE Engage to specific ATT&CK techniques ensures that each activity is directly informed by observed adversary behavior. For instance, if an adversary demonstrates the Remote System Discovery technique (T1018), they may be vulnerable to collecting, observing, or manipulating deceptive system artifacts or information. Armed with this knowledge, defenders can strategize and employ tactics such as using lures to elicit desired behaviors from the adversary, leveraging additional or advanced capabilities against the target, or influencing the adversary's dwell time within the compromised environment [5].

**CWE** [3] is a collection of weaknesses found in software and hardware. These weaknesses can arise in various aspects such as architecture, design, code, or implementation, and can potentially lead to exploitable security vulnerabilities. The purpose of CWE is to provide a standardized language for describing these weaknesses, serving as a benchmark for security tools targeting these weaknesses, and establishing a common standard for identifying, mitigating, and preventing weaknesses. In essence, a weakness refers to a condition in a software, firmware, hardware, or service component that, in specific circumstances, could contribute to the introduction of vulnerabilities.

**CVE** [9] is a comprehensive list of publicly known vulnerabilities. Each entry in the Common Vulnerabilities and Exposures (CVE) database, includes an identification number, a description, and references to publicly known cybersecurity vulnerabilities. The entries may also provide additional information such as fixes, severity scores, impact ratings based on the Common Vulnerability Scoring System (CVSS), and links to exploit and advisory information. Weaknesses are errors that can lead to vulnerabilities [3], therefore, a connection can be established between CWE and CVE entries. This relationship between CVE and CWE implies that the Vulnerability is an example of the (type of) Weakness [11].

## 3   Ontological Design

Our ontology builds upon the work presented by Akbar et al. [2] and extends its scope by incorporating the MITRE D3FEND and ENGAGE framework. Furthermore, in contrast to their approach of associating vulnerability information solely through the CVETag property, our work takes it a step further by integrating CWE weaknesses and CVE vulnerabilities as distinct classes. This expansion provides access to additional properties such as CVSS scores and information about specific products affected by the vulnerabilities. By incorporating these elements, our approach offers a more comprehensive representation of weaknesses, vulnerabilities, countermeasures and adversary engagements, enhancing the overall knowledge representation within the ontology.

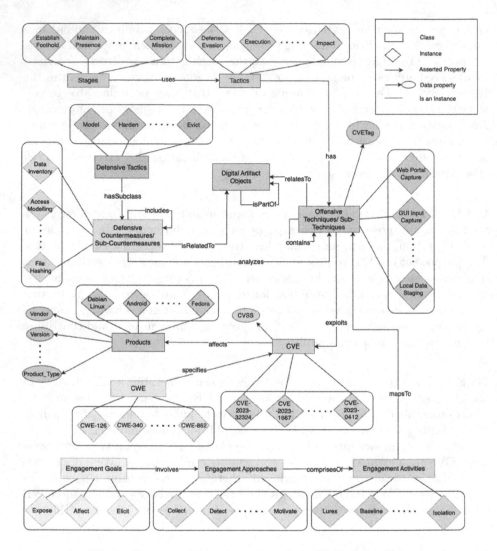

**Fig. 1.** Conceptual Representation of the Unified Ontology

## 3.1   WAVED: Unified Ontology

Figure 1 illustrates the conceptual representation of our proposed ontology –
WAVED (**W**eakness, **A**tt&ck, **V**ulnerability, **E**ngage, **D**3fend). Our extended
ontology encompasses a total of 14 classes – Stages, Tactics, Techniques, Sub-
Techniques, CWE, CVE, Products, DAO (Digital Artifact Object), Defensive

Tactics, Countermeasures, Sub Countermeasures, Engagement Goals, Engagement Approaches and Engagement Activities. These classes represent different entities within the ontology and are linked to each other. Table 1 provides an overview of the classes that were used to build the ontology and the number of instances for each class. Table 2 provides an overview of the object properties that links these classes together.

The relationships among the instances of these classes are defined below:

1. **uses:** APT attack employs attack tactics in different stages of the kill chain.
2. **has:** Each attack tactic can be accomplished via different attack techniques.
3. **contains:** Each attack technique may or may not contain sub-techniques.
4. **relatesTo:** This relationship links offensive techniques and sub-techniques to Digital Artifact Objects (DAOs).
5. **isRelatedTo:** Countermeasures and sub-countermeasures are linked to DAOs through this relationship.
6. **isPartOf:** Digital Artifact Objects (DAOs) form a hierarchical structure, with certain DAOs being part of other DAOs.
7. **analyzes:** This provides a direct link between defensive countermeasures/ sub-countermeasures and offensive techniques/sub-techniques.
8. **hasSubclass:** Countermeasures are a subclass of defense tactics.
9. **includes:** Countermeasures may be further specified into sub-countermeasures.
10. **exploits:** Offensive techniques/sub-techniques exploit vulnerabilities documented in the CVE.
11. **affects:** A product is affected by one or more vulnerabilities listed in the CVE.
12. **specifies:** This relationship links CWE entries to CVE entries.
13. **mapsTo:** Engagement activities are mapped to attack techniques/sub-techniques.
14. **comprisesOf:** Engagement activities are organized under engagement approaches.
15. **involves:** Engagement approaches are organized under engagement goals.

**Table 1.** Overview of Ontology classes.

| Class | Instances | Description |
|---|---|---|
| Stages | 7 | The seven stages of the APT kill chain: 1) Initial Compromise, 2) Establish Foothold, 3) Escalate Privileges, 4) Internal Reconnaissance, 5) Move Laterally, 6) Maintain Presence, and 7) Complete Mission |
| Tactics | 14 | Refers to tactics from the attack matrix. An attack tactic refers to a high-level category or strategy used by threat actors to achieve their objectives. It represents a broad approach or methodology employed in a cyber attack |
| Techniques | 196 | The means by which threat actors achieve their tactical objectives. These techniques represent specific actions, methods, or tools used by adversaries to carry out their attacks. Each technique is associated with a particular tactic |
| Sub-Techniques | 411 | ATT&CK techniques can be further categorized into sub-techniques |
| Defensive Tactics | 6 | The elements of the D3FEND matrix are classified into six high-level categories: Model, Harden, Detect, Isolate, Deceive, and Evict. These categories serve as a framework for organizing and classifying the various techniques and countermeasures available to defenders |
| Countermeasures | 22 | Each defensive tactic contains several techniques that describe how to implement appropriate strategies to counter cyber threats |
| Sub-Countermeasures | 154 | Countermeasures can be further classified into sub-countermeasures |
| DAO | 521 | The D3FEND matrix uses the concept of digital artifacts to establish connections between the defensive techniques with the offensive techniques from the ATT&CK framework |
| CWE | 1395* | List of publicly known weaknesses found in software and hardware |
| CVE | 206798* | List of publicly known cybersecurity vulnerabilities |
| Products | 37465* | List of products that are affected by one or more vulnerabilities documented in the CVE database |
| Engagement Goals | 3 | ENGAGE matrix provides 3 engagement goals – Expose, Affect, and Elicit that describe the desired outcomes of adversary engagement operations |
| Engagement Approaches | 7 | High-level methods or strategies used to engage the adversary |
| Engagement Activities | 23 | Concrete techniques or actions used to implement the engagement approaches |

* To demonstrate the use case of our ontology, only a subset of these instances were utilized in its construction.

**Table 2.** Object Properties of the Ontology

| Property | Domain | Range |
|----------|--------|-------|
| uses | Stages | Tactics |
| has | Tactics | Techniques |
| contains | Techniques | Sub-techniques |
| relatesTo | Techniques, Sub-Techniques | DAO |
| isRelatedTo | Countermeasures, Sub-Countermeasures | DAO |
| isPartOf | DAO | DAO |
| hasSubclass | Defensive-Tactics | Countermeasures |
| includes | Countermeasures | Sub-Countermeasures |
| analyzes | Countermeasures, Sub-Countermeasures | Techniques, Sub-Techniques |
| exploits | Techniques, Sub-Techniques | CVE |
| affects | CVE | Products |
| specifies | CWE | CVE |
| mapsTo | Engagement-Activities | Techniques, Sub-Techniques |
| comprisesOf | Engagement-Approaches | Engagement-Activities |
| involves | Engagement-Goals | Engagement-Approaches |

# 4   Querying Ontology for Security Insights

Semantic query language can be used to explore and make inferences from the ontology. In this section, we showcase examples of sparql queries that can be applied to our unified ontology to gain security insight and help analysts combat cyber threats.

SPARQL is a valuable tool for querying ontologies due to its capabilities in handling complex joins and relationships among entities and properties within the ontology. It enables the execution of analytic query operations, such as joins, sorting, aggregation, and filtering. SPARQL's flexibility and functionality make it well-suited for querying ontologies and extracting meaningful insights from the data they represent.

## 4.1   Simple Queries

In this section, we will explore some simple SPARQL queries that can be used to retrieve information from classes of a single datasource or to retrieve combined information by joining two datasources. An overview of these queries are presented in Table 3. The first column presents the queries expressed in English, while the second column presents the corresponding queries implemented in SPARQL.

**Table 3.** Examples of simple SPARQL queries

| Query | SPARQL |
|---|---|
| **Q1.** Retrieve CVE tags for a certain adversarial technique (Command and Scripting Interpreter) | PREFIX WAVED: <ontologyURI><br>SELECT ?technique ?value<br>WHERE {<br>    ?technique WAVED:CVETag ?value.<br>    FILTER(?technique=<ontologyURI<br>               #Command_and_Scripting_Interpreter>).<br>} |
| **Q2.** Retrieve products that might contain a particular vulnerability (CVE-2022-24663) | PREFIX WAVED: <ontologyURI><br>SELECT ?CVE ?Products<br>WHERE {<br>    ?CVE WAVED:affects ?Products.<br>    FILTER(?CVE=<ontologyURI#CVE-2022-24663>).} |
| **Q3.** Retrieve specifics of a certain product (Chrome) | PREFIX WAVED: <ontologyURI><br>SELECT ?Products ?Product_Type ?Vendor ?Product<br>       ?Edition ?Language ?Version ?Update<br>WHERE {<br>    ?Products WAVED:Product_Type ?Product_Type.<br>    ?Products WAVED:Vendor ?Vendor.<br>    ?Products WAVED:Product ?Product.<br>    ?Products WAVED:Version ?Version.<br>    ?Products WAVED:Update ?Update.<br>    ?Products WAVED:Edition ?Edition.<br>    ?Products WAVED:Language ?Language.<br>    FILTER(?Products=<ontologyURI#Chrome>).<br>} |
| **Q4.** Retrieve APT stage, tactic, technique/ sub-technique associated with a specific CVE Tag (CVE-2019-1943) | PREFIX WAVED: <ontologyURI><br>SELECT ?stage ?tactic ?technique ?sub-technique<br>WHERE {<br>    ?stage WAVED:uses ?tactic.<br>    ?tactic WAVED:has ?technique.<br>    ?technique WAVED:contains ?sub-technique.<br>    ?technique WAVED:CVETag  "CVE-2019-1943".<br>} |
| **Q5.** Retrieve defensive countermeasures that are related to the same attack technique | PREFIX WAVED: <ontologyURI><br>SELECT ?countermeasure1 ?attack_technique1<br>WHERE {<br>    ?countermeasure1 WAVED:analyzes ?attack_technique1<br>    {<br>      SELECT ?countermeasure2 ?attack_technique2<br>      WHERE {<br>        ?countermeasure2 WAVED:analyzes<br>                    ?attack_technique2.<br>      }<br>    }<br>    FILTER(?attack_technique1= ?attack_technique2).<br>} |

*(continued)*

**Table 3.** (*continued*)

| Query | SPARQL |
|---|---|
| **Q6.** Retrieve all defensive countermeasures for a certain attack technique (Boolkit) | PREFIX WAVED: <ontologyURI><br>SELECT ?countermeasures<br>WHERE {<br>    ?technique WAVED:analyzes ?attack_techniques.<br>    FILTER(?attack_techniques =<ontologyURI<br>               #Boolkit>).<br>} |
| **Q7.** Retrieve all connected attack techniques to a defensive countermeasure (Bootloader Authentication) | PREFIX WAVED: <ontologyURI><br>SELECT ?attack_techniques<br>WHERE {<br>    ?countermeasures WAVED:analyzes ?attack_techniques.<br>    FILTER(?countermeasures =<ontologyURI<br>            #Bootloader_Authentication>).<br>} |
| **Q8.** Associate defensive countermeasures with attack techniques through DAOs | PREFIX WAVED: <ontologyURI><br>SELECT ?countermeasure ?attack_technique<br>WHERE {<br>    ?countermeasure WAVED:isRelatedTo ?dao.<br>    ?attack_technique WAVED:relatesTo ?dao.<br>} |
| **Q9.** Retrieve countermeasures when a specific attack technique is detected (Valid Accounts) | PREFIX WAVED: <ontologyURI><br>SELECT ?attack_techniques<br>WHERE {<br>    ?countermeasures WAVED:analyzes ?attack_techniques.<br>    FILTER(?attack_techniques=<ontologyURI<br>            #Valid_Accounts>).<br>} |
| **Q10.** Retrieve engagement activity mapped to a certain adversarial technique (Remote System Discovery) | PREFIX WAVED: <ontologyURI><br>SELECT ?technique ?engagement-activity<br>WHERE {<br>    ?technique WAVED:mapsTo ?engagement-activity.<br>    FILTER(?technique=<ontologyURI<br>            #Remote_System_Discovery>).<br>} |
| **Q11.** Retrieve CWE entry associated to a specific CVE (CVE-2009-1699) | PREFIX WAVED: <ontologyURI><br>SELECT ?CWE ?CVE<br>WHERE {<br>    ?CWE WAVED:specifies ?CVE.<br>    FILTER(?CVE=<ontologyURI#CVE-2009-1699>).<br>} |
| **Q12.** Retrieve all CVE entries associated to a specific CWE (CWE-611) | PREFIX WAVED: <ontologyURI><br>SELECT ?CWE ?CVE<br>WHERE {<br>    ?CWE WAVED:specifies ?CVE.<br>    FILTER(?CWE=<ontologyURI#CWE-611>).<br>} |

Q1 demonstrates how our ontology enables us to query and retrieve vulnerabilities that are susceptible to specific adversarial techniques. Conversely, we can also perform reverse queries to obtain information about adversarial stages, tactics, techniques, and sub-techniques linked to a particular CVE tag, as demonstrated in Q4 using the example "CVE-2019-1943". The result of this query is presented in Table 4. This highlights the bidirectional nature of our ontology in providing insights into the relationship between adversarial techniques and vulnerabilities.

**Table 4.** Result from SPARQL Query Q4

| Stage | Tactic | Technique | Sub-Technique |
|---|---|---|---|
| Completed Mission | Impact | Data Manipulation | Transmitted Data Manipulation |
| Completed Mission | Impact | Data Manipulation | Stored Data Manipulation |
| Completed Mission | Impact | Data Manipulation | Runtime Data Manipulation |
| .... | ..... | ...... | ..... |

Our ontology also enables the identification of products that may be affected by specific vulnerabilities. Q2 exemplifies this by querying for such products. By delving deeper into the information, as shown in Q3, security analysts can obtain comprehensive details about the involved products. This knowledge empowers them to evaluate whether a specific version of a product is present in their system and take appropriate actions if any vulnerability associated with that version is detected.

Q5 provides a comprehensive list of defensive countermeasures organized by attack techniques. This query can be further refined to focus on specific attack techniques of interest. For example, Q6 retrieves the countermeasures associated with the "Boolkit" attack technique. By reviewing the list of defensive countermeasures linked to a particular attack technique, security analysts can explore alternative approaches if one countermeasure proves ineffective. This query empowers analysts to make informed decisions and adapt their defensive strategies based on the available options and their effectiveness in countering specific attack techniques. Conversely, Q7 focuses on retrieving all attack techniques connected to a specific defensive countermeasure, specifically those associated with "Bootloader Authentication". Table 5 presents a subset of the list of attack techniques linked to this defensive countermeasure, providing valuable insights into the potential threats that this countermeasure aims to mitigate.

**Table 5.** Result from SPARQL Query Q7

| Attack Techniques |
| --- |
| Software Packing |
| AppCert DLLs |
| Dynamic-Link Library Injection |
| Thread Execution Hijacking |
| File Deletion |
| Application Layer Protocol |
| ... |

The ontology leverages Digital Artifact Objects (DAOs) to establish connections between defensive countermeasures or sub-countermeasures and offensive techniques or sub-techniques. Q8 is designed to retrieve this mapping, showcasing the relationship between countermeasures and attack techniques. A snippet of the result from this query is provided in Table 6, offering a glimpse into the interconnectedness of defensive measures and offensive techniques within the ontology.

**Table 6.** Result from SPARQL Query Q8

| Countermeasures | Attack Techniques |
| --- | --- |
| Credential Compromise Scope Analysis | OS Credential Dumping |
| Authentication Cache Invalidation | Additional Cloud Credentials |
| Credential Revoking | Unsecured Credentials |
| Decoy Session Token | Unsecured Credentials |
| ...... | ...... |

By correlating engagement activities in MITRE Engage with specific ATT&CK techniques, we can determine the appropriate engagement activity to exploit vulnerabilities demonstrated by adversaries. Q10 demonstrates this by retrieving the engagement activity associated with the use of the Remote System Discovery technique by adversaries.

A CWE entry is associated with a collection of CVE vulnerability entries. This connection allows for the identification of similar vulnerabilities across different operating systems and applications, which can occur due to shared software development practices or coding styles. When anticipating an upcoming attack stage, it is crucial to not only focus on individual vulnerabilities but also understand the underlying weaknesses present in the system. By analyzing the weakness associated with a vulnerability, it becomes possible to proactively assess the potential presence of other vulnerabilities that may stem from the same weakness. This holistic approach, rather than addressing vulnerabilities in isolation, allows for a more comprehensive understanding of the system's security landscape. By querying the ontology, Q11 demonstrates how the weakness associated with a specific vulnerability can be retrieved, while Q12 showcases how all vulnerabilities organized under a particular weakness can be retrieved. These capabilities enable security analysts to take preemptive actions and mitigate potential risks before they can be exploited.

## 4.2    Advanced Queries

To fully unlock the potential of our ontology, having access to a complete and comprehensive context is vital. This underscores the importance of being able to execute a single query that can instantly retrieve information from multiple data sources. In this section, we explore complex queries that facilitate such capabilities.

The primary use case of our ontology is focused on detecting and mitigating Advanced Persistent Threat (APT) campaigns. When a specific stage of an APT campaign is detected in a system, it indicates that the attacker may advance to the next stage at any time. To effectively mitigate these threats, prompt identification and patching of vulnerabilities in the system is essential. It is not only crucial to identify the vulnerabilities that may be exploited but also to identify appropriate analysis tools to defend against or mitigate an imminent attack.

Figure 2 illustrates an example query in which the adversary has already established a foothold in the system. The next stage anticipated is "Escalate Privileges". By using this query, we can retrieve information about the vulnerabilities that the adversary is likely to exploit in the next stage. Additionally, the query allows us to identify the appropriate countermeasures that can be taken to defend against these vulnerabilities and hinder the adversary's progress.

```
PREFIX owl: <http://www.w3.org/2002/07/owl#>
PREFIX rdf: <http://www.w3.org/1999/02/22-rdf-syntax-ns#>
PREFIX rdfs: <http://www.w3.org/2000/01/rdf-schema#>
PREFIX WAVED: <OntologyURI>

SELECT ?Stage ?Vulnerability ?Countermeasure
WHERE{
            ?Stage WAVED:uses ?Tactic.
            ?Tactic WAVED:has ?Technique.
            ?Technique WAVED:CVETag ?Vulnerability.
            ?Countermeasure WAVED:analyzes ?Technique.
            FILTER(?Stage = <OntologyURI#Escalate_Privileges>).
}
```

**Fig. 2.** Retrieve Vulnerabilities and Countermeasures associated with the APT Stage "Escalate Privileges"

However, with the proliferation of technology across various domains, the number of vulnerabilities has significantly increased, posing a challenge in determining which vulnerabilities should be addressed without significant delays. Our ontology addresses this challenge by providing a list of associated vulnerabilities that require immediate attention. By extending the ontology to include severity scores of CVEs and information on software prone to these vulnerabilities, security analysts can prioritize and address the most critical vulnerabilities promptly.

Figure 3 demonstrates how when a weakness (CWE-125) is identified within a system, we can retrieve the vulnerability, attack technique and countermeasures associated with it in descending order of CVSS Score so that the most critical vulnerabilities may be tackled first.

In summary, our ontology plays a vital role in detecting APT campaigns, prioritizing vulnerability patching, identifying appropriate analysis tools, and selecting defensive countermeasures and engagement activities to effectively defend against sophisticated cyber threats. Its holistic approach to vulnerability management and threat mitigation enhances the effectiveness of cybersecurity efforts in addressing complex and evolving threats.

```
PREFIX owl: <http://www.w3.org/2002/07/owl#>
PREFIX rdf: <http://www.w3.org/1999/02/22-rdf-syntax-ns#>
PREFIX rdfs: <http://www.w3.org/2000/01/rdf-schema#>
PREFIX WAVED: <OntologyURI#>
SELECT ?CVE ?CWE ?CVSS  ?attacktechnique ?countermeasure

WHERE{
            ?CWE WAVED:specifies ?CVE.
            ?CVE WAVED:CVSS_Score ?CVSS.
            ?attacktechnique WAVED:exploits ?CVE.
            ?countermeasure WAVED:analyzes ?attacktechnique.
            FILTER(?CWE = <OntologyURI#CWE-125>).
}
ORDER BY DESC(?CVSS)
```

**Fig. 3.** Retrieve CVE, Attack Techniques and Countermeasures for a given weakness (CWE-125) in descending order of CVSS Score

## 5   Related Work

Ontologies have proven to be effective and robust solutions for representing domain-specific knowledge, integrating data from diverse sources, and enabling various semantic applications [19]. This is evident in various domains, including the Internet of Things (IoT) [16] and Information Selection [13,14], where ontology-based approaches have been applied to enhance data integration, knowledge representation, and semantic reasoning.

According to the study conducted by JASON [8], constructing a common language and a set of basic concepts within the cybersecurity research community is vital for making significant progress in the field. As cybersecurity deals with adversaries, these concepts may evolve over time, but having a shared language and agreed-upon experimental protocols will facilitate hypothesis testing and concept validation.

Threat intelligence plays a crucial role in enhancing security operations by providing evidence-based knowledge about current and potential cyber threats. This leads to improved efficiency and effectiveness in detecting and preventing such threats. To effectively organize and represent this knowledge, tools like taxonomies, sharing standards, and ontologies are used. However, upon analyzing existing taxonomies, sharing standards, and ontologies, it becomes apparent that a comprehensive threat intelligence ontology is lacking [15]. This underscores the need for the development of a more encompassing ontology to address this gap and enable more cohesive and coherent cybersecurity research efforts.

In the domain of network security, several existing ontologies have been developed to capture domain-specific concepts and relationships. Obrst et al. [17] proposed a methodology for creating ontologies based on well-defined ones that can be used as modular sub-ontologies. They emphasized the usefulness of existing schemas, dictionaries, glossaries, and standards as a means of knowledge acquisition for defining an ontology.

Oltramari et al. [18] introduced a three-layer cyber security ontology called CRATELO with the goal of improving the situational awareness of security analysts and enabling optimal operational decisions through semantic representation. They built upon existing ontologies, extending them to include security-related middle-level ontology (SECCO) and low-level sub-ontology (OSCO) for capturing domain-specific scenarios related to threats, vulnerabilities, attacks, countermeasures, and assets.

STUCCO [12] is another notable example of a network security ontology that collects data from security systems and integrates it into a network security knowledge graph. It consolidates information from various structured data sources and establishes relationships among different entity types, such as software, vulnerabilities, and attacks.

The Unified Cybersecurity Ontology (UCO) [22], developed by Syed et al., focuses on integrating various cybersecurity ontologies, heterogeneous data schemes, and common cybersecurity standards to facilitate the sharing and exchange of cyber threat intelligence. UCO aims to unify the representation of threat and vulnerability data within knowledge graphs and ontologies.

Similarly, BRON [11] utilizes a single bidirectional graph to connect entries from different sources, ranging from tactics to vulnerable software. This relational approach enables the representation and analysis of various aspects of network security.

Our ontology improves upon existing implementations by integrating a more diverse and comprehensive range of data sources. It goes beyond just capturing attacks and vulnerabilities to include countermeasures and adversary engagement techniques, providing a broader scope for analysis. Additionally, our paper highlights how our ontology enriches the context and enhances inferential capabilities by leveraging semantic query language to explore the extensive and diverse data sources integrated within the ontology.

# 6    Limitations and Future Work

This paper primarily focuses on the modeling and querying of a cybersecurity ontology. However, there is room for future work beyond the scope of this paper that could explore semi-automating the construction process of the ontology. The manual effort required for establishing associations between classes within the ontology, such as defensive and offensive techniques, as well as linking attack techniques with CVE tags, does come with its limitations. It's worth noting that even existing frameworks like D3FEND rely on manual knowledge base generation, which demands significant human effort. The challenge becomes more evident when trying to associate new defensive techniques with existing attack techniques or zero-day attack methods. This underscores the pressing need for automation in the association process, where machine learning and data-driven approaches could offer substantial assistance [1].

Additionally, there may be gaps and missing links within the ontology that require attention. This presents an opportunity for future enhancement by incorporating natural language processing (NLP) techniques. The automation potential of NLP can prove invaluable in predicting and establishing these missing links within the ontology, significantly boosting its overall completeness and accuracy. Moreover, NLP can be leveraged to extract pertinent information from diverse sources such as reports, blogs, and threat report websites. By doing so, we can enrich the ontology with up-to-date insights and data. Through the synergistic integration of NLP and diverse data sources, the ontology can be expanded and improved upon.

To bolster the paper's contributions and provide tangible evidence of the ontology's effectiveness in real-world cybersecurity scenarios, empirical studies are imperative. At present, empirical validation is an aspect that remains unaddressed, yet it is absolutely vital for gauging the practical applicability of the proposed ontology. Looking ahead, we have concrete plans to take action in this regard. Specifically, we are committed to releasing an all-encompassing tool that incorporates our current ontology. This tool will be meticulously designed to assist security analysts in their day-to-day tasks. This practical tool will enable us to collect empirical evidence regarding the utility and real-world impact of our ontology.

# 7    Conclusion

The importance of curated knowledge in the cybersecurity field cannot be overstated. In the face of attack incidents that demand immediate and impactful actions, effective knowledge management plays a crucial role in providing guidance to security analysts. Whether it is an individual or an organization, minimizing the damage caused by cyber attacks hinges on the proper dissemination of information. Our ontology serves as a valuable tool for curating knowledge and assisting security analysts in effectively mitigating the continued spread of ongoing cyber attacks.

**Acknowledgement.** The research reported herein was supported in part by NIST Award # 60NANB23D007, NSF awards DMS-1737978, DGE-2039542, OAC-1828467, OAC-1931541, and DGE-1906630, ONR awards N00014-17-1-2995 and N00014-20-1-2738.

**Disclaimer.** Certain equipment, instruments, software, or materials are identified in this paper in order to specify the experimental procedure adequately. Such identification is not intended to imply recommendation or endorsement of any product or service by NIST, nor is it intended to imply that the materials or equipment identified are necessarily the best available for the purpose.

# References

1. Akbar, K.A., Halim, S.M., Hu, Y., Singhal, A., Khan, L., Thuraisingham, B.: Knowledge mining in cybersecurity: from attack to defense. In: Sural, S., Lu, H. (eds.) DBSec 2022. LNCS, vol. 13383, pp. 110–122. Springer, Cham (2022). https://doi.org/10.1007/978-3-031-10684-2_7
2. Akbar, K.A., Halim, S.M., Singhal, A., Abdeen, B., Khan, L., Thuraisingham, B.: The design of an ontology for ATT&CK and its application to cybersecurity. In: Proceedings of the Thirteenth ACM Conference on Data and Application Security and Privacy [Poster Presentation], pp. 295–297 (2023)
3. MITRE Corporation: Common weakness enumeration. https://cwe.mitre.org/
4. MITRE Corporation: A knowledge graph of cybersecurity countermeasures. https://d3fend.mitre.org/
5. MITRE Corporation: Mapping the engage matrix to MITRE ATT&CK. https://engage.mitre.org/wp-content/uploads/2022/05/Mapping-Engage-to-ATTCK.pdf
6. MITRE Corporation: MITRE ATT&CK. https://attack.mitre.org/
7. MITRE Corporation: MITRE engage. https://engage.mitre.org/
8. MITRE Corporation: Science of cyber-security. https://irp.fas.org/agency/dod/jason/cyber.pdf
9. MITRE Corporation: The ultimate security vulnerability data source. https://www.cvedetails.com
10. NIST CSRC: Advanced persistent threat. https://csrc.nist.gov/glossary/term/advanced_persistent_threat
11. Hemberg, E., et al.: Linking threat tactics, techniques, and patterns with defensive weaknesses, vulnerabilities and affected platform configurations for cyber hunting. arXiv preprint arXiv:2010.00533 (2020)
12. Iannacone, M., et al.: Developing an ontology for cyber security knowledge graphs. In: Proceedings of the 10th Annual Cyber and Information Security Research Conference, pp. 1–4 (2015)
13. Khan, L., McLeod, D., Hovy, E.: Retrieval effectiveness of an ontology-based model for information selection. VLDB J. **13**, 71–85 (2004)

14. Luo, F.: Ontology construction for information selection. In: 2002 Proceedings of the 14th IEEE International Conference on Tools with Artificial Intelligence (ICTAI 2002), pp. 122–127. IEEE (2002)

15. Mavroeidis, V., Bromander, S.: Cyber threat intelligence model: an evaluation of taxonomies, sharing standards, and ontologies within cyber threat intelligence. In: 2017 European Intelligence and Security Informatics Conference (EISIC), pp. 91–98. IEEE (2017)

16. Mozzaquatro, B.A., Agostinho, C., Goncalves, D., Martins, J., Jardim-Goncalves, R.: An ontology-based cybersecurity framework for the internet of things. Sens. (Basel Switz.) **18**(9), 3053 (2017). https://doi.org/10.3390/s18093053

17. Obrst, L., Chase, P., Markeloff, R.: Developing an ontology of the cyber security domain. In: Semantic Technologies for Intelligence, Defense, and Security (STIDS), pp. 49–56 (2012)

18. Oltramari, A., Cranor, L.F., Walls, R.J., McDaniel, P.D.: Building an ontology of cyber security. In: Semantic Technologies for Intelligence, Defense, and Security (STIDS), pp. 54–61 (2014)

19. Salatino, A.A., Thanapalasingam, T., Mannocci, A., Birukou, A., Osborne, F., Motta, E.: The computer science ontology: a comprehensive automatically-generated taxonomy of research areas. Data Intell. **2**(3), 379–416 (2020)

20. Shlapentokh-Rothman, M., Kelly, J., Baral, A., Hemberg, E., O'Reilly, U.M.: Coevolutionary modeling of cyber attack patterns and mitigations using public datasets. In: Proceedings of the Genetic and Evolutionary Computation Conference, pp. 714–722 (2021)

21. Strom, B.E., et al.: Finding cyber threats with ATT&CK-based analytics. The MITRE Corporation, Bedford, MA, Technical report No. MTR170202 (2017)

22. Syed, Z., Padia, A., Finin, T., Mathews, L., Joshi, A.: UCO: a unified cybersecurity ontology. UMBC Student Collection (2016)

23. Tomaszuk, D., Hyland-Wood, D.: RDF 1.1: knowledge representation and data integration language for the web. Symmetry **12**(1), 84 (2020)

24. World Wide Web Consortium (W3C): OWL web ontology language guide. Technical report, World Wide Web Consortium (2004). https://www.w3.org/TR/owl-guide/

25. World Wide Web Consortium (W3C): SPARQL query language for RDF. Technical report, World Wide Web Consortium (2008). https://www.w3.org/TR/rdf-sparql-query/

26. World Wide Web Consortium (W3C): Resource description framework (RDF). Technical report, World Wide Web Consortium (2014). https://www.w3.org/RDF/

27. Zou, Q., Sun, X., Liu, P., Singhal, A.: An approach for detection of advanced persistent threat attacks. Computer **53**(12), 92–96 (2020)

# Big Data Forensics on Apache Kafka

Thomas Mager[(✉)]

Bonn, Germany
kafkaforensics@tom84.anonaddy.com

**Abstract.** There is a growing demand for information exchange in the age of the Internet of Things. One common scenario involves transferring data from distributed devices in the field to central servers or cloud environments. However, little research has been done on the possibilities for forensic investigation of supporting infrastructure such as Apache Kafka, which plays a crucial role in modern big data architectures.

In this paper, we present our work on the forensic investigation of Apache Kafka. We use methodologies of reverse engineering to infer the data formats that Apache Kafka uses server-side. The results help us to implement a new module that is able to read Apache Kafka log files. An investigator can load the module in the open-source forensic platform "Autopsy". We highlight possibilities and limitations regarding encryption and data retention in Apache Kafka and suggest to store data decentralized when it comes to sensitive data. As a result of these measures, applications become more resilient to attacks and are able to provide increased security, ethical standards, and freedom for the application users. This can be a unique selling point in future data driven applications.

## 1 Introduction

In our new world of the Internet of Things, there is an ever increasing demand for information exchange. A typical scenario is to transfer data from distributed devices in the field to either central servers on-premises or to cloud environments. However, currently, there is little research about the possibilities for forensic investigation of the supporting infrastructure. We shed light on methods and possibilities for forensic investigation of one essential component in nowadays architectures: Apache Kafka. This enables forensic specialists to perform investigations and leads to approaches that are legally sound and withstand challenges before the court.

Originally developed at LinkedIn [32], the Apache Kafka platform offers functionality not only to process data transfers with extremely high throughput but also provides a way to ease coupling between application components. It can play the role of a software bus where data consumers and producers can join and leave the system at any time and, hence, be the backbone for world wide data movement. Compared to some of its alternatives, such as RabbitMQ, RocketMQ, ActiveMQ, or Pulsar, it offers much greater throughput [1] with great

V. Muthukkumarasamy et al. (Eds.): ICISS 2023, LNCS 14424, pp. 42–56, 2023.
https://doi.org/10.1007/978-3-031-49099-6_3

ability to scale. Also for its reliability and ability to run on common hardware, Apache Kafka is a component of high value in modern big data infrastructures. It is used in the areas of the automotive industry, banks, insurances, logistic services, media, retail, and in the public sector [2]. In a common scenario, Kafka is connected upstream to other big data systems for distributed storage and processing. This includes S3 object storage or HDFS, as well as setups for analytics and artificial intelligence such as the Hadoop ecosystem, Apache Spark [38], TensorFlow, and Keras [37].

In this paper, we provide insights into Apache Kafka's storage internals and enable investigators to perform forensic inspections of clusters running the software.

We first show in Sect. 2 related work in the area of digital infrastructure investigation. Subsequently, in Sect. 3 we give an overview on the general architectural concepts of Apache Kafka. Section 4 outlines our methodologies for reverse engineering Apache Kafka data formats, as well as providing internals of the files holding message payloads. This transparency is crucial for investigators to interpret confiscated data effectively. We discuss security features of Apache Kafka for data in transit and at rest in Sect. 5. In addition, we describe the capabilities and limitations related to deleting messages within the system in Sect. 6.1. We introduce our new Autopsy module for forensic investigation in Sect. 7, followed by a conclusion in Sect. 8.

## 2 Related Work

There are numerous publications in the area of forensic analysis of database systems, including work by Wagner et al. [3] on relational database forensics with a focus on page-based data storage mechanisms. Khanuja et al. [5] have developed a framework specifically for MySQL database forensic analysis, while Beyers et al. [6] have focused on PostgreSQL databases. Pereira [4] has published approaches to recover deleted entries from SQLite databases used in many user applications such as Mozilla Firefox. Chivers et al. [7] have investigated the recovery of database records of Windows Search. Yoon et al. [8] have conducted a forensic case study on the distributed NoSQL database MongoDB.

For general storage analysis e.g. The Sleuth Kit [9] and other tools offer functionality for many file systems. There are also numerous books and studies available specifically for particular file systems, including FAT [11], NTFS [10], EXT2/3/4 [12–15], or XFS [12,16–18].

For forensic analysis of big data systems, Asim et al. [25] have published a detailed approach for the widely used Hadoop Distributed File System (HDFS). While files in HDFS can easily be browsed, viewed, hashed and exported in an operating cluster via HDFS command line, the open source project "Hadoop distributed file system forensics toolkit (HDFS FTK)" [19] also provides insights into a cluster that is offline. HDFS FTK relies not only on the acquired data of Hadoop data nodes, but also requires the metadata stored on name nodes. However, as these studies have focused on the open source release of Hadoop, the work does not consider the implications of the administrative tooling used for cluster rollout and management, such as Apache Ambari [45] or Cloudera Manager. Vulnerabilities of such tool potentially might allow intruders full access [43,43] to the cluster and its data. Bhathal et al. [21] have assessed the security of Hadoop in their conclusion by stating "there is a need to upgrade the complete Hadoop system released with all security features without installing and to configure it separately". The complexity and the missing [21] security features of countless components within Hadoop's ecosystem, its international open source nature dating back to 2005, suggest inconsistency between holding personal-related data within this system and meeting region specific laws such as the GDPR standards of 2018. As of 2023, we have not found any scientific studies or final discussions [20] that contradict the international concerns on the technical security of Hadoop. While a firewall around all involved components improves security, it doesn't offer complete separation between different tenants or their respective processes operating within the cluster. For investigating HDFS, secure deletion tools [23] should be taken into account. Additionally, when dealing with large amounts of data, ethical considerations become relevant and require responsible political and judicial discourse [22].

There are several publications that explain Apache Kafka's general architecture [29,33,36]. Among various use cases described by its inventors back in 2011 [32], numerous papers have used Apache Kafka as an infrastructure component in their system setups for a variety of applications such as recommender systems [31], Security Information and Event Management (SIEM) systems [30], Industrial IoT installations [35], and forensic image classification systems [34].

Despite its widespread use in various applications and systems, to our knowledge there is no study that specifically focuses on forensic inspection of an Apache Kafka cluster.

In general, forensic investigations are likely to involve systems that fall under shadow IT within an organisation. Mallmann et al. [24] provide a comprehensive overview on this topic.

## 3    Architectural Overview on Apache Kafka

The software Apache Kafka typically runs on several interconnected hosts which we call Kafka *brokers*. Together these brokers form one Kafka *cluster* that provides a unified and highly available platform for processing real-time data feeds. Bare-metal systems for brokers are a popular setup to increase performance in deployment scenarios with high throughput. As exemplified in Fig. 1, an arbitrary number of *producers* send messages to the cluster while an arbitrary number of *consumers* read messages from the cluster. Apache Kafka offers developers a basic unit called *topic* to help group and manage similar types of messages. Topics have unique names for identification, given at the time of their creation. As Kafka persists the messages on disk, producers and consumers are not required to be connected with Kafka at the same time.

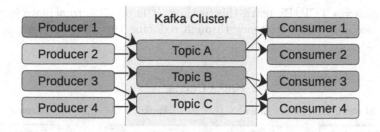

**Fig. 1.** Exemplary data flow from producers to consumers via Kafka topics

Apache Kafka allows developers to add messages to a topic using an immutable appending operation but does not provide functionality for selective removal or modification of existing messages in place. As a result, topics in Apache Kafka can also be referred to as distributed append-only logs.

### 3.1  Data Placement Strategy in Kafka

For forensic investigation it is essential to know where Kafka stores its data within the cluster. This section provides an overview of the data placement strategy as indicated in the Apache Kafka online documentation [27], which will help us better comprehend the internal data placement strategy used by Kafka for fast and scalable data processing.

In Fig. 2 Kafka broker 0 to $b$ form a single distributed *cluster* that stores message data for one exemplary topic $A$. Kafka splits the data of the topic into partitions 0 to $n$ and elects one broker as a *leader* from which other brokers, the so-called *followers*, receive a replica of the partition. Depending on the requirements for broker failure tolerance and performance, a developer can specify the individual number of partitions and replicas for a topic at topic creation time. By default, Kafka creates a total of three partition replicas on different brokers within the same cluster. As a result of this placement strategy and depending on the parameters used by the developer, each broker stores zero or more partitions per topic. In Kafka, producers create messages in the form of tuples consisting of keys and values. An application can use the key to group messages e.g. by an identifier for the origin source of a message. By default, the Kafka producer first calculates the hash value of such key. This hash value modulo the total number of partitions deterministically results in the partition in which Kafka stores the message [28]. In case there is no key provided with a message, Kafka falls back to a round robin approach for partitioning.

Each message within a partition has a unique sequence number, called *offset*. The offset allows to sustain the order of arriving messages. Kafka stores this offset together with the message and a timestamp for creation time.

Kafka employs message serialization as a means of storing and transferring messages. By avoiding additional copies in memory, also known as "zero-copying", data can be passed directly from the read buffer to the socket buffer for transmission via TCP. By using this method, it is possible to achieve improved performance and reduced latency through reducing the number of unnecessary copies.

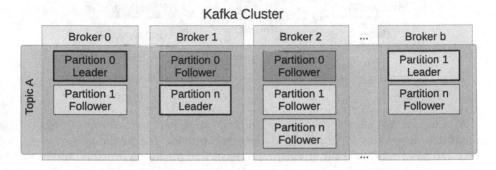

**Fig. 2.** Exemplary Partition Placement for One Topic in Kafka

## 4    Kafka Forensics

In this section, we describe our methodological approach for investigating the inner workings of Apache Kafka and identifying relevant data, which enables us to provide insight into its underlying data structures.

### 4.1    Methodological Approach

In the following we outline our system setup we use to infer our insights. To facilitate our investigation, we utilize CentOS within VirtualBox, allowing us to easily return the system to its original state. Our test system starts a Kafka cluster with three brokers, which is a common setup for production scenarios. Our test system is configured to run Kafka 3.0.0, using the standard configuration. We deploy Apache ZooKeeper for failover handling and specify dedicated ports for each Kafka broker. We perform our analysis on the open source version of Apache Kafka. In our analysis we do not cover vendor specific tools for cluster management (c.f. Sect. 2), Kafka clients, and specific Kafka features involving additional setups such as Kafka Streams or KSQL.

For data generation we use different bash scripts. The first script creates an empty topic with three partitions and two replicas. Subsequently, another script acts as a Kafka producer for the topic and generates iterative data input with incremental key-value pairs.

After the scripts complete, we check the local data folders of the brokers for changes. With the help of a hex editor we inspect the created data via binary reverse engineering. We further utilize the shell script kafka-run-class.sh that Apache Kafka provides. Together with the Java class kafka.tools.DumpLogSegments the script prints the content of the Kafka data files to console. This output allows the comparison with the binary view. Additionally, we perform verifications against the source code [26] of Apache Kafka.

## 4.2   Data of Interest

Depending on the replication setting of topics, one Kafka broker potentially holds all data required for investigation. If no disk encryption is in place, it is possible to power off a broker and remove it from the cluster, while the cluster continues operating. Always securing the data of all Kafka brokers, however, is recommended. We identify the following files and folders of particular interest to secure for investigation:

- The file zookeeper.properties holds the configuration of ZooKeeper, e.g. its data directory and listening port
- Folder dataDir as specified in zookeeper.properties (default is /tmp/zookeeper)
- The file server.properties holds the configuration of a Kafka server such as log directory and listening port
- Folder log.dirs as specified in server.properties (default is /tmp/kafka)

The file meta.properties in the log.dirs contains a unique cluster identifier with a length of 22 Bytes.

We further investigate data of Zookeeper in order to determine all brokers of a Kafka cluster. Zookeeper stores its metadata about the cluster in the log-file within the dataDir directory. This file contains JSON-formatted data. We can search the file for the keyword "host" to find all broker hostnames of the Kafka cluster. The keyword "topics" provides us with the names of the topics which the cluster holds.

Since Kafka version 2.8 we see the preview of the new consensus mode KRaft, which will render an additional Zookeeper setup obsolete. With the release of Kafka version 3.6 KRaft will be production ready. When we see our setup uses KRaft, we can inspect the dedicated topic "_cluster_metadata" to get the topic and hostname information of the cluster. We can do so via the script kafka-dump-log.sh that comes with Kafka and pass the option −cluster-metadata-decoder. Alternatively we inspect the log file of the topic as described in the following section.

## 4.3   Kafka Storage Internals

In the data directory of a Kafka broker we find a folder for each topic in the form "[topic-name]-[partition-number]". Within such partition folder, Kafka generates files for **segments** with a maximum size, which an administrator can configure via log.segment.bytes. The file names of such segment contain the offset of the first message within the file. We call this offset of a segment its *base offset* which reaches a high value in case of high throughput. As we outline more detailed in the following, each segment consists of a log file, an index file, and a timeindex file.

| Log File | |
| --- | --- |
| Field description | Length (Bytes) |
| Batch headers (multiple per log file) | |
| Base offset | 8 |
| Batch length | 4 |
| Partition leader epoch | 4 |
| Magic number | 1 |
| CRC-32C of following bytes in batch | 4 |
| Attributes (e.g. compression type) | 2 |
| Last offset in batch | 4 |
| Create time first record | 8 |
| Create time batch | 8 |
| Producer identifier | 8 |
| Producer epoch | 2 |
| Base sequence | 4 |
| Number of records in batch | 4 |
| Record entries (multiple per batch) | |
| Record length × 2 | 1 |
| Sequence of 0xFF | 1 |
| Time offset in ms | 1 |
| Offset from base offset | 1 |
| Length of key | runlength-encoded |
| Key content | variable length |
| Length of value | runlength-encoded |
| Value content | variable length |
| Sequence of 0x00 | 1 |

**Log Files.** The log file holds the data of messages that a Kafka topic stores in a segment. Kafka tries to write several messages to a log file in a batch. This avoids disk seeks and therefore increases the write performance of Kafka. In the following table we provide an overview on the different fields we find in a log file. In a log file we see batch headers which hold the metadata of batches. The metadata supports seeking and verifying data within the log file by providing information such as offsets, lengths, and a CRC checksum. Kafka achieves data consistency in failover scenarios by using epoch information for partition leaders and producers. By default, Kafka operates with disabled compression and persists keys and values in the same binary representation as they arrive from a receiver. After a batch header we find multiple record entries which hold the actual payload of messages together with its offset and time information.

**Index Files.** The index files enable fast data retrieval from specific topic offsets. They serve as a mapping table of offsets to absolute positions within the log file of the same segment. By default, Kafka adds an offset entry to the index file for every 4 KiB of data in the corresponding log file. Because the offsets in the index file are sorted by design, binary searches within the file enable fast lookups.

| Index File | |
| --- | --- |
| Field description | Length (Bytes) |
| Offset | 4 |
| Position in log file | 4 |

**Timeindex Files.** Timeindex files allow fast lookups of messages with specific timestamps. They provide a mapping table of timestamps to offsets within the same segment. Kafka adds entries to the timeindex file at fixed time intervals. As Kafka writes entries ordered in time, binary searches are possible within the file. After Kafka locates the offset corresponding to a timestamp, it leverages the index file to determine the absolute position within the log file of the same segment.

| Timeindex File | |
| --- | --- |
| Field description | Length (Bytes) |
| Timestamp | 8 |
| Offset | 4 |

# 5 Data Security

In this section we will explore the various methods available to secure Apache Kafka, including data transmission encryption and encryption at rest. The availability of these features may be critical for effective investigation and analysis following an external security breach or incident.

## 5.1 Encryption in Transit

Apache Kafka supports classic SSL/TLS encryption for data transfer between participants. As TCP/UDP protocols do not provide authentication and authorization, we need a secure setup for the following tasks and components:

- certificate/key distribution and management

- a certificate authority (CA)
- a Kerberos setup (KDC)
- management of service users and their Kerberos keytabs
- maintenance of access control lists (ACLs) for topic specific permissions
- drawing and renewing Kerberos ticket-granting tickets (TGTs) with Kerberos keytabs

Apache Kafka falls short in providing these features which increase the system complexity significantly. Vendor-specific Kafka cluster management tools, such as those offered by Cloudera [51], can support the ACL maintenance. Nevertheless, we require additional effort for automation or manual intervention. The individual infrastructure environment also determines if and how e.g. privileged remote system access via SSH can be used for the distribution of keys and credentials.

With activated encryption via SSL/TLS, Kafka suffers a small loss in performance as it cannot profit from zero-copying anymore [50].

If there are unencrypted ports in a distributed software such as Apache Kafka, the system has high exposure to advanced persistent threats (APT): malicious actors may use a man-in-the-middle attack to infiltrate the cluster and move from one broker to another. When combined with privilege escalation, malicious actors can gain complete access and potentially obscure any trace of their actions. In this situation, the data stored on the brokers of the cluster loses its consistency and security properties and can only be seen as circumstantial evidence. We therefore denote it negligent to hold sensitive personal-related data in such environment. These considerations are especially relevant if the unencrypted ports affect the cluster management system with its full control over the cluster brokers. As a countermeasure, full isolation via perimeter security and tenant separation can enhance data security.

## 5.2   Encryption at Rest

Encryption at rest is a standard measure when it comes to storing confidential or sensitive personal-related data. Unfortunately, Kafka does not provide means for data encryption at rest. Using whole volume encryption as part of the infrastructure is an option, however, primarily reserved to public cloud infrastructures with other security constraints [40,44]. Vendor-specific management systems can also support in providing encrypted folders, where Kafka may transparently store its data. These solutions share a common challenge related to managing encryption keys [39,41].

As promoted at Kafka Summit Europe 2021 [42], client-side encryption of all messages can be an option. It provides data privacy to customers and compliance with data protection laws to system owners. Furthermore, with client-side encryption, a data thief can not obtain the data of all system participants at once. This significantly reduces the risk for system owners concerning extortion attempts in case data gets in control of criminals.

With client-side encryption, for a server-side forensic analysis, we can only focus on the origin, size and timing of messages. We can not inspect the message contents in this case.

# 6  Data Removal in Kafka

This section explains how and why messages are deleted from Kafka topics, as well as the potential locations where forensic investigators may be able to find remaining traces.

## 6.1  Data Retention

One of Kafka's main features is the possibility to specify data retention for topics. After reaching the retention criteria, messages are eventually removed from a topic. This gives the system engineer a measure to limit the overall size of a Kafka cluster and e.g. meet performance requirements. Generally, Kafka deletes a message after a certain time or topic size limit, which we can specify via log.retention.[ms,minutes,hours] or log.retention.bytes. However, some details related to deletion are important when it comes to forensic analysis.

First, Kafka does only remove whole segments from disks, not single messages. Kafka will not remove a message from the segment it currently writes to, even if the message meets the deletion criteria.

Second, when a segment is complete, Kafka will only delete it after the last message within the segment meets the deletion criteria. Meanwhile, older messages still reside on disk.

Further, the setting log.retention.check.interval.ms specifies how frequent Kafka performs retention checks. The setting defaults to five minutes which implies that data resides on disk during this time window.

Finally, even when Kafka deletes a segment, there is a period the segment remains available on disk. Before Kafka deletes a segment, it adds the string ".deleted" to the segments filename. The file is released in the file system only after the period log.segment.delete.delay.ms, which defaults to one minute.

We see that Kafka might also be used as a long term storage system, comparable to a database [46]. It is technically feasible to store virtually infinite amounts of data in Kafka [47]. This is extended by features like tiered storage [48] which allows to decrease storage costs as it supports cheap and scalable object storage. For less frequently accessed data, such as historical data, the costs are even lower.

## 6.2  Limited Capabilities for Targeted Deletion

Kafka does not provide targeted deletion capabilities, which are relevant for ensuring the "right to be forgotten", as enforced by the European GDPR and similar privacy laws [52,53]. The design of Kafka does not prioritize meeting these requirements for deleting messages in a targeted and timely manner, especially with longer retention times or high topic sizes. Due to the focus on fast sequential reads and writes, Kafka brokers do not offer delete operations to consumers or producers.

In certain application architectures, activating log compaction [49] via the setting log.cleanup.policy can be used to eventually remove messages from Kafka topics. However, this option is inactive by default due to its limitations and high performance requirements. When active, selective message removal from a topic partition is possible for producers through appending a new message with corresponding key and a null value (called tombstone-message). Previous records with same key and the tombstone record will be eventually deleted on the broker during a subsequent log compaction process. Removal by key only works at the partition level, not the topic level. Additionally, consumers may miss a tombstone message if they are disconnected for longer than log.cleaner.delete.retention.ms, which defaults to one day. The compaction process sequentially operates on every segment, but it is unable to remove records from the most recent segment because of potential write conflicts with incoming messages.

Messages that are still present in the system can be accessed and analyzed through the log files.

## 7    Autopsy Module

The forensic software "The Sleuth Kit" [9] and the related project "Autopsy" have an extensible architecture. An author can create a new module by imple-

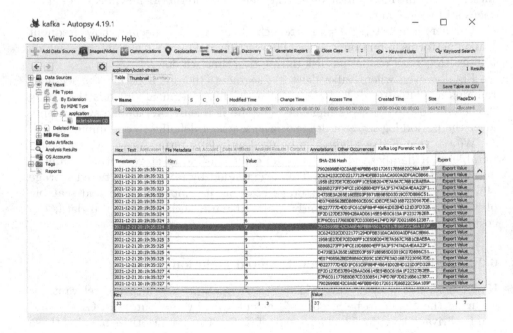

**Fig. 3.** Autopsy Plugin

menting Java classes and compiling them into a NetBeans Module (NBM) package. With the knowledge from our analysis above, we implement a first file content viewer module for Kafka log files. The module parses a Kafka log file by iterating over batches and extracting properties of contained messages.

The module allows to view basic features for forensic investigation such as the message timestamp, the key-value-pair in string format, and calculates a checksum. For binary data, a hex view is available at the bottom of the screen. For subsequent analysis and archival, the investigator can export values of any type from the user interface into a file.

Figure 3 shows Autopsy running our module on an exemplary Kafka log file. We contribute the plugin to the public by releasing the code as open source.

## 8   Conclusion

In this paper, we have discussed various aspects related to the use of Apache Kafka in big data processing systems and its role as a software bus for worldwide data movement. We have also highlighted the importance of forensic investigation of supporting infrastructure in modern architectures and proposed methods and possibilities for investigating an Apache Kafka cluster.

We believe that this paper can contribute to a deeper understanding of Apache Kafka's role in big data processing systems, as well as its potential value for forensic investigations.

We also hope that our findings and our Autopsy module will be useful for both researchers and practitioners, and we encourage ongoing collaboration through the sharing of experience.

Although Apache Kafka has less components and therefore a lower complexity than Apache Hadoop, we draw a conclusion similar to Bhathal et al. [21]: there is a need to upgrade Apache Kafka with complete security features and bundle them together into one release. Additionally, implementing an "in place" delete operation can help project managers meet compliance standards.

Meanwhile, in order to increase system resilience against any issues with security, availability, and confidentiality, we strongly encourage to use decentralized system designs for applications with sensitive data. If a single-point-of-failure cannot be avoided to provide certain application features, we recommend to consider data minimisation and, whenever possible, to use client-side encryption. This approach is not only in the interest of users to protect them as individuals against data leakage and unintentionally being part of potential artificial intelligence applications, it can also be a unique selling point for organisations when made transparent. If public institutions like to support ethical [22] transparency in this matter, applications reaching a certain number of affected users could be rated based on criteria such as the complexity of central components, data center location, measures for internal tenant isolation, and amount of data that is accessible to operators and scientists, e.g. for artificial intelligence.

**Acknowledgement.** We would like to extend our heartfelt appreciation to all those who have supported us throughout this work.

# References

1. Fu, G., Zhang, Y., Yu, G.: A fair comparison of message queuing systems. IEEE Access **9**, 421–432 (2021)
2. Zelenin, A., Kropp, A.: Apache Kafka: Von den Grundlagen bis zum Produktiveinsatz, 1st edition. Carl Hanser Verlag (2021)
3. Wagner, J., Rasin, A., Grier, J.: Database forensic analysis through internal structure carving. Digit. Investig. **14**, S106–S115 (2015)
4. Pereira, M.: Forensic analysis of the Firefox 3 Internet history and recovery of deleted SQLite records. Digit. Investig. **5**, 93–103 (2009)
5. Kaur, K., Adane, D.: A framework for database forensic analysis. Comput. Sci. Eng.: Int. J. **2**, 27–41 (2012)
6. Beyers, H., Olivier, M., Hancke, G.: Assembling metadata for database forensics. In: Peterson, G., Shenoi, S. (eds.) DigitalForensics 2011. IAICT, vol. 361, pp. 89–99. Springer, Heidelberg (2011). https://doi.org/10.1007/978-3-642-24212-0_7
7. Chivers, H., Hargreaves, C.: Forensic data recovery from the windows search database. Digit. Investig. **7**, 114–126 (2011)
8. Yoon, J., Jeong, D., Kang, C., Lee, S.: Forensic investigation framework for the document store NoSQL DBMS: MongoDB as a case study. Digit. Investig. **17**, 53–65 (2016)
9. Carrier, B., et al.: The Sleuth Kit/Autopsy (2021). https://www.sleuthkit.org
10. Lin, X.: Introductory Computer Forensics: A Hands-On Practical Approach. Springer, Cham (2018). https://doi.org/10.1007/978-3-030-00581-8
11. Arnes, A.: Digital Forensics. Wiley, Hoboken (2018)
12. Kim, H., Kim, S., Shin, Y., Jo, W., Lee, S., Shon, T.: Ext4 and XFS file system forensic framework based on TSK. Electronics **2021**, 10 (2021)
13. Lee, S., Shon, T.: Improved deleted file recovery technique for Ext2/3 filesystem. J. Supercomput. **2014**(70), 20–30 (2014)
14. Fairbanks, K.: An analysis of Ext4 for digital forensics. Digit. Investig. **9**, S118–S13 (2012)
15. Lee, S., Jo, W., Eo, S., Shon, T.: ExtSFR: scalable file recovery framework based on an Ext file system. Multimed. Tools Appl. **79**, 16093–16111 (2019)
16. Ahn, J., Park, J., Lee, S.: The research on the recovery techniques of deleted files in the XFS filesystem. JKII Secur. Cryptol. **24**, 885–896 (2014)
17. Park, Y., Chang, H., Shon, T.: Data investigation based on XFS file system metadata. Multimed. Tools Appl. **75**, 14721–14743 (2015)
18. Majore, S., Lee, C., Shon, T.: XFS file system and file recovery tools. Int. J. Smart Home **7** (2013)
19. Lim, E., et al.: Hadoop Distributed File System Forensics Toolkit (HDFS FTK) (2018). https://github.com/edison0xyz/hadoop_ftk
20. Big Data Community Forum (2017). https://archive.today/qpHBt
21. Bhathal, G., Singh, A.: Big Data: Hadoop framework vulnerabilities, security issues and attacks. Array **1-2** (2019)
22. Zuber, N., Kacianka, S., Gogoll, J.: Big data ethics, machine ethics or information ethics? Navigating the maze of applied ethics in IT. arXiv:2203.13494 (2022)
23. Agrawal, B., Hansen, R., Rong, C., Wiktorski, T.: SD-HDFS: secure deletion in hadoop distributed file system. In: IEEE BigData Congress 2016, pp. 181–189 (2016)

24. Mallmann, G.L., de Vargas Pinto, A., Maçada, A.C.G.: Shedding light on shadow IT: definition, related concepts, and consequences. In: Ramos, I., Quaresma, R., Silva, P., Oliveira, T. (eds.) Information Systems for Industry 4.0. LNISO, vol. 31, pp. 63–79. Springer, Cham (2019). https://doi.org/10.1007/978-3-030-14850-8_5
25. Asim, M., McKinnel, D.R., Dehghantanha, A., Parizi, R.M., Hammoudeh, M., Epiphaniou, G.: Big data forensics: hadoop distributed file systems as a case study. In: Dehghantanha, A., Choo, K.-K.R. (eds.) Handbook of Big Data and IoT Security, pp. 179–210. Springer, Cham (2019). https://doi.org/10.1007/978-3-030-10543-3_8
26. Apache Kafka Contributors. Apache Kafka Git Repository (2021). https://github.com/a0x8o/kafka
27. Apache Software Foundation. Apache Kafka Online Documentation (2022). https://kafka.apache.org/documentation/
28. Confluent Inc. Confluent Developer Portal (2023). https://developer.confluent.io/learn-kafka/apache-kafka/partitions/
29. Raptis, T., Passarella, A.: On efficiently partitioning a topic in apache Kafka. In: CITS 2022, pp. 1–8 (2022)
30. Vielberth, M., Pernul, G.: A security information and event management pattern. SLPLoP 2018 Chile (2018)
31. Choudhary, C., Singh, I., Kumar, M.: A real-time fault tolerant and scalable recommender system design based on Kafka. In: IEEE I2CT 2022 India (2022)
32. Kreps, J., Narkhede, N., Rao, J.: Kafka: a distributed messaging system for log processing. In: NetDB Workshop 2011 (2011)
33. Dobbelaere, P., Esmaili, K.: Kafka versus RabbitMQ: a comparative study of two industry reference publish/subscribe implementations: industry Paper. In: ACM DEBS 2017, Spain, pp. 19–23 (2017)
34. Silva, I., Valle, J., Souza, G., Budke, J.: Using micro-services and artificial intelligence to analyze images in criminal evidences. In: DFRWS 2021 USA, Digital Investigation, vol. 37 (2021)
35. Braunisch, N., Schlesinger, S., Lehmann, R.: Adaptive industrial IoT gateway using Kafka streaming platform. In: INDIN 2022 Australia (2022)
36. Narkhede, N., Shapira, G., Palino, T.: Kafka: The Definitive Guide: Real-time Data and Stream Processing at Scale. O'Reilly (2017)
37. Google Brain Team. Robust machine learning on streaming data using Kafka and Tensorflow-IO (2022). https://www.tensorflow.org/io/tutorials/kafka
38. Apache Software Foundation. Apache Spark - Kafka Integration Guide (2022). https://spark.apache.org/docs/latest/structured-streaming-kafka-integration.html
39. Kamaraju, A., Ali, A., Deepak, R.: Best practices for cloud data protection and key management. In: Arai, K. (ed.) FTC 2021. LNNS, vol. 360, pp. 117–131. Springer, Cham (2022). https://doi.org/10.1007/978-3-030-89912-7_10
40. Alouffi, B., Hasnain, M., Alharbi, A., et al.: A systematic literature review on cloud computing security: threats and mitigation strategies. IEEE Access 9, 57792–57807 (2021)
41. Giblin, C., Rooney, S., Vetsch, P., Preston, A.: Securing Kafka with encryption-at-rest. In: IEEE International Conference on Big Data (2021)
42. Barnes, R.: Kafka Summit 2021. https://www.confluent.io/events/kafka-summit-europe-2021/encrypting-kafka-messages-at-rest-to-secure-applications/
43. Hashemi, S., Zarei, M.: Internet of Things backdoors: resource management issues, security challenges, and detection methods. Trans. Emerg. Telecommun. Technol. 32(2), e4142 (2021)

44. FISA Report of the Research Section of the German Federal Parliament 2020. https://www.bundestag.de/resource/blob/796102/ ea53ffe8e08a9ab11e270719263d8c53/WD-3-181-20-pdf-data.pdf
45. Apache Software Foundation. Apache Ambari (2022). https://ambari.apache.org
46. Kleppmann, M.: Is Kafka a database. Kafka Summit London 2019 Keynote (2019). https://www.youtube.com/watch?v=BuE6JvQE_CY
47. Confluent Inc., Blog. It's Okay to Store Data in Kafka (2017). https://www.confluent.io/blog/okay-store-data-apache-kafka/
48. Confluent Inc., Blog. Infinite Storage in Confluent Platform (2020). https://www.confluent.io/blog/infinite-kafka-storage-in-confluent-platform/
49. Apache Software Foundation. Apache Kafka Online Documentation on Compaction (2023). https://kafka.apache.org/documentation/#compaction
50. Ismael Juma (Confluent Inc.) on Twitter (2019). https://twitter.com/ StephaneMaarek/status/1161173028627202049
51. Cloudera Inc.: Kafka Security (2021). https://docs.cloudera.com/documentation/ enterprise/latest/topics/kafka_security.html
52. Official Journal of the European Union. Right to be forgotten. GDPR, Chapter 3, Section 2 (2016). https://eur-lex.europa.eu/legal-content/EN/TXT/HTML/? uri=CELEX:32016R0679#d1e2606-1-1
53. National Privacy Commission Philippines. Data Privacy Act of 2012 (2016). https://privacy.gov.ph/implementing-rules-regulations-data-privacy-act-2012/#34

# A Survey on Security Threats and Mitigation Strategies for NoSQL Databases

## MongoDB as a Use Case

Surabhi Dwivedi[✉], R. Balaji, Praveen Ampatt, and S. D. Sudarsan

Centre for Development of Advanced Computing (C-DAC), 68-Electronic City,
Bengaluru 560100, India
{surabhi,balaji,apraveen,sds}@cdac.in

**Abstract.** With the advent of IoT devices, cloud computing, accessible mobile devices, social networking sites and other advancements in technology a huge amount of data is being generated. NoSQL databases were evolved to provide a better storage capability, scalability, improved performance for read and write operations for the enormous data generated by various systems which are continuously being read and written by large number of users. Initially it was believed to provide better security in comparison to the traditional relational database management system (RDBMS), but in due course of time NoSQL databases were also exposed to various security breaches and vulnerabilities. In this paper we studied in detail the various security vulnerabilities of MongoDB, along with the need to secure the interfaces being used to access MongoDB. We analyzed the prevention and mitigation strategies for the same. The study of this paper can be used as a best practice to secure NoSQL or MongoDB database. It suggests how to secure the queries and all the interfaces that are being used to access the database.

**Keywords:** NoSQL · MongoDB · NoSQL Injection · Data Masking

## 1 Introduction

Due to technological advancements, there are varieties of data, of different sizes available from diverse possible resources like IoT devices, social networking, mobile devices, cloud computing etc. There is also a significant decrease in storage cost, due to which more data is available. Data is available in different shapes and sizes like structured, semi-structured, or unstructured. It was realized that traditional relational database management systems (RDBMS) are not able to cater to the immense requirements of scalability, high availability, dynamic schema design, elasticity and high performance. It gave rise to the popularity of NoSQL databases which, is also called as 'Not only SQL' or 'Non-SQL' database. Along with providing storage capability for the modern application it provides lots of flexibility for the developers to store huge amounts of data. It is very adaptable to the rapidly changing agile requirements. Any new requirements can be easily incorporated in these databases without affecting the high availability of the

V. Muthukkumarasamy et al. (Eds.): ICISS 2023, LNCS 14424, pp. 57–76, 2023.
https://doi.org/10.1007/978-3-031-49099-6_4

databases. The RDBMS systems are based on ACID properties namely atomicity, consistency, isolation and durability. The NoSQL databases are based on BASE properties which are defined as basically available, soft state and eventual consistent. The NoSQL databases do not require any standard languages like structured query language (SQL) of RDBMS. Data manipulation can happen via object-oriented application programming interface (API). Though each NoSQL database has their own query language interface with a syntax like any popular programming languages.

The CAP theorem for databases was introduced for by Portland [1]. According to this theorem a distributed system can deliver two of the following three properties at any given point of time. 1) Consistency (C): All clients should see the same data at the given time; 2) Availability (A): If a client makes a request for data, it should get a response, even if one or more nodes are down. System can run even if parts have failed via replication; 3) Partitions Tolerance (P): The database cluster must continue to work despite any number of communication breakdowns between nodes in the system.

Based on the above three properties there are different types of databases like CP database, CA database and AP database. Most of the RDBMS databases like PostgreSQL, MySQL etc. are CA databases. CA databases are non-fault tolerant and deliver consistency and availability across all connected nodes. NoSQL Databases like MongoDB, Redis, HBase are CP databases. CP databases, deliver consistency and partition tolerance at the expense of availability. When a partition occurs between any two nodes, the system shuts down the non-consistent node (i.e., make it unavailable) until the partition is resolved. Some NoSQL databases like Cassandra, CouchDB [37] and Riak are AP databases. AP databases forego consistency to provide availability and partition tolerance. In case of partition all the nodes will be available and the one at the wrong end of partition will continue to return the old version of data.

NoSQL databases are broadly categorized into four different types namely 1) Column oriented databases 2) Document oriented databases 3) Key value databases 4) Graph databases.

Though NoSQL (Not only SQL) are very efficient to handle the structured and unstructured data generated from real time applications but there is still a lack of standard security mechanism in NoSQL. Although the query model of NoSQL databases makes the known SQL injection attack irrelevant, attackers now try with new vulnerable codes to breach. In this work we are analyzing the security features of NoSQL databases with an example of MongoDB database, which is a document-oriented database. MongoDB is the most popular NoSQL database and fifth most popular database as per a survey [2]. Many popular companies including eBay, Foursquare, Adobe, Uber, and LinkedIn etc., have adopted MongoDB. In this study we will use MongoDB to illustrate the NoSQL security attacks, prevention and mitigation strategies. MongoDB stores the information in collections and documents. Collections and documents are analogous to tables and rows respectively of RDBMS. MongoDB is available in community, enterprise (commercial edition) and Atlas (multi-cloud developer data platform) editions.

This study is based on extensive analysis of 18 quality research papers, MongoDB manuals and experiments. Section 2 explains the similar study done by the other authors and the motivation to write this paper; Sect. 3 discusses various NoSQL database-based security breach incidences that happened during the last five years. Section 4 and its subsections explain the various NoSQL security breaches techniques followed by the attackers. Section 5 explains about the various strategies and measures to prevent NoSQL security attacks. Section 6 concludes the paper.

## 2 Literature Survey

There are many research work highlighting the significant security issues in NoSQL databases. Okman et al. [3] reviewed the most popular NoSQL databases, MongoDB (document oriented), Cassandra (column family) and analyzed the security features such as authentication, authorization, auditing, and injection attacks etc. The research work done by Sicari et al. [4] analyses the security and privacy solutions of NoSQL databases, particularly Redis, Cassandra, MongoDB, and Neo4j and analyses the security requirements in terms of authentication, authorization, access control, privacy, policy enforcement, integrity, and confidentiality. Fahd et al. in the research paper [5] also studies the security issues of Redis, Cassandra, MongoDB and Neo4j in terms of authentication/authorization, auditing, encryption and NoSQL injection attack scenarios. They also propose a framework for NoSQL database security. Ron et al. [6] have also analyzed NoSQL vulnerabilities and mitigation mechanism.

There is no comprehensive study available which analyses to secure all the interface being used to access MongoDB along with the security issues of MongoDB. It is important to have the overall security requirements of MongoDB along with securing the API being used to access the database, network interfaces, prevention of NoSQL injections, required data privacy and encryption techniques, authentication and role-based access control mechanism etc., to provide a comprehensive solution for the MongoDB database security. This work will provide an exhaustive detail of the possible NoSQL injection scenarios, the available authentication mechanisms in MongoDB, strength of available cypher suites, certificates, protocols, requirements of data masking for data privacy and security along with securing the API being used to access the database.

## 3 Attack Incidences on NoSQL Databases

As Zdnet news [7] reported that 590 million resumes' were leaked by a company. Most of the resume' leaks occurred because of poorly secured MongoDB databases and Elasticsearch servers that have been left exposed online without a password.

One media streaming platform also reported a data breach, where a 72 GB MongoDB JSON dump containing information of almost 44 million users and 7,455,926 unique email addresses, were leaked over a social network [8].

Another incident was identified in April 2019 where almost 275 million records containing detailed personally identifiable information were exposed by MongoDB database [9].

Toyota connected service faced a decade long data leak, spanning from January 2012 to April 2023, which exposed 2.15 million customers data and it was based on NoSQL database [10].

The distribution of exposed data by RDBMS and NoSQL database is shown in Fig. 1 [11]. The major portion of the exposed data is from Redis 37.5% and MongoDB 30.9% and Elasticsearch 29.3%, all are NoSQL database.

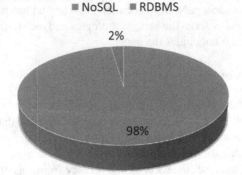

**Fig. 1.** Distribution of exposed Databases by type [11]

# 4 NOSQL Security Breaches

This section describes various scenarios where NoSQL database can be vulnerable.

## 4.1 NoSQL Injection Vulnerabilities

NoSQL-Injection is a security vulnerability where the attackers take control of database queries through the unsafe use of user input or appending a malicious code/query to a legal NoSQL query statement [12]. Although it is believed that SQL injections are hard to perform on NoSQL databases as these databases use different query language than traditional SQL. NoSQL, queries and data are mostly represented in JSON format, which is better than SQL in terms of security because it is well defined, very simple to encode/decode and has good native implementations in most of the programming language [13]. Still, it is being exploited by many attackers to append a malicious script into a query statement. Injection for NoSQL database is same as injection in SQL database, the difference is only in the syntax [14]. It can affect the database significantly by reducing the system performance, making unauthorized changes, modifying the user privileges and permissions.

Malicious queries can be injected using the input boxes of web applications or in the URL of web applications. The paper [6] describes the five types of malicious query injections 1) Tautology expression 2) NoSQL OR injections 3) Java script injection 4) Piggybacking queries.

**Tautologies Expressions:** Tautology expressions are generated in a conditional statement which is always true. It can facilitate authentication bypass. The attackers can access the database without valid credentials. The following JSON input is an example of malicious code.

> *Malicious Query:*
> *{*
> *"Username": {"$ne": "1"}, "Password": {"$ne": "1 "}*
> *}*

The above statement compares password with an empty string for $ne function, which will always be true and so login authentication will be bypassed.

Table 1 describes some more operators that can be used to bypass the authentication. In place of valid credentials, the login authentication will be bypassed by using these operators as payloads which will always be evaluated as true.

**Table 1.** Vulnerable MongoDB payloads

| $ne | Not equal to |
| --- | --- |
| $eq | Equal to |
| $gt | Greater than |
| $lt | Less than |
| $regex | regular expression |

**NoSQL OR Injections:** Another form of malicious queries are NoSQL OR injections or Union queries. An OR condition will be used to bind an empty expression to the input. Since an empty expression is always valid, it renders the password check ineffective. The following example illustrates a scenario [15].

> *Original Query:*
> *{ username: 'admin',password: 'welcome' }*
>
> *Injection Query :*
> *{*
> *username= 'admin', $or:[{},{'a': 'a', password=''}],*
> *$comment:'successful MongoDB injection'*
> *}*

The above query will succeed if the username is correct, the password part will become redundant. The empty query will always be true, and unauthorized access will be granted to the system.

**Java Script Injections** For NoSQL databases JavaScript enables to query the database. A web application becomes vulnerable if $where query operator is being used and user inputs are not validated. It exposes illegal data extraction or alteration and can also introduce denial of service attacks by making the server inaccessible for a given time. The following example demonstrates the scenario of such vulnerability. The following example illustrate a vulnerable query, to fetch the name [16]

*Original Query:*
*db.students.find({*
*$where: function ()*
*{return (this.name == $Name)}});*

The above query will search for a document in student collection, java script function is used as the value of $where field. The function compares name field in each document with a variable/parameter called $Name.

The following query will inject a sleep function call within the $where java script function. It will pause the server for 8 s if the injection was successful.

*Injection Query:*

*db.collection.find({$where: function()*

*{return (this.name == 'test'; sleep(8000) ) } } );*

It can introduce denial-of-service (DoS) attacks, by making the server unavailable by the specified time. Use of other operators like MapReduce, group by of MongoDB can also enable Java Script injection if query is not sanitized.

The following example demonstrates a vulnerable code while using a group by operator of MongoDB.

*Original Query :*
*db.orders.aggregate([*
*{    $group: { _id: "$items",totalQuantity: { $sum: "$quantity" }    } }]);*

The above query performs aggregation on orders collection. It groups the documents by the "item" field and calculates the total quantity for each product using the $sum. In this example, the query will become vulnerable if the input values product and quantity are provided from user without a proper validation. The following example illustrate an injection query.

*Injection Query :*
*var injectionInput = "item'; db.orders.deleteMany({}) //";*
*db.orders.aggregate([ {*
*    $group: { _id: injectionInput, totalQuantity: { $sum: "$quantity" }*
*} }]);*

The injection input has the value "item'; db.orders.deleteMany({})//'". This input contains a potential injection payload. The _id field in the $group stage will set to the value of insecure Input. The insecure input "item'; db.orders.deleteMany({}) //'" code will delete all documents in the "orders" collection, which can be highly destructive.

**Piggybacked Queries:** Piggybacked queries can be used by attackers to inject additional queries or commands within a legitimate query.

Escape sequences and special characters like carriage return [CR], line feed [LF], closing braces, semicolons can be used to end a query and then insert additional malicious queries. Following example explains a scenario of piggybacked query [15].

> *Original Query:*
> *db.student.find({ username: 'testuser'});*
>
> *Injection Query:*
> *db.student.find({ username: 'testuser'}); db.dropDatabase();*
> *db.insert({username: 'malicious ', password: 'malicioustext'});*

The injection query injects additional malicious query after a semicolon. Which will drop the database if user access management is not taken care of, and it will also insert a new malicious user.

### 4.2 Absence of Strong Authentication and Authorization

Authorization and authentication are not enabled by default in MongoDB. It exposes the vulnerability to anyone who has access to the database server and then could modify the database and its content. Some malicious queries (as explained in Sect. 4.1) like tautology and union queries can be used to gain unauthorized access to the database. In absence of strong authentication login can be bypass for MongoDB on PHP, NodeJS and JAVA Script [17].

### 4.3 Insecure REST API

NoSQL databases expose HTTP REST APIs so that applications can use this database without need of any additional driver for the programming languages.

The exposure of REST API also introduces various risks if it's not configured properly, and queries are not sanitized. The risk includes Cross-Site Request Forgery (CSRF) attack, click jacking attack etc. Anyone who has access to the secure network can perform queries against the database. The attacker uses the victim's browser to generate requests which are considered genuine by the application/server. As a response to these requests, the application can return unauthorized data or can execute various data manipulation task [18].

Cross site scripting introduces a harmful or malicious script to a vulnerable web application using a malicious link. The user information can be affected by stealing cookies, phishing, or attacking an organization's entire network [19].

The cross-side scripting attacks can be categorized into stored and reflected categories. The stored type of attack stores the malicious scripts into the database and whenever the stored information is requested, malicious scripts are returned to the victim. Reflected kind of attacks reflects the injected scripts on the web servers in the form of error message or search result.

Figure 2 explains CSRF attack, it is derived from "NoSQL No Injection" [13]. 1) A victim browses a malicious website 2) Injection script gets executed and it submits HTML from with an action URL of a NoSQL database which is internal to the organization 3) The action will get executed as employee has access to the internal network and it can reset the values of the database.

These attacks can be executed provided following conditions are satisfied [6].

- The attacker controls the website either from exploiting a vulnerable website or it is hosted by the attacker.
- Trick the victim either by phishing technique or injecting a malicious script into a site that victim visits frequently.
- Another very common API based attack is click jacking attack. If the content of the main website is embedded into another website using <frame>, <iframe> or < embed> option, it can trick the main website users to unwillingly click on malicious links. If a user clicks on these links the attackers get the confidential information and access the database as well.

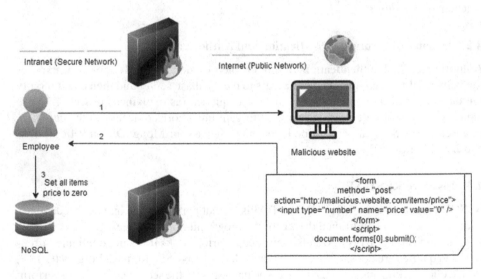

**Fig. 2.** CSRF via NoSQL API [13]

## 4.4 Vulnerable Database Access Security

The clients and servers, including the database servers, are connected to each other over a network. The secure socket layer (SSL) and Transport layer security (TLS), secure the data between the client and the database server in a network. It is very important to provide a safe mechanism to access the database.

**Vulnerable Cipher Suites.** A cipher suite consists of the following [20].

1) Encryption protocol (e.g., Data encryption standard (DES), Rivest Cipher4 (RC4), Advance encryption standard (AES) etc.)
2) Encryption key length (e.g., 40, 56, or 128 bits)
3) Hash algorithm (e.g., SHA, MD5) used for integrity checking.

As per OWASP [20] any one of the following conditions can constitute a weak cipher suite combination.

1) Less than 128 bits encryption key length
2) Not NULL ciphers suite
3) Absence of encryption
4) Weak protocols like SSLv2 etc.

If the database is not configured with a strong cipher suite, it will be vulnerable to attacks. Table 2 describes a set of vulnerability for encryption protocols and the hash algorithms.

**Vulnerable Certificate.** If certificates are not obtained from a valid source, or certificate management is not appropriate such as self-signed or expired, it can also introduce vulnerabilities. The certificate key length must be strong and must be signed with secure hashing algorithms. If non secure algorithms like md5 (as discussed in the previous sub section) are used for signing, it can introduce vulnerability.

**Table 2.** Protocols/Algorithms Vulnerability

| Protocol/ Algorithms | Vulnerability |
| --- | --- |
| MD5 | Known collision attacks [21] |
| RC4 | Crypto Analytical attack [22] |
| SSL v2 | Weakness in protocol design |
| DES | Brute force attacks |
| AES | Brute force attacks, Man in the middle attack |

**Absence of Strong Encryption.** Data encryption plays a crucial role for data protection. Encryption facilitates the security of data at rest and data in motion. MongoDB encrypts the network traffic (data-in-transit) using TLS/SSL. The community edition does not have encryption available for data-at rest [23].

### 4.5 Meow Attack

The insecure installation of MongoDB is prone to Meow attack also known as automated attack. As per a study [24] 4000 unsecured databases were deleted by this attack. This is a scripted bot attack that scrambles the data & indexes of victim MongoDB by overriding it with numbers and appending the string 'meow'. [25]. There could be several reasons for this kind of attack such as 1) The firewall being used is not secure 2) SSL encrypted mechanism is not being used appropriately, 3) Public access port of the database is open without proper authentication settings, 4) Plain clear text to access the password. As per the report [26] "meow" attacks only affected the free Community version of MongoDB database, not the MongoDB Enterprise Advanced or MongoDB Atlas products.

# 5 NOSQL Attacks – Prevention and Mitigation

## 5.1 Enable Access Control and Authentication

Authentication should always be enabled whenever using any NoSQL database including MongoDB and appropriate access should be given to the identified users based on their identified roles.

Access control policies are mainly classified into three well-known categories, as following [27].

- Discretionary Access Control (DAC): Individual users can be the owner of some resources and objects. They grant or revoke privileges to the other users, for the object or resources own by them.
- Mandatory Access Control (MAC): This is used in a high security environment. Access decisions are made by the administrator. It restricts access to resources based on the security classification of the resources and the clearance level of the users or processes attempting to access them.
- Role Based Access Control (RBAC): The users will be granted permission based on the organizational roles assigned to users.

MongoDB provides built-in roles in addition to the user defined roles. The various options for different roles are shown in Table 3 [28].

The MongoDB supports the following authentication mechanism:

- SCRAM-SHA-256 (MongoDB 4.0 and later)
- SCRAM-SHA-1 (MongoDB 3.0, 3.2, 3.4, and 3.6)
- MONGODB-CR (MongoDB 2.6 and earlier)
- MongoDB-AWS
- X.509

SCRAM-SHA-256 and SCRAM-SHA-1 uses username and password and encrypt it with SHA-256 and SHA-1 algorithm respectively to authenticate the users. MOGNOGODB-CR uses username and password for authentication. MONGODB-AWS authentication mechanism uses Amazon Web Services Identity and Access Management (AWS IAM) credentials to authenticate the user. The X.509 authentication mechanism uses TLS with X.509 certificates to authenticate the users [28]. The enterprise edition of MongoDB supports additional authentication mechanisms like GSSAPI/Kerberos, LDAP (Plain).

**Appropriate Input Validations.** Proper input validations should be added to all the user inputs. User field should be carefully analyzed to give privilege for appropriate strings, integers or date type to prevent the input of any malicious and unwanted characters along with the user inputs.

**Table 3.** MongoDB Built-in roles

| Users | Built-in Roles |
|---|---|
| DB user | read, readWrite |
| DB administrator | dbAdmin, dbOwner, userAdmin |
| Cluster Administration | clusterAdmin,clusterManager, clusterMonitor, hostManager |
| Backup and Restoration | backup, restore |
| All database roles | readAnyDatabase,readWriteAnyDatabase, userAdminAnyDatabase,dbAdminAnyDatabase |
| Super user roles | Root |

String manipulation can be avoided by type casting of the input parameters. The following example illustrates a method of type casting.

*{'password': req.param.password.toString()}.*

### 5.2  Enable Collection/Document Level Access

MongoDB offers collection-level access control. A role will be specific to a collection in a particular database. This can limit the user's privilege to a specific collection. So, depending upon the requirements, the users should be exposed to limited collections.

The following code snippet defines the collection level access control for a particular database [29].

```
privileges: [
{resource: { db: "course", collection: "student" },
 actions: [ "find", "update", "insert" ] },
{resource: { db: "course", collection: "faculty" },  actions: [ "find" ] }]
```

The above example defines find, update and insert on student collection and find privilege on faculty collection of a database named as course.

MongoDB also provides field level restrictions. This will restrict the contents of a document based on the information stored in the document itself. Multiple access levels for the same data are enabled via an access field, best set to an array of arrays. Each array element contains a required set of tags that a user needs to have to be allowed to access the data.

## 5.3  Output Encoding

If the application has any regular texts in the user generated content, it should be properly encoded before it is displayed in HTML templates or dynamically generated web pages. The encoding will convert the characters into a format that can be transmitted over the internet. Any unsafe characters can be replaced by % followed by two hexadecimal digits. It will prevent any potential interpretation of data.

## 5.4  Query Sanitizations

Query sanitization is a process to validate the user supplied data before using it in software application. Any special characters that can introduce vulnerability should be avoided.

To prevent Java script injection the MongoDB versions 4.4 onwards, use of $where is not supported [29]. MongoDB operators like where, mapReduce, or group with user supplied data can be avoided. Where clauses should be re-written as normal queries, using the expr operator, that does not use JavaScript. JavaScript enabled options can be set to false in mongod.conf, to disable JavaScript execution in MongoDB instance and prevent these kinds of attacks. It is available for both mongod (server component) as well as mongos (used for sharded cluster).

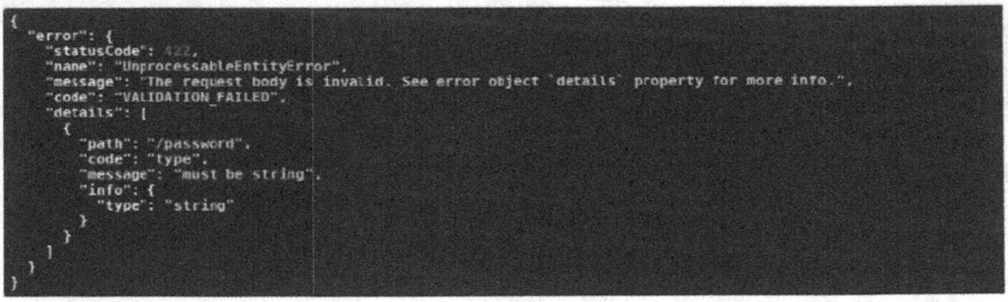

**Fig. 3.** Failed NoSQL injection with sanitized user input field.

Figure 3 shows an output where injections were tried to perform using the fields in the JSON format on a NodeJS application. Username is an email which is a validated field which should satisfy the criteria of e-mail validation and the password should be of string, minimum length 4 and blank space and $ not allowed as a filed.

*{ "username": "admin@xyz.com"}, "password": { "$ne": "1"}}*

Since the input was sanitized we got the output as shown in Fig. 3, while testing with loopback API explorer. So unauthorized access can be prevented at this portal with appropriate user input sanitizations and validations.

## 5.5 Data Masking Techniques

Data masking is a popular technique used to protect sensitive data and along with being useable. Although personal identifiable information or financial data can be hidden by use of data masking technique. This will hide the original data with some random character or data. The authors [30] describes five laws of data masking.

1. Masking must not be reversible. The original sensitive data should not be retrieved by use of masking.
2. The data should resemble the original data so that functionality of the application remains the same even after masking the data.
3. Referential integrity must be maintained. If any field is declared as a primary key and it is linked as data referencing, all the referred data should also be masked.
4. It is only advisable to mask the sensitive data rather than masking everything.
5. The development and test data should be close to the real production data.

Some of the popular data masking techniques are described as following [31].

1. Substitution: Replace original value with the other value and the replaced data should not have any correlation with the original data.
2. Shuffling: This technique uses existing data for masking. For example, replacing one row of a particular column with the data of the other row of the same column. This technique is useful when the data is large.
3. Number and Date variance: Numeric or number data can be masked using this technique. The data is increased by some random percent of the original data. For example, the birthdates can be increased by ± 80 days.
4. Masking Out: This is a very popular technique to replace the original data with some mask characters. For example, the credit card numbers are masked with some XXX characters.
5. Hashing: This technique takes data and creates hash of the data. The hash of a given data will always be same. This is used in storing passwords.
6. Tokenization: Using tokenization sensitive data will be replaced with randomly generated tokens. The mapping between the original data and tokens is maintained in a secure lookup table or service.

Data masking can be further described using the following example taken from gitHub [32]. The sample collection contains some dummy payment related information. Figure 4 shows the collection before masking and the masked collection is show in Fig. 5.

The collection has been masked using MongoDB aggregation pipeline. The sensitive information is masked using various techniques like 1) Name and Card number is masked out using partial obfuscation by retaining the last word and characters 2) Card expiry date is masked by taking the current date time and adding a random amount up to one year 3) Transaction date is obfuscated by adding or subtracting a random time amount up to one hour max 4) Transaction amount is masked by partial number obfuscation by adding or subtracting a random percent of its value, up to 10% max 5) Transaction id is masked by using md5 of its hash value.

```
MongoDB Enterprise > db.payments.find().pretty();
{
        "_id" : ObjectId("649ec681a1ae9329b0dac292"),
        "card_name" : "Mrs. Jane A. Doe",
        "card_num" : "1234567890123456",
        "card_expiry" : ISODate("2023-08-31T23:59:59Z"),
        "card_sec_code" : "123",
        "card_provider_name" : "Credit MasterCard Gold",
        "card_type" : "CREDIT",
        "transaction_id" : "eb1bd77836e8713656d9bf2debba8900",
        "transaction_date" : ISODate("2021-01-13T09:32:07Z"),
        "transaction_curncy_code" : "GBP",
        "transaction_amount" : NumberDecimal("501.98"),
        "settlement_id" : "9ccb27aeb8394c2b3547521bcd52a367",
        "settlement_date" : ISODate("2021-01-21T14:03:53Z"),
        "settlement_curncy_code" : "DKK",
        "settlement_amount" : NumberDecimal("4255.16"),
        "reported" : false,
        "customer_info" : {
                "category" : "SENSITIVE",
                "rating" : 89,
                "risk" : 3
        }
}
{
        "_id" : ObjectId("649ec681a1ae9329b0dac293"),
        "card_name" : "Jim Smith",
        "card_num" : "9876543210987654",
        "card_expiry" : ISODate("2022-12-31T23:59:59Z"),
        "card_sec_code" : "987",
        "card_provider_name" : "Debit Visa Platinum",
        "card_type" : "DEBIT",
        "transaction_id" : "634c416a6fbcf060bb0ba90c4ad94f60",
        "transaction_date" : ISODate("2020-11-24T19:25:57Z"),
        "transaction_curncy_code" : "EUR",
        "transaction_amount" : NumberDecimal("64.01"),
        "settlement_id" : "d53799f94d7ad72f698c5a4f04c031a6",
        "settlement_date" : ISODate("2020-12-04T11:51:48Z"),
        "settlement_curncy_code" : "USD",
        "settlement_amount" : NumberDecimal("76.87"),
        "reported" : true,
        "customer_info" : {
                "category" : "NORMAL",
                "rating" : 78,
                "risk" : 55
        }
}
```

**Fig. 4.** MongoDB collection before data masking

### 5.6 Ensure the REST API Security.

The API which is being used to access the database should also be secure to prevent any unauthorized access to the database. Allow trusted resource for Cross origin resource sharing (CORS). It will enable only the listed resource to execute JavaScript and interact with the page [33]. If CORS configuration is not secure any website can send requests with the user's credentials and perform malicious activities.

X-XSS-Protection Header is responsible for toggling off the XSS filter implemented by most current browsers [34]. It should be disabled to prevent cross side scripting (XSS) attack, as discussed in Sect. 4.3. The setup of appropriate content security policy prevents cross side scripting (XSS) attack and click jacking attack.

Strict-Transport-Security (HSTS) header should be enabled to access the website only using HTTPS. It will allow secure access to the website.

X-Frame response header can be set appropriate options of DENY or SAMEORIGIN access to prevent any click jacking attack.

Table 4 describes the preventive measures by setting appropriate security header option to prevent a vulnerability using API's.

```
MongoDB Enterprise > db.payments.aggregate(pipeline).pretty();
{
    "_id" : ObjectId("649ec681a1ae9329b0dac292"),
    "card_name" : "Mx. Xxx Doe",
    "card_num" : "XXXXXXXXXXX3456",
    "card_expiry" : ISODate("2024-04-17T10:34:26.494Z"),
    "card_sec_code" : "861",
    "card_provider_name" : "Credit MasterCard Gold",
    "card_type" : "CREDIT",
    "transaction_id" : "c830b5c72e480793f371063b618e9acc",
    "transaction_date" : ISODate("2021-01-13T10:09:14.590Z"),
    "transaction_curncy_code" : "GBP",
    "transaction_amount" : NumberDecimal("516.78726575600056264000000000000000"),
    "settlement_id" : "9ccb27aeb8394c2b3547521bcd52a367",
    "settlement_date" : ISODate("2021-09-02T21:03:20.675Z"),
    "settlement_curncy_code" : "DKK",
    "settlement_amount" : NumberDecimal("4255.16"),
    "reported" : true
}
{
    "_id" : ObjectId("649ec681a1ae9329b0dac293"),
    "card_name" : "Mx. Xxx Smith",
    "card_num" : "XXXXXXXXXXX7654",
    "card_expiry" : ISODate("2024-06-27T11:06:58.968Z"),
    "card_sec_code" : "148",
    "card_provider_name" : "Debit Visa Platinum",
    "card_type" : "DEBIT",
    "transaction_id" : "b6c35a9130598f98287288855e9b5ff6",
    "transaction_date" : ISODate("2020-11-24T18:49:22.032Z"),
    "transaction_curncy_code" : "EUR",
    "transaction_amount" : NumberDecimal("66.05476959916344105400000000000000"),
    "settlement_id" : "d53799f94d7ad72f698c5a4f04c031a6",
    "settlement_date" : ISODate("2021-11-17T00:31:20.620Z"),
    "settlement_curncy_code" : "USD",
    "settlement_amount" : NumberDecimal("76.87"),
    "reported" : false,
    "customer_info" : {
            "category" : "NORMAL",
            "rating" : 78,
            "risk" : 55
    }
}
```

**Fig. 5.** MongoDB collection after data masking

**Table 4.** Security Header Options for API security

| Threats | HTTP Security Header Options |
|---|---|
| Cross side scripting (XSS) | Content Security Policy (CSP) |
| | X-XSS-Protection Header- disable |
| Click jacking attack | Content Security Policy (CSP) |
| | X-Frame response header options |
| Insecure access | Strict-Transport-Security (HSTS) header |

## 5.7 Use Strong Network Security and Encryption Techniques

Weaker cipher suites as discussed in Sect. 4.4 should be avoided, to protect the vulnerability of data at rest and data in motion. This will also prevent the recent Meow attack. Encryption of stored data and the data floating across the network can protect the relevant accounts, passwords, and encryption keys.

The support of TLS 1.0 encryption (weaker technique) is disabled in the latest version of MongoDB. MongoDB's TLS/SSL encryption only allows use of strong TLS/SSL ciphers with a minimum of 128-bit key length for all connections.

In MongoDB encryption is available only in the Enterprise edition. The default encryption mode is the AES256-CBC via OpenSSL. AES-256 uses a symmetric key, i.e. the same key to encrypt and decrypt text [28].

Table 5 describes various provisions available for network security in MongoDB in version 6.0.

**Table 5.** Network Security in MongoDB [35]

| Forward Secrecy | Ephemeral Elliptic Curve Diffie-Hellman (ECDHE) | A new session key gets generated for each message of the communication. Once the communication is over key cannot be used to decrypt a message |
|---|---|---|
| | Ephemeral Diffie-Hellman (DHE) | |
| Certificate Expiry Warning | A warning is issued if x.509 certificate is about to expire in next 30 days | |
| OCSP (Online Certificate Status Protocol) | The use of OCSP eliminates the need to periodically download certificate revocation list | |

MongoDB supports Client-Side Field Level Encryption (CSFLE) to encrypt data the application before sending it over the network. MongoDB community edition supports explicit encryption to perform encrypted read and write operations through MongoDB driver's encryption library. The developer needs to specify the logic for encryption in the application. [36]. Table 6 describes the overall security features and their availability in MongoDB version 6.0.

### 5.8  Prevention of Meow Attack

Meow kind of automated attack can be prevented by taking care of appropriate authentication mechanism, encryption technique and security as discussed in Sect. 5.1 and 5.7 respectively. The database should use strong password and encryption. Use firewall and access control mechanism to allow only authorized users to access the database. Database auditing and monitoring mechanisms should be placed appropriately to monitor any unauthorized behaviors.

**Table 6.** MongoDB Security Features and Status

| Security Features | Status |
|---|---|
| Encryption at rest | Only available for enterprise edition. WiredTiger Storage Engine |
| Authentication | SCRAM, X.509(Community Edition) |
| | LDAP proxy, Kerberos(Enterprise edition) |
| Authorization | Not enabled by default<br>Can be enabled using the --auth or the securty.authorization setting [29] |
| Role base access control (RBAC) | Built-in and user defined roles are available if authentication is enabled |
| Audit log | Available on only in enterprise edition |

# 6 Conclusion

In this paper we studied in detail the NOSQL database security vulnerability and prevention strategies. We took examples of the most popular NoSQL database MongoDB for illustrations of various security breaches and prevention strategies. We can leverage the benefits of NoSQL databases and MongoDB by following the appropriate mitigation strategies. With each version of the NoSQL databases, security features are being enhanced. One can use the study of this paper to secure all the interface being used to access the NoSQL databases like prevent the NoSQL injection vulnerabilities using Input validation, query sanitization, output encoding and data masking techniques. Secure the channels being used to access the database by using strong cipher suites, appropriate certificates and certificates policies, use strong encryption, authentication and authorization. If the REST API is being used to access the database, appropriate security headers should be enabled to prevent any kind of vulnerabilities. Table 7 summarizes the various possible security breaches and prevention strategies using MongoDB database.

**Table 7.** Summary of Security Threats and Mitigation Strategies of NoSQL Databases

| Security Threats | | Mitigation Strategy |
|---|---|---|
| Injection Vulnerabilities | Tautologies expressions | Input validation |
| | NoSQL OR Injections | Query Sanitization |
| | JavaScriptInjections | Dynamic code analysis |
| | | Output encoding |
| | Piggybacked queries | Data masking and anonymization |
| Access control, Authentication/Authorization | | Enable Authentication |
| | | Enable Role based access control |
| REST API Security | | X-Frame response header |
| | | Enable CSP |
| | | X-XSS-Protection Header |
| | | Strict-Transport-Security (HSTS) |
| | | White listing of IP |
| Cryptographic Security | Vulnerable Cipher | Strong Ciphers - Forward Secrecy |
| | Vulnerable certificate | OCSP, Certificate expiry policy, Use of strong hashing algorithm |
| | Absence of Strong Encryption | AES256-CBC (Enterprise edition) |
| | | Client-Side Field Level Encryption |

# References

1. Brewer, E.A.: Towards robust distributed systems. In: PODC, vol. 7 (2000)
2. Db engines. https://db-engines.com/en/ranking. Accessed 02 Sept 2022
3. Okman, L., Gal-Oz, N., Gonen, Y., Gudes, E., Abramov, J.: Security Issues in NoSQL Databases. In: 10th International Conference on Trust, Security and Privacy in Computing and Communications, Changsha, China, 2011 (2011)
4. Sicari, S., Rizzardi, A., Coen-Porisini, A.: Security& privacy issues and challenges in NoSQL databases. Comput. Netw. Int. J. Comput. Telecommun. Netw. **206**(C), 341 (2022)
5. Fahd, K., Venkatraman, S., Hammeed, F.K.: A comparative study of NOSQL system vulnerabilities with big data. Int. J. Managing Inf. Technol. (IJMIT), **11**(4), 1–19 (2019)
6. Ron, A., Shulman-Peleg, A., Puzanov, A.: Analysis and mitigation of NoSQL injections. IEEE Secur. Priv. **14**(2), 30–39 (2016)
7. Zdnet. https://www.zdnet.com/article/chinese-companies-have-leaked-over-590-million-res umes-via-open-databases/. Accessed 02 July 2023
8. Bleeping computer. https://www.bleepingcomputer.com/news/security/russian-streaming-platform-confirms-data-breach-affecting-75m-users/. Accessed 09 July 2023
9. Bleeping computer. https://www.bleepingcomputer.com/news/security/over-275-million-rec ords-exposed-by-unsecured-mongodb-database/. Accessed 09 July 2023
10. Cpomagazine. https://www.cpomagazine.com/cyber-security/toyota-connected-service-dec ade-long-data-leak-exposed-2-15-million-customers/. Accessed 18 July 2023
11. Bleeping computer. https://www.bleepingcomputer.com/news/security/redis-mongodb-and-elastic-2022-s-top-exposed-databases/. Accessed 18 July 2023

12. Imam, A.A., Basri, S., González-Aparicio, M.T., Balogun, A.O., Kumar, G.: NoInjection: preventing unsafe queries on NoSQL-document-model databases. In: 2nd International Conference on Computing and Information Technology (ICCIT) (2022)
13. Ron, A., Shulman-Peleg, A., Bronshtein, E: No SQL, No Injection? Examining NoSQL Security
14. Hou, B., Qian, K., Li, L., Shi, Y., Tao, L., Liu, J.: MongoDB NoSQL Injection Analysis and Detection. In: IEEE 3rd International Conference on Cyber Security and Cloud Computing (CSCloud), 2016 (2016)
15. A survey on detection and prevention of SQL and NoSQL injection attack on server-side applications. Int. J. Comput. Appl. (0975 - 8887), **183** (2021)
16. Invicti. https://www.invicti.com/blog/web-security/what-is-nosql-injection/. Accessed 07 Nov 2022
17. Spiegel, P.: NoSQL injection fun with objects and arrays (2022). https://owasp.org/www-pdf-archive/GOD16-NOSQL.pdf
18. Databases security issues - a short analysis on the emergent security problems generated by NoSQL databases. Economic Computation and Economic Cybernetics Studies and Research **53**(3) (2019)
19. Rodríguez, G.E., Torres, J.G., Flores, P., Benavides, D.E.: Cross-site scripting (XSS) attacks and mitigation: a survey. Comput. Netw. **166**, 106960 (2020)
20. OWASP. https://owasp.org/www-project-web-security-testing-guide/v41/4-Web_Application_Security_Testing/09-Testing_for_Weak_Cryptography/01-Testing_for_Weak_SSL_TLS_Ciphers_Insufficient_Transport_Layer_Protection. Accessed 28 July 2023
21. Wang, X., Yu, H.: How to break MD5 and other hash functions. In: Cramer, R. (ed.) EUROCRYPT 2005. LNCS, vol. 3494, pp. 19–35. Springer, Heidelberg (2005). https://doi.org/10.1007/11426639_2
22. Qualys. https://blog.qualys.com/product-tech/2013/03/19/rc4-in-tls-is-broken-now-what. Accessed 09 July 2023
23. Zugaj, W., Beichler, A.S.: Analysis of standard security features for selected NoSQL systems. Am. J. Inf. Sci. Technol. (2019)
24. Meow attack. https://www.bleepingcomputer.com/news/security/new-meow-attack-has-deleted-almost-4-000-unsecured-databases/. Accessed 02 Oct 2023
25. Hackernoon. https://hackernoon.com/learnings-from-the-meow-bot-attack-on-our-mongodb-databases-y22q3zs8. Accessed 12 Oct 2023
26. Techtarget. https://www.techtarget.com/searchsecurity/news/252486971/Meow-attacks-continue-thousands-of-databases-deleted. Accessed 9 Oct 2023
27. Osborn, S.L., Servos, D., Shermin, M.: Issues in access control and privacy for big data. In: Meyers, R.A. (eds.) Encyclopedia of Complexity and Systems Science, pp. 1–9. Springer, Heidelberg (2018). https://doi.org/10.1007/978-3-642-27737-5_752-1
28. MongoDB docs. https://www.mongodb.com/docs/drivers/go/current/fundamentals/auth/. Accessed 22 June 2023
29. MongoDB manual. https://www.mongodb.com/docs/manual/. Accessed 22 June 2023
30. Ajayi, O.O., Adebiyi, T.O.: Application of data masking in achieving information privacy. IOSR J. Eng. (IOSRJEN) **4**(2), 13–21 (2014)
31. Cuzzocrea, A., Shahriar, H.: Data masking techniques for NoSQL database security: a systematic review. In: 2017 IEEE International Conference on Big Data (Big Data), Boston, MA, USA (2017)
32. Git hub Data masking. https://github.com/pkdone/mongo-data-masking. Accessed 06 July 2023
33. Mozilla docs. https://developer.mozilla.org/en-US/docs/Web/HTTP/CORS. Accessed 18 July 2023

34. Lavrenovs, A., Melón, F.J.R.: HTTP security headers analysis of top one million websites. In: 10th International Conference on Cyber Conflict (CyCon), Tallinn, Estonia (2018)
35. MongoDB manual. https://www.mongodb.com/docs/manual/core/security-transport-encryption/. Accessed 04 July 2023
36. MongoDB manual, CSFLE. https://www.mongodb.com/docs/manual/core/csfle/. Accessed 16 July 2023
37. CouchDB homepage. https://couchdb.apache.org/. Accessed 19 June 2023

# Theoretical Enumeration of Deployable Single-Output Strong PUF Instances Based on Uniformity and Uniqueness Constraints

Venkata Sreekanth Balijabudda[1]($\boxtimes$), Kamalesh Acharya[2],
Rajat Subhra Chakraborty[1], and Indrajit Chakrabarti[1]

[1] Indian Institute of Technology Kharagpur, West Bengal, India
sreekanthbv@iitkgp.ac.in, rschakraborty@cse.iitkgp.ac.in,
indrajit@ece.iitkgp.ac.in
[2] VIT Chennai, Tamil Nadu, India

**Abstract.** *Uniqueness* and *Uniformity* are two important quality metrics that determine the practical usability of a strong Physically Unclonable Function ("strong PUF") instance, or an ensemble of strong PUF instances. In this paper, we consider the strong PUF instance as a Boolean function, and theoretically enumerate the total number of usable single-output practical strong PUF instances, assuming commonly acceptable thresholds of the Uniqueness and Uniformity metrics. We have computed the number of possible strong PUF instances with ideal Uniformity (= 0.50), and Uniformity within an acceptable range of the ideal value, and the same for Uniqueness. Additionally, given an ideal Uniformity, we have enumerated the number of strong PUF instances with ideal Uniqueness (= 0.50), and Uniqueness within an acceptable range. Our analysis is completely generic and applicable to any PUF variant, independent of its structure and operating principle.

**Keywords:** Boolean function · Combinatorics · Physically Unclonable Function · Uniformity · Uniqueness

## 1 Introduction

A semiconductor Physical Unclonable Function (PUF) [5,10] is an electronic circuit embedded in a physical device, which has (ideally) unclonable instance-specific output characteristics. A PUF instance acts as digital "fingerprint generator", where the fingerprint consists of either a bit-string obtained automatically on power-on without the application of any input stimuli for a "weak PUF", or the input-output ("challenge-response") truth-table of the PUF instance for a "strong PUF". PUF circuit behavior is the manifestation of unpredictable and unavoidable manufacturing process variations for modern nanometre-scale CMOS devices. PUF has emerged as an important hardware security primitive,

V. Muthukkumarasamy et al. (Eds.): ICISS 2023, LNCS 14424, pp. 77–87, 2023.
https://doi.org/10.1007/978-3-031-49099-6_5

and have found widespread application in numerous problems, ranging from integrated circuit (IC) identification to device authentication [4, 7]. PUFs are particularly suitable for resource-constrained platforms such as the Internet of Things (IoTs), where they help to efficiently substitute computationally-expensive cryptographic operations.

Unfortunately, in practice, not all PUF instances are usable. For example, if the power-on signature of a weak PUF instance is 1 in all the bits or 0 in all the bits, i.e. $1111 \cdots 11111$ or $0000 \cdots 0000$, it is not usable because of low-entropy. However, the issue of determining whether a given PUF instance is usable in practice is more complicated for a strong PUF, since whether a strong PUF instance is usable or not can be decided only after extensive experimental characterization. A strong PUF instance with $n$-bit input challenges and $m$-bit output responses can be considered to be a Boolean function $f : \{0, 1\}^n \rightarrow \{0, 1\}^m$. Given that typically $n \geq 64$ in practice, exhaustive enumeration of the truth table for each of the $m$ outputs of a given strong PUF instance is practically infeasible. Hence, the challenge-response characterization is limited to a small subset of the truth table, typically building a database of only a few thousand challenge-response pairs (CRPs). Additional experimental characterization is performed to evaluate several statistical performance metrics of the PUF. Some of these metrics – e.g. *Uniformity* which measures the fraction of 1 s in the truth table of a PUF instance, are applicable for an individual strong PUF instance, while some metrics, e.g. *Uniqueness* which measures the distinguishability of individual PUF instances, apply to an ensemble of PUF instances of the same type (precise definition of these metrics are given later in the paper). The practical acceptability of a given strong PUF instance, or a strong PUF ensemble, is based on the obtained metric values. Those PUF instances or a PUF ensemble with the individual metric values within specified limits are accepted for practical deployment, while the others are rejected. For example, a strong PUF instance with Uniformity value in the range $[0.45, 0.55]$ and a strong PUF ensemble with Uniqueness value in the same range can be considered suitable for practical deployment for most application scenarios.

In this paper, we aim to solve the interesting open problem of theoretically estimating the number of practically deployable instances of a given strong PUF variant, based on its experimentally determined Uniformity and Uniqueness metrics. **Our treatment is based purely on combinatorial arguments, while being completely agnostic of the physical nature, electrical characteristics, operating principle, and type of a given PUF design.**

These estimates are useful in taking a call about the degree of practical usefulness of a proposed new PUF variant, or an ensemble of an existing PUF variant, based on a count of deployable PUF instances. We expect this work would make estimation of the number of deployable unique instances an important consideration while deciding upon a PUF choice.

## 2  Background

### 2.1  Related Works and Motivation

The idea of Physical one-way functions for cryptography applications was introduced in [12]. More useful constructions of PUF circuits which are economical to widely available devices are proposed in [5]. Mathematical representations of these PUF circuits are established in [2,3]. Nevertheless, it is the authors of [13] who had proposed the first theoretical study exploring the sampling spaces of Boolean functions and PUF models. However, a drawback of this incomprehensive study is that, although the security of arbiter PUF in a restricted *domain* of Boolean functions is provided from [11], a combinatorial analysis of the usable PUF instances based on their performance metrics (i.e., *range* of Boolean functions) is not performed. In our work, we overcome this drawback and perform a detailed combinatorial analysis of the total usable PUF instances with ideal and practical quality metrics. An emphasis on *Uniformity* and *Uniqueness* metrics is laid in choosing the PUF instances from the space of Boolean functions. The results are obtained for any $n$-bit PUF, also encompassing the noise in real-world scenarios.

Most current works usually consider the robustness of a given strong PUF variant to *Model Building Attacks* [9], as the most important factor in deciding the practical acceptability of a PUF. **However, to the best of our knowledge, combinatorial analysis of PUFs to enumerate the number of practically deployable PUF instances based on statistical performance metrics have not been attempted.**

### 2.2  PUF Performance Metrics

The performance of any PUF implementation is evaluated using several statistical performance metrics [8]. Among them, two of the most commonly used metrics are *Uniformity* and *Uniqueness*, and are defined below (for simplicity, we assume the PUF has a single output bit, i.e. $m = 1$).

The **Uniformity** of a strong PUF instance measures the relative frequency of 1's in its response. It is given by:

$$Uniformity = \tfrac{1}{R}\sum_{l=1}^{R} r_l \tag{1}$$

where $R$ is the total number of applied challenges for which the PUF instance was characterized, and $r_l \in \{0,1\}$ is the response obtained for the $l$-th challenge. Its ideal value is 0.50 (or 50%).

The **Uniqueness** metric, on the other hand, provides a measure of distinguishability among two PUF instances of the same type. Consider an ensemble of $k$ strong PUFs of the same type, two separate PUF instances $i$ and $j$ belonging to this ensemble, and each PUF instance of the ensemble have been characterized for the same set of $R$ challenges. Then, the *Uniqueness* metric is defined as:

$$Uniqueness = \tfrac{2}{k(k-1)}\sum_{i=1}^{k-1}\sum_{j=i+1}^{k} \frac{\mathrm{HD}(R_i,R_j)}{R} \tag{2}$$

where $R_i$ and $R_j$ represent the $R$-bit concatenated responses to the $R$-applied challenges for the $i$-th and $j$-th PUF instances, and HD( ) represents the *Hamming Distance* between two $R$-bit vectors. Again, ideal Uniqueness value for an ensemble of strong PUFs is 0.50 (or 50%).

It should be noted that in practical implementations, usually these ideal values of the performance metrics are not attained. Hence, we have to consider ranges of values that are close to ideal, in general in the range $[0.50 - \epsilon, 0.50 + \epsilon]$, where $\epsilon$ is a small positive constant, whose value is decided based on the application scenario.

## 3  Enumeration of Deployable PUF Instances Based on Uniformity and Uniqueness

Each strong PUF instance with $n$-bit challenge and a single-bit response can be represented by an $n$-variable Boolean function. Hence, the terms "Boolean function" and "PUF instance" have been used interchangeably below.

### 3.1  PUF Instances with Ideal Uniformity

**Theorem 1.** *The total number of possible PUF instances with n-bit challenges and Uniformity = 0.50 is* $\binom{2^n}{2^{n-1}}$.

*Proof.* For Uniformity to be 0.50, the number of 1's in the truth table of a strong PUF instance with $n$-bit challenges should be exactly $2^n/2 = 2^{n-1}$. There are exactly $\binom{2^n}{2^{n-1}}$ distinct choices of $2^{n-1}$ entries in a truth table of size $2^n$. Hence, the number of distinct PUF instances with Uniformity value exactly 0.5 is $\binom{2^n}{2^{n-1}}$.                                                                     □

### 3.2  PUF Instances with Uniformity in the Range $[0.50 - \epsilon, 0.50 + \epsilon]$

Before proceeding to the next major result, a useful recursion is proved below:

**Lemma 1.** *Let $N$ and $r$ be positive integers with $r < N$ and*

$$f(N,r) = \binom{N}{0} + \binom{N}{1} + \ldots + \binom{N}{r-1}, \quad r < N \tag{3}$$

$$\textit{Then,} \quad f(N,r) = \quad 2f(N-1,r) - \binom{N-1}{r-1} \tag{4}$$

*Proof.* Applying *Pascal's Identity* [6], $\binom{N}{k} = \binom{N-1}{k-1} + \binom{N-1}{k}$, $k > 0$, repeatedly, and since $\binom{N}{0} = \binom{N-1}{0} = 1$, we get,

$$\begin{aligned} f(N,r) &= \quad \binom{N}{0} + \binom{N}{1} + \binom{N}{2} + \ldots + \binom{N}{r-1} \\ &= 2\left[\binom{N-1}{0} + \binom{N-1}{1} + \ldots + \binom{N-1}{r-1}\right] - \binom{N-1}{r-1} \\ &= \quad 2f(N-1,r) - \binom{N-1}{r-1} \end{aligned} \tag{5}$$

**Theorem 2.** *Assuming $2^{n-1}(1 - 2\epsilon)$ to be a positive integer for an $\epsilon > 0$, the number of n-bit PUF instances with Uniformity in the range $[0.50 - \epsilon, 0.50 + \epsilon]$ is given by:*

$$X = \binom{2^n}{2^{n-1}(1-2\epsilon)} + \binom{2^n}{2^{n-1}(1-2\epsilon)+1} + \ldots + \binom{2^n}{2^{n-1}} +$$

$$\ldots + \binom{2^n}{2^{n-1}(1+2\epsilon)} = 2^N - 2f(N, r) \tag{6}$$

*where $N = 2^n$, $r = (N/2) \cdot (1 - 2\epsilon)$ and $f(N, r)$ is given by Eq. (3).*

*Proof.* For an Uniformity value $0.50 - \epsilon$, we need $2^n(0.50 - \epsilon) = 2^{n-1}(1 - 2\epsilon)$ number of 1's in the PUF instance's truth table. Hence, the number of such Boolean functions, i.e. distinct PUF instances is $\binom{2^n}{2^{n-1}(1-2\epsilon)}$. Similarly, for a Uniformity value $0.50 + \epsilon$, we need $2^n(0.50 + \epsilon) = 2^{n-1}(1 + 2\epsilon)$ number of 1's in the PUF instance's truth table. Hence, the number of such Boolean functions are $\binom{2^n}{2^{n-1}(1+2\epsilon)}$. Extrapolating in the same way, the total number of PUF instances with Uniformity in the range $[0.50 - \epsilon, 0.50 + \epsilon]$ is given by:

$$X = \binom{2^n}{2^{n-1}(1-2\epsilon)} + \binom{2^n}{2^{n-1}(1-2\epsilon)+1} + \ldots + \binom{2^n}{2^{n-1}} + \ldots + \binom{2^n}{2^{n-1}(1+2\epsilon)} \tag{7}$$

Let $2^n = N$ and $r = (N/2) \cdot (1 - 2\epsilon)$; then, the above expression can be written as:

$$X = \binom{N}{r} + \binom{N}{r+1} + \ldots + \binom{N}{N/2} + \ldots + \binom{N}{N-r} \tag{8}$$

Let $X_1 = \left[\binom{N}{r} + \ldots + \binom{N}{N/2}\right]$. Using the basic identity $\binom{N}{i} = \binom{N}{N-i}$, $0 \leq i \leq N$, Eq. (8) can be rewritten as:

$$X = 2\left[\binom{N}{r} + \ldots + \binom{N}{N/2}\right] - \binom{N}{N/2} = 2X_1 - \binom{N}{N/2} \tag{9}$$

We now derive an expression for $X_1$ as follows: Since,

$$\binom{N}{0} + \binom{N}{1} + \ldots + \binom{N}{N/2} + \binom{N}{N/2+1} + \ldots + \binom{N}{N} = 2^N$$

$$\Rightarrow \quad 2\left[\binom{N}{0} + \binom{N}{1} + \ldots + \binom{N}{N/2}\right] - \binom{N}{N/2} = 2^N \tag{10}$$

After some rearrangement of terms,

$$\left[\binom{N}{r} + \ldots + \binom{N}{N/2}\right] = 2^{N-1} + \tfrac{1}{2}\binom{N}{N/2} - f(N)$$

$$\Rightarrow \quad X_1 = 2^{N-1} + \tfrac{1}{2}\binom{N}{N/2} - f(N, r) \tag{11}$$

Substituting this value of $X_1$ in Eq. (9), we have the total number of PUF instances as,

$$X = 2\left[2^{N-1} + \tfrac{1}{2}\binom{N}{N/2} - f(N,r)\right] - \binom{N}{N/2} = 2^N - 2f(N,r) \quad \square \quad (12)$$

## 3.3  PUF Instances Having Ensemble Uniqueness = 0.50

We assume that each PUF instance in the ensemble is exhaustively enumerated, i.e. number of applied challenges $R = 2^n$, where each challenge is $n$-bit long. We consider the following cases: the first case of exact analysis for a small ensemble of only two PUF instances ($k = 2$), and the second case of a more general analysis with more instances ($k > 2$).

**k = 2**: To obtain an Uniqueness value of 0.50 in an ensemble of $k = 2$ PUF instances, we need to have the Hamming distance to be $R/2$, i.e., the responses bitstrings for the two PUF instances must differ at exactly $R/2$ positions. Note that $R/2$ distinct positions in a $R$-bit bitstring can be chosen in $\binom{R}{R/2}$ ways. These distinct positions can be covered in $(2^{R/2})/2$ ways (either all-ones or all-zeros, resulting in the division by 2), while the remaining positions have $2^{R/2}$ different choices. Hence, the total number of possible PUF instances is:

$$Y_{k=2} = \frac{\binom{R}{R/2} 2^{R/2} (2^{R/2})}{2} = \binom{R}{R/2} 2^{R-1} \tag{13}$$

**k > 2**: Let $M = \binom{k}{2}/2$. To achieve Uniqueness 0.50, we can rewrite Eq. (2):

$$\frac{1}{\binom{k}{2}} \frac{\sum_{i=1}^{k-1} \sum_{j=i+1}^{k} HD(R_i, R_j)}{R} = 0.50 \Rightarrow \sum_{i=1}^{k-1} \sum_{j=i+1}^{k} HD(R_i, R_j) = \frac{R\binom{k}{2}}{2} = M \cdot R \tag{14}$$

where $HD(R_i, R_j)$ represents the Hamming distance between two PUF $R$-bit response strings $R_i$ and $R_j$, for PUF instances $i$ and $j$ respectively. Note that this Hamming distance for a pair of distinguishable PUF instances lies in the range $[1, R]$. There are $2M$ Hamming distances, corresponding to $2M$ PUF instance pairs. To get the sum of these Hamming distances to be $MR$ is equivalent to obtaining the solution of the equation $a_1 + a_2 + \ldots + a_{2M} = M \cdot R$, for the $2M$ unknowns $a_1, a_2, \ldots a_{2M} \in [1, R]$. Let us consider the polynomial $(x^1 + x^2 + \ldots x^R)^{2M}$. It contains terms of the form $c_i \cdot x^{a_1 + a_2 + \ldots a_{2M}}$, where $c_i$ is a positive integer. Hence, the total number of solutions to the equation $a_1 + a_2 + \ldots + a_{2M} = M \cdot R$, which is also the required number of PUF instances, is:

$$Y_{k>2} = \text{coefficient of } x^{MR} \text{ in } (x^1 + x^2 + \ldots + x^R)^{2M}$$
$$= \text{coefficient of } x^{MR} \text{ in } (1 - x)^{2M}(x^1 + x^2 + \ldots + x^R)^{2M}/(1 - x)^{2M}$$
$$= \text{coefficient of } x^{MR} \text{ in } (1 - x^R)^{2M} x^{2M} (1 - x)^{-2M}$$

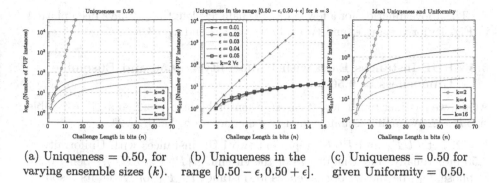

(a) Uniqueness = 0.50, for varying ensemble sizes ($k$).    (b) Uniqueness in the range $[0.50 - \epsilon, 0.50 + \epsilon]$.    (c) Uniqueness = 0.50 for given Uniformity = 0.50.

**Fig. 1.** Number of $n$-bit PUF Instances with various performance metrics.

The results for a few values of $n$ and $k$ are plotted in Fig. 1a. It must be noted that an exact numerical result is derived for $k = 2$, while a lower bound or minimum usable instances is obtained for $k > 2$. This relaxation applies to all successive evaluations.

### 3.4  PUF Instances with Uniqueness In Range $[0.50 - \epsilon, 0.50 + \epsilon]$

As previously done, we consider two separate cases, for different ensemble sizes.

**k = 2**: To achieve a Uniqueness value of $0.50 - \epsilon$, the response strings for two PUF instances must have Hamming distance $m_1 = (R/2)(1 - 2\epsilon)$, where $R$ is the number of applied challenges and $\epsilon > 0$. Hence, the number of such cases is $\binom{R}{m_1} 2^{R-1}$. Similarly, to have Uniqueness $0.50 + \epsilon$, the response strings must have Hamming distance $m_2 = (R/2)(1 + 2\epsilon)$. Thereby, the number of such cases is $\binom{R}{m_2} 2^{R-1}$. Hence, the total number of PUF instances is $\sum_{i=m_1}^{m_2} \binom{R}{i} 2^{R-1}$, assuming $m_1$ and $m_2$ are positive integers, and $R = 2^n$.

**k > 2**: To obtain Uniqueness in the range of $[0.50 - \epsilon, 0.50 + \epsilon]$, the value of $\sum_{j=1}^{k-1} \sum_{i=j+1}^{k} HD(R_i, R_j)$ must lie in the range $[M \cdot r_1, M \cdot r_2]$, where $M = \frac{1}{2}\binom{k}{2}, r_1 = R(1 - 2\epsilon), r_2 = R(1 + 2\epsilon)$. From the analysis presented in Sect. 3.3 for the case $k > 2$, it is apparent that if $\sum_{i=1}^{k-1} \sum_{j=i+1}^{k} HD(R_i, R_j)$ is $M \cdot R$, then the approximate number of possible choices are (assuming $r_1$ and $r_2$ are integers):

$$= \binom{MR-1}{MR-2M} - \binom{2M}{1}\binom{(M-1)R-1)}{(M-1)R-2M} + \ldots (M \text{ terms}). \tag{15}$$

Hence adding all such choices in the range of $[M \cdot r_1, M \cdot r_2]$, we have the approximate number of total PUF instances as:

$$= \binom{Mr_1-1}{Mr_1-2M} - \binom{2M}{1}\binom{(M-1)r_1-1}{(M-1)r_1-2M} + \binom{2M}{2}\binom{(M-2)r_1-1}{(M-2)r_1-2M} \ldots$$

$$+ \binom{Mr_2-1}{Mr_2-2M} - \binom{2M}{1}\binom{(M-1)r_2-1}{(M-1)r_2-2M} + \binom{2M}{2}\binom{(M-2)r_2-1}{(M-2)r_2-2M} \ldots$$

$$= \sum_{i=Mr_1}^{Mr_2} \binom{i-1}{i-2M} - \binom{2M}{1} \sum_{i=(M-1)r_1}^{(M-1)r_2} \binom{i-1}{i-2M} + \ldots (M \text{ terms}) \tag{16}$$

The above function for a few values of challenge lengths $(n)$ have been plotted in Fig. 1b for varying $\epsilon$, and two values of $k = 2$ and $k = 3$.

### 3.5 PUF Instances Each with Uniformity $= 0.50$ and Ensemble Uniqueness $= 0.50$

Again, we consider two different cases: (a) ensemble size $k = 2$, and, (b) ensemble size $k > 2$. We again assume exhaustive enumeration, i.e. $R = 2^n$.

**k = 2**: Let $PUF_A$ and $PUF_B$ represent two PUF instances with Uniformity $= 0.50$ individually, and Uniqueness of the ensemble $\{PUF_A, PUF_B\}$ being 0.50. Suppose, $C_{1A}$ be the set of challenges for instance $PUF_A$ for which its response is 1, and $C_{0A} = \{0,1\}^n \setminus C_{1A}$ be the set of challenges for instance $PUF_A$ for which its response is 0. Similarly, let $C_{1B}$ and $C_{0B} = \{0,1\}^n \setminus C_{1B}$ be the corresponding challenge sets for PUF instance $PUF_B$. Then, given the Uniformity and Uniqueness values of 0.50 each, and $k = 2$, we have the following properties:

1. $|C_{1A}| = |C_{0A}| = |C_{1B}| = |C_{0B}| = R/2$
2. $|C_{1A} \setminus C_{1B}| = |C_{0A} \setminus C_{0B}| = R/4$

The second property can be argued based on the fact that for every challenge $c_1 \in C_{1A} \setminus C_{1B}$, there must be exactly one challenge $c_2 \in C_{1B} \setminus C_{1A}$, to ensure property-1. Considering all possible ways to construct sets $C_{1A}$, $C_{0A}$, $C_{1B}$ and $C_{0B}$, and remembering that the number of possible $n$-variable Boolean functions with Uniformity $= 0.50$ is $\binom{R}{R/2}2^{R-1}$, the total number of possible PUF instances in this case is:

$$Z_{k=2} = \binom{R/2}{R/4}\binom{R/2}{R/4}\binom{R}{R/2}2^{R-1} = \binom{R/2}{R/4}^2\binom{R}{R/2}2^{R-1} \tag{17}$$

**k > 2**: Let $M = \frac{1}{2}\binom{k}{2}$. To achieve Uniqueness as 0.50, we must have (from Eq. 14):

$$\Rightarrow \sum_{i=1}^{k-1}\sum_{j=i+1}^{k} HD(R_i, R_j) = \frac{R\binom{k}{2}}{2} = M \cdot R \tag{18}$$

Note that since we are considering PUF instances each of which have an even number ($= R/2 = 2^{n-1}, n > 1$) of 1's and 0's in its truth table (because of Uniformity $= 0.50$), Hamming distance between each pair must be even, i.e. $HD(R_i, R_j) \in \{2, 4, \ldots R\}$, $i \neq j$. There are $2M$ possible PUF instance pairs. Finding the choices for all the Hamming Distance values which sum to $M \cdot R$ is equivalent to obtaining a solution to the equation $a_1 + a_2 + \ldots + a_{2M} = M \cdot R$, where $a_1, a_2, \ldots a_{2M}$ values lies in $\{2, 4, \ldots, R\}$. Let us consider the polynomial $(x^2 + x^4 + \ldots x^R)^{2M}$. It contains terms of the form $c_i \cdot x^{a_1 + a_2 + \ldots a_{2M}}$ and its co-efficient will give the required result. Hence, the approximate number of PUF instances is = coefficient of $x^{MR}$ in $(x^2 + x^4 + \ldots + x^R)^{2M}$ = coefficient of $X^{MR/2}$ in $(1 - X)^{2M}(X^1 + X^2 \ldots + X^{R/2})^{2M}/(1-x)^{2M}$ = coefficient of $X^{MR/2}$ in $(1 - X^{R/2})^{2M}X^{2M}(1 - X)^{-2M}$

The results for a few values of $n$ are shown in Fig. 1c for different number of $k$ instances in the ensemble.

## 3.6 PUF Instances Each with Uniformity 0.50 and Ensemble Uniqueness in the Range $[0.50 - \epsilon, 0.50 + \epsilon]$

Again, we consider two separate cases, as follows:

$k = 2$: Given Uniformity of 0.50, we had earlier derived the number of PUF instances with Uniqueness 0.50, in Eq. (17), as $\binom{R/2}{R/4}^2 \binom{R}{R/2} 2^{R-1}$. Let $T_1 = \binom{R}{R/2} 2^{R-1}$. Similarly, for Uniqueness $= 0.50 - \epsilon$ it would be $\binom{R/2}{l_1}^2 T_1$ and for Uniqueness $= 0.50 + \epsilon$ it would be $\binom{R/2}{l_2}^2 T_1$, where $l_1 = R(0.50 - \epsilon)/2$, and $l_2 = R(0.50 + \epsilon)/2$. Hence for Uniqueness $[0.50 - \epsilon, 0.50 + \epsilon]$, the total number of functions are:

$$\binom{R/2}{l_1}^2 + \ldots + \binom{R/2}{R/4}^2 + \ldots + \binom{R/2}{l_2}^2 = \sum_{i=l_1}^{l_2} \binom{R/2}{i} \cdot T_1. \qquad (19)$$

$k > 2$: To obtain Uniqueness in $[0.50 - \epsilon, 0.50 + \epsilon]$, the value of $\sum_{i=j+1}^{M} \sum_{j=1}^{M-1} HD(P_i, P_j)$ must lie in $[MR_1, MR_2]$ where, $M = \frac{1}{2}\binom{k}{2}$, $R_1 = R(1 - 2\epsilon)$, and $R_2 = R(1 + 2\epsilon)$. From previous result, it is apparent that if $\sum_{i=j+1}^{M} \sum_{j=1}^{M-1} HD(P_i, P_j)$ is $MR$, then the approximate number of possible cases are:

$$= \binom{MR/2-1}{MR/2-2M} - \binom{2M}{1}\binom{(M-1)(R/2)-1}{(M-1)(R/2)-2M} + \ldots (M \text{ terms}). \qquad (20)$$

Hence. adding all such choices in the range of $[MR_1, MR_2]$, we have the approximate number of total PUF instances as:

$$= \binom{MR_1/2-1}{MR_1/2-2M} - \binom{2M}{1}\binom{(M-1)(R_1/2)-1}{(M-1)(R_1/2)-2M} \ldots (M \text{ terms}) +$$

$$\binom{MR_2/2-1}{MR_2/2-2M} - \binom{2M}{1}\binom{(M-1)(R_2/2)-1}{(M-1)(R_2/2)-2M} \ldots (M \text{ terms})$$

$$= \sum_{i=MR_1/2}^{MR_2/2} \binom{i-1}{i-2M} - \binom{2M}{1} \sum_{i=(M-1)(R_1/2)}^{(M-1)(R_2/2)} \binom{i-1}{i-2M} + \ldots$$

$$+(-1)^{l-1}\binom{2M}{l-1} \sum_{i=(M-(l-1))(R_1/2)}^{(M-(l-1))(R_2/2)} \binom{i-1}{i-2M} + \ldots (M \text{ terms}). \qquad (21)$$

Note that if some $(M - (l - 1))(R_i/2) - (2M) < 0$, where $1 \leq l \leq M$, and $i \in \{1, 2\}$, then we will not add that corresponding term. It is obvious that the number of terms is less than or equal to $M$ (except the $k = 3$ case where there are $\lceil M \rceil$ terms).

## 4 Discussions

To make our analysis mathematically tractable, we were forced to make an impractical assumption that each PUF instance is characterized exhaustively for all its possible input challenges. However, our analysis should also be approximately valid for PUF implementations where each instance has undergone a more common incomplete characterization (for only a small subset of the possible challenges). Although closed-form expressions are not provided for those cases involving the Uniqueness metric, the coefficient results can be easily obtained using computer algebra systems like *SAGE* or *MAPLE*, from which exact numerical values can be obtained by evaluating the expressions.

Practical validation of the derived results through analysis of actual data obtained from silicon PUF implementations is difficult, because while we have control over the number of challenges, given the very characteristics of PUFs, we have no *a priori* control over the nature of the Boolean function that corresponds to an implemented strong PUF instance.

# 5   Conclusions

We have theoretically derived the total number of deployable $n$-bit strong PUF instances, based on constraints set by Uniformity and Uniqueness values. Such analysis is useful in deciding the relative usability of different PUF variants while being independent of the nature of the PUF in practical scenarios. This work has produced a valuable metric to evaluate the yield of a PUF design, especially during the manufacturing process. Our future work would be directed toward extending our analysis to include other common performance metrics such as *Bit-aliasing* [1] and *Reliability*.

# References

1. Feiten, L., Sauer, M., Becker, B.: On metrics to quantify the inter-device uniqueness of PUFs. Cryptology ePrint Archive, Paper 2016/320 (2016). https://eprint.iacr.org/2016/320
2. Ganji, F.: On the Learnability of Physically Unclonable Functions. Springer, Cham (2018). https://doi.org/10.1007/978-3-319-76717-8
3. Ganji, F., Tajik, S., Fäßler, F., Seifert, J.-P.: Strong machine learning attack against PUFs with no mathematical model. In: Gierlichs, B., Poschmann, A.Y. (eds.) CHES 2016. LNCS, vol. 9813, pp. 391–411. Springer, Heidelberg (2016). https://doi.org/10.1007/978-3-662-53140-2_19
4. Gassend, B., Clarke, D., van Dijk, M., Devadas, S.: Controlled physical random functions. In: 18th Annual Computer Security Applications Conference, 2002. Proceedings, pp. 149–160 (2002). https://doi.org/10.1109/CSAC.2002.1176287
5. Suh, G.E., Devadas, S.: Physical unclonable functions for device authentication and secret key generation. In: Proceedings of the Design Automation Conference (DAC) (2007)
6. Harne, S., Badshah, V., Verma, V.: Fibonacci and Lucas polynomial identities, binomial coefficients and pascal's triangle. Int. J. Math. Res. **7**(1), 7–13 (2015)
7. Herder, C., Yu, M.D., Koushanfar, F., Devadas, S.: Physical unclonable functions and applications: a tutorial. Proc. IEEE **102**(8), 1126–1141 (2014)

8. Hori, Y., Yoshida, T., Katashita, T., Satoh, A.: Quantitative and statistical performance evaluation of arbiter physical unclonable functions on FPGAs. In: 2010 International Conference on Reconfigurable Computing and FPGAs, pp. 298–303 (2010)

9. Lim, D., Devadas, S.: Extracting secret keys from integrated circuits. S.M. Thesis, Massachusetts Institute of Technology (2004). https://hdl.handle.net/1721.1/18059

10. Lim, D., Lee, J.W., Gassend, B., Suh, G.E., van Dijk, M., Devadas, S.: Extracting secret keys from integrated circuits. IEEE Trans. Very Large Scale Integr. (VLSI) Syst. **13**(10), 1200–1205 (2005)

11. Maitra, S., Mandal, B., Martinsen, T., Roy, D., Stănică, P.: Analysis on Boolean function in a restricted (Biased) domain. IEEE Trans. Inf. Theory **66**(2), 1219–1231 (2020). https://doi.org/10.1109/TIT.2019.2932739

12. Ravikanth, P.S., Benton, S.A.: Physical one-way functions. Science **297**, 2026–2030 (2001)

13. Roy, A., Roy, D., Maitra, S.: How do the arbiter PUFs sample the Boolean function class? In: AlTawy, R., Hülsing, A. (eds.) SAC 2021. LNCS, vol. 13203, pp. 111–130. Springer, Cham (2022). https://doi.org/10.1007/978-3-030-99277-4_6

# Network Security

# Detection and Hardening Strategies to Secure an Enterprise Network

Preetam Mukherjee$^{(\boxtimes)}$ (ID), Sabu M. Thampi (ID), N. Rohith,
Bishwajit Kumar Poddar, and Ipshita Sen

Digital University Kerala, Thiruvananthapuram, Kerala, India
preetam.mukherjee@duk.ac.in

**Abstract.** In today's IT enterprises, security strategy determination
has become exponentially complex with the increasing complexity of the
network infrastructure. Various types of defenses are available with a
security administrator, viz., harden, detect, isolate, deceive, and evict.
These defenses have their specific purposes. Separate strategies are
required for implementing each type of defense in the context of an enterprise network. The existing defense strategy selection schemes do not
have explicit strategies for different classes of defenses. In this paper, we
propose two separate strategies to determine the point of deployment of
harden and detect defenses. These strategies would be useful in providing
a better return on security investments.

**Keywords:** Attack Graph · Mitre D3FEND · Mitre ATT&CK ·
Defense Strategies

## 1 Introduction

Cyber security has become an essential nonfunctional requirement in the modern
day scenario. Organizations are investing a large portion of their budget to secure
assets from cyber attackers. Accurate distribution of this security budget as per
the requirements is a real challenge considering the large number of vulnerabilities and their complex causal relationships. Understanding these relationships is
essential for effectively mitigating vulnerabilities and preventing attacks. It also
helps to implement best security practices and develop comprehensive defense
strategies.

Causal relationship among the vulnerabilities can be modelled using various
attack modelling techniques like, attack tree, attack graph [1,22,23,26,27]. One
can use these techniques to describe the attackers' reachability in an enterprise
network. The generated models can be analyzed to find the crucial most attack
points that need immediate attention from the security team. These crucial attack
points need to be secured to get the best return on security investment [7,8,35].

Security administrators follow one interesting thumb rule in big enterprises.
They made the core networks more secure than the outer or perimeter networks.
In contrast, administrators put more effort into monitoring the perimeter networks than the core network. The logic behind this is "Late detection is equivalent to not detecting the case at all." As detecting and reacting to a security

V. Muthukkumarasamy et al. (Eds.): ICISS 2023, LNCS 14424, pp. 91–108, 2023.
https://doi.org/10.1007/978-3-031-49099-6_6

incident takes time, security administrators always want to detect the problem at the earliest. On the other hand, in the case of hardening, the goal is to secure all the valuables. Even company insiders may launch attacks on the company's core data centre. To deal with such risks it is crucial to concentrate on the core, to protect the valuables. This approach will also reduce the financial burden of implementing security, as the core network will have a limited attack surface.

Existing research uses various optimization techniques to find the best possible defenses within budget [2,5,7,8,13,19,23,25,29,30,35], but they have not included the "hardened core and monitored perimeter" in the strategy. Due to that deficiency, those methods will fall short in choosing the best defenses.

This paper has formulated two different types of crucial attack point identification techniques for enterprise networks. One type requires strict monitoring, and the other requires hardening of the security. The contribution of this paper is threefold,

- identification of critical vulnerabilities for which hardening is required
- identification of vulnerabilities in urgent need of monitoring/detection
- mapping of vulnerability to the proper type of defense technique(s)

The rest of the paper is structured as follows, Sect. 2 discusses the related research in attack-defense modeling, security metrics, various knowledge bases, etc. Section 3 discusses various repositories and their relationships. Attack modeling is elaborated in Sect. 4. Section 5 presents hardening and detection strategies, illustrated with examples and accompanied by a high-level algorithm. Section 6 elaborates on the defense strategy determination with a detailed example. Section 7 contains the discussion, and Sect. 8 concludes the paper.

## 2   Related Work

Vulnerability databases like CVE[1], CWE[2] are used to find the vulnerabilities/weaknesses associated with IT assets. These databases help find the possible attacks on the network of concern. For the last few years, security researchers started using the latest knowledge repositories like Mitre ATT&CK[3], Mitre D3FEND[4], Mitre CREF navigator[5], etc. [12,28,32,36]. A lot of effort is going into mapping these knowledge bases, which would be helpful in case of analysis and for taking actionable decisions [9,15].

The vulnerabilities identified in an enterprise network can be causally connected. Various attack modeling techniques viz. attack graph [1,22,27], attack trees [26], bayesian attack graph [23] are available to capture these causal dependencies. Attack modeling languages like meta attack language (MAL) [11] are also developed to simulate attacks in the modeled networks.

---

[1] cve.mitre.org.
[2] cwe.mitre.org.
[3] attack.mitre.org.
[4] d3fend.mitre.org.
[5] crefnavigator.mitre.org/navigator.

Different security metrics are generated to help find the critical path from the generated attack models. A few metrics count the number of vulnerabilities between the attacker and target to compute the security strength of a path. These metrics are called Counting metrics, viz. shortest path metric [20,22], weakest-adversary security metric [21]. While computing these metrics, the difficulty of exploiting the vulnerabilities is not considered. Another set of metrics, called Difficulty based metrics, includes difficulty values. A few example difficulty based metrics are attack resistance [34], probabilistic security [33], attack difficulty [16], and diversity metric [4].

Adding the defenses in the attack model to show the possible way of countering the attack steps is the obvious next step toward security related decision making. Attack-defense tree [14], attack countermeasure tree [24], protection tree [6], defense tree [3] are a few example modeling schemes where possible defenses are also included along with the attacks. Attack modeling languages are also extended to add defense mechanisms with the corresponding attack steps. With this extension, it is possible to simulate attack models along with the defense suggestions for the given network.

Adding defenses to the attack model will help identify the defenses quickly but do not provide us with much decision making power. A security officer requires an optimal strategy by using which (s)he can implement the best security within budget (or best return on investment). Existing processes use a variety of optimization techniques to solve the problem of defense strategy identification. In [30] authors proposed a heuristic approach for selecting the countermeasures. A cost-impact analysis-based countermeasure selection approach is proposed in [29]. The selection of optimal countermeasures can be represented as a single and multi-objective optimization problem [23] or a min-max optimization problem [13]. Authors also use mixed integer linear programming to solve the optimization problem for selecting the best defense strategy [25]. In [37], the authors take maximum vulnerability coverage as the main factor, and a stochastic programming-based solution is proposed. Countermeasures can be selected in such a way that the maximum number of attacks can be countered in the high risk attack paths [7,8,35]. Business scenarios can also be added to find out the impact of attacks. Business impact analysis can help determine the network's riskiest assets. Research studies are combining the attack modeling with the business impact analysis [17,18,31] to increase the decision making capacity of security officers.

Even though there is a lot of exciting research ongoing to find the optimal set of defenses within budget, these studies are not including the fundamental idea of securing the core first.

Monitoring strategies should also be set according to the attack scenarios. Positioning properly configured intrusion detection systems (IDS) and other monitoring devices will help detect malicious activities in the initial phases of the attack. Optimal placement of detection mechanisms is a well-researched problem [2,5]. Optimal placement of IDS sensor devices according to attack modelling is also studied [19]. In the existing research works, researchers mainly focused on finding a minimum set of detection systems covering the whole network but they have not included the necessity of early detection of the attack.

# 3  Background

This section has elaborated on several critical knowledge bases that assist security practitioners in making informed security-related decisions.

## 3.1  CVE

The common vulnerabilities and exposures (CVE) system provides a reference method for publicly disclosed cybersecurity vulnerabilities. It is used to identify, define and catalog vulnerabilities. Each security flaw is assigned a CVE ID number. National Vulnerability Database (NVD) assigns the CVE Ids and maintains the list of vulnerabilities[6].

## 3.2  MITRE ATT&CK

Mitre ATT&CK is a knowledge base of adversary tactics and techniques. The ATT&CK knowledge base is used as a foundation for the generation of threat models for real-life attack scenarios. Mitre ATT&CK offers a standard knowledge base for various types of attacks on enterprise assets (viz. Windows, Linux, MacOS, cloud systems, networks, and containers), mobile assets (viz. Android, iOS), and industrial control systems. Attack techniques are classified into separate tactics like reconnaissance, initial access, execution, persistence, privilege escalation, lateral movement, command and control.

## 3.3  MITRE D3FEND

Mitre D3FEND[7] is a framework of a countermeasure knowledge base. A countermeasure can be any process that counteracts or neutralizes cyber attacks. D3FEND has managed to classify all possible countermeasures into five different Tactics.

- Harden: It is used to increase the cost of the exploitation or attack and is generally conducted before a system is online and operational, like application configuration hardening, message encryption, etc.
- Detect: This tactic is used to identify malicious activities on computer networks, like dynamic file analysis, operating system monitoring, etc.
- Isolate: The isolation tactic creates logical or physical barriers which reduce the further access/activities of the attacker in a system/network, like IO port restriction or network traffic filtering.

---

[6] nvd.nist.gov.
[7] d3fend.mitre.org.

- Deceive: Deceiving is based on the fact of attracting potential attackers and giving them entrance to a monitored or restricted environment, like the implementation of honeynet, decoy session tokens, etc.
- Evict: The eviction tactic is used to remove an adversary from a computer network, like account locking or process termination.

According to the Mitre D3FEND knowledge base, every tactic listed above can have a variety of techniques and sub-techniques.

## 3.4 Mappings

**CVE to MITRE ATT&CK.** A vulnerability (identified by the CVE Id) can be exploited by one or more exploitation techniques. A diverse set of attack techniques are enumerated in the Mitre ATT&CK. Thus we can map the CVE record to corresponding ATT&CK techniques which is/are used to exploit the same. For example, CVE-2019-15976 is a vulnerability in the authentication mechanisms of the Cisco data center network manager (DCNM) that could allow an unauthenticated, remote attacker to bypass authentication and execute arbitrary actions with administrative privileges on an affected device. The Mitre ATT&CK technique for the corresponding CVE record is T1190 (exploit public-facing application). Various researcher groups have taken initiatives to map the CVE Ids to Mitre ATT&CK techniques like Centre for Threat-Informed Defense (Mitre Engenuity)[8], Voyager18 (Vulcan)[9].

**MITRE ATT&CK to MITRE D3FEND.** After the CVE - Mitre ATT&CK mapping, we can map the Mitre ATT&CK techniques to Mitre D3FEND, which allows defenders to check for suitable countermeasures based on the cyber security situation. Mitre D3FEND is already mapped to the ATT&CK techniques; recently, Mitre has taken another initiative to accurately map attacks to defenses using ATT&CK extractor[10], but it is under development. The ATT&CK technique T1190, taken in the earlier example, can be detected by the D3FEND techniques D3-RTSD (remote terminal session detection), D3-ISVA (inbound session volume analysis), etc. The mapping will also provide possible hardening, isolation, deceiving or eviction techniques for the corresponding ATT&CK techniques.

## 4   Attack Modeling

In a general scenario, an attacker from the internet can't exploit a vulnerability in the data centre directly due to obvious access restrictions. The attacker may only reach the goal by exploiting multiple causally connected vulnerabilities on

---

[8] github.com/center-for-threat-informed-defense/attack_to_cve.
[9] vulcan.io/voyager18/mitre-mapper.
[10] d3fend.mitre.org/tools/attack-extractor.

its way. Attack modeling techniques will help security administrators figure out all possible paths using which an attacker can reach valuable assets. XploitMAP is a software solution developed to generate attack models represented as attack graphs.

## 4.1   Attack Graph

An Attack Graph is a graphical representation that shows an attacker's possible ways to reach the target. It represents the relationships among the asset vulnerabilities. An attacker who gains the required preconditions for attacking a vulnerability can attempt to exploit the vulnerability. After a successful exploit, the attacker may gain new conditions to perform further exploit(s). The attacker continues the process until it reaches the goal. An Attack Graph can model these multihop attack sequences. It can investigate the potential dangers to a given asset and the range of possible outcomes if an attack is successful [22].

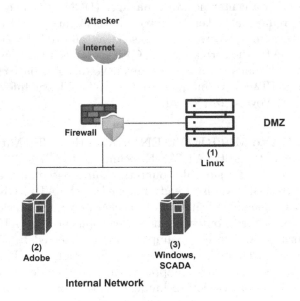

**Fig. 1.** Example network

## 4.2   Tool: XploitMAP

A web-based, interactive security application called XploitMAP is developed to generate and visualize an attacker's reachability to the target. Attack graphs generated by the XploitMAP tool can be used for a multitude of security analyses. Network topology, firewall rules, and the list of vulnerabilities on every host machine are fed to the XploitMAP for generating an attack graph.

Figure 1 represents a simplistic enterprise network with a few servers and computers for running a SCADA testing and reporting platform. The Firewall restricts connectivity from the internet to the Internal network, but the Linux server in DMZ is accessible from outside. Connectivity is also allowed between the Linux server and the Internal network. Software applications running in the infrastructure have multiple vulnerabilities, as shown in Table 1.

**Table 1.** List of vulnerabilities of the software running in the example enterprise network

| Host ID | Software | CVE ID |
|---------|----------|--------|
| (1) | Linux (Kernel version 3.15) | CVE-2015-1805 |
| (2) | Acrobat Adobe Reader 8.1 | CVE-2008-0655 |
| (3) | Windows 7 SP1 | CVE-2014-4077 |
| (3) | LAquis SCADA 4.3 | CVE-2019-10980 |

Connectivity and vulnerability information for this simple network is fed to the XploitMAP tool for generating all possible attack scenarios. Figure 2 shows a snapshot from the tool. In the figure, vulnerabilities are shown in blue and conditions in yellow. The directed arrows connect the required precondition(s) to the vulnerabilities and vulnerabilities to the post-condition(s). The conditions are various access levels (generally user or root access) in the software running on the networked servers and computers. User access to the Linux OS running on the host(1) is the default initial condition here and the goal condition is to get the User access to the LAquis SCADA software on the host(3). Host(3) is the most important asset in the network as it supports the most crucial business activity of the SCADA testing platform. Possible paths following which an outside attacker can reach the goal condition starting from the initial condition are shown in the figure.

## 5 Methodology

This paper proposes a scheme for finding the crucial vulnerabilities in the generated attack graph. Two types of vulnerabilities are identified 1) Critical vulnerabilities, which are in need of Harden defenses, and 2) Vulnerabilities in urgent need of Detect defenses. The whole process, along with the generation of the attack graph using XploitMAP, is shown in Fig. 3.

### 5.1 Hardening Defense

**Identification of Critical Vulnerabilities Which Need Hardening.** Budget constraints make it impossible to plug all the vulnerabilities in an enterprise. Finding critical vulnerabilities would be very important from the security

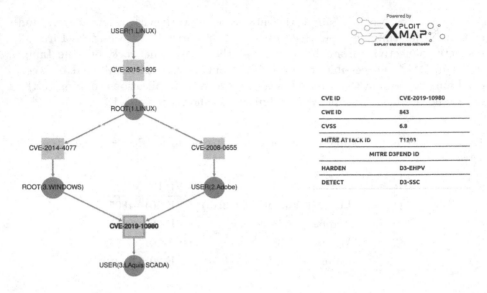

**Fig. 2.** Attack Graph generated by XpolitMAP tool

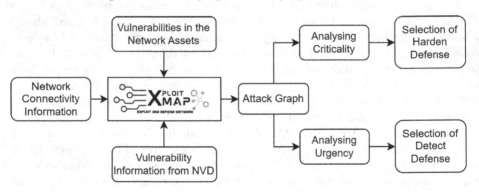

**Fig. 3.** Process of selecting necessary defenses

analysis point of view. Plugging a critical vulnerability may make the system more secure than plugging multiple non-critical vulnerabilities. By using the XploitMAP tool, it is possible to identify the most critical vulnerability in the generated attack graph.

To compute the criticality of a vulnerability, a criticality metric is proposed.

- Let $A$ be the set of all the assets in the target network.
- Let $C$ be the set of all possible user access levels in assets, e.g. user, admin, etc. These access levels can be initial access conditions from where the attacker may start the multihop attack, e.g. the user of a public web server (anyone from the internet can become a user). After executing an attack successfully,

an attacker may gain new access conditions. These derived conditions are also included in set $C$.

- $Num$ is a function mapping an access level to the corresponding numeric value. These values will be given by experts, e.g. root access may get a numeric value of 2, and user access may get a numeric value of 1.5. One may refer to the common vulnerability scoring system (CVSS)[11] or any information security risk management standards like ISO 27005 [10] to check how numeric values are allocated for qualitative parameters related to security.
- Let $V$ be the set of all the vulnerabilities in the assets.
- $Imp$ is a function mapping an asset to the importance levels; generally, we use three levels high(H), medium(M), and none(N) depending on their business impact. Experts can set the corresponding numeric values, e.g. high will get a value of 3, medium 2, and none 1. All the assets in an enterprise network are not important. Security officers' priority should be to defend the most important/valuable assets; like in an IT enterprise, the assets in a data centre are considered the most valuable.
- $Dist$ is a function, and it will measure the distance between two points in an attack graph. The meaning of distance may vary; it can be as simple as counting the number of vulnerabilities on the shortest path between the source and the destination and will provide a positive integer value. Complex distance measures may include the difficulty of exploiting the vulnerabilities.

In the simplest case, let's assume there is only one initial access permission $(c_I \in C)$ from which the attacker can start a multihop attack and only one important asset $(a \in A)$ is there with a single reachable access level $(c_a \in C)$. It is also assumed that the generated attack graph includes both $c_I$ and $c_a$.

To fulfil our goal of hardening the core, we propose two different metrics for any vulnerability, **Impact value** and **Criticality value**. Impact value $(v^{Impact})$ represents the effect if the vulnerability $(v)$ is exploited. It depends on the reachability of various access permissions of the important assets from the vulnerability $v$. By normalizing the impact value depending on the vulnerability's reachability from the initial access conditions, we can compute the criticality value $(v^{Criticality})$.

For a vulnerability $v$ $(v \in V)$ on the attack graph,

$$v^{Criticality} = \frac{v^{Impact}}{Dist(c_I,\ v)}$$

$$and,\ v^{Impact} = \frac{Imp(a) \times Num(c_a)}{e^{Dist(v,\ c_a)}}$$

$$therefore,\ v^{Criticality} = \frac{\frac{Imp(a) \times Num(c_a)}{e^{Dist(v,\ c_a)}}}{Dist(c_I,\ v)}$$

---

[11] www.first.org/cvss/specification-document.

The closer the vulnerability to an important asset, the more the requirement for hardening. Accordingly, while computing the `Criticality`, we divide the value by $e$ raised to the power of the distance between the vulnerability and target access level.

In the case of multiple important assets,

$$v^{Impact} = \sum_i \frac{Imp(a_i) \times Num(c_{a_i})}{e^{Dist(v,\ c_{a_i})}} \tag{1}$$

In the case of multiple initial access conditions,

$$v^{Criticality} = \sum_j \frac{v^{Impact}}{Dist(c_j,\ v)} = \sum_j \frac{\sum_i \frac{Imp(a_i) \times Num(c_{a_i})}{e^{Dist(v,\ c_{a_i})}}}{Dist(c_j,\ v)} \tag{2}$$

The vulnerability with the highest $v^{Criticality}$ will be taken as the critical most vulnerability, and the corresponding asset needs hardening.

**Example.** One example attack graph is shown in Fig. 4 developed in the XploitMAP tool to elaborate the concept. To explain the concept properly in the example attack graph, only conditions are shown, not vulnerabilities. We are finding the most critical conditions instead of the most critical vulnerabilities. All other calculations will remain the same. Initial conditions are shown with $I_j$; four initial conditions are in the example attack graph. Goal conditions are represented with $G_i$, and three goal conditions are in the graph. The importance of all the assets (with goal conditions) is high (H) and has a numeric value of 3. The access levels of all the goal conditions have a numeric value 2. Distance is calculated by counting the number of vulnerabilities on the shortest path from source to destination. The calculation shows red colored nodes are the most critical and require hardening. $v^{Criticality}$ value for these conditions are as follows, $(G_2) : 7.1, (G_3) : 6.8, (8) : 4.41.$

**Counter Measure Selection.** Following the procedure above, we can identify the critical vulnerabilities. Once the vulnerabilities are identified, the security administrator would like to remove/neutralize them from the system. In the attack graph created by the XploitMAP tool, vulnerabilities are represented by CVE Ids. In Sect. 3.4, we discussed how CVE Ids could be mapped to the Mitre ATT&CK Techniques. We also discussed how to map Mitre ATT&CK and Mitre D3FEND. Using these two mappings, it is possible to find the possible defense technique(s) that can be implemented to counter the attack technique(s)

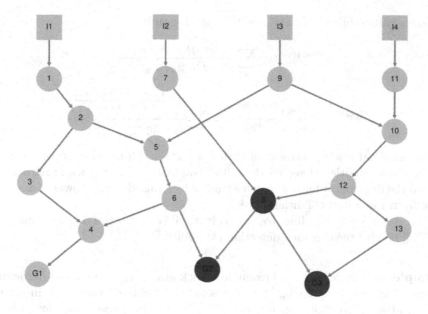

**Fig. 4.** Critical nodes in the example attack graph requiring hardening

exploiting the critical vulnerabilities. These defense techniques will be essentially from the `Harden` tactic in the D3FEND knowledge base.

There are a number of security hardening techniques. One may harden applications, credentials, messages, or platforms depending on the need.

## 5.2 Detection Defense

**Identification of the Vulnerabilities in Urgent Need of Attack Detection.** Attack monitoring involves checking out for attackers' activity on networks and systems. As we discussed earlier, any security administrator needs early detection of the attack. We are proposing two different metrics for any vulnerability, `Proximity value` and `Urgency value`. Proximity value ($v^{Proximity}$) will represent the effect if the vulnerability ($v$) is not detected. Urgency value ($v^{Urgency}$) can be calculated by normalizing the proximity value with the distance of the vulnerability from the initial attack conditions.

For a vulnerability $v$ $(v \in V)$ on the attack graph,

$$v^{Proximity} = \sum_i \frac{Imp(a_i) \times Num(c_{a_i})}{Dist(v,\ c_{a_i})} \tag{3}$$

$$v^{Urgency} = \sum_j \frac{v^{Proximity}}{e^{Dist(c_j,\ v)}} = \sum_j \frac{\sum_i \frac{Imp(a_i) \times Num(c_{a_i})}{Dist(v,\ c_{a_i})}}{e^{Dist(c_j,\ v)}} \tag{4}$$

Our goal is to detect attacks in their early stage. Monitoring is more urgent for the vulnerabilities closer to the initial conditions. For the same reason, we divided the Urgency value of the vulnerability by $e$ raised to the power of distance value from the initial conditions.

The asset corresponding to the vulnerability with the highest value of $v^{Urgency}$ needs urgent attack detection capability.

**Example.** In Fig. 5, the same example attack graph used in case of hardening defense (Fig. 4) is used again. In this case, the red colored nodes are in urgent need of attack detection capability. $v^{Urgency}$ value for these conditions are as follows, $(I_3) : 6.3$, $(I_2) : 4$, $(I_4) : 3.6$, $(I_1) : 3.4$, $(9) : 2.94$.

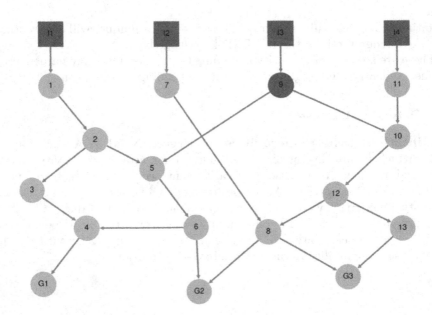

**Fig. 5.** Crucial nodes in the example attack graph requiring urgent detection capability

**Attack Detection Techniques.** Successful prevention of an attack requires timely and efficient detection mechanisms. It is not possible to detect all types of attacks using a single detection technique. Security officers need to select proper detection mechanisms from the multitude of mechanisms available.

Just like hardening defense (Subsect. 5.1), in case of detection, we can use the mappings between CVE to Mitre ATT&CK and Mitre ATT&CK to Mitre D3FEND. For monitoring, we need to use defenses from the `Detect` tactic. File analysis, identifier analysis, message analysis, network traffic analysis, platform monitoring, process analysis, and user behaviour analysis are the example detection approaches.

## 5.3   Algorithm

A high level algorithm is presented for computing the criticality and urgency values for vulnerabilities of the attack graph.

---

**Algorithm 1.** Computation of criticality and urgency of vulnerabilities

---
**Input**
>    Attack Graph
>    Initial conditions
>    Goal conditions

**Output**
>    Vulnerabilities annotated with $v^{Criticality}$ and $v^{Urgency}$

**while** new `initial condition` exists **do**
>    depth first search (DFS) starting from that initial condition
>                                      ▷ traversing the attack graph in the given directions
>    **for** each vulnerability that can be reached from the initial condition **do**
>                        ▷ possible to reach a vulnerability following different paths
>        store the shortest distance (hop count) from the specific initial condition
>    **end for**
**end while**
**while** new `goal condition` exists **do**
>    depth first search (DFS) from that goal condition
>                                ▷ traversing the attack graph in the opposite directions
>    **for** each vulnerability that can be reached from the goal condition **do**
>                    ▷ possible to reach back to a vulnerability following different paths
>        store the shortest distance (hop count) from the specific goal condition
>    **end for**
**end while**
**while** new vulnerabilities left to annotate **do**
>    calculate the value of $v^{Impact}$, $v^{Criticality}$, $v^{Proximity}$, $v^{Urgency}$
**end while**

---

## 6   Practical Example

We are using the attack scenario illustrated in Fig. 6 to show the implementable harden and detect defenses against the CVE Ids.

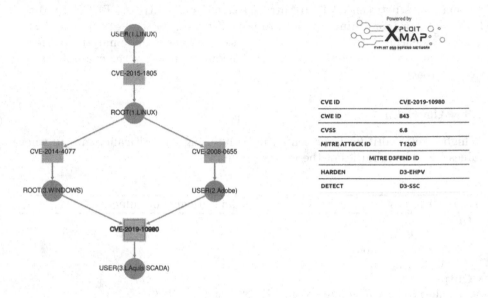

**Fig. 6.** Selection of defense in the example attack scenario

Each CVE Id used in the attack graph is first mapped to the `exploitation techniques` of the Mitre ATT&CK, shown in Table 2. The exploitation techniques are then mapped to the harden and detect defense techniques from Mitre D3FEND.

**Table 2.** Example mapping of CVE ID - MITRE ATT&CK - MITRE D3FEND

| CVE ID | Exploitation Technique | Harden Technique | Detect Technique |
|---|---|---|---|
| CVE-2015-1805 | T1068 | D3-PSEP | D3-DA |
| CVE-2014-4077 | T1553 | D3-DLIC | – |
| CVE-2019-10980 | T1203 | D3-EHPV | D3-SSC |
| CVE-2008-0655 | T1068 | D3-SU | – |

In Fig. 6 the vulnerability CVE-2019-10980 (execute code vulnerability in the SCADA software LAquis SCADA) is the vulnerability with the highest

`Criticality value.` To counter this vulnerability or to make the system hardened, D3-EHPV, i.e. exception handler pointer validation defense can be implemented. According to the attack graph, CVE-2015-1805 (denial of service vulnerability in the Linux kernel) is the vulnerability having the highest `Urgency value`. To detect the exploitation efforts to this vulnerability, D3-DA, i.e. dynamic analysis can be implemented in the sandbox environment to detect files with malicious programs.

## 7 Discussion

Hardening the core and monitoring the perimeter is the proposed idea. While identifying the point of deploying the hardening or detection defenses, we gave weightage to the reachability of those points from the initial conditions and the reachability of the goal conditions from those points. In the described methodology, the distance between two nodes is computed by counting the number of hops between them. More complex metrics like attack resistance, probabilistic security, or attack difficulty can also be used to include other allied factors along with the hop count. DFS is used for traversing the generated attack graphs; in future, more intelligent and better-performing algorithms can be used while computing the criticality and urgency values. The computation also includes the importance of the target assets and the reachable access labels. The importance of an asset is a crucial factor for security-related decision-making.

Different interesting scenarios will come up with the varying importance of the harden and detect mechanism deployment, within a fixed budget. Business impact analysis is another factor that can also be added while making decisions. A defensive mechanism negatively impacting the business of the enterprise may not be implemented in a normal condition.

## 8 Conclusion

This paper proposed two main concepts, the first is identifying the critical attack points that need to be hardened immediately, and the second is identifying the attack points that urgently need attack detection capability. Earlier works regarding defense strategy selection have not considered two security thumb rules; one is detection should be done as early as possible, and the other one is protection should be done as close to the valuable assets as possible. The paper has also elaborated on the way of identifying applicable defenses from the vulnerability identifiers. Existing knowledge bases can be used to find suitable defense techniques.

In this work, we are not considering the cases of disjunction or conjunction of multiple attack paths to propose this new idea in an uncomplicated manner. In the future, we will include AND/OR scenarios in the attack graph and modify the equations for calculating criticality and urgency accordingly. The paper elaborates on the methodology of applying Harden and Detect defenses. We would also like to extend the present work to include other defense tactics from Mitre D3FEND, i.e. isolate, deceive, and evict, to develop comprehensive defense strategies.

# References

1. Ammann, P., Wijesekera, D., Kaushik, S.: Scalable, graph-based network vulnerability analysis. In: Proceedings of the 9th ACM Conference on Computer and Communications Security, Washington, DC, USA, pp. 217–224. ACM (2002)
2. Anjum, F., Subhadrabandhu, D., Sarkar, S., Shetty, R.: On optimal placement of intrusion detection modules in sensor networks. In: First International Conference on Broadband Networks, pp. 690–699. IEEE (2004)
3. Bistarelli, S., Fioravanti, F., Peretti, P.: Defense trees for economic evaluation of security investments. In: First International Conference on Availability, Reliability and Security (ARES'06), pp. 8-pp. IEEE (2006)
4. Bopche, G.S., Rai, G.N., Mehtre, B.M.: Inter-path diversity metrics for increasing networks robustness against zero-day attacks. In: Thampi, S.M., Madria, S., Wang, G., Rawat, D.B., Alcaraz Calero, J.M. (eds.) SSCC 2018. CCIS, vol. 969, pp. 53–66. Springer, Singapore (2019). https://doi.org/10.1007/978-981-13-5826-5_4
5. Chen, H., Clark, J.A., Shaikh, S.A., Chivers, H., Nobles, P.: Optimising IDS sensor placement. In: 2010 International Conference on Availability, Reliability and Security, pp. 315–320. IEEE (2010)
6. Edge, K.S., Dalton, G.C., Raines, R.A., Mills, R.F.: Using attack and protection trees to analyze threats and defenses to homeland security. In: MILCOM 2006–2006 IEEE Military Communications Conference, pp. 1–7. IEEE (2006)
7. Fila, B., Wideł, W.: Exploiting attack-defense trees to find an optimal set of countermeasures. In: Proceedings of the 33rd IEEE Computer Security Foundations Symposium, CSF 2020, Boston, MA, USA, 22–26 June 2020, pp. 395–410. IEEE (2020)
8. George, G., Thampi, S.M.: A graph-based security framework for securing industrial IoT networks from vulnerability exploitations. IEEE Access 6, 43586–43601 (2018)
9. Grigorescu, O., Nica, A., Dascalu, M., Rughinis, R.: CVE2ATT&CK: BERT-based mapping of CVEs to MITRE ATT&CK techniques. Algorithms 15(9), 314 (2022)
10. Information security, cybersecurity and privacy protection - Guidance on managing information security risks. Standard, ISO/IEC, Geneva, CH, October 2022
11. Johnson, P., Lagerström, R., Ekstedt, M.: A meta language for threat modeling and attack simulations. In: Proceedings of the 13th International Conference on Availability, Reliability and Security, ARES 2018, Hamburg, Germany, 27–30 August 2018, pp. 38:1–38:8. ACM (2018)
12. Kaloroumakis, P.E., Smith, M.J.: Toward a knowledge graph of cybersecurity countermeasures. Corporation, Editor (2021)
13. Khouzani, M.H.R., Liu, Z., Malacaria, P.: Scalable min-max multi-objective cybersecurity optimisation over probabilistic attack graphs. Eur. J. Oper. Res. 278(3), 894–903 (2019)
14. Kordy, B., Mauw, S., Radomirović, S., Schweitzer, P.: Foundations of attack–defense trees. In: Degano, P., Etalle, S., Guttman, J. (eds.) FAST 2010. LNCS, vol. 6561, pp. 80–95. Springer, Heidelberg (2011). https://doi.org/10.1007/978-3-642-19751-2_6

15. Kuppa, A., Aouad, L., Le-Khac, N.A.: Linking CVE's to MITRE ATT&CK techniques. In: The 16th International Conference on Availability, Reliability and Security, pp. 1–12 (2021)
16. Mukherjee, P., Mazumdar, C.: Attack difficulty metric for assessment of network security. In: Proceedings of the 13th International Conference on Availability, Reliability and Security, pp. 1–10 (2018)
17. Mukherjee, P., Mazumdar, C.: "Security Concern" as a metric for enterprise business processes. IEEE Syst. J. **13**(4), 4015–4026 (2019)
18. Mukherjee, P., Sengupta, A., Mazumdar, C.: "Security Gap" as a metric for enterprise business processes. Secur. Priv. **5**(6), e263 (2022)
19. Noel, S., Jajodia, S.: Optimal IDS sensor placement and alert prioritization using attack graphs. J. Netw. Syst. Manag. **16**, 259–275 (2008)
20. Ortalo, R., Deswarte, Y., Kaâniche, M.: Experimenting with quantitative evaluation tools for monitoring operational security. IEEE Trans. Softw. Eng. **25**(5), 633–650 (1999)
21. Pamula, J., Jajodia, S., Ammann, P., Swarup, V.: A weakest-adversary security metric for network configuration security analysis. In: Proceedings of the 2nd ACM Workshop on Quality of Protection, pp. 31–38 (2006)
22. Phillips, C., Swiler, L.P.: A graph-based system for network-vulnerability analysis. In: Proceedings of the 1998 Workshop on New Security Paradigms, pp. 71–79 (1998)
23. Poolsappasit, N., Dewri, R., Ray, I.: Dynamic security risk management using Bayesian attack graphs. IEEE Trans. Dependable Secure Comput. **9**(1), 61–74 (2011)
24. Roy, A., Kim, D.S., Trivedi, K.S.: Cyber security analysis using attack countermeasure trees. In: Proceedings of the Sixth Annual Workshop on Cyber Security and Information Intelligence Research, pp. 1–4 (2010)
25. Sawik, T.: Selection of optimal countermeasure portfolio in IT security planning. Decis. Support Syst. **55**(1), 156–164 (2013)
26. Schneier, B.: Attack trees. Dr. Dobb's J. **24**(12), 21–29 (1999)
27. Sheyner, O., Haines, J.W., Jha, S., Lippmann, R., Wing, J.M.: Automated generation and analysis of attack graphs. In: Proceedings of the IEEE Symposium on Security and Privacy, Berkeley, California, USA, pp. 273–284. IEEE Computer Society (2002)
28. Shin, Y., Kim, K., Lee, J.J., Lee, K.: Focusing on the weakest link: a similarity analysis on phishing campaigns based on the ATT&CK matrix. Secur. Commun. Netw. **2022**, 1–12 (2022)
29. Soikkeli, J., Muñoz-González, L., Lupu, E.: Efficient attack countermeasure selection accounting for recovery and action costs. In: Proceedings of the 14th International Conference on Availability, Reliability and Security, pp. 1–10 (2019)
30. Stan, O., et al.: Heuristic approach towards countermeasure selection using attack graphs. arXiv preprint arXiv:1906.10943 (2019)
31. UcedaVelez, T., Morana, M.M.: Risk Centric Threat Modeling: Process for Attack Simulation and Threat Analysis. John Wiley & Sons, Hoboken (2015)
32. van Leeuwen, R.: Cyber-Attack Containment through Actionable Awareness. Doctoral dissertation, Master's thesis. Technical University of Eindhoven (2022)
33. Wang, L., Islam, T., Long, T., Singhal, A., Jajodia, S.: An attack graph-based probabilistic security metric. In: Atluri, V. (ed.) DBSec 2008. LNCS, vol. 5094, pp. 283–296. Springer, Heidelberg (2008). https://doi.org/10.1007/978-3-540-70567-3_22

34. Wang, L., Singhal, A., Jajodia, S.: Measuring the overall security of network configurations using attack graphs. In: Barker, S., Ahn, G.-J. (eds.) DBSec 2007. LNCS, vol. 4602, pp. 98–112. Springer, Heidelberg (2007). https://doi.org/10.1007/978-3-540-73538-0_9
35. Widel, W., Mukherjee, P., Ekstedt, M.: Security countermeasures selection using the meta attack language and probabilistic attack graphs. IEEE Access **10**, 89645–89662 (2022)
36. Xiong, W., Legrand, E., Åberg, O., Lagerström, R.: Cyber security threat modeling based on the MITRE enterprise ATT&CK matrix. Softw. Syst. Model. **21**(1), 157–177 (2022)
37. Zheng, K., Albert, L.A., Luedtke, J.R., Towle, E.: A budgeted maximum multiple coverage model for cybersecurity planning and management. IISE Trans. **51**(12), 1303–1317 (2019)

# Attack Graph Based Security Metrics for Dynamic Networks

Ayan Gain(✉) and Mridul Sankar Barik

Jadavpur University, Kolkata, India
ayan.gain2010@gmail.com, mridulsankar.barik@jadavpuruniversity.in

**Abstract.** Evaluating network attack graphs in today's dynamic networks poses a challenge. Conventional metrics used for attack graph based risk assessment are inadequate due to their inability to consider temporal evolution of networks. To address this limitation, we introduce the notion of temporal attack graph, which incorporates the temporal characteristics of network configurations and vulnerabilities. It provides a notion for risk assessment by providing a more precise depiction of the network's security state over time. In addition, we introduce two security metrics based on temporal attack graphs. By effectively capturing the temporal features of dynamic networks, these metrics enable accurate measurement of network security over time. Path-based metrics analyze whether an attacker can reach a target along a specific temporal path. These metrics help in evaluating overall robustness of the network and adopting appropriate security counter measures beforehand.

**Keywords:** Dynamic Networks · Temporal Attack Graph · Security Metrics · Path Based Metrics

## 1 Introduction

Today's enterprise networks are highly dynamic, i.e. their configurations frequently change over time. As a result, keeping track of changing security posture of such networks is challenging. Attack graph is a widely used formalism for enumerating all possible attack paths of a given network configuration. Also, different attack graph based security metrics help in determining both qualitative and quantitative security measures of the network. But these metrics are computed based on a static view of a network at any point of time and hence fail to capture its dynamic and evolving nature. Among the state-of-the-art in attack graph based security analysis [1–4], very few works have considered dynamic or evolving nature of enterprise networks.

Also, in recent years, intensive research in understanding the properties of dynamic systems such as delay-tolerant networks, opportunistic-mobility networks, social networks etc. have produced solid theoretical foundation around time varying graphs (also known as evolving graphs or temporal graphs). Existing metrics based on static graphs are not able to capture the temporal features

V. Muthukkumarasamy et al. (Eds.): ICISS 2023, LNCS 14424, pp. 109–128, 2023.
https://doi.org/10.1007/978-3-031-49099-6_7

of dynamic networks, whereas temporal graph metrics represent a powerful tool for analyzing such real world networks.

The primary contribution of this paper is to introduce the idea of temporal attack graphs, and to introduce the concept of temporal attack paths. Additionally, we have introduced two security metrics i.e. characteristic temporal attack path length and shortest temporal attack path length in temporal attack graphs. Furthermore, in this paper we provide evaluation of the proposed security metrics by analyzing them on an example network.

This paper is organized as follows: In Sect. 2, we review the existing literature and discuss its limitations in analyzing the security of complex computer systems within dynamic networks and the concept of temporal metrics. We look into the various formalisms of temporal graphs and temporal networks in Sect. 3. In Sect. 4 we discuss the previously proposed metrics of temporal graphs. The concepts proposed by various researchers about attack graphs are discussed in Sect. 5. Section 6 introduces the concept of temporal attack graphs, including temporal attack paths along with a detailed example of a network and it's corresponding temporal attack graph. Section 7 presents the notion of temporal security metrics, Results of applying the metrics along with the interpretation of temporal paths and path-based temporal metrics are given in Sect. 8. Concluding remarks are provided in Sect. 9, followed by a discussion on the future scope of our work in Sect. 10.

## 2   Related Works

Numerous significant concepts have been identified in assessing dynamic networks, often assigned specific names and occasionally formally defined. A growing realization indicates that these concepts are intricately intertwined. In several cases, disparate concepts labeled differently by various researchers are, in fact, synonymous. For instance, the concept of temporal distance, as outlined in [5], aligns with reachability time, information latency, and temporal proximity. Similarly, the notion of a journey has been alternatively referred to as a schedule-conforming path, time-respecting path, and temporal path. Hence, the discoveries stemming from these investigations can be perceived as constituent components of a unified conceptual topic, while the existing formalisms aimed at expressing specific concepts can be regarded as fragments of a broader, all-encompassing formal description of this topic.

Static security metrics fail to capture the changing security posture, adapt to evolving threats and network conditions - hence, they are inadequate for assessing security of dynamic enterprise networks. To effectively address security challenges, dynamic enterprise networks require adaptable and scalable security metrics and strategies that can capture real-time changes and emerging threats. Dynamic security metrics, leveraging continuous monitoring, threat intelligence, and adaptive security controls, offer a more accurate and up-to-date view of the network's security state [6, 7].

A pivotal commonality across various domains in the context of enterprise networks is the temporal variability inherent in the system's structure, specifically the dynamic nature of the network topology. Furthermore, the rate and magnitude of these fluctuations generally surpass the previous notion that when network faults or failures occur then only the network needs to be looked at. In these systems, changes are not anomalies but rather an inseparable and integral element intricately woven into the fabric of the system's essence. Time plays a vital role in shaping network topologies. The mathematical formalism used to describe time-evolving networks is a critical issue to address.

To effectively allocate security resources and optimize network hardening, security analysts require vital information about vulnerabilities and their enabling conditions. Recent research focuses on obtaining hardening recommendations from attack graphs [8].

However, previously proposed attack graph-based security metrics [9–11] do not measure the temporal variation in the network, which is essential to identify problems early and take corrective actions. Without proper metrics to detect variation in attack graphs, significant network or security events causing change in the network will remain undetected, preventing analysts from gaining awareness of the temporal aspects of network security. Therefore, it is imperative to develop metrics that can detect variation in the attack surface and enable analysts to gain timely insight into network security [12–14].

The attack graph of the network is subject to constant change due to the discovery of new vulnerabilities, misconfigured hardware or software components, and loose access control policies. Neglecting the temporal aspects of security poses significant risks. To ensure optimal network security, regular monitoring is recommended by guidelines such as [15] and [16]. Appropriate metrics are vital for assessing the security state of the network which may be impacted by events resulting in compromise of critical resources.

## 3 Temporal Graphs

A number of formalisms have emerged to capture the essence of evolving networks (not necessarily information networks), while retaining their complete informational content. Notable among them are: temporal networks [17], time-varying graphs [18–20], interaction networks [21,22], link streams and stream graphs [23,24], which have gained significant popularity. In this context, various authors have adopted the term "temporal networks" as an umbrella term encompassing all these formalisms. Temporal networks serve as models for dynamic structures where nodes and edges appear and vanish over time.

According to *Rossetti et al.* [22] the definition to establish a formal understanding of temporal graphs is as follows: In the topic of network representation, a temporal network is defined as a graph denoted by $G = (V, E, T)$, where $V$ constitutes a set of triplets in the form $(v, t_s, t_e)$. In this context, $v$ represents a vertex within the graph, while $t_s$ and $t_e$, belonging to the set $T$, signify the initial and final timestamps of the associated vertices, adhering to the condition

$t_s \leq t_e$. Furthermore, $E$ represents a set of quadruplets $(u, v, t_s, t_e)$, where $u$ and $v$ are vertices from $V$, and $t_s$ and $t_e$, also belonging to $T$, indicate the initial and final timestamps of the corresponding edge, satisfying the condition $t_s \leq t_e$.

Undirected temporal networks (TNs) or directed temporal networks (DTNs) can be dealt with depending on the interaction semantics. The high-level definition proposed encompasses nodes and edges with or without duration (if $t_s = t_e$). Often, a strong distinction is made between these two categories. Networks without edge durations are often referred to as contact sequences, and those with durations are referred to as interval graphs [25].

Frequently, the history of a network is divided into a sequence of snapshots, where each snapshot represents either the network's state at a specific time (referred to as a relation network) or the collection of observed interactions during a particular period (referred to as an interaction network).

*Rossetti et al.* [22] also put forward the concept of a snapshot graph $\mathcal{G}_\tau$ as characterized by an ordered set of snapshots $G_1, G_2...G_t$, where each snapshot $G_i = (V_i, E_i)$ is uniquely identified by the node set $V_i$ and edge set $E_i$.

Basically a temporal graph is a mathematical representation that depicts the evolving nature of a network across time. It comprises a sequence of snapshots or *"time slices"* that portray the network's topology at various time points. Put simply, a temporal graph is a collection of graphs, each of which characterizes the network at a specific time instance [19,26].

## 4  Temporal Metrics

In the following subsections, we will explore several metrics that are employed to quantify temporal distances. Holme and Saramaki [25] presents an overview of these metrics used in the analysis of temporal networks. Additionally, Tang et al. [20] offer a detailed exploration of the potential applications for these metrics.

### 4.1  Path Based Temporal Metrics

Based on the definition provided in [19,27], the concept of a temporal path in a directed temporal graph can be summarized as follows:

**Temporal Path:** A *temporal path*, represented as $p_{ij}^h = (n_0^{W_0}, \ldots, n_\eta^{W_\eta})$, originates from node $i = n_0$ and terminates at node $j = n_\eta$ within the time interval specified in the temporal graph $\mathcal{G}^w(t_{min}, t_{max})$. This path comprises a series of $\eta$ number of edges through different nodes $n_a^{W_a}$ at specific time windows $W_a$, where a node $n_a$ is considered part of the path only if there exists a directed edge between $n_{a-1}$ and $n_a$ at time window $W_{a-1} \leq W_a$, with $0 \leq W_a < \tau$ [19], where $\tau$ is the maximum delivery time in the temporal graph.

Let $Q_{ij}$ denote the set comprising all temporal paths connecting nodes $i$ and $j$. In the absence of a temporal path between $i$ and $j$, i.e., when $Q_{ij} = \emptyset$, it can be inferred that the node pair $(i, j)$ is temporally disconnected, and thus the distance is assigned an infinite value, represented as $l_{ij} = \infty$.

Introducing the function $D(p_{ij})$, which represents the estimated time duration to traverse a given path $p_{ij}$ within the time window $W_\eta$, we can calculate
the shortest temporal path length, denoted as $d_{ij}$, between nodes $i$ and $j$. This
corresponds to the minimum delivery time among all feasible paths $p_{ij}$ in the
set $Q_{ij}$. This approach enables the identification of the most efficient delivery
route that satisfies the temporal constraints of the problem. Specifically, it can
be expressed as the length of the shortest path:

$$d_{ij} = min(D(p_{ij})), \forall p_{ij} \in Q_{ij} \tag{1}$$

Given that $Q_{ij}$ represents the set containing all feasible paths connecting
nodes $i$ and $j$, due to the potential non-uniqueness of the shortest temporal
path, we define the set $S_{ij}$ to encompass all such shortest temporal paths from
node $i$ to node $j$. More precisely, $S_{ij}$ can be expressed as:

$$S_{ij} = \{p_{ij} \in Q_{ij} : (D(p_{ij}) = d_{ij})\} \tag{2}$$

The concept of temporal shortest path length, in terms of efficiency, is discussed in [28]. The temporal efficiency $E_{ij}$ between nodes $i$ and $j$ is defined to
avoid potential divergence and is given as follows:

$$E_{ij} = \frac{1}{d_{ij} + 1} \tag{3}$$

**Characteristic Temporal Path Length:** The temporal shortest path refers
to the shortest path between node $i$ and node $j$ in terms of time duration. It
is the path that connects $i$ to $j$ and has the minimum duration. Similarly, the
temporal distance $d_{ij}$ represents the duration of the shortest temporal path from
$i$ to $j$.

In the context of time-varying graphs, the characteristic temporal path length
is an extension of the average geodesic distance. It is calculated by averaging the
temporal distances between all pairs of nodes in the graph. This concept is
defined as the average temporal distance over the entire set of node pairs in
the graph, as explained in [29,30]. The equation of characteristic temporal path
length $L$, where $N$ is the number of nodes in the temporal graph, is given as:

$$L = \frac{1}{N(N-1)} \sum_{ij} d_{ij} \tag{4}$$

In general, it is assumed that information has a finite lifespan. Hence, when
nodes $i$ and $j$ become disconnected over a time duration, a value of $d_{ij} = w\tau$,
where $w$ is the length of each time window and $\tau$ is the maximum delivery time
in the temporal graph.

If a node $j$ is not reachable from node $i$ in terms of time, the temporal distance $d_{ij}$ is considered to be infinity, and as a result, the characteristic temporal
path length becomes divergent. To prevent this divergence, the temporal global

efficiency of a time-varying graph has been defined. This concept is formulated as follows [28]:

$$E = \frac{1}{N(N-1)} \sum_{ij} \frac{1}{d_{ij}} \qquad (5)$$

The work presented in Tang et al. [19] highlights important differences between static and temporal analyses of shortest paths. Their findings show that static graphs, which do not consider the ordering of time, tend to overestimate the availability of links and underestimate the actual lengths of shortest paths. Interestingly, the research also reveals a counter-intuitive discovery, indicating that even networks with slow evolution can exhibit properties that enable rapid information dissemination between nodes in temporal networks.

## 5    Attack Graph

Understanding the various ways in which the attackers can compromise our cyber infrastructures is crucial in adopting different proactive and reactive security measures. Researchers have proposed many attack modelling techniques for this purpose [31]. Attack graphs and attack trees [32] are the two most popularly used graphical attack modelling techniques.

Attack graphs provide a representation of existing knowledge about vulnerabilities, their dependencies, and network connectivity. There are two approaches to representing an attack graph. The first approach involves explicitly listing all possible sequences of vulnerabilities that an attacker can exploit to reach their target, encompassing all potential attack paths. However, this method can result in a large number of attack paths, leading to a combinatorial explosion. The second approach to attack graph representation employs a monotonicity assumption, assuming that an attacker never loses acquired capabilities. This representation captures vulnerability dependencies and preserves implicit attack paths, retaining all information while avoiding duplicate vertices. As a result, the size of this attack graph is polynomial, meaning it is proportional to the number of vulnerabilities multiplied by the number of connected pairs of hosts [33].

Attack graphs serve to depict system states and attacker actions. They are generated using model checking algorithms like SMV [34] or NuSMV [2]. However, as the size of the system increases, the graphs grow exponentially. To mitigate this issue, the monotonicity assumption [1] proposes that one attack cannot invalidate the precondition of another. However, it is important to note that this assumption is not always valid, as certain vulnerabilities rely on others. For instance, if an attacker exploits a network service vulnerability, rendering it unavailable, other vulnerabilities that depend on that service become unexploitable.

The tool TVA (Topological Vulnerability Analysis) [35, 36] automates the construction of an attack graph by utilizing attack scenarios, a collection of identified vulnerabilities in the system, and network models. Vulnerabilities can be automatically identified using scanning tools such as Nessus [37] or Retina [38]. The attack graph consists of nodes representing exploits and the security conditions accessible to the attacker. Edges connecting precondition nodes to vulnerability nodes indicate the necessary conditions for exploiting the vulnerability. Conversely, an arc from a vulnerability node to a condition node represents the impact of vulnerability exploitation. The size of the attack graph grows quadratically in relation to the system's size.

The MulVAL [39] (Multihost, multistage Vulnerability Analysis) framework generates an attack graph using a list of system vulnerabilities, asset configurations, user access rights, and potential interactions and policies. The system is modeled using the Datalog language [40], while interactions are represented by Horn clauses. The XSB [41] environment is utilized to derive new information about the system state.

According to the definition provided in [4], an attack graph, denoted as $G$, is a directed graph $G = (E \cup C, R_r \cup R_i)$. The vertex set $E \cup C$ represents the collection of exploits and security conditions, while the edge set $R_r \cup R_i$ represents the require and imply relations. Here, $R_r \subseteq C \times E$ and $R_i \subseteq E \times C$. Exploits are represented as $v(h_s, h_d)$, for exploits on local hosts, they are denoted as $v(h)$.

Security conditions are predicates of the form $c(h_s, h_d)$, which signify the fulfillment of a security-related condition $c$ involving the source host $h_s$ and the destination host $h_d$. In cases where the condition only pertains to a single host, it is represented as $c(h)$. Examples of security conditions include existence of vulnerabilities on a specific host or connections between two hosts etc.

Vulnerability scanner tools like OVAL [42] automatically detects vulnerabilities in a network and links them to the elements in the network environment. But, the decision on the frequency of its usage should be determined by the network administrator as these tools inflict considerable overhead in terms of additional network traffic. The reports generated by the vulnerability scanner tool form one of the input to the attack graph generation tool.

## 6   Temporal Attack Graph

Present day enterprise networks comprise of resources that are provisioned dynamically, on-demand. These are mostly cloud based virtual resources i.e. compute, network, storage etc. which are made available on the fly. New compute nodes with services and network connectivity as per the application requirements are provisioned dynamically through software. Conglomeration of such on-premise and off-premise resources evolve continuously with time. Attack graph based security analysis must consider such time evolving nature of the networks. The notion of temporal attack graph takes into consideration such time dependent features.

**Definition 1 (Temporal Attack Graph).**
   *A Temporal Attack Graph $\mathcal{G}^a(t_{min}, t_{max})$ is defined as a sequence of graphs $(G_0, G_1, \ldots, G_{\tau-1})$, such that:*

- $G_t = (V_t, E_t)$ is an attack graph $AG_t$ of the snapshot of the network taken at time instance $t$
- $\tau = ((t_{max} - t_{min})/w) = \mid \mathcal{G}^a(t_{min}, t_{max}) \mid$ is the number of graphs in the sequence or the number of time windows
- $w$ is the duration of each time window
- $|E \cup C| = \sum_{w=1}^{\tau} |E^w \cup C^w|$ is the total number of vertices across all time windows in the temporal Attack Graph $\mathcal{G}^a$;
- $|R_r \cup R_i| = \sum_{w=1}^{\tau} |R_r^w \cup R_i^w|$ is the total number of edges across all time windows in the Temporal Attack Graph $\mathcal{G}^a$.
- $(E^w \cup C^w)$ is the vertex set and $(R_r^w \cup R_i^w)$ is the edge set of attack graph at time window $w$;

We assume that, the system parameters are sampled and the corresponding attack graphs are generated (or incrementally updated) at the beginning of each time window, i.e. at time instances $t_0, t_1, \ldots t_{\tau-1}$, where $t_0 = t_{min}$ and $t_\tau = t_{max}$ and $t_i = t_{min} + w \times i$, for $0 < i < \tau$.

It may be noted that the window size ($w$) depends on number of factors, like: how frequently the network configuration changes, the cost of attack graph generation etc. The security administrator has to consider all these facts and choose the window length accordingly.

## 6.1  A Motivating Example

Let us consider a simplified example network depicted in Fig. 1. The internal network consists of a File Server, along with Hosts A, B, and C. Host C holds significant importance as it serves as the main server. In this scenario, there is a malicious entity, referred to as an attacker who is operating from the external network. The attacker's objective is to obtain root-level privileges on Host C. Therefore, our main concern is whether the attacker can achieve this goal. To mitigate potential threats, firewalls have been placed in strategic locations, which allow all internal to external connection requests. However, inbound requests are only permitted to access the file server. In simpler terms, the FIREWALL 1 grants access to any unidentified user solely for the purpose of accessing service(s) running on the file server. Access to all other services running on different machines is denied or blocked. The internal hosts within the network, including the File Server, Hosts A, B, and C, are restricted to connecting only to specific ports or services based on the firewall policies outlined in Table 1. These policies define the limitations on connectivity. The term "All" indicates that a source host is allowed to connect to a destination host on any port to access the services running on those ports. Conversely, "None" indicates that a source host is forbidden from accessing any services on the destination host. In our example network, we assume that the hosts initially have certain vulnerabilities, which are summarized in Table 2 along with time windows in which they exist and indexed by their CVE numbers.

Within our example network, the File Server is open to access by all unidentified external users. Additionally, it possesses a vulnerability of the SAP service known as CVE-2021-44235. If this vulnerability is successfully exploited, an

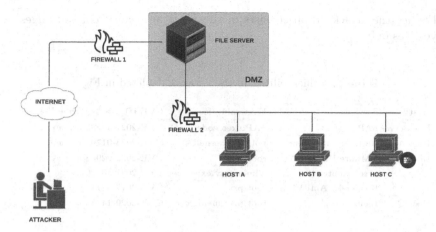

**Fig. 1.** An Example Network

attacker can gain root-level privileges on the File Server. Host C has a host based firewall which has such a policy that it only allows to connect to a particular port and the particular service running on that port can only be exploited from only Host B at the particular time window $w_2$. Figure 2 presents an attack graph for this particular network configuration, showcasing all the possible attack paths an intruder can take to reach the desired target, which is Host C. The graph illustrates these attack paths across different time windows, namely $w_0$, $w_1$, and $w_2$.

**Table 1.** Firewall policies of the network depicted in Fig. 1

| Host | Attacker | File Server | HostA | HostB | HostC |
|------|----------|-------------|-------|-------|-------|
| Attacker | localhost | All | None | None | None |
| File Server | All | localhost | All | Kaspersky Cisco Router | None |
| HostA | All | All | localhost | Vmware | None |
| HostB | All | All | All | localhost | All |
| HostC | All | All | All | All | localhost |

In Fig. 2 we can see the temporal attack graph of three time windows $w_0, w_1, w_2$. The graph is color coded in such a way that the attack graph generated at 3 timestamps are represented together. To give a better idea:

– For $w_0$ the attack graph consists of the *black* and *blue* colored edges and vertices only
– For $w_1$ the attack graph consists of the *black*, *blue* and *red* colored edges and vertices only

– For $w_2$ the attack graph consists of the *black* and *green* colored edges and vertices only

**Table 2.** Vulnerabilities in the network depicted in Fig. 1

| Host | Services | Vulnerabilities | CVE ID | Time Window |
|------|----------|-----------------|--------|-------------|
| File Server | SAP | SAP_exec_code | CVE-2021-44235 | $w_0, w_1, w_2$ |
| Host A | Netfilter subsystem | bof_linuxkernell | CVE-2023-0179 | $w_0, w_1$ |
| Host B | VMware Horizon Agent | root_priv | CVE-2022-22964 | $w_0, w_1$ |
| | Cisco Router | admin_priv_exec_code | CVE-2021-40120 | $w_1$ |
| | Kaspersky Anti-Virus | root_priv | CVE-2017-9811 | $w_2$ |
| Host C | Linux kernel | root_priv_mem_corr | CVE-2020-14386 | $w_2$ |

At time $w_0$, the attacker can exploit vulnerabilities in the File server, Host A, and Host B, thereby obtaining root access to all of them. At time $w_1$, despite these vulnerabilities still existing, a new service starts in Host B, introducing the CVE-2021-40120 vulnerability, which can only be exploited from the File service. Consequently, a new attack path is created to gain root access to Host B. Moving to time $w_2$, all previously existing vulnerabilities in Host A and Host B have been patched. However, a new Kaspersky Antivirus service running on Host B introduces the CVE-2017-9811 vulnerability, which allows the attacker to gain root access to Host B. Additionally, at this timestamp, the firewall policy permits the attacker to access the vulnerability in Host C's Linux kernel service, identified as CVE-2020-14386, thereby granting root access to Host C. Ultimately, the attacker successfully achieves the objective of gaining root access to Host C.

In general, the starting point in an attack graph corresponds to the assumed initial location of the attacker and the ending point corresponds to the location of any critical resource in the network. And, there has to exist some initial conditions before an attack graph is generated. Because the first exploitation of a vulnerability is enabled by the initial conditions only. It generates intermediate conditions which in combination with other initial conditions may further enable more exploits.

## 6.2 Temporal Attack Paths

**Definition 2 (Temporal Attack Path).**

*A temporal attack path, $p_{ij}^a = (n_0^{W_0}, \ldots, n_{\eta-1}^{W_k})$, starting at node $i = n_0$ and finishing at node $j = n_{\eta-1}$ is defined over a Temporal Attack Graph $\mathcal{G}^a(t_{min}, t_{max})$ as a sequence of $\eta$ hops via distinct nodes $n_h^{W_p}$ at time window $W_p$, node $n_h$ is visited if and only if there is an edge between $n_{h-1}$ and $n_h$ at time window $W_{p-1} \leq W_p$; and $0 \leq W_p < \tau$.*

$Q_{ij}^a$ is the set of all temporal attack paths between nodes $i$ and $j$. If a temporal attack path between $i$ and $j$ does not exist, i.e., $Q_{ij}^a = \phi$ we can deduce that $(i, j)$ is a temporally disconnected node pair, and we set the distance $l_{ij}^a = \infty$.

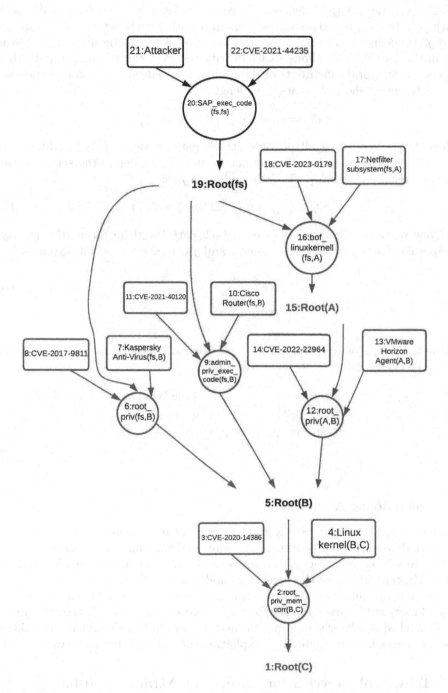

**Fig. 2.** Temporal Attack Graph of the network shown in Fig. 1 (Color figure online)

The function $D^a(p_{ij}^a)$ denotes the set of nodes in a given temporal attack path $p_{ij}^a$. To calculate the shortest temporal path length between two points $i$ and $j$, we define $d_{ij}^a$ as the minimum number of hops among all feasible paths $p_{ij}^a$ in the set $Q_{ij}^a$. This allows us to identify the most efficient attack path that meets the temporal constraints of the problem. Specifically, it can be expressed as the temporal shortest attack path length:

$$d_{ij}^u = min(|D^a(p_{ij})|), \forall\, p_{ij} \in Q_{ij}^a \tag{6}$$

where $Q_{ij}^a$ is the set of all possible attack paths between $i$ and $j$. Since the shortest temporal attack path may not be unique, we define the set $S_{ij}^a$ of all shortest temporal attack paths from node $i$ to $j$ as:

$$S_{ij}^a = \left\{ p_{ij} \in Q_{ij}^a : \left( D^a(p_{ij}) = d_{ij}^a \right) \right\} \tag{7}$$

Now we define Temporal shortest attack path length in terms of efficiency, temporal efficiency $E_{ij}^a$ between nodes $i$ and $j$ can be expressed as given as:

$$E_{ij}^a = \frac{1}{d_{ij}^a + 1} \tag{8}$$

**Table 3.** Example of Temporal Attack Paths Present in the network depicted in Fig. 1 and in its corresponding temporal attack graph in Fig. 2.

| Attack Path | Time Windows |
|---|---|
| 20, 19, 9, 5, 2, 1 | $w_0, w_1, w_2$ |
| 20, 19, 16, 15, 12, 5, 2, 1 | $w_0, w_1, w_2$ |

### 6.3   Simplifying Assumption

We have considered only attack graphs wherein the number of nodes across all time windows may vary, or remain the same and the number of edges may also vary. We will be referring to the set of nodes in a temporal attack graph as $V^a = V_w, \forall \epsilon [0, \tau)$, hence the number of nodes is $N = |V^a|$.

We assume that when an attacker has exploited a vulnerability and has gained root/user access on a host/server/workstation etc, even if the vulnerability is patched at a later timestamp the attacker would still retain the capabilities and privileges he had acquired by exploiting the vulnerability earlier.

## 7   Temporal Metrics for Temporal Attack Graphs

In static graphs, the shortest path length metric gives the number of hops between any two nodes. But, the shortest temporal path length gives an idea about the speed (in terms of number of time intervals) at which the attacker can reach from a source node to a destination node.

Previously in Sect. 4 we saw how Temporal Metrics for normal temporal graphs was defined by various other authors, now we will define temporal metrics for attack graphs.

## 7.1 Characteristic Temporal Attack Path Length

From the above temporal metrics, we define the characteristic temporal attack path length $L^a$ as:

$$L^a = \frac{1}{N(N-1)} \sum_{ij} d_{ij}^a \tag{9}$$

where $N$ is the total number of nodes across all time windows in the attack graph and it is to be mentioned that there maybe no link between two nodes in the Temporal Attack Graph (even considering the temporal aspect) those nodes may be called as unreachable nodes from a particular node, then in this case the value of $d_{ij}^a = \tau$ representing the maximum time windows in the Temporal Attack Graph i.e. if there are 2 time windows and a node is unreachable from $i$ then its $d_{ij}^a = 2$.

Temporal global efficiency of the Temporal Attack Graph $\mathcal{G}^a$ to prevent potential divergence may be defined as:

$$E^a = \frac{1}{N(N-1)} \sum_{ij} \frac{1}{d_{ij}^a} \tag{10}$$

# 8    Results and Discussions

For the temporal attack graph of three time windows depicted in Fig. 2 we have used the Mulval [39] tool for attack graph generation and then loaded the graphs into Neo4j[1] graph database for calculation of the proposed metrics.

It may be noted that a temporal attack graph is defined as a sequence of attack graphs corresponding to a series of network configurations in defined time windows. We assume that attack graphs in different time windows are faithfully generated using existing tools like MulVAL. Hence, there is no need of a separate temporal attack graph generation tool.

## 8.1 Generating Temporal Attack Graphs

We have used the MulVAL [39] tool to generate an attack graph at a particular timestamp. The input information on network topology, vulnerabilities, fire rules etc. are coded in an input file as required by MulVAL. The generated attack graph is produced in many forms, i.e. a pdf file for visualization, xml/csv

---

[1] https://neo4j.com/.

files containing the graph information. We have taken the two output csv files: one containing node data and another containing information about edges. We have then loaded the sequence of attack graphs into the Neo4j graph database and labeled them as $w_0, w_1, \ldots, w_{n-1}$ i.e. the time window at which they were generated. Finally we have used cypher graph queries over this database of the attack graphs to compute the proposed security metrics.

However, if for a given network configuration the final attack goal cannot be reached, then the corresponding attack graph would not be generated. This is true for all attack graph generation tools, including MulVAL. Our work is based on a particular attack goal which remains fixed through out all the time windows.

The reason for using the Neo4j graph database as a storage for the temporal attack graph is that we can use Neo4j's built-in query language cypher for efficient computation of the proposed security metrics. Cypher supports queries related to various graph analytic tasks.

## 8.2    Pre-processing of Temporal Attack Graph

Before loading the temporal attack graph generated by MulVAL [39], we need to do some pre-processing as we need not load all the nodes and edges for applying our metrics.

The nodes in the temporal attack graphs representing initial security conditions may be ignored for the purpose of computing temporal metrics as they may result in large anomalies in the desired results. We can observe that in characteristic temporal attack path length $L^a$, when we are calculating $\sum_{ij} d^a_{ij}$ we are basically calculating the sum of shortest temporal attack path length from every node to every other node in the temporal attack graph. Now the said nodes are always unreachable as they have no incoming edges. Hence, they always will have the value $\tau$, thus effectively increasing the characteristic temporal attack path length proportionately. In the context of attack graphs these nodes are security conditions which act as pre-conditions for a vulnerability to be exploited. So we are ignoring these nodes and omitting them before loading them into Neo4j for calculation of various metrics. We assume that these pre-conditions are satisfied to get the values of our metrics in correct order, so that they can be interpreted correctly for further applications and use.

## 8.3    Importing Data into Neo4j

To load the temporal attack graph into Neo4j graph database, we have used the csv output file generated by the MulVAL tool and invoked cypher queries to import the nodes and edges into the database. We have labelled each attack graph as $w_0, w_1, \ldots, w_{n-1}$ - thus, we have a temporal attack graph in Neo4j graph database. We have implemented the temporal metric computation as a Python module.

The temporal attack graph depicted in Fig. 2 after preprocessing and loading into the Neo4j Graph database is shown in Fig. 3 and Table 3.

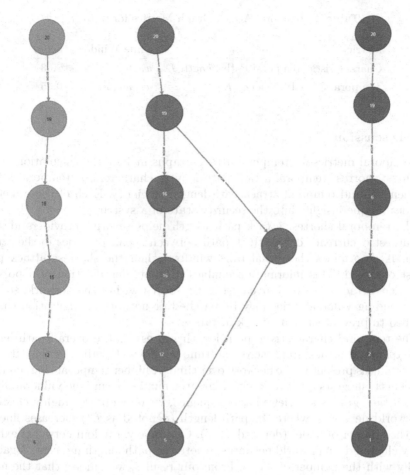

**Fig. 3.** Temporal Attack Graph represented in Graph Database Neo4j for network depicted in Fig. 1, Cyan depicts $w_0$, Red depicts $w_1$ and Blue depicts $w_2$ (Color figure online)

## 8.4  Temporal Attack Graph of Three Time Windows

In this part we have taken a temporal attack graph of three time windows, the same is depicted in Fig. 2.

Here the temporal attack graph $\mathcal{G}^a(t_0, t_3)$ consists of attack graphs starting at time window $w_0$ and ending at time window $w_2$. The visualisation of Temporal Attack Graph loaded into and extracted from Neo4j database is shown in Fig. 3. After loading our temporal attack graphs into the graph database we compute the metrics given previous sections and the results are recorded and they are shown in Table 4.

**Table 4.** Temporal Attack Graph Metrics for $\mathcal{G}^a(t_0, t_3)$

| Metric | Time Windows | Score |
|---|---|---|
| Characteristic Temporal Path Length $L^a$ | $w_0, w_1, w_2$ | 2.63 |
| Temporal Global Efficiency $E^a$ | $w_0, w_1, w_2$ | 0.45 |

## 8.5  Discussion

Our temporal metrics for temporal attack graphs include the calculation of key measures: shortest temporal attack path length, characteristic temporal attack path length, and temporal attack path length efficiency. Each of these metrics provides unique insights into the security state of a system.

The temporal shortest attack path length helps security providers identify the earliest occurrence of an attack path between a pair of nodes in the attack graph. It determines the initial time window when the shortest attack path is first observed. This information enables prompt identification of a possible multistage attack path to a given critical resource within the network, so that corresponding vulnerabilities may be patched or network configuration can be modified to prevent such an attack instance.

The temporal characteristic path length represents the overall path length of the temporal attack graph across all time windows. It indicates the extent of vulnerabilities present in the network over time. A higher temporal characteristic path length suggests a network with a greater number of unique vulnerabilities. When attack graphs are viewed as a sequence, we may observe highly clustered large-world networks, where the path length (denoted as $L^a$) increases linearly with the number of nodes (denoted as $N$). Conversely, random networks exhibit poorly clustered small-world networks, where the path length increases logarithmically with the number of nodes. From our results, we can see that the motivating example had a considerable number of vulnerabilities spread out across all time windows, and that resulted in a fairly higher temporal characteristic path length of 2.63. It is to be noted that this value is always within the threshold of the number of time windows present in a temporal attack graph.

Temporal global efficiency provides insight into the network's overall robustness. It is inversely related to the temporal attack path length ($L^a$), meaning that low values of $L^a$ correspond to high values of efficiency ($E^a$), and vice versa. Thus, a network with fewer vulnerabilities over time exhibits greater temporal efficiency, indicating a higher level of security. In our results, we can see that high $L^a$ resulted in an efficiency value of 0.45 (45%) which indicates the overall robust nature of the given network and the same is also in sync with the mathematical formulations.

## 9  Conclusion

Attack graph-based security metrics are a valuable approach for assessing the security of enterprise networks. These metrics provide insights into potential attack routes and vulnerabilities within the network. Temporal attack graph based metrics offer significant advantages in evaluating network security. They account for the dynamic nature of modern networks, which continuously evolve in terms of topology and configurations. By considering these changes over time, these metrics provide a more accurate and up-to-date assessment of a network's security.

The path-based metrics introduced in this paper offer a new perspective for analyzing dynamic networks, effectively filling the existing gap in assessing their security. Nonetheless, in order to unlock their full potential, it is imperative to apply these metrics to real-world datasets and make necessary adaptations to account for distinct network characteristics and unique security requirements. By doing so, we can harness the true power of these metrics and obtain comprehensive insights into the dynamics and vulnerabilities of real-world networks.

## 10  Future Work

The security metrics proposed in this paper hold immense promise for advancing network security evaluation. However, their efficacy needs to be rigorously tested through empirical studies, and appropriate algorithms should be developed to facilitate their implementation. We could not evaluate our proposal due to non-availability of public dataset of attack graphs. One possible avenue of future work would involve generation of synthetic attack graphs to test the efficacy of the proposed security metrics.

Furthermore, it is worth exploring the potential of centrality-based temporal attack graph metrics, as they could provide deeper insights into the security of dynamic networks. By delving into these areas, we can further enhance our understanding and assessment of network security in dynamic environments.

**Acknowledgement.** Authors would like to express their sincere thanks to the anonymous reviewers for their invaluable feedback.

## References

1. Ammann, P., Wijesekera, D., Kaushik, S.: Scalable, graph-based network vulnerability analysis. In: Proceedings of the 9th ACM Conference on Computer and Communications Security, CCS 2002, pp. 217–224. Association for Computing Machinery, New York (2002). https://doi.org/10.1145/586110.586140
2. Sheyner, O., Haines, J.W., Jha, S., Lippmann, R., Wing, J.M.: Automated generation and analysis of attack graphs. In: Proceedings 2002 IEEE Symposium on Security and Privacy, pp. 273–284 (2002)
3. Albanese, M., Jajodia, S., Pugliese, A., Subrahmanian, V.S.: Scalable analysis of attack scenarios. In: Atluri, V., Diaz, C. (eds.) ESORICS 2011. LNCS, vol. 6879, pp. 416–433. Springer, Heidelberg (2011). https://doi.org/10.1007/978-3-642-23822-2_23. http://dl.acm.org/citation.cfm?id=2041225.2041255
4. Albanese, M., Jajodia, S., Noel, S.: Time-efficient and cost-effective network hardening using attack graphs. In: IEEE/IFIP International Conference on Dependable Systems and Networks (DSN 2012), pp. 1–12 (2012)

5. Xuan, B.B., Ferreira, A., Jarry, A.: Computing shortest, fastest, and foremost journeys in dynamic networks. Int. J. Found. Comput. Sci. **14**, 267–285 (2003)
6. Yusuf, S.E., Ge, M., Hong, J.B., Alzaid, H., Kim, D.S.: Evaluating the effectiveness of security metrics for dynamic networks. In: 2017 IEEE Trustcom/BigDataSE/ICESS, pp. 277–284 (2017)
7. Enoch, S.Y., Ge, M., Hong, J.B., Alzaid, H., Kim, D.S.: A systematic evaluation of cybersecurity metrics for dynamic networks. Comput. Netw. **144**, 216–229 (2018). https://www.sciencedirect.com/science/article/pii/S1389128618306285
8. Bopche, G.S., Mehtre, B.M.: Attack graph generation, visualization and analysis: issues and challenges. In: Mauri, J.L., Thampi, S.M., Rawat, D.B., Jin, D. (eds.) SSCC 2014. CCIS, vol. 467, pp. 379–390. Springer, Heidelberg (2014). https://doi.org/10.1007/978-3-662-44966-0_37
9. Noel, S., Jajodia, S.: A suite of metrics for network attack graph analytics. In: Wang, L., Jajodia, S., Singhal, A. (eds.) Network Security Metrics, pp. 141–176. Springer, Cham (2017). https://doi.org/10.1007/978-3-319-66505-4_7
10. Frigault, M., Wang, L., Jajodia, S., Singhal, A.: Measuring the overall network security by combining CVSS scores based on attack graphs and Bayesian networks. In: Wang, L., Jajodia, S., Singhal, A. (eds.) Network Security Metrics, pp. 1–23. Springer, Cham (2017). https://doi.org/10.1007/978-3-319-66505-4_1
11. Noel, S., Jajodia, S.: Metrics suite for network attack graph analytics. In: Proceedings of the 9th Annual Cyber and Information Security Research Conference, CISR 2014, pp. 5–8. Association for Computing Machinery, New York (2014). https://doi.org/10.1145/2602087.2602117
12. Wang, L., Jajodia, S., Singhal, A., Cheng, P., Noel, S.: k-zero day safety: evaluating the resilience of networks against unknown attacks. In: Wang, L., Jajodia, S., Singhal, A. (eds.) Network Security Metrics, pp. 75–93. Springer, Cham (2017). https://doi.org/10.1007/978-3-319-66505-4_4
13. Wang, L., Islam, T., Long, T., Singhal, A., Jajodia, S.: An attack graph-based probabilistic security metric. In: Atluri, V. (ed.) DBSec 2008. LNCS, vol. 5094, pp. 283–296. Springer, Heidelberg (2008). https://doi.org/10.1007/978-3-540-70567-3_22
14. Enoch, S.Y., Hong, J.B., Ge, M., Kim, D.S.: Composite metrics for network security analysis. CoRR abs/2007.03486 (2020). https://arxiv.org/abs/2007.03486
15. ISO/IEC 27005: Information technology-security techniques-information security risk management. ISO/IEC 44 (2008)
16. Popov, O.: Priorities for research on current and emerging network technologies. ENISA (European Network and Information Security Agency) (2010)
17. Holme, P.: Network reachability of real-world contact sequences. Phys. Rev. E **71**, 046119 (2005). https://doi.org/10.1103/PhysRevE.71.046119
18. Casteigts, A., Flocchini, P., Quattrociocchi, W., Santoro, N.: Time-varying graphs and dynamic networks. CoRR abs/1012.0009 (2010). http://arxiv.org/abs/1012.0009
19. Tang, J.K.: Temporal network metrics and their application to real world networks. Ph.D. thesis, Robinson College, University of Cambridge (2011)
20. Tang, J., et al.: Applications of temporal graph metrics to real-world networks. In: Holme, P., Saramäki, J. (eds.) Temporal Networks, pp. 135–159. Springer, Heidelberg (2013). https://doi.org/10.1007/978-3-642-36461-7_7
21. Rossetti, G., Guidotti, R., Pennacchioli, D., Pedreschi, D., Giannotti, F.: Interaction prediction in dynamic networks exploiting community discovery. In: Proceedings of the 2015 IEEE/ACM International Conference on Advances in Social

Networks Analysis and Mining 2015, ASONAM 2015, pp. 553–558. Association for Computing Machinery, New York (2015). https://doi.org/10.1145/2808797. 2809401

22. Rossetti, G., Cazabet, R.: Community discovery in dynamic networks: a survey. ACM Comput. Surv. **51**, 1–37 (2018). https://doi.org/10.1145/3172867

23. Viard, T., Latapy, M., Magnien, C.: Computing maximal cliques in link streams. Theor. Comput. Sci. **609**, 245–252 (2016)

24. Latapy, M., Viard, T., Magnien, C.: Stream graphs and link streams for the modeling of interactions over time. Soc. Netw. Anal. Min. **8**, 1–29 (2018). https://doi.org/10.1007/s13278-018-0537-7

25. Holme, P., Saramäki, J.: Temporal networks. Phys. Rep. **519**, 97–125 (2012). https://www.sciencedirect.com/science/article/pii/S0370157312000841

26. Casteigts, A., Meeks, K., Mertzios, G.B., Niedermeier, R.: Temporal graphs: structure, algorithms, applications (dagstuhl seminar 21171). In: Dagstuhl Reports, vol. 11. Schloss Dagstuhl-Leibniz-Zentrum für Informatik (2021)

27. Grindrod, P., Parsons, M.C., Higham, D.J., Estrada, E.: Communicability across evolving networks. Phys. Rev. E **83**, 046120 (2011)

28. Latora, V., Marchiori, M.: Efficient behavior of small-world networks. Phys. Rev. Lett. **87**, 198701 (2001). https://doi.org/10.1103/PhysRevLett.87.198701

29. Watts, D.J., Strogatz, S.H.: Collective dynamics of 'small-world' networks. Nature **393**, 440–442 (1998)

30. Tang, J., Musolesi, M., Mascolo, C., Latora, V.: Characterising temporal distance and reachability in mobile and online social networks. ACM SIGCOMM Comput. Commun. Rev. **40**, 118–124 (2010)

31. Noel, S.: A review of graph approaches to network security analytics. In: Samarati, P., Ray, I., Ray, I. (eds.) From Database to Cyber Security. LNCS, vol. 11170, pp. 300–323. Springer, Cham (2018). https://doi.org/10.1007/978-3-030-04834-1_16

32. Lallie, H.S., Debattista, K., Bal, J.: A review of attack graph and attack tree visual syntax in cyber security. Comput. Sci. Rev. **35**, 100219 (2020). https://www.sciencedirect.com/science/article/pii/S1574013719300772

33. Wang, L., Liu, A., Jajodia, S.: Using attack graphs for correlating, hypothesizing, and predicting intrusion alerts. Comput. Commun. **29**, 2917–2933 (2006). https://doi.org/10.1016/j.comcom.2006.04.001

34. Ritchey, R.W., Ammann, P.: Using model checking to analyze network vulnerabilities. In: Proceeding 2000 IEEE Symposium on Security and Privacy, S&P 2000, pp. 156–165. IEEE (2000)

35. Jajodia, S., Noel, S.: Topological vulnerability analysis: a powerful new approach for network attack prevention, detection, and response. In: Algorithms, Architectures and Information Systems Security, pp. 285–305. World Scientific (2009)

36. Jajodia, S., Noel, S., O'berry, B.: Topological analysis of network attack vulnerability. In: Kumar, V., Srivastava, J., Lazarevic, A. (eds.) Managing Cyber Threats: Issues, Approaches, and Challenges, vol. 5, pp. 247–266. Springer, Boston (2005). https://doi.org/10.1007/0-387-24230-9_9

37. A Nessus scanner. https://www.tenable.com/products/nessus

38. A Retina IoT (RIoT). https://sss.gd/uvAbx

39. Ou, X., Govindavajhala, S., Appel, A.W.: MulVAL: a logic-based network security analyzer. In: Proceedings of the 14th Conference on USENIX Security Symposium, SSYM 2005, vol. 14, p. 8. USENIX Association (2005)

40. Ceri, S., Gottlob, G., Tanca, L., et al.: What you always wanted to know about datalog (and never dared to ask). IEEE Trans. Knowl. Data Eng. **1**, 146–166 (1989)

41. Sagonas, K., Swift, T., Warren, D.S.: XSB as an efficient deductive database engine. ACM SIGMOD Rec. **23**, 442–453 (1994)
42. Ingols, K., Chu, M., Lippmann, R., Webster, S., Boyer, S.: Modeling modern network attacks and countermeasures using attack graphs. In: 2009 Annual Computer Security Applications Conference, pp. 117–126 (2009)

# An Energy-Conscious Surveillance Scheme for Intrusion Detection in Underwater Sensor Networks Using Tunicate Swarm Optimization

Sunil Kumar Kammula$^{(\boxtimes)}$, Veena Anand, and Deepak Singh

Department of Computer Science and Engineering, National Institute of Technology Raipur,
Raipur, Chhattisgarh, India
{kskumar.phd2020.cse,vanand.cs,dsingh.cs}@nitrr.ac.in

**Abstract.** The underwater environment is crucial for various scientific applications, including naval bases, offshore installations, and military surveillance. Precise intruder detection in such environments via underwater acoustic sensor networks (UASN) with minimal network resources is quite challenging in safeguarding the territorial marine environment. Moreover, the unavailability of GPS, poor visibility, and diverging network scenarios make it more complicated than terrestrial sensor networks. Hence, this article addresses an energy-efficient surveillance scheme using only one beacon -node for intrusion detection subject to location precision, energy restrictions, and network overhead constraints. The proposed energy-conscious surveillance scheme monitors the chosen region of interest (ROI) with a single beacon node using its Boolean perception probability to find an intruder node in its area of responsibility. Next, a low-cost centroid technique is applied to calculate the estimated location coordinates of the intruder node. Estimated intruder coordinates are further enhanced using a rapid convergent Tunicate swarm algorithm (TSO). Thorough findings from simulations reveal that the proposed technique reduces the overhead of employing numerous beacon nodes while substantially improving the intruder position accuracy compared to its contemporary schemes.

**Keywords:** Energy efficient · Surveillance scheme · Target detection · UASN

## 1 Introduction

UASNs consist of underwater sensors and nodes using acoustic waves for communication. They're tailored for aquatic settings due to the limitations of RF wireless communication. Vital for naval, offshore, and defense applications, UASNs enhance border security by detecting intruders in maritime and coastal areas [1]. The sensors in an intrusion detection network only need to be able to spot the intruder once they enter the monitored area rather than at every step along the journey. The spatial identification of intruder position has become a crucial factor in improving situational awareness, decision-making, and secure usage of the aquatic environment. Identified location information assists in preventing illicit or unauthorized fishing, poaching, and other activities [2] that exploit

V. Muthukkumarasamy et al. (Eds.): ICISS 2023, LNCS 14424, pp. 129–138, 2023.
https://doi.org/10.1007/978-3-031-49099-6_8

underwater resources. Precise marine localization aids responsible resource management, prevents overfishing, and aids in emergencies, benefiting research, conservation, and protection efforts [3–5].

Earlier works have put a substantial amount of effort into solving the sensor node's resource utilization problem using a variety of genetic algorithms. Numerous beacon nodes can enhance UASN detection precision and coverage [6]. However, such solutions have adverse cost, energy, communication, and deployment effects. To stay in place and communicate, beacon nodes must run continually [7]. As beacon nodes rise, network energy usage does, too. This may shorten the network lifespan. Many beacon nodes might strain the constrained resources, impacting the network's overall performance. Therefore, for optimized energy requirements and overhead complications, the suggested methodology uses a single beacon node architecture with the assistance of the centroid technique. In addition, this article also proposes a quick convergent and robust explorative Tunicate Swarm Optimization (TSO) -based intrusion detection mechanism for IoUT applications, which solves the issue of maximizing the accuracy of target node detection while minimizing energy consumption.

The article makes the following contributions:

• The proposed single beacon-node surveillance scheme seeks to increase intruder nodes' identification precision by minimizing the number of reference nodes.
• To estimate the location coordinates of the intruder, a centroid technique that is less susceptible to chaotic measurements is utilized.
• A novel fitness function based on TSO is developed with residual energy, precision, and proximity to estimated coordinates for more precise intruder accuracy.
• We have combined the beacon node scheme with the TSO method to attain precise accuracy by reducing the network's complexity.

## 2 Related Works

Localization and target tracking in underwater acoustic sensor networks are interdependent, as accurate localization aids intruder detection, and effective tracking enhances localization precision.

Several surveillance schemes for UASNs have been devised based on measurements of localization techniques. For example, to perform continuous tracking and quantization of the local estimates, a surveillance scheme using an extended Kalman filter (EKF) and global nearest neighbor (GNN) mechanism was proposed in [8]. The technique uses optimal quantization of the sensed information over linear quantization to address bandwidth and computational load constraints. To address the expedition of limited energy sources of a sensor node during the accurate localization of intruder nodes, Inam and Chenn [7] presented a range-free localization scheme using angle-based and distance-based metrics. The procedure helps reduce the localization error gap to improve the detection process's accuracy.

Previous works have considered localization schemes using some machine learning algorithms to detect the intruder nodes in the underwater environment precisely. In [9], a privacy-preserving localization technique using deep reinforcement learning (DRL) has been proposed to conceal the private location coordinates of the anchor and target nodes.

Muhammad Irshad et al. [10] have used a decision tree method by improving the J48 algorithm to assess localization accuracy, precision, and computational cost parameters. The information gain and entropy values are calculated with the help of the J48 algorithm for efficient splitting of the decision trees. In [11], an efficient method for localization of the target nodes using Support Vector Regression (SVR) is proposed. The SVR scheme only uses the proposed methodology to identify static target nodes, leaving the mobility constraints behind.

Energy efficiency for target detection or tracking in UASNs has been the subject of numerous previous studies. In reference [12], an energy-efficient intruder tracking system with asynchronous clocks and Bayesian filtering is presented, enhancing sensor network longevity through duty cycles. In [13], the adverse effect of reference node failure because of natural calamities and obstacles on limited energy reserves is addressed. Reference [14] introduces a self-adaptive AUV-based scheme for target node detection, enhancing identification accuracy while reducing computational overhead in sparse networks.

The literature review highlights existing solutions for intruder node detection, suggesting a novel, resource-efficient UASN surveillance scheme that balances accuracy and energy efficiency using a minimal number of anchor nodes.

## 3 Preliminaries

### 3.1 Node Sensing and Distribution Model

The sensor nodes' perception ability in UASNs allows it to detect, sense, or perceive an event or phenomenon occurring in their surroundings. Considerations for node perception probability include the detecting capability of each deployed node, the quality of the sensor itself, the state of the environment, and the overall reliability of the nodes' capacity to communicate with the centralized base station [15]. In this article, only the sensing range $(R_s)$ of a sensor node is used to detect and perceive the surrounding area in its vicinity. Manhattan distance [13] is used as a catalyst in determining the spatial gap separating the beacon node and the event or intruder. Whenever an event $e$ occurs within the sensing range of the beacon node [16], the perception probability of the sensor $(s_i)$ for the event $e$ is 1; otherwise, the perception probability is 0. This phenomenon is called the Boolean perception probability model, and the mathematical representation is shown in Eq. 1

$$f(e, s_i) = \begin{cases} 1 & d(e, s_i) \leq R_s \\ 0 & d(e, s_i) > R_s \end{cases} \tag{1}$$

where $f(e, s_i)$ represents the probability of a sensor node detecting the event happened in its sensing range and $d(e, s_i)$ denotes the distance between event $e$ and node $s_i$.

### 3.2 Tunicate Swarm Optimization Algorithm

The algorithm draws inspiration from tunicates' jet propulsion, swarm behavior, and remarkable survival skills in deep ocean environments. Tunicates locate food underwater, aided by their unique attributes and interconnected gelatinous tunics [17]. The four stages mentioned below explain the jet propulsion behaviors of tunicates [18].

**Conflict Free Distribution of Search Agents:** Vector M guides new agent positions, minimizing conflicts and sensing overlap while optimizing node placement in the ROI. The new position can be represented as given below.

$$\vec{M} = \frac{\vec{G}}{\vec{F}} \tag{2}$$

$$\vec{G} = a_2 + a_3 - \vec{W} \tag{3}$$

$$\vec{F} = 2.a_1 \tag{4}$$

where $\vec{M}$ stands for a vector of new agent locations, $\vec{G}$ stands for gravity, $\vec{W}$ for deep ocean water flow, and $a_1$ through $a_3$ stands for three random quantities [19]. In deep oceans there exists some internal force amongst agents because of external factors, those forces will be stored in a new vector $\vec{Y}$, denoted by:

$$\vec{Y} = [Z_{mi} + a_1.Z_{ma} - Z_{mi}] \tag{5}$$

In the equation $Z_{mi} = 1$ and $Z_{ma} = 4$ talk about first and second subordinate speeds, which help to make social interaction, respectively.

**Converging Toward the Best Neighbor:** Each particle advances to the best neighboring particle after averting the collision with neighboring particles.

$$\overrightarrow{PD} = \left| \overrightarrow{LF} - r_{rnd}.\overrightarrow{P_p(x)} \right| \tag{6}$$

In the above equation $\overrightarrow{PD}$ is the separation value between location of the food source and the current particle. The parameter x describes the current iteration and $\overrightarrow{LF}$ is the current global optimal solution specifying about the position of the food sources. Similarly, $\overrightarrow{P_p(x)}$ denotes the current position of tunicate and a random number in between 0,1 is represented by $r_{rnd}$. The particles move in such a way that, they reduce the distance between estimated and actual coordinates of the intruder node.

**Moving to Global Optimum:** In each iteration, search agents will keep moving in the direction of the optimal position, which is described by using the below equation.

$$\overrightarrow{P_p(x)} = \begin{cases} \overrightarrow{LF} + \vec{M}.\overrightarrow{PD}, & \text{if } r_{rnd} \geq 0.5 \\ \overrightarrow{LF} - \vec{M}.\overrightarrow{PD}, & \text{if } r_{rnd} < 0.5 \end{cases} \tag{7}$$

At iteration x, Eq. 7 gives the updated locations of the agent as $\overrightarrow{P_p(x)}$ in comparison to the optimal scored location $\overrightarrow{LF}$. The continuous movement of these particles towards the optimal position helps in identify the intruder coordinates more precisely.

**Swarm Behavior:** Initial two solutions become current best. Others adjust positions based on ideal particle coordinates using specified equations [20].

$$\overrightarrow{P_p(x+1)} = \frac{\overrightarrow{P_p(x)} + \overrightarrow{P_p(x+1)}}{2+a_1} \tag{8}$$

The last position would be at random, either a cylindrical or cone-shaped region defined by tunicate position. A few crucial aspects of the TSA algorithm are as follows:

- The modifications in vectors $M$, $G$, and $F$ provide the potential for enhanced exploration and exploitation phases.
- The tunicate's jet propulsion and swarm behavior in a particular ROI describe the proposed TSA algorithm's collaborative behavior.

## 4 Energy Conscious a Single Beacon Node-Based Intrusion Detection Mechanism for IoUT Application

In UASN intrusion detection, pinpointing intruders in their area of responsibility is essential to prevent exploitation of location methods. Intruders may seek unauthorized access for nefarious activities like illegal fishing or environmental harm. To counter this, a single beacon node with known coordinates monitors the chosen ROI using Boolean perception probability, accurately identifying intruders during the invasion through a defined procedure.

### 4.1 Precise Detection of the Intruder Node Through the Calculation of Spatial Coordinates

The spatial coordinates of the intruder node can be calculated by using the following procedure: A single beacon node empowered with an initial energy of 50 units and threshold energy of 10 units is initialized in the 15 * 15 grid for surveillance of the chosen ROI. The spatial coordinates of the beacon node are considered as (5.5, 5.5) to assist in the identification of intruder nodes. Also, three intruder nodes were deployed in the same ROI with distinctive sensing and transmission ranges compared to beacon node. Regarding intrusion detection, it is not necessary to identify moving objects at all times along the trajectory; instead, it is sufficient that the beacon detects the intruder in its ROI. The beacon node is fixed in the environment with known spatial coordinates, and intruder nodes will exhibit a random movement within the considered ROI. The underwater environment's ocean currents, tidal waves, and noise characteristics will continuously relocate the target nodes from their initial positions. When intruder nodes come under the vicinity of the beacon's sensing range, a position estimation process is initiated to calculate the computed coordinates of the intruder. Manhattan distance and a centroid technique are used along with the known location coordinates of the beacon node to estimate the intruder coordinates.

$$\text{Manhattan distance } d = |x_b - x_i| + |y_b - y_i| \tag{9}$$

In the above formula $(x_i, y_i)$, $(x_b, y_b)$ are the spatial coordinates of the intruder and beacon node respectively. Two emulated beacon nodes are also deployed in the ROI with the same d distance to estimate the intruder nodes' position precisely.

Ecological conditions, poor visibility, and the noise generated from the hostile environment of the UASN will affect the accuracy of intruder nodes position. The distance calculation between beacon and target node pair also considers the ecological noise during the deployment of the emulated anchor nodes. But, throughout the surveillance scheme this noise is considered as a gaussian noise for simplicity.

$$(x_m, y_m) = \left( \frac{x_b + x_{ea1} + x_{ea2}}{3}, \frac{y_b + y_{ea1} + y_{ea2}}{3} \right) \tag{10}$$

Here, $(x_m, y_m)$ indicate the calculated centroid coordinates with the assistance of emulated anchor nodes. Similarly, $(x_b, y_b)$, $(x_{ea1}, y_{ea1})$, and $(x_{ea2}, y_{ea2})$ represents the beacon and two emulated anchor node position coordinates.

The calculated centroid coordinates $(x_m, y_m)$, are used as initial guess during the estimation of intruder node coordinates. Tunicate particles are distributed around the centroid coordinates to assist in the calculation of estimated coordinates. Intruder nodes, whenever entered into the sensing range of the beacon node will localize itself by finding its coordinates as $f(x_q, y_q)$ by executing tunicate particles iteratively. The ultimate goal is to reduce the error in estimated sensor node placements relative to their real locations

$$\text{Fitness function } (f(x_q, y_q)) = \frac{1}{r} \sum_{a=1}^{r} \left( \sqrt{(x_{et} - x_b)^2 + (y_{et} - y_b)^2} - d \right)^2 \tag{11}$$

where $(x_{et}, y_{et})$ represents the estimated coordinates of the intruder node and $(x_b, y_b)$ are the spatial coordinates of the beacon node. The Manhattan distance between beacon and intruder node is given by $d$ and the minimum number of required beacon and emulated beacon nodes to estimate the intruder coordinates is given by r. Figure 1 describes the intruder node estimation process using the centroid technique and tunicate particles. Minimizing the spatial gap between estimated and actual intruder coordinates enhances precise intruder detection and identification.

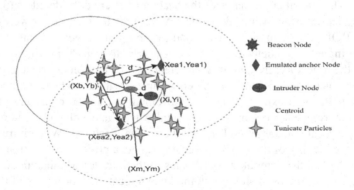

**Fig. 1.** Intruder node estimation process with the assistance of tunicate particles

# 5  Simulation Analysis

In this section, the efficacy of the proposed methodology in identifying the position coordinates of the intruder node is examined using MATLAB R2021a. The proposed methodology considered a single beacon node with known location coordinates (5.5, 5.5) and three intruder nodes with unknown locations. The beacon node is deployed randomly on a 15 * 15 gird sensing region, with fixed nature in the environment, whereas intruder nodes will exhibit a random displacement. Table 1 indicates the simulation parameters used for the evaluation purpose.

Simulation process for the intruder position estimation: The effectiveness of the proposed intrusion detection mechanism, as presented in Sect. 4.1, is examined here to identify the intruder coordinates. The deployed tunicate particles around the estimated node position help reduce the distance gap between the intruder node and the calculated node. Only 30 tunicate particles were deployed in the process, and the simulation ran for 40 iterations to acquire the intruder coordinates preciously. By executing Eq. 3 at each iteration, particles converge towards the best neighbor by reducing the separation value $d$. Also, the propagation probability ($P_p$) of 0.5 is considered in the network to mimic the ocean environment drifting nature towards the installed nodes while addressing the detection of intruder node positions.

**Table 1.** Simulation parameters

| Parameter | Values |
|---|---|
| Monitoring Area (ROI) | 15 * 15 Grid |
| Sensing Range | 75 m |
| No of Beacon node | 1 |
| No of Intruder nodes | 3 |
| Initial Energy | 50 J |
| Simulation Time | 150 s |
| Min and Max drifting of the nodes | 0 to 3 m/s |
| Propagation Probability ($P_p$) | 0.5 |

The initial population of 30 tunicates around the estimated node is shown in Fig. 2(a) and 2(b). During execution, when the process is evaluated for 40 iterations, the interme- diate results of the estimated node moving towards the global optimum of the intruder node are represented in Fig. 2(c) to Fig. 2(j). Figure 2(k) and 2(l) indicate the total con- vergence of tunicate particles towards the global optimum estimated node for the precise detection of the intruder node. In this case, the separation distance value $d$, as mentioned in Eq. 9, becomes zero at the 29th iteration with a convergence time of 0.8329 s to exactly match the coordinate values.

Analysis of the accurate position estimation of the proposed methodology is described in Fig. 3. Here, a single beacon node which is static in the environment

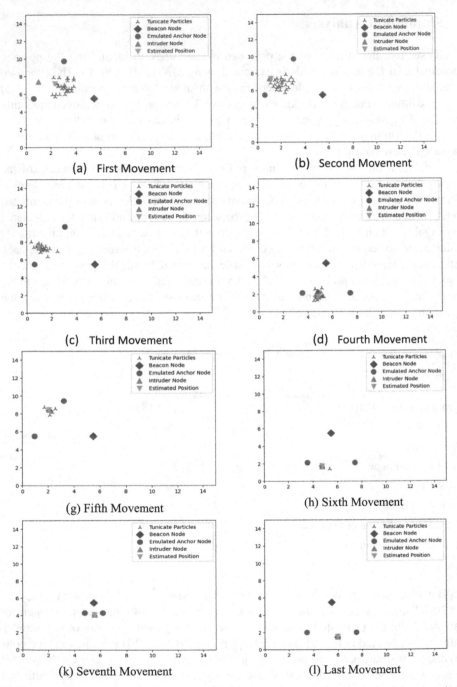

**Fig. 2.** Precise detection of the intruder node with the assistance of tunicate particles at various iteration phases.

with position coordinates of (5.5, 5.5), and three intruder nodes which are dynamic with some random mobility, are considered. The beacon nodes' Boolean perception ability helps identify intruder node entries in their surrounding area. Minimized fitness function value at each iteration, defined in Eq. 11, will reduce the spatial differentiation between authentic and computed coordinates so that there exists an exact match between both coordinates to give precise coordinates of the intruder. Here a sample of only three intruder nodes and one beacon node with a sensing range of 75 m were considered to illustrate the effectiveness of the proposed methodology. Increased sensing range of the beacon node may help in enhancing the surveillance scheme, but it will adversely affect the nodes' energy levels, which eventually leads to a reduced network lifetime.

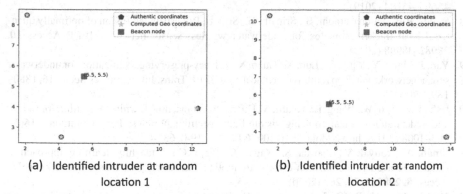

(a)  Identified intruder at random
        location 1

(b)  Identified intruder at random
        location 2

**Fig. 3.** Identification of location coordinates of three intruder nodes at different places using a single beacon node.

## 6  Conclusion

The article tackles intruder detection in underwater acoustic sensor networks (UASNs) through the use of the TSO application. It introduces a centroid-based identification approach for estimating intruder node positions during an intrusion. To enhance accuracy, a rapid-convergence TSO algorithm is applied to improve the estimated coordinates, minimizing the gap between estimated and true positions. The method also addresses energy conservation by utilizing a single beacon node in the region of interest, extending network longevity. This strategy strikes a balance between precise intruder detection and reduced energy consumption, crucial in UASNs. Future work could expand the scheme for continuous 3D tracking of intruders in complex underwater environments.

## References

1. Luo, J., Yang, Y., Wang, Z., Chen, Y.: Localization algorithm for underwater sensor network: a review. IEEE Internet Things J. **8**(17), 13126–13144 (2021)
2. Kumar, M., Mondal, S.: Recent developments on target tracking problems: a review. Ocean Eng. **236**, 109558 (2021)

3. Zade, N., Deshpande, S., Kamatchi Iyer, R.: Target tracking based on approximate localization technique in deterministic directional passive sensor network. J. Ambient Intell. Human. Comput. **12**(11), 10171–10181 (2021). https://doi.org/10.1007/s12652-020-02783-5

4. Nain, M., Goyal, N.: Energy efficient localization through node mobility and propagation delay prediction in underwater wireless sensor network. Wireless Pers. Commun. **122**(3), 2667–2685 (2021). https://doi.org/10.1007/s11277-021-09024-8

5. Feng, H., Cai, Z.: Target tracking based on improved square root cubature particle filter via underwater wireless sensor networks. IET Commun. **13**(8), 1008–1015 (2019)

6. Ullah, I., Liu, Y., Su, X., Kim, P.: Efficient and accurate target localization in underwater environment. IEEE Access **7**, 101415–101426 (2019)

7. Ullah, I., Chen, J., Su, X., Esposito, C., Choi, C.: Localization and detection of targets in underwater wireless sensor using distance and angle-based algorithms. IEEE Access **7**, 45693–45704 (2019)

8. Reddy, B.B., Pardhasaradhi, B., Srinath, G., Srihari, P.: Distributed fusion of optimally quantized local tracker estimates for underwater wireless sensor networks. IEEE Access **10**, 38982–38998 (2022)

9. Yan, J., Meng, Y., Yang, X., Luo, X., Guan, X.: Privacy-preserving localization for underwater sensor networks via deep reinforcement learning. IEEE Trans. Inf. Forensics Secur. **16**, 1880–1895 (2020)

10. Irshad, M., Liu, W., Wang, L., Khalil, M.U.R.: Cogent machine learning algorithm for indoor and underwater localization using visible light spectrum. Wireless Pers. Commun. **116**(2), 993–1008 (2019). https://doi.org/10.1007/s11277-019-06631-4

11. Singh, A., Kotiyal, V., Sharma, S., Nagar, J., Lee, C.C.: A machine learning approach to predict the average localization error with applications to wireless sensor networks. IEEE Access **8**, 208253–208263 (2020)

12. Yan, J., Zhao, H., Pu, B., Luo, X., Chen, C., Guan, X.: Energy-efficient target tracking with UASNs: a consensus-based Bayesian approach. IEEE Trans. Autom. Sci. Eng. **17**(3), 1361–1375 (2019)

13. Kumari, S., Mishra, P.K., Anand, V.: Fault-resilient localization using fuzzy logic and NSGA II-based metaheuristic scheme for UWSNs. Soft. Comput. **25**(17), 11603–11619 (2021). https://doi.org/10.1007/s00500-021-05975-z

14. Ojha, T., Misra, S., Obaidat, M.S.: SEAL: self-adaptive AUV-based localization for sparsely deployed Underwater Sensor Networks. Comput. Commun. **154**, 204–215 (2020)

15. Yan, J., Zhao, H., Luo, X., Wang, Y., Chen, C., Guan, X.: Asynchronous localization of underwater target using consensus-based unscented Kalman filtering. IEEE J. Oceanic Eng. **45**(4), 1466–1481 (2019)

16. Kumari, S., Gupta, G.P.: Target localization algorithm in a three-dimensional wireless sensor networks. In: Smys, S., Bestak, R., Chen, J.-Z., Kotuliak, I. (eds.) International Conference on Computer Networks and Communication Technologies. LNDECT, vol. 15, pp. 33–42. Springer, Singapore (2019). https://doi.org/10.1007/978-981-10-8681-6_5

17. Kaur, S., Awasthi, L.K., Sangal, A.L., Dhiman, G.: Tunicate Swarm Algorithm: a new bio-inspired based metaheuristic paradigm for global optimization. Eng. Appl. Artif. Intell. **90**, 103541 (2020)

18. Srinivas, P., Swapna, P.: Quantum tunicate swarm algorithm-based energy aware clustering scheme for wireless sensor networks. Microprocess. Microsyst. **94**, 104653 (2022)

19. Li, J., Li, G.C., Chu, S.C., Gao, M., Pan, J.S.: Modified parallel tunicate swarm algorithm and application in 3D WSNs coverage optimization. J. Internet Technol. **23**(2), 227–244 (2022)

20. Lin, Y., Zhang, Z., Najafabadi, H.E.: Underwater source localization using time difference of arrival and frequency difference of arrival measurements based on an improved invasive weed optimization algorithm. IET Sig. Process. **16**(3), 299–309 (2022)

# Security Using AI/ML

# STN-Net: A Robust GAN-Generated Face Detector

Tanusree Ghosh[✉][ID] and Ruchira Naskar[ID]

Department of Information Technology, Indian Institute of Engineering Science and
Technology, Shibpur 711103, India
2021itp001.tanusree@students.iiests.ac.in, ruchira@it.iiests.ac.in

**Abstract.** Massive advancements in Generative Artificial Intelligence
in the recent years, have introduced hyper-realistic fake multimedia content. Where such technologies have become a boon to industries such as
entertainment and gaming, malicious uses of the same in disseminating
fabricated information eventually have invited serious social perils. Generative Adversarial Network (GAN) generated images, especially non-
existent human facial images, lately have widely been used to dissemi-
nate propaganda and fake news in Online Social Networks (OSNs), by
creating fake OSN profiles. Being visually indistinguishable from authentic images, GAN-generated image detection has become a massive challenge to the forensic community. Even though countermeasure solutions
based on various Machine Learning (ML) and Deep Learning (DL) techniques have been proposed recently, most of their performance drops
significantly for OSN-compressed images. Also, DL solutions based on
Convolutional Neural Networks (CNN) tend to be highly complex and
time-consuming for training.

This work proposes a solution to these problems by introducing *STN-
Net*, a CNN classifier with an extremely reduced set of parameters, which
adopts a carefully crafted minimal image feature set, computed based on
*Sine Transformed Noise (STN)*. Despite having a much-reduced feature
set compared to other State-of-the-Art (SOTA) CNN-based solutions,
our model achieves very high detection accuracy (*average* $\geq$ 99%). It
also achieves promising detection performance on post-processed images,
which mimic real-world OSN contexts.

## 1 Introduction

Although the origins of image forgery and manipulation can be traced in history
as far back as the 1840s [19], contemporary technological advancements have
eased forgery creation to a great extent. The invention of Generative Adversarial Networks (GANs) in 2014 [9] is considered one of the milestones in artificial
image generation. Eventually, other GAN architectures like PGGAN [13], Style-
GAN [15], StyleGAN2 [16], StyleGAN3 [14] etc. have further advanced the capabilities of GANs in generating hyper-realistic and high-quality images. Through
easily accessible interfaces[1], anyone can generate synthetic images in a matter of

---

[1] https://thispersondoesnotexist.com/.

© The Author(s), under exclusive license to Springer Nature Switzerland AG 2023
V. Muthukkumarasamy et al. (Eds.): ICISS 2023, LNCS 14424, pp. 141–158, 2023.
https://doi.org/10.1007/978-3-031-49099-6_9

seconds. Whereas such technologies have brought immense progress in various fields like the entertainment and gaming industries, illicit uses of the same have also raised concerns regarding the authenticity and trustworthiness of digital content[2]. Moreover, the prevalence of fake images has become a significant issue due to the ever-increasing presence of Online Social Networks (OSNs) in our daily lives. Illicit users often utilize OSN to spread disinformation and propaganda, potentially harming individuals and society as a whole[3,4].

While earlier AI-generated face detection was highly dependent on visual inconsistency, like different eye colours in both eyes, asymmetric face shapes, irregular pupil shapes, etc. [5], with the technological advancements of Style-GAN, such artifacts have been largely omitted. A recent study [21] found that regular human observers find AI-generated faces more trustworthy than real faces. Having human accuracy of identifying synthetic faces around ≈50%–60% makes them highly vulnerable to trusting fake content online. Hence, to identify GAN-generated images, automated detectors that rely on apparently 'hidden' characteristics of visually indistinguishable hyper-realistic GAN-generated synthetic images are of paramount need in the multimedia forensics community.

A few successful detectors have already been proposed in the literature.

Most of them almost accurately (average detection accuracy as high as 99%) detect synthetic faces in the lab environment, where the training and testing dataset is pre-known [4,7]. However, deploying these detectors in real-world scenarios remain challenging, as they often face performance degradation for OSN-circulated images. It happens due to the fact that images circulated through OSNs go through various compression algorithms and transformations, which can alter their statistical features and make them more difficult to detect using traditional methods. The specific operations performed by any OSN on images are usually unknown, posing a challenge for designing detectors that can successfully handle various image modifications encountered in real-life situations. A few recent works [22,23,31] have addressed this issue and studied the performance of their solutions on post-processed images. They use complex feature sets with deep CNN-based classifiers, which makes them hard to implement in resource-constrained platforms like edge devices. In this work, we formulate the synthetic image detection problem as a binary classification problem between real and fake faces. We propose a solution based on a hand-crafted feature set followed by a well-designed CNN. Our solution achieves a high average accuracy of 99.53% for images from our test set. We evaluate the performance of our solution on post-processed images to understand its real-world usability. Consisting of a minimal feature set compared to SOTA CNN-based solutions, our solution performs well in the context of post-processed images. Specifically, the main contributions of this paper are:

---

[2] https://www.npr.org/2022/12/15/1143114122/ai-generated-fake-faces-have-become-a-hallmark-of-online-influence-operations.

[3] https://edition.cnn.com/2020/02/28/tech/fake-twitter-candidate-2020/index.html.

[4] https://edition.cnn.com/2020/02/20/tech/fake-faces-deepfake/index.html.

(a) Real                    (b) StyleGAN2                    (c) StyleGAN3

**Fig. 1.** Example of Real and GAN-generated images from dataset (https://github.com/NVlabs/ffhq-dataset), (https://github.com/NVlabs/stylegan2), (https://github.com/NVlabs/stylegan3)

- We introduce a novel feature set *Sine Transformed Noise (STN)* that enhances differentiating features between real and synthetic images. Our feature set, STN is of size $m \times n \times 1$ for an RGB image of size $m \times n \times 3$. STN is the minimal-sized feature map compared to existing feature sets for detecting fake images using any CNN-based network.
- We introduce *STN-Net*, a CNN-based detector utilising STN feature set and augmented STN feature set, which uses very few parameters compared to existing CNN-based detectors while maintaining high detection accuracy. We compare STN-Net with several well-known CNN detectors in the field.
- Proposed STN-Net is tested on various post-processing conditions such as Median filtering, Gaussian Noise addition, Contrast Limited Adaptive Histogram Equalization (CLAHE), Average Blurring, Gamma Correction and Resizing with different parameters, as well as JPEG compression. Our extensive experimental results prove the effectiveness of the proposed network in the presence of such post-processing operations that images undergo in real-world scenarios.

The rest of this paper is organised as follows. Section 2 reviews the relevant related works in the field of GAN image detection. Section 3 presents the proposed STN-Net approach, including the generation of the STN feature set and the architecture of the proposed CNN-based detector. Section 4 presents the experimental setup and evaluation results, comparing STN-Net with other state-of-the-art detectors, while Sect. 5 concludes the paper and provides directions for future research in the field.

## 2   Related Works

While the primary GAN model [9] was able to generate synthetic images that were identifiable with bare eyes, the advanced GAN model StyleGAN and their variants [14–16] generated images have become visually hardly distinguishable from authentic images. The existing community of Digital Image Forensics started synthetic image detection. GAN image detection is considered a binary classification problem, similar to binary detection of forged images [28]. Having a strong similarity with traditional image forgery detection, most of the earlier solutions consisted of steganalysis-based features like Co-occurrence matrix [20], SRM [17] etc. Later, semantic inconsistency-related features like Corneal specular highlight [18], Landmark locations [32], Irregular pupil shape [11] etc. were explored to identify GAN-faces. Once explored, such artefacts could be used by regular users in their daily lives to some extent to identify fakes. However, with improvements in GAN architecture, such visual inconsistency-based artefacts have been reduced to a great extent, making synthetic images hard to detect.

Another approach to GAN-image detection is purely deep neural network-based. Automatically learned features by DL-based classifiers [4] have been proven to be very successful in detecting synthetic faces. However, a major hurdle for such classifiers is the architectural setting of GAN models. GANs simultaneously use a generator and a discriminator network to learn the data distribution of real datasets and mimic them to generate new data. If a purely DL-based GAN image detector is used as a discriminator inside GAN architecture, eventually, the generator module of GAN will be trained to fool the discriminator, making the DL-based detector useless. As a result, using hand-crafted features in conjunction with deep neural networks (DNN) has gained traction as a prevalent solution method in contemporary contexts [3,22,23]. Spatial domain features are primarily used in such solutions. From a different perspective, symmetries in GAN-faces in the frequency domain have also been explored [7,30].

However, even though progress in GAN image detection is gaining momentum lately, the performance of existing GAN-image detectors in real-world scenarios remains a big challenge. Marra et al. [17] first explored the problem of performance degradation of synthetic image detectors while tested on OSN-like compressed images. Recently, Chen et al. [3] proposed the inclusion of two modules from multiple colour domains, named block attention module and a multi-layer feature aggregation module, into the Xception model to increase robustness against such post-processing degradation. Lately, another problem domain related to GAN-image detection has been explored: The generalisation problem [6]. In real-world scenarios, guessing the exact source model of any GAN image is difficult. Hence, any practical detector should be capable of detecting fake faces even though the training and test datasets mismatch. The work [10] contains a performance comparison between existing solutions.

Recently, the study of anti-forensics in the context of detecting GAN-generated images has gained significance. Carlini et al. [1] explored the anti-forensics aspect of GAN-generated image detectors. They explored five white-box and black-box attack scenarios that severely degraded the performance of GAN-image detection. As our scope for this work is to propose a GAN-image detector that performs well in OSN-context, we consider only common OSN-specific perturbations, as discussed in earlier similar studies [22,23]. The study of the detector's robustness against additional white-box and black-box attacks is reserved for future research endeavours.

We can infer from the high detection performance of existing solutions that detecting GAN faces is not a big hurdle these days while training and testing dataset matches. The bigger problem remains maintaining the detection performance while test images have different statistical characteristics due to unknown manipulation. Hence, we aim to propose a GAN-generated face detection solution robust to image manipulations. In that direction, we design a reliable GAN-face detector combining hand-crafted features with a DNN-based classifier, implementable in real-world scenarios.

## 3    Proposed Methodology

As shown in Fig. 2, our proposed solution consists of two major blocks of operations: *Preprocessing and Feature Extraction* followed by *Deep-Learning-based Classifier*.

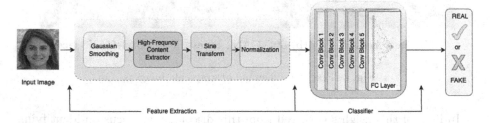

**Fig. 2.** Proposed Framework

### 3.1    Preprocessing

Given an input RGB image $I(x, y)$, which represents the intensity of the image at coordinates $x$ and $y$ in the spatial domain, we first convert it to grayscale using the Eq. 1. The grayscale value at a pixel location $(x, y)$ is denoted as $I_{gray}(x, y)$, and it is calculated as a weighted sum of the red, green, and blue channels.

$$I_{gray}(x, y) = 0.2989 \times R(x, y) + 0.5870 \times G(x, y) + 0.1140 \times B(x, y) \quad (1)$$

where $R(x, y)$, $G(x, y)$, and $B(x, y)$ are the red, green, and blue intensity values of the pixel at coordinates $(x, y)$, respectively.

Although a few earlier works [2,8,20,22] have explored strong discriminating features in colour-domain statistics, such methods usually have large feature sizes. We convert a three-channel RGB image to a one-channel grayscale image based on the finding in Fig. 3, which we explain below. Here, we calculate pixel-wise mean values from 400 real images (Fig. 3a), 400 StyleGAN2 generated

146    T. Ghosh and R. Naskar

images (Fig. 3b) and 400 StyleGAN3 generated images (Fig. 3c). As all synthesised images use the same FFHQ dataset for generating synthetic images, it is trivial that generated photos from both generative architectures look similar to originals, as depicted in Fig. 1. However, as shown in Fig. 3, there are visible differences between the three mean images. GAN-generated images possess much more structure than real ones, especially the mean of StyleGAN2 images, which have a visible common structure. This hints towards the presence of model-specific similar high-frequency components in each type of GAN, which are different from other GAN models and real images. Hence, it is shown that even single-channel grayscale images possess visually discriminating features.

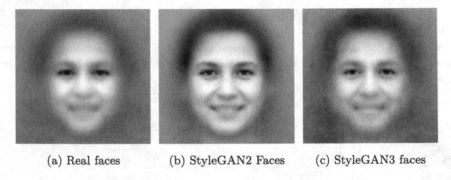

(a) Real faces        (b) StyleGAN2 Faces        (c) StyleGAN3 faces

**Fig. 3.** Pixel-wise average of grayscale images

In light of the insights gathered from this discourse, we focus on identifying robust feature representations with high-frequency content in grayscale images generated by GANs. Laplacian of Gaussian (LoG) is a well-known method in image processing for high-frequency image feature extraction in the context of faces [24, 29].

Hereby, we employ Gaussian Blur with kernel size 3 × 3 and 0 standard deviation ($\sigma$) followed by Laplacian kernel to extract high-frequency information. Gaussian kernel, as shown in Eq. 2, is computed using the Gaussian distribution formula. Smoothened image $I_{smoothed}(x, y)$ is generated by convolving this kernel with $I_{gray}(x, y)$, using Eq. 3, where $i$ and $j$ are the indices of the kernel's rows and columns, respectively. Here Gaussian blur is used to mitigate the influence of random high-frequency noise on images.

$$kernel(i,j) = \frac{1}{2\pi\sigma^2} \exp\left(-\frac{i^2 + j^2}{2\sigma^2}\right) \tag{2}$$

$$I_{smoothed}(x,y) = \sum_{i=-1}^{1} \sum_{j=-1}^{1} I_{gray}(x+i, y+j) \times kernel(i,j) \tag{3}$$

On smoothened image $I_{smoothed}(x, y)$, the Laplacian operator is applied to compute the *Laplacian Response*, which denotes the second order derivative of the image intensity, for the spatial coordinates $x$ and $y$, hence obtaining rate of intensity change.

Mathematically, the Laplacian kernel (L) is defined as:

$$L = \begin{bmatrix} 0 & 1 & 0 \\ 1 & -4 & 1 \\ 0 & 1 & 0 \end{bmatrix}$$

The Laplacian response $(I_{laplacian}(x,y))$ at a pixel location $(x,y)$ is calculated by convolving the smoothened image $I_{smoothed}(x,y)$ with the Laplacian kernel using Eq. 4.

$$I_{laplacian}(x,y) = \sum_{i=-1}^{1} \sum_{j=-1}^{1} I_{smoothed}(x+i, y+j) \times L(i,j) \qquad (4)$$

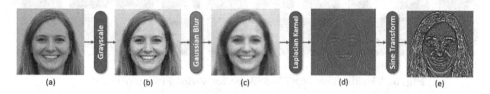

**Fig. 4.** Visualisation of STN-Feature evolution: (a) Input RGB Image; (b) Grayscaled Image; (c) Gaussian Blurred Image; (d) Laplacian Transformed Image; (f) Sine Transformed Feature

### 3.2   Sine-Transformed Noise

Primarily, sine transformations are used in the frequency domain accompanied by Fourier Transform. However, we use sine transformation on direct pixel values obtained by $I_{laplacian}(x,y)$ using Eq. 5. As shown in Fig. 4, Sine transformation preserves texture and high-frequency information at the pixel level. After extensive experiments with different frequencies, we found the best performance with frequency ten. We have shown a visual representation of feature $I_{STN}(x,y)$ in Fig. 5 for varying frequencies from 1 to 50.

$$I_{STN}(x,y) = \sin\left(2\pi \times frequency \times \frac{I_{laplacian}(x,y)}{255.0}\right) \qquad (5)$$

We utilize the normalized form of the $I_{STN}(x,y)$ as feature, as shown in Eq. 6.

$$I_{STN_{Normalized}}(x,y) = \frac{I_{STN}(x,y) - \min(I_{STN}(x,y))}{\max(I_{STN}(x,y)) - \min(I_{STN}(x,y))} \times 255.0 \qquad (6)$$

Given an RGB image, the evolution of feature $I_{STN}(x,y)$ is pictorially shown in Fig. 4.

It is evident from the visualisation that for frequency 1, the feature set visually depicts merely high-frequency edge information. As the frequency increases to 10, the features get much more accentuated.

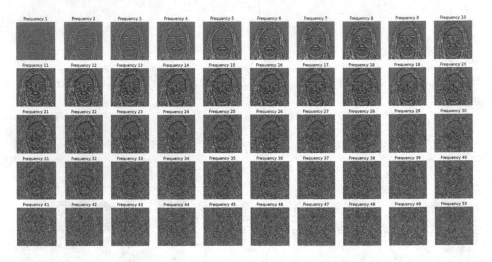

**Fig. 5.** Visualisation of STN-feature for various frequency values

### 3.3  Classifier

Convolutional Neural Networks (CNN) are conventionally used for image classification for their efficient capability of extracting features hierarchically. As shown in Fig. 6, our proposed CNN-based classifier consists of five convolution blocks. Each block consists of a *Convolutional Layer* with $3 \times 3$ sized kernel, followed by a *Batch Normalization* layer and *Max Pooling Layer* with window size $2 \times 2$. The batch Normalization layer is used to increase stability in training, whereas the Max Pooling Layer is used to downsample the feature size after each convolution for computational efficiency.

The number of filters in the convolutional layer varies in each block. Block 1 has 8 filters, Block 2 has 16 filters, Block 3 has 32 filters, Block 4 has 64 filters, and Block 5 has 128 filters. It is because, with deeper levels, the network needs to capture more complex and abstract features, which require a larger number of filters. In each block, 'ReLU' is used as an activation function to induce non-linearity. The last convolution block is followed by a flattening layer, which reshapes the high-dimensional feature maps into a one-dimensional vector, then connected to a fully connected (dense) layer with 64 neurons. The final dense layer consists of a single neuron, representing the output layer of the classifier with the sigmoid activation function.

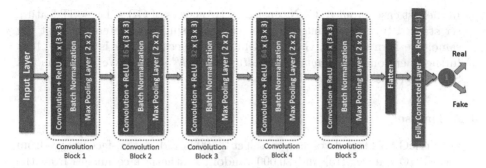

**Fig. 6.** STN-Net Architecture

## 4 Experimental Results and Analysis

We study the detection performance of our solutions on two versions of StyleGAN-generated images. StyleGAN2-generated images are widely available throughout the OSN and easily accessible to ordinary people, whereas Style-GAN3 is the improved version of StyleGAN2, with exceptionally good hyper-photorealism. Detection of both StyleGAN model-generated images is essential in identifying manipulated or fake images on online social networks in current time.

### 4.1 Solution Models

We experiment with our proposed feature set and CNN in three different settings:

- In the Baseline configuration, our proposed CNN model is utilized for binary classification without preprocessing. In this case, the input provided to our model consists of only grayscaled image $I_{gray}(x, y)$. The performance of this model serves as an indicator of the effectiveness and quality of our CNN framework. It is further mentioned as *'Only CNN'* setting.
- In the second case, we examine the influence of various preprocessing stages: Gaussian Blurring (GB), Laplacian Transformation (LT) and Sine Transformation (ST) separately. In all cases, the classifier is fixed. It is further mentioned as *'Feature + CNN'* setting.
  - GB + ST: Sine Transformation is directly applied on Gaussian Blur operated grayscaled image.
  - LT + ST: The input grayscaled image undergoes two transformations: the Laplacian Transformation and the Sine Transformation.
  - GB + LT: The grayscaled image undergoes Gaussian blur and subsequent Laplacian transformation without any sine transformation applied.
  - GB + LT + ST: Input image in preprocessed with all above-discussed operations. Along with CNN, this model is STN-Net (Single Layer).

- In the last case, input to CNN consists of two layers of GB + LT + ST feature set stacked together. While all other preprocessing parameters are kept the same, the kernel for the Gaussian Blur of the second layer is set to 5. It is further mentioned as *'Augmented Feature + CNN'* setting. We call this model STN-Net (Dual Layer).

## 4.2  Dataset

- For StyleGAN2 face detection, we select 20,000 random real-face images from the FFHQ dataset [15] and 20,000 random synthetic face images from the StyleGAN2 dataset [16]. We divide these 40,000 images: 28,000 for training, 8,000 for validation and 4,000 for testing. We consider image size $256 \times 256$ for all experiments.
- For StyleGAN3 face detection, we select 1,592 StyleGAN3 face images generated from the FFHQ dataset, provided by official dataset [14], and we collect the same number of images from the FFHQ dataset as real face images. We further divide these images: 2,228 for training, 638 for validation and 318 for testing. We use $256 \times 256$ sized images in all experiments.

## 4.3  Settings

We use the 'Adam' optimizer and 'Binary Cross-Entropy' loss function for all experiments. We train our classifier for 40 epochs for each case of StyleGAN2 and 100 epochs for StyleGAN3 detector. We use a Learning Rate (LR) scheduler for efficient convergence. For the first ten epochs, LR is set to $1 \times 10^{-3}$; for the subsequent ten epochs, LR is multiplied by $1 \times 10^{-1}$; while for the last 20 epochs, LR is multiplied by $1 \times 10^{-3}$.

## 4.4  Performance Evaluation

For detection performance evaluation, we consider five metrics: Accuracy, Area Under the ROC Curve (AUC) Score, Precision, Recall and F-1 Score. *Accuracy*, the most common metric for classification tasks, is the ratio of correctly predicted instances to the total number of instances in the test dataset. *Precision* is the ratio of correctly predicted positive instances, called true positives to the total number of predicted positive instances (sum of true positives and false positives). *Recall*, also known as Sensitivity or True Positive Rate, is the ratio of correctly predicted positive instances (true positives) to the total number of actual positive instances (sum of true positives and false negatives). The ROC curve plots the True Positive Rate (Recall) against the False Positive Rate. AUC measures the area under this curve, providing a single value that represents the overall discriminative power of a model. An AUC of 1 indicates perfect separation between the classes, while an AUC of 0.5 indicates random guessing. In the context of our problem of detecting real and synthetic images, as discussed earlier, we utilize a balanced dataset for training and testing our models. Hence, accuracy is considered a suitable metric. However, as our main focus is not to misclassify any fake images as real, 'Recall' is chosen as a metric. Higher precision signifies fewer 'fake' predictions that are 'real'.

As shown in Table 1, our baseline model, with only grayscaled image as input, performs quite well in discriminating StyleGAN2 images from Real images with an average accuracy greater than 91%, while performing exceptionally well in

**Table 1.** Detection Performances

| Detector type | GB | LT | ST | StyleGAN2 | | | | | StyleGAN3 | | | | |
|---|---|---|---|---|---|---|---|---|---|---|---|---|---|
| | | | | Accuracy | AUC | Precision | Recall | F1-Score | Accuracy | AUC | Precision | Recall | F1-Score |
| Baseline (Gray) | - | - | - | 91.79 | 97.51 | 94.04 | 89.49 | 91.47 | 80.90 | 88.70 | 75.64 | **89.96** | 81.77 |
| 1-layer (Gray) | Y | - | Y | 98.19 | 99.80 | 98.11 | 98.31 | 98.14 | 80.80 | 90.90 | 77.78 | 86.21 | 81.31 |
| | - | Y | Y | 89.89 | 95.86 | 92.23 | 85.34 | 88.33 | 80.77 | 86.66 | 80.25 | 81.63 | 80.54 |
| | Y | Y | - | 98.39 | 99.88 | 98.97 | 97.76 | 98.26 | 81.38 | 84.53 | 77.15 | 89.23 | 82.37 |
| | Y | Y | Y | 99.38 | 99.96 | 99.45 | 99.08 | 99.24 | **84.21** | 92.34 | **82.14** | 87.35 | **84.28** |
| 2-layer (Augmented) | Y | Y | Y | **99.53** | **99.97** | **99.55** | **99.28** | **99.43** | 83.49 | **93.17** | 80.18 | 88.71 | 83.85 |

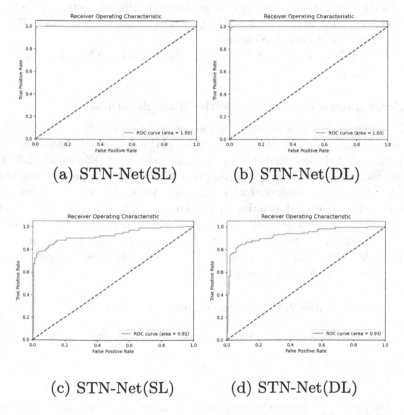

(a) STN-Net(SL)          (b) STN-Net(DL)

(c) STN-Net(SL)          (d) STN-Net(DL)

**Fig. 7.** ROC curve for Single Layer and Dual Layer STN-Net: (a) and (b) for Style-GAN2 dataset, (c) and (d) for StyleGAN3 dataset

terms of Precision and Recall for StyleGAN3 images. As discussed earlier, this result proves the strength of our designed CNN.

It is very evident from Table 1 that models with Gaussian Blur transformation bring significant performance enhancement to CNN model. While Sine transformation is constant in the first two cases of 'Feature + CNN' setting, only LT transformed models face sharp performance degradation, compared with only GB models for both StyleGAN2 and StyleGAN3. We may take the insight that LT alone enhances high-frequency components, many of which may be unnecessary, while GB smoothens them, making CNN learn more generalised features. GB + LT performs slightly better than GB + ST in most of the metrics for StyleGAN2 images. For StyleGAN3 we perform similar tests. Even though GB + LT performed well together compared to their single transformation performance, GB + LT + ST outperformed them, proving the effectiveness of the proposed Sine Transformation on synthetic image detection. For StyleGAN3 image detection, this feature pipeline achieves the best performance with an average accuracy of 84.21%.

Following the earlier result proving the effectiveness of GB transformation, in 'Augmented Feature + CNN' case, we use two layers of GB + LT + ST feature as discussed earlier. It achieves the best performance for all metrics with 99.53% average accuracy for StyleGAN2 case. For StyleGAN3, two layers of GB + LT + ST feature achieve best AUC score.

We show ROC curve for STN-Net for both StyleGAN2 and StyleGAN3 datasets in Fig. 7.

### 4.5   Performance Comparison with Other Solutions

Table 2 compares detection performance for StyleGAN2 images with other State-of-the-art (SOTA) solutions. Our best model performs better than most SOTA models, only slightly less than the solution proposed by Qiao et al. [23]. However, our model attains such performance with the minimum size feature set of 1 grayscale channel compared with other solutions. While their solution [23] utilizes colour domain information with ten channels through a CNN, other works [20,22] utilize co-occurrence and cross co-occurrence metrics with three channels and six channels features respectively. Chen et al. [3] fuse information from multiple colour domains with a six channels-sized feature set. Frank et al. [7] use frequency domain artefacts.

**Table 2.** Performance comparison with SOTA

| Metric | Ours (Best Model) | Qiao [23] | Nowroozi [22] | Nataraj [20] | Chen [3] | Frank [7] |
|---|---|---|---|---|---|---|
| Accuracy (%) | 99.53 | 99.80 | 99.33 | 96.11 | 97.70 | 98.58 |

As shown in Fig. 8, we compare the performance of our two models, STN-Net (Single-Layer) and STN-Net (Dual-Layer) with other available transfer-learning-based models: XceptionNet [4], ResNet50 [12], VGG-16 [25], InceptionV3 [26]

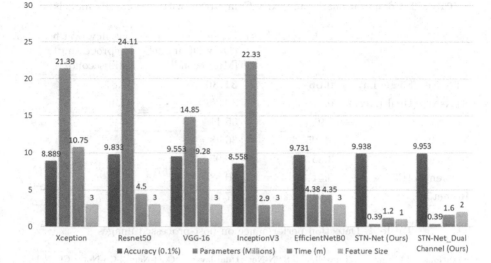

**Fig. 8.** Comparison with other CNNs

and EfficientNetB0 [27] for StyleGAN2 image detection. In all these cases, we import pre-trained models from the Keras library. We use weights from 'imagenet'. For all these models, on top of base pre-trained models, we add a *Global Average Pooling Layer* followed by a Fully Connected Layer with 256 neurons. The final layer of the model is added, consisting of a single neuron, which is activated using the sigmoid activation function. Raw RGB image is provided as input in every case. All models are compiled using the Adam optimizer and the binary cross-entropy loss function.

In Fig. 8, Accuracy is multiplied by 0.1 for better visibility in the chart. Parameters are shown in millions, and the Average time to train per epoch is shown in minutes. Among transfer learning models, ResNet50 performs best with the detection accuracy of 98.33%, having the largest number of parameters, 24.11 million and three channels of feature space. Our model having ≈1.61% parameters of ResNet50, with grayscale images, achieves 99.53% detection accuracy.

As shown in Table 3, we further compare the computational complexity of the above-mentioned transfer learning-based models with our proposed solutions regarding Floating point operations (FLOPs) and Average Latency. We have calculated the Average Latency as the average inference time for 500 test samples in all cases. Further, for both our solutions, we have calculated latency with the preprocessing steps included, i.e., the calculation of the STN feature. It is evident from both Fig. 8 and Table 3 that our solutions obtain excellent performance despite having the lowest number of model parameters, training time, FLOPs and output latency.

**Table 3.** Computational Complexity Comparison with other CNN models

| Model | FLOPs (Billion) | Latency (Only DL model) [Millisecond] | Latency (With Preprocessing) [Millisecond] |
|---|---|---|---|
| STN-Net (Single Layer) | **0.06** | **31.30** | 32.87 |
| STN-Net (Dual Layer) | 0.07 | 33.36 | 34.46 |
| Xception | 5.95 | 35.11 | – |
| VGG-16 | 20.05 | 36.48 | – |
| InceptionV3 | 3.85 | 36.95 | – |
| EfficientNetB0 | 0.51 | 60.88 | – |
| Resnet50 | 5.04 | 87.74 | – |

**Table 4.** Detection performance on post-processed images

| Operations | Parameters | Baseline Model | STN-Net | Dual layer STN-Net | CSC-Net [23] | Co-Net [20] | CC-Net [22] |
|---|---|---|---|---|---|---|---|
| Median Filter | 3 × 3 | 91.62 | 96.92 | 98.78 | **99.35** | 81.48 | 85.13 |
| | 5 × 5 | 91.12 | 63.77 | 78.92 | **93.80** | 75.98 | 83.65 |
| Gaussian Noise | 1.0 | 91.82 | 99.21 | **99.38** | 94.43 | 76.35 | 93.68 |
| | 2.0 | 91.84 | 99.28 | **99.33** | 74.25 | 76.73 | 96.80 |
| CLAHE | 3 × 3 | 85.54 | 97.10 | **98.99** | 94.70 | 51.43 | 50.32 |
| Average Blurring | 3 × 3 | 91.37 | 86.11 | 94.84 | **97.30** | 93.68 | 86.90 |
| | 5 × 5 | **90.40** | 50.12 | 53.77 | 82.68 | 88.23 | 76.63 |
| Gamma Correction | 0.8 | 90.10 | **99.28** | 99.26 | 95.08 | 82.28 | 83.15 |
| | 0.9 | 91.69 | 99.23 | **99.45** | 98.00 | 87.23 | 90.98 |
| | 1.2 | 89.56 | **99.40** | 99.36 | 96.90 | 87.20 | 85.53 |
| Resizing | 0.5 | 91.42 | 72.40 | 86.31 | 79.80 | 57.93 | **92.47** |
| Average | – | 90.58 | 87.53 | **91.67** | 91.48 | 78.04 | 84.11 |

## 4.6 Performance in the Context of OSN

As previously discussed, the exact operations of OSN platforms on images are unknown but must be investigated further by the research community to develop any solution for fake image detection in practical cases. Hence, to check the robustness of our solutions, we apply common post-processing operations like Median filtering, Gaussian Noise addition, Contrast Limited Adaptive Histogram Equalization (CLAHE), Average Blurring, Gamma Correction and Resizing with different parameters on StyleGAN2 dataset as shown in Table 4. The best performance of each operation is marked in bold, and the second-best performance is underlined. We examine performances in terms of detection accuracy for our three models: Baseline (Only CNN), STN-Net (Single Layer) and STN-Net (Dual Layer). Our model STN-Net (Dual Layer) achieves the best average accuracy of

91.67%, closely followed by CSC-Net [23]. Both versions of STN-Net perform exceptionally well on Gaussian noise-added images. While for Gaussian noise with a standard deviation of 2.0, Single layer STN has a performance drop of 0.10%, Dual-Layer STN has 0.20% performance drops. Interestingly, our baseline model has a much smaller performance drop than others. Detailed results are shown in Table 4.

## 4.7    Performance in the Context of JPEG Compression

As discussed earlier, even though mostly GAN-generated images are by default in PNG format, they are commonly converted into JPEG format while uploaded or downloaded to or from OSNs. Unlike lossless PNG images, JPEG images use lossy compression, which enables discarding of some image data to reduce file size. This can lead to a loss of image quality and a change in the statistical properties of images.

**Table 5.** Performance on JPEG Compression

| Quality Factor | Base Model | STN-Net | Dual-Layer STN-Net | CSC-Net [23] | Cross Co-Net [22] | Co-Net [20] |
|---|---|---|---|---|---|---|
| 90 | 91.38 | 99.33 | **99.33** | 97.53 | 94.50 | 95.58 |
| 80 | 91.37 | 98.71 | **99.08** | 97.44 | 88.66 | 94.93 |
| 70 | 91.29 | 97.99 | **98.69** | 97.23 | 83.50 | 94.03 |
| 60 | 91.34 | 96.90 | **98.26** | 96.83 | 94.00 | 94.65 |
| 50 | 91.22 | 96.88 | **97.89** | 96.51 | 80.05 | 96.66 |

CNN models learn abstract information from provided training data. Most CNN-based GAN-image detectors face performance drop issues when training data is from PNG images and testing data from JPEG images. We check the performance of our models on JPEG quality factors: 90, 80, 70, 60 and 50 and compare their performance with SOTA solutions. As shown in Table 5, the Dual layer variant of our proposed STN model performs best for all mentioned JPEG compression levels.

## 4.8    Generalization Performance

We further explore the generalization capability of our proposed solutions: STN-Net with both single-layer and dual-layer variations. We show results using ROC curve, as shown in Fig. 9. Firstly, we test StyleGAN3-generated faces on models trained on the StyleGAN2 dataset (Fig. 9a, Fig. 9b). Next, we test StyleGAN2-generated faces on models trained on StyleGAN3 dataset (Fig. 9c, Fig. 9d). As shown in Fig. 9, while the training set is from StyleGAN3, in both single-layer and dual-layer versions, detection performance for StyleGAN2 images is satisfactory

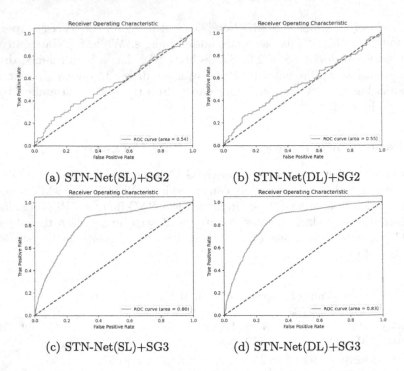

(a) STN-Net(SL)+SG2        (b) STN-Net(DL)+SG2

(c) STN-Net(SL)+SG3        (d) STN-Net(DL)+SG3

**Fig. 9.** Generalization Performance: (a) and (b) trained on StyleGAN2 while tested on StyleGAN3, (c) and (d) trained on StyleGAN3 while tested on StyleGAN2

with AUC score $\geq 80\%$. While the training set is from StyleGAN2, in both single-layer and dual-layer versions, the detection performance for StyleGAN3 images is worse than the previous case. However, it still performs better than random guesses.

We may infer that StyleGAN3-trained models learn more generalised features than StyleGAN2-trained models. StyleGAN3 is an improved version of StyleGAN2. Hence, it is possible that models that learn statistical features of StyleGAN3 images naturally cover many of StyleGAN2 features.

## 5    Concluding Remarks

In this work, we propose a solution to identify authentic and GAN-generated face images in the context of OSNs. Hence, we test our proposed detector's performance against standard perturbation in OSN. However, we have not included the study of other sophisticated black-box and white-box attacks [1] like adaptive attacks in this work. We wish to include such studies in future work.

In this work, we introduce a feature *Sine Transformed Noise (STN)* that is highly capable of discriminating between real and GAN images. Accompanied by a well-designed deep neural network, STN is capable of performing at par with SOTA solutions in ideal scenarios and achieves prominent performance for post-processed and compressed images. Compared with other SOTA solutions, STN-Net uses lightweight CNN with fewer parameters, lesser computational complexity and high inference time. All these advantages make STN-Net very usable in real-world scenarios.

# References

1. Carlini, N., Farid, H.: Evading deepfake-image detectors with white-and black-box attacks. In: Proceedings of the IEEE/CVF Conference on Computer Vision and Pattern Recognition Workshops, pp. 658–659 (2020)
2. Chen, B., Ju, X., Xiao, B., Ding, W., Zheng, Y., de Albuquerque, V.H.C.: Locally GAN-generated face detection based on an improved Xception. Inf. Sci. **572**, 16–28 (2021)
3. Chen, B., Liu, X., Zheng, Y., Zhao, G., Shi, Y.Q.: A robust GAN-generated face detection method based on dual-color spaces and an improved Xception. IEEE Trans. Circ. Syst. Video Technol. **32**(6), 3527–3538 (2021)
4. Chollet, F.: Xception: deep learning with depthwise separable convolutions. In: Proceedings of the IEEE Conference on Computer Vision and Pattern Recognition, pp. 1251–1258 (2017)
5. Ciftci, U.A., Demir, I., Yin, L.: FakeCatcher: detection of synthetic portrait videos using biological signals. IEEE Trans. Pattern Anal. Mach. Intell. (2020). https://doi.org/10.1109/TPAMI.2020.3009287
6. Cozzolino, D., Gragnaniello, D., Poggi, G., Verdoliva, L.: Towards universal GAN image detection. In: 2021 International Conference on Visual Communications and Image Processing (VCIP), pp. 1–5. IEEE (2021)
7. Frank, J., Eisenhofer, T., Schönherr, L., Fischer, A., Kolossa, D., Holz, T.: Leveraging frequency analysis for deep fake image recognition. In: International Conference on Machine Learning, pp. 3247–3258. PMLR (2020)
8. Fu, Y., Sun, T., Jiang, X., Xu, K., He, P.: Robust GAN-face detection based on dual-channel CNN network. In: 2019 12th International Congress on Image and Signal Processing, BioMedical Engineering and Informatics (CISP-BMEI), pp. 1–5. IEEE (2019)
9. Goodfellow, I., et al.: Generative adversarial nets. In: Advances in Neural Information Processing Systems, vol. 27 (2014)
10. Gragnaniello, D., Cozzolino, D., Marra, F., Poggi, G., Verdoliva, L.: Are GAN generated images easy to detect? A critical analysis of the state-of-the-art. In: 2021 IEEE International Conference on Multimedia and Expo (ICME), pp. 1–6. IEEE (2021)
11. Guo, H., Hu, S., Wang, X., Chang, M.C., Lyu, S.: Eyes tell all: irregular pupil shapes reveal GAN-generated faces. In: ICASSP 2022–2022 IEEE International Conference on Acoustics, Speech and Signal Processing (ICASSP), pp. 2904–2908. IEEE (2022)
12. He, K., Zhang, X., Ren, S., Sun, J.: Deep residual learning for image recognition. In: Proceedings of the IEEE Conference on Computer Vision and Pattern Recognition, pp. 770–778 (2016)
13. Karras, T., Aila, T., Laine, S., Lehtinen, J.: Progressive growing of GANs for improved quality, stability, and variation. arXiv preprint arXiv:1710.10196 (2017)

14. Karras, T., et al.: Alias-free generative adversarial networks. In: Advances in Neural Information Processing Systems, vol. 34, pp. 852–863 (2021)
15. Karras, T., Laine, S., Aila, T.: A style-based generator architecture for generative adversarial networks. In: Proceedings of the IEEE/CVF Conference on Computer Vision and Pattern Recognition, pp. 4401–4410 (2019)
16. Karras, T., Laine, S., Aittala, M., Hellsten, J., Lehtinen, J., Aila, T.: Analyzing and improving the image quality of StyleGAN. In: Proceedings of the IEEE/CVF Conference on Computer Vision and Pattern Recognition, pp. 8110–8119 (2020)
17. Marra, F., Gragnaniello, D., Cozzolino, D., Verdoliva, L.: Detection of GAN-generated fake images over social networks. In: 2018 IEEE Conference on Multimedia Information Processing and Retrieval (MIPR), pp. 384–389. IEEE (2018)
18. Matern, F., Riess, C., Stamminger, M.: Exploiting visual artifacts to expose deep-fakes and face manipulations. In: 2019 IEEE Winter Applications of Computer Vision Workshops (WACVW), pp. 83–92. IEEE (2019)
19. Mishra, M., Adhikary, F.: Digital image tamper detection techniques-a comprehensive study. arXiv preprint arXiv:1306.6737 (2013)
20. Nataraj, L., et al.: Detecting GAN generated fake images using co-occurrence matrices. arXiv preprint arXiv:1903.06836 (2019)
21. Nightingale, S., Agarwal, S., Härkönen, E., Lehtinen, J., Farid, H.: Synthetic faces: how perceptually convincing are they? J. Vis. 21(9), 2015–2015 (2021)
22. Nowroozi, E., Mekdad, Y.: Detecting high-quality GAN-generated face images using neural networks. In: Big Data Analytics and Intelligent Systems for Cyber Threat Intelligence, pp. 235–252 (2023)
23. Qiao, T., et al.: CSC-Net: cross-color spatial co-occurrence matrix network for detecting synthesized fake images. IEEE Trans. Cogn. Dev. Syst. (2023). https://doi.org/10.1109/TCDS.2023.3274450
24. Sharif, M., Mohsin, S., Javed, M.Y., Ali, M.A.: Single image face recognition using Laplacian of Gaussian and discrete cosine transforms. Int. Arab J. Inf. Technol. 9(6), 562–570 (2012)
25. Simonyan, K., Zisserman, A.: Very deep convolutional networks for large-scale image recognition. arXiv preprint arXiv:1409.1556 (2014)
26. Szegedy, C., Vanhoucke, V., Ioffe, S., Shlens, J., Wojna, Z.: Rethinking the inception architecture for computer vision. In: Proceedings of the IEEE Conference on Computer Vision and Pattern Recognition, pp. 2818–2826 (2016)
27. Tan, M., Le, Q.: EfficientNet: rethinking model scaling for convolutional neural networks. In: International Conference on Machine Learning, pp. 6105–6114. PMLR (2019)
28. Verdoliva, L.: Media forensics and deepfakes: an overview. IEEE J. Sel. Top. Sig. Process. 14(5), 910–932 (2020)
29. Wan, J., He, X., Shi, P.: An iris image quality assessment method based on Laplacian of Gaussian operation. In: MVA, pp. 248–251 (2007)
30. Wang, B., Wu, X., Tang, Y., Ma, Y., Shan, Z., Wei, F.: Frequency domain filtered residual network for deepfake detection. Mathematics 11(4), 816 (2023)
31. Xia, Z., Qiao, T., Xu, M., Zheng, N., Xie, S.: Towards DeepFake video forensics based on facial textural disparities in multi-color channels. Inf. Sci. 607, 654–669 (2022)
32. Yang, X., Li, Y., Qi, H., Lyu, S.: Exposing GAN-synthesized faces using landmark locations. In: Proceedings of the ACM Workshop on Information Hiding and Multimedia Security, pp. 113–118 (2019)

# MDLDroid: Multimodal Deep Learning Based Android Malware Detection

Narendra Singh[⊠] and Somanath Tripathy

Department of Computer Science and Engineering, Indian Institute of Technology
Patna, Dayalpur Daulatpur, India
{narendra_2021cs21,som}@iitp.ac.in

**Abstract.** In the era of Industry 5.0, there has been tremendous usage
of android platforms in several handheld and mobile devices. The open-
ness of the android platform makes it vulnerable for critical malware
attacks. Meanwhile, there is also dramatic advancement in malware
obfuscation and evading strategies. This leads to failure of traditional
malware detection methods. Recently, machine learning techniques have
shown promising outcome for malware detection. But past works utilizing machine learning algorithms suffer from several challenges such
as inadequate feature extraction, dependency on hand-crafted features,
and many more. Thus, existing machine learning approaches are inefficient in detecting sophisticated malware, thus require further enhancement. In this paper, we extract behavioural characteristics of system calls
and dynamic API features using our proposed multimodal deep learning model (*MDLDroid*). Our model extracts system call features using
LSTM layers and extracts dynamic API features using CNN. Further,
both the features are fused in a vector space which is finally classified for
benign and malign categories. Comparison with several state-of-the-art
approaches on two dataset shows a significant improvement of 4–12% by
the metric accuracy.

**Keywords:** Android · Malware detection · Dynamic Analysis ·
System call · Dynamic API

## 1 Introduction

There is a surge in uses and applications of Android platforms. There are more
than 2.5 billion active android devices [4] which are used by users of different
demography. Android development platforms are open platforms which makes
it prone to several security threats such as confidential information leakage and
device hijacking. Often, android users do not pay heed to security permissions
and warnings and end up installing malicious applications which expose not only
the user but also other connected users. It is reported [1] that over 12,000 new
malware incidents are reported daily.

At this, there has been signification advances in detecting malicious applications such as Google *Bouncer*, Google Play Protect [2] and many more to

V. Muthukkumarasamy et al. (Eds.): ICISS 2023, LNCS 14424, pp. 159–177, 2023.
https://doi.org/10.1007/978-3-031-49099-6_10

detect malicious applications on android. These approaches often fail due to ever-sophisticating android malware. There are many signature based and heuristics based approaches which are also ineffective for malware with integrated evasion methods [32,37].

Recently, machine learning based approaches have shown promising results in identifying malware. The effectiveness of machine learning based approaches is highly dependent on the considered features and the quality of extracted features. The feature can be categorized in three categories i. static ii. dynamic, and iii. hybrid. The past approaches [20,34,36] relying on static features under-perform for obfuscated malware. Past approaches using [6,21,37] dynamic and hybrid features are more promising as compared to static feature. But appropriate representation of features is challenging. There is still a scope of improvement in representation of these features which can boost the performance of malware detection.

In this paper, we propose a multi-modal deep learning model MDLDroid, which uses dynamic features composed of system call features and dynamic API features. The analysis of system call sequences embedded in a running application is essential for understanding the dynamic behavior of the application. This natural language-based information can be harnessed to distinguish between malicious and harmless applications. We adopt the Word2Vec concept to construct system call embedding for each system call. This feature vector not only encompasses the co-occurrence patterns of system calls but also encapsulates their semantic significance. We also utilize dynamic API features as API call sequences which contain all the activities that take place during application execution. However, in order to initiate malicious behavior, a substantial volume of investigative operations is essential. These operations will generate notably extensive API call sequences. A sliding window method is used to construct N-grams from the extracted API sequences and finaly generated feature image.

We propose *MDLDroid*, a Multimodal Deep Learning framework that better captures inherent features of android malware and fuses relevant information to accurately detect unknown malwares. We observed that our proposed methodology outperforms the state-of-the-art by 4–12% by accuracy.

The key contributions are as follows.

- We propose *MDLDroid*, a multi-modal deep learning framework uses the run-time behavior features (N-grams) from dynamic APIs and fuses with System Call embedding feature. These fuses vector help to classify the behavior of unseen malware effectively.
- We created several malicious payloads and embedded into benign android apps to generate obfuscated backdoors. We could observe that the existing detection mechanisms in Virustotal fail to detect our created obfuscated backdoors, but, MDLDroid is successful to identify those backdoors.
- On experimentation with two dataset, we observe a significant improvement of 4–12% as compared to existing approaches. Our proposed model outperform static feature capturing approaches as well as hybrid feature capturing approaches.

The remaining part of this article is organized as follows. In Sect. 2, the existing research works on android malware detection are discussed. The proposed method is described in Sect. 3. Section 4 discusses the experimental results. Section 5 concludes this work.

**Table 1.** Summary of existing malware detection method

| Similar Work | Feature Type | Feature Used | Algorithm Used | Dataset Used with Accuracy | UMDR |
|---|---|---|---|---|---|
| Chatchai et al. [26] | Static | N-gram | MLP/C4.5/ SVM | VX Heavens Virus Collection\96.64% | ✗ |
| Daniel Arp et al. [8] | Static | Hardware components Restricted API call | SVM | Drebin\94% | ✗ |
| Santanu et al. [13] | Dynamic | System Calls | SVM with Conformal Pred | Genome Project, Drebin\94% | ✗ |
| Hou et al. [19] | Static | API Calls | DBN | Comodo Cloud Security Center\96.66% | ✓ |
| Kim el at. [22] | Static | Permission Opcode, API String, Shared library | Multimodal (DNN) | VirusShare Google Play Store Malgenome project\98% | ✗ |
| Arora et al. [7] | Hybrid | Network Traffic Permissions | FP-Growth Algorithm | Genome FP-Growth Algorithm dataset\94.2% | ✗ |
| Kelkar et al. [21] | Dynamic | HTTP-based information | ✗ | Trustlook repository | ✗ |
| Wang et al. [41] | Dynamic | Network Traffic | Multi-level Network | Drebin\97.89% | ✓ |
| Fan et al. [14] | Dynamic | API | Unsupervised Leraning | Genome project Drebin\ . . . | ✗ |
| Lou et al. [29] | Static | Data Flow(source, sink) | SVM | Drebin dataset Google Play Store Contagio\93.7% | ✗ |
| Alzaylaee et al. [6] | Hybrid | Permission, API call | w-FM for DL-Droid | McAfee Security Labs\98.82% | ✓ |
| Millar et al. [31] | Static | Permission Opcode, API | multi-view CNN | AMD dataset Drebin dataset\99.29% | 91% |
| *MDLDroid* (Prop.) | Dynamic | Multimodal LSTM+CNN | System Call Dynamic APIs | Andozoo Dataset CICMalDroid2020\99.23% | 98.45% |

UMDR: Unseen Malware Detection Rate

## 2    Related Work

Our work is based on three broad category of past works namely i. Static Analysis ii. Dynamic Analysis iii. Multi-modal Learning. Next we give overview of these categories of past works.

### 2.1    Static Analysis Techniques

Static analysis a technique that design the features of the application by examining the code and properties without executing it. A large set of literature has used static analysis to detect malware as this is comparatively simple and straightforward. Static analysis consists of extraction of static feature, which are fed into different types of classifier for predicting malign and non-malign applications. Past works have used machine learning based classifiers, deep learning based classifiers, and graph based classifiers for classifying the static features of an applications.

**Machine Learning Based Classification:** There are a number of past works [24,44] which uses static feature and a machine learning algorithms to detect malware. The idea is to treat the problem as a classification problem and classify in two classes of malware and non-malware. There is a heavy use of off the shelf machine learning classifiers like SVM [29], Decision Trees [33], Bagging [27] are used for classification. However, the advances in deep learning has surpassed the prediction results. next, we present past works utilizing deep learning.

### 2.2 Deep Learning Based Approaches

For efficient feature capturing, many past deep learning models [8,10,19,22] have helped. The work by Drebin et. al. [8] is a simple approach for detection of malicious applications on mobile devices. It collects as many characteristics as possible from an Android application and embeds them into a single feature vector so that common features of malicious applications can be extracted. Another study [10] utilize the behaviour of data flow of malicious applications on sensitive sources of benign applications. The motivation behind this is that the malicious applications act differently as compared to benign applications in terms of sensitive sources of benign applications. So, the data flow from sensitive sources of benign Android applications is mined and compared with the data flows identified in malicious applications to find similarities. Millar et al. [31] proposed a multi-view deep learning model composed of Convolutional Neural Network (CNN) using only static analysis to detect android malware. It uses features from permissions, opcode, and android API package. We also mention that the use of deep learning models are not limited to static features only. The works by Kim et al. [22] utilizes a vast range of features such as string, method opcode, method API, shared library function opcode, permission, App component and environmental features. The use of deep learning technique for malware detection of is not limited to android devices but have wide applicability for IOT devices [9,28]. Additionally, graph-based malware detection algorithms [14,16] have also got attention in past works for delivering good performance.

### 2.3 Dynamic Analysis Techniques

There are malicious applications which do have any static specifications and hence cannot be detected using static analysis. So, there have been a quest to utilize run-time behaviours of the applications known as dynamic analysis. In dynamic analysis, run-time behaviour of applications are captures by executing them suing emulators. Using dynamic features requires additional work, so the utilization of dynamic feature is grey zoned in past literature. However, a few past works [15,18,45] have utilized dynamic features showing outstanding improvement in prediction accuracy. Riskranker [15] proposed a dynamic analysis based technique which observes whether a given application acts harmful behavior with root exploits or sending SMS messages in the background. This output is then used to prioritize reduced applications for further examination. [25] takes advantage of bytecode to facilitate detection of android malware. The bytecode of an app includes accurate information on the program's behavior, which can offer sufficient information about the application's intended behavior. Similarly, malicious apps have a common pattern of bytecodes that distinguishes them from benign applications. Droiddetector [45] uses deep neural networks to analyse three distinct sets of features, including necessary permissions, sensitive APIs, and dynamic behaviour. Hou et al. [18] developed Deep4MalDroid, an automated Android malware detection system that uses the Genymotion emulator to dynamically retrieve system calls. DroidScribe [13] is another dynamic analysis technique, which demonstrates how supervised classification algorithms can be utilized to automatically identify Android malware into different malware families based on their runtime behavior, without the need for any additional training data. As system calls alone do not give adequate semantic information for classification on Android systems, it employs a lightweight virtual machine to recreate inter-process communication on Android systems to do successful analysis. Kelkar et al. [21] developed a method for detecting malicious Android applications that exfiltrate data through HTTP. They focused on the leaked information, locations to which it had been exfiltrated, and the relationships between these factors and categories of sensitive information. There a few unsupervised approaches also which help predicting malwares. GefDroid [14] carried out graph embedding using unsupervised learning. In order to abstract program semantics, they use a fine-grained behavioral model to create sub-graphs that evaluate analysis of android malware family. Wang et al. [41] implemented a multi-level network traffic analysis, aggregating and combining network characteristics with machine learning algorithm that can identify Android malware accurately.

**Hybrid Analysis.** In order to utilize the key features from static as well as dynamic analysis past works [6,12,30] have also used hybrid analysis. The DL-Droid [6] framework employed stateful input generation with the commonly used stateless approach for deep learning-based android malware classification. They observed a performance boost by including both the features as compared to either static or dynamic features. [30] have used a fusion of both the feature and also a ensemble classifier for predicting malware. There is also a comprehensive study [12] claiming that use of hybrid feature boosts performance only in a few cases. Recently, there has been significant advancement in machine learning which can help removing this bottleneck. We present an overview of a few past research works highlighting the used features, types of features, used methodology and the dataset in Table 1. In this paper, we use multi-modal machine learning on hybrid features in order to deliver a consistent better performance.

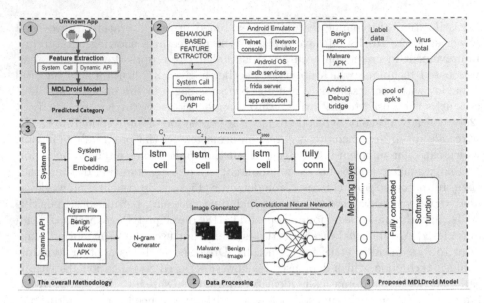

**Fig. 1.** The figure shows 1. Our Proposed Methodology 2. Data pre-processing steps 3. Proposed Multi-Modal Deep Learning Model Architecture

## 2.4   Multi-modal Learning

A malware is characterized by multiple static and dynamic features. For a better identification of malware, multiple features needs to be captured simultaneously. Multi-modal deep learning models [39,42,43] have achieved a great success in capturing better feature representation for scenario of multiple category of features. Motivated from this a few recent approaches [17,23] also applied multi-modal models for malware detection. However, to the best of our knowledge we can there is still a chance of improvement prediction results using a multi-modal model. In this, paper we propose a multi-modal model capturing dynamic API features and system call features.

## 3   MDLDroid: The Proposed Malware Detection Technique

The overview of our proposed methodology is shown in Fig. 1-1. For predicting whether an unknown app is malign or benign, we first extract relevant features(system call and dynamic API) of the app. Then we feed these features to our proposed MDLDroid model for predicting the category of the app. Next, we elaborate the steps of feature extraction and our proposed MDLDroid model.

### 3.1   Feature Extraction

In this paper, we propose to use multiple behavioural features of apps. As found from the past works [30], dynamic features can be indicative of a malware. So, we use features composed of static system calls and dynamic API calls of an app. Next we detail the feature extraction methodology of both the type of feature.

**Behaviour Based Feature Extraction.** The analysis of Android APK files is automated using a script. The Genymotion emulator is run on a Windows 10 desktop. Consequently, an APK file folder is established as the sample repository for analysis. Finally, an output repository folder containing analysis results from files is obtained. After the initialization step, a python script is run to handle all the analysis operations to provide runtime environment with all the necessary commands. The Android Debug Bridge (ADB) communicates between the python script and the runtime environment. Following the initialization, the python script executes for each android application to collect dynamic characteristics.

**System Call Extraction.** During the execution of an Android application, we use the Linux strace tool to record system call invocations to capture the behavior of android application. Genymotion is an emulator of the Android OS that we use to analyze Android applications dynamically. Following that, we run a sequence of user interaction events using the Monkey framework provided by Android SDK. While the app is running, we also engage in other activities like making phone calls and sending SMS.

In order to record system call invocation, an android APK file is selected from the input repository and installed in the genymotion emulator. *pidof* command is run to retrieve the zygote process's PID. Simultaneously, strace command is run to record zygote and descendant process system calls. The zygote process is a common task that runs in the Dalvik Virtual Machine which is a part of the Android OS. When an application is executed in the emulator, zygote creates an associated process for the application, assigns it a PID, and records dynamic characteristics (system calls) of all the android samples that will start later from the instance then the zygote has been created. The application is executed on the emulator for 200 s uninterruptedly. Next, obtain the application PID and package name using *pidof* command, and start capturing the system calls. In parallel, user interactions are simulated with monkey tool kit, producing 100 random events, including touches, motions, trackballs, navigation, system key events, and activity launches. We also simulate phone call events and send SMS events for 300 s. The strace process is terminated, and the output logs are saved to the output repository.

**Dynamic APIs Extraction.** Frida[1] is a dynamic instrumentation framework for monitoring user-selected APIs, during app execution. User can choose to monitor a predefined list of APIs as shown in Table 2. It stores the invoked API, the parameters, the return value, and the file from which it was called. For this,

---

[1] https://frida.re/.

**Table 2.** Dynamic API listed under various categories.

| Sno. | Dyanmic API | # of API | Sno. | Dynamic API | # of API |
|------|-------------|----------|------|-------------|----------|
| 1 | Device Data | 12 | 10 | DeviceInfo | 9 |
| 2 | Shared Preferences | 14 | 11 | IPC | 6 |
| 3 | SMS | 2 | 12 | Database | 19 |
| 4 | System Manager | 4 | 13 | SharedPreferences | 3 |
| 5 | Base64 encode/decode | 3 | 14 | WebView | 11 |
| 6 | Dex Class Loader | 6 | 15 | Java Native Interface | 2 |
| 7 | Network | 8 | 16 | Command | 3 |
| 8 | Crypto - Hash | 4 | 17 | Process | 3 |
| 9 | Binder | 3 | 18 | FileSytem - Java | 4 |

we use the latest version of 'frida-server' [2] for the arm64 architecture. This file is extracted, and pushed to the genymotion emulator for execution. Each android app is placed into the emulator using adb command. Next, push Frida server into the emulator, change its permission, and execute it. Now, start importing the Frida library and retrieve device id. Then, invoke the spawn() function to start the messenger to extract the application PID. Finally, create a Frida session using PID and Hook JavaScript code to monitor specified Dynamic API during the application execution.

### 3.2 Feature Vector Generation

**System Call Embedding.** Word embedding is the the process of incorporating words into vectors, preserving the syntactic and semantic relationships between words. Our work is motivated by TWEET2VEC [40] and ATTACK2VEC [38], which use word embedding approach to convert tweets, assaults, and system call (word) to feature vectors.

Since the system calls are in string format, they cannot be directly fed into the LSTM network. So we convert each system call (Represent as $x_i$ in Fig. 2) into numerical vectors. The word2vec (Continuous Bag Of Word algorithm) technique is used to obtain the vector representation, which captures the semantic significance. Here for example, inter related system calls ("send" and "receive") would have similar vector representations.

To implement the Continuous Bag Of Word (CBOW) algorithm, an exhaustive system calls vocabulary (V) is created, which comprises with 113 distinct system calls. Then a one-hot encoded vector for each system call in V is generated. For each system call, the input layer receives 113-dim one-hot encoded vector. The hidden layer contains 100 neurons that simply transfers the input's weighted sum to the output layer. Let W (113 × 100) and W' (100 × 113) are the weight matrices that transfer the input x (113 × 100 dimension matrix) to the

---

[2] https://github.com/frida/frida/releases.

hidden layer and outputs to the final output layer (100 × 113 dimension matrix) receptively. The softmax computations are in the output layer of a 113-dim vector, as shown in Fig. 2.

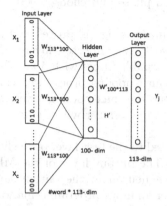

**Fig. 2.** System call embedding

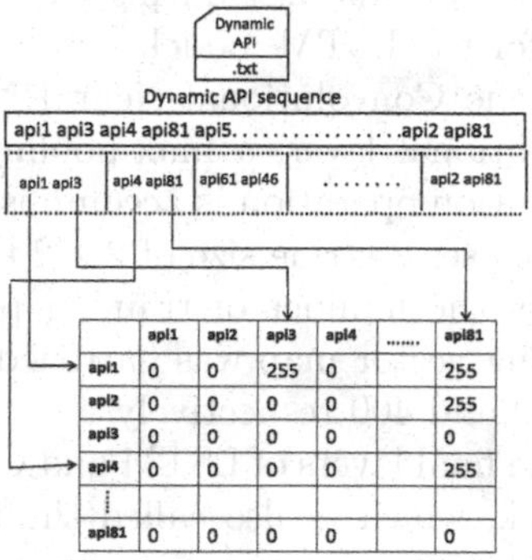

**Fig. 3.** N-gram File and Image Generation

**Feature Image Generation. a. N-gram Pair Generation:** N-grams are sequences [35] of 'N' consecutive bytes, where 'N' is the predetermined number of bytes. In the proposed approach, we made successive pairs of the dynamic API sequence, as in Fig. 3. A sliding window method is used to construct N-grams from the extracted API sequences. Each N-grams is considered as a feature. The repeated N-grams would affect the amount of space available, the processing time required, and the classifier's effectiveness. So duplicates N-gram are removed.

**b. Feature Image Generation:** The image is generated based on whether an N-gram is present or absent in the N-gram pairs ('0' indicates the absence of an N-gram, whereas '255' indicates its presence). The generated image is used to test the effectiveness of the proposed method. As shown in Figs. 4 and 5, the generated images of malware applications have visual similarities, and they differ significantly from the images that belong to benign applications.

## 3.3  MDLDroid Model

*MDLDroid Architecture:* It uses two feature vectors, each of which is input into the initial networks, including Long Short-Term Memory (LSTM) and Convolutional Neural Network (CNN). Both networks are independent of each other, and their final layers are connected to the merger layer, which is the first layer of the final network. Multilayer Perceptron (MLP) is the final network that categorizes benign and malignant applications.

LSTM network input layer uses the embedding matrix generated by the word2vec algorithm, instead of learning weights for mapping each system call into its vector representation. We assume that the input $X$ has 3000-time steps and reshape the input accordingly. The data for each time step $X(i)$ is supplied into the LSTM cell. Notably, each inner fully connected layer of the LSTM cell has thirty-two hidden units. Additionally, we examine the system call distribution in our dataset during the data preparation phase and choose 3000-time steps for the LSTM model.

In the Convolutional Neural Network, each input image is processed by a convolutional layer, a max-pooling layer and two fully connected layers. The convolution operation is accomplished using 32 learnable filters with $4 \times 4$. Further, it uses a stride size of $2 \times 2$ throughout the max-pooling procedure, which reduces the number of training parameters. After the max-pooling layer, the resulting vector map was flattened and joined to a dense layer with dimensions of 1600 and 400 respectively.

The final layers of LSTM and CNN are connected to the first layer of the final network, which is also called the merging layer. The output layer of the MLP network generates the classification results. Each neuron in the output layer employs the sigmoid function to determine whether an input program is malware or not. ReLU activation function is used, as it avoids the vanishing gradient problem during training and significantly increases the computing efficiency of our model.

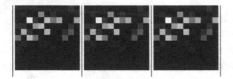   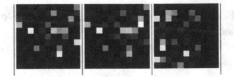

**Fig. 4.** Generated Malware Images      **Fig. 5.** Generated Benign Images

*MDLDroid Training:* *MDLDroid* is a multimodal deep learning-based Android malware detector which discovers inherent information of android malware and fuses complementary information. In *MDLDroid*, LSTM (Long Short Term Memory) is used to learn from System Call Embedding features, while CNN (Convolution Neural Network) is used to learn from images of N-gram pairs, as shown in Fig. 1. This multimodal learning strategy improves the overall performance of *MDLDroid* and helps to detect unseen malware effectively.

Hyperparameters are tuned through several experiments with different learning rates. The dataset is split into train and test data, and then the training data is divided into training and validation using scikit Stratified Shuffle Split to generate random training and validation sets. The proposed framework is trained on the training set and evaluated with the validation dataset for each learning rate, maintaining the batch size of 32. We find that 0.001 was the best learning rate. Dropout regularization [11] is used on our multimodal deep learning model to prevent overfitting. During the hyperparameter tuning process, we determined that the optimal dropout rate for our proposed model is 0.3.

**Table 3.** Performance comparison(Androzoo)

| Methodology | Performance Metric | System Call | Dynamic API | System Call and Dynamic API |
|---|---|---|---|---|
| [22] | Acc.(%) | 94.72 | 91.94 | 94.16 |
| | Pre.(%) | 96.80 | 92.59 | 91.42 |
| | Rec.(%) | 91.42 | 89.60 | 94.45 |
| | F1-Sc(%) | 93.97 | 91.04 | 93.64 |
| | Time(Sec.) | 0.412 | 0.219 | 0.443 |
| [19] | Acc.(%) | 94.72 | 91.94 | 92.77 |
| | Pre.(%) | 96.80 | 92.59 | 91.46 |
| | Rec.(%) | 91.42 | 89.62 | 92.23 |
| | F1-Sc(%) | 93.97 | 91.04 | 92.18 |
| | Time(Sec.) | 0.420 | 0.331 | 0.502 |
| [41] | Acc.(%) | 94.16 | 92.50 | 92.22 |
| | Pre.(%) | 96.18 | 93.25 | 90.85 |
| | Rec.(%) | 90.81 | 90.20 | 92.63 |
| | F1-Sc(%) | 93.35 | 91.66 | 91.56 |
| | Time(Sec.) | 0.389 | 0.293 | 0.391 |
| [6](S.F) | Acc.(%) | 95.00 | 92.77 | 91.4 |
| | Pre.(%) | 97.75 | 93.34 | 90.08 |
| | Rec.(%) | 91.42 | 90.81 | 92.02 |
| | F1-Sc(%) | 94.42 | 92.01 | 91.26 |
| | Time(Sec.) | 0.510 | 0.341 | 0.532 |
| [6] (S.L) | Acc.(%) | 94.12 | 92.22 | 91.94 |
| | Pre.(%) | 96.80 | 93.19 | 91.34 |
| | Rec.(%) | 91.42 | 89.60 | 91.42 |
| | F1-Sc(%) | 93.97 | 91.33 | 91.20 |
| | Time(Sec.) | 0.473 | 0.431 | 0.492 |
| MDLDroid | Acc.(%) | 96.11 | 94.72 | 99.23 |
| | Pre.(%) | 96.94 | 96.26 | 99.56 |
| | Rec.(%) | 94.50 | 92.02 | 98.62 |
| | F1-Sc(%) | 95.64 | 94.01 | 99.05 |
| | Time(Sec.) | 0.671 | 0.491 | 1.481 |

# 4 Experimental Analysis

## 4.1 Data Collection

In order to train *MDLDroid*, we use AndroZoo [5] dataset, which continues to grow with over 12 million applications at last count. Out of these, 28,805 android samples are selected randomly from AndroZoo's repository, where 13,469 are benign and 15336 are malware, as identified by VirusTotal. Further, CICMal-Droid[3] 2020 Android Malware dataset is used only for testing as unseen malware samples. We have used 11,598 Android samples for CICMalDroid, in which 1795 are benign samples, while the rest are malign samples.

**Data Description.** We used 28,805 android applications from AndroZoo data repository [5]. Each application is labelled through VirusTotal [3], which generates a JSON file that contains reports from 62 anti-malware vendors. If no anti-malware program in VirusTotal identifies an application as dangerous, it is considered to be benign. Thus, 13,469 apps were identified as benign, and 15336 were classified as malware. We used the CICMalDroid 2020[4] dataset, for testing as unseen samples. This dataset contains 9803 Android malware samples classified into four categories: Adware, Banking, SMS malware, and Riskware. The benign sample contained 1795 applications from popular application genres such as life, leisure, and social commerce.

The System Call and Dynamic API features were extracted from the android application, as explained in Sects. 3.1 and 3.1. As System calls are sequential in nature, we opted word2vec (continuous bag of word) embedding algorithm and set the dimension to 100. The Dynamic API features were extracted from each android application. We generated 81 N-gram pairs and constructed an image with 81/$times$81 dimensions using the Dynamic API features.

**Evaluation Setup:** We used Anaconda[5], Scikit-learn, Keras[6], and TensorFlow[7] libraries. We configured Windows 10 with Processor Intel® Core™ i7-7700 CPU E3-1225 v5 @ 3.30GHz, and 8 GB RAM with 1 TB Memory.

**Evaluation Metrics:** Accuracy, F-measure, precision, and recall were used to evaluate the proposed approach against state of art android model. Precision is the ratio of true positives to actually positive. Recall is the ratio of predicted positive to predicted correctly. F-measure gives a single value: the harmonic mean of precision and recall. Accuracy is the ratio of predicted data which points correctly to total data points.

$$Precision(Pre.) = \frac{TP}{(TP+FP)} \tag{1}$$

$$Recall(Rec.) = \frac{TP}{(TP+FN)} \tag{2}$$

$$F-measure(F1-sc) = 2 \times \frac{Pre. \times Rec.}{(Pre.+Rec.)} \tag{3}$$

---

[3] https://www.unb.ca/cic/datasets/maldroid-2020.html.
[4] https://www.unb.ca/cic/datasets/maldroid-2020.html.
[5] https://docs.anaconda.com/anaconda/install/index.html.
[6] https://anaconda.org/conda-forge/keras.
[7] https://docs.anaconda.com/anaconda/user-guide/tasks/tensorflow/.

**Table 4.** Performance Comparison(CICMalDroid2020)

| Methodology | Performance Metric | System Call | Dynamic API | System Call and Dynamic API |
|---|---|---|---|---|
| [22] | Acc.(%) | 87.7 | 86.34 | 84.02 |
| | Pre.(%) | 86.36 | 83.45 | 84.73 |
| | Rec.(%) | 88.94 | 90.52 | 83.15 |
| | F1-Sc(%) | 87.55 | 86.71 | 83.64 |
| | Time(Sec.) | 0.530 | 0.341 | 0.552 |
| [19] | Acc.(%) | 87.61 | 86.34 | 85.05 |
| | Pre.(%) | 86.36 | 83.45 | 86.03 |
| | Rec.(%) | 88.94 | 90.52 | 83.68 |
| | F1-Sc(%) | 87.55 | 86.71 | 84.58 |
| | Time(Sec.) | 0.450 | 0.381 | 0.492 |
| [41] | Acc.(%) | 86.58 | 85.31 | 84.27 |
| | Pre.(%) | 85.07 | 81.99 | 84.77 |
| | Rec.(%) | 88.42 | 90.52 | 83.68 |
| | F1-Sc(%) | 86.57 | 85.88 | 83.91 |
| | Time(Sec.) | 0.519 | 0.377 | 0.397 |
| [6](S.F) | Acc.(%) | 86.58 | 85.31 | 84.54 |
| | Pre.(%) | 85.07 | 81.99 | 85.96 |
| | Rec.(%) | 88.42 | 90.52 | 82.63 |
| | F1-Sc(%) | 86.57 | 85.88 | 83.90 |
| | Time(Sec.) | 0.479 | 0.317 | 0.518 |
| [6] (S.L) | Acc.(%) | 87.87 | 86.07 | 84.53 |
| | Pre.(%) | 86.17 | 83.85 | 84.85 |
| | Rec.(%) | 90.00 | 89.47 | 84.21 |
| | F1-Sc(%) | 87.91 | 86.32 | 84.22 |
| | Time(Sec.) | 0.499 | 0.301 | 0.528 |
| MDLDroid | Acc.(%) | 88.66 | 88.90 | 98.45 |
| | Pre.(%) | 86.73 | 91.33 | 99.46 |
| | Rec.(%) | 91.05 | 85.78 | 97.26 |
| | F1-Sc(%) | 88.75 | 88.35 | 98.30 |
| | Time(Sec.) | 0.395 | 0.539 | 1.109 |

$$Accuracy(Acc.) = \frac{(TP+TN)}{(TP+TN+FN+FP)} \qquad (4)$$

**Results:** It can be observed from Table 3, that the proposed approach achieves accuracy, precision, recall, and F-Measure values of 99.23%, 99.56%, 98.62%, and 99.05%, respectively for combined features. On the other hand, the existing methodology like Kim el at. [22], Hou et al. [19], Wang et al. [41], and Alzaylaee et al. [6] achieve accuracy of 94.16%, 92.77%, 92.22%, and 91.40%, respectively, using the combined system call embedding and N-grams pairs features. The Kim el at. [22] achieves the best accuracy among the above proposed methods, with Precision, Recall, and F-Measure values of 96.80%, 91.42%, and 93.77%, respectively.

Table 4 presents the experimental observations over CICMalDroid 2020 dataset as unseen data. We compare our model with similar existing Android malware detection models, which illustrates that the proposed method outperforms the state-of-the-art methodologies. The Hou et al. [19] achieves a higher accuracy of 85.05% among the other existing Android malware detection models when the combine feature is used, along with Precision, Recall, and F-Measure value of 86.03%, 83.68%, and 84.58% respectively. Meanwhile, *MDLdroid* achieves accuracy, precision, recall, and F-Measure values of 98.45%, 99.46%, 97.26%, and 98.30%, respectively for unseen malware.

We further evaluated the time taken by *MDLDroid* for identifying malicious behaviour. We considered 1000 applications of different sizes in range of (1 KB–100 KB), (100 KB–1 MB) and (1 MB–72 MB) separately, the average detection time for them are found to be 0.432, 0.578 and 0.793 respectively. Table 5 lists down the time consumed for pre-processing (APK to System Call Embedding and Image File Conversion) and detection. WE noticed athat *MDLDroid* requires nearly 0.5 s to analyse small applications, while up to 1.5 s to analyse large applications.

**Table 5.** Time to detect unknown applications of different size by MDLdroid.

| Process step/Apk Size | Time (Sec) taken | | |
|---|---|---|---|
| | 1 KB–100 KB | 100 KB–1 MB | 1 MB–72 MB |
| APK to System Call Embedding | 0.080 | 0.116 | 0.318 |
| APK to Image File Conversion | 0.160 | 0.346 | 0.618 |
| Avg. detection Time | 0.432 | 0.578 | 0.793 |
| Total Time | 0.592 | 0.924 | 1.411 |

***Detection Efficiency Against Obfuscated Backdoor:*** To find the efficiency of *MDLdroid* and other existing techniques, we created 1700 backdoor applications using Msfvenom[8] as shown in Fig. 6. Msfvenom is a command-line utility of Metasploit that is used to create malicious payloads in different format and encode them using other encoder modules. A benign APK file is downloaded and extracted from Google Play Store. Both malicious payload and original APK files are decompiled, using the APK tool[9]. The required permissions are embedded into the original APK. Then APK is reassembled with embedded payload via apktool. The recompiled application (backdoor) is installed on an android device.

[8] https://www.offensive-security.com/metasploit-unleashed/msfvenom/.
[9] https://ibotpeaches.github.io/Apktool/.

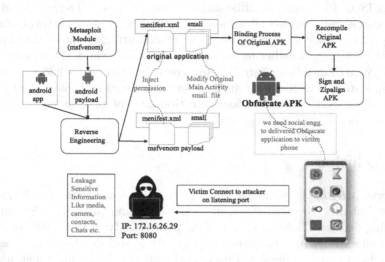

**Fig. 6.** Backdoor Creation

**Table 6.** Backdoor Analysis for 100 application

| D-Rate | AV | D-Rate | AV | D-Rate | AV | D-Rate | AV |
|---|---|---|---|---|---|---|---|
| 57% | AhnLab-V3 | 26% | eScan | 0% | NANO-Antivirus | 39% | Arcabit |
| 50% | Avast | 41% | ESET-NOD32 | 0% | Rising | 21% | Emsisoft |
| 40% | Avast-Mobile | 3% | F-Secure | 0% | TACHYON | 0% | Panda |
| 42% | Avira (nocloud) | 27% | Gridinsoft | 0% | TrendMicro-Housec | 60% | AVG |
| 3% | Ad-Aware | 27% | GData | 0% | Tencent | 46% | Fortinet |
| 0% | Alibaba | 0% | Jiangmin | 17% | Trellix (FireEye) | 0% | TrendMicro |
| 0% | ALYac | 43% | K7GW | 0% | Trustlook | 0% | Antiy-AVL |
| 58% | BitDefenderFalx | 0% | K7AntiVirus | 39% | Sophos | 51% | Kaspersky |
| 0% | Baidu | 0% | Kingsoft | 0% | Symantec Mobile | 33% | Sangfor Engine Zero |
| 42% | CAT-QuickHeal | 0% | MAX | 0% | VirIT | 2% | BitDefenderTheta |
| 63% | Cynet | 0% | MaxSecure | 0% | VBA32 | 0% | Lionic |
| 0% | Cyren | 0% | Microsoft | 0% | ViRobo | 0% | SUPERAntiSpyware |
| 0% | Comodo | 0% | McAfee | 0% | Zillya | 0% | ClamAV |
| 36% | DrWeb | 0% | McAfee-GW-Edition | 2% | ZoneAlarm | 0% | Yandex |
| 0% | Malwarebytes | 98.98% | *MDLDroid(Our Method)* | | | | |

The obfuscated backdoors are submitted to VirusTotal, which generates a report (a JSON file) from 57 mobile anti-malware programs. The generated backdoors[10] successfully bypass all anti-malware programs in VirusTotal. Further, creating a Metasploit session between victim and attacker shows that all anti-malwares fail to detect malicious payloads compromising android device security fortunately, *MDLdroid* successfully categorizes the created backdoor as a malicious application. The backdoor analysis report is listed in Table 6 of Appendix. It can be observed that the backdoor detection rates of existing mobile antivirus vendors are nearly half of the proposed approach.

## 5    Conclusion

We propose *MDLDroid*, a multi-modal deep learning framework uses the runtime behavior features (N-grams) from dynamic APIs and fuses with System Call embedding feature. These fuses vector help to classify the behavior of unseen malware effectively. In this work, we proposed a Multimodal Deep Learning-based android malware detection framework called *MDLDrroid* which uses the runtime behaviour features (N-grams) from dynamic APIs and fuses with System Call embedding feature. To measure the effectiveness of our proposed approach, Various experiments were carried out with a total of 40,403 samples(Androzoo + CICMalDroid 2020 dataset). We observe a significant improvement of 4–12% as compared to existing approaches. Our proposed model outperforms static feature capturing approaches as well as hybrid feature capturing approaches. Further, we created a backdoor app which could fool all 57-antimalware programs used in Virustotal, but could successfully detect the generated backdoors.

**Acknowledgment.** We acknowledge the Government of India, Ministry of Home Affairs, Bureau of Police Research and Development for funding this research.

## References

1. Cyber attacks on android devices on the rise 11 July 2018. https://www.gdatasoftware.com/blog/2018/11/31255-cyber-attacks-on-android-devices-on-the-rise
2. Global smartphone shipments by OS 2016–2022, statistic. google play protect. android2018 (2018). https://android-developers.googleblog.com/2019/02/google-play-protect-in-2018-new-updates.html
3. Operating system market share worldwide. https://gs.statcounter.com/os-market-share. Accessed 12 June 2019
4. Stephanie cuthbertson - director, android - google I/0 2019 keynote speech. https://www.youtube.com/watch?v=lyRPyRKHO8M. Accessed Apr 2020
5. Allix, K., Bissyandé, T.F., Klein, J., Le Traon, Y.: Androzoo: collecting millions of android apps for the research community. In: 2016 IEEE/ACM 13th Working Conference on Mining Software Repositories (MSR), pp. 468–471. IEEE (2016)

---

[10] md5 hash: 9428c569daddeaf815d48768e259ee27.

6. Alzaylaee, M.K., Yerima, S.Y., Sezer, S.: DL-droid: deep learning based android malware detection using real devices. Comput. Secur. **89**, 101663 (2020)
7. Arora, A., Peddoju, S.K.: Ntpdroid: a hybrid android malware detector using network traffic and system permissions. In: 2018 17th IEEE International Conference on Trust, Security and Privacy in Computing and Communications/12th IEEE International Conference on Big Data Science and Engineering (TrustCom/BigDataSE), pp. 808–813. IEEE (2018)
8. Arp, D., Spreitzenbarth, M., Hubner, M., Gascon, H., Rieck, K., Siemens, C.: Drebin: effective and explainable detection of android malware in your pocket. In: NDSS, vol. 14, pp. 23–26 (2014)
9. Asam, M., et al.: IoT malware detection architecture using a novel channel boosted and squeezed CNN. Sci. Rep. **12**(1), 15498 (2022)
10. Avdiienko, V., et al.: Mining apps for abnormal usage of sensitive data. In: 2015 IEEE/ACM 37th IEEE International Conference on Software Engineering, vol. 1, pp. 426–436. IEEE (2015)
11. Baldi, P., Sadowski, P.J.: Understanding dropout. Adv. Neural. Inf. Process. Syst. **26**, 2814–2822 (2013)
12. Damodaran, A., Troia, F.D., Visaggio, C.A., Austin, T.H., Stamp, M.: A comparison of static, dynamic, and hybrid analysis for malware detection. J. Comput. Virol. Hacking Tech. **13**, 1–12 (2017)
13. Dash, S.K., et al.: Droidscribe: classifying android malware based on runtime behavior. In: 2016 IEEE Security and Privacy Workshops (SPW), pp. 252–261. IEEE (2016)
14. Fan, M., et al.: Graph embedding based familial analysis of android malware using unsupervised learning. In: 2019 IEEE/ACM 41st International Conference on Software Engineering (ICSE), pp. 771–782. IEEE (2019)
15. Grace, M., Zhou, Y., Zhang, Q., Zou, S., Jiang, X.: Riskranker: scalable and accurate zero-day android malware detection. In: Proceedings of the 10th International Conference on Mobile Systems, Applications, and Services, pp. 281–294 (2012)
16. Gülmez, S., Sogukpinar, I.: Graph-based malware detection using opcode sequences. In: 2021 9th International Symposium on Digital Forensics and Security (ISDFS), pp. 1–5. IEEE (2021)
17. Guo, J., Xu, Y., Xu, W., Zhan, Y., Sun, Y., Guo, S.: Mdenet: multi-modal dual-embedding networks for malware open-set recognition. arXiv preprint arXiv:2305.01245 (2023)
18. Hou, S., Saas, A., Chen, L., Ye, Y.: Deep4maldroid: a deep learning framework for android malware detection based on linux kernel system call graphs. In: 2016 IEEE/WIC/ACM International Conference on Web Intelligence Workshops (WIW), pp. 104–111. IEEE (2016)
19. Hou, S., Saas, A., Chen, L., Ye, Y., Bourlai, T.: Deep neural networks for automatic android malware detection. In: Proceedings of the 2017 IEEE/ACM International Conference on Advances in Social Networks Analysis and Mining 2017, pp. 803–810 (2017)
20. Kang, B., Yerima, S.Y., McLaughlin, K., Sezer, S.: N-opcode analysis for android malware classification and categorization. In: 2016 International Conference on Cyber Security and Protection of Digital Services (cyber Security), pp. 1–7. IEEE (2016)
21. Kelkar, S., Kraus, T., Morgan, D., Zhang, J., Dai, R.: Analyzing HTTP-based information exfiltration of malicious android applications. In: 2018 17th IEEE International Conference on Trust, Security and Privacy in Computing and Communica-

tions/12th IEEE International Conference on Big Data Science and Engineering (TrustCom/BigDataSE), pp. 1642–1645. IEEE (2018)

22. Kim, T., Kang, B., Rho, M., Sezer, S., Im, E.G.: A multimodal deep learning method for android malware detection using various features. IEEE Trans. Inf. Forensics Secur. **14**(3), 773–788 (2018)

23. Li, S., Li, Y., Wu, X., Al Otaibi, S., Tian, Z.: Imbalanced malware family classification using multimodal fusion and weight self-learning. IEEE Trans. Intell. Transp. Syst. (2022)

24. Li, W., Ge, J., Dai, G.: Detecting malware for android platform: an SVM-based approach. In: 2015 IEEE 2nd International Conference on Cyber Security and Cloud Computing, pp. 464–469. IEEE (2015)

25. Liang, S., Du, X.: Permission-combination-based scheme for android mobile malware detection. In: 2014 IEEE International Conference on Communications (ICC), pp. 2301–2306. IEEE (2014)

26. Liangboonprakong, C., Sornil, O.: Classification of malware families based on n-grams sequential pattern features. In: 2013 IEEE 8th Conference on Industrial Electronics and Applications (ICIEA), pp. 777–782. IEEE (2013)

27. Liu, K., Xu, S., Xu, G., Zhang, M., Sun, D., Liu, H.: A review of android malware detection approaches based on machine learning. IEEE Access **8**, 124579–124607 (2020)

28. Liu, X., Du, X., Zhang, X., Zhu, Q., Wang, H., Guizani, M.: Adversarial samples on android malware detection systems for IoT systems. Sensors **19**(4), 974 (2019)

29. Lou, S., Cheng, S., Huang, J., Jiang, F.: TFDroid: android malware detection by topics and sensitive data flows using machine learning techniques. In: 2019 IEEE 2nd International Conference on Information and Computer Technologies (ICICT), pp. 30–36. IEEE (2019)

30. Martín, A., Lara-Cabrera, R., Camacho, D.: Android malware detection through hybrid features fusion and ensemble classifiers: the andropytool framework and the omnidroid dataset. Inf. Fusion **52**, 128–142 (2019)

31. Millar, S., McLaughlin, N., del Rincon, J.M., Miller, P.: Multi-view deep learning for zero-day android malware detection. J. Inf. Secur. Appl. **58**, 102718 (2021)

32. Moser, A., Kruegel, C., Kirda, E.: Limits of static analysis for malware detection. In: Twenty-Third Annual Computer Security Applications Conference (ACSAC 2007), pp. 421–430. IEEE (2007)

33. Peiravian, N., Zhu, X.: Machine learning for android malware detection using permission and API calls. In: 2013 IEEE 25th International Conference on Tools with Artificial Intelligence, pp. 300–305. IEEE (2013)

34. Rahali, A., Lashkari, A.H., Kaur, G., Taheri, L., Gagnon, F., Massicotte, F.: Didroid: android malware classification and characterization using deep image learning. In: 2020 the 10th International Conference on Communication and Network Security, pp. 70–82 (2020)

35. Reddy, D.K.S., Pujari, A.K.: N-gram analysis for computer virus detection. J. Comput. Virol. **2**(3), 231–239 (2006)

36. Rosmansyah, Y., Dabarsyah, B., et al.: Malware detection on android smartphones using API class and machine learning. In: 2015 International Conference on Electrical Engineering and Informatics (ICEEI), pp. 294–297. IEEE (2015)

37. Shan, Z., Wang, X.: Growing grapes in your computer to defend against malware. IEEE Trans. Inf. Forensics Secur. **9**(2), 196–207 (2013)

38. Shen, Y., Stringhini, G.: Attack2vec: leveraging temporal word embeddings to understand the evolution of cyberattacks. In: 28th {USENIX} Security Symposium {USENIX} Security 2019), pp. 905–921 (2019)

39. Suzuki, M., Matsuo, Y.: A survey of multimodal deep generative models. Adv. Robot. **36**(5–6), 261–278 (2022)
40. Vosoughi, S., Vijayaraghavan, P., Roy, D.: Tweet2vec: learning tweet embeddings using character-level CNN-LSTM encoder-decoder. In: Proceedings of the 39th International ACM SIGIR conference on Research and Development in Information Retrieval, pp. 1041–1044 (2016)
41. Wang, S., Chen, Z., Yan, Q., Yang, B., Peng, L., Jia, Z.: A mobile malware detection method using behavior features in network traffic. J. Netw. Comput. Appl. **133**, 15–25 (2019)
42. Xu, P., Zhu, X., Clifton, D.A.: Multimodal learning with transformers: a survey. IEEE Trans. Pattern Anal. Mach. Intell. (2023)
43. Yang, Z., et al.: i-code: an integrative and composable multimodal learning framework. In: Proceedings of the AAAI Conference on Artificial Intelligence, vol. 37, pp. 10880–10890 (2023)
44. Yerima, S.Y., Sezer, S., Muttik, I.: Android malware detection using parallel machine learning classifiers. In: 2014 Eighth International Conference on Next Generation Mobile Apps, Services and Technologies, pp. 37–42. IEEE (2014)
45. Yuan, Z., Lu, Y., Xue, Y.: Droiddetector: android malware characterization and detection using deep learning. Tsinghua Sci. Technol. **21**(1), 114–123 (2016)

# A Cycle-GAN Based Image Encoding Scheme for Privacy Enhanced Deep Neural Networks

David Rodriguez[✉] and Ram Krishnan[✉]

Department of Electrical and Computer Engineering, University of Texas at San Antonio, San Antonio, TX 78249, USA
david.rodriguez3@my.utsa.edu, ram.krishnan@utsa.edu

**Abstract.** Deep learning model training on cloud platforms typically require users to upload raw input data. However, uploading raw image data to cloud service providers raises serious privacy concerns. To address this problem, we propose a Cycle-Gan based-image transformation scheme that leverages convolutional autoencoder image encoding for domain translation. Our Cycle-GAN based image transformation scheme enhances privacy of deep neural networks while preserving model utility. In this paper, we demonstrate that our Cycle-GAN based image transformation scheme protects visual feature information of sensitive image data. We evaluate the effectiveness of our proposed method to preserve model utility using classification accuracy and robustness against reconstruction attacks using structural similarity index measure (SSIM). The classification accuracy of encoded images using our proposed method is 92.48, 91.05, 90.37 for Chest X-ray, Dermoscopy and OCT datasets, respectively. The SSIM scores for reconstruction attacks where the attacker only has access to the encoded data and corresponding labels are 0.1002, 0.0995 and 0.0329 for Chest X-ray, Dermoscopy and OCT datasets, respectively. Our results demonstrate that the Cycle GAN based encoding scheme effectively enhance privacy while preserving model utility.

**Keywords:** Cycle-GAN · Deep Neural Networks · Convolutional Autoencoder · Privacy · Utility

## 1 Introduction

The amount of data generated by worldwide data sources has increased exponentially. Nevertheless, the utilization of big data is suboptimal without proper computing resources to extract patterns and vital information from zetabytes of data. Consequently, many businesses have switched to cloud service providers for computationally expensive tasks using large and complex datasets [1,2]. As a

Research supported in part by NSF CREST Grant HRD-1736209 (RK) and NSF CAREER Grant CNS-1553696 (RK).

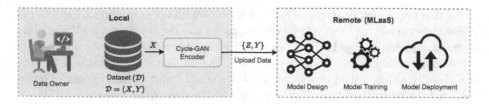

**Fig. 1.** Cycle-GAN based image transformation for privacy enhanced DNNs. Where $X$ is the data owner's original dataset and $\{Z, Y\}$ are the data owner's encoded images and corresponding class labels. The encoded images and labels are uploaded to MLaaS provider for DNN model development and deployment while keeping the original image data private.

result, there has been a surge in the demand for cloud services. Cloud services are often categorized into Infrastructure as a Service (IaaS), Platform as a Service (PaaS), and Software as a Service (SaaS) and IaaS offers infrastructure such as servers, virtual machines (VMs), storage, networks, operating systems on a pay-as-you-go basis. PaaS offers on-demand environments for developing, testing, delivering, and managing software applications. SaaS offers on-demand software applications over the internet which are typically on a subscription basis.

Additionally, machine learning-as-a-service (MLaaS) includes a variety of machine learning tools offered by cloud service providers such as Amazon, Google and Microsoft. MLaaS enables efficient model development and deployment at low cost. However, the adoption of MLaaS raises several data privacy concerns. This is especially true with sensitive image data e.g., suppose that a data owner uploads sensitive image data to an MLaaS provider for the purpose of developing a deep learning model but a curious MLaaS developer may also want to learn some additional sensitive information that could lead to identity theft, financial fraud, disease misdiagnosis [3–5]. Therefore, sensitive image data privacy plays an essential role in the deep learning life cycle.

The deep learning life cycle includes a training phase for model development and a testing phase for model deployment. Deep learning is susceptible to several attack methods during training and testing phase such as data poisoning attacks, model extraction attacks, model inversion attacks and adversarial attacks. However, in this work, we focus on protecting the privacy of sensitive image data for privacy enhanced deep neural networks (DNNs) during the training phase. Several image transformation methods have been proposed to protect the privacy of image data during the training phase of a deep learning life cycle [6–8]. However, a major challenge in transforming image data to enhance the privacy of DNNs is the trade-off between privacy and utility [9]. Typically, DNN model performance on original images degrades as images are transformed for privacy protection. To address this problem, we evaluate the effectiveness of Cycle-GAN [10] to preserve model utility using classification accuracy and robustness against reconstruction attacks using structural similarity index measure (SSIM).

In this paper, we propose a Cycle-GAN based image transformation scheme to enhance privacy of DNN model development and deployment on MLaas platforms as depicted in Fig. 1. Our Cycle-GAN method leverages autoencoder obfuscated images for domain translation. First, the autoencoder is trained to output visually unrecognizable versions of the original input image. Second, Cycle-GAN is trained to translate original images to the corresponding encoded image domain. We evaluate the robustness of our Cycle-GAN method to reconstruction attacks. In our results, we demonstrate that the proposed Cycle-GAN method enhances the privacy of image data while preserving model utility using Chest X-ray, Dermoscopy and OCT datasets.

In summary our contributions are as follows:

- We develop a Cycle-GAN based image transformation scheme for privacy enhanced deep neural networks.
- We enhance privacy of sensitive image data while maintaining classification accuracy.

The remainder of this paper is organized as follows. In Sect. 2, we provide an overview of related works for privacy enhancing methods in machine learning. In Sect. 3, we discuss the proposed Cycle-GAN method formulation and loss function. In Sect. 4, we describe the data sets, network architecture and training procedure. In Sect. 5, we evaluate our proposed Cycle-GAN method by analyzing the trade-off between privacy-utility and robustness to reconstruction attacks. Finally, we conclude our paper in Sects. 6.

## 2    Related Works

The security and privacy of machine learning models is usually concerned with the model's input, the model's output or the model itself. There are many proposed methods in the literature e.g., secure multi-party computation, homomorphic encryption, federated learning, visual image protection and learnable image encryption. Secure multi-party computation is a set of cryptographic protocols that allow multiple parties to evaluate a function to perform computation over each parties private data such that only the result of the computation is released among participants while all other information is kept private [11]. Secure multi-party computation methods have been applied in machine learning among multiple parties by computing model parameters using gradient descent optimization without revealing any information beyond the computed outcome [12–15]. The proposed Cycle-GAN image encoding scheme does not require multiple parties to compute the gradient descent of each model individually which is computationally expensive but instead enables users to encode private data individually and develop privacy enhanced deep neural networks with greater efficiency.

Homomorphic encryption is a type of encryption that allows multiple parties to perform computations on its encrypted data without having access to the original data [16–18]. It provides strong privacy but is computationally expensive requiring significant overhead to train machine learning models [19–21]. The proposed Cycle-GAN image encoding method does not use computationally expensive encryption operations or specialized primitives during model development.

Federated learning allows multiple parties to train a machine learning model without sharing data [22–24]. For example, in centralized federated learning a central server sends a model to multiple parties to train locally using their own data, then each participant sends it's own model update back to the central server to update the global model which is again sent to each party to obtain the optimal model without access to the local data by iterating through this process [25]. Essentially, federated learning builds protection into the model. Nevertheless, federated learning requires that each user have enough computing resources to train locally using their own data. The proposed Cycle-GAN image encoding method allows multiple parties to share obfuscated data for model training without the computational resource requirement of each participant.

Visual image protection methods transform plain images to unrecognizable encoded images while preserving important feature information for model utility. A few examples are pixelation, blurring, P3 [26], InstaHide [27] and NueraCrypt [28] which aim at preserving privacy and utility—a model trained on an encoded dataset should be approximately as accurate as a model trained on the original dataset [29,30]. InstaHide mixes multiple images together with a linear pixel blend and randomly flips the pixel signs. NeuraCrypt encodes data instances through a neural network with random weights and adds position embeddings to keep track of image structure then shuffles the modified output in blocks of pixels. However, [31] showed that position information, permutation order and image-encoding pairs could be learned given an unordered set of images and corresponding encodings. The proposed Cycle-GAN image encoding method inherently generates encoded images by learning a mapping function between original images and distorted images while reducing data leakage during domain translation.

Learnable image transformation methods obfuscate image data such that the encoded versions are useful for classification [6–8,32,33]. However, in some cases network adjustments are required to process learnable image transformations such as blockwise adaptation [6]. Our proposed Cycle-GAN encoding scheme does not require any particular changes to the network to develop models using the encoded data. Our work is most closely related to [34] but instead of transforming image data using adversarial perturbations for domain translation we develop our encoding model leveraging obfuscated autoencoder output. The key benefit in our method is that the autoencoder is specifically optimized to generate transformed images that retain image features that are useful for model utility.

## 3 Cycle-GAN Image Transformation Formulation

We aim to transform image data using a Cycle-GAN based approach to obfuscate sensitive feature information while preserving classification accuracy. The proposed method allows participants within a network to share sensitive image data while protecting privacy and maintaining model utility. We consider features that do not highly contribute to the classification task as sensitive features.

For example, in chest x-ray images the features that do not highly contribute to the classification of the pneumenia disease are considered sensitive features. On the other hand, we consider features that highly contribute to the classification task as non-sensitive features. For example, in chest x-ray images the features that highly contribute to the classification of the pneumenia disease are considered non-sensitive features. Our goal is to transform image data such that non-sensitive features are preserved for image classification. We aim to preserve classification accuracy of transformed images similar to original images.

Our goal is to enhance the privacy of deep neural networks by transforming image data using Cycle-GAN for image-encoding domain translation. Let $\mathcal{X}$ be the set of all images in the data domain, $X \subseteq \mathcal{X}$ is the local subset of private images and $Y$ is the corresponding label set. Given the private image dataset $\{x_i\}_{i=1}^N$ where $x_i \in X$, the images are transformed using the private Cycle-GAN encoding function $G_Z(x)$. The encoded images and corresponding labels can be safely uploaded to remote MLaaS providers for deep learning model development using visibly unrecognizably images. The proposed Cycle-GAN method is similar to [34] but instead of transforming image data using adversarial perturbations for domain translation we develop our encoding model leveraging modified autoencoder output. The proposed method consists of a classification model to distinguish between non-sensitive features. Additionally, our methods consists of an autoencoder model for initial image transformation. Finally, the encoding network consists of a Cycle-GAN model for final image transformation. The training objective is to optimize the model parameters of generator $G_Z$ to transform original images into encoded images.

## 3.1    Overview

First, the classification model is trained to classify original images using a constructed dataset that follows the probability distribution of the original dataset and their respective class labels. Our objective function for the classification model has a loss term for classifying non-sensitive features. The goal is to classify non-sensitive features of a given image with high classification accuracy. Second, the classification model loss function is used to optimize the model parameters of a randomly initialized autoencoder network given it's output to generate distorted versions of the input image while preserving important feature information for model utility. Third, the Cycle-GAN network is used to transform original images to the distorted images. Our Cycle-GAN based image transformation final objective function follows original Cycle-GAN [10] objective which contains three loss terms: adversarial loss for mapping original images to encoded images, adversarial loss for mapping encoded images to original images and cycle consistency loss to prevent the learned mappings from contradicting each other. We aim to learn a mapping function from original images to distorted images to transform private data while preserving important feature information for model utility.

Our proposed Cycle-GAN image transformation scheme consists of a non-sensitive feature loss, distortion loss, adversarial loss and cycle consistency loss.

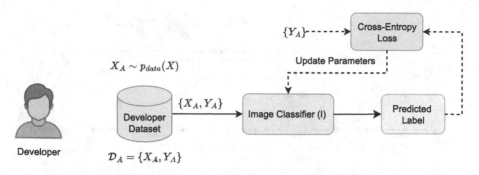

**Fig. 2.** Image classification model training phase. Where $X_A$ is the developer's constructed data set that follows the probability distribution of the original dataset and $Y_A$ are the corresponding class labels. Standard DNN image classification model training is conducted to predict the labels of non-sensitive image features.

First, we develop a classification model to classify non-sensitive features using a non-sensitive feature loss as depicted in Fig. 2. Second, we develop an autoencoder model to distort images using an image distortion loss as depicted in Fig. 3. The networks are trained using a constructed dataset that follows the probability distribution of the original dataset i.e., $x_a \sim p_{data}(x)$. The non-sensitive feature loss is used to minimize the error between the true label and the classifier's predicted label for non-sensitive features. For example, the true label of a chest x-ray image is the correct class assigned to the image which specifies whether the image has pneumonia disease or not. The distortion loss is used to minimize the error between the true label and the pre-trained classifier's predicted output label given the autoencoder distorted image for each sample in the constructed dataset. The aim is to distort image data and classify non-sensitive features with high classification accuracy. Third, we train Cycle-GAN to using adversarial loss and cycle consistency loss to learn a mapping function from images to distorted images as depicted in Fig. 4.

## 3.2  Non-sensitive Feature Loss

The non-sensitive feature loss function $L_n$ uses cross-entropy to measure the performance of the image classifier $I$ which is trained to classify non-sensitive features.

$$L_n(I, X_A, Y_A) = -\frac{1}{N} \sum_{i=1}^{N} Y_{A_i} log(I(X_{A_i})) \tag{1}$$

where $X_{A_i}$ is the $i^{th}$ image and $Y_{A_i}$ is the corresponding ground truth identity label. $I(X_{A_i})$ is the image classifier's predicted output for the $i^{th}$ image.

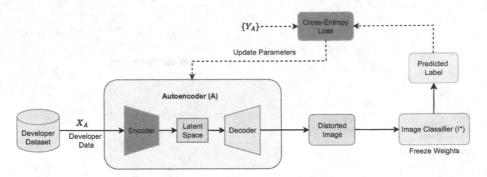

**Fig. 3.** Distortion model training phase. An autoencoder network $A$ is optimized to generate distorted images that preserve important feature information for model utility given the developer input data. The pre-trained classifier $I^*$ model parameters are frozen to ensure they remain constant during the distortion model training. The error between the predicted output label of $I^*$ given distorted images and the true label is minimized. The model parameters of the $A$ are updated based on the gradient of the crossentropy loss.

### 3.3 Non-sensitive Feature Loss Objective

The goal is to find the classification model $I$ parameters that minimize the error between the true label and predicted label.

We aim to solve:

$$I^* = \operatorname*{argmin}_{I} L_n(I, X_A, Y_A) \tag{2}$$

### 3.4 Distortion Loss

The distortion loss function $L_d$ uses cross-entropy to distort feature information in sensitive image data.

$$L_d(A, I^*, X_A, Y_A) = -\frac{1}{N} \sum_{i=1}^{N} Y_{A_i} log(I^*(A(X_{A_i}))) \tag{3}$$

where $A$ is a randomly initialized autoencoder network and $I^*$ is a pre-trained image classification function. $I(A(X_{A_i}))$ is the image classifier's predicted output given the $i^{th}$ distorted image.

### 3.5 Distortion Loss Objective

The goal is to find the autoencoder model $A$ parameters that minimize the error between the true label and the image classifier $I$ predicted output given the $i^{th}$ distorted image i.e., $I^*(A(X_{A_i}))$.

We aim to solve:

$$A^* = \operatorname*{argmin}_{A} L_d(A, I^*, X_A, Y_A) \tag{4}$$

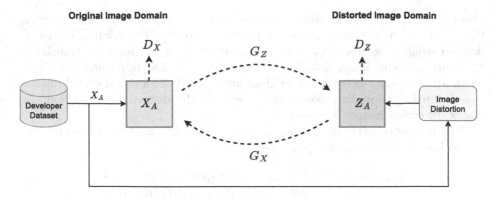

**Fig. 4.** Cycle-GAN based image transformation for privacy enhanced DNNs. Where $X_A$ is the developer data set and $Z_A$ is the corresponding distorted image generated using the pre-trained distortion model $A^*$. Generator $G_Z$ learns a mapping function from $X_A$ to $Z_A$ and generator $G_X$ learns a mapping function from $Z_A$ to $X_A$. Discriminator $D_X$ distinguishes between real and fake images while discriminator $D_Z$ distinguishes between real and fake distorted images.

### 3.6 Adversarial Loss

The full adversarial loss consists of a loss term from generators $(G_Z, G_X)$ and discriminators $(D_Z, D_X)$. The following equations describe the adversarial loss term.

$$
\begin{aligned}
L_{GAN}(G_Z, D_Z, X_A, Z_A) = \ &\mathbb{E}_{z_a \sim p_{enc}(z_a)}[\log D_Z(z_a)] \\
&+ \mathbb{E}_{x_a \sim p_{data}(x_a)}[\log(1 - D_Z(G_Z(x_a)))]
\end{aligned}
\tag{5}
$$

where $G_Z$ tries to generate encoded images $G_Z(x_a)$ that are similar to distorted autoencoder images i.e., $z_a = A^*(x_a)$. $D_Z$ distinguishes between real autoencoder distorted images $z_a$ and generated encoded images $G_Z(x_a)$. $G_Z$ minimizes the objective while $D_Z$ maximizes the objective, $\min_{G_Z} \max_{D_Z}$ $L_{GAN}(G_Z, D_Z, X_A, Z_A)$.

$$
\begin{aligned}
L_{GAN}(G_X, D_X, Z_A, X_A) = \ &\mathbb{E}_{x_a \sim p_{data}(x_a)}[\log D_X(x_a)] \\
&+ \mathbb{E}_{z_a \sim p_{enc}(z_a)}[\log(1 - D_X(G_X(z_a)))]
\end{aligned}
\tag{6}
$$

where $G_X$ tries to images $G_X(z_a)$ that are similar to original images $x_a$, while $D_X$ distinguishes between the real original images and generated images $G_X(z_a)$. $G_X$ minimizes the objective while $D_X$ maximizes the objective, $\min_{G_X} \max_{D_X}$ $L_{GAN}(G_X, D_X, Z_A, X_A)$.

### 3.7 Cycle Consistency Loss

The cycle consistency loss term is computed using generator $G_Z$ and generator $G_X$. First, the original images $X$ are translated into the distorted image domain $Z_A$ using generator $G_Z$. Then the generated distorted image is translated back into the original image domain using generator $G_X$ i.e., forward cycle. Second, the autoencoder distorted image $Z_A$ is translated into the original image $X$ domain using generator $G_X$. Then the generated original image is translated back into distorted image domain using generator $G_Z$ i.e., backward cycle. The mean absolute error between the original images and the forward cycled images is computed. The mean absolute error between the distorted images and the backward cycled images is computed.

The computed cycle consistency loss values for the original images and distorted images are summed together below.

$$
\begin{aligned}
L_{cyc}(G_Z, G_X) = \; & \mathbb{E}_{x_a \sim p_{data}(x_a)}[\|G_X(G_Z(x_a)) - x_a\|_1] \\
& + \mathbb{E}_{z_a \sim p_{enc}(z_a)}[\|G_Z(G_X(z_a)) - z_a\|_1]
\end{aligned}
\tag{7}
$$

$G_X(G_Z(x_a))$ is the forward cycled original image and $G_Z(G_X(z_a))$ is the backward cycled distorted image. The error between the cycled images and real images is minimized and summed to compute the total cycle consistency loss.

### 3.8  Cycle-GAN Encoding Full Objective

The adversarial and cycle consistency loss terms are summed together for the full objective. The full objective for the Cycle-GAN encoding loss consists of an adversarial loss term and cycle consistency loss term.

The full objective is:

$$
\begin{aligned}
L(G_Z, G_X, D_X, D_Z) = \; & L_{GAN}(G_Z, D_Z, X_A, Z_A) \\
& + L_{GAN}(G_X, D_X, Z_A, X_A) \\
& + \lambda L_{cyc}(G_Z, G_X)
\end{aligned}
\tag{8}
$$

where $\lambda$ controls the importance of the objectives. We solve the following optimization problem:

$$
G_Z^*, G_X^* = \underset{G_Z, G_X}{\text{argmin}} \; \underset{D_Z, D_X}{\max} \; L(G_Z, G_X, D_X, D_Z)
\tag{9}
$$

## 4  Methods

### 4.1  Dataset

In this work, we use three publicly available medical image datasets to develop our Cycle-GAN encoding scheme, which include Chest X-Ray, Dermoscopy and Optical Coherence Tomography (OCT). The Chest X-ray dataset [35] consists of 5,863 grayscale chest radiograph images used to diagnose thorax disease. It includes two classes, where each image is labeled as "Pneumonia" or "Normal". The Dermoscopy dataset [36] contains 17.8K color images of skin lesions, which are used to diagnose melanoma skin cancer. It includes two classes, where each image is labeled as "Melanoma" or "NotMelanoma". We consider all non-melanoma images to be part of the NotMelanoma class [37]. The OCT dataset

[35] consists of 84,495 grayscale images with four classes—including "Choroidal Neovascularization (CNV)", "Drusen", "Diabetic macular edema (DME)", and "Normal". It utilizes light waves to take cross-section imagery of the retina to assist in diagnosing retina disease and disorders in the optic nerve.

## 4.2 Network Architecture

The Cycle-GAN based image encoding architecture consists of three parts: a Resnet-50 for image classification, a standard convolutional autoencoder (CAE) for image distortion and a Cycle-GAN for image encoding. Resnets are large state-of-the-art DL architectures that consist of several blocks of residual modules and skip connections [38]. The classification model architecture consists of a Resnet-50 network trained to classify non-sensitive features i.e., features that highly contribute to the classification task. The CAE network consists of three convolution layers with 32, 64 and 128 filters, respectively. The kernel size is $3 \times 3$ with a stride of 2 and a latent space of 128. Each convolution layer consists of a leaky relu activation function with alpha 0.2 followed by a batch normalization layer. The decoder network consists of three transposed convolution layers with 128, 64 and 32 filters, respectively. The kernel size is $3 \times 3$ with a stride of 2 and output size of $224 \times 224 \times 3$. Each transposed convolution layer consists of a leaky relu activation function with alpha 0.2 followed by a batch normalization layer.

The Cycle-GAN network consists of two generators $(G_Z, G_X)$, two discriminators $(D_Z, D_X)$. The generator networks contain three convolutions, 9 residual blocks [38], two transpose convolutions and one convolution that maps features to RGB. Also, we use instance normalization [39]. Similar to [10] we use $70 \times 70$ PatchGANs for the discriminator networks. Generator $G_Z$ is used to translate original images to the distorted image domain and generator $G_X$ is used to translate distorted images to original image domain. Discriminator $D_Z$ is used to distinguish between real and fake distorted images and discriminator $D_X$ is used to distinguish between the real and fake original images.

## 4.3 Training Procedure

**Image Classification Model.** Our training procedure consists of an image classification phase to classify non-sensitive features, an image distortion phase to obfuscate sensitive image data and an image encoding phase to reduce the risk of data leakage. First, in the image classification phase we train a Resnet-50 model from randomly initialized parameters using the original image dataset and corresponding class labels for non-sensitive features. We train using binary crossentropy loss function for dataset with two classes. Additionally, we train using categorical crossentropy loss function for dataset with more than two classes. We wish to classify non-sensitive features for a given data set i.e., features that are strongly correlated with the class label. The classification model loss function is used to optimize our image distortion model.

**Image Distortion Model.** Second, in the image distortion phase we randomly initialize the CAE model parameters and add its output to the pre-trained Resnet-50 classification model input for each of the given original images. We freeze the Resnet-50 classifier model parameters to ensure that the weights do not change during training for the image distortion phase. During training we use the classification model loss function to find the CAE model parameters that minimize the error between the true label and the image classifier predicted label given the distorted image for the original image dataset. We wish to preserve non-sensitive feature information while reconstructing an unrecognizable version of the original image. The reconstructed image is a distorted version of the original image that is useful for classification. It is generated to obfuscate sensitive image data. To obfuscate sensitive image data we use the output of the image classifier to optimize the CAE model with crossentopy loss function.

**Cycle-GAN Encoding Model.** Third, in the Cycle-GAN encoding phase we learn a mapping function between original images and distorted images. The distorted images are generated using the pre-trained autoencoder i.e., $Z_A = A^*(X_A)$. The Cycle-GAN adversarial loss is computed using generator $G_Z$, generator $G_X$, discriminator $D_Z$ and discriminator $D_X$. Generator $G_Z$ is used as a mapping function from the original image domain $X_A$ to the distorted image domain $Z_A$. Discriminator $D_Z$ is a binary classifier used to distinguish between real distorted images $Z_A$ and generated distorted images $G_Z(X_A)$. Generator $G_Z$ wishes to minimize the probability of $G_Z(X_A)$ being classified as generated distorted images by discriminator $D_Z$ while $D_Z$ aims to maximize the probability of the real distorted images $Z_A$ being classified as real and generated distorted images $G_Z(X_A)$ being classified as fake. The aim is to learn a generator $G_Z$ that translates original images $X_A$ into the distorted image domain.

Discriminator $D_X$ is a binary classifier used to distinguish between real and generated original images. We obtain generated original images using generator $G_X$ given distorted images as input to generator $G_X$, i.e. $G_X(Z_A)$. Generator $G_X$ wishes to minimize the probability of $G_X(Z_A)$ being classified as a generated original image by discriminator $D_X$ while $D_X$ aims to maximize the probability of the real original images $X_A$ being classified as a real and generated original images $G_X(Z_A)$ being classified as fake. As a result, we learn a generator that translates original images into the distorted image domain.

Generator $G_Z$ and generator $G_X$ are used to compute the cycle consistency loss. The original images are translated into the distorted image domain and then back to the original image domain which is called a forward cycle i.e., $G_X(G_Z(X_A))$. Then the distorted images are translated into the original image domain and then back to the distorted image domain which is called a backward cycle i.e., $G_Z(G_X(Z_A))$. The mean absolute error between the original images and the forward cycled images is computed. The mean absolute error between the distorted images and the backward cycled images is computed. Both values are summed to ensure that the real and generated images remain similar.

All networks were trained using the adam optimizer with a batch size of 32. We utilize check points to save the model with the highest validation accuracy during model development. The classification and autoencoder models were trained for 100 epochs and Cycle-GAN network was trained for 200 epochs. During Cycle-GAN training we set $\lambda = 10$. All images were resized to $224 \times 224$ and normalized between 0 and 1. Each dataset was randomly shuffled and split ten times to generate multiple subsets of the train, test and validation set. Each network was trained ten times for a given dataset to assess the average performance of all models across multiple subsets of the data.

## 5   Evaluation

### 5.1   Evaluating Privacy/Utility Trade-Off

We develop classification models using Resnet-50 architecture as described in Sect. 4.2 and encoded images generated by the proposed Cycle-GAN encoding scheme. Additionally, we also develop classification models using Resnet-50 architecture and original images to evaluate the trade-off between privacy and model utility, i.e. we measure the change in classification accuracy for a network trained with original images compared to a network trained with encoded images. First, we transform the original images using our Cycle-GAN image transformation method. Second, we compare the classification accuracy of original images and the transformed images. The classification accuracy of networks trained using Cycle-GAN transformed images exhibits a slight performance decrease compared to networks trained using original images. To quantify the trade-off between privacy and utility we measure the reduction in classification accuracy for the network trained using original images and the network trained using encoded images. Additionally, we measure the SSIM score between original images and encoded images. SSIM measures similarities within pixels i.e., it checks whether the pixels in the images line up and or if the images have similar pixel density values. In our experiments, we demonstrate that the proposed Cycle-GAN method allows us to maintain high classification accuracy of $92.48 \pm 1.53\%, 91.05 \pm 1.10\%, 90.37 \pm 2.06\%$ for Chest X-ray, Dermoscopy and OCT datasets, respectively, compared to models trained using plain images with classification accuracy of $96.90 \pm 1.26\%, 95.20 \pm 0.85\%, 95.20 \pm 2.71\%$ for Chest X-ray, Dermoscopy and OCT datasets, respectively which is similar to original images as shown in Table 1. Additionally, we demonstrate that the proposed Cycle-GAN method enhances privacy using SSIM scores between original and encoded images. The SSIM scores closer to zero indicate that the images are highly dissimilar. The SSIM scores in our privacy versus utility experiments were 0.0935, 0.0582, 0.0277 for Chest X-ray, Dermoscopy and OCT datasets, respectively,

**Table 1.** Trade-off between privacy and model utility for medical image deep learning models. Classification accuracy slightly decreases for networks trained using encoded medical images compared to networks trained using plain images i.e., original images. The proposed scheme enhances privacy of medical image DNNs while preserving model utility.

| Encoding Scheme | Classification Acc.% | | |
|---|---|---|---|
| | Chest X-ray | Dermoscopy | OCT |
| Plain Images | $96.90 \pm 1.26$ | $95.20 \pm 0.85$ | $95.20 \pm 2.71$ |
| Proposed Method | $92.48 \pm 1.53$ | $91.05 \pm 1.10$ | $90.37 \pm 2.06$ |

## 5.2  Evaluating Robustness to Attacks

**Model Stealing Attack.** We evaluate the robustness of our proposed Cycle-GAN based image encoding method against reconstruction attacks given the assumption that the data owner's Cycle-GAN encoder is publicly available to an attacker. The goal of an attacker is to learn $G_X$ given $G_Z$. In this case, the attacker begins training Cycle-GAN by querying $G_Z$ using his own constructed dataset $X_B$ to obtain the predicted output. $G_Z(X_B)$ is used to train the attacker's generator $F_X$ which is a randomly initialized version of $G_X$. Additionally, the attacker randomly initializes two discriminators $Q_X$ to distinguish between real and fake images and $Q_Z$ to distinguish between real and fake distortions. Following the previously discussed Cycle-GAN standard training procedure, the attacker learns a mapping function $F_X^*$ to reconstruct the data owner's original image dataset. During training, we freeze the weights of the data owner's original encoder $G_Z$.

**Model Stealing Attack Results.** We evaluate the performance of the model stealing attack using structural similarity index measure (SSIM). The SSIM values that are closer to 1 indicate that the reconstructed images are similar to the original images and values closer to 0 indicate that reconstructed images are poor quality compared to original images. The model stealing attack SSIM scores are shown in row 1 of Table 2. The model stealing attack SSIM scores for Chest X-ray, Dermoscopy and OCT datasets are 0.6064, 0.7783 and 0.5981, respectively. It is evident from our SSIM results that the attacker can reconstruct the data owner's original dataset with poor quality given that he has access to data owner's original encoder $G_Z$. The model stealing attacks is a baseline attack method with the strong assumption that an attacker has access to the data owner's original encoding function.

**Minimal Data Subset Attack.** We evaluate the robustness of our proposed Cycle-GAN image encoding method against minimal data subset attacks where the adversary is granted access to a subset of the data owner's original image

**Table 2.** Proposed Cycle-GAN image reconstruction attack SSIM results. SSIM scores near 1 indicate high quality image reconstruction whereas scores closer to 0 indicate poor quality imge reconstruction.

| Attack Method | Attacker's Knowledge | SSIM Score | | |
|---|---|---|---|---|
| | | Chest X-ray | Dermoscopy | OCT |
| Model Stealing | $G_Z, Z, Y$ | 0.6064 | 0.7783 | 0.5981 |
| Min. Data Subset (FT) | $X, Z, Y$ | 0.7582 | 0.8154 | 0.7109 |
| Min. Data Subset (RI) | $X, Z, Y$ | 0.7461 | 0.8033 | 0.7082 |
| Cycle GAN Recon | $Z, Y$ | 0.1002 | 0.0995 | 0.0329 |

dataset and corresponding encoded images. The goal is to develop a deep learning model to reconstruct original images given encoded images. The attack is performed by incrementally updating the model parameters using a single image-encoding pair from the data owner's original dataset and corresponding encoded images i.e., $\{X, Z\}$. Image-encoding pairs are gradually included during the training process until SSIM saturates. The image reconstruction model parameters are updated by minimizing the mean squared error between original images and reconstructed images given the encoded samples. At the conclusion of each training step, we measure the SSIM score of the data owner's original images and the reconstructed images. First, the attacker develops a randomly initialized (RI) reconstruction model with a subset of the data owner's original image-encoding pair. Second, the attacker pre-trains a reconstruction model using his constructed dataset $X_B$ and later fine-tunes the network (FT) with a subset of the data owner's original image-encoding pair. Afterwards, the reconstruction model is used to reconstruct the data owner's original image dataset.

**Minimal Data Subset Attack Results.** The reconstruction model performance is evaluated using SSIM. The SSIM results reflect the model performance as SSIM scores begins to saturate. The fine-tuned reconstruction model SSIM scores are shown in row 2 of Table 2. The fine-tuned SSIM scores for Chest X-ray, Dermoscopy and OCT datasets are 0.7582, 0.8154 and 0.7109, respectively. The randomly initialized reconstruction model SSIM scores are shown in row 3 of Table 2. The fine-tuned SSIM scores for Chest X-ray, Dermoscopy and OCT datasets are 0.7461, 0.8033 and 0.7082, respectively. The SSIM scores are indicative of good quality image reconstruction. The minimal data subset attack is a baseline attack method in which the attacker has access to a subset of the original image-encoding pairs.

**Reconstruction Cycle GAN Attack.** We evaluate the robustness of our proposed method against Cycle-GAN reconstruction attacks. In this case, an attacker constructs a dataset that follows the probability distribution of the data owner's original dataset i.e., $x_b \sim p_{data}(x)$ and attempts to reconstruct the original dataset by learning his own mapping function using a Cycle-Gan based approach. First, the attacker develops his own image classification model using the constructed dataset and corresponding class labels by following the previously mentioned procedure from our proposed method. Second, the attacker develops a distortion model using the constructed dataset and corresponding class labels by following the previously mentioned procedure from our proposed method. Third, the attacker develops a Cycle-GAN encoding model using the constructed dataset and corresponding class labels by following the previously mentioned procedure from our proposed method. The goal is to learn a mapping function between the attacker's constructed dataset and the attacker's distorted dataset. We assume an attacker only has access to the data owner's encoded dataset and corresponding labels.

The attacker's reconstruction Cycle-GAN attack network consists of the same components of the proposed method i.e., two generators $(F_Z, F_X)$, two discriminators $(Q_Z, Q_X)$. The attacker's distorted dataset $Z_B$ is generated using pre-trained distortion model $Z_B = A_B^*(X_B)$. Generator $F_Z$ is used to translate the attacker's constructed images to the distorted image domain and generator $F_X$ is used to translate distorted images to the attacker's constructed image domain. Discriminator $Q_Z$ is used to distinguish between the real and fake distorted images and discriminator $Q_X$ is used to distinguish between the attacker's real and fake constructed images.

**Reconstruction Cycle-GAN Adversarial Loss.** The adversarial loss term is computed using generator $F_Z$, generator $F_X$, discriminator $Q_Z$ and discriminator $Q_X$. Discriminator $Q_Z$ is a binary classifier used to distinguish between the distorted set $Z_B$ and the generated distorted set $F_Z(X_B)$. First, generator $F_Z$ is used as a mapping function from the attacker's constructed image domain to the distorted image domain $Z_B' = F_Z(X_B)$. Generator $F_Z$ wishes to minimize the probability of $Z_B'$ being classified as a generated distorted image by discriminator $Q_Z$ while $Q_Z$ aims to maximize the probability of the real distorted images $Z_B$ being classified as real and generated distorted images $Z_B'$ being classified as fake. The attacker learns a generator $F_Z$ that translates constructed images $X_B$ into the distorted image domain.

Discriminator $Q_X$ is a binary classifier used to distinguish between real and generated constructed images. We obtain $X_B'$ using generator $F_X$ given the distorted set as input to generator $F_X$, i.e. $X_B' = F_X(Z_B)$. Generator $F_X$ wishes to minimize the probability of $X_B'$ being classified as a generated construct image by discriminator $Q_X$ while $Q_X$ aims to maximize the probability of real constructed images $X_B$ being classified as a real and generated constructed images $X_B'$ being classified as fake. The attacker learns a generator $F_X$ that translates distorted images into the attacker's constructed image domain.

The full adversarial loss consists of a loss term from generators $(F_Z, F_X)$ and discriminators $(Q_Z, Q_X)$. The following equations describe the adversarial loss term.

$$L_{GAN}(F_Z, Q_Z, X_B, Z_B) = \mathbb{E}_{z_b \sim p_{enc}(z_b)}[\log Q_Z(z_b)]$$
$$+\mathbb{E}_{x_b \sim p_{data}(x_b)}[\log(1 - Q_Z(F_Z(x_b)))] \tag{10}$$

where $F_Z$ tries to generate distorted images $F_Z(x_b)$ that are similar to the real distorted images $z_b$, while $Q_Z$ distinguishes between real distorted images $z_b$ and generated distorted images $F_Z(x_b)$. $F_Z$ minimizes the objective while $Q_Z$ maximizes the objective, $\min_{F_Z} \max_{Q_Z} L_{GAN}(F_Z, Q_Z, X_B, Z_B)$.

$$L_{GAN}(F_X, Q_X, Z_B, X_B) = \mathbb{E}_{x_b \sim p_{data}(x_b)}[\log Q_X(x_b)]$$
$$+\mathbb{E}_{z_b \sim p_{enc}(z_b)}[\log(1 - Q_X(F_X(z_b)))] \tag{11}$$

where $F_X$ tries to generate constructed images $F_X(z_b)$ that are similar to the attacker's constructed images $x_b$, while $Q_X$ distinguishes between the attacker's real constructed data and generated $F_X(z_b)$ constructed data. $F_X$ minimizes the objective while $Q_X$ maximizes the objective, $\min_{F_X} \max_{Q_X} L_{GAN}(F_X, Q_X, Z_B, X_B)$.

**Reconstruction Cycle-GAN Cycle Consistency Loss.** Next, we compute the cycle consistency loss terms using generator $F_Z$ and generator $F_X$. First, the attacker translates his constructed data set $X_B$ into the distorted image domain using generator $F_Z$. Then the generated distorted image is translated back into the attacker's constructed image domain using generator $F_X$. Second, the attacker translates distorted images $Z_B$ into the constructed image domain using generator $F_X$. Then the generated construct image set is translated back into distorted image domain using generator $F_Z$. The mean absolute error between the constructed images and the cycled constructed images are computed. Additionally, the mean absolute error between the distorted images and the cycled distorted images are computed.

The computed cycle consistency loss values for the constructed and distorted data are summed together below.

$$L_{cyc}(F_Z, F_X) = \mathbb{E}_{x_b \sim p_{data}(x_b)}[|||F_X(F_Z(x_b)) - x_b||_1]$$
$$+\mathbb{E}_{z_b \sim p_{enc}(z_b)}[|||F_Z(F_X(z_b)) - z_b||_1] \tag{12}$$

$F_X(F_Z(x_b))$ is the attacker's cycled constructed data and $F_Z(F_X(z_b))$ is the attacker's cycled distorted data. The error between the cycled constructed data and real constructed data is minimized. Also, the error between the cycled distorted data and real distorted data is minimized. Both values are combined to compute the total cycle consistency loss.

**Reconstruction Cycle-GAN Attack Full Objective.** All of the previously discussed loss terms are summed together for the full objective. The full objective for the attack consists of two adversarial loss terms and a cycle consistency loss term.

The full objective is:

$$L(F_Z, F_X, Q_X, Q_Z) = L_{GAN}(F_Z, Q_Z, X_B, Z_B)$$
$$+ L_{GAN}(F_X, Q_X, Z_B, X_B) \tag{13}$$
$$+ \lambda L_{cyc}(F_Z, F_X)$$

where $\lambda$ controls the importance of each objective. In our experiments, $\lambda = 10$. We solve the following optimization problem:

$$F_Z^*, F_X^* = \underset{F_Z, F_X}{\text{argmin}} \ \underset{Q_Z, Q_X}{\max} \ L(F_Z, F_X, Q_X, Q_Z) \tag{14}$$

**Reconstruction Cycle-GAN Attack Results.** The reconstruction Cycle-GAN attack results demonstrate an attacker's ability to reconstruct the data owner's original image dataset using the learned mapping function $F_X^*$ given the data owner's encoded dataset $Z$ i.e., $F_X^*(Z)$. Generator $F_X^*$ was optimized to translate encoded images to plain images. The translated images are expected to consist of inherent features from the distorted image domain as Cycle-GAN learns a mapping from one domain to another. Thus, we translate the data owner's encoded set to the attacker's constructed plain image domain $F_X(Z)$ to reconstruct the data owner's original image given the data owner's encoded images. The SSIM score between the reconstructed images and the original images are shown in row 5 of Table 2. We report SSIM scores using $X$ and $F_X(Z)$ for Chest X-ray, Dermoscopy and OCT datasets. Our results demonstrate that image reconstruction exhibits poor quality given that only the encoded set and corresponding labels are available to an attacker. Consequently, given that an attacker's knowledge is restricted to $\{Z, Y\}$ it is evident that the reconstructed images consist of poor quality when compared to original private images.

## 6 Conclusion

We proposed a Cycle-GAN image transformation scheme that leverages autoencoder image encoding for domain translation to enhance the privacy of deep neural networks. The visible image feature information is encoded using autoencoder and Cycle-GAN to reduce the risk of information leakage. The important feature information is retained for image classification while obfuscating the sensitive image features. In this paper, we demonstrated that the proposed Cycle-GAN image encoding method successfully enhances the privacy of sensitive image data while preserving model utility with high classification accuracy. In our experiments, we evaluated the effectiveness of our Cycle-GAN encoding scheme by assessing the privacy versus model utility trade-off using classification accuracy. Additionally, we show that our proposed method is robust against reconstruction attacks when an attacker only has access to encoded data and corresponding class labels using SSIM.

# References

1. Atallah, M.J., Pantazopoulos, K.N., Rice, J.R., Spafford, E.E.: Secure outsourcing of scientific computations. In: Advances in Computers, vol. 54, pp. 215–272. Elsevier (2002)
2. Yuan, X., Wang, X., Wang, C., Squicciarini, A., Ren, K.: Enabling privacy-preserving image-centric social discovery. In: Proceedings of the 2014 IEEE 34th International Conference on Distributed Computing Systems, ser. ICDCS 2014, pp. 198–207. IEEE Computer Society, USA (2014). https://doi.org/10.1109/ICDCS. 2014.28
3. Wu, Z., Huang, Y., Wang, L., Wang, X., Tan, T.: A comprehensive study on cross-view gait based human identification with deep CNNs. IEEE Trans. Pattern Anal. Mach. Intell. **39**(2), 209–226 (2016)
4. Packhäuser, K., Gündel, S., Münster, N., Syben, C., Christlein, V., Maier, A.: Is medical chest X-ray data anonymous? arXiv preprint arXiv:2103.08562 (2021)
5. Ma, X., et al.: Understanding adversarial attacks on deep learning based medical image analysis systems. Pattern Recognit. **110**, 107332 (2021). https://doi.org/10. 1016/j.patcog.2020.107332
6. Tanaka, M.: Learnable image encryption. In: 2018 IEEE International Conference on Consumer Electronics-Taiwan (ICCE-TW), pp. 1–2 (2018)
7. Sirichotedumrong, W., Maekawa, T., Kinoshita, Y., Kiya, H.: Privacy-preserving deep neural networks with pixel-based image encryption considering data augmentation in the encrypted domain. In: 2019 IEEE International Conference on Image Processing (ICIP), pp. 674–678 (2019)
8. Sirichotedumrong, W., Kiya, H.: A GAN-based image transformation scheme for privacy-preserving deep neural networks (2020). https://arxiv.org/abs/2006.01342
9. Li, T., Li, N.: On the tradeoff between privacy and utility in data publishing. In: Proceedings of the 15th ACM SIGKDD International Conference on Knowledge Discovery and Data Mining, pp. 517–526 (2009)
10. Zhu, J.-Y., Park, T., Isola, P., Efros, A.A.: Unpaired image-to-image translation using cycle-consistent adversarial networks (2020)
11. Yao, A.C.: Protocols for secure computations. In: 23rd Annual Symposium on Foundations of Computer Science (SFCS 1982), pp. 160–164. IEEE (1982)
12. Chase, M., Gilad-Bachrach, R., Laine, K., Lauter, K., Rindal, P.: Private collaborative neural network learning. Cryptology ePrint Archive (2017)
13. Mohassel, P., Zhang, Y.: Secureml: a system for scalable privacy-preserving machine learning. In: 2017 IEEE Symposium on Security and Privacy (SP), pp. 19–38 (2017)
14. Wagh, S., Gupta, D., Chandran, N.: Securenn: 3-party secure computation for neural network training. Proc. Priv. Enhancing Technol. **2019**(3), 26–49 (2019)
15. Nikolaenko, V., Weinsberg, U., Ioannidis, S., Joye, M., Boneh, D., Taft, N.: Privacy-preserving ridge regression on hundreds of millions of records. In: 2013 IEEE Symposium on Security and Privacy, pp. 334–348 (2013)
16. Aono, Y., Hayashi, T., Trieu Phong, L., Wang, L.: Scalable and secure logistic regression via homomorphic encryption. In: Proceedings of the Sixth ACM Conference on Data and Application Security and Privacy, pp. 142–144 (2016)
17. Bonte, C., Vercauteren, F.: Privacy-preserving logistic regression training. BMC Med. Genomics **11**(4), 13–21 (2018)
18. Crawford, J.L.H., Gentry, C., Halevi, S., Platt, D., Shoup, V.: Doing real work with FHE: the case of logistic regression. Cryptology ePrint Archive, Paper 2018/202 (2018). https://eprint.iacr.org/2018/202

19. Graepel, T., Lauter, K., Naehrig, M.: ML confidential: machine learning on encrypted data. In: Kwon, T., Lee, M.-K., Kwon, D. (eds.) ICISC 2012. LNCS, vol. 7839, pp. 1–21. Springer, Heidelberg (2013). https://doi.org/10.1007/978-3-642-37682-5_1

20. Kim, M., Song, Y., Wang, S., Xia, Y., Jiang, X., et al.: Secure logistic regression based on homomorphic encryption: design and evaluation. JMIR Med. Inform. **6**(2), e8805 (2018)

21. Nandakumar, K., Ratha, N., Pankanti, S., Halevi, S.: Towards deep neural network training on encrypted data. In: Proceedings of the IEEE/CVF Conference on Computer Vision and Pattern Recognition Workshops (2019)

22. Li, T., Sahu, A.K., Talwalkar, A., Smith, V.: Federated learning: challenges, methods, and future directions. IEEE Signal Process. Mag. **37**(3), 50–60 (2020)

23. Bonawitz, K., et al.: Towards federated learning at scale: system design. Proc. Mach. Learn. Syst. **1**, 374–388 (2019)

24. Zhao, Y., Li, M., Lai, L., Suda, N., Civin, D., Chandra, V.: Federated learning with non-IID data, arXiv preprint arXiv:1806.00582 (2018)

25. Konečný, J., McMahan, H.B., Yu, F.X., Richtárik, P., Suresh, A.T., Bacon, D.: Federated learning: strategies for improving communication efficiency (2016). https://arxiv.org/abs/1610.05492

26. McPherson, R., Shokri, R., Shmatikov, V.: Defeating image obfuscation with deep learning, arXiv preprint arXiv:1609.00408 (2016)

27. Huang, Y., Song, Z., Li, K., Arora, S.: InstaHide: instance-hiding schemes for private distributed learning. In: Daume III, H., Singh, A. (eds.) Proceedings of the 37th International Conference on Machine Learning, ser. Proceedings of Machine Learning Research, vol. 119, pp. 4507–4518. PMLR (2020). https://proceedings.mlr.press/v119/huang20i.html

28. Yala, A., et al.: Neuracrypt: hiding private health data via random neural networks for public training (2021). https://arxiv.org/abs/2106.02484

29. Carlini, N., et al.: Is private learning possible with instance encoding? (2020). https://arxiv.org/abs/2011.05315

30. Raynal, M., Achanta, R., Humbert, M.: Image obfuscation for privacy-preserving machine learning (2020). https://arxiv.org/abs/2010.10139

31. Carlini, N., Garg, S., Jha, S., Mahloujifar, S., Mahmoody, M., Tramer, F.: Neuracrypt is not private (2021)

32. Sirichotedumrong, W., Kinoshita, Y., Kiya, H.: Pixel-based image encryption without key management for privacy-preserving deep neural networks. IEEE Access **7**, 177844–177855 (2019)

33. Chen, Z., Zhu, T., Xiong, P., Wang, C., Ren, W.: Privacy preservation for image data: a GAN-based method. Int. J. Intell. Syst. **36**(4), 1668–1685 (2021)

34. Sirichotedumrong, W., Kiya, H.: A GAN-based image transformation scheme for privacy-preserving deep neural networks (2020)

35. Kermany, D.S., et al.: Identifying medical diagnoses and treatable diseases by image-based deep learning. Cell **172**(5), 1122–1131 (2018)

36. Scarlat, A.: dermoscopic pigmented skin lesions from ham10k (2019). https://www.kaggle.com/drscarlat/melanoma. Accessed 02 May 2020

37. Rasul, M.F., Kumar Dey, N., Hashem, M.: A comparative study of neural network architectures for lesion segmentation and melanoma detection (2020)

38. He, K., Zhang, X., Ren, S., Sun, J.: Deep residual learning for image recognition (2015). https://arxiv.org/abs/1512.03385

39. Ulyanov, D., Vedaldi, A., Lempitsky, V.: Instance normalization: the missing ingredient for fast stylization (2017)

# Secure KNN Computation on Cloud

Tikaram Sanyashi[1]([✉]) [ID], Nirmal Kumar Boran[2] [ID], and Virendra Singh[3] [ID]

[1] Department of Information Security and Communication Technology, NTNU,
Trondheim, Norway
tikaram.sanyashi@ntnu.no
[2] Department of Computer Science and Engineering, NIT Calicut, Kozhikode, India
nirmalkboran@nitc.ac.in
[3] Department of Computer Science and Engineering, IIT Bombay, Mumbai, India
viren@cse.iitb.ac.in

**Abstract.** Cloud computing has emerged as a trend of outsourcing database and query services to a powerful cloud to ease local storage and computing pressure. However, private data storage and computation in the cloud come with a risk of losing the privacy and confidentiality of the data. Thus, sensitive applications running on the cloud require to be encrypted before storing it in the cloud. Additionally, to run some data mining algorithms, viz., $k$-NN requires the data to be in the encrypted domain computation-friendly ciphertext form. Thus, data are encrypted using a searchable encryption scheme before outsourcing it into the cloud. Asymmetric scalar-product-preserving encryption (ASPE) scheme provides secure *k-nearest neighbors* computation that is designed to provide both *Data Privacy* and *Query Privacy*. However, this scheme assumed that the query users were trusted entities. Enhancements to this work further showed that trusted query user assumption is no longer necessary if we use the Paillier cryptosystem. In this work, we have shown that even if we do not use the Paillier cryptosystem, query privacy in the cryptosystem can be achieved using the ASPE technique alone. Using ASPE for query encryption reduces the query encryption time, further improving the practicality of the encryption scheme.

**Keywords:** Privacy preserving · $k$-NN · Cloud computing · Encrypted Data

## 1  Introduction

The rapid progress of cloud computing has sparked a burgeoning movement towards migrating databases to cloud-based environments. The cloud also provides users with a query service to ease the cloud storage and computing pressure. Typically, a data owner delegates their databases to a cloud service for management, leveraging the cloud's resources and flexibility to decrease database maintenance expenses [1,15,16]. The cloud performs both database maintenance and outsourced computation. Nonetheless, this presents a challenge concerning

V. Muthukkumarasamy et al. (Eds.): ICISS 2023, LNCS 14424, pp. 197–216, 2023.
https://doi.org/10.1007/978-3-031-49099-6_12

data security and privacy. As a result, safeguarding data privacy in external-ized databases has gained significant attention in recent times, driving intensive research efforts in this domain.

Considering a practical scenario involving location-based services, a local ser-vice provider (LSP) hosts an extensive geospatial database containing compre-hensive information about numerous locations. In this setup, a user can transmit her current location to the LSP, prompting the LSP to furnish query results such as the top five closest hotels. A prevalent approach among LSPs is to entrust their geospatial database to a robust public cloud, thereby availing geospa-tial database storage and location-based query processing capabilities. Cloud computing, acknowledged as the next-generation computing paradigm, promises LSPs many advantages, including reduced operational costs and enhanced per-formance.

However, this adoption of cloud services introduces a conundrum regarding data security and privacy. The act of outsourcing geospatial data to a public cloud deprives LSPs of direct data control, consequently giving rise to security concerns that impede the widespread adoption of this novel computing paradigm. One pressing issue is the potential for the cloud to gather and track the location of the data user (i.e., the querier), thereby compromising user privacy. Moreover, the ominous possibility of a cloud breach exists, leading to the unauthorized exposure of stored data. Such a breach could empower malicious actors with commercial gains or unfair advantages.

To safeguard the data privacy of LSPs, it becomes imperative to encrypt geospatial data before transmitting it to the cloud. This, however, introduces a pertinent question: which encryption schemes should be employed for this pur-pose? Traditional encryption methods lack the ability to perform computations in the encrypted domain, and while homomorphic encryption schemes exist, their efficiency for real-world data computations might be questionable [14].

In such places, searchable encryption [2,4,7,18,19,23] plays a significant role viz., a client encrypts a collection of sensitive data for privacy protection and delegates the encrypted database to a server capable of effectively responding to search queries without requiring decryption of the database. Established method-ologies address intricate and comprehensive queries [7,8] within the structural encryption (STE) conceptual framework [5]. More information can be obtained from the survey paper by Fuller et al. [9].

Computation of $k$-nearest neighbor ($k$-NN) of a given query vector finds wide application in many fields, such as location-based services, data mining, $e$-healthcare, etc. The ($k$-NN) query seeks to identify the closest $k$ neighbors to a specified query vector. Nevertheless, the outcome of a $k$-NN query is intimately tied to a user's preferences and interests. Consequently, scholarly exploration has been into devising secure $k$-NN query processing algorithms that simulta-neously uphold data privacy and query confidentiality. One such scheme is the asymmetric scalar-product-preserving encryption (ASPE) technique introduced by Wong et al. [23]. It finds many applications in secure cloud computation, including $k$-NN, fuzzy keyword search, content-based image retrieval, keyword matching, etc.

In [23], Wong treated the cloud as an untrusted entity while the query users as a trusted entity; thus, the data encryption key is shared with them, which in real-world scenarios may not be an acceptable assumption to consider. Later, Zhu et al. [26] addressed this issue and presented a way to achieve query privacy without sharing the secret key with the query users. However, they used the help of Paillier cryptosystem, which requires comparatively higher encryption and decryption time for query encryption and decryption. This work replaces the Paillier encryption scheme using the ASPE technique and has shown that query privacy of the encryption can also be achieved using the ASPE technique. The use of ASPE reduces the query encryption time, making the encryption scheme more efficient and practical at the same time.

The rest of the paper is organized as follows: Sect. 2 introduces the background, and Sect. 3 related work. Section 4 presents the system model, while Sect. 5 presents the proposed encryption scheme. Section 6 presents the performance evaluation of the proposed encryption scheme, and Sect. 7 presents the proposed work's empirical evaluation. Finally, Sect. 8 concludes the paper.

Mathematical notations used in the paper can be found in Table 1.

## 2   Background

This section will briefly review the ASPE encryption scheme [26]. In the ASPE encryption scheme, given a database $\mathcal{D} = (p_1, p_2, \cdots, p_m)$ of $d$-dimension with $i^{th}$ tuple as $(p_{i_1}, p_{i_2}, \cdots, p_{i_d})$. The database is encrypted first and stored in the cloud as $\mathcal{D}' = (p'_1, p'_2, \cdots, p'_m)$. ASPE encryption scheme increases the dimension of each data vector by $(1+c+\epsilon)$-dimension. Thus given a $d$-dimensional data vector $(p_{i_1}, p_{i_2}, \cdots, p_{i_d})$ the encrypted data vector results into $(d+1+c+\epsilon)$-dimensional vector as $(p'_{i_1}, p'_{i_2}, \cdots, p'_{i_{(d+1+c+\epsilon)}})$. Positive integers $c$ and $\epsilon$ are the dimensions added to maintain the security of the encryption scheme.

ASPE encryption scheme can be modularized into four modules: key generation, data encryption, query encryption, and query processing. Below, we have covered each of these modules in brief.

*Key Generation:* In this step, the data owner (DO) generates the data encryption key as follows

- $s = (s_1, s_2, \cdots, s_{d+1}) \in \mathbb{R}^{d+1}$ and $\tau \in \mathbb{R}^c$, fixed long-term secrets.
- $v_i \in \mathbb{R}^\epsilon$ is a per-tuple ephemeral secret while $r^{(q)} \in \mathbb{R}^c$ and $\beta_q \in \mathbb{R}$ are per-query ephemeral secrets.
- $M$ is an invertible matrix with $(d+1+c+\epsilon)$ rows/columns and with elements drawn uniformly at random from $\mathbb{R}$.
- $\pi$ a secret permutation function of length $(d+1+c+\epsilon)$.
- The resultant secret key consist of $(M, s, \tau, \pi)$.

**Table 1.** Table of Notations

| Notation | Meaning |
|---|---|
| **A** - **Z** | matrices |
| **a** - **z** | vectors |
| a - z | constants |
| $\mathcal{D}$ | database of vectors |
| $\mathbf{p}_i$ | $i^{th}$ data vector |
| **q** | query vector |
| $d$ | dimension of data and query vector |
| $\mathbf{p}_i'$ | encrypted data vector $\mathbf{p}_i$ |
| $\mathcal{D}'$ | database $\mathcal{D}$ in encrypted form |
| $\mathbf{p}_i''$ | computed from $\mathbf{p}_i'$ for $k$-NN computation |
| $\mathcal{D}''$ | database created for $k$-NN computation |
| $\dot{\mathbf{q}}$ | encrypted query vector by Query User |
| $\hat{\mathbf{q}}$ | encrypted query vector by Data Owner |
| $\tilde{\mathbf{q}}_{vec}$ | query encrypted for $k$-NN computation |
| $\mathbf{M}_{base}^{\eta \times \eta}$ | invertible base secret matrix |
| $\mathbf{M}_t^{\eta \times \eta}$ | invertible temporary secret matrix |
| $\mathbf{E}^{\eta \times \eta}$ | error matrix used for encryption |
| $\mathbf{N}^{d \times d}$ | diagonal matrix used for query encryption by QU |
| $\mathbf{N}'^{\eta \times \eta}$ | diagonal matrix used for query decryption by QU |
| $ED(\mathbf{p}_i) = \|\mathbf{p}_i\|$ | $\sqrt{\sum_{l=0}^{d} p_{il}^2}$ |
| $ED(\mathbf{p}_i, \mathbf{q})$ | $\sqrt{\sum_{l=0}^{d} (p_{il} - q_l)^2}$ |
| $c, \epsilon$ | security parameters $> 0$ |
| $\eta = (d + 1 + c + \epsilon)$ | encrypted data/query vector length |
| **s** | $(d+1)$-dimensional vector of reals |
| $\boldsymbol{w}$ | $c$-dimensional fixed real vector |
| $\boldsymbol{z}$ | $\epsilon$-dimensional data encryption ephemeral vector |
| $\boldsymbol{x}$ | $c$-dimensional query encryption ephemeral vector |
| $\beta_1, \beta_2$ | random real numbers used for encryption |

*Data Encryption:* In this step, the database of vectors is encrypted row-wise. For encryption, the following steps are performed.

- It starts by shifting each tuple of data vector $\boldsymbol{p}_i$ by the shifting vector $\boldsymbol{s}$ later augmented by two secrets, long-term secret $\boldsymbol{\tau}$ and per tuple ephemeral secret $\boldsymbol{v}_i$ creating the shifted data vector as

$$\hat{p}_i = (s_1 - 2p_{i_1}, \cdots, s_d - 2p_{i_d}, s_{d+1} + \|\boldsymbol{p}_i\|^2, \boldsymbol{\tau}, \boldsymbol{v}_i)$$

– The shifted vector is later encrypted using the secret encryption matrix as

$$\boldsymbol{p}'_i = \hat{\boldsymbol{p}}_i \hat{\boldsymbol{M}}^{-1}$$

Here, $\hat{\boldsymbol{M}} = \pi(\boldsymbol{M})$, is the matrix obtained by permuting the columns of $\boldsymbol{M}$ using the permutation function $\pi$.

*Query Encryption:* For query encryption, interaction between the DO and query user (QU) is needed. The query user performs the first step of query encryption. In this step, QU encrypts the query vector using the Paillier cryptosystem and forwards it to the DO for its encryption. In the second step, DO re-encrypts the encrypted query vector and reverts it to the QU. QU performs the third and final step of query encryption. In this step, QU removes his encryption layer and forwards the encrypted query vector encrypted with only DO's secret key to the cloud service provider (CSP) for $k$-NN computation. The encryption scheme presented in this work removes the Paillier encryption scheme for query encryption and uses the ASPE techniques instead. Thus, understanding the query encryption of Zhu et al. [26] in detail is optional for the present work. In general, the encrypted query $q'_{enc}$ have a form of

$$q'_{enc} = \beta_q.\hat{\boldsymbol{M}}\hat{q}_*$$

where $\hat{q}_* = (q_1, q_2, \cdots, q_d, 1, r^{(q)}, \boldsymbol{0}_{(\epsilon)})$

*k-NN Computation:* In its simplest form, solving the $k$-nearest neighbors problem involves computing the distance, $D(\boldsymbol{p}_i, \boldsymbol{q})$ between the query vector, $\boldsymbol{q}$ and each database vector, $\boldsymbol{p}_i$. However, in the current context, we are dealing with an encrypted query vector and an encrypted database. Fortunately, a comparison between the distances, $D(\boldsymbol{p}_i, \boldsymbol{q})$ and $D(\boldsymbol{p}_j, \boldsymbol{q})$ reduces to a simple comparison in the encrypted domain as derived below:

$$
\begin{aligned}
& D(\boldsymbol{p}_i, \boldsymbol{q}) > D(\boldsymbol{p}_j, \boldsymbol{q}) \\
\Leftrightarrow\ & \|\boldsymbol{p}_i - \boldsymbol{q}\|^2 > \|\boldsymbol{p}_j - \boldsymbol{q}\|^2 \\
\Leftrightarrow\ & \|\boldsymbol{p}_i\|^2 - 2\boldsymbol{p}_i\boldsymbol{q} + \|\boldsymbol{q}\|^2 > \|\boldsymbol{p}_j\|^2 - 2\boldsymbol{p}_j\boldsymbol{q} + \|\boldsymbol{q}\|^2 \\
\Leftrightarrow\ & -2\sum_{k=1}^{d} p_{ik}q_k + \|\boldsymbol{p}_i\|^2 > -2\sum_{k=1}^{d} p_{jk}q_k + \|\boldsymbol{p}_j\|^2 \\
\Leftrightarrow\ & \sum_{k=1}^{d}(s_k - 2p_{ik})q_k + s_{d+1} + \|\boldsymbol{p}_i\|^2 + \boldsymbol{\tau}.r^{(q)} \\
& > \sum_{k=1}^{d}(s_k - 2p_{jk})q_k + s_{d+1} + \|\boldsymbol{p}_j\|^2 + \boldsymbol{\tau}.r^{(q)} \\
\Leftrightarrow\ & \boldsymbol{p}'_i\boldsymbol{q}' > \boldsymbol{p}'_j\boldsymbol{q}'
\end{aligned}
$$

Thus, as presented above, we can safely compute the k-NN in the encrypted domain using the ASPE technique.

This completes the brief description of the ASPE encryption scheme and is sufficient to understand the work in this paper.

## 3  Related Work

This section reviews the existing works on privacy-preserving secure $k$-NN computation. Privacy-preserving secure $k$-NN computation – retrieval of top-$k$ database records satisfying the smallest distances to a given query vector in the encrypted domain. It finds many applications in various fields, viz., data mining, pattern recognition, e-healthcare, location-based services, and signal processing, to name a few. Due to its ubiquitous application in various fields, it finds considerable attention from both industries and academia. Thus, it remains an active field of research in the outsourced computation environment, preserving data and query privacy.

In literature, different $k$-NN computing techniques are available, viz., matrix encryption, homomorphic encryption, private information retrieval, and other privacy preservation techniques. ASPE based on matrix multiplication initially presented by Wong et al. [23] in 2009 is used to realize $k$-NN computation. It focuses on the privacy of the database and query vector from the CSP while the QUs are treated as trusted users; thus, the data encryption key is shared with them for query encryption, which might not be a reasonable assumption to consider. Zhu et al. [26] improved the encryption scheme by treating query users as non-trusted entities and provided a privacy-preserving $k$-NN query computation using the Paillier encryption scheme. The scheme requires the DO's active participation in the query encryption process. Over time, many privacy-preserving schemes have been designed based on the ASPE scheme.

Additionally, many similarity range query schemes have also been proposed viz., [3,11,20,21,24,26]. Later, it was shown that such a scheme could not resist known-plaintext attacks as mentioned in [13]. The key confidentiality claim of the encryption scheme [26] is later breached by the work of [17]. However, [17] also present a way to enhance the scheme and a technique to restrict known plaintext attack on the encryption scheme and shows a way to securely compute $k$-NN queries, keeping data privacy and query privacy intact. A variant of the $k$-NN problem is the reverse $k$-NN problem that produces $k$ data vectors whose query vector is the $k$-NN. Li et al. [12] used the ASPE technique and other methods to realize the same.

Meanwhile, many schemes leverage homomorphic encryption techniques to protect data and query privacy viz., [10,25]. In addition, some privacy-preserving $k$-NN query computing schemes [6,22] were also designed by employing other privacy preservation techniques, e.g., private information retrieval. ASPE, however, still finds an active place in all these techniques due to its computation speed in the encrypted domain.

## 4    System Model

The security model of secure $k$-NN computation consists of three entities: a data owner (DO), a cloud service provider (CSP), and a group of query users (QU). Here, the DO encrypts its database intended to be stored in the cloud using a searchable encryption scheme and stores it in the cloud as shown in Fig. 1. A QU intending to compute $k$-NN of its query vector encrypts its query vector using the encryption scheme mentioned in Sect. 5 and sends it to DO for query re-encryption by the DO's secret key. On receiving the query vector from a QU, DO re-encrypts it using the procedure mentioned in Sect. 5 and sends it back to the QU. On receiving an encrypted query vector from the DO, QU removes his encryption layer as mentioned in Sect. 5 and sends the encrypted query vector for $k$-NN computation to the CSP. CSP checks the *user_id* and uses the corresponding data for $k$-NN calculation. The data prepared using the temporary secret key $M_t$ uses the Euclidean distance as the distance metric to obtain $k$ data vector. The computed $k$ data labels are later forwarded to the QU as the obtained $k$-NN. The data labels may correspond to different disease names in the case of healthcare data and nearby restaurant names in the case of LSP and usually depend on the data type and query under consideration.

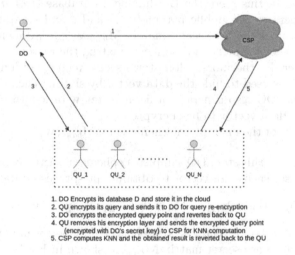

1. DO Encrypts its database D and store it in the cloud
2. QU encrypts its query and sends it to DO for query re-encryption
3. DO encrypts the encrypted query point and revertes back to QU
4. QU removes his encryption layer and sends the encrypted query point
   (encrypted with DO's secret key) to CSP for KNN computation
5. CSP computes KNN and the obtained result is reverted back to the QU

**Fig. 1.** Secure $k$-NN computation model in the cloud computation environment. In the figure, DO represents the data owner, QU represents the query users, and CSP represents the cloud service provider.

A semi-honest threat model has been considered in the proposed encryption scheme. Here, the cloud is the semi-honest adversary (a.k.a., honest-but-curious), viz., it does not deviate from the defined protocol. However, it uses the legitimately received data to infer other private or sensitive information. For instance, the cloud may want to infer the DO's geospatial data and the QU's query locations.

Consequently, to protect the DO's geospatial location data and QU's query location data, both the geospatial data and query location should be encrypted before sending it to the public cloud. The QU also behaves as a semi-honest entity; however, to gain information about the secret key used for data encryption, he tries to frame queries of his choice. Here, we assume that the CSP and QU are non-colluding entities.

# 5   Proposed Scheme

This section will discuss the proposed enhanced encryption scheme. The proposed encryption scheme can be modularized into the following four modules, similar to the previous work: key generation, data encryption, query encryption, and secure $k$-NN computation. Query encryption is performed in three steps: query encryption by QU, query encryption by DO, and finally, query encryption by QU. The encrypted query is later sent to the CSP for secure $k$-NN computation. The CSP computes the $k$-NN in the encrypted domain and reverts the obtained label to the query user. Below, each module mentioned above has been discussed in more detail.

*Key Generation:* In this step, the DO having a database $\mathbb{D}$ of $n$ vectors with $d$-dimension generates the public parameters $c$ and $\epsilon$ and computes $\eta$ as $\eta = d + 1 + c + \epsilon$. Samples the base secret matrix $\mathbf{M}_{base}$ of $\eta \times \eta$-dimension, here we have termed the secret matrix as base secret matrix; the reason behind this will be discussed later. Furthermore, a long-term secret vector $\mathbf{s}$ of length $(d + 1)$ is also generated; it is used to hide the data vector by shifting each data vector by this secret vector. DO also generates a fixed vector $\mathbf{w}$ of length $c$ uniformly at random for each data vector to be encrypted.

The secret key of the encryption scheme is $(\mathbf{s}, \mathbf{M}_{base}, \mathbf{w})$.

*Data Encryption:* In this step, DO samples a ephemeral secret vector $\mathbf{z}$ of length $\epsilon$ and pre-processes each data vector to obtain a pre-processed data vector as

$$\tilde{\mathbf{p}}_i = (s_1 - 2p_{i1}, \cdots, s_d - 2p_{id}, s_{d+1} + ||\mathbf{p}_i||^2, \mathbf{w}, \mathbf{z})$$

The pre-processed data vector is later encrypted by performing vector-matrix multiplication with base secret matrix $\mathbf{M}_{base}$ as shown in Eq. 1.

$$\mathbf{p}'_i = \tilde{\mathbf{p}}_i \mathbf{M}_{base}^{-1} \tag{1}$$

Encrypted data vectors are later stored in the cloud, where the rest of the query computations are performed. DO also computes the Euclidean norm (EN) of data vectors and stores the maximum norm as $Max\_norm = Max(EN(\boldsymbol{p}_1), \cdots, EN(\boldsymbol{p}_m))$, which will be used for query encryption later.

Performing the computation as mentioned above and storing the database in the cloud, DO can drop the database $\mathbf{D}$ from the local storage. In the future, if the database is needed, he can download it from the cloud and decrypt it to get the database in the plaintext format.

*Query Encryption:* Interaction between the QU and the DO is required to perform query encryption. Different steps performed by the DO and the QU are divided into three steps. Each of these three steps has been covered below.

– Step 1: QU performs the first step of query encryption. A QU having a query vector $\mathbf{q}$ of $d$-dimension samples a diagonal matrix $\mathbf{N}^{d \times d}$ of real numbers and computes the encrypted query $\dot{\mathbf{q}}$ as

$$\dot{\mathbf{q}} = \beta_1 \cdot \mathbf{q} \cdot \mathbf{N}$$

Here, $\beta_1$ is an encryption constant and is a real number. The encrypted query $\dot{\mathbf{q}}$ obtained above is later sent to the DO along with query user id as $(user\_id, \dot{\mathbf{q}})$ to obtain a doubly encrypted query vector $\hat{\mathbf{q}}$. This completes step 1 of query encryption.

– Step 2: This step of query encryption is performed by the DO. Here the DO at first computes the largest number present in the encrypted query vector $\dot{\mathbf{q}}$ as $q_{max} = max(\dot{\mathbf{q}})$. Next, it samples a temporary secret matrix $\mathbf{M}_t^{\eta \times \eta}$, with all elements except the diagonal elements of matrix $\mathbf{M}_t$ uniformly at random larger than $q_{max}$. In contrast, the diagonal elements are sampled uniformly at random larger than $Max\_norm$. Later, matrix $\mathbf{M}_t$ is multiplied with $\mathbf{M}_{base}$ to obtain a temporary secret matrix for the query encryption as $\mathbf{M}_{sec} = \mathbf{M}_t \mathbf{M}_{base}$.

The obtained query vector $\dot{\mathbf{q}}$ is appended to obtain a new query vector $\mathbf{q}'$ of $\eta$-dimension as

$$\mathbf{q}' = (\dot{\mathbf{q}}, 1, \mathbf{x}, \mathbf{0}_\epsilon)$$

where $\mathbf{x}$ is an ephemeral integer vector of length $c$ and $\mathbf{0}_\epsilon$ is a zero vector of length $\epsilon$. Next it uses the operator $O_e$ to convert vector $\mathbf{q}'$ into a $\eta \times \eta$ dimensional diagonal matrix $\mathbf{q}_{\eta\eta}$ as follows

$$O_e : \mathbf{q}' \to \mathbf{q}_{\eta\eta} \quad with \quad q_{ii} = q'_i$$

Next, it performs computation as presented by Eq. 2 below

$$\hat{\mathbf{q}} = \beta_2(\mathbf{M}_{sec}\mathbf{q}_{\eta\eta} + \mathbf{E}) \tag{2}$$

Here the error matrix $\mathbf{E}^{\eta \times \eta}$ is used to hide the secret matrix $\mathbf{M}_{sec}$ from QU and the real number $\beta_2$ is a DO encryption constant. Elements of the error matrix $\mathbf{E}$ are sampled uniformly at random larger than $q_{max}$. The reason is that the QU should not learn any content of the secret matrix by looking into the obtained doubly encrypted query vector. It is to be noted that the elements of the matrix $\mathbf{E}$ are sampled in such a way that the correctness of the $k$-NN computation remains intact; in the later section, we will discuss it further.

DO returns the doubly encrypted query matrix $\hat{\mathbf{q}}$ to the QU and send the temporary secret matrix and $user\_id$ to the CSP as $(user\_id, \mathbf{M}_t)$. The CSP prepares the temporary database $\mathbf{D}''$ for the query user $user\_id$ for computing $k$-NN computation as

$$\mathbf{p}''_i = \mathbf{p}'_i \mathbf{M}_t^{-1}$$
$$\mathbf{p}''_i = \tilde{\mathbf{p}}_i \mathbf{M}_{base}^{-1} \mathbf{M}_t^{-1}$$

This completes the step 2 of query encryption.

- Step 3: This step of query encryption is performed by the QU. In this step, QU removes his encryption layer to obtain $\tilde{\mathbf{q}}_{enc}$. QU constructs a diagonal matrix $\mathbf{N}'^{\eta \times \eta}$ with first $d$ diagonal elements same as that of the matrix $\mathbf{N}^{d \times d}$ and rest all 1. Computes its inverse and uses it to remove his encryption layer as follows

$$\tilde{\mathbf{q}}_{enc} = \hat{\mathbf{q}}\mathbf{N}'^{-1}$$
$$= \beta_2(\mathbf{M}_{sec}\mathbf{q}''_{\eta\eta}\mathbf{N}' + \mathbf{E}) \cdot \mathbf{N}'^{-1}$$
$$= \beta_2(\mathbf{M}_{sec}\mathbf{q}''_{\eta\eta} + \mathbf{E} \cdot \mathbf{N}'^{-1})$$

where $\mathbf{q}''_{\eta\eta}$ is a diagonal matrix with diagonal element $(\beta_1\mathbf{q}, 1, \mathbf{x}, \mathbf{0}_\epsilon)$.

The encrypted query matrix $\tilde{\mathbf{q}}_{enc}$ is converted to a vector $\tilde{\mathbf{q}}_{vec}$ using an operator $O_r$ as presented below.

$$O_r : \tilde{\mathbf{q}}_{enc} \to \tilde{\mathbf{q}}_{vec}$$

Here $\tilde{\mathbf{q}}_{vec_j} = \sum_{i=1}^{\eta} \tilde{\mathbf{q}}_{enc_{ji}}$, for $j \in \{1, \eta\}$ viz., the $j^{th}$ element of vector $\tilde{\mathbf{q}}_{vec}$ is obtained by adding all columns of row $j$ of matrix $\tilde{\mathbf{q}}_{enc}$. In short

$$\tilde{\mathbf{q}}_{vec} = \beta_2(\mathbf{M}_{sec}\mathbf{q}''_{\eta} + err)$$

where $\mathbf{q}''_{\eta}$ is a vector of $\eta$ elements as $(\beta_1\mathbf{q}, 1, \mathbf{x}, \mathbf{0}_\epsilon)$ and $err$ is a vector obtained by computing $Row\_Sum(\mathbf{E} \cdot \mathbf{N}'^{-1})$. The encrypted vector $\tilde{\mathbf{q}}_{vec}$ is later sent to the CSP for $k$-NN computation. This completes stage 3 of query encryption and, as a whole, query encryption as well.

*Decryption:* Decryption of encrypted data vectors is straightforward and is performed as

$$\tilde{\mathbf{p}}_i = \mathbf{p}'_i\mathbf{M}_{base}$$

From $\tilde{\mathbf{p}}_i$ data tuples are recovered by following

$$p_{ij} = s_j - \tilde{\mathbf{p}}_{ij}$$

*k-NN Computation:* The cloud performs the $k$-NN computation by performing multiplication of encrypted data vectors $\mathbf{p}''_i$ from the temporary database $\mathbf{D}''$ and an encrypted query vector $\tilde{\mathbf{q}}_{enc}$ as follows

$$\mathbf{p}''_i\tilde{\mathbf{q}}_{vec} = \beta_2[\tilde{\mathbf{p}}_i\mathbf{M}_{base}^{-1}\mathbf{M}_t^{-1}(\mathbf{M}_{sec}\mathbf{q}''_{\eta} + err)]$$
$$= \beta_2(\tilde{\mathbf{p}}_i\mathbf{q}''_{\eta} + \tilde{\mathbf{p}}_i \cdot \mathbf{M}_{base}^{-1}\mathbf{M}_t^{-1} \cdot err)$$
$$= \beta_2(\tilde{\mathbf{p}}_i\mathbf{q}''_{\eta} + err'_i) \qquad [err'_i = \tilde{\mathbf{p}}_i \cdot \mathbf{M}_{base}^{-1}\mathbf{M}_t^{-1} \cdot err]$$

The proposed encryption scheme performs correct $k$-NN computation provided it satisfies

$$(\tilde{\mathbf{p}}_i - \tilde{\mathbf{p}}_j)\mathbf{q}''_{\eta} > (err'_i - err'_j)$$

This is ensured by selecting parameters as discussed in step 2 of query encryption.

## 5.1   Correctness Analysis

The correctness of the encryption scheme needs two-fold proof. First, we need to show that the decryption of the encrypted data produces consistent plaintext data. This has already been shown in the decryption part above. Second, we must show that the encryption scheme produces correct $k$-NN computation in the encrypted domain. For this, it is sufficient to prove the Lemma 1 presented below.

**Lemma 1.** *Comparison of multiplication result of encrypted data vector $\mathbf{p}_i''$ and encrypted query vector $\tilde{\mathbf{q}}_{vec}$ is sufficient for $k$-NN computation.*

*Proof.* The encrypted data vector $\mathbf{p}_i''$ when multiplied with encrypted query vector $\tilde{\mathbf{q}}_{vec}$ it gives rise to

$$\mathbf{p}_i'' \tilde{\mathbf{q}}_{vec} = \beta_2 (\tilde{\mathbf{p}}_i \mathbf{q}_\eta'' + err_i')$$

Here,

$$\mathbf{p}_i'' \tilde{\mathbf{q}}_{vec} = \beta_1 \beta_2 [(s_1 q_1 + \cdots + s_d q_d + s_{d+1}) - 2(p_{i1} q_1 + \cdots + p_{id} q_d) + ||\mathbf{p}_i||^2]$$
$$+ \beta_2 \cdot \mathbf{wx} + \beta_2 \cdot err_i'$$

Similarly,

$$\mathbf{p}_j'' \tilde{\mathbf{q}}_{vec} = \beta_1 \beta_2 [(s_1 q_1 + \cdots + s_d q_d + s_{d+1}) - 2(p_{j1} q_1 + \cdots + p_{jd} q_d) + ||\mathbf{p}_j||^2]$$
$$+ \beta_2 \cdot \mathbf{wx} + \beta_2 \cdot err_j'$$

Thus,

$$(\mathbf{p}_i'' - \mathbf{p}_j'') \tilde{\mathbf{q}}_{vec} = \beta_1 \beta_2 [(||\mathbf{p}_i||^2 - 2p_{i1} q_1 - \cdots - 2p_{id} q_d + ||\mathbf{q}||^2)$$
$$- (||\mathbf{p}_j||^2 - 2p_{j1} q_1 - \cdots - 2p_{jd} q_d + ||\mathbf{q}||^2)] + \beta_2 (err_i' - err_j')$$
$$= \beta_1 \beta_2 [(p_{i1} - q_1)^2 - (p_{j1} - q_1)^2 + \cdots + (p_{id} - q_d)^2 - (p_{jd} - q_d)^2]$$
$$+ \beta_2 (err_i' - err_j')$$

The above term evaluates to correct comparison provided it satisfies the inequality given below

$$(err_i' - err_j') < \beta_1 [(p_{i1} - q_1)^2 - (p_{j1} - q_1)^2 + \cdots + (p_{id} - q_d)^2 - (p_{jd} - q_d)^2]$$
$$\beta_1 (\tilde{\mathbf{p}}_i - \tilde{\mathbf{p}}_j) \mathbf{q}_\eta'' > (\tilde{\mathbf{p}}_i - \tilde{\mathbf{p}}_j) \mathbf{M}_{base}^{-1} \mathbf{M}_t^{-1} \cdot err$$
$$\beta_1 \mathbf{q}_\eta'' > \mathbf{M}_{base}^{-1} \mathbf{M}_t^{-1} \cdot Row\_Sum(\mathbf{E} \cdot \mathbf{N}'^{-1}) \tag{3}$$

In Eq. 3 above, by choosing elements of $\mathbf{E}$ and $\mathbf{M}_t$ as mentioned in step 2 of query encryption makes $\mathbf{M}_{base}^{-1} \mathbf{M}_t^{-1} \cdot Row\_Sum(\mathbf{E} \cdot \mathbf{N}^{-1})$ negligible. This is because elements of matrix $\mathbf{M}_t$ are large, making elements of matrix $\mathbf{M}_t^{-1}$ quite small. Furthermore, it further gets multiplied with elements of matrix $\mathbf{M}_{base}^{-1}$ making overall multiplication negligible, which when multiplied with vector $Row\_Sum(\mathbf{E} \cdot \mathbf{N}'^{-1})$, the resultant vector have negligibly large values. Thus the overall result becomes quite small, which enforces the evaluation of correct $k$-NN.

## 5.2   Security Analysis

The proposed encryption scheme is claimed to hold following properties: *Key Confidentiality, Data Privacy, Query Privacy* and *Known Plaintext Attack*. We will discuss each of these properties one by one below.

*Data Privacy:* DO outsource its database in the encrypted form to the CSP. Thus, CSP can access the DO's private data other than the DO. Privacy of the DO's private data remains intact if encrypted data does not leak any information about the plaintext data. So, it is sufficient to prove Lemma 2 presented below.

**Lemma 2.** *Without the knowledge of secret matrix $M_{base}$, encrypted database $D'$ behaves as a random number.*

*Proof.* In the presented encryption scheme an encrypted data vector $\mathbf{p}'_i$ is obtained by performing computation as

$$\mathbf{p}'_i = \tilde{\mathbf{p}}_i \mathbf{M}^{-1}_{base}$$

where the initial data vector $\mathbf{p}_i$ is pre-processed to obtain $\tilde{\mathbf{p}}_i$ as

$$\tilde{\mathbf{p}}_i = (s_1 - 2p_{i1}, \cdots, s_d - 2p_{id}, s_{d+1} + ||\mathbf{p}_i||^2, \mathbf{w}, \mathbf{z})$$

In the pre-processed data vector $\tilde{\mathbf{p}}_i$, an ephemeral random vector $\mathbf{z}$ of length $\epsilon$ is used. The use of ephemeral random vector $\mathbf{z}$ for encrypting $\mathbf{p}_i$ makes it random even if the same data vector is encrypted for the second time, resulting in a semantically secure encryption scheme. Thus, no information about the plaintext data can be derived from the ciphertext data unless the secret key of the encryption scheme is known. This completes the proof of the lemma.

*Query Privacy:* Query Privacy of the encryption scheme needs to be established from the DO and the CSP. We will discuss each of these two cases separately.

- Case1: Query privacy against DO – It is established by encrypting the data vector by the QU. The encrypted query vector $\dot{\mathbf{q}}$ received by the DO have a form of

$$\dot{\mathbf{q}} = \beta_1 \cdot \mathbf{q} \cdot \mathbf{N}$$

Here query vector $\mathbf{q}$ is multiplied with a diagonal random matrix $\mathbf{N}$ and a real number $\beta_1$ to obtain the encrypted query vector $\dot{\mathbf{q}}$. Each element of query vector $\dot{\mathbf{q}}$ looks something like

$$\dot{q}_i = \beta_1 \cdot q_i \cdot n_{ii}$$

In the above equation, the $i$-th diagonal element $n_{ii}$ and $\beta_1$ are unknown real numbers. Without their knowledge, retrieval of $q_i$ is infeasible.

- Case2: Query privacy against CSP – It comes from the query encryption performed by the DO. The query vector sent for $k$-NN computation to the CSP has a form of

$$\tilde{\mathbf{q}}_{vec} = \beta_2(\mathbf{M}_{sec}\mathbf{q}''_\eta + err) \qquad (4)$$

where $\mathbf{q}''_\eta = (\beta_1\mathbf{q}, 1, \mathbf{x}, \mathbf{0}_\epsilon)$ and $err$ is a vector obtained by computing $Row\_Sum(\mathbf{E} \cdot \mathbf{N}'^{-1})$. The $i^{th}$ element of $\tilde{\mathbf{q}}_{vec}$ is computed as

$$\tilde{\mathbf{q}}_{vec_i} = \beta_2(\mathbf{M}_{sec_i}\mathbf{q}''_\eta + err_i) \qquad (5)$$

From Eq. 4 and 5, it is clear that retrieval of $\mathbf{q}''_\eta$ from $\tilde{\mathbf{q}}_{vec}$ requires the knowledge of $\beta_2$, $\mathbf{M}_{sec}$ and $err_i$. Thus, without the knowledge of $\beta_2$, $\mathbf{M}_{sec}$ and $err_i$ retrieval of the plain query is infeasible. In short, encryption performed by the DO can successfully withstand the query privacy against the CSP.

*Key Confidentiality:* Key confidentiality of the encryption scheme means the data encryption key should not be revealed to anyone and should remain confidential. Key confidentiality of the encryption scheme from CSP is straightforward as the DO only stores its encrypted database in the CSP, which looks completely random. Furthermore, for each query user interested in performing $k$-NN computation, a temporary key $\mathbf{M}_t$ is sent to the CSP to prepare data for the query user. This new temporary key $\mathbf{M}_t$ keeps on changing for each new $k$-NN computation request and is entirely independent of $\mathbf{M}_{base}$. Thus, by looking into the random-looking encrypted database and $\mathbf{M}_t$, no information about the base key $\mathbf{M}_{base}$ can be derived.

Additionally, as discussed in the *query privacy* part above, CSP can not figure out the data encryption key used for database encryption by looking into the encrypted database $\mathbf{D}'$ this is due to the use of the ephemeral secret vector $\mathbf{z}$, which makes the encrypted data vector pseudorandom. Thus by using database $\mathbf{D}'$ and query $\tilde{\mathbf{q}}_{enc}$ only $k$-NN can be computed, and no further information about the secret key matrix $\mathbf{M}_{base}$ can be obtained unless the error term $err$ and constant $\beta_1$ and $\beta_2$ are known.

*Key confidentiality* against the QU comes from the fact that the encrypted query vector sent to the QU is of the form of Eq. 2. When QU multiplies matrix $\mathbf{N}'^{-1}$ to Eq. 2 the equation evaluates to

$$\hat{\mathbf{q}}\mathbf{N}'^{-1} = \beta_2(\mathbf{M}_{sec}\mathbf{q}''_{\eta\eta} + \mathbf{E} \cdot \mathbf{N}'^{-1}) \qquad (6)$$

Here $\mathbf{q}''_{\eta\eta}$ is a diagonal matrix with diagonal elements $(\beta_1\mathbf{q}, 1, \mathbf{x}, \mathbf{0}_\epsilon)$.

In Eq. 6, query user knows matrix $\mathbf{q}''_{\eta\eta}$ and $\mathbf{N}'^{-1}$. As the QU can ask queries of any form, he can construct a query of his choice to extract maximum information about the secret key matrix used for the data encryption. Below we tried to cover each possible queries a QU can frame and tried to analyze key confidentiality against the query user.

- Case 1: Query user constructs a query with all query elements set to 1 and send the query vector as shown below for encryption

$$\dot{\mathbf{q}} = \mathbf{1N}$$

The received query after the removal of $\mathbf{N}$ will be of the following form

$$\tilde{\mathbf{q}} = \beta_2(\mathbf{M}_{sec}\mathbf{1} + \mathbf{EN}'^{-1})$$

Here the value of $\mathbf{E}$ and $\beta_2$ are unknown to the QU. So he can not get meaningful information about the secret key matrix $\mathbf{M}_{sec}$.
- Case 2: The QU constructs a query by setting the first element to non-zero, rest all zeros, and sends it for encryption. On the received encrypted query, when the QU removes his encryption layer by multiplying $\mathbf{N}'^{-1}$, the obtained query has a form as shown below.

$$
\begin{aligned}
\tilde{\mathbf{q}} = \beta_2 &\begin{pmatrix} m_{11} & m_{12} & \cdots & m_{1\eta} \\ m_{21} & m_{22} & \cdots & m_{2\eta} \\ \vdots & \vdots & \ddots & \vdots \\ m_{\eta 1} & m_{\eta 2} & \cdots & m_{\eta\eta} \end{pmatrix} \begin{pmatrix} 1 \\ 0 \\ \vdots \\ 0 \end{pmatrix} + \beta_2 \begin{pmatrix} E_{11}N_{11}^{-1} & E_{12}N_{22}^{-1} & \cdots & E_{1\eta}N_{\eta\eta}^{-1} \\ E_{21}N_{11}^{-1} & E_{22}N_{22}^{-1} & \cdots & E_{2\eta}N_{\eta\eta}^{-1} \\ \vdots & \vdots & \ddots & \vdots \\ E_{\eta 1}N_{11}^{-1} & E_{\eta 2}N_{22}^{-1} & \cdots & E_{\eta\eta}N_{\eta\eta}^{-1} \end{pmatrix} \\
= \beta_2 &\begin{pmatrix} m_{11} + E_{11}N_{11}^{-1} & E_{12}N_{22}^{-1} & \cdots & E_{1\eta}N_{\eta\eta}^{-1} \\ m_{21} + E_{21}N_{11}^{-1} & E_{22}N_{22}^{-1} & \cdots & E_{2\eta}N_{\eta\eta}^{-1} \\ \vdots & \vdots & \ddots & \vdots \\ m_{\eta 1} + E_{\eta 1}N_{11}^{-1} & E_{\eta 2}N_{22}^{-1} & \cdots & E_{\eta\eta}N_{\eta\eta}^{-1} \end{pmatrix}
\end{aligned} \tag{7}
$$

From Eq. 7 without the knowledge of error matrix $\mathbf{E}$ and constant $\beta_2$ no information about the secret matrix $\mathbf{M}_{base}$ can be retrieved. Furthermore, for each new query secret matrix $\mathbf{M}_{sec}$ keeps on changing making the secret key retrieval impossible.

*Known Plaintext Attack:* Assuming a CSP with an encrypted database has access to a polynomial number of plaintext data vectors, he can perform a known plaintext attack as shown in [13]. However, the same attack is not possible in the proposed encryption scheme; this is because in [13], ASPE computes the exact value of $\mathbf{p}_i \cdot \mathbf{q}$ to compare $k$-NN, which is later exploited using known plaintext data vectors to break the query confidentiality and later data privacy of the encryption scheme. However, extending this to the proposed encryption scheme is impossible because we do not compute the exact distance to compute $k$-NN in the proposed encryption scheme. In the proposed encryption scheme, only the relative distance is compared to find the $k$-NN, as shown below.

$$
\begin{aligned}
(\mathbf{p}_i'' - \mathbf{p}_j'')\tilde{\mathbf{q}}_{vec} &= \beta_1\beta_2[(||\mathbf{p}_i||^2 - 2p_{i1}q_1 - \cdots - 2p_{id}q_d + ||\mathbf{q}||^2) - (||\mathbf{p}_j||^2 - 2p_{j1}q_1 \\
&\quad - \cdots - 2p_{jd}q_d + ||\mathbf{q}||^2)] + \beta_2(err_i' - err_j') \\
&= \beta_1\beta_2[||\mathbf{p}_i||^2 - 2p_{i1}q_1 - \cdots - 2p_{id}q_d + 2p_{j1}q_1 + \cdots + 2p_{jd}q_d \\
&\quad - ||\mathbf{p}_j||^2] + \beta_2(err_i' - err_j')
\end{aligned}
$$

From the above equations, without the knowledge of $\beta_1, \beta_2$ and $(err'_i - err'_j)$, the CSP can not frame linear equations to retrieve the query vector $\mathbf{q}$ uniquely. Thus, we can not retrieve $\mathbf{q}$ from the above equations.

# 6  Performance Evaluation

This section will analyze the cost of our proposed encryption scheme, viz., the computation and communication costs.

## 6.1  Computation Cost

The computational complexity of different steps of the proposed encryption scheme is presented in Table 2. DO generates different secrets for the key generation step, including the secret matrix $\mathbf{M}_{base}$. Thus, the computational complexity of the KeyGen step of the proposed encryption evaluates to $O(\eta^2)$. For the database encryption, DO multiplies $m$ data vectors–each enhanced to $\eta$-dimensional vector for security, with the secret matrix $\mathbf{M}_{base}^{-1}$. Thus, the total computational complexity of database encryption evaluates to $O(m\eta^2)$.

Query encryption is performed in three steps, with QU performing the first step. In this step, the QU samples the diagonal matrix $\mathbf{N}$ and multiplies it with the query vector. This requires multiplication of $d$ diagonal elements with $d$-dimensional query vector. So, the total computational cost evaluates to $O(d)$. The DO performs the second step of the query encryption by sampling a secret matrix $\mathbf{M}_t$ and multiplying it with the base secret key matrix $\mathbf{M}_{base}$, which is later multiplied with the query vector – enhanced to $\eta$ dimension. Thus, the total computational complexity of this step evaluates to $O(\eta^3)$. The third and final step of query encryption is performed by the QU, which multiplies $\mathbf{N}'^{-1}$ to the received query vector, evaluating the total computational cost of this step to $O(\eta^3)$. Thus, the overall computational complexity of the query encryption evaluates to $O(\eta^3)$.

The computational cost of $k$-NN evaluation using the proposed encryption scheme evaluates to $O(m\eta \log k)$. This is because it requires the multiplication of $m$ data vectors with $\eta$-dimension with a query vector of the same dimension and comparing the distances to figure out the $k$-NN.

**Table 2.** Computation complexity of the proposed encryption scheme

| Process | DO | QU | CSP | Total |
|---|---|---|---|---|
| Key Generation | $O(\eta^2)$ | $O(1)$ | - | $O(\eta^2)$ |
| Database Encryption | $O(m\eta^2)$ | - | - | $O(m\eta^2)$ |
| Query Encryption | $O(\eta^3)$ | $O(\eta^3)$ | - | $O(\eta^3)$ |
| $k$-NN Computation | - | - | $O(m\eta \log k)$ | $O(m\eta \log k)$ |

## 6.2    Communication Cost

Considering the proposed encryption scheme's communication cost, the initial key generation and database encryption involve only DO. Thus, zero communication cost is required in this step. Considering each tuple of encrypted query vectors as $\log n$ bits, QU sends $d$-dimensional encrypted query to the DO. DO encrypts it and sends the encrypted matrix of $\eta^2$ elements. Thus, the total communication cost between DO and QU equals $O(\eta^2 \log n)$ bits. The encrypted query vector is then sent to CSP for $k$-NN computation with a communication cost of $O(\eta \log n)$ bits. Finally, CSP returns computed $k$-NN result with communication cost equivalent to $O(kc)$ bits, where $c = \lceil \log(\mathbb{L}) \rceil$, here $L$ represents the total number of labels in the database.

## 7    Empirical Evaluation

This section will cover the empirical performance of the proposed encryption scheme presented in Sect. 5, it also covers performance analysis in detail with respect to the earlier encryption schemes, viz. Zhu et al. [26] for varying dimensions and the number of samples considering synthetic database generated using some computer programs.

### 7.1    Experiment Setup

We have implemented the encryption scheme proposed in Sect. 5 and Zhu et al. [26] in Python. The security parameters of both the encryption schemes have been fixed to $c = 5$ and $\epsilon = 5$. Paillier encryption scheme with a key size of 1024 bits is used to maintain query privacy between QU and DO in the case of Zhu et al. All experiments are performed on an Intel Core $i7 - 8700$ CPU @$3.20GHz \times 12$ with 32 GB RAM running Ubuntu 22.04.

### 7.2    Experiments Performed

To better analyze the encryption scheme, we have performed five experiments. Each of these experiments has been covered in detail below.

*Encryption Time-Varying Dimension:* To compare the encryption time of the proposed encryption schemes, we have created a database for varying dimensions starting from 10 up to 100 in a step of 10, keeping the number of samples fixed to 100, 000. The behavior of the encryption schemes has been plotted and is shown in Fig. 2a. The figure shows that the run time of the proposed encryption scheme increases linearly with dimension and behaves almost similarly to that of the Zhu encryption scheme. The minute difference in the figure is caused by removing the permutation function used in the Zhu et al. [26].

*Encryption Time Varying Samples:* To compare the data encryption time of the proposed encryption scheme, we have kept the dimension of the encryption

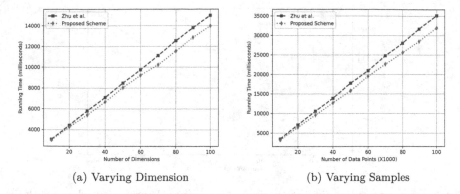

(a) Varying Dimension          (b) Varying Samples

**Fig. 2.** Comparison of the data encryption time of the proposed encryption scheme with that of the Zhu encryption scheme for varying dimensions with data samples fixed to $n = 100,000$ (a) and varying number of data samples with data dimension fixed to $d = 10$ (b).

scheme fixed as 10 and varied the number of samples starting from $100,000$ to $1,000,000$ in the step of $100,000$. The behavior of the encryption scheme has been plotted and is shown in Fig. 2b. From Fig. 2b, it is clear that with an increase in the number of samples keeping the dimension fixed, both the encryption schemes behave similarly, and the slight difference in the encryption time between the two is caused by the permutation function used in the Zhu encryption scheme.

*Query Encryption Time-Varying Dimension:* The main contribution of this work lies in query encryption; thus, it is most important to show the outcome of the new way of encrypting the query vector. Figure 3 shows the same for varying dimensions in a step of 10. From Fig. 3, it is clear that the new way of encrypting the query vector significantly reduces the query encryption time compared to the earlier encryption scheme. This is because it involves simple matrix multiplication operations, compared to the operation involved in the Zhu et al. [26], which requires query encryption by the Paillier encryption scheme.

*k-NN Computation Time for Varying Number of Samples and Dimensions:* Figure 4a and 4b shows the secure $k$-NN computation time for varying number of samples and dimensions and is also compared with that of the plaintext $k$-NN computation time. The figures show that $k$-NN computation in the encrypted environment remains almost similar for both encryption schemes and is slightly higher than that of the plaintext computation time. From Fig. 4a and 4b, it is clear that the computational overhead of computing $k$-NN in the encrypted domain is negligible in comparison to the plaintext domain. Thus, the proposed encryption scheme perfectly suits for the practical applications.

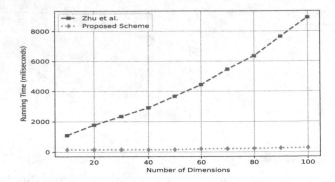

**Fig. 3.** Query encryption time comparison of the proposed encryption scheme with the Zhu encryption scheme for varying dimensions in a step size 10.

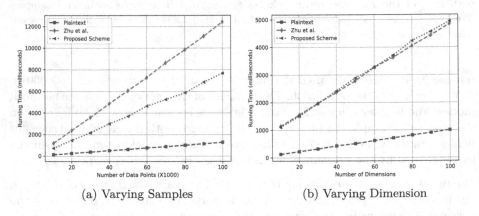

(a) Varying Samples                    (b) Varying Dimension

**Fig. 4.** $k$-nearest neighbor computation time for a varying number of data samples keeping dimension fixed to $d = 10$ (a) and varying number of data dimensions keeping data samples fixed to $n = 100,000$) (b) for $k = 20$.

## 8    Conclusion

The work presented in this paper suggests performing query encryption in an untrusted query user setting of the ASPE encryption scheme without compromising the query privacy of the QU. The new way of performing query encryption replaces the Paillier encryption technique used in the earlier work, which required comparatively higher computation time; as a result, it may not be suggestable for real-world applications. This work tries to fix this issue by removing the Pailler cryptosystem used for query encryption and using the ASPE technique instead. Using the ASPE technique for query encryption increases the overhead of CSP's computation in the cloud, which requires preparing a temporary database for $k$-NN computation. However, this step can be avoided by directly multiplying the query obtained from the QU with the temporary matrix and using the obtained vector for $k$-NN computation. The work of this paper shows that query privacy using ASPE alone is achievable, and the experimental result indicates a considerable reduction in query encryption time. Using the ASPE technique for query encryption instead of the Paillier Cryptosystem performs better and is achievable without compromising the security requirements.

**Acknowledgments.** This work was supported by AI powered adaptive cyber defense framework and solution for national critical information infrastructure, National Cyber Security Council, Government of India.

# References

1. Ahmad, A., et al.: Parallel query execution over encrypted data in database-as-a-service (DaaS). J. Supercomput. **75**, 2269–2288 (2019)
2. Bost, R.: $\sum$ οφος: forward secure searchable encryption. In: Proceedings of the 2016 ACM SIGSAC Conference on Computer and Communications Security, pp. 1143–1154 (2016)
3. Cao, N., Wang, C., Li, M., Ren, K., Lou, W.: Privacy-preserving multi-keyword ranked search over encrypted cloud data. IEEE Trans. Parallel Distrib. Syst. **25**(1), 222–233 (2013)
4. Cash, D., et al.: Dynamic searchable encryption in very-large databases: data structures and implementation. Cryptology ePrint Archive (2014)
5. Chase, M., Kamara, S.: Structured encryption and controlled disclosure. In: Abe, M. (ed.) ASIACRYPT 2010. LNCS, vol. 6477, pp. 577–594. Springer, Heidelberg (2010). https://doi.org/10.1007/978-3-642-17373-8_33
6. Choi, S., Ghinita, G., Lim, H.S., Bertino, E.: Secure KNN query processing in untrusted cloud environments. IEEE Trans. Knowl. Data Eng. **26**(11), 2818–2831 (2014)
7. Demertzis, I., Papadopoulos, S., Papapetrou, O., Deligiannakis, A., Garofalakis, M.: Practical private range search revisited. In: Proceedings of the 2016 International Conference on Management of Data, pp. 185–198 (2016)
8. Faber, S., Jarecki, S., Krawczyk, H., Nguyen, Q., Rosu, M., Steiner, M.: Rich queries on encrypted data: beyond exact matches. In: Pernul, G., Ryan, P.Y.A., Weippl, E. (eds.) ESORICS 2015. LNCS, vol. 9327, pp. 123–145. Springer, Cham (2015). https://doi.org/10.1007/978-3-319-24177-7_7
9. Fuller, B., et al.: SoK: cryptographically protected database search. In: 2017 IEEE Symposium on Security and Privacy (SP), pp. 172–191. IEEE (2017)
10. Guan, Y., Lu, R., Zheng, Y., Shao, J., Wei, G.: Toward oblivious location-based k-nearest neighbor query in smart cities. IEEE Internet Things J. **8**(18), 14219–14231 (2021)
11. Li, H., Yang, Y., Luan, T.H., Liang, X., Zhou, L., Shen, X.S.: Enabling fine-grained multi-keyword search supporting classified sub-dictionaries over encrypted cloud data. IEEE Trans. Dependable Secure Comput. **13**(3), 312–325 (2015)
12. Li, X., Xiang, T., Guo, S., Li, H., Mu, Y.: Privacy-preserving reverse nearest neighbor query over encrypted spatial data. IEEE Trans. Serv. Comput. **15**(5), 2954–2968 (2021)
13. Lin, W., Wang, K., Zhang, Z., Chen, H.: Revisiting security risks of asymmetric scalar product preserving encryption and its variants. In: 2017 IEEE 37th International Conference on Distributed Computing Systems (ICDCS), pp. 1116–1125. IEEE (2017)

14. Liu, J., Wang, C., Tu, Z., Wang, X.A., Lin, C., Li, Z.: Secure KNN classification scheme based on homomorphic encryption for cyberspace. Secur. Commun. Netw. **2021**, 1–12 (2021)
15. Oh, D., Kim, I., Kim, K., Lee, S.M., Ro, W.W.: Highly secure mobile devices assisted with trusted cloud computing environments. ETRI J. **37**(2), 348–358 (2015)
16. Raja, J., Ramakrishnan, M.: Confidentiality-preserving based on attribute encryption using auditable access during encrypted records in cloud location. J. Supercomput. **76**, 6026–6039 (2020)
17. Sanyashi, T., Menezes, B.: Secure computation over encrypted databases. CoRR abs/2308.02878 (2023). https://doi.org/10.48550/arXiv.2308.02878
18. Song, D.X., Wagner, D., Perrig, A.: Practical techniques for searches on encrypted data. In: Proceeding 2000 IEEE Symposium on Security and Privacy, S&P 2000, pp. 44–55. IEEE (2000)
19. Stefanov, E., Papamanthou, C., Shi, E.: Practical dynamic searchable encryption with small leakage. Cryptology ePrint Archive (2013)
20. Sun, W., et al.: Privacy-preserving multi-keyword text search in the cloud supporting similarity-based ranking. In: Proceedings of the 8th ACM SIGSAC Symposium on Information, Computer and Communications Security, pp. 71–82 (2013)
21. Wang, B., Yu, S., Lou, W., Hou, Y.T.: Privacy-preserving multi-keyword fuzzy search over encrypted data in the cloud. In: IEEE INFOCOM 2014-IEEE Conference on Computer Communications, pp. 2112–2120. IEEE (2014)
22. Wang, B., Hou, Y., Li, M.: Practical and secure nearest neighbor search on encrypted large-scale data. In: IEEE INFOCOM 2016-The 35th Annual IEEE International Conference on Computer Communications, pp. 1–9. IEEE (2016)
23. Wong, W.K., Cheung, D.W.l., Kao, B., Mamoulis, N.: Secure KNN computation on encrypted databases. In: Proceedings of the 2009 ACM SIGMOD International Conference on Management of Data, pp. 139–152 (2009)
24. Yu, J., Lu, P., Zhu, Y., Xue, G., Li, M.: Toward secure multikeyword top-k retrieval over encrypted cloud data. IEEE Trans. Dependable Secure Comput. **10**(4), 239–250 (2013)
25. Zheng, Y., Lu, R., Shao, J.: Achieving efficient and privacy-preserving k-NN query for outsourced ehealthcare data. J. Med. Syst. **43**, 1–13 (2019)
26. Zhu, Y., Huang, Z., Takagi, T.: Secure and controllable k-NN query over encrypted cloud data with key confidentiality. J. Parallel Distrib. Comput. **89**, 1–12 (2016)

# A Multi-stage Multi-modal Classification Model for DeepFakes Combining Deep Learned and Computer Vision Oriented Features

Arnab Kumar Das[✉], Soumik Mukhopadhyay, Arijit Dalui,
Ritaban Bhattacharya, and Ruchira Naskar

Department of Information Technology, Indian Institute of Engineering Science and
Technology, Shibpur 711103, India
{2020itp008_arnab,510819102.soumik,510819100.arijit,510819101.ritaban}
@students.iiests.ac.in, ruchira@it.iiests.ac.in

**Abstract.** Recent advances in deep learning have empowered media synthesis and alteration to achieve levels of realism that were previously unheard of. Artificial intelligence is a potent tool that may be used to modify digital data, such as images, videos, and audio files, through the use of emerging deepfake technologies. Deepfake technology has the potential to significantly affect the reliability of multimedia data through the synthesis of fake media. Significant ramifications arise from this for individuals, organizations, and society at large. With the pace and accessibility of social media, convincing deepfakes can swiftly reach millions of people and adversely influence public opinion. To this end, we propose a multi-modal feature-based classification model that can distinguish between deepfake and real videos efficiently. We have used prefabricated image features as well as a variety of Convolutional Neural Network (CNN) model-generated features, including ResNet50, ResNet101, VGG16, and VGG19. The fake videos are taken up for further investigation to detect their source of origin. We propose a CNN-based classifier for deepfake detection and also explore the efficiency of multiple feature-based classifiers in this respect. This enables us to evaluate the comparative performance of both. The proposed model achieves an accuracy of 99.06% on deepfake classification and 98.75% on source identification when tested on a publicly available FaceForensics++ dataset.

**Keywords:** Artificial Intelligence · Convolutional Neural Network · Digital Forensics · Deepfakes · Faceforensics

## 1 Introduction

Digital manipulation of human facial images or videos involves superimposing artificial or synthetic features or expressions onto the face of an individual to generate a synthetic image or video of the person. This is done using powerful artificial intelligence (AI) tools and techniques, preliminary among which in today's date is Generative Adversarial Network (GAN) based tools. One of the most popular GAN-based synthetic video creation tools in today's date is *DeepFake*, which is capable of superimposing an individual's facial movement and speech onto another [1]. Such synthetic videos are prone to be misused in personal defamation cases, child pornography-related crimes, and in misleading court cases and the society at large. Deepfakes were born in 2017 when a Reddit user of the same name posted doctored porn clips on the site [2]. The videos swapped the faces of celebrities - Gal Gadot, Taylor Swift, Scarlett Johansson, and others - onto porn performers. Deepfake videos have recently been reported to have been used as a political weapon during elections. During the run-up to the 2020 US elections, Facebook banned Deepfake and its synthesized videos in order to stop the spread of misinformation [3]. Shin et al. [4] showed how the use of deepfake video, as opposed to genuine video in a news piece, influences the behavior common mass. For stakeholders, the fraudulent, false, and abusive use of this technology has created more risks than opportunities and this was studied by Kwok et al. in [5].

Among the recent studies on challenges of deepFake detection, the one by Lyu [6] is among one of the most noteworthy. With the metaverse gaining popularity rapidly, concerns about the adverse impacts of deepfakes have grown paramount. Tariq et al. in [7], have explored the effects of deepfakes on the metaverse including security risks and impersonations in online meetings. Researchers in recent times have started exploring possibilities of detecting deepfakes from multiple modes. On similar lines, among the very recent works, Yang et al. [8] proposed an audio-visual joint learning platform for detecting deepfakes, where the authors have adopted a temporal-spatial encoder for deepfake detection.

In this paper, we present a blind deepFake video detection system, where we investigate the efficiency of both feature-based and deep neural network-based classifiers. For this purpose, we propose a multimodal detection technique by combining an efficient set of prefabricated *Histogram of Oriented Gradients* (HOG) based features, and a set of features automatically learned by Convolutional Neural Networks (CNNs). Our contributions in this paper may be summarized as follows: (1) Development of a multimodal DeepFake detection scheme combining both deep learning and traditional computer vision techniques, hence optimizing performance efficiency. (2) We propose a multi-stage classification approach, for identifying a DeepFake video, followed by identifying its source network using the above set of features. (3) We explore and investigate the roles of both deep neural network-based and feature-based classifiers.

The rest of the paper is organized as follows. The proposed multi-stage multimodal deepfake classification architecture is presented in Sect. 2. Experimental results and discussion are presented in Sect. 3. The paper is concluded in Sect. 4.

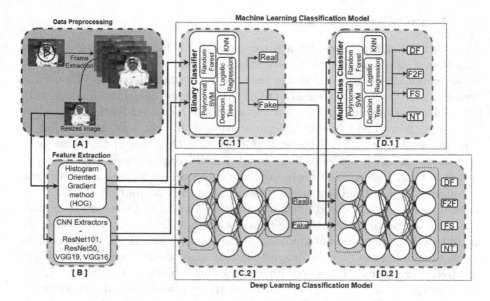

**Fig. 1.** Workflow of the proposed method having 4 stages. **(A) Data Pre-processing**: Extracts frames from a video and resize them into 64 × 128 pixels. **(B) Feature Extraction**: Extract features from the frames using HOG and CNN models. **(C and D) Classification using Machine Learning and Proposed Deep Learning approaches**: A binary classifier followed by a multi-class classifier to distinguish between a real and a fake image and further identify the fake as Deepfakes, Face2Face, FaceSwap, or NeuralTextures.

## 2 Proposed Multi-stage Multi-modal DeepFake Video Identification

We have divided the present task of identifying DeepFakes, into two distinct stages. The first stage consists of detecting whether a contentious video is fake or real; and the second stage of investigation involves identifying the source of a video, in case the video has been detected to be fake. In this paper, we consider four sources of deepfake videos provided by the FaceForensics++ [9] dataset, viz. *DeepFake* [10], *NeuralTexture* [11], *FaceSwap* [12], and *Face2Face* [12].

Summarily, in order to accurately determine if a video is real or fraudulent, we construct a feature extraction module and classification module, to operate on individual video frames (Module I). If this module predicts that the test video is fake, we combine the feature extraction module from Module I with a second multilevel classification module to accurately identify the type of fake video (Deepfake, NeuralTexture, FaceSwap, or Face2Face video). The architecture and major components of the modposed modules have been presented Fig. 1.

## 2.1   Feature Extraction Module

As evident from Fig. 1, we use a feature extraction block to create a feature map from a video. In this work, we combine both deep-learned features as well as conventional prefabricated image features for deepfake detection. We use the Histogram of Oriented Gradients (HOG) [13] feature descriptors, along with four different Convolutional Neural Network (CNN) based feature extractors for this purpose. The CNN architectures explored in this work are: ResNet-50 [14], ResNet-101 [15], VGG-16, and VGG-19 [16]. Our aim in this work is to investigate the effectiveness of both prefabricated image features (as the HOG) and deep CNN-learned features in deepfake detection. HOG features have been prevalently used in the literature for determining the distribution of image gradient orientations in focused areas of an image [13]. HOG features are capable of identifying patterns and texture information in an image, by computing the magnitude and orientation of gradients of the pixels. It calculates the image gradient. Combining the image is magnitude and angle yields the gradient. $\mathcal{GR}_{(x)}$ and $\mathcal{GR}_{(y)}$ are initially calculated for each pixel in a block of $3 \times 3$ pixels. $\mathcal{IM}$ is for an image, while $r,c$ stands for the respective row and column. Equation 1 is used to compute $\mathcal{GR}_{(x)}$ and $\mathcal{GR}_{(y)}$ first for each pixel value, and then magnitude $(\mathcal{MA})$ and angle $(\Theta)$ of each pixel are calculated using Eq. 2.

$$\mathcal{GR}_{(x)} = \mathcal{IM}(r, c+1) - \mathcal{IM}(r, c-1); \mathcal{GR}_{(y)} = \mathcal{IM}(r-1, c) - \mathcal{IM}(r+1, c) \quad (1)$$

$$\mathcal{MA} = \sqrt{\mathcal{GR}_{(x)}^2 + \mathcal{GR}_{(y)}^2}; \Theta = \left| tan^{-1} \frac{\mathcal{GR}_{(y)}}{\mathcal{GR}_{(x)}} \right| \quad (2)$$

The next mode of feature extraction in this work is the features learned in an automated way by deep CNNs. The ResNet architecture involves a number of residual blocks, each of which has a batch normalization layer, a Rectifier Linear Unit (ReLU) [17] activation function, and one or more convolutional layers. ResNet50 [14] and ResNet101 [15] are 50- and 101-layer deep convolutional neural network architectures, respectively. Deep convolutional neural network architectures VGG-16 and VGG-19 [16], combine a deep stack of convolutional layers with tiny filters. These models can capture both local and global features in an image, including edges, textures, and object forms, making them useful for feature extraction in synthesized frames. The above CNNs are used here as feature extractors by removing the last classification layer and passing test video frames through the network, to obtain a fixed-length feature vector. This feature vector is later used in our classification step, to distinguish between fake and authentic videos.

## 2.2   Feature Based Classification

The classification module is responsible for performing a binary classification between fake and real videos, as well as for detecting the source of a deepfake

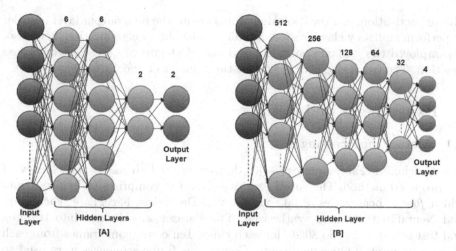

**Fig. 2.** Proposed CNN. [A] Model for deepFake detection. [B] Model for source classification.

video by performing a four-way classification. The proposed classification module uses five different classifiers - Polynomial Kernel SVM [18], Random Forest [19], Decision Tree [20], K Nearest Neighbor (KNN) [21], Logistic Regression [22]. In this paper, we introduced two different CNN models for binary and multiclass classification purposes. We also highlight the distinctions between the proposed CNN model classifier and the machine learning classifier.

For classification, we use the feature maps generated by the CNNs presented in Sect. 2.1 as well as the HOG features. Once the model determines a frame to be fake, it undergoes multi-way classification to determine whether it is Deepfake [10], Face2Face [23], FaceSwap [12] or NeuralTextures [11]. Our experimental results with related discussions are presented next.

## 2.3 Deep Learning-Based Classification

For deepfake classification as well as source identification, we adopt a one-dimensional convolutional neural network (CNN) shown in Fig. 2. We use the "glorot_uniform" as a kernel initializer for deepfake detection and source classification. During training, vanishing and exploding gradients can be an issue; "glorot_uniform" helps to alleviate this. Gradients in deep neural networks can become extremely small (vanishing) or extremely huge (exploding), which makes training difficult. The weights are kept within a range using "glorot_uniform", which helps to prevent these problems. In both classification techniques, we use the 3 × 3 kernel size. For deepfake detection, we employed three hidden layers, the "ReLu" activation function, and the "SoftMax" function at the final output. The loss function used is "Categorical Cross Entropy", and the optimizer used is "Adam" optimizer, in our model. In deepfake classification, we use batch sizes 16 and 50 epochs. For source classification, we employed five hidden layers, the

222    A. K. Das et al.

"ReLu" activation, and the "SoftMax" function for the final output layer in order to perform multiway classification. Similar to the binary classification, here also, we employed the "Adam" optimizer and the "Categorical Cross Entropy" loss function. The batch size here is 32, and the number of epochs is 100.

# 3  Experiments and Results

## 3.1  Data Preprocessing

The benchmark FaceForensics++ [9] dataset is used to assess the efficacy of the proposed method. The FaceForensics++ dataset comprises real videos, from which *four* subcategories of fake videos, viz. Deepfakes, Face2Face, FaceSwap, and NeuralTextures were synthesized. The dataset was divided into training and test sets in the ratio 80:20, for each class. Ten contiguous frames from each video were used in our experiments. Contiguous frame sequences were used so as to exploit the synchronization factor of frame edges. Among the two different compression rates available, we have chosen the c23 version here. The frames were further downsized from their original $720 \times 1080$ resolution to $64 \times 128$.

## 3.2  Feature Extraction

We generate a feature map containing 3780 features per video frame using HOG. The retrieved features from ResNet and VGG were substantially more numerous and may have had several outliers. In order to extract principle features in each of these extracted feature maps, we reduced the dimensionality using PCA [24] to 1500, while keeping computational power constraints and outliers in mind. PCA maximizes the variance along each axis, or principle component, by transforming

**Fig. 3.** Confusion Matrices of best results of Fake Video Detection. **[A]** HOG Polynomial SVM **[B]** ResNet101 Polynomial SVM **[C]** ResNet50 Random Forest **[D]** VGG16 Random Forest **[E]** VGG19 Random Forest **[F]** Proposed CNN Classifier.

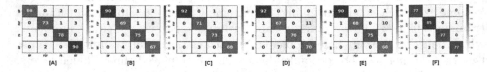

**Fig. 4.** Confusion Matrices of best results of Source Classification. **[A]** HOG Polynomial SVM **[B]** ResNet101 Logistic Regression **[C]** ResNet50 Logistic Regression **[D]** VGG16 Logistic Regression **[E]** VGG19 Logistic Regression **[F]** Proposed CNN Classifier.

**Table 1.** Feature-based binary classification results for fake vs. real video detection.

| Extractor | Polynomial kernel SVM | | Decision Tree | | Random Forest | | Logistic Regression | | KNN | |
|---|---|---|---|---|---|---|---|---|---|---|
| | Accuracy | FI-Score | Accuracy | FI-Score | Accuracy | FI-Score | Accuracy | FI-Score | Accuracy | FI-Score |
| HOG | 98.91% | 98.12 | 94.87% | 95.93 | 95.75% | 97.49 | 92.11% | 92.13 | 98.25% | 99.37 |
| VGG-16 | 98.59% | 99.69 | 97.56% | 96.87 | 98.91% | 99.37 | 96.68% | 98.68 | 96.62% | 95.92 |
| VGG-19 | 98.09% | 98.44 | 96.88% | 95.61 | 98.44% | 100 | 98.03% | 98.02 | 96.72% | 96.55 |
| ResNet 50 | 98.59% | 99.69 | 97.69% | 97.81 | 98.81% | 98.44 | 98.68% | 96.68 | 98.62% | 97.81 |
| ResNet 101 | 98.91% | 98.13 | 98.00% | 98.00 | 98.75% | 99.37 | 96.08% | 96.07 | 98.22% | 97.81 |

**Table 2.** Feature-based multi-way classification results for source detection of fake videos.

| Extractor | Polynomial kernel SVM | | Decision Tree | | Random Forest | | Logistic Regression | | KNN | |
|---|---|---|---|---|---|---|---|---|---|---|
| | Accuracy | FI-Score | Accuracy | FI-Score | Accuracy | FI-Score | Accuracy | FI-Score | Accuracy | FI-Score |
| HOG | 98.56% | 97.18 | 71.86% | 74.28 | 95.56% | 94.99 | 68.61% | 69.26 | 69.79% | 66.50 |
| VGG-16 | 81.74% | 79.24 | 81.11% | 81.45 | 97.50% | 97.48 | 98.44% | 97.49 | 84.24% | 82.36 |
| VGG-19 | 58.79% | 22.14 | 60.48% | 61.50 | 87.49% | 9.60 | 95.12% | 95.62 | 78.42% | 76.23 |
| ResNet 50 | 70.54% | 68.52 | 55.29% | 57.22 | 82.74% | 88.77 | 95.31% | 94.97 | 79.11% | 77.33 |
| ResNet 101 | 66.29% | 64.70 | 58.72% | 59.88 | 83.62% | 86.24 | 94.93% | 93.73 | 76.30% | 76.89 |

the data into a new coordinate system. To ascertain which is best, the resulting feature maps were examined using both binary and multi-class classifiers using different types of machine learning models and proposed deep learning models.

### 3.3  Fake Video Detection and Source Classification

**Feature-Based Detection and Classification Results.** The classification results for both stages, binary and four-way, are presented in Table 1 and Table 2, respectively. All results presented are outcomes of a 15-fold cross-validation. The best results were seen obtained for binary fake vs. actual video classification with the Polynomial SVM classifier on HOG and Resnet-101 extracted features, with an accuracy of 98.91% and F1-score of 98.12 and 98.13 respectively. For source identification, that is four-way classification, the best results were obtained with the Polynomial SVM classifier on HOG extracted features, with an accuracy of 98.56% and F1-score of 97.18.

To further analyze the performance of the best classification models with the most efficient sets of features in our work, we present the confusion matrices generated through our experiments for select sets of classifiers with the best feature sets in Fig. 3 and Fig. 4. Also, a comparison of performances of the above classifier-feature pairs has been presented in the form of a bar chart in Fig. 5.

**Classification Results Obtained by Proposed CNN Model.** The performance evaluation results of the proposed deep neural network have been presented in Table 3. We found that the ResNet101 feature extraction strategy produced the best results for deepfake detection in our model with an accuracy of 99.06% and F1 score of 99.06. For source classification, the VGG19 feature

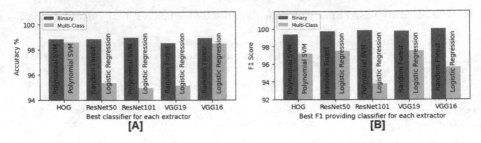

**Fig. 5.** Comparing the best results obtained in binary classification and source detection models for each feature extractor. **[A]** Accuracy Comparison **[B]** F1-Score Comparison

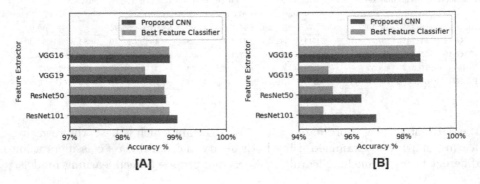

**Fig. 6.** Performance of proposed deep CNN model vs. the best classifier for corresponding feature set. **[A]** Deepfake detection performance. **[B]** Source classification performance.

**Table 3.** Proposed deep learning model's performance for both fake video identification and source classification.

| Problem | Extractor | | | | | | | |
|---------|-----------|---|---|---|---|---|---|---|
| | ResNet101 | | ResNet50 | | VGG19 | | VGG16 | |
| | Accuracy | F1 Score | Accuracy | F1 Score | Accuracy | F1 Score | Accuracy | F1 Score |
| Deepfake Detection | 99.06% | 99.06 | 98.44% | 98.38 | 98.75% | 98.75 | 98.44% | 98.42 |
| Source Classification | 95.94% | 95.62 | 94.38% | 94.37 | 98.75% | 98.75 | 98.44% | 98.44 |

extractor produced the best results in our model, with an accuracy of 98.75% and F1 score of 98.75. The confusion matrices for fake video detection and source classification are presented in Fig. 3 and Fig. 4, respectively. The comparison of the best feature-based classifier against the proposed CNN classifiers (both fed on CNN generated features), is done and reported in Fig. 6.

# 4   Conclusion

In this paper, we propose a multi-stage approach for detecting deepfake media followed by its source generator network investigation, using a combination of deep network learned and prefabricated image features. We employ both feature based classification, as well as deep learning based CNN to solve the above problems. Our observation is that the proposed CNN model outperforms the feature based classifier, in most cases. However, with the HoG texture features, the polynomial SVM classifier obtains the best performance. Our experiments show that different feature extraction methods can successfully recover local and global image data, including texture and structural elements that are helpful in differentiating between real and synthetic media. Additionally, we demonstrate different classifiers' and proposed CNN model's strengths in learning complicated decision boundaries in the given problem, in a high-dimensional feature space. We have performed 15-fold cross-validation to overcome over-fitting. The future scope of work in this direction will include the development of dedicated recurrent neural network for investigating features enabling the classification of deepfakes generated by newer classes of generative adversarial network-based synthetic media-generating models.

# References

1. Goodfellow, I.J., et al.: Generative adversarial networks (2014)
2. Flynn, A., Clough, J., Cooke, T.: Disrupting and preventing deepfake abuse: exploring criminal law responses to AI-facilitated abuse. In: Powell, A., Flynn, A., Sugiura, L. (eds.) The Palgrave Handbook of Gendered Violence and Technology, pp. 583–603. Palgrave Macmillan, Cham (2021). https://doi.org/10.1007/978-3-030-83734-1_29
3. Temir, E.: Deepfake: new era in the age of disinformation & end of reliable journalism. Selçuk İletişim **13**(2), 1009–1024 (2020)
4. Shin, S.Y., Lee, J.: The effect of deepfake video on news credibility and corrective influence of cost-based knowledge about deepfakes. Digit. Journal. **10**(3), 412–432 (2022)
5. Kwok, A.O.J., Koh, S.G.M.: Deepfake: a social construction of technology perspective. Curr. Issue Tour. **24**(13), 1798–1802 (2021)
6. Lyu, S.: Deepfake detection: current challenges and next steps. In: 2020 IEEE International Conference on Multimedia & Expo Workshops (ICMEW), pp. 1–6. IEEE (2020)
7. Tariq, S., Abuadbba, A., Moore, K.: Deepfake in the metaverse: security implications for virtual gaming, meetings, and offices. arXiv preprint arXiv:2303.14612 (2023)
8. Yang, W., et al.: Avoid-DF: audio-visual joint learning for detecting deepfake. IEEE Trans. Inf. Forensics Secur. **18**, 2015–2029 (2023)
9. Rossler, A., Cozzolino, D., Verdoliva, L., Riess, C., Thies, J., Nießner, M.: Faceforensics++: learning to detect manipulated facial images. In: Proceedings of the IEEE/CVF International Conference on Computer Vision, pp. 1–11 (2019)
10. Westerlund, M.: The emergence of deepfake technology: a review. Technol. Innov. Manag. Rev. **9**(11) (2019)

11. Thies, J., Zollhöfer, M., Nießner, M.: Deferred neural rendering: image synthesis using neural textures. ACM Trans. Graph. (TOG) **38**(4), 1–12 (2019)

12. Korshunova, I., Shi, W., Dambre, J., Theis, L.: Fast face-swap using convolutional neural networks. In: Proceedings of the IEEE International Conference on Computer Vision, pp. 3677–3685 (2017)

13. Dalal, N., Triggs, B.: Histograms of oriented gradients for human detection. In: 2005 IEEE Computer Society Conference on Computer Vision and Pattern Recognition (CVPR 2005), vol. 1, pp. 886–893. IEEE (2005)

14. Koonce, B.: Convolutional Neural Networks with Swift for Tensorflow: Image Recognition and Dataset Categorization. Springer, Cham (2021). https://doi.org/10.1007/978-1-4842-6168-2

15. He, K., Zhang, X., Ren, S., Sun, J.: Deep residual learning for image recognition. In: Proceedings of the IEEE Conference on Computer Vision and Pattern Recognition, pp. 770–778 (2016)

16. Simonyan, K., Zisserman, A.: Very deep convolutional networks for large-scale image recognition. arXiv preprint arXiv:1409.1556 (2014)

17. Agarap, A.F.: Deep learning using rectified linear units (ReLU). arXiv preprint arXiv:1803.08375 (2018)

18. Patle, A., Chouhan, D.S.: SVM kernel functions for classification. In: 2013 International Conference on Advances in Technology and Engineering (ICATE), pp. 1–9. IEEE (2013)

19. Breiman, L.: Random forests. Mach. Learn. **45**, 5–32 (2001)

20. Rokach, L., Maimon, O.: Decision trees. In: Data Mining and Knowledge Discovery Handbook, pp. 165–192 (2005)

21. Guo, G., Wang, H., Bell, D., Bi, Y., Greer, K.: KNN model-based approach in classification. In: Meersman, R., Tari, Z., Schmidt, D.C. (eds.) OTM 2003. LNCS, vol. 2888, pp. 986–996. Springer, Heidelberg (2003). https://doi.org/10.1007/978-3-540-39964-3_62

22. Abramovich, F., Grinshtein, V., Levy, T.: Multiclass classification by sparse multinomial logistic regression. IEEE Trans. Inf. Theory **67**(7), 4637–4646 (2021)

23. Thies, J., Zollhofer, M., Stamminger, M., Theobalt, C., Nießner, M.: Face2face: real-time face capture and reenactment of RGB videos. In: Proceedings of the IEEE Conference on Computer Vision and Pattern Recognition, pp. 2387–2395 (2016)

24. Jolliffe, I.T., Cadima, J.: Principal component analysis: a review and recent developments. Philos. Trans. R. Soc. A Math. Phys. Eng. Sci. **374**(2065), 20150202 (2016)

# Privacy

# Security and Privacy in Machine Learning

Nishanth Chandran$^{(\boxtimes)}$

Microsoft Research, Bengaluru, India
nichandr@microsoft.com

**Abstract.** Machine learning technologies have the potential to transform and revolutionize various industries, such as drug discovery by finding new molecules, medical diagnosis by analyzing images and signals, fraud prevention by detecting anomalies, and security by recognizing faces and objects. However, training and utilizing machine learning models requires handling large volumes of sensitive and private data. In this article, we discuss some of the security and privacy challenges in this process. We focus mainly on how we can securely compute machine learning algorithms over sensitive data, but we also describe data privacy problems in this domain and how we can mitigate them.

## 1 Introduction

Machine learning (ML) is a powerful technology that enables computers to learn from data and perform tasks that normally require human intelligence [5]. ML has applications in various domains, such as healthcare, finance, and governmental, where it can help improve diagnosis, treatment, prevention, and management of diseases [61]; optimize trading strategies, risk assessment, and fraud detection [46]; and enhance public services, security, and policy making [85]. However, ML also poses significant challenges for the security and privacy of data, as it often relies on sensitive and personal information from patients, customers, and citizens [94]. In this article, we will explore some of the main challenges and some solutions for ensuring the security and privacy of data for use in ML. We will specifically focus on secure computation [57,122] for machine learning and will also highlight some of the open challenges in ensuring a secure and private end-to-end machine learning pipeline.

One of the key challenges in ML is data sharing. Data is the fuel of ML, and more data usually leads to better performance and generalization. However, data sharing also entails risks of data leakage, misuse, or abuse. For example, in healthcare, data sharing can enable collaborative research and innovation among different hospitals, clinics, or researchers. However, it can also expose patients' confidential medical records or genomic data to unauthorized parties or malicious attacks. Similarly, in finance, data sharing can facilitate cross-border transactions and regulatory compliance. However, it can also compromise customers' financial information or transaction history. In governmental applications, data sharing can improve public administration and decision making. However, it can

V. Muthukkumarasamy et al. (Eds.): ICISS 2023, LNCS 14424, pp. 229–248, 2023.
https://doi.org/10.1007/978-3-031-49099-6_14

also violate citizens' privacy rights or reveal sensitive national security informa-tion. Therefore, there is a need for secure and privacy-preserving ML techniques that can enable data sharing without compromising data security or privacy.

## 1.1    Data Protection At-Rest and In-Transit

Traditional security techniques such as encryption and authentication [102] can provide data protection at-rest (e.g. while the data is stored on local machines or in the cloud) or while in-transit (e.g. while moving data from one machine to another). Authenticated Encryption [13] ensures that, as long as the decryption key is kept hidden, an attacker can neither learn anything about the contents of the message nor modify the contents of the message. Symmetric-key encryption mechanisms such as AES-128, AES-256 [36] are used when the two end points for communication can share the same key that is used both for encryption and decryption. On the other hand, public-key encryption such as RSA [10,105] and elliptic curve cryptography (ECC) [74] are used when the sender only has the recipient's public encryption key.

## 1.2    Data Protection for Machine Learning Tasks

While data protection at-rest and in-transit is a minimum requirement to protect data used in machine learning applications, there are several other considerations when computation on sensitive data must be performed. We first outline some of these security issues below:

1. **ML Training.** Typically, multiple entities contribute data to train a machine learning model. In the consumer context this could be end users (e.g. while training a model for auto completion [30]), while in the enterprise context this could be customers pooling in their data to derive better insights (e.g. while training a model for healthcare from multiple hospitals [92]). While training a model using data from such multiple sources, several security and privacy questions arise. Some of these include: a) where will the model be trained? b) is that compute region trusted by all entities?; and c) what does the model trained reveal about the raw data?

2. **ML Inference.** Once an ML model is trained, one would like to offer this model for inference to multiple entities. However, here too there are data secu-rity concerns. E.g. typically model publishers would not want to reveal their models in the clear to external entities in order to protect their intellectual property. At the same time, model consumers want the inference results of the model on sensitive input data. Hence, an important question is: can model publishers offer inference-as-a-service to model consumers while protecting their intellectual property while at the same time offering input privacy to the consumers [17,80,89]?

3. **Evaluation.** An intermediate step between training and inference is that of evaluation. While an ML model may have been trained on data from one geography (or one type of data), one may eventually want to use it in a

different geography or domain. In order to do this, one may have to choose the best model from many different models. To choose a good model, consumers would need to validate or evaluate the accuracy of the ML model on test datasets that they have curated. However, this test dataset itself may have to be kept private for several reasons (e.g. it may contain sensitive data or the consumer may be concerned about the model being contaminated with the test dataset itself). Hence, another question is: can models be evaluated on private datasets while protecting the intellectual property of the model [110]?

## 1.3 Security and Privacy Techniques

Security, in the context of machine learning applications, deals with protecting sensitive information from unauthorized access while computing certain desired outcomes or functions. For example, if multiple entities pool in data to train an ML model, then a requirement could be that the entities all only learn the final trained model and that no entity learns anything beyond this [67,73,89,98,115,120]. This constitutes providing data security. Another example in the context of inference is to ensure that the model consumer only learns the inference output on its input data point and nothing else about the model, while model publishers learn nothing about the input data point [17,80,89,101]. Examples of techniques that aim to provide security guarantees include enclave-based confidential computing (such as Azure Confidential Computing [86], Amazon Nitro Enclaves [6]), fully homomorphic encryption [52,93,108], and secure multi-party computation [17,57,89,101,122].

Privacy, in the context of ML applications, deals with providing guarantees on what can be learned by attackers from the end-results of the computations above. For example, when multiple entities pool in data to train an ML model, what does the ML model itself reveal about individual user's data present with the entities [35,103]? Can guarantees be provided to users about this information? Examples of techniques that aim to provide privacy guarantees include differential privacy [1,48,97].

An orthogonal technique, that can help with reducing information leakage when training machine learning models over sensitive data, is that of federated learning [75]. Federated learning, while itself not a privacy or security technique, indirectly aids in the process of protecting sensitive data, as only aggregate information about data (and not the raw data itself) is used in computations (e.g. in the training of ML models). This technique is often combined with security [15] and privacy [121] techniques to provide better guarantees to user data.

## 1.4 Organization

The rest of this article will be organized as follows. In Sect. 2, we shall describe some of the security and privacy challenges in ML computations and formally define the goals that we wish to achieve. Section 3 will provide a broad overview of the security and privacy techniques. In Sect. 4, we will specifically focus on the problem of securing computation in ML workloads (during training, inference and evaluation). Section 5 will conclude by briefly discussing a few aspects not covered in this article and presenting some important open challenges.

## 2    ML Security and Privacy Goals

One can abstract out the main challenges in protecting data in machine learning applications into security and privacy goals. We describe them below.

### 2.1    Security Goals

To provide data security, at a very high level, multiple entities $P_1, \cdots P_n$ have private inputs $x_1, \cdots x_n$ respectively. They wish to compute a function $w = M(x_1, \cdots, x_n)$, where, typically $M$ is a publicly agreed upon function or model architecture. They wish to do so in such a way that only $w$ is revealed to the parties (or a subset of the parties). For example, in the context of machine learning training, $P_1, \cdots, P_n$ are $n$ parties, each having training data (in the same format) – $P_i$ holds $x_i$. They wish to train some machine learning model $M$ (e.g. a neural network, decision tree, or transformer) on this data to obtain the weights of the model $w$ and only $w$ must be learned by $P_i$, for all $i \in [n]$. This problem is known as the problem of *secure training*, which is a specific case of the well-studied problem of secure multi-party computation [57,122]. In the context of ML inference, $P_1$ holds a pre-trained ML model with weights $w$. The model architecture/function $M$ (i.e. the neural network structure, or decision tree structure etc.) are known to both $P_1$ and a party $P_2$ who holds a private input $x$. $P_1$ and $P_2$ wish to compute $y = M(w, x)$, which is the inference results of model $M$ with weights $w$ on input $x$. The output results should be revealed to $P_2$ (and perhaps also $P_1$). $P_2$ should learn nothing else, while $P_1$ should learn nothing. Formalizing the notion that $P_2$ learns nothing more than $y$ is non-trivial and was first done so in the seminal works of [56,57]. In order to formalize security, one first needs to specify what the adversary can do and we shall go into this into a bit more detail in the next section. An important take away here is that security goals protect the computation itself with an end goal of collaboratively computing some function without sharing the raw data with untrusted entities.

### 2.2    Privacy Goals

At a very high level, privacy addresses the question: "*Was my data used in the training of an ML algorithm?*". In more detail, say that an ML algorithm $M$ has been trained on data points $x_1, x_2, \cdots, x_\ell$, to obtain the weights of the model $w$. Can an adversary, who has some form of access to $M$ (either given its weights $w$ or given black-box inference access to the model $M$ with weights $w$), tell whether a particular data point $x_j$ was used in the training process? Informally, privacy guarantees ensure that an adversary cannot determine this. This guarantee for examples assures an individual patient that their data was not revealed through access to an ML model trained on data (including theirs). Furthermore, one may also want to provide such a privacy guarantee to a collection of users. That is, we want to ensure that an adversary cannot determine whether a collection of data points $x_{t_1}, \cdots, x_{t_k}$ was used to obtain the model $M$ with weights $w$. Typically privacy guarantees are provided through the technique of differential privacy [48] and we shall formalize these guarantees in the next section.

# 3 Techniques for Security and Privacy

In this section, we shall provide an overview of the various security and privacy techniques deployed in the context of machine learning.

## 3.1 Security Techniques

Security techniques can broadly be divided into two categories – enclave based security and cryptographic techniques. At a very high level, enclave based security provides security guarantees through restricting access to the computation from the adversary, while cryptographic solutions transform the computation mathematically and are based on cryptographic hardness assumptions.

**Enclave Based Security.** Enclaves can be of different varieties - confidential virtual memories (VMs) [7,32], Intel SGX [65], and so on. At a high level, enclaves are protected computation regions that cannot be accessed by even the operating system of the machine on which the region is hosted. In this security technique, the enclave holds a (private, public) key pair for a public-key encryption system – denote this key pair by (pk, sk), while every party holds a corresponding key pair (pk$_i$, sk$_i$). Now, every party $P_i$ will encrypt $x_i$ with pk to produce $c_i = \mathsf{Enc}(\mathsf{pk}, x_i)$ and sends this to the enclave. The enclave will decrypt $c_i$ for all $i \in [n]$, compute $w = M(x_1, \cdots, x_n)$, encrypt $w$ under pk$_i$ and send it to $P_i$. Furthermore, in order to ensure that the outputs of the computation are indeed correct, that $P_i$'s input was faithfully used and so on, further checks are put in place. For example, every entity (parties and the enclave) also have a verification key/signing key pair (vk, $\sigma$) for a signature scheme. Additionally, party $P_i$ will sign $c_i$ using $\sigma$ and this signature will be verified inside the enclave. Furthermore, the enclave will sign the results of the computation (along with all the signed and encrypted inputs it received from the $n$ parties) as well as the description of the function, $M$, to provide a guarantee that the computation was indeed done correctly and on the right inputs provided by the parties. Since enclaves can be susceptible to different types of side channel attacks (such as read access patterns, timing and so on), various techniques are also sometimes employed to protect against these. For more details on enclave based security techniques, we refer the read to [91,106,115,116].

**Homomorphic Encryption.** Homomorphic encryption is a special kind of encryption that supports computations on encrypted data. While earlier homomorphic encryption schemes supported limited types of computations (e.g. either only additions or only multiplications), Gentry [52] provided the first construction of a fully homomorphic encryption scheme that supports arbitrary polynomial time computations. We first present the formal definition of homomorphic encryption schemes and then outline how it can be used in the context of providing security for machine learning applications. $\kappa$ is the cryptographic security parameter (typically set to 128).

**Definition 1.** *A homomorphic encryption scheme for a function family* F, HE = (HE.KeyGen, HE.Enc, HE.Dec, HE.Eval) *is a set of four probabilistic polynomial time algorithms as follows:*

- HE.KeyGen($1^\kappa$) *outputs* (pk, sk, evk), *where* pk *is the public key,* sk *is the secret key and* evk *is the evaluation key.*
- $c = $ HE.Enc(pk, $x$) *is the (randomized) ciphertext produced while encrypting message $x$ with public key* pk.
- $x' = $ HE.Dec(sk, $c$) *is the decryption of ciphertext $c$ with secret key* sk *to produce $x'$.*
- *For a function $f \in $ F, $c_f = $ HE.Eval(evk, $f, c_1, \cdots, c_\ell$) is the output of the evaluation algorithm on $\ell$ ciphertexts (with $c_i$ encrypting $x_i$) on function $f$ using the evaluation key* evk.

*The scheme satisfies the following two properties:*

- **Correctness.** *For all functions $f \in $ F and for $c_i = $ HE.Enc(pk, $c_i$), $\forall i \in [\ell]$, we have that HE.Dec(sk, HE.Eval(evk, $f, c_1, \cdots, c_\ell$)) = $f(x_1, \cdots, x_\ell)$, except with probability negligible in $\kappa$. Furthermore, the size of HE.Eval(evk, $f, c_1, \cdots, c_\ell$) is required to be independent of the size of $f$ as well as $\ell$.*
- **Security.** *The standard notion of semantic security applies. That is for any two adversarially chosen $x_0$ and $x_1$, no adversary (given pk, evk) can distinguish between HE.Enc(pk, $x_0$) and HE.Enc(pk, $x_1$) with probability significantly better than $\frac{1}{2}$.*

When only 2 participants have inputs to the computation (e.g. in the inference scenario described earlier where $P_1$ has weights $w$ to an ML model and $P_2$ has input $x$), then homomorphic encryption can be used directly to provide security. $P_2$ encrypts $x$ using pk (public key of a homomorphic encryption scheme for which only $P_2$ knows sk) and provides $P_1$ with $c = $ HE.Enc(pk, $x$) and pk, evk. $P_1$ computes $d = $ HE.Enc(pk, $w$) and $z = $ HE.Eval(evk, $M, c, d$) and sends back $z$ to $P_2$. $P_2$ computes $y = $ HE.Dec(sk, $z$) which is $M(w, x)$. This provides security as long as we trust $P_1$ to perform the right computation (and also trust $P_2$ to compute $c$ correctly). When more than 2 parties are involved, the protocol to provide security is more complex and based on threshold fully homomorphic encryption [16]. At a high level, this allows the $n$ parties to sample a pk, evk for a homomorphic encryption scheme such that no subset of these parties learn anything about sk. Then, all participants can create encryptions of their inputs which can be provided to one of the parties to perform the encrypted computation and produce the encrypted results of the computations. Using the properties of the threshold encryption scheme, all participants can collectively decrypt the results to obtain the results of the computation.

While homomorphic encryption has been used in machine learning applications [14,41,47,53,54,72], typically it is efficient only if the underlying ML operations are purely arithmetic in nature (e.g. matrix multiplications or convolutions) and non-linear activation functions, such as ReLU (defined as $\mathsf{ReLU}(x) = \max(x, 0)$), have to be approximated using some polynomial. This can sometimes affect the underlying accuracy of the ML model.

**Multi-party Computation.** Secure multi-party computation (or MPC for short) is a cryptographic technique introduced through the seminal works of Yao [122] and Goldreich, Micali, and Wigderson [57]. At a high level, MPC allows $n$ parties $P_1, \cdots, P_n$ with $P_i$ having private input $x_i$ to collectively compute a publicly agreed upon function, $M$ to obtain the output $w = M(x_1, \cdots, x_n)$ through an interactive protocol. In this interactive protocol, every party performs computation, exchanges messages with other participants and this process continues several times iteratively. At the end of this interaction, participants are guaranteed to only learn the outputs of the computation. MPC is an area that has seen rich and extensive research over the last 40 years. Papers have explored its round complexity (i.e., how many times do the participants have to talk back and forth with each other) [9,11,39,50], its communication complexity (how much information must the parties exchange with each other) [21,33,52], and various notions of security. Some variants of security include considering - the threshold of corrupted parties, semi-honest, malicious, static, and adaptive. Typically in an $n$-party computation, it is assumed that up to $t < n$ of the participants, known as the threshold, can be corrupted. These $t$ parties can collectively coordinate and try to figure out something more about the information that the remaining $n - t$ honest parties hold (beyond the function output $w$ itself) or they may simply try to disrupt the computation and force the honest parties to compute some other function. Semi-honest (or passive) adversaries are adversaries that are assumed to follow the protocol specification faithfully, but may try to learn additional information about the honest parties' inputs, while no such assumptions are made about malicious adversaries. Protocols that are secure only against static adversaries assume that the list of corrupted parties is specified by the adversary at the beginning of the protocol while protocols secure against adaptive adversaries make no such assumptions.

*MPC Security.* Defining each of these notions of security is beyond the scope of this article; however, we shall provide a formal definition of security against static, semi-honest adversaries below. The popular paradigm to define security is that of the simulation paradigm [27,56,79]. In this paradigm, security is modeled through two worlds - a *real world* and the *ideal world*. In the real world, all participants interact with each other through the MPC protocol $\pi$. The adversary $\mathcal{A}$ is allowed to corrupt a set $\mathcal{C}$ of parties (of size up to $t < n$) of the parties and observe their complete internal state - this includes inputs, outputs, any randomness sampled during the protocol execution and all messages sent and received by these $t$ parties. This is known as the *view* of the adversary, denoted by $\mathsf{view}_{\mathsf{real},\kappa,\mathcal{C}}$ for security parameter $\kappa$. In the ideal world, all participants in the protocol provide their inputs to a trusted ideal functionality that computes the functionality faithfully and provides the participants with the outputs of the functionality. In the above scenario, this functionality would take as inputs $x_i$ from $P_i$, compute $w = M(x_1, \cdots, x_n)$ and provide $w$ to every $P_i$. The adversary, in this world known as the simulator $\mathsf{S}$ observes the inputs and outputs of the $t$ corrupted parties. This is the view of the adversary in the ideal world, denoted by $\mathsf{view}_{\mathsf{ideal},\kappa,\mathcal{C}}$.

**Definition 2.** *We say that a protocol $\pi$ securely realizes* functionality $\mathcal{M}$ *(which takes* $x_1, \cdots, x_n$ *as inputs from parties* $P_1, \cdots, P_n$ *respectively and outputs* $w = M(x_1, \cdots, x_n)$ *to all parties) in the presence of semi-honest adversaries if for all probabilistic polynomial time adversaries* $\mathcal{A}$, *for all corrupted sets* $\mathcal{C}$, *there exists a simulator* $\mathsf{S}$, *such that the views* $\mathsf{view}_{\mathsf{real},\kappa,\mathcal{C}}$ *and* $\mathsf{view}_{\mathsf{ideal},\kappa,\mathcal{C}}$ *are indistinguishable to any environment denoted by* $\mathcal{Z}$ *(except with probability negligible in* $\kappa$*).*

### 3.2  Privacy Techniques

At a high level, privacy in machine learning addresses the question of what can an adversary learn about data used to train a machine learning model if they had access to the model in some form? In this section, we shall present a high level overview of the technique of differential privacy that helps address questions of this form. We shall also briefly discuss some methodologies that are applied to attack machine learning models so as to understand what an adversary can learn from them.

**Differential Privacy.** The technique of differential privacy was introduced in the seminal work of Dwork, McSherry, Nissim, and Smith [48]. The setting is as follows: say an entity holds a dataset D comprising of $n$ records. This entity wishes to release some aggregate statistics about the data that can provide insights about the entire set of $n$ records (a machine learning model is a (complex) example of such an aggregate statistic). By releasing a noisy version of this statistic, differential privacy focusses on ensuring that the privacy of individual records in this database are preserved. We shall present the formal definition of $\epsilon$-differential privacy below.

**Definition 3.** *Let* $\epsilon > 0$ *and let* $\mathcal{M}$ *be a randomized algorithm that takes as input a dataset D and outputs values in the image of* $\mathcal{M}$, *denoted by* $\widehat{\mathcal{M}}$. *Algorithm* $\mathcal{M}$ *is said to provide* $\epsilon$-*differential privacy if for all datasets* $D_1$ *and* $D_2$ *that differ on a single record, and all subsets* $S \in \widehat{\mathcal{M}}$,

$$\Pr[\mathcal{M}(D_1) \in \mathcal{S}] \leq \exp(\epsilon)\Pr[\mathcal{M}(D_2) \in \mathcal{S}]$$

*where the probability is over the randomness of* $\mathcal{M}$.

At a high level, this definition says that if we considered an individual record in a dataset (corresponding to an individual user's data) and an adversary could only observe the output of $\mathcal{M}$ on the dataset, then whatever they could tell about the dataset cannot differ by more than $\exp(\epsilon)$ whether the individual record was present in the dataset or not. Hence, no individual's data can be "leaked" through this process. Analyzing differential privacy for simple functions such as aggregates and so on are relatively easier, while doing so for more complex algorithms such as machine learning training algorithms [1] require an analysis invoking the composition theorem for differential privacy [84].

**Attacks.** While not a privacy technique as such, several works have also considered what information can an adversary obtain given some form of access to an ML model. For example, given either black-box access to or the weights of a model $M$ trained on data points $x_1, \cdots x_n$, can an adversary determine whether a specific data point $x^*$ was used to train $M$ or not? Or in other words, was $x^* = x_j$ for some $j \in [n]$? The process of attacking an ML model to determine this is known as a *membership inference attack* (see [109] for more details). The reader may recognize that the technique of differential privacy described earlier can be used as a defence mechanism to protect against membership inference attacks. Another form of attack is where an adversary, given only black-box access to the model $M$ (i.e. can make only inference queries to the model), tries to then develop another model that has the same performance characteristics (say, inference accuracy) as the original model. This attack is known as a *model extraction attack* [113]. A *data poisoning attack* aims to provide an ML model with corrupted data during training such that the ML model so obtained then underperforms in some specific way [12], while *evasion attacks* aim to provide a pretrained ML model with artificially created data for inference that may lead the model to perform in undesired ways [37,82].

## 4    Secure Computation for Machine Learning

In this section, we will provide an overview of various works on securely computing ML algorithms based on cryptographic techniques (some of these works are based on homomorphic encryption, some on secure multi-party computation, and others combine the two techniques as well). We will split this section into 3 parts covering the problems of inference, evaluation, and training. While the computations that must be supported by these 3 problems are not fundamentally very different, works in the literature have considered these problems separately. Unless explicitly specified, the works here considered the threat model of semi-honest secure adversaries. In the two party setting (naturally) at most one party can be corrupt, while in the multi-party setting various thresholds of corruptions have been considered.

### 4.1    Inference

In *secure inference*, a model owner holds the weights $w$ of a pre-trained model with public architecture $M$, while a model consumer holds an input point $x$. The goal is for the consumer to learn $y = M(w, x)$ and nothing else, while the owner should not learn anything. While generic secure computation protocols [34, 40, 57, 122] can be used to solve the problem of secure inference, much gains can be obtained by considering specialized cryptographic protocols for the task of machine learning inference.

*Decision Trees.* Perhaps the first work that considered such protocols in the context of machine learning was that of Lindell and Pinkas [80] with a focus on decision tree algorithms for training and classification. While this work provided a theoretical analysis of the efficiency of their protocol, perhaps the first work to show a concretely efficient implementation of secure machine learning classification was that of Bost *et al.* [17]. Their focus was also on decision trees and Naïve Bayes classification. A long line of works have considered such secure computation of decision trees (see [2, 3, 38, 42]) with the currently most efficient protocol being that due to Hamada *et al.* [62]. Since decision tree algorithms typically traverse a path of the tree (during classification) that depends on the input, this traversal must be kept hidden from both model owner and consumer (to provide security). Hence, the techniques for computing decision tree algorithms securely rely on techniques such as oblivious RAM and oblivious shuffle [58].

*Neural Networks.* On the other hand, neural networks typically have an uniform access pattern (that is independent of the input data point) and hence the techniques to compute such algorithms securely are a bit different. The first work to consider the secure inference of neural networks was that of SecureML [89] who provided a generalization of the Beaver multiplication triples [8] to matrices that helped bring down the overheads of computing linear layers securely. They showed how to evaluate 3-layer networks securely over the MNIST dataset [45]. Furthermore, cleartext machine learning algorithms are typically written using floating-point arithmetic [90], while secure multi-party computation is much more efficient when computation is over fixed-point numbers (with a fixed bitwidth and precision). The work of SecureML also showed how to emulate ML algorithms written in floating point using fixed-point arithmetic (albeit with loss of accuracy). The work of EzPC [29] showed how to create a programmable C-like framework for computing various algorithms (including ML inference) and used it in conjunction with the ABY cryptographic backend [43], showing better performance than SecureML. ABY3 [88] and SecureNN [118] considered the problem of secure inference (as well as training) in the weaker threat model where there is an additional party in the computation (with no input) that is trusted not to collude with either the model owner or the consumer. In this setting, they showed (naturally) more performant protocols for similar kinds of benchmarks from SecureML. A long line of works have also explored the setting of secure computation with more number of parties (e.g. 4 or 5) [26, 76, 96], but these have an even weaker threat model (assuming that no party colludes with another).

CrypTFlow [77] was the first work to demonstrate secure inference at the scale of real world ML benchmarks (e.g. ImageNet [44] scale). This work also assumed an additional party in the computation. It provided protocols for semi-honest secure computation as well as a generic compiler to convert any semi-honest protocol into a malicious secure protocol while assuming hardware enclaves. This work provided the first framework to compile ML inference algorithms written in TensorFlow directly into secure computation protocols (while also accounting for bitwidth and precision through an automatic compiler). Falcon [119] improved upon the works of [77,88,118] and provided better secure inference protocols (via better comparison protocols) once again in the setting with an additional party. The work of Gazelle [68] focussed on specialized 2-party protocols based on homomorphic encryption for computing convolutional layers while Delphi [87] optimized the computation of non-linear layers through the modification of the underlying ML algorithms. CrypTFlow2 [101] gave new specialized protocols for comparisons, ReLUs, and truncations (required in fixed-point arithmetic) and through these gave improved 2-party secure inference protocols. While being the first 2-party work to execute ImageNet scale benchmarks securely, CrypTFlow2 also provided support to compute the linear layers through either oblivious transfer based protocols [81,89] or homomorphic encryption based protocols [68,87] (along with their corresponding non-linear layer protocols) thus offering flexibility when running the protocols in various bandwidth settings (e.g. homomorphic encryption protocols being more communication frugal perform better in low bandwidth settings). Cheetah [64] improved upon CrypTFlow2 and showed how to eliminate expensive rotations that were required when computing linear layers through homomorphic encryption in [68,87,101] and further optimized the non-linear computations as well through the use of Silent OTs [19]. An orthogonal line of work has explored modifying the underlying ML algorithms to make them either more MPC friendly or suitable for computation using homomorphic encryption (see e.g. [41,54,104]).

The first work to consider secure inference of recurrent neural networks was SiRNN [100]. The main challenge in handling such networks was in the design of precise and secure protocols for computing transcendental functions such as exponentiation, reciprocal square root, sigmoid and tanh. SiRNN designed approximations for these functions that were both precise (formally defined through the notion of Unit-in-the-Last-Place (ULP) error [55]) as well as had low computing cost through MPC protocols. The works of Muse [78] and SIMC [28] consider a setting wherein the model consumer could potentially be malicious (and is not assumed to be semi-honest). Finally, an orthogonal line of work shows how to emulate floating-point arithmetic securely in the two-party setting [99] including for machine learning inference. For a somewhat recent survey on the state-of-the-art in secure inference (not covering works below), we refer the reader to [83].

*Preprocessing model.* A popular model for secure 2-party computation is that of the preprocessing model - in this there are 2 phases: 1) The preprocessing/offline phase: Here, the 2 parties obtain correlated randomness (either through a pre-processing secure computation protocol or through a dealer party) that is inde-pendent of all inputs to the computation. 2) The online phase: Here, the 2 parties use their inputs (as well as the correlated randomness from the preprocessing phase) to run the secure computation of the function required. Several works have explored the cost of 2PC in such a setting [31,70,89,95]. A new line of work shows how to construct secure 2-party computation protocols [18,23] in the preprocess-ing model using the technique of function secret sharing (FSS) [20,22].Through these class of protocols, overheads of 2-party secure computation protocols shift from communication to computation. The work of [18] show how to build secure computation protocols for emulating fixed-point arithmetic. Llama [60] and Ari-aNN [107] show how to build an end-to-end secure inference library based on FSS techniques (with Llama also providing support for evaluating transcen-dental functions and hence recurrent neural networks, thus improving upon SiRNN [100]). Pika [117] showed how to use lookup tables to compute transcen-dental functions at the expense of larger compute using FSS techniques, while Grotto [111] showed how to do the same without such an increase in compute. The works of CrypTen [73], CryptGPU [112] and Piranha [120] showed how to accelerate MPC protocols on GPUs. A very recent system, Orca [67] shows how to accelerate FSS-based MPC protocols and for this system, the online time overheads of running secure inference (over the corresponding cleartext code) can be as low as 2×. The work of Iron [63], building upon [100], showed how to construct secure computation protocols for transformer models [114], while most recently, Sigma [59] shows how to provide FSS-based secure computation pro-tocols for large transformer models such as Generative Pre-trained Transformer (GPT) models [24,25].

## 4.2   Evaluation

In the problem of model evaluation (also known as AI validation), a dataset owner wishes to evaluate a model from a model publisher on its dataset to evaluate its accuracy. The dataset owner does not wish to make the dataset public (for fear of model contamination and/or to protect the privacy of the dataset), while the model publisher does not want to reveal the model to the dataset owner. At a very high level, let $M$ be the model architecture (that is public), let $w$ be the weights of this model held by the model owner, let $(x_1, \ell_1), \cdots, (x_t, \ell_t)$ be the private set of $t$ points in the dataset along with their labels. Let $f$ be an evaluation metric that takes as input $y_j = (x_j, \ell_j, M(w, x_j))$ for all $j \in [t]$ and outputs a score. For example an evaluation metric could simply be one that counts the number of datapoints on which $M(w, x_j)$ and $\ell_j$ agree (i.e., $y_j = 1$ iff $\ell_j = M(w, x_j)$ and $f(y_1, \cdots, y_t) = \sum_{j=1}^{t} y_j$). We want to design a secure computation protocol for this task. The reader may observe that this task is fairly similar to performing secure inference – except that the outputs from the secure inference must be fed in a secure manner into another secure computation (that is the computation of the function $f$). Secure AI validation was explored in the work of Soin *et al.* [110] through an experiment performed between Stanford University hosting the CheXpert model [66] and CARING Research hosting a test dataset of 500 chest x-ray images. The evaluation metric used was the Area Under the Receiver Operating Characteristics (AUROC) score and the model was shown to have a score of 0.9 (out of a maximum of 1) on the test dataset.

## 4.3   Training

In the context of decision trees, training algorithms are somewhat different in structure from their classification counterparts. The works discussed above [2, 62,80] all consider the training of decision tree algorithms that are practical up to a small tree depth and a small number of attributes. Neural network training algorithms were considered in the works of SecureML [89], ABY3 [88], SecureNN [118], Quotient [4,69], and Piranha [120] to name a few. The work of Keller and Sun [71] provides an overview of the various methods used in fixed-point secure machine learning training algorithms. The current state-of-the-art to train ML models in the two-party setting is Orca [67]. The work of Beacon [98] shows how to train ML models in the two-party setting over floating-point arithmetic.

## 5   Conclusion

In this article, we discussed some of the privacy and security challenges in machine learning. We described various security techniques in detail - enclave based security, homomorphic encryption, and secure multi-party computation and focussed on cryptographic works that have aimed to provided solutions to the problems of secure inference, evaluation and training. We also briefly outlined the technique of differential privacy that helps protect the privacy of individual data in ML training. There are topics not addressed in this work - e.g. the notion of federated learning. Federated learning is a technique in which $n$ entities, each holding some amount of training data, iteratively train an ML model by locally training models on their data and then exchanging some information (e.g. the collective gradients) in order to combine the models. Federated learning, by itself, does not provide privacy guarantees. However, since raw data is not directly used while interacting with other data providers, this technique may provide some attractive properties. Furthermore, while individual gradients from participants can be protected through techniques such as secure aggregation [15] when there are many data providers involved, such techniques provide absolutely no guarantees when the number of data providers is small (e.g. say with 2 data providers). Furthermore data privacy techniques described in this article only protect the privacy of individuals in the data, but do not help prove anything about information that may be leaked about a collection of individuals present in a dataset (while differential privacy can also be used in this context, the noise added to obtain reasonable privacy bounds is too high to derive utility from the function being computed). To see the dangers of information leakage from a collection of data points, consider an ML model trained for auto completion from 2 different enterprise customers $A$ and $B$. If this model were to auto complete a sentence for an employee in $B$ based on sensitive information from a collection of employees in $A$, then this could have disastrous consequences. Providing training mechanisms that can guarantee no such information leakage is one of the greatest unsolved challenges today. Finally, data regulation today (such as GDPR [49] and Data Protection Act [51]) does not consider various types of privacy and security techniques described in this article. By relying on the latest technologies, regulation can potentially be amended to provide stronger privacy and security guarantees to end users.

# References

1. Abadi, M., et al.: Deep learning with differential privacy. In: Weippl, E.R., Katzenbeisser, S., Kruegel, C., Myers, A.C., Halevi, S. (eds.)Proceedings of the 2016 ACM SIGSAC Conference on Computer and Communications Security, Vienna, Austria, 24–28 October 2016, pp. 308–318. ACM (2016)
2. Abspoel, M., Escudero, D., Volgushev, N.: Secure training of decision trees with continuous attributes. Proc. Priv. Enhancing Technol. **2021**(1), 167–187 (2021)
3. Adams, S., et al.: Privacy-preserving training of tree ensembles over continuous data. Proc. Priv. Enhancing Technol. **2022**(2), 205–226 (2022)
4. Agrawal, N., Shahin Shamsabadi, A., Kusner, M.J., Gascón, A.: QUOTIENT: two-party secure neural network training and prediction. In: CCS (2019)
5. Alpaydin, E.: Introduction to Machine Learning (Adaptive Computation and Machine Learning ). MIT Press, Cambridge (2004)
6. AWS. AWS Nitro Enclaves (2023). https://aws.amazon.com/ec2/nitro/nitro-enclaves/
7. Microsoft Azure. DCasv5 and ECasv5 series confidential VMs (2023). https://learn.microsoft.com/en-us/azure/confidential-computing/confidential-vm-overview
8. Beaver, D.: Efficient multiparty protocols using circuit randomization. In: Feigenbaum, J. (ed.) CRYPTO 1991. LNCS, vol. 576, pp. 420–432. Springer, Heidelberg (1992). https://doi.org/10.1007/3-540-46766-1_34
9. Beaver, D., Micali, S., Rogaway, P.: The round complexity of secure protocols (extended abstract). In: Ortiz, H. (ed.) Proceedings of the 22nd Annual ACM Symposium on Theory of Computing, 13–17, May 1990, Baltimore, Maryland, USA, pp. 503–513. ACM (1990)
10. Bellare, M., Rogaway, P.: Optimal asymmetric encryption. In: De Santis, A. (ed.) EUROCRYPT 1994. LNCS, vol. 950, pp. 92–111. Springer, Heidelberg (1994). https://doi.org/10.1007/bfb0053428
11. Benhamouda, F., Lin, H.: $k$-round multiparty computation from $k$-round oblivious transfer via garbled interactive circuits. In: Nielsen, J.B., Rijmen, V. (eds.) EUROCRYPT 2018. LNCS, vol. 10821, pp. 500–532. Springer, Cham (2018). https://doi.org/10.1007/978-3-319-78375-8_17
12. Biggio, B., Nelson, B., Laskov, P.: Poisoning attacks against support vector machines. In: Proceedings of the 29th International Conference on Machine Learning, ICML 2012, Edinburgh, Scotland, UK, June 26 - July 1, 2012. icml.cc/Omnipress (2012)

13. Black, J.: Authenticated encryption. In: van Tilborg, H.C.A., Jajodia, S. (eds.) Encyclopedia of Cryptography and Security, 2nd edn., pp. 52–61. Springer, Boston (2011). https://doi.org/10.1007/978-1-4419-5906-5_548

14. Blatt, M., Gusev, A., Polyakov, Y., Rohloff, K., Vaikuntanathan, V.: Optimized homomorphic encryption solution for secure genome-wide association studies. IACR Cryptol. ePrint Arch., p. 223 (2019)

15. Bonawitz, K.A., et al.: Practical secure aggregation for privacy-preserving machine learning. In: Thuraisingham, B., Evans, D., Malkin, T., Xu, D. (eds.) Proceedings of the 2017 ACM SIGSAC Conference on Computer and Communications Security, CCS 2017, Dallas, TX, USA, October 30 - November 03, 2017, pp. 1175–1191. ACM (2017)

16. Boneh, D., et al.: Threshold cryptosystems from threshold fully homomorphic encryption. In: Shacham, H., Boldyreva, A. (eds.) CRYPTO 2018. LNCS, vol. 10991, pp. 565–596. Springer, Cham (2018). https://doi.org/10.1007/978-3-319-96884-1_19

17. Bost, R., Popa, R.A., Tu, S., Goldwasser, S.: Machine learning classification over encrypted data. In: NDSS (2015)

18. Boyle, E., et al.: Function secret sharing for mixed-mode and fixed-point secure computation. In: Canteaut, A., Standaert, F.-X. (eds.) EUROCRYPT 2021. LNCS, vol. 12697, pp. 871–900. Springer, Cham (2021). https://doi.org/10.1007/978-3-030-77886-6_30

19. Boyle, E., et al.: Efficient two-round OT extension and silent non-interactive secure computation. In: CCS (2019)

20. Boyle, E., Gilboa, N., Ishai, Y.: Function secret sharing. In: Oswald, E., Fischlin, M. (eds.) EUROCRYPT 2015. LNCS, vol. 9057, pp. 337–367. Springer, Heidelberg (2015). https://doi.org/10.1007/978-3-662-46803-6_12

21. Boyle, E., Gilboa, N., Ishai, Y.: Breaking the circuit size barrier for secure computation under DDH. In: Robshaw, M., Katz, J. (eds.) CRYPTO 2016. LNCS, vol. 9814, pp. 509–539. Springer, Heidelberg (2016). https://doi.org/10.1007/978-3-662-53018-4_19

22. Boyle, E., Gilboa, N., Ishai, Y.: Function secret sharing: improvements and extensions. In: CCS (2016)

23. Boyle, E., Gilboa, N., Ishai, Y.: Secure computation with preprocessing via function secret sharing. In: Hofheinz, D., Rosen, A. (eds.) TCC 2019. LNCS, vol. 11891, pp. 341–371. Springer, Cham (2019). https://doi.org/10.1007/978-3-030-36030-6_14

24. Brown, T.B., et al.: Language models are few-shot learners. In: Larochelle, H., Ranzato, M., Hadsell, R., Balcan, M.F., Lin, H.T. (eds.) Advances in Neural Information Processing Systems, vol. 33. Annual Conference on Neural Information Processing Systems 2020, NeurIPS 2020, 6–12 December 2020, virtual (2020)

25. Brown, T.B., et al.:. Language models are few-shot learners (2020)

26. Byali, M., Chaudhari, H., Patra, A., Suresh, A.: FLASH: fast and robust framework for privacy-preserving machine learning. Proc. Priv. Enhancing Technol. **2020**(2), 459–480 (2020)

27. Canetti, R.: Security and composition of multiparty cryptographic protocols. J. Cryptology **13**, 143–202 (2000)

28. Chandran, N., Gupta, D., Obbattu, S.L.B., Shah, A.: SIMC: ML inference secure against malicious clients at semi-honest cost. In: USENIX Security Symposium (2022)

29. Chandran, N., Gupta, D., Rastogi, A., Sharma, R., Tripathi, S.: EzPC: programmable and efficient secure two-party computation for machine learning. In:2019 IEEE European Symposium on Security and Privacy (EuroS&P), pp. 496–511 (2019)

30. Chen, M.X., et al.: Gmail smart compose: real-time assisted writing. In: Teredesai, A., Kumar, V., Li, Y., Rosales, R., Terzi, E., Karypis, G. (eds.) Proceedings of the 25th ACM SIGKDD International Conference on Knowledge Discovery & Data Mining, KDD 2019, Anchorage, AK, USA, 4–8 August 2019, pp. 2287–2295. ACM (2019)

31. Chen, V., Pastro, V., Raykova, M.: Secure computation for machine learning with SPDZ. In: Workshop on PPML at NeurIPS (2018)

32. Google Cloud. Confidential Computing concepts (2023). https://cloud.google.com/confidential-computing/confidential-vm/docs/about-cvm

33. Couteau, G.: A note on the communication complexity of multiparty computation in the correlated randomness model. In: Ishai, Y., Rijmen, V. (eds.) EUROCRYPT 2019. LNCS, vol. 11477, pp. 473–503. Springer, Cham (2019). https://doi.org/10.1007/978-3-030-17656-3_17

34. Cramer, R., Damgård, I., Escudero, D., Scholl, P., Xing, C.: SPDℤ$_{2^k}$: efficient MPC mod $2^k$ for dishonest majority. In: Shacham, H., Boldyreva, A. (eds.) CRYPTO 2018. LNCS, vol. 10992, pp. 769–798. Springer, Cham (2018). https://doi.org/10.1007/978-3-319-96881-0_26

35. De Cristofaro, E.: A critical overview of privacy in machine learning. IEEE Secur. Priv. 19(4), 19–27 (2021)

36. Daemen, J., Rijmen, V.: The Design of Rijndael - The Advanced Encryption Standard (AES). Information Security and Cryptography, 2nd edn. Springer, Heidelberg (2020). https://doi.org/10.1007/978-3-662-60769-5

37. Dalvi, N., Domingos, P., Mausam, Sanghai, S., Verma, D.: Adversarial classification. In: Kim, W., Kohavi, R., Gehrke, J., DuMouchel, W. (eds.) Proceedings of the Tenth ACM SIGKDD International Conference on Knowledge Discovery and Data Mining, Seattle, Washington, USA, 22–25 August 2004, pp. 99–108. ACM (2004)

38. Damgård, I., Escudero, D., Frederiksen, T., Keller, M., Scholl, P., Volgushev, N.: New primitives for actively-secure MPC over rings with applications to private machine learning. In: 2019 IEEE Symposium on Security and Privacy, SP 2019, San Francisco, CA, USA, 19–23 May 2019, pp. 1102–1120. IEEE (2019)

39. Damgård, I., Ishai, Y.: Constant-round multiparty computation using a black-box pseudorandom generator. In: Shoup, V. (ed.) CRYPTO 2005. LNCS, vol. 3621, pp. 378–394. Springer, Heidelberg (2005). https://doi.org/10.1007/11535218_23

40. Damgård, I., Pastro, V., Smart, N., Zakarias, S.: Multiparty computation from somewhat homomorphic encryption. In: Safavi-Naini, R., Canetti, R. (eds.) CRYPTO 2012. LNCS, vol. 7417, pp. 643–662. Springer, Heidelberg (2012). https://doi.org/10.1007/978-3-642-32009-5_38

41. Dathathri, R., et al.: CHET: an optimizing compiler for fully-homomorphic neural-network inferencing. In: PLDI (2019)

42. de Hoogh, S., Schoenmakers, B., Chen, P., op den Akker, H.: Practical secure decision tree learning in a teletreatment application. In: Christin, N., Safavi-Naini, R. (eds.) FC 2014. LNCS, vol. 8437, pp. 179–194. Springer, Heidelberg (2014). https://doi.org/10.1007/978-3-662-45472-5_12

43. Demmler, D., Schneider, T., Zohner, M.: ABY-a framework for efficient mixed-protocol secure two-party computation. In: NDSS (2015)

44. Deng, J., Dong, W., Socher, R., Li, L.-J., Li, K., Fei-Fei, L.: ImageNet: a large-scale hierarchical image database. In: CVPR (2009)
45. Deng, L.: The MNIST database of handwritten digit images for machine learning research. IEEE Signal Process. Mag. **29**(6), 141–142 (2012)
46. Dixon, M.F., Halperin, I., Bilokon, P.: Machine Learning in Finance. Springer, Cham (2020). https://doi.org/10.1007/978-3-030-41068-1
47. Dowlin, N., Gilad-Bachrach, R., Laine, K., Lauter, K.E., Naehrig, M., Wernsing, J.: Manual for using homomorphic encryption for bioinformatics. Proc. IEEE **105**(3), 552–567 (2017)
48. Dwork, C., McSherry, F., Nissim, K., Smith, A.: Calibrating noise to sensitivity in private data analysis. In: Halevi, S., Rabin, T. (eds.) TCC 2006. LNCS, vol. 3876, pp. 265–284. Springer, Heidelberg (2006). https://doi.org/10.1007/11681878_14
49. European Commission. Regulation (EU) 2016/679 of the European Parliament and of the Council of 27 April 2016 on the protection of natural persons with regard to the processing of personal data and on the free movement of such data, and repealing Directive 95/46/EC (General Data Protection Regulation) (Text with EEA relevance) (2016)
50. Garg, S., Srinivasan, A.: Two-round multiparty secure computation from minimal assumptions. In: Nielsen, J.B., Rijmen, V. (eds.) EUROCRYPT 2018. LNCS, vol. 10821, pp. 468–499. Springer, Cham (2018). https://doi.org/10.1007/978-3-319-78375-8_16
51. Gazette of India. The digital personal data protection act (2023)
52. Gentry, C.: Fully homomorphic encryption using ideal lattices. In: Mitzenmacher, M. (ed.) Proceedings of the 41st Annual ACM Symposium on Theory of Computing, STOC 2009, Bethesda, MD, USA, May 31 - June 2, 2009, pp. 169–178. ACM (2009)
53. Geva, R., et al.: Collaborative privacy-preserving analysis of oncological data using multiparty homomorphic encryption. In: IACR Cryptol. ePrint Arch., p. 1203 (2023)
54. Gilad-Bachrach, R., Dowlin, N., Laine, K., Lauter, K., Naehrig, M., Wernsing, J.: CryptoNets: applying neural networks to encrypted data with high throughput and accuracy. In: Balcan, M.F., Weinberger, K.Q. (ed.) ICML (2016)
55. Goldberg, D.: What every computer scientist should know about floating-point arithmetic. ACM Comput. Surv. **23**, 5–48 (1991)
56. Goldreich, O.: The Foundations of Cryptography - Volume 2: Basic Applications. Cambridge University Press, Cambridge (2004)
57. Goldreich, O., Micali, S., Wigderson, A.: How to play any mental game or a completeness theorem for protocols with honest majority. In: STOC (1987)
58. Goldreich, O., Ostrovsky, R.: Software protection and simulation on oblivious rams. J. ACM **43**(3), 431–473 (1996)
59. Gupta, K., et al.:. SIGMA: secure GPT inference with function secret sharing. Cryptology ePrint Archive, Paper 2023/1269 (2023). https://eprint.iacr.org/2023/1269
60. Gupta, K., Kumaraswamy, D., Chandran, N., Gupta, D.: Llama: a low latency math library for secure inference. In: PETS (2022)
61. Habehh, H., Gohel, S.: Machine learning in healthcare. **22**(4), 291–300 (2021)
62. Hamada, K., Ikarashi, D., Kikuchi, R., Chida, K.: Efficient decision tree training with new data structure for secure multi-party computation. Proc. Priv. Enhancing Technol. **2023**(1), 343–364 (2023)
63. Hao, M., Li, H., Chen, H., Xing, P., Guowen, X., Zhang, T.: Iron: private inference on transformers. In: NeurIPS (2022)

64. Huang, Z., Lu, W.J., Hong, C., Ding, J.: Cheetah: lean and fast secure two-party deep neural network inference. In: USENIX Security Symposium (2022)
65. Intel. Intel Software Guard Extensions (2020). https://www.intel.com/content/www/us/en/developer/tools/software-guard-extensions/overview.html
66. Irvin, J., et al.: CheXpert: a large chest radiograph dataset with uncertainty labels and expert comparison. In: The Thirty-Third AAAI Conference on Artificial Intelligence, AAAI 2019, The Thirty-First Innovative Applications of Artificial Intelligence Conference, IAAI 2019, The Ninth AAAI Symposium on Educational Advances in Artificial Intelligence, EAAI 2019, Honolulu, Hawaii, USA, January 27 - February 1, 2019, pp. 590–597. AAAI Press (2019)
67. Jawalkar, N., Gupta, K., Basu, A., Chandran, N., Gupta, D., Sharma, R.: Orca: FSS-based secure training with GPUs. In: IEEE S&P (2024)
68. Juvekar, C., Vaikuntanathan, V., Chandrakasan, A.: GAZELLE: a low latency framework for secure neural network inference. In USENIX Security Symposium (2018)
69. Kelkar, M., Le, P.H., Raykova, M., Seth, K.: Secure poisson regression. In: USENIX Security Symposium (2022)
70. Keller, M.: MP-SPDZ: a versatile framework for multi-party computation. In: CCS (2020)
71. Keller, M., Sun, K.: Secure quantized training for deep learning. In: ICML (2022)
72. Kim, M., Lauter, K.E.: Private genome analysis through homomorphic encryption. BMC Med. Inform. Decis. Mak. $15$-S(5), 1–12 (2015)
73. Knott, B., Venkataraman, S., Hannun, A., Sengupta, S., Ibrahim, M., van der Maaten, L.: CrypTen: secure multi-party computation meets machine learning. In: NeurIPS (2021)
74. Koblitz, A.H., Koblitz, N., Menezes, A.: Elliptic curve cryptography: the serpentine course of a paradigm shift. In: IACR Cryptol. ePrint Arch., p. 390 (2008)
75. Konečný, J., McMahan, B., Ramage, D.: Federated optimization: distributed optimization beyond the datacenter. CoRR, abs/1511.03575 (2015)
76. Koti, N., Pancholi, M., Patra, A., Suresh, A.: SWIFT: super-fast and robust privacy-preserving machine learning. In: USENIX Security Symposium (2021)
77. Kumar, N., Rathee, M., Chandran, N., Gupta, D., Rastogi, A., Sharma, R.: CrypTflow: secure tensorflow inference. In: IEEE S&P (2020)
78. Lehmkuhl, R., Mishra, P., Srinivasan, A., Popa, R.A.: Muse: secure inference resilient to malicious clients. In: USENIX Security Symposium (2021)
79. Lindell, Y.: How to simulate it – a tutorial on the simulation proof technique. In: Tutorials on the Foundations of Cryptography. ISC, pp. 277–346. Springer, Cham (2017). https://doi.org/10.1007/978-3-319-57048-8_6
80. Lindell, Y., Pinkas, B.: Privacy preserving data mining. J. Cryptol. $15$(3), 177–206 (2002)
81. Liu, J., Juuti, M., Yao, L., Asokan, N.: Oblivious neural network predictions via MiniONN transformations. In: CCS (2017)
82. Lowd, D., Meek, C.: Adversarial learning. In: Grossman, R., Bayardo, R.J., Bennett, K.P. (eds.) Proceedings of the Eleventh ACM SIGKDD International Conference on Knowledge Discovery and Data Mining, Chicago, Illinois, USA, 21–24 August 2005, pp. 641–647. ACM (2005)
83. Mann, Z.A., Weinert, C., Chabal, D., Bos, J.W.: Towards practical secure neural network inference: the journey so far and the road ahead. In: IACR Cryptol. ePrint Arch., p. 1483 (2022)

84. McSherry, F.: Privacy integrated queries: an extensible platform for privacy-preserving data analysis. In: Çetintemel, U., Zdonik, S.B., Kossmann, D., Tatbul, N. (eds.) Proceedings of the ACM SIGMOD International Conference on Management of Data, SIGMOD 2009, Providence, Rhode Island, USA, June 29 - July 2, 2009, pp. 19–30. ACM (2009)
85. Mehr, H.: Artificial intelligence for citizen services and government. Harvard Kennedy School (2017)
86. Microsoft. Azure confidential computing (2023). https://azure.microsoft.com/en-in/solutions/confidential-compute/
87. Mishra, P., Lehmkuhl, R., Srinivasan, A., Zheng, W., Popa, R.A.: DELPHI: a cryptographic inference service for neural networks. In: USENIX Security Symposium (2020)
88. Mohassel, P., Rindal, P.: ABY$^3$: a mixed protocol framework for machine learning. In: CCS (2018)
89. Mohassel, P., Zhang, Y.: SecureML: a system for scalable privacy-preserving machine learning. In: IEEE S&P (2017)
90. Muller, J.M., et al.: Handbook of Floating-Point Arithmetic. 2nd edn. Springer, Cham (2018)
91. Ohrimenko, O., et al.: Oblivious multi-party machine learning on trusted processors. In: Holz, T., Savage, S. (eds.) 25th USENIX Security Symposium, USENIX Security 16, Austin, TX, USA, 10–12 August 2016, pp. 619–636. USENIX Association (2016)
92. Oldenhof, M., et al.:. Industry-scale orchestrated federated learning for drug discovery. In: Williams, B., Chen, Y., Neville, J. (eds.) Thirty-Seventh AAAI Conference on Artificial Intelligence, AAAI 2023, Thirty-Fifth Conference on Innovative Applications of Artificial Intelligence, IAAI 2023, Thirteenth Symposium on Educational Advances in Artificial Intelligence, EAAI 2023, Washington, DC, USA, 7–14 February 2023, pp. 15576–15584. AAAI Press (2023)
93. OpenFHE. OpenFHE (2022). https://www.openfhe.org/
94. Papernot, N., McDaniel, P., Sinha, A., Wellman, M.P.: SoK: security and privacy in machine learning. In: 2018 IEEE European Symposium on Security and Privacy, EuroS&P 2018, London, United Kingdom, 24–26 April 2018, pp. 399–414. IEEE (2018)
95. Patra, A., Schneider, T., Suresh, A., Yalame, H.: ABY2.0: improved mixed-protocol secure two-party computation. In: USENIX Security Symposium (2021)
96. Patra, A., Suresh, A.: BLAZE: blazing fast privacy-preserving machine learning. In: NDSS (2020)
97. Ponomareva, N., et al.: How to DP-FY ML: a practical guide to machine learning with differential privacy. J. Artif. Intell. Res. **77**, 1113–1201 (2023)
98. Rathee, D., Bhattacharya, A., Gupta, D., Sharma, R., Song, D.: Secure floating-point training. In: 32nd USENIX Security Symposium (USENIX Security 23), pp. 6329–6346. USENIX Association, Anaheim, CA (2023)
99. Rathee, D., Bhattacharya, A., Sharma, R., Gupta, D., Chandran, N., Rastogi, A.: SecFloat: Accurate floating-point meets secure 2-party computation. In: IEEE S&P (2022)
100. Rathee, D., et al.: SIRNN: a math library for secure inference of RNNs. In: IEEE S&P (2021)
101. Rathee, D., et al.: CrypTFlow2: practical 2-party secure inference. In: CCS (2020)
102. Rescorla, E.: The transport layer security (TLS) protocol version 1.3. RFC 8446 (2018)

103. Microsoft Research. Privacy preserving machine learning: maintaining confidentiality and preserving trust (2021). https://shorturl.at/guFLM
104. Riazi, M.S., Samragh, M., Chen, H., Laine, K., Lauter, K., Koushanfar, F.: XONN: XNOR-based Oblivious Deep Neural Network Inference. In: USENIX Security (2019)
105. Rivest, R.L., Shamir, A., Adleman, L.M.: A method for obtaining digital signatures and public-key cryptosystems. Commun. ACM **21**(2), 120–126 (1978)
106. Russinovich, M., et al.: Toward confidential cloud computing. Commun. ACM **64**(6), 54–61 (2021)
107. Ryffel, T., Pointcheval, D., Bach, F.: ARIANN: Low-interaction privacy-preserving deep learning via function secret sharing. In: PETS (2022)
108. Microsoft SEAL (release 4.1) (2023). https://github.com/Microsoft/SEAL. Microsoft Research, Redmond, WA
109. Shokri, R., Stronati, M., Song, C., Shmatikov, V.: Membership inference attacks against machine learning models. In: 2017 IEEE Symposium on Security and Privacy, SP 2017, San Jose, CA, USA, 22–26 May 2017, pp. 3–18. IEEE Computer Society (2017)
110. Soin, A., et al.: Multi-institution encrypted medical imaging AI validation without data sharing (2021)
111. Storrier, K., Vadapalli, A., Lyons, A., Henry, R.: Grotto: screaming fast $(2+1)$-pc for $\mathbb{Z}_{2^n}$ via $(2, 2)$-DPFs. In: CCS (2023)
112. Tan, S., Knott, B., Tian, Y., Wu, D.J.: CryptGPU: fast privacy-preserving machine learning on the GPU. In: IEEE S&P (2021)
113. Tramèr, F., Zhang, F., Juels, A., Reiter, M.K., Ristenpart, T.: Stealing machine learning models via prediction APIs. In: Holz, T., Savage, S. (eds.) 25th USENIX Security Symposium, USENIX Security 16, Austin, TX, USA, 10–12 August 2016, pp. 601–618. USENIX Association (2016)
114. Vaswani, A., et al.: Attention is all you need. In: NeurIPS (2017)
115. Vaswani, K., et al.: Confidential computing within an AI accelerator. In: Lawall, J., Williams, D. (eds.) 2023 USENIX Annual Technical Conference, USENIX ATC 2023, Boston, MA, USA, 10–12 July 2023, pp. 501–518. USENIX Association (2023)
116. Volos, S., Vaswani, K., Bruno, R.: Graviton: trusted execution environments on GPUs. In: Arpaci-Dusseau, A.C., Voelker, G. (eds.) 13th USENIX Symposium on Operating Systems Design and Implementation, OSDI 2018, Carlsbad, CA, USA, 8–10 October 2018, pp. 681–696. USENIX Association (2018)
117. Wagh, S.: Pika: secure computation using function secret sharing over rings. In: PETS (2022)
118. Wagh, S., Gupta, D., Chandran, N.: SecureNN: 3-party secure computation for neural network training. PoPETs **2019**, 26–49 (2019)
119. Wagh, S., Tople, S., Benhamouda, F., Kushilevitz, E., Mittal, P., Rabin, T.: Falcon: honest-majority maliciously secure framework for private deep learning. In: PoPETs (2021)
120. Watson, J.-L., Wagh, S., Popa, R.A.: Piranha: a GPU platform for secure computation. In: USENIX Security Symposium (2022)
121. Yang, Y., Hui, B., Yuan, H., Gong, N., Cao, Y.: PrivateFL: accurate, differentially private federated learning via personalized data transformation. In: 32nd USENIX Security Symposium (USENIX Security 23), pp. 1595–1612. USENIX Association, Anaheim, CA (2023)
122. Yao, A.: How to generate and exchange secrets (extended abstract). In: FOCS (1986)

# Attack on the Privacy-Preserving Carpooling Service TAROT

Meghana Vargheese$^{(\boxtimes)}$ (ID) and Srinivas Vivek (ID)

IIIT Bangalore, Bengaluru, India
{meghana.pv,srinivas.vivek}@iiitb.ac.in

**Abstract.** The widespread popularity of carpooling services has brought about several privacy concerns, including the collection and use of user location data by service providers. To address these concerns, various carpooling service schemes based on homomorphic encryption have been proposed. TAROT, proposed by Xu *et al.* (IEEE IOT Journal 2022), aims to be an efficient, accurate, and privacy-preserving carpooling service scheme. In this paper, we show that there is a leakage of location data for users in TAROT. Specifically, we examine a Goldwasser-Micali (homomorphic encryption scheme)-based Equality Determination Algorithm (GMEDA) used in TAROT and propose passive attacks, where honest-but-curious users collude to steal the location information of other users.

**Keywords:** Privacy-preserving · Carpooling services · TAROT · Homomorphic encryption · Hamming weight

## 1 Introduction

Ride-Hailing Services (RHS) are a type of transportation services that aim to connect passengers and drivers through a mobile app, by allowing passengers to request a ride, and nearby drivers to accept or reject the offered ride. These services offer convenient, affordable, and flexible transportation options to users, and have become increasingly popular in recent years. Examples of popular ride-hailing services include Uber, Lyft, DiDi, and Ola, among others.

Apart from RHS, carpooling services also exist, which allow passengers travelling on the same route to connect with each other and share vehicles and transportation costs. The main advantages of these services are that they are economical and ecological. It not only saves money for the individuals involved, but it also helps reduce traffic congestion and decrease carbon emissions. Some popular carpooling services include Waze Carpool, BlaBlaCar, Scoop, etc.

In this paper, we consider carpooling services and examine one particular privacy-preserving protocol called TAROT [10]. TAROT is one among many recent privacy-preserving carpooling service protocols proposed. In any carpooling service, there are mainly two entities, the Carpooling Service Provider (CSP) and the Carpooling Users (CUs). Initially, CUs send carpooling queries to the

V. Muthukkumarasamy et al. (Eds.): ICISS 2023, LNCS 14424, pp. 249–258, 2023.
https://doi.org/10.1007/978-3-031-49099-6_15

CSP and in return, the CSP sends the carpooling group matching. Using this result, CUs finally get a group of matching users to share the ride. The carpooling queries sent by the CUs contain private location information of the CUs such as starting points, destinations, travel routes, and others. This might lead to privacy leakage. Therefore, it is challenging to design a privacy-preserving carpooling service scheme. The goal is to provide a convenient and secure way for people to carpool with one another, without compromising their privacy. Aiming at these goals, in 2022, Xu *et al.* [10] proposed an efficient, accurate, and privacy-preserving route matching scheme for carpooling services named TAROT.

In TAROT, Xu *et al.* propose a *Dissimilar Route Filter Algorithm* [10, Algorithm 2] to filter the dissimilar routes and outputs a list of candidate CUs. They also propose an *Accurate Similarity Computation Algorithm* (ASCA) [10, Algorithm 3] to compute the accurate similarity between two routes in a privacy-friendly manner. This algorithm further uses Goldwasser-Micali (GM) based Equality Determination Algorithm (GMEDA) [10, Algorithm 1]. The GM algorithm [3] is a probabilistic public-key encryption algorithm that encrypts only one bit at a time and satisfies the XOR homomorphic property. GMEDA is used to determine whether the location points of two users are identical or not in a privacy-friendly manner. The users apply the GM algorithm to encrypt their respective location points. One of the users performs a Hadamard product on both encrypted points, where the Hadamard product of two vectors is defined to be the element-wise multiplication of the two vectors, and permutes the elements to preserve privacy and sends the result to the other user. On decryption, the other user can determine whether their respective location points are identical or not. By employing this method, a user can identify if their location point matches that of the other user, without directly knowing the other user's location point.

## 1.1 Threat Model

We consider the same threat model as in TAROT [10] where the CSP and CUs are honest in executing the protocol. The CUs send legitimate requests by encrypting their precise location points to the CSP during the query phase and to other CUs to compute the accurate similarity between their corresponding routes. Also, the CSP will honestly adhere to the protocol when providing CUs with carpooling query services. The CSP and CUs are both honest but have a sense of curiosity within the protocol. The CSP wants to learn more about the CUs' private location information, while the CUs want to know more about other CUs' private location information.

The TAROT protocol aims to preserve the location privacy of CUs from both the CSP and from other CUs. The authors assume that there is no collusion between the CSP and CUs in TAROT as otherwise it would be possible for the CSP to learn about the location of other CUs in a straightforward way. Our passive attacks on GMEDA utilizes the fact that the honest-but-curious CUs collude within themselves to steal the location information of other CUs. These colluding CUs can include anyone taking part in the TAROT protocol and not just the CUs who have already matched successfully. Therefore, our attacks are valid in the threat model considered in [10]. We stress that honest-but-curious CUs that collude is a realistic threat as an adversary could always hire two or more CUs to work for it.

## 1.2  Our Contribution

The authors in [10] claim that GMEDA preserves the privacy of CUs. In Sect. 2, we present two variants of passive attacks on GMEDA where some of the honest-but-curious CUs collude to steal the sensitive location details of other CUs. In the first variant, the colluding adversary CUs choose location points of their choice. The second variant is a more efficient attack where the location points of the colluding adversary CUs are arbitrarily placed. That is, these location points may be placed anywhere, which may not always be of the CUs' choice.

As mentioned previously, in the GMEDA protocol, one of the users performs a Hadamard product on both the encrypted location points and permutes the elements. However, this leaks the Hamming weight of the XOR values of the location points of both users. We make use of this fact to mount passive attacks on GMEDA. We model the passive attacks where colluding CUs are considered adversaries and the goal is to recover the location information of the target user. Our Attack-1 uses $l + 1$ honest-but-curious adversary CUs in collusion and Attack-2 uses at least $l$ honest-but-curious adversary CUs in collusion, where $l$ is the number of bits in the bit representation of the location points of the users. We provide algorithms for the proposed Attack-1 and Attack-2 in Algorithm 2 and Algorithm 3, respectively. Our experiments show that we can recover the secret location points of all the users with a 100% success rate in both Attack-1 and Attack-2. Our Attack-1 algorithm runs in $\mathcal{O}(nl)$ time and the Attack-2 algorithm runs in $\mathcal{O}(nLl)$ time, where $n$ is the number of users in the post-filtering stage of the TAROT protocol, $l$ is the number of bits in the bit representation of the location points of the users and $L$ is the number of users in collusion.

In our attacks on GMEDA, we make use of the leaked Hamming weights of the XOR values of the location points of the users. Interestingly, problems related to the extraction of values using the Hamming weights have been addressed in a different context in the side-channel implementations. For instance, in [11] the authors use the Hamming weight of the intermediate values of the ARX-based block cipher's state to analyse the standard side-channel leakage from the power consumption or electromagnetic radiation of the cipher's execution. The paper [2] discusses a side-channel analysis of multiplications in $GF(2^{128})$. The authors show that the secret multiplier can be efficiently recovered by utilizing the least significant bit of the Hamming weight of the multiplication result. As a follow-up work, the paper [1] presents a novel side-channel attack against the multiplication in $GF(2^{128})$ which utilizes the most significant bits of the Hamming weight of the multiplication result. However, the variant in our attacks utilizing the Hamming weights does not seem to be investigated to the best of our knowledge.

The attack we present in this work is another addition to the recent cryptanalytic attacks in [4–9] on PP-RHS protocols.

## 1.3    Outline of the Paper

Section 2 describes the preliminaries required to understand GMEDA - a privacy-preserving equality determination algorithm used in the TAROT protocol and provides two variants of passive attacks on GMEDA.

## 2    GMEDA - Privacy-Preserving Equality Determination Algorithm

This section briefly explains the steps involved in TAROT. It also provides a detail explanation of the steps involved in GMEDA, a privacy-preserving equality determination algorithm used in TAROT and proposes passive attacks on GMEDA, where honest-but-curious users collude to steal the private location information of other users.

### 2.1    TAROT

In this section, we briefly explain the steps involved in the TAROT protocol [10]. In TAROT, each route is represented by a set of location points, which is also considered as a vector and each location is represented as a point on a grid. The following are the steps involved in TAROT:

1. **Initialization:** In this step, the CSP publishes the public parameters, and each user publishes their respective public keys.
2. **Query Token Generation:** In this step, each user generates their carpooling queries and sends them to the CSP.
3. **Dissimilar Route Filter:** On receiving the carpooling query tokens, the CSP uses Dissimilar Route Filter Algorithm (DRFA) [10, Algorithm 2] to filter the dissimilar routes among the CUs and outputs a list of candidate CUs for further analysis.
4. **Accurate Similarity Computation:** Accurate Similarity Computation Algorithm (ASCA) [10, Algorithm 3] is run between the candidate CUs to accurately compute the similarities between their respective routes. After the computations, the CUs send their corresponding results to the CSP.
5. **CU Grouping:** Based on the results sent by the CUs, the CSP outputs the CU grouping results.

### 2.2    GMEDA

In the fourth step of TAROT, the candidate CUs use Accurate Similarity Computation Algorithm (ASCA) to compute their corresponding route similarities. This algorithm further uses, Goldwasser-Micali-based Equality Determination Algorithm (GMEDA). GMEDA is an algorithm proposed by Xu *et al.* [10] to determine whether two location points are identical. It is based on Goldwasser-Micali (GM), a probabilistic public-key encryption algorithm that encrypts only one bit at a time. The GM algorithm satisfies the XOR homomorphic property.

That is, $\mathrm{Enc}(m_1) \times \mathrm{Enc}(m_2) \to \mathrm{Enc}(m_1 \oplus m_2)$. The GMEDA protocol involves two users $\mathrm{CU}_i$ and $\mathrm{CU}_j$ who each have an integer value $A$ and $B$, respectively, encoded as an $l$-bit integer, and want to determine whether $A$ equals $B$. The steps in GMEDA are as follows and are given in Algorithm 1.

1. Let, $[\![\,]\!]$ represent encryption in the GM algorithm.
2. $\mathrm{CU}_i$ generates public key $pk_i$ and secret key $sk_i$ as in GM algorithm. $\mathrm{CU}_i$ uses $pk_i$ to encrypt $A$ as $[\![A]\!]$.
3. $\mathrm{CU}_i$ sends $pk_i$ and $[\![A]\!]$ to $\mathrm{CU}_j$.
4. $\mathrm{CU}_j$ generates $[\![B]\!]$ by encrypting $B$ with $pk_i$.
5. $\mathrm{CU}_j$ computes the Hadamard product of $[\![A]\!]$ and $[\![B]\!]$, denoted by $[\![A]\!] \circ [\![B]\!]$.
6. $\mathrm{CU}_j$ then randomly permutes the elements of $[\![A]\!] \circ [\![B]\!]$ to obtain $[\![A]\!][\![B]\!]$, and sends it to $\mathrm{CU}_i$.
7. $\mathrm{CU}_i$ decrypts each element of $[\![A]\!][\![B]\!]$ using $sk_i$ and outputs $A = B$ if the decryption result is 0, and $A \neq B$ otherwise.

---

**Algorithm 1.** GMEDA [10, Algorithm 1]

```
1: procedure ENC                                              ▷ by CUᵢ
2:     (pkᵢ, skᵢ) ← KeyGen(κ)                     ▷ public and private key
3:     A ← ⟨a₁, a₂, …, aₗ⟩₂                          ▷ express A in binary
4:     ⟦A⟧ = (⟦a₁⟧, ⟦a₂⟧, …, ⟦aₗ⟧)                      ▷ encrypt A with pkᵢ
5:     send ⟦A⟧ to CUⱼ
6: end procedure

7: procedure MULTIENC                                         ▷ by CUⱼ
8:     B ← ⟨b₁, b₂, …, bₗ⟩₂                          ▷ express B in binary
9:     ⟦B⟧ = (⟦b₁⟧, ⟦b₂⟧, …, ⟦bₗ⟧)                      ▷ encrypt B with pkᵢ
10:    ⟦A⟧ ∘ ⟦B⟧ ← (⟦a₁⟧ × ⟦b₁⟧, ⟦a₂⟧ × ⟦b₂⟧, …, ⟦aₗ⟧ × ⟦bₗ⟧)
11:    ⟦A⟧⟦B⟧ ← randomly permute ⟦A⟧ ∘ ⟦B⟧
12:    send ⟦A⟧⟦B⟧ to CUᵢ
13: end procedure

14: procedure GETEQUALITY                                     ▷ by CUᵢ
15:    for e ∈ ⟦A⟧⟦B⟧ do
16:        if Dec(skᵢ, e) = 1 then
17:            send A ≠ B to CUⱼ
18:        end if
19:    end for
20:    if all Dec(skᵢ, e) = 0 then
21:        send A = B to CUⱼ
22:    end if
23: end procedure
```

---

As mentioned earlier, TAROT uses GMEDA to compute the accurate similarity between two routes. In [10, Section IV A] the authors claim that the step where the user $CU_j$ permutes the elements in the Hadamard product of $[\![A]\!]$ and $[\![B]\!]$ in GMEDA is the key to achieving privacy preservation. However, it is a practical possibility that CUs can collude with each other to steal other CUs' private location information. In this regard, we consider a case where some of the honest-but-curious CUs collude to steal the location information of other CUs and propose passive collusion attacks. We consider the following two variants of the passive attacks:

1. **Attack-1:** In this variant, the honest-but-curious CUs collude and choose location points of their choice.
2. **Attack-2:** In this variant, the honest-but-curious CUs collude and their location points are arbitrarily placed.

Consider the step in the GMEDA protocol where $CU_j$ sends the permuted elements of the Hadamard product of $[\![A]\!]$ and $[\![B]\!]$. In practice if User $CU_i$ is honest-but-curious, then it could choose zero as its location point. Suppose $CU_i$ encrypts zero and sends it to $CU_j$. Then, $CU_j$ outputs $[\![0]\!][\![B]\!]$ by randomly permuting the elements of the Hadamard product of $[\![0]\!]$ and $[\![B]\!]$. Because of the XOR homomorphic property of the GM algorithm, $[\![0]\!][\![B]\!]$ is equivalent to the result obtained by permuting the elements of $[\![0 \oplus B]\!]$, which is the same as the permuted elements of $[\![B]\!]$. On decryption, the user $CU_i$ determines the number of 1 s in $B$. Hence, $CU_i$ learns the Hamming weight of $B$. Our goal is to recover $B$ considering $CU_j$ as the target user for any $j$.

Both our attacks assume that there are sufficiently many honest-but-curious adversaries who pass the dissimilar route filtering stage in TAROT. This is feasible in practice since the colluding adversaries may possess knowledge of the general area in which the target user resides, even if they do not have precise location information. By positioning attackers in proximity to the known area, it becomes feasible to gather a sufficient number of attackers to potentially bypass the filtering stage.

### 2.3   Attack on GMEDA (Attack-1)

In this section, we consider a passive collusion attack where honest-but-curious CUs collude and choose the location points of their choice. Suppose the location point of the target user is an $l$-bit string $k$, we need $l + 1$ honest-but-curious CUs in collusion to recover the secret location point $k$. Our attack is similar to a key recovery attack in the Chosen Plaintext Attack (CPA) model for encryption schemes.

For each $i, 0 \leq i \leq l$, let $m_i$ represent the location point chosen by the colluding user $CU_i$. During the query phase of the GMEDA protocol, each $CU_i$ encrypts $m_i$ and sends it to the target user $CU_j$. In return, $CU_j$ sends the randomly permuted elements of the Hadamard product of $[\![m_i]\!]$ and $[\![k]\!]$, which is equivalent to the randomly permuted elements of $[\![m_i \oplus k]\!]$ due to the XOR homomorphic property of the GM algorithm. Upon decryption, each $CU_i$ in collusion learns the Hamming weight of $m_i \oplus k$ denoted as $HW(m_i \oplus k)$. To recover the unknown location $k$ the CUs in collusion use the following strategies:

1. $CU_0$ sends the encryption of zero as its query to the target user $CU_j$. As a result, $CU_0$ learns $HW(0 \oplus k) = HW(k)$ and denotes it as $c_0$.
2. For each $i, 1 \le i \le l$, $CU_i$ sends the encryption of $e_i$ to the target user $CU_j$, where $e_i$ has 1 in the $i^{th}$ position and zeroes everywhere else. As a result, each $CU_i$ learns $HW(e_i \oplus k)$ and denotes it as $c_i, 1 \le i \le l$.

Note that $HW(e_i \oplus k) < HW(k)$ if $k$ has a 1 in the $i^{th}$ position, and $HW(e_i \oplus k) > HW(k)$ if $k$ has a 0 in the $i^{th}$ position. Therefore, by comparing $c_0$ with each $c_i$, where $1 \le i \le l$, the colluding CUs can recover the secret location point $k$ of the target user $CU_j$. The algorithm to recover the secret location point $k$ using Attack-1 is given in Algorithm 2. It is clear from the algorithm that, if $l+1$ users collude, then they can recover the location points of all the users with 100% success rate. Our algorithm is efficient and runs in $\mathcal{O}(nl)$ time, where $n$ is the number of users in the post-filtering stage of the TAROT protocol and $l$ is the number of bits in the bit representation of the location points of the users.

---

**Algorithm 2.** Attack-1

---

1: **procedure**
2:     **Input** : $K \leftarrow \{0,1\}^l$                    ▷ Location point of any target user $CU_j$
3:     **Output** : $K'$ such that $K = K'$
4:     $M \leftarrow null$                    ▷ List to store the queries $m_i$
5:     $temp \leftarrow$ list of zeroes of length $l$
6:     **for** $i \leftarrow 1$ to $l$ **do**                    ▷ Generating $e_i$ bit strings
7:         $temp[i] = 1$
8:         Add $temp$ to $M$
9:         $temp \leftarrow$ list of zeroes of length $l$                    ▷ Re-initializing to 0
10:     **end for**
11:     **return** $M$
12:     $C \leftarrow$ list of zeroes of length $l+1$        ▷ List to store the result of GMEDA
13:     $C[0] \leftarrow HW(K)$
14:     **for** $i \leftarrow 1$ to $l$ **do**
15:         $C[i+1] \leftarrow HW(M[i] \oplus K)$        ▷ Computing the result of GMEDA
16:     **end for**
17:     $K' \leftarrow$ list of zeroes of length $l$        ▷ List to store the recovered secret
18:     **for** $i \leftarrow 1$ to $l$ **do**
19:         **if** $C[i+1] < C[0]$ **then**
20:             $K'[i] = 1$
21:         **else**
22:             $K'[i] = 0$
23:         **end if**
24:     **end for**
25:     **return** $K'$                    ▷ The recovered location point
26: **end procedure**

---

## 2.4   A More Efficient Attack on GMEDA (Attack-2)

In this section, we consider a passive collusion attack where honest-but-curious CUs collude and their location points are arbitrarily placed. Let the location point of the target user $CU_j$ be an $l$-bit string $k$. Let $L$ many honest-but-curious users collude to recover the secret location point $k$. In this collusion attack, when the CUs collude they know their arbitrarily placed $l$-bit location points $m_i$ and their corresponding results obtained at the end of the GMEDA protocol, $c_i = HW(m_i \oplus k)$. Our goal is to recover the secret location point $k$ with the knowledge of these known pair of values $(m_i, c_i), 1 \le i \le L$. Our attack is similar to the Known Plaintext Attack (KPA) model on encryption schemes. In this attack model, the adversary is weaker than the adversary in Attack-1, hence this is a more powerful attack.

For each $i, 1 \le i \le L$, $c_i$ is the sum of XOR of each bit of $m_i \oplus k$. Let $c_i = \langle c_{i1}, c_{i2}, \dots, c_{il} \rangle_2$, $m_i = \langle m_{i1}, m_{i2}, \dots, m_{il} \rangle_2$ and $k = \langle k_1, k_2, \dots, k_l \rangle_2$ be the bit representations of $c_i$, $m_i$ and $k$, respectively. Then,

$$c_i = HW(m_i \oplus k) = \sum_{j=1}^{l}(m_{ij} \oplus k_i).$$

Here, $m_{ij}$'s and $c_i$'s are known, and the $k_i$'s are unknown. That is, we have $L$ equations in $l$ unknowns. Solving these equations, if possible, reveals the secret $k$. Each equation contains both a Boolean sum and an integer sum which makes it tricky to solve them. To simplify solving these equations, we rewrite the Boolean sum as an integer sum as follows:

$$c_i = \sum_{j=1}^{l}(m_{ij} \oplus k_i) = \sum_{j=1}^{L}((-1)^{m_{ij}} k_j + m_{ij}), \forall 1 \le i \le L.$$

Now, we have $L$ linear system of equations over integers in $l$ unknowns. Solving this system of equations, if possible, recovers the unknown location point $k$ completely. The variable $L$ has to be at least $l$ for a unique solution to the above system of equations to exist. That is, we require at least $l$ users to collude to recover the secret location point of the target user. This is practically possible since the number of bits in the bit representation of the location points is not large.

We represent the above system of equations in the matrix form $AK' = B$, where $A$ represents the coefficient matrix, $K'$ represents the variable matrix and $B$ represents the constant matrix. We use the Row-Reduced Echelon Form method to solve the system $AK' = B$. The algorithm to recover the secret location point $k$ using Attack-2 is given in Algorithm 3. Our algorithm is efficient and runs in $\mathcal{O}(nLl)$ time, where $n$ is the number of users in the post-filtering stage of the TAROT protocol, $l$ is the number of bits in the bit representation of the location points of the users and $L$ is the number of users in collusion.

Let us consider the following example to understand Attack-2. Let, $k = \langle 1, 0 \rangle_2$ be the location point of the target user, and $m_1 = \langle 1, 1 \rangle_2$ and $m_2 = \langle 0, 1 \rangle_2$ be the location points of the colluding users $CU_1$ and $CU_2$, respectively. Then, $A = \begin{bmatrix} -1 & -1 \\ 1 & -1 \end{bmatrix}$, $B = \begin{bmatrix} -1 \\ 1 \end{bmatrix}$. Now, solving the system, $AK' = B$, we get, $K' = \begin{bmatrix} 1 \\ 0 \end{bmatrix} = k$, the location point of the target user.

---

**Algorithm 3. Attack-2**

---

1: **procedure**
2:     **Input** : $K \leftarrow \{0,1\}^l$                    ▷ Location point of any target user $CU_j$
            $m_i \xleftarrow{\$} \{0,1\}^l, 1 \leq i \leq L$     ▷ Location point of the adversary user $CU_i$
            $c_i \leftarrow \mathrm{HW}(m_i \oplus k), 1 \leq i \leq L$     ▷ Result sent by $CU_j$ in the GMEDA
3:     **Output** : $K'$ such that $K = K'$

4:     $K \leftarrow \langle k_1, k_2, \ldots, k_l \rangle_2$                    ▷ Bit representation of $K$
5:     $m_i \leftarrow \langle m_{i1}, m_{i2}, \ldots, m_{il} \rangle_2$ for each $1 \leq i \leq L$     ▷ Bit representation of $m_i$
6:     $c_i \leftarrow \mathrm{HW}(m_i \oplus k) = \sum_{j=1}^{l}(m_{ij} \oplus k_j)$
7:     $c_i \leftarrow \sum_{j=1}^{l}((-1)^{m_{ij}} k_j + m_{ij})$     ▷ Re-writing Boolean sum as integer sum
8:     $A \leftarrow (a_{ij})$ such that $a_{ij} = (-1)^{m_{ij}}$     ▷ Coefficient matrix of order $L \times l$
9:     $B \leftarrow (b_i)$ such that $b_i = c_i - \mathrm{HW}(m_i)$     ▷ Constant matrix of order $L \times 1$
10:    $K' \leftarrow (k'_i)$                    ▷ Variable matrix of order $l \times 1$
11:    Solve $AK' = B$
12:    **return** $K'$                    ▷ The recovered location point
13: **end procedure**

---

Since the location points $m_i$ are randomly generated, in certain cases, even when $L \geq l$, the system $AK' = B$ may become undetermined or yield multiple solutions. This occurrence is attributed to the presence of dependent rows in the augmented matrix $[A : B]$, resulting in non-pivot columns and, consequently, multiple solutions. As the number of rows, denoted as $L$, increases, the likelihood of non-pivot columns decreases, thereby enhancing the success rate. To estimate the number of colluding users required to completely recover the secret location point $k$ of the target user $CU_j$, we ran experiments for different values of $l$ and $L$. For each value of $L$, we considered 100 runs and estimated the success rate. From Table 1, it is clear that in all the cases, we could recover $k$ with a success rate close to 100. Therefore, for an appropriate $L$, if $L \geq l$ users collude, then they can recover the location points of all the users with 100% success rate.

**Table 1.** Estimate of Success for Attack-2

| $L$ | $l = 10$ | | | | $l = 11$ | | | | $l = 12$ | | | |
|---|---|---|---|---|---|---|---|---|---|---|---|---|
| | 10 | 11 | 12 | 13 | 11 | 12 | 13 | 14 | 12 | 13 | 14 | 15 |
| Success rate (%) | 92 | 95 | 97 | 100 | 84 | 97 | 100 | 100 | 88 | 99 | 100 | 100 |

**Acknowledgements.** This work was funded by the Infosys Foundation Career Development Chair Professorship grant for Srinivas Vivek.

# References

1. Belaïd, S., Coron, J.-S., Fouque, P.-A., Gérard, B., Kammerer, J.-G., Prouff, E.: Improved side-channel analysis of finite-field multiplication. In: Güneysu, T., Handschuh, H. (eds.) CHES 2015. LNCS, vol. 9293, pp. 395–415. Springer, Heidelberg (2015). https://doi.org/10.1007/978-3-662-48324-4_20
2. Belaïd, S., Fouque, P.-A., Gérard, B.: Side-channel analysis of multiplications in $GF(2^{128})$. In: Sarkar, P., Iwata, T. (eds.) ASIACRYPT 2014. LNCS, vol. 8874, pp. 306–325. Springer, Heidelberg (2014). https://doi.org/10.1007/978-3-662-45608-8_17
3. Goldwasser, S., Micali, S.: Probabilistic encryption. J. Comput. Syst. Sci. **28**(2), 270–299 (1984). https://doi.org/10.1016/0022-0000(84)90070-9
4. Kumaraswamy, D., Murthy, S., Vivek, S.: Revisiting driver anonymity in ORide. In: AlTawy, R., Hülsing, A. (eds.) SAC 2021. LNCS, vol. 13203, pp. 25–46. Springer, Cham (2022). https://doi.org/10.1007/978-3-030-99277-4_2
5. Kumaraswamy, D., Vivek, S.: Cryptanalysis of the privacy-preserving ride-hailing service TRACE. In: Adhikari, A., Küsters, R., Preneel, B. (eds.) INDOCRYPT 2021. LNCS, vol. 13143, pp. 462–484. Springer, Cham (2021). https://doi.org/10.1007/978-3-030-92518-5_21
6. Murthy, S., Vivek, S.: Driver locations harvesting attack on pRide. In: Yuan, X., Bai, G., Alcaraz, C., Majumdar, S. (eds.) NSS 2022. LNCS, vol. 13787, pp. 633–648. Springer, Cham (2022). https://doi.org/10.1007/978-3-031-23020-2_36
7. Murthy, S., Vivek, S.: Passive triangulation attack on ORide. In: Beresford, A.R., Patra, A., Bellini, E. (eds.) CANS 2022. LNCS, vol. 13641, pp. 167–187. Springer, Cham (2022). https://doi.org/10.1007/978-3-031-20974-1_8
8. Vivek, S.: Attacks on a privacy-preserving publish-subscribe system and a ride-hailing service. In: Paterson, M.B. (ed.) IMACC 2021. LNCS, vol. 13129, pp. 59–71. Springer, Cham (2021). https://doi.org/10.1007/978-3-030-92641-0_4
9. Vivek, S.: Attack on "a privacy-preserving online ride-hailing system without involving a third trusted server". In: Proceedings of the 18th International Conference on Availability, Reliability and Security, ARES 2023, pp. 59:1–59:3. ACM (2023). https://doi.org/10.1145/3600160.3605040
10. Xu, Q., Zhu, H., Zheng, Y., Zhao, J., Lu, R., Li, H.: An efficient and privacy-preserving route matching scheme for carpooling services. IEEE Internet Things J. **9**(20), 19890–19902 (2022). https://doi.org/10.1109/JIOT.2022.3168661
11. Yan, Y., Oswald, E., Vivek, S.: An analytic attack against ARX addition exploiting standard side-channel leakage. In: Mori, P., Lenzini, G., Furnell, S. (eds.) Proceedings of the 7th International Conference on Information Systems Security and Privacy, ICISSP 2021, pp. 89–97. SCITEPRESS (2021). https://doi.org/10.5220/0010223600890097

# Democracy in Your Hands!: Practical Multi-key Homomorphic E-Voting

Tanusree Parbat[1]($\boxtimes$)(iD), Aniket Banerjee[2], and Ayantika Chatterjee[1](iD)

[1] Indian Institute of Technology Kharagpur, Kharagpur, India
tanusree.parbat@iitkgp.ac.in
[2] Indian Institute of Engineering Science and Technology, Shibpur, Shibpur, India

**Abstract.** Digitization of elections demands end-to-end security of the overall process and hence, cyber security for elections is an important issue. Distributed blockchain technology in e-voting can only provide verification advantages. However, voters' authenticity, data confidentiality, and intermediaries represent other major concerns in this regard. Existing secure voting frameworks either provide final voting results with the help of trusted intermediaries or provide vote verifiability in an unencrypted domain. At present, there is no such realistic mechanism to assure full security of vote casting and result declaration from cyber threats. Even Microsoft's ElectionGuard is not free from postquantum attacks due to additive ElGamal cryptosystem. To achieve effective guards against cyberattacks, we propose a voting framework, which reduces vote transmission overhead on a per-voter basis and supports post-quantum secure automated vote counting and winner selection without any manual intervention with the aid of multi-key homomorphic encryption. Along with suitable preventive measures against double voting, vote rigging, and coercion effects, we include a secure result deciphering process evading the possibility of result alteration using multi-key approach. Though our scheme is scalable for smaller as well as large organizations/communities, encrypted processing is inherently performance-costly. Hence, to reduce the overall timing overhead, encrypted hierarchical processing with zonal segregation and parallel computation have been incorporated. Our proposed scheme demonstrates party-specific vote counting without rank generation within 4 days and 22 h and vote counting with winner rank calculation within 5 days (for four candidates and one hundred thousand voters) without any manual intervention with the support of suitable distributed computing.

**Keywords:** E-voting · Security · Privacy · Homomorphic Encryption · Multi-key

## 1 Introduction

Security is a major concern for both online and offline voting. Secret vote suffrage and vote transmitting to the server through internet may be convenient and

© The Author(s), under exclusive license to Springer Nature Switzerland AG 2023
V. Muthukkumarasamy et al. (Eds.): ICISS 2023, LNCS 14424, pp. 259–271, 2023.
https://doi.org/10.1007/978-3-031-49099-6_16

appealing in both voting systems, but they come with added concern of security. In fact, traditional ballot-based voting is also not free from device exploitation, through which attackers gain access to voting-related critical information. Recent research shows that blockchain-based security solutions only provide vote or voter verifiability, which is not enough to provide minimal election security requirements like ballot secrecy and contestability [18].

Several research works [1,5,13,16] have explored the e-voting scheme with blockchain to resolve the security issues in existing paper based voting schemes, but they are either lacking integrity [1] or confidentiality. In 2021, Mccrory et al. [16] proposed an end-to-end secure e-voting over blockchain but this work suffers from scalability issues. Some online voting platforms like "Follow My Vote", "Polyas", "Luxoft", "Voatz", "Polys", "Agora" etc., are already adapted by several countries like US and Europe. These platforms encounter a lack of voters' authenticity and scalability issues due to the usage of blockchain technology in a straightforward way. From a recent study [20], it is known that "Voatz" mobile app suffers from severe security flaws that allow attackers to observe the vote casting and alter the ballot. Few other research efforts [6,17] provide solutions for voter-verifiability, and contestability but ballot secrecy is not supported in those schemes. In this work, we implement a practical voting framework in encrypted domain that supports ballot confidentiality and voting result computation without any manual intervention. In case of traditional encryption, encrypted plaintext must be decrypted before processing over it. So, data may be leaked during computation because of intermediate decryption. To provide outsourced data security during computation without any intermediate decryption, homomorphic encryption (HE) [12] is a conventional solution, which is adapted in this case. Along with providing security, proposed framework is also meaningful to reduce the gross overhead of manual vote counting. Moreover, our proposed solution can also be easily adapted for traditional EVM-based vote counting with the support of additional processing hardware like Raspberry Pi.

## Limitations of Additive Homomorphic-Based Voting Framework

Existing few works proposed secure e-voting scheme with automated vote counting by additive homomorphic encryption [2,14,19]. Recently, Microsoft ElectionGuard [15] has proposed end-to-end vote verifiability and homomorphic aggregation of votes using ElGamal cryptosystem. However, there are some recent reported attacks against additive homomorphic schemes like Paillier, ElGamal cryptosystem as they are not post-quantum secure [10]. Chillotti et al. [10] proposed a post-quantum resistant e-voting scheme which offers a publicly verifiable ciphertext trapdoor instead of zero-knowledge proof and intermediate processing assuming an honest bulletin board. Here, we highlight more technically the limitations of additive homomorphic encryption-based YES-NO elections where 'YES' means 1 and 'NO' means 0. Let us consider there is a $\ell$ number of election candidates. While a voter selects his/her preferred candidate, it is considered as 1, whereas the remaining $(\ell - 1)$ candidates' votes are automatically considered to be 0. Now, all these votes are encrypted and transmitted to respective homomorphic adders in the server. According to the vote aggregation, only *Total vote* count of selected candidate (whose received vote is encrypted 1) will be added with 1 and other $(\ell - 1)$ candidates' *Total vote* count will be added with 0. This method requires transmitting all encrypted votes for each candidate for every voter, leading to increased transmission overhead as the number of candidates grows. To reduce this overhead, a more efficient approach involves transmitting only the selected candidate's ID as the vote for each voter.

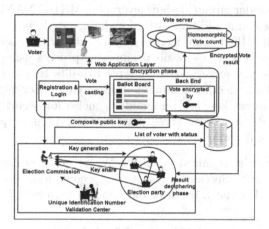

**Fig. 1.** System model for voting

In this context, our motivation is to develop a secure automated voting system using multi-key homomorphic encryption (MK-HE), eliminating the need for transmitting $\ell$ encrypted votes per voter. Instead of YES-NO votes, we assign binary codes (candidate's ID) to each candidate and transmit only the chosen candidate's encrypted code as the vote. In the subsequent section, we will detail this decoding framework to process the encrypted vote in server and discuss the associated overhead. Our framework is generic and can be adapted for smaller organizations as well as can be scaled for larger organizations/requirements with suitable parallelization techniques. We specifically choose MK-TFHE library [9] to alleviate the requirement of intermediate trusted authority with the support of multi-key encryption. This MK-TFHE scheme follows a number of polynomial-time algorithms: Setup(), KeyGen(), Enc(), Eval(), PartDec(), and Merge() to process multi-key computation (see the reference [8] for more details). However, the main challenge in this work is to implement the circuit-based representation of vote count and final winner declaration using basic supported gates, specifically MK-TFHE-based NAND gates (MKHE_NAND). Our contributions are as follows:

1. To maintain the ballot secrecy we propose a new voting scheme with multi-key homomorphic encryption. Instead of YES-NO voting, we transmit only the

encrypted code of the selected candidate to the server. Now, server follows a circuit-based homomorphic decoding with MKHE_NAND operations to identify encrypted votes, reducing performance overhead in decision-making.

2. Second, We propose an optimized addition method for counting votes automatically. As encrypted votes passes through the decoding technique, it generates a 1-bit vote (i.e., Encrypted 0 for all candidates except chosen candidate who received Encrypted 1) for each candidate. So, we require to add this 1 bit vote with $k$ bits total vote count for each candidate. But its circuit-based representation is challenging in homomorphic domain. To address this, we use a bit-wise half-adder circuit design, leveraging MKHE_NAND operations for the desired vote count addition. Additionally, we apply homomorphic sorting technique in MK-HE domain to declare rank-wise winner selection.

3. Finally, we present a secure result deciphering process using multi-key computation, where the server sends encrypted results to all parties, including candidates and the election commission. Each party decrypts the result partially with its secret key, adds a smudging noise for security, and shares it with others. After receiving these partially decrypted outputs, each party computes the final voting results.

The remaining paper is organized as follows. We introduce our system model and threat model in Sect. 2. Section 3 presents our scheme followed by performance evaluation in Sect. 4. Finally, we draw our conclusion in Sect. 5.

## 2    System Model and Threat Model

Our system model consists of four significant entities - 1) Election Commission (EC), 2) Number of Voters, denoted as $\nu = \{\nu_1, \ldots \nu_n\}$, 3) Election candidate, denoted as $\xi = \{\xi_1, \ldots \xi_\ell\}$, and 4) Vote Server. Figure 1 depicts our proposed system model. **Election Commission** (EC) is responsible for voter validation, tracking voter status, and announcing the election winner. In this model, EC shares a common security parameter with election candidates to generate their key pairs. It forms a joint public key ($j\_pk$) from all candidates' public keys, including its own, and a joint evaluation key ($j\_ek$). EC stores $j\_pk$ in an encryption unit (EU)/encryption module (EM) for vote encryption and sends $j\_ek$ to the vote server for homomorphic evaluation. Encrypted votes are then transmitted from EU/EM to the server for further processing. **Voters** receive a ballot board with a list of election candidates $\{\xi_1, \ldots \xi_\ell\}$, including corresponding candidate IDs, to cast their votes after proving their authenticity. Before casting their votes, they need to confirm their authenticity with the help of unique identification number (UIN) and fingerprint template following proposed validation protocol. **Election Candidates** $\xi_i$ share their $pk_i$ and $ek_i$ sequentially with EC to form a $j\_pk$ and $j\_ek$ keeping secret keys private with them. Each candidate will participate to decrypt voting results by combining partially decrypted results from all other parties (whose $pk$ is involved in $j\_pk$). **Vote Server** is only responsible for adding a casting vote with the appropriate candidate's vote under homomorphic environment and storing this computed result.

Our proposed solution is adaptable to both offline and online voting systems. In offline voting, a Raspberry Pi-based hardware encryption unit (EU) can be added to traditional EVMs for encryption. In online voting, individuals can cast their votes using mobile devices or laptops with a software-based encryption module (EM) integrated into the voting platform. The output from the hardware encryption unit or software encryption module is then transmitted to the vote server for processing and result generation.

Based on the key generation by participating candidates, EC forms a joint public key and joint evaluation key after receiving public and evaluation keys sequentially from the candidates. This assumption is reasonable due to multi-key processing over the encrypted vote count in the server. In this model, EC, vote server, election candidates are considered to be semi-honest, which means they follows the proposed scheme but may be curious to know private information. However, like traditional paper voting, our model ensures that voters cannot cast multiple votes during the same voting session to prevent coercion.

## 3   Encrypted Voting Framework Implementation

Our proposed scheme improves the voting system by enhancing the security requirements of six phases related to traditional voting framework. Subsequent sections describe the phases in detail.

### 3.1   Key Generation Phase

In this phase, EC generates two types of keys - MK-HE related key (joint public key $j\_pk = [pk_{EC}, \{pk_1, pk_2, \ldots, pk_\ell\}_{pk_i | \ell \in candidate}]$ and joint evaluation key $j\_ek = [ek_{EC}, \{ek_1, ek_2, \ldots, ek_\ell\}_{ek_i | \ell \in candidate}])$ for encrypted computation and ECC-based key (EC's public $Epk_{EC}$ and private key $Esk_{EC}$)) for confidential data transmission. In general, to avoid MK-HE based transmission overhead and ciphertext-related memory requirement we use ECC encryption with low overhead for securely storing voter information.

EC also chooses a hash function $H(.)$, which follows $H : \{0,1\}^* \longrightarrow \{0,1\}$. At the end of key generation, public keys ($Epk_{EC}$, base point of ECC curve $E_p$ i.e. $P$ and hash function $H(.)$ are publicly available for ECC-based data transmission.

### 3.2   Voter Registration Phase

In this phase, before applying for voter registration, a citizen should have a unique identification number (UIN) and key-token ($S1$) from unique identification number validation center (UINVC). If a citizen doesn't have it, s/he applies for a UIN number with his/her fingerprint template (which will be collected by UINVC using MINDTCT tool [21]). UINVC derives fingerprint key ($f_k$) from fingerprint template [3] along with generating UIN number and a $k$-bit random number for the applicant. UINVC encrypts UIN and DOB separately

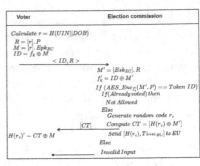

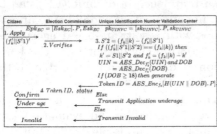

(a) voter Registration        (b) Voter verification phase

**Fig. 2.** Voter registration and login phase

by $f_k$ using AES encryption technique. It stores $(f_k||k)$, $AES\_Enc_{fk}(UIN)$, $AES\_Enc_{fk}(DOB)$ and key-token $S1$ after dividing $k$ bit number into $S1$ and $S2$. Here, UINVC stores these information as per applicant encrypted by its public key i.e., $pk_{UINVC} = sk_{UINVC}.P$ (where $sk_{UINVC}$ indicates secret key of UINVC). At last, it sends $UIN$ and key-token $S1$ to the applicant. While a citizen applies for voter registration with fingerprint template and the key-token i.e., $(f_k'||S'1)$, the registration process follows the steps depicted in Fig. 2a.

### 3.3 Voter Verification Phase

Aim of this phase is to authenticate the voters, resist double voting issues, and avoid vote rigging and coercion effects. This phase requires a finger sensing module (MINDTCT) to capture the fingerprint template. Figure 2b depicts the voter authenticity validation protocol, which will be followed to verify a voter in both online/offline voting systems. In offline voting system, voter verification is performed in the polling booth following Fig. 2b. In online voting, voter login to the voting portal with UIN and DOB along with fingerprint template captured by MINDTCT. Fingerprint key $f_k$ is extracted from fingerprint template following algorithm [3] at login portal.

### 3.4 Vote Casting Phase

In this phase, eligible voters can choose their preferred candidates upon successful login, using a ballot board displaying candidate code numbers. Voters select one choice, and the chosen candidate code is encrypted with $j_{pk}$ in EU/EP and sent to the vote server. Simultaneously, a randomly generated passcode is sent to EC and the voter, updating the voter's status in the database. This passcode confirms the successful addition of the vote and prevents coercion or rigging. Our method ensures data confidentiality through multi-key encryption and maintains an encrypted voting record as a chain of blocks using blockchain technology. Block generation follows an exponential distribution model, optimizing block creation based on time requirements. Unlike traditional blockchains, our vote-counting process is independent of block creation, ensuring efficiency. The vote server receives encrypted votes before generating a new block and initiates automated vote counting. We aim to preserve immutable voting records in the blockchain, facilitating future vote recounts. Detailed descriptions of the circuit-based secure vote counting and result deciphering process are provided in subsequent sections.

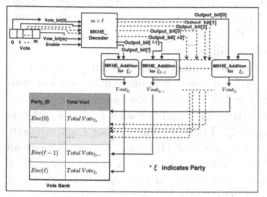

(a) Vote counting phase in homomorphic domain

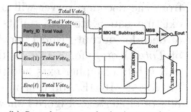

(b) Sorted encrypted winning result generation.

**Fig. 3.** Vote counting and winner selection

## 3.5   Automated Vote Counting Phase

In this phase, a vote bank stores total vote count information for each election candidate, initially encrypted as zeros (i.e., $Enc(0,...)$). To implement vote counting efficiently, our scheme encrypts only the chosen candidate's code as a vote for each voter, reducing transmission overhead. The server's responsibility is to increment the selected candidate's vote count by 1 while leaving other vote counts unchanged. However, identifying the selected candidate's vote in the encrypted domain is challenging and performance-intensive. Therefore, we focus on designing an encrypted decoder module to identify the selected candidate's vote and increment the party-specific vote count.

### Decoder-Based Automated Vote Count

1. **Identification of Selected candidate:** In order to find out the vote recipient party, generally, we require costly encrypted decision-making modules (MKHE_MUX). To alleviate the requirement, we implement an $m \times \ell$ encrypted MKHE_Decoder using the basic MKHE_NAND operations to reduce the performance overhead, where $2^m = \ell$, and $m$ represents number of bits present in encrypted candidate ID (i.e., Party_ID), and $\ell$ indicates a number of election candidate. Once the server receives an encrypted input vote

($Enc(Vote)$), it follows a bit-wise decoder implementation (shown in Fig. 3a) in encrypted domain. Bit-wise vote input (i.e., $Vote\_bit[0], \ldots, Vote\_bit[m]$) is fed into MKHE_Decoder as decoder inputs. Based on the given vote input $Enc(Vote)$, one of the $\ell$ output lines of encrypted decoder will be activated i.e., $Output\_bit[i] = Enc(1)$ (where $0 \le i \le \ell$) that indicates the given vote is only for that specific $i$-th candidate, whereas remaining output lines will be low i.e., $Enc(0)$. In this case, only the $i$-th candidate vote will be increased, but $Enc(0)$ will be added to other candidates' total votes. Figure 4 shows implementation details of $2 \times 4$ MKHE_Decoder with 2-bits vote representation for four election candidates. Here, we require only 12 MKHE_NAND operations to identify the selected candidate's vote.

2. **Optimized MKHE_Addition for vote counts:** After getting all $\ell$ outputs from the decoder, server will perform bitwise $\ell$ homomorphic addition with existing candidate vote counts using MKHE_Addition module. Here, 1 bit of decoder output ($Enc(1)$ or $Enc(0)$) will be added with $k$ number of bits of $Total\ Vote_{\xi_i}$ for a $i$-th candidate $\xi$. Therefore, we do not require costly two $k$ bits of ciphertexts addition module. For this case, We implement an improved MKHE_Addition module which will add 1 bit ciphertext with $k$ bits of ciphertext. Figure 4 shows our optimized MKHE_Addition module in comparison to full adder MKHE_Addition using 5 MKHE_NAND operations. In this case, only a specific candidate's (for which decoder $Output\_bit[i] = Enc(1)$) $Total\ Vote_{\xi_i}$ will be increased by 1. For other candidates, $Enc(0)$ will be added with previous vote count results $Vout_{\xi_{\ell-i}}$. However, total execution time for per vote counting is $4(12 \times 2.19675) + 4(5 \times 2.19675 \times k) = (105.444 + 43.935k)$ *sec*. At the end of the voting session, server will obtain $Total\ Vote_{\xi_i}$ for each candidate (shown in Fig. 3a) and send this result to all candidates including EC to disclose the voting result.

## Automated Vote Count with Winner Selection

The objective of our election scheme is to find out the winner among the candidates. This phase discloses encrypted rank of candidates, which assures the correctness of the decrypted voting result. If some parties collude to decrypt wrong result, they also have to alter all ranks to produce the proof because two candidates may not have same rank. Here, to find out the respective rank of multiple candidates, server will re-arrange $Total\ Vote_{\xi_i}$ homomorphically in sorted order. As it is proven in [7], partition-based sort incurs extra overhead in the encrypted domain than comparison-based sort. In this implementation, we consider comparison-based sorting technique to finalize the winner, second winner, and subsequent positions of the parties following Fig. 3b.

## 3.6    Result Deciphering Phase

EC and candidates will receive all $Total\ Vote_{\xi_i}$ from the server to reveal the candidates' vote. But, Only EC will receive rank-wise winner list in encrypted form.

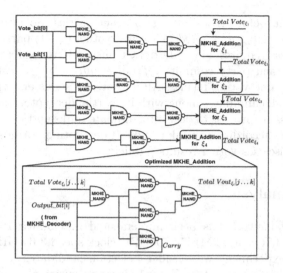

**Fig. 4.** $2 \times 4$ MKHE_Decoder and Vote Aggregation

Our proposed model employs a multi-key computation procedure to decrypt these encrypted votes, with all candidates' secret keys, including EC's, needed to retrieve the results. The idea is that each party performs partial decryption of encrypted *result* by its secret key $sk_i$ and then transmits that partially decrypted result to all other parties. If there is $\chi$ number of parties (including EC), each party computes $result' = ParDec(result, sk_i)$ in their local system and adds a small smudging noise $e_{sm_i}$ such that $[err < e_{sm_i} < 1]$ (where $err$ indicates the error attached with an input ciphertext) to avoid the

**Table 1.** Execution time of vote count with and without winner rank generation

| No. of votes | CPU (MK-TFHE) (sec) | | CPU ∥ (MK-TFHE) with 4 cores (sec) | |
|---|---|---|---|---|
| | Encrypted party specific Vote count computation | Encrypted vote count with rank declaration | Encrypted party specific Vote count computation | Encrypted vote count with rank declaration |
| 16 | 1642.62 | 2233.82 | 919.866 | 1224.55 |
| 32 | 3946.18 | 4669.27 | 2299.58 | 2662.02 |
| 64 | 9219.52 | 10053.62 | 5346.85 | 5776.59 |
| 128 | 21224.7 | 22210.65 | 12462.9 | 12960.1 |
| 256 | 48729.7 | 49902.6 | 28604.9 | 29166.6 |
| 512 | 111017 | 112242.99 | 63488.4 | 64116.5 |
| 1024 | 182300.8 | 183646.462 | 140880 | 141582 |

secret key leakage before transmitting to other parties. So after adding $e_{sm_i}$, $result' = result - a_i sk_i + e_{sm_i} (mod\ 1)$ is sent to other $(\chi - 1)$ parties. This partial decryption process requires $\chi(\chi - 1)$ data transmissions to obtain final voting results. At last, each party computes: $final\_result = \sum_{i=1}^{\chi} result'_i | \chi \in party$ and obtains the same voting results. After that, EC sends encrypted rank-wise candidate list to all candidates along with its partial decrypted result. All candidates follow the same process to decrypt candidate ranks and verify whether voting result appears according to rank or not. If decrypting voting result matches with rank, EC discloses voting results publicly.

## 4   Result Analysis

The proposed framework has been implemented in Ubuntu 16.04.3 platform where 64 bit Intel(R) core(TM) i7-7700CPU clock speed 3.60 GHz, with 64 GB memory. In this experiment, we consider 4 election candidates and variable number of voters in the voting system. Table 1 shows execution time of party-specific vote count and vote count with rank generation with respect to number of voters. It is clear from Table 1 that if the number of voters increases, the bit-size of Total Vote$_{\xi_i}$ for each candidate also increases, leading to performance challenges in a homomorphic environment. To address these issues, zonal segregation-based vote counting with the support of multiple vote servers is an effective solution to overcome these bottlenecks. In this approach, we divide voters into polling zones, each of polling zones is associated with zone-specific vote server. With $n$ voters and $p$ polling zones, each zone handles $n/p$ votes concurrently. Furthermore, if each server has $k$ cores, they process votes in parallel within multi-core platforms. After the voting session, each server produces encrypted total vote counts, $Total\ Vout_{\xi_i}$, specific to its polling zone and candidate IDs, which are then sent to a central server for aggregation and homomorphic sorting. The central server generates a sorted encrypted voting result, which is later decrypted by individual parties. Using this method, our scheme takes approximately 4 days and 22 h for party-specific 100000 vote counts without ranking, and 5 days for counting 100000 votes with candidates' rank generation, adding 25 polling zone-specific 4-core vote servers. With the support of zonal segregation-based vote counting, if we increase the polling vote servers to perform parallel execution, our proposed mechanism will be scalable for large election. Figure 5b illustrates the execution time for zonal-specific votes in single and multi-core systems. MK-TFHE [9] supports homomorphic computations over multi-key-encrypted ciphertexts, which is extension of TFHE library [11]. But under LWE assumption, MK-HE computations become noisy as the number of parties increases. The library defines a bootstrapping key's standard deviation parameter, $bk\_stdev$, as $3.72e\text{-}9$ [9] for a 1-bit MKHE_NAND operation. Due to this standard deviation, the bootstrapping phase is unable to reduce the noise within a certain threshold range for more than certain consecutive bit operations and produces erroneous results. Experimentally we set $bk\_stdev = 1.27e\text{-}9$ to perform arbitrary error-free homomorphic computations for one hundred thousand votes. We have shown a comparison

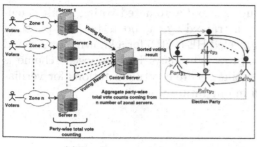 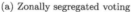

(a) Zonally segregated voting

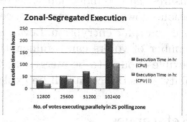

(b) Zonal-wise Parallel Execution time with single and multi-core system

**Fig. 5.** Zonal-segregated voting

**Table 2.** Comparison of our scheme with other schemes

| E-voting Scheme | Underlying Technology | Vote privacy | Voter privacy | Rank-wise Winner | Post quantum secure | Limitations |
|---|---|---|---|---|---|---|
| Shinde et al. [19] | Additive homomorphic encryption | ✓ | X | X | X | security issues |
| Anggriane et al. [2] | Paillier homomorphic encryption | ✓ | X | X | X | Single key issue |
| Mccory et al. [16] | Blockchain | ✓ | X | X | X | Privacy and Scalability issues |
| Bistarelli et al. [4] | Blockchain | ✓ | poor | X | X | No dataconfidentiality |
| Jabbar et al. [14] | Homomorphic encryption | X | poor | X | X | Double voting issue |
| Chillotti et al. [10] | Fully Homomorphic encryption | ✓ | ✓ | X | ✓ | Follows honest bulletin board |
| Microsoft ElectionGuard [15] | ElGamal encryption | ✓ | ✓ | X | X | vote verifiability |
| Our scheme | Multi-key homomorphic encryption and blockchain | ✓ | ✓ | ✓ | ✓ | No information leakage except Performance issue |

Table 2, which demonstrates that our scheme supports end-to-end confidentiality. All the complex computations are implemented using basic MKHE gates underneath from the standard library [8], hence security assumptions of this framework also follow the security analysis given in [8].

## 5    Conclusion

This work introduces an MKHE-supported voting framework with multi-key decryption to address security concerns in e-voting systems. The framework ensures data confidentiality, secret suffrage, and automated voting result calculation. However, the performance is constrained by the bootstrapping phase of homomorphic encryption. Leveraging leveled HE (LHE) for a known or restricted number of voters can significantly improve efficiency. The proposed scheme is flexible enough to be merged with existing secure e-voting solutions for verifiability. This direction will be explored in our future work.

# References

1. Anane, R., Freeland, R., Theodoropoulos, G.: E-voting requirements and implementation. In: The 9th IEEE International Conference on E-Commerce Technology and The 4th IEEE International Conference on Enterprise Computing, E-Commerce and E-Services (CEC-EEE 2007), pp. 382–392. IEEE (2007)
2. Anggriane, S.M., Nasution, S.M., Azmi, F.: Advanced e-voting system using paillier homomorphic encryption algorithm. In: 2016 International Conference on Informatics and Computing (ICIC), pp. 338–342. IEEE (2016)
3. Barman, S., Chattopadhyay, S., Samanta, D.: Fingerprint based symmetric cryptography. In: 2014 International Conference on High Performance Computing and Applications (ICHPCA), pp. 1–6. IEEE (2014)
4. Bistarelli, S., Mantilacci, M., Santancini, P., Santini, F.: An end-to-end voting-system based on bitcoin. In: Proceedings of the Symposium on Applied Computing, pp. 1836–1841 (2017)
5. Blaze, M., Braun, J., Hursti, H., Jefferson, D., MacAlpine, M., Moss, J.: DEF CON 26 voting village: Report on cyber vulnerabilities in us election equipment, databases, and infrastructure. DEF CON **26** (2018)
6. Boyen, X., Haines, T., Müller, J.: Epoque: practical end-to-end verifiable post-quantum-secure e-voting. In: 2021 IEEE European Symposium on Security and Privacy (EuroS&P), pp. 272–291. IEEE (2021)
7. Chatterjee, A., Sengupta, I.: Sorting of fully homomorphic encrypted cloud data: can partitioning be effective? IEEE Trans. Serv. Comput. **13**(3), 545–558 (2020)
8. Chen, H., Chillotti, I., Song, Y.: Multi-Key homomorphic encryption from TFHE. In: Galbraith, S.D., Moriai, S. (eds.) ASIACRYPT 2019. LNCS, vol. 11922, pp. 446–472. Springer, Cham (2019). https://doi.org/10.1007/978-3-030-34621-8_16
9. Chillotti, I.: https://github.com/ilachill/MK-TFHE
10. Chillotti, I., Gama, N., Georgieva, M., Izabachène, M.: A homomorphic LWE based E-voting scheme. In: Takagi, T. (ed.) PQCrypto 2016. LNCS, vol. 9606, pp. 245–265. Springer, Cham (2016). https://doi.org/10.1007/978-3-319-29360-8_16
11. Chillotti, I., Gama, N., Georgieva, M., Izabachène, M.: TFHE: fast fully homomorphic encryption over the torus. J. Cryptol. **33**(1), 34–91 (2020)
12. Gentry, C.: A fully homomorphic encryption scheme. Stanford University (2009)
13. Hardwick, F.S., Gioulis, A., Akram, R.N., Markantonakis, K.: E-voting with blockchain: an e-voting protocol with decentralisation and voter privacy. In: 2018 IEEE International Conference on Internet of Things (iThings) and IEEE Green Computing and Communications (GreenCom) and IEEE Cyber, Physical and Social Computing (CPSCom) and IEEE Smart Data (SmartData), pp. 1561–1567. IEEE (2018)
14. Jabbar, I., Alsaad, S.N.: Design and implementation of secure remote e-voting system using homomorphic encryption. Int. J. Netw. Secur. **19**(5), 694–703 (2017)
15. Masiarek, A., lprichar, L.R.: https://github.com/microsoft/electionguard

16. Mccorry, P., Mehrnezhad, M., Toreini, E., Shahandashti, S.F., Hao, F.: On secure e-voting over blockchain. Digit. Threats Res. Pract. (DTRAP) **2**(4), 1–13 (2021)
17. Olembo, M.M., Renaud, K., Bartsch, S., Volkamer, M.: Voter, what message will motivate you to verify your vote. In: Workshop on Usable Security, USEC (2014)
18. Park, S., Specter, M., Narula, N., Rivest, R.L.: Going from bad to worse: from internet voting to blockchain voting. J. Cybersecur. **7**(1), tyaa025 (2021)
19. Shinde, S.S., Shukla, S., Chitre, D.: Secure e-voting using homomorphic technology. Int. J. Emerg. Technol. Adv. Eng. **3**(8), 203–206 (2013)
20. Specter, M.A., Koppel, J., Weitzner, D.: The ballot is busted before the blockchain: a security analysis of voatz, the first internet voting application used in {US}. Federal elections. In: 29th USENIX Security Symposium (USENIX Security 2020), pp. 1535–1553 (2020)
21. Watson, C.I., et al.: User's guide to NIST biometric image software (NBIS) (2007)

# Cryptography

Typography

# Secured Collaboration with Ciphertext Policy Attribute Based Signcryption in a Distributed Fog Environment for Medical Data Sharing

G. A. Thushara[(✉)] and S. Mary Saira Bhanu

Department of CSE, National Institute of Technology Tiruchirappalli,
Tiruchirappalli 620015, Tamil Nadu, India
thusharagopinath25@gmail.com, msb@nitt.edu

**Abstract.** Smart hospitals are leveraging cloud computing as a practical platform for storing and sharing medical data, enhancing medical analyses. However, entrusting sensitive medical data to third parties poses risks to patient privacy. Cloud-based data sharing also leads to many hazards, including latency challenges and bandwidth concerns when accessing data through cloud storage. To address these security flaws inherent in centralized cloud systems, this study proposes employing ciphertext policy-sensitive attribute-based signcryption with verifiable designcryption within a spatially distributed fog environment. This method signs messages using sensitive attributes and access entitlements, organized in a tree structure alongside non-sensitive attributes. The proposed approach integrates attribute-based encryption, ensuring fine-grained access control and digital signatures to guarantee data authenticity and secrecy. Unlike conventional cloud computing, the data distribution occurs in fog computing, facilitating swift data analysis. Spatial data distribution via fog nodes offers advantages such as low latency, optimized bandwidth usage, offline capabilities, enhanced privacy and security, scalability, and improved redundancy. These benefits position fog computing as a crucial element in real-time, location-based data processing for data sharing applications. The proposed method incorporates secure data authentication, access controls, and resistance against message attacks. To assess its effectiveness, a comparative analysis is conducted with existing methods, focusing primarily on computational efficiency. This scientific evaluation aims to offer insights into the advantages and limitations of the proposed approach.

**Keywords:** Data sharing · Security · Access control · Signcryption · Fog computing

## 1 Introduction

The cloud computing combines resources for secure medical data sharing to enhance medical analysis due to open-source nature. Computing servers assert

© The Author(s), under exclusive license to Springer Nature Switzerland AG 2023
V. Muthukkumarasamy et al. (Eds.): ICISS 2023, LNCS 14424, pp. 275–294, 2023.
https://doi.org/10.1007/978-3-031-49099-6_17

control over user data storage and processing, reducing operational cost, maintenance expenses, and optimizes energy usage [1]. However, cloud servers often outsource the management of confidential medical data to some third parties, compromising patient privacy [2]. Cloud-based data sharing poses various risks, including security, latency, and bandwidth issues when accessing data through cloud storage. To address these concerns, in 2015, Cisco launched a fog computing environment [3] positioned between data users and the cloud. Fog computing brings information processing and connectivity closer to the user, improving network performance [4]. By situating computation nearer to the information source, fog computing reduces latency and optimizes bandwidth usage, particularly beneficial in scenarios with resource-limited sensors, such as in Internet of Things (IoT) applications [5]. Data sharing has become crucial in various fields, especially in shared medical systems. Imagine a scenario where a patient and doctor are geographically distant, but the doctor can access the patient's data through data sharing. In this situation, the doctor can make informed decisions about patient's treatment. By exchanging data, doctors can ensure patients receive appropriate tests and treatments while avoiding unnecessary or ineffective ones. However, when data is transferred to the cloud or processed by fog nodes, the data owner loses control, potentially leading to the unauthorized disclosure of the sensitive information.

Attribute-based signcryption (ABSC) offers advantages in sharing sensitive information, as it combines an access policy with the efficiency of digital signature and the adaptability of attribute-based encryption (ABE) [7]. Signcryption is a secure method that combines encryption with signatures, providing with low processing and transmission costs, enabling primary data verification, and ensuring secrecy [8]. However, basic ABSC has significant drawbacks that limit its use in resource-constrained systems. ABSC processes are more expensive to designcrypt than to encrypt because they involve several comparing and computational operations for evaluation and conversion back to the original plaintext. Signed messages need to be re-encrypted when adding or revoking a user or attribute from the system, requiring the redistribution of the user secret key by a trusted authority [9]. To address these issues, the proposed method divides the signcrypted file into blocks and distributes them among different fog nodes. The technique utilizes a master fog node (MFN), which maintains the file's metadata, and worker fog nodes (WFN), which store chunks of files using an indexed-based allocation and designcrypt the file upon request from the MFN. During the system's intended activation phase, the data owner gathers medical files and categorizes file attributes into two groups: sensitive (e.g., medical history, medication records, HIV/AIDS status) for the signature phase and non-sensitive attributes (e.g., patient age group, blood type, gender) for constructing the encryption phase's predicate. This approach enhances security in medical data sharing by employing multiple predicates for signing and encryption rather than relaying on a single set of attributes.

Traditional data sharing methods involves sending data to a centralized cloud server for processing and analysis, which can strain network bandwidth, especially with large datasets. The proposed approach tackles this problem by distributing computing resources across various fog nodes. Locally on these fog nodes, data can be pre-processed, filtered, and aggregated, reducing the volume of data that needs transmission to the cloud. This optimized data transmission decreases bandwidth, easing network congestion. Distributed fog computing offers advantages, including reduced latency, optimized bandwidth usage, offline capabilities, edge intelligence, improved privacy and security, scalability, flexibility, and redundancy compared to cloud computing. Coupled with ciphertext policy-attribute-based signcryption (CP-ABSC) and index-based file-block storage and access, an additional layer of security is provided for medical data sharing.

Summary of the proposed approach:

- Access Control: The proposed method explores the possibility of integrating CP-ABSC in a distributed fog environment to provide authorized granular access control, scalability, and efficiency. It also enables index-based storage and access of file blocks.
- Complex predicate: The attributes are categorized into two different classes (sensitive and non-sensitive) to generate two different predicate for both signature and encryption process.
- Data Confidentiality: The proposed approach ensures confidentiality for encrypted data, by allowing only authorized users who meet specified attribute conditions to verify, decrypt, and access the data.
- Data Integrity: The signcryption component of ABSC offers the ability to verify the integrity of data, ensuring it has not been tampered with during sharing or storage. This safeguard protects the data from unauthorized modifications and guarantees its authenticity.
- Low Latency: Unlike sending files to a centralized cloud server, fog nodes minimize the latency that files must traverse. Due to their proximity, the communication of medical data occurs more rapidly and with better bandwidth.
- Bandwidth Optimization: Distributing file blocks across fog nodes helps optimize network bandwidth usage. Files can be cached and replicated across multiple fog nodes, reducing the need for repetitive file transfer over the network. This optimized file distribution minimizes bandwidth requirements and helps for fast and secure medical data sharing.

The paper is structured as follows: Sect. 2 summarizes relevant studies on secure medical data sharing in a cloud and fog environment. Section 3 describes The system design and security requirements for medical data sharing in a distributed fog environment. The security proof and effectiveness of the proposed method evaluates in detail in Sect. 4 and Sect. 5, respectively. Section 6 concludes with reflections on the findings and offer recommendations for future research trajectories.

## 2   Literature Review

To securely communicate medical records with multiple professionals in a distributed storage setting, Yang et al. [10] introduced a blockchain-assisted verifiable outsourced ABSC system (BVOABSC). This system revealed the secret of crucial medical records and ensured the patient's safety by employing public blockchain and property-based attribute encoding algorithms. Cloud experts completed the cipher model computation, and clients validated the ciphertext produced for the flawed cipher design. Evaluators could jointly verify the validity of the modified medical records by evaluating their overall productivity within a comparative context. However, concerns regarding its falsity and leakage have arisen. Deng et al. [11] provides an ABSC method that uses broadcast encryption and key division technologies to achieve user revocation. Under specific plaintext attacks, it also proves to be unforgeable and confidential. Along with user revocation, consideration might be given to attribute revocation. Bao et al. [6] introduced a secure method for sharing medical data, addressing the issue of encrypted data retrieval inconvenience for data users. They achieved this by employing attribute-based searchable encryption, enabling access control for data users and provided them with the capability to perform keyword searches. However, it is important to note that this system does not verify data authenticity, and its substantial storage requirements could pose challenges when implementing IoT systems.

In a separate study by Bao et al. [21], proposed a solution for access control and keyword-based searching in medical data sharing. Their approach includes a revocation mechanism to deter unauthorized access and introduces a unique pseudo-identity-based signature for data authenticity. While this scheme successfully guarantees data privacy and authenticity, it is worth noting that it incurs a relatively high transmission cost, which may not be practical in real time scenarios. Liu et al. [22] proposed a privacy-preserving data aggregation method to address security issues in sharing multidimensional health data within IoT systems. This approach, utilizing multi-secret sharing and symmetric homomorphic cryptography, enhances data security and privacy. However, it does not verify the retrieved data, leaving data authenticity unverified. Elayan et al. [23] introduced a novel deep federated learning framework to tackle the challenge of safeguarding data privacy amid the dispersion of medical data and the decentralized structure commonly found in existing models used for medical data monitoring and analysis. Yu et al. [12] revised the lightweight hybrid policy ABSC (LH-ABSC) employing the CP-ABE and key policy- attribute based signature (KP-ABS). The data owner can directly decode the details based on the attributes embedded in the ciphertext. LH-ABSC responds to open accounting and maintains a consistent signature size, essential for IoT devices.

For a cloud-based medical data sharing system offering fine-grained access control and public verifiability, Rao et al. [13] proposed a provably secure CP-ABSC approach. However, frequent pairing and modular exponentiation operations result in significant computational costs during the CP-ABSC designcryption process. Deng et al. [14] devised a transfer strategy to address the issue of the designcryption process' low performance and high computational cost. They developed a system that transforms plaintext into a ciphertext during a portion of the process, requiring the user of medical records to perform additional processing to enhance security. Hong et al. [15] combined CP-ABE and ABSC to create an efficient data sharing scheme with a linear secret-sharing system instead of a tree structure, eliminating the need for repeated iterations of the recursive method. Nevertheless, this effort must handle with attribute revocation more skillfully. In 2020, Yu et al. [16] proposed a lightweight ABSC that combines CP-ABE and KP-ABS and maintains a constant signature size. Their primary objective was to make IoT devices' connectivity costs more affordable. However, there is a fully trusted centralized authority raises potential security issues in the future. As medical data must be shared with several organizations for cloud storage, this could threaten patient privacy by making it accessible to unauthorized individuals or groups. To address this security vulnerability, Liu et al. [17] suggest a possible strategy that employs attribute-based signature (ABS) and CP-ABE to tackle attribute revocation challenges and thwart message and ciphertext assaults. The gaps in research identified through the literature review are outlined below.

- Transferring data between cloud layer and IoT devices proves to be a time-consuming endeavor, making it unsuitable for medical data sharing that require real-time responsiveness. The delay in data transmission hampers the seamless flow of information, hindering the effectiveness of treatment that relies on instant data processing and analysis.
- In order to maintain high confidentiality levels for sensitive data, it is imperative to have fine-grained accessibility and analysis capabilities. Traditional encryption methods do not support detailed access control, creating challenges in managing encryption keys during data transmission.
- In addition to innovative encryption methods, digital signatures are also essential for ensuring the authenticity of authorized users.
- Relying on centralized cloud server systems for data sharing poses a significant risk due to the potential occurrence of centralized failures. In such a scenario, where all data is stored and managed in one central location, any failure in this system could lead to a complete loss of data that might be unrecoverable.
- Areas with limited network access necessitate local, resource-efficient computing for processing and transmitting data. Implementing efficient data distribution through fog computing is crucial for enhancing fault tolerance and mitigating various network-related threats.

## 3    Proposed Methodology

### 3.1    Preliminaries

The following features are part of the CP-ABSC scheme.

- Key Generation: The key authority (KA) generates the master key $(MK)$ and the public parameters $(PP)$ for the CP-ABSC scheme. The KA also generates attribute-based secret keys $(SK)$ for each user based on their access policies.

- Signcryption: The data owner (DO) wants to signcrypt a $(MK)$ with a specific access policy $\mathbb{A}$ and attributes. The DO uses the CP-ABSC algorithm to signcrypt the message by combining hashing and ABE techniques. It generates a ciphertext that includes both the encrypted message and a digital signature over the message.
- Encryption: The CP-ABSC algorithm takes the $(M)$, $\mathbb{A}$, $(PP)$, and $(SK)$ as inputs. It generates a signciphertext $(CT)$ that is associated with the specified $\mathbb{A}$ and signed by the DO. The $(CT)$ contains the encrypted message, the access structure information, and the digital signature.
- Key Extraction: Data users (DU) who want to access the $(CT)$ request a $(SK)$ from the KA. The KA verifies the user's attributes and generates a corresponding $(SK)$ for the DU.
- Decryption and Verification: A DU with a valid $(SK)$ can attempt to decrypt and verify the $(CT)$. The decryption process involves evaluating the $\mathbb{A}$ against the DU's attributes to recover the encrypted message. The DU can then verify the digital signature using the DO's public key.

## 3.2    Architecture Overview

The following entities are involved in the proposed system architecture shown in Fig. 1: DO, KA, Cloud Server(CS), Master Fog Node (MFN), Worker Fog Nodes (WFNs) and a group of DU.

- KA: System keys are distributed and managed by KA for all system entities. In the event of a security compromise, the KA enables the revocation of the system's public and private keys, preventing any entity from accessing the service. The KA typically generates a public-private key pair in the proposed work for each authorized piece of equipment in the proposed work. The public key is widely disseminated and accessible to all system entities. The device protects the privacy of the private key and uses it to verify the legitimacy of requests for system services.
- DO: The DO gathers patient-submitted or IoT device-collected data for healthcare use. After being signcrypted, the $CT$ is shared and sent to the appropriate MFN with the proper $\mathbb{A}$. The DO uses the KA to design the $\mathbb{A}$ for an authorized DU. The data is encrypted with the proper $\mathbb{A}$ and signed with an attribute-generated key before being sent to the MFN.
- MFN and WFNs: Both the MFN and WFNs possess the capability to transmit and store medical data. The technologies utilized by MFN and WFNs for data processing are well-established. Metadata can be added to the CS after a predetermined amount of time by MFN. The $CT$ blocks are created and separated by MFN, then stored in the authorized WFNs. The file blocks follow an index-based allocation in each WFN.
- CS: The CS is a remote server owned by a third party with substantial storage capacity. The metadata sent by the MFN is managed and tracked by the CS. An MFN can only store metadata temporarily before seamlessly sharing it with the CS. Any modified files on the CS will impact the corresponding MFN.

– DU: Medical experts, academics, insurance businesses, and pharmaceutical firms are examples of DU. Their user-specific attributes enable access to the ciphertext. Data exchange is crucial for institutions to acquire medical data and offer medical services. For system access, each DU must register with KA using their ID. They can utilize their properties to get the $CT$ from the nearby MFN. The $CT$ can only be accessed when the group key and attribute of the DU meet the necessary conditions.

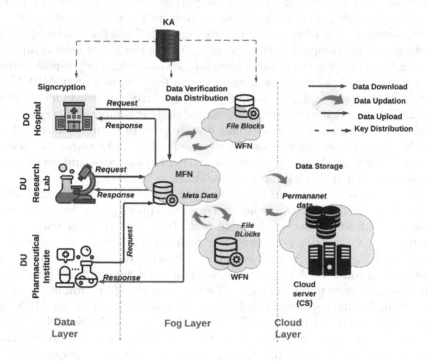

**Fig. 1.** System Architecture.

### 3.3 System Description

This section introduces the system design and provides an overview of the proposed work. The proposed system comprises six entities: the Data Owner (DO), Master Fog Node (MFN), Worker Fog Nodes (WFNs), Cloud Server (CS), Key Authority (KA), and Data Users (DUs). In the system architecture depicted in Fig. 1, the first scenario involves centralized servers, including the cloud and fog layers. Communication within the fog layer is limited to a single cloud environment, while the data layer is confined to a single MFN. Medical data is transmitted through e-hospitals and other medical-related organizations, such as research institutions and pharmaceutical firms, for comprehensive medical analysis. Data sharing processes are expedited as all entities operate within a unified fog environment. The DO, situated in the data layer, employs a CP-ABSC scheme to perform signcryption and generate a $CT$ before transmitting the data to the MFN. The MFN periodically updates its metadata, which is subsequently transferred to the CS for long-term archival purposes. Alongside the $CT$, the DO creates user-specific policy attributes $\mathbb{A}$. To decrypt the $CT$, the DU must provide the necessary sensitive attributes, aligning with the defined access policies. By integrating fog computing, the system optimizes the use of local computing resources within the fog layer, minimizing latency and enhancing responsiveness. The cornerstone of the system's security lies in the adoption of the CP-ABSC scheme. This cryptographic technique provides robust safeguards for ensuring the confidentiality and integrity of transmitted data. It combines encryption and digital signature functionalities, enabling data to be both securely encrypted and digitally signed before transmission. This ensures that only authorized parties with the appropriate decryption keys and attributes can access and decipher the data, protecting it from unauthorized disclosure or tampering.

Inaccuracies in the CS metadata can trigger changes in the associated MFN. The DO has the capability to construct an encryption policy based on user-specific attributes and encrypt the plain text ($PT$) using the designated access structure ($\mathbb{A}$). Only DUs possessing the required attributes can successfully decrypt the $CT$. The CP-ABESC scheme employed in this context enables fine-grained access control, offering greater flexibility and expressiveness compared to conventional encryption methods. The distributed fog environment plays a vital role in facilitating flexible and secure data sharing, where an MFN and WFNs exist within the fog layer. To access data on the WFNs, DUs initiate requests to the neighboring MFN. The MFN checks the metadata to confirm if the requested data is accessible. If it is, the MFN directs the requests to the relevant WFNs. The MFN maintains essential details such as location identifiers, file names, and WFNs identifications for each file. Before retrieving data from the MFN, DUs from different locations must authenticate their identities. In essence, the proposed approach leverages the CP-ABESC scheme for precise access control and harnesses the capabilities of the distributed fog environment for secure and adaptable data sharing. The collaboration between MFN and WFNs, coupled with appropriate authentication mechanisms, ensures efficient management and retrieval of data within the distributed fog architecture.

---

**Algorithm 1.** System Setup

   **Input:** $1^\lambda$
   **Output:** $MK, PP$

1: Generate the pairing, $e : G_1 * G_1 \rightarrow G_2$
2: Consider two random variables $a, b \in \mathbb{Z}_P^*$
3: Generate a hash function $H : (0,1)^* \rightarrow \mathbb{Z}_P^*$
4: Generate public parameter $(PP)$ from the above assumption.
5: $PP = (G_1, G_2), g_1, g_2, P, \lambda, H, u = g_1^a, v = e(g_1, g_2)^b$
6: The master key $(MK)$ of the system which KA keep secret is:
7: $MK = (b^\lambda, g_2^a)$

---

## 3.4   System Design

### System Setup:

Algorithm 1 represents the system initialization process overseen by a trusted KA. The setup procedure requires a security parameter $\lambda$ as input. The system employs two multiplicative cyclic groups, $G1$ and $G2$, which are mathematical structures with specific properties and operations and an attribute universe $(W)$. The groups are defined within the system with generators indicated as $g_1$ and $g_2$, respectively. Algorithm 1 describes a cryptographic system based on bilinear pairings and prime order groups. The system involves generating two random variables, $a$ and $b$, from a set of integers with prime order $(Z_p^*)$. A hash function $(H)$ is utilized to generate a cryptographic hash from input data. Public parameters $(PP)$ are then computed, including elements from the groups, $G1$ and $G2$, along with generator elements $(g_1, g_2)$, a large prime number (P), $(\lambda)$, and the $H$. The master key (MK), kept confidential by the KA, consists of two parts: $(b^\lambda)$ and $((g_2)^a)$. These components are crucial for ensuring the security and confidentiality of the system. The algorithm's security relies on the complexity of certain mathematical problems, particularly those related to bilinear pairings and the discrete logarithm problem in the prime order groups. Algorithm 1 involves several key operations. Pairing generation, which depends on the size of involved groups, is denoted as $O(f(N))$. Random variable generation and hash function creation have constant time complexity $(O(1))$. Public parameter and master key generation also depend on the group size $(O(f(N)))$. The overall time complexity of Algorithm 1 is $O(f(N))$, where $N$ represents the size of the groups involved.

### Key Generation:

During the key generation phase, outlined in Algorithm 2, the KA is tasked with assigning each user with their unique user identification $(u_{id})$ for system access and a file-specific secret key $(S_k)$. The $(u_{id})$ enables individuals to authenticate themselves and access the system, while the $(S_k)$ is employed by the DO to provide authenticity and integrity for specific files. Additionally, the KA generates two important keys: the decryption key $(D_k)$ and the verification key $(V_k)$. The $D_k$ is derived from the non-sensitive attributes associated with a user. Each non-sensitive attribute $t$ from the attribute universe $T$ has been used to generates a components of $D_k$, named as $R_t$ and $R'_t$. This key is utilized to decrypt encrypted data and access the corresponding information based on the user's attribute set. The $V_k$ is generated from the sensitive attributes associated with a user to verify the authenticity and integrity of data. The time complexity of the Algorithm 2 is determined by the size of the attribute set ($|T|$), making it $O(|T|)$.

---

**Algorithm 2.** Key Generation
___

    **Input:** $PP, MK, T$
    **Output:** $S_k, D_k, V_k$
1: Choose two random numbers $r_1, r_2 \in Z_P^*$
2: Calculate the $u_{id} = (g_2^{(a+r_1)/b})$
3: Calculate the $S_k = (g_2^{(a+r_2)/b})$
4: **while** $t \in T$ **do**
5:    Choose a random number $R_t = (g_2^{(r_1)} * g_2^{(H(t)*r_t)})$
6:    Consider $R'_t = g_2^{r_t}$
7: **end while**
8: Calculate the $D_k = (S_k, \forall t \in T : R_t, R'_t)$
9: Calculate the $V_k = g_2^{(r_2)}$

---

**File Uploading:**

To securely share data with external entities, the DO employs the "signcrypt" process as part of the encryption procedure. This process combines signing and encryption operations to provide confidentiality, integrity, and authenticity for the shared data. The inputs for the signcryption process include the $PP$, which helps ensure the security and correctness of the signcryption process, the message $M$ that the DO intends to encrypt and share with external parties, and the access policy ($\rho$) defines the set of attributes or conditions that external entities must possess or fulfill to access the encrypted data. This policy establishes a fine-grained access control mechanism, enabling the DO to specify who can decrypt and access the shared information based on their attributes or other criteria. The $S_k$ is generated from the sensitive attributes, used for signing the message ($M$). By signing the $M$, the DO provides a digital signature that ensures the authenticity and integrity of the file content. This helps verify that the data has not been tampered with during transmission and that it originates from the DO. The final product of signcryption must be signed ciphertext $CT_{sign}$. The Algorithm 3 selects a polynomial $P(x)$ that fulfills the specified access policy ($\rho$). For each non-sensitive attribute ($t$), a random variable ($r_i$) is chosen and assigned such that it makes $P_r(x) = t$. To fully describe the polynomial $P(x)$, another random variable $r_j$ is selected from $Z_P^*$. The use of multiple random variables in the polynomial allows for a more flexible and complex access control policy. The time complexity of this Algorithm 3 is polynomial and depends on the size of the attribute set ($|T|$) and the complexity of the access tree predicate

$\Theta$. Specifically, it can be expressed as $O(|T|^k)$, where k represents the degree of the polynomial used in the algorithm.

The $CT$) is generated along with the access tree predicate $\Theta$, where the encryption randomness $\rho$ is crucial to ensure that each encryption of the same plaintext ($M$) yields a different $CT$, enhancing security. $M'$ represents the CT obtained by XOR $M$ with the attribute set $t$. $t''$ is the result of applying a cryptographic hash function $H$ to $t$. This can be useful when it is not necessary to reveal the exact attribute value, but its presence is required for access control decisions. For each attribute $t$ in the attribute universe $T$, the polynomial's constant term $P_x(0)$ is encrypted using a generator $g_1$ from group $G1$, ensuring that each attribute in the access tree has an associated ciphertext component. $M'_t$ represents the ciphertext component for each attribute $t$, but with an additional step. Here, the constant term $P_x(0)$ is hashed using $H$ before being encrypted with the generator $g_1$ from group $G1$. This extra hashing step further conceals the specific attribute values in the ciphertext, providing an added layer of security.

---

**Algorithm 3.** File Uploading

**Input:** $PP, M, \rho, S_k$
**Output:** $CT_{sign}$

1: Choose a polynomial $P(x)$ which satisfies the $\rho$.
2: Select a random variable $r_i \in Z_P^*$ and sets $P_r(0) = t \ \forall t \in T$
3: Select another random variable $r_j \in Z_P^*$ to fully describe the $P(x)$
4: The CT can be generated depends on the access tree predicate $\Theta$.
5: $CT = (\rho, M' = M \oplus t, M'' = H^t, \forall t \in T : M_t = g_1^{P_x(0)}, M'_t = g_1^{H(P_x(0))}))$
6: Calculate $\Delta_a = H(\rho|M)$ and $\Delta_b = g_2 * r_i * \Delta_a$
7: $CT_{sign} = (\rho, M', M'', \forall t \in T : M_t, M'_t, Y = (g_1 * S_k, \Delta_a, \Delta_b))$

---

**File Distribution:**
Upon receiving the $CT_{sign}$ from the DO, the MFN stores its metadata, including details such as the file name, size, number of blocks, and hashed index values. The neighboring WFNs hold the $CT_{sign}$ after it gets converted to various blocks. A hash value is generated for each block to ensure the integrity of the contents. During retrieval, the MFN can utilize these hash values to verify the consistency of the blocks. The unique block identifiers (hash values) and their respective storage locations are connected through a mapping that the MFN maintains and keep up-to-date. MFN stores this mapping in a separate index file during block distribution. MFN duplicates the blocks across WFNs to handle redundancy and data replication based on the desired level of fault tolerance.

**File Downloading:** The MFN needs to query the WFNs when it receives a request from DU, after verifying the file location and index values. Once the user attributes are confirmed, the MFN sends the $CT$ to the respective DU as outlined in Algorithm 4. The verification process conducted by the MFN reduces the overhead for the DU. $M$ represents the decrypted plaintext, obtained by decrypting the $CT$ using the decryption key $D_k$. Here, $M'$ denotes the result of a bilinear pairing operation between the $CT$ and the decryption key $D_k$, with the additional input of the plaintext $M$. The equation $\rho' = (e(CT, \Delta_a))/e(CT, V_k) * M'$ involves the calculation of a new value $\rho'$ in a cryptographic context. The equation combines the results of two bilinear pairings and multiplies it by $M'$. The first bilinear pairing $e(CT, \Delta_a)$ involves the $CT$ and $\Delta_a$ from the Algorithm 3, which serves to introduce additional factors or constraints in the cryptographic scheme. The second bilinear pairing $e(CT, V_k)$ involves elements $CT$ and $V_k$, where $V_k$ is derived from the Algorithm 2. The overall complexity of Algorithm 4 is $O(|CT_{sign}| + |M|)$, where $|CT_{sign}|$ is the size of the ciphertext and $|M|$ is the size of the processed data.

---

**Algorithm 4.** File Downloading

---

    **Input:** $CT_{sign}, D_k, V_k$
    **Output:** $CT, M$
1:  $M = Dec(CT, D_k)$
2:  $M' = e(CT, D_k|M)$
3:  Compute $\rho' = (e(CT, \Delta_a))/e(CT, V_k) * M'$
4:  **if** $H(\rho'|M = \Delta_b)$ **then**
5:     Allow for downloading
6:  **else**
7:     Reject the request
8:  **end if**

---

## 4    Security Proof

In accordance with the indistinguishable nature of chosen plaintext attack (CPA) and chosen ciphertext attack (CCA), the proposed approach for secure medical data sharing in a distributed fog environment is secure from CPA and CCA. To prove that CP-ABSC in a distributed fog environment is CPA secure, the proposed system illustrates that even when an adversary has access to an encryption oracle, cannot differentiate between two ciphertexts corresponding to different plain texts. Here's a high-level outline of the proof for both CPA and CCA:

**CPA Security Proof:**

- Assume that there exists an adversary $\mathbb{A}$ that can distinguish between two ciphertexts $CT$ and $CT'$ corresponding to different plain texts $PT$ and $PT'$ with a non-negligible advantage.
- Proposed system use $\mathbb{A}$ to construct an adversary $(B)$ that can break the security of the underlying encryption or signature scheme (on which CP-ABSC is built), which contradicts the assumed security of the underlying schemes.

- A receives a public key and attribute set from the KA of the system and can act as encryption oracle, where it encrypts any plain texts of its choice using the proposed scheme.
- If A can distinguish between $CT$ and $CT'$, corresponding to different $PT$ and $PT'$, (B) will be able to break the security of the underlying encryption or signature scheme. This would imply that either the encryption or signature scheme is insecure, which contradicts proposed approach's assumption of their security. It will be more challenging to produce the same ciphertext for the same plaintext even if the proposed method, unlike the existing CP-ABSC scheme, uses two different sets of attributes for the signature and encryption process.
- Assisted signature verification by MFN with input Attribute $a$ revoked from the attribute set $S$, $u_{id}$
- Initialization Phase: $(1^\delta \rightarrow pp, msk)$
  Assumed that the security variable $(\delta)$ would provide both the master secret key $msk$ and the public parameters $pp$.
- Key Generation Phase: $(pp, msk, s)$
  In this stage, the specified algorithm generates three unique private keys for each user. To produce the sign secret key $(s_k)$, decryption secret key $(d_k)$, and verification secret key $(v_k)$, consider the random numbers $q_1, q_2, q_3, and q_4 \in Z_p$. The probability of creating the correct secret key is reduced by randomness.
- Signcryption Phase: $(pp, s_k, s, \lambda_i, \lambda_j, M) \rightarrow M'$
  It is executed by the DO with public parameter $(PP)$, $s_k$, attribute set $(s)$, predicate formed from the sensitive attributes $\lambda_i$, predicate formed from the non-sensitive attributes $\lambda_j$, and plaintext $M$. It generates a signed ciphertext $M'$.
- Predicate Updating Phase: Update $(pp, s', M', \xi)$: This phase runs by the MFN on demand from the DO.
  Calculate $\xi = revoke(a)$ and $s'$ be the updated attribute set for new predicates.
  Then $s \cap s' = 0$ if $\xi = add(a) \forall a \in s$. Otherwise $s \subset s'$ if $\xi = revoke(a) \forall a \in s$.

## CCA Security Proof:

- Assume that there exists an adversary A that can distinguish between two ciphertexts corresponding to different plain texts with a non-negligible advantage, even with access to a decryption oracle.
- A can construct an adversary B that can break the security of the underlying encryption or signature scheme which contradicts the assumed security of the underlying schemes.
- B can acts as decryption oracle for getting the $CT$ and $CT'$, returns to A
- This can be formalized as:

$$(B) = |Pr[A(c) = 1|c = Enc(PK, PT, CT)] - Pr[A(c) = 1|c = Enc(PK, PT', CT')]|$$

- By the assumption that $\mathbb{A}$ can distinguish $CT$ and $CT'$ corresponding to different $PT$ and $PT'$ with a non-negligible advantage, $\mathbb{B} > \epsilon$ for some non-negligible $\epsilon$.
- Data Accessing Phase: $(pp, u_{id}, \lambda_i) \rightarrow Q$ This phase achieved through MFN with a set of attributes attains $\lambda_i$. Then MFN generates the transformation key $Q = (Q_p, Q_q)$ identified with $u_{id}$ and available publically.
- Designcryption Phase: $(pp, Q_i, \lambda_i, \lambda_j, M' \rightarrow M'')$
  This phase executes by the $(B)$. $Dec(Q_j, M'' \rightarrow (M' - u_{id}))$, this performs decryption to recover $M$. $(B)$ partially process the data $M''$ as input addition and outputs $M$. Since attributes are not matching, $M''$ and $M$ shows the corruption.

## 5  Performance Evaluation

To assess the performance of the proposed method, signature and encryption values were calculated and compared against the average system. The proposed solution employed the Java pairing-based cryptography library (JPBC) and the Netbeans 8.1 IDE for the system implementation. Utilizing pairing on an elliptic curve, $y2 = x3 + x$ over a field $F_q$, where $q$ 3 mod 4 is some prime, the JPBC technique created a bilinear map. This pairing is symmetric as $G_1$ and $G_2$ are collections of points from $E(F_q)$. The length of the parameter $p$, representing the relationship between $G_1$ and $G_2$, was set at 160 bits. The system expanded the number of attributes in the access policy, ranging from 2 to 20 with a step length of 2, to determine the average time taken by each technique. The system was designed to handle different types of data, including text, images, and multimedia, in various sizes and formats. During testing, the proposed method employed file sizes ranging from 1 MB to 500 MB, allowing for a comprehensive evaluation of its performance across different data sizes. The experiments were conducted on a 64-bit Linux Professional system with specific hardware specifications. The computer utilized in the testing equipped an Intel(R) Core(TM) i5-4210U processor running at clock speeds of 1.70 GHz and 2.40 GHz, supported by 8 GB of DDR3 RAM.

Figures 2, 3, 4 and 5 provides insights into the expressiveness and performance of the proposed CP-ABESC scheme compared to other existing schemes [18,19], and [20]. Figure 2 specifically focuses on illustrating the access policy's expressiveness by using the proposed CP-ABESC scheme alongside the mentioned schemes. The Fig. 2 visually represents how the proposed scheme offers a high degree of flexibility and granularity in defining access policies for secure medical data sharing. The signcryption time for a file is plotted against the number of attributes in the system in Fig. 3. As seen in the Fig. 3, the system has a little shorter signcryption time than the [18,19], and [20] schemes. The amount of time required for designcryption versus the number of attributes used is shown in Fig. 4. It illustrates how close the designcryption time is to that of [20]. Since users rather than fog nodes must decrypt in the schemes [18], and [19], the designcryption algorithms have higher processing costs. The figures demonstrate that the designcryption procedure takes longer than the signcryption process. In Fig. 5, the impact of the number of attributes on the authentication time for various procedures is investigated. The Fig. 5 reveals that the authentication process is not significantly affected by the number of system attributes. Regardless of the range of attributes considered, from 2 to 20, the average time for authentication remains consistent at 200 milliseconds. The signcryption, designcryption and authentication time for the proposed method and the existing methods during execution is represented in the table data that is attached to each fig. [20] introduced a CP-ABSC based encryption technique to achieve secure fine-grained access control for multi-recipient communication between the utility control center and a collection of smart meters with a pairing-free elliptic curve cryptosystem. The proposed system achieved relative computing speed in the authentication, signcryption, and designcryption processes owing to the distributed fog nodes, even if [20] used faster elliptic curve point multiplication operations instead of the complicated bilinear pairing procedures.

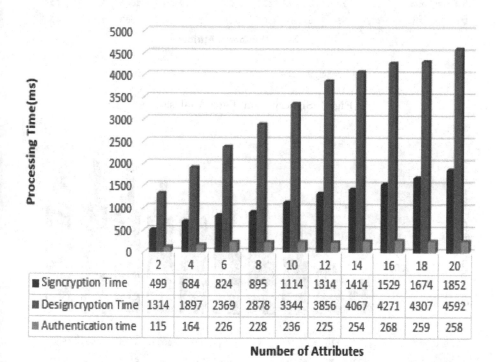

| | 2 | 4 | 6 | 8 | 10 | 12 | 14 | 16 | 18 | 20 |
|---|---|---|---|---|---|---|---|---|---|---|
| Signcryption Time | 499 | 684 | 824 | 895 | 1114 | 1314 | 1414 | 1529 | 1674 | 1852 |
| Designcryption Time | 1314 | 1897 | 2369 | 2878 | 3344 | 3856 | 4067 | 4271 | 4307 | 4592 |
| Authentication time | 115 | 164 | 226 | 228 | 236 | 225 | 254 | 268 | 259 | 258 |

**Number of Attributes**

**Fig. 2.** Performance Efficiency of the Proposed System.

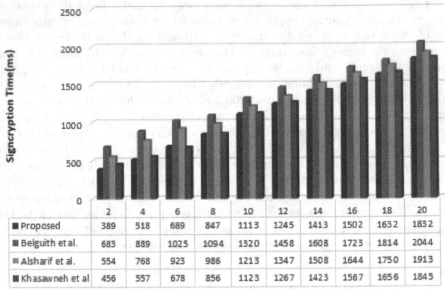

| | 2 | 4 | 6 | 8 | 10 | 12 | 14 | 16 | 18 | 20 |
|---|---|---|---|---|---|---|---|---|---|---|
| Proposed | 389 | 518 | 689 | 847 | 1113 | 1245 | 1413 | 1502 | 1632 | 1832 |
| Belguith et al. | 683 | 889 | 1025 | 1094 | 1320 | 1458 | 1608 | 1723 | 1814 | 2044 |
| Alsharif et al. | 554 | 768 | 923 | 986 | 1213 | 1347 | 1508 | 1644 | 1750 | 1913 |
| Khasawneh et al | 456 | 557 | 678 | 856 | 1123 | 1267 | 1423 | 1567 | 1656 | 1845 |

**Number of Attributes**

■ Proposed    ■ Belguith et al.    ■ Alsharif et al.    ■ Khasawneh et al

**Fig. 3.** Signcryption Time Analysis

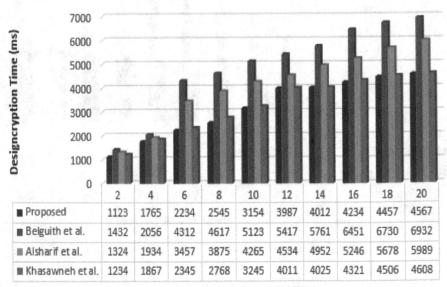

| | 2 | 4 | 6 | 8 | 10 | 12 | 14 | 16 | 18 | 20 |
|---|---|---|---|---|---|---|---|---|---|---|
| Proposed | 1123 | 1765 | 2234 | 2545 | 3154 | 3987 | 4012 | 4234 | 4457 | 4567 |
| Belguith et al. | 1432 | 2056 | 4312 | 4617 | 5123 | 5417 | 5761 | 6451 | 6730 | 6932 |
| Alsharif et al. | 1324 | 1934 | 3457 | 3875 | 4265 | 4534 | 4952 | 5246 | 5678 | 5989 |
| Khasawneh et al. | 1234 | 1867 | 2345 | 2768 | 3245 | 4011 | 4025 | 4321 | 4506 | 4608 |

**Number of Attributes**

**Fig. 4.** Designcryption Time Analysis

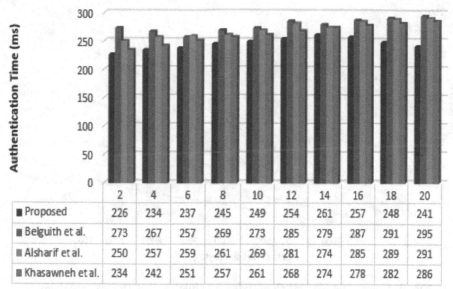

| | 2 | 4 | 6 | 8 | 10 | 12 | 14 | 16 | 18 | 20 |
|---|---|---|---|---|---|---|---|---|---|---|
| ■ Proposed | 226 | 234 | 237 | 245 | 249 | 254 | 261 | 257 | 248 | 241 |
| ■ Belguith et al. | 273 | 267 | 257 | 269 | 273 | 285 | 279 | 287 | 291 | 295 |
| ■ Alsharif et al. | 250 | 257 | 259 | 261 | 269 | 281 | 274 | 285 | 289 | 291 |
| ■ Khasawneh et al. | 234 | 242 | 251 | 257 | 261 | 268 | 274 | 278 | 282 | 286 |

**Number of Attributes**

**Fig. 5.** Authentication Time Analysis

$$\text{Latency} = a \cdot \text{PS} + b \cdot \text{dR} + c \cdot \text{pS}, \quad \forall a, b, c \text{ are constants} \tag{1}$$

$$\text{Latency} = \left( \frac{\text{PS}}{\text{Network speed}} \right) + \text{dR} \tag{2}$$

Apart from the algorithm execution time, examining the fog server performance is essential, especially when considering varying delay ratios, processing speeds. The system being studied evaluates packet sizes (PS) ranging from 1000 bytes to 10,000 bytes to evaluate overall performance. In this study, the fog server count is set at four times the number of cloud servers plus one, denoted as $N_{fs} = 4*N_{cs}+1$. The ratio of 1:4 between cloud servers and fog servers in edge computing is a flexible configuration choice, not a strict standard. It is often used due to its effectiveness in distributing data processing tasks. Cloud servers handle high-level processing, while fog servers manage localized tasks, ensuring reduced latency, redundancy, scalability, resource optimization, and cost efficiency. The specific ratio varies based on factors such as the fault tolerances, network conditions, and geographic distribution of devices. Their processing power is merely 10 percent of their cloud counterparts ($P_{fs} = P_{cs} * 0.1$). The average delay ratio (dR) is varied from 0.01 to 0.75. Figure 6 illustrates the latency outcomes of the proposed system based on the Eq. 1. It is evident that as the average delay ratio increases from 0.01 to 0.75, fog latency rises until it surpasses cloud latency. This suggests that relying solely on cloud servers for data sharing is not suitable for real-time applications. Fog servers need to be easily accessible to users, indicating they should be closer than cloud servers. In the analysis of processing speed, based on the Eq. 2, the

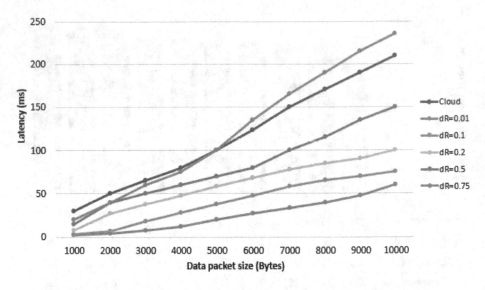

**Fig. 6.** Comparing fog and cloud latency while varying the average delay.

average delay, denoted as $D$, is 0.01. The processing speed (pS) varies at rates of 0.03, 0.05, 0.07, 0.1, and 0.2. According to the results depicted in Fig. 7, reducing the processing speed ratio from 0.2 to 0.03 leads to an increase in latency for fog nodes. Eventually, it reaches a point where it surpasses the latency of cloud nodes. This indicates that fog servers exhibit slow processing capabilities. Despite their proximity to the edge compared to cloud resources, fog servers result in higher latency due to their sluggish processing speeds.

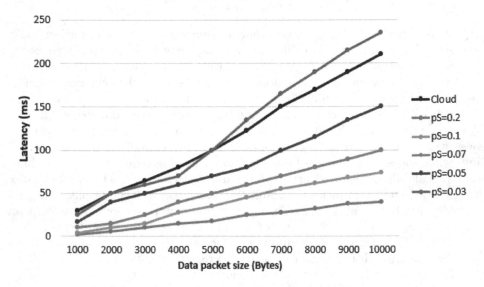

**Fig. 7.** Compare fog and cloud latency while varying the processing speed in the fog layer.

# 6  Conclusion

This paper introduces a novel scheme designed to ensure authenticity, fine-grained access control, and confidentiality for secure medical data exchange in a distributed fog environment. The scheme utilizes a cryptographic technique known as CP-ABSC, which is extensively presented and discussed in this study. In a fog environment, requiring minimal computing and communication compared to a cloud-based infrastructure, the proposed method leverages bilinear pairing-based CP-ABSC to achieve its security objectives. By employing this technique, the research demonstrates how the proposed approach effectively addresses the security requirements of confidentiality and integrity, surpassing the limitations of CPA and CCA scenarios. Furthermore, an efficiency analysis of the proposed scheme indicates its suitability for resource-constrained Internet of Things (IoT) contexts. This suggests that the proposed approach can be successfully implemented in environments with limited computational and communication resources while still ensuring robust security measures. In future work, it is recommended to explore and evaluate the indistinguishability features of the proposed approach to further demonstrate its value. Additionally, efforts should be made to simplify the implementation of bilinear pairing through the use of elliptic curve cryptography. By doing so, the overall complexity of the cryptographic operations involved in the scheme can be reduced, enhancing its practicality and efficiency.

# References

1. Debnath, S., Nunsanga, M.V.L., Bhuyan, B.: Study and scope of signcryption for cloud data access control. In: Biswas, U., Banerjee, A., Pal, S., Biswas, A., Sarkar, D., Haldar, S. (eds.) Advances in Computer, Communication and Control. LNNS, vol. 41, pp. 113–126. Springer, Singapore (2019). https://doi.org/10.1007/978-981-13-3122-0_12
2. Iqbal, J., Umar, A.I., Amin, N., Waheed, A.: Efficient and secure attribute-based heterogeneous online/offline signcryption for body sensor networks based on blockchain. Int. J. Distrib. Sens. Netw. 15(9) (2019)
3. Zahmatkesh, H., Al-Turjman, F.: Fog computing for sustainable smart cities in the IoT era: caching techniques and enabling technologies-an overview. Sustain. Cities Soc. 59, 102139 (2020)
4. Alli, A.A., Alam, M.M.: The Fog cloud of things: a survey on concepts, architecture, standards, tools, and applications. Internet Things 9, 100177 (2020)
5. Jalali, F., Hinton, K., Ayre, R., Alpcan, T., Tucker, R.S.: Fog computing may help to save energy in cloud computing. IEEE J. Sel. Areas Commun. 34(5), 1728–1739 (2016)
6. Bao, Y., Qiu, W., Cheng, X.: Secure and lightweight fine-grained searchable data sharing for IoT-oriented and cloud-assisted smart healthcare system. IEEE Internet Things J. 9(4), 2513–2526 (2021)
7. Wang, Y., Pang, H., Deng, R.H., Ding, Y., Wu, Q., Qin, B.: Securing messaging services through efficient signcryption with designated equality test. Inf. Sci. 490, 146–165 (2019)

8. Lin, X.J., Sun, L., Qu, H.: Generic construction of public key encryption, identity-based encryption and signcryption with equality test. Inf. Sci. **453**, 111–126 (2018)
9. Zhang, R., Wang, J., Song, Z., Wang, X.: An enhanced searchable encryption scheme for secure data outsourcing. Sci. China Inf. Sci. **63**(3) (2020)
10. Yang, X., Li, T., Xi, W., Chen, A., Wang, C.: A blockchain-assisted verifiable outsourced attribute based signcryption scheme for EHRs sharing in the cloud. IEEE Access **8**, 170713–170731 (2020)
11. Deng, F., Wang, Y., Peng, L., Lai, M., Geng, J.: Revocable cloud-assisted attribute-based signcryption in personal health system. IEEE Access **7**, 120950–120960 (2019)
12. Yu, J., Liu, S., Wang, S., Xiao, Y., Yan, B.: LHABSC: a lightweight hybrid attribute-based signcryption scheme for cloud-fog assisted IoT. IEEE Internet Things J. **7**(9), 7949–7966 (2020)
13. Rao, Y.S.: A secure and efficient ciphertext-policy attribute-based signcryption for personal health records sharing in cloud computing. Future Gener. Comput. Syst. **67**, 133–151 (2017)
14. Deng, F., Wang, Y., Li Peng, H., Xiong, J.G., Qin, Z.: Ciphertext-policy attribute-based signcryption with verifiable outsourced designcryption for sharing personal health records. IEEE Access **6**, 39473–39486 (2018)
15. Hong, H., Sun, Z.: An efficient and secure attribute based signcryption scheme with LSSS access structure. Springerplus **5**(1), 1–10 (2016)
16. Yu, J., Liu, S., Wang, S., Xiao, Y., Yan, B.: LH-ABSC: a lightweight hybrid attribute-based signcryption scheme for cloud-fog-assisted IoT. IEEE Internet Things J. **7**(9), 7949–7966 (2020)
17. Liu, J., Huang, X., Liu, J.K.: Secure sharing of personal health records in cloud computing: ciphertext-policy attribute-based signcryption. Futur. Gener. Comput. Syst. **52**, 67–76 (2015)
18. Belguith, S., Kaaniche, N., Mohamed, M., Russello, G.: C-ABSC: cooperative attribute based signcryption scheme for internet of things applications. In: IEEE International Conference on Services Computing (SCC), pp. 245–248. IEEE (2018)
19. Alsharif, A., Shafee, A., Nabil, M., Mahmoud, M., Alasmary, W.: A multi-authority attribute-based signcryption scheme with efficient revocation for smart grid down-link communication. In: International Conference on Internet of Things and IEEE Green Computing and Communications (GreenCom) and IEEE Cyber, Physical and Social Computing (CPSCom) and IEEE Smart Data (SmartData), pp. 1025–1032. IEEE (2019)
20. Khasawneh, S., Kadoch, M.: ECS-CP-ABE: a lightweight elliptic curve signcryption scheme based on ciphertext-policy attribute-based encryption to secure down-link multicast communication in edge envisioned advanced metering infrastructure networks. Trans. Emerg. Telecommun. Technol. **32**(8), e4102 (2021)
21. Bao, Y., Qiu, W., Tang, P., Cheng, X.: Efficient, revocable, and privacy-preserving fine-grained data sharing with keyword search for the cloud-assisted medical IoT system. IEEE J. Biomed. Health Inf. **26**(5), 2041–2051 (2021)
22. Liu, H., Gu, T., Shojafar, M., Alazab, M., Liu, Y.: OPERA: optional dimensional privacy-preserving data aggregation for smart healthcare systems. IEEE Trans. Ind. Inform. **19**(1), 857–866 (2022)
23. Elayan, H., Aloqaily, M., Guizani, M.: Sustainability of healthcare data analysis IoT-based systems using deep federated learning. IEEE Internet Things J. **9**(10), 7338–7346 (2021)

# Verifiable Timed Accountable Subgroup Multi-signatures

Duygu Özden$^{(\boxtimes)}$ and Oğuz Yayla

Middle East Technical University, Çankaya, 06800 Ankara, Turkey
duyguozden91@gmail.com, oguz@metu.edu.tr

**Abstract.** Accountable subgroup multi-signature (ASM) is a form of multi-signature scheme that permits any subgroup of a group to sign a message on behalf of the group while ensuring that the signers are accountable for the multi-signature. Since the accountability principle cannot be provided in many multi-signature schemes, an ASM algorithm makes a difference by providing this feature. ASM has many application areas, especially due to its practical and efficient usage in blockchain or legacy systems. On the other hand, timed signatures allow one to send information to the future which is also necessary for many applications such as blockchain, secure communication, or proof of ownership. In this paper, we propose a timed version of a multi-signature scheme with the help of linearly homomorphic time-lock puzzles (LHTLP) using the method constructed by Thyagarajan *et al.* Also, we slightly modified the ASM scheme constructed by Boneh *et al.* to adapt it to the verifiable timed commitment schemes.

**Keywords:** accountable · multi-signature · proof of ownership · timed signatures · verifiable

## 1 Introduction

Cryptography applications heavily rely on digital signature schemes. Perhaps one of the most important of these is the role of digital signatures in the blockchain mechanism, which has many application areas in today's world. They are a way of providing proof of ownership of the messages used in underlying construction. There are many known types of digital signature algorithms and the preferred type varies according to the usage area or need. Multi-signature schemes are an important type of digital signature that enables multiple parties to jointly produce a signature that is used to sign a shared document, transaction, etc. In a standard way of creating a digital signature, a single private key is used to sign messages or authenticate data. However, in many real-world applications, a single key may not be sufficient enough to provide the required security features. For example, in a corporate business, multiple people/departments/executives may need to sign off on a document; in a distributed system, multiple nodes may need to approve information. Multi-signature schemes solve these types

V. Muthukkumarasamy et al. (Eds.): ICISS 2023, LNCS 14424, pp. 295–305, 2023.
https://doi.org/10.1007/978-3-031-49099-6_18

of scenarios by allowing multiple parties to collaborate in generating a multi-signature. Similar to other digital signature schemes, it generally has a public key that can be used to verify signatures created by any member of the group. In such a scheme, each member provides their own signature on a pre-agreed message. The signatures are aggregated into a single signature verifiable by anyone using the public key. However, not all multi-signature schemes provide accountability which is a very important security principle to make signers responsible for their activities. Accountable subgroup multi-signature (ASM) schemes are a type of multi-signature scheme in which a subgroup of a group can sign a document instead of whole members of the group while ensuring accountability. When we consider a transaction or a mechanism involving multiparty computation, it is possible to say that ASM brings accountability and efficiency which are desired properties for most such systems. Although there are various ASM constructions, the ASM scheme recently introduced by Boneh *et al.* [1] is quite efficient and the subgroup selection is possible after users generate their individual signatures. A timed commitment, on the other hand, is another important cryptographic construction. It allows one party to deliver information to the future. It guarantees that the receiver can extract the committed information after some predetermined time $T$. One of the most important security properties for timed commitments is the notion of "verifiability" to ensure that the construction of timed commitment holds reliable information and is well-formed.

**Our Motivation and Contribution.** This paper concentrates on the significance and effectiveness of timed structures in applications that utilize multi-signatures. We introduce a timed version of an ASM, that holds considerable potential for real-world implementations. We also show that the design we constructed is sound, private, and unforgeable as the desired security features of timed signatures and multi-signatures. Also, as the underlying scheme is pairing-based, we calculated the computational complexity of our scheme to be able to show it with the VT-BLS [3] which is also a pairing-based algorithm. To the best of our knowledge, there is currently no version of the multi-signature that incorporates a time component that would be applicable to schemes containing information intended for future use. For this reason, the performance calculation with VT-BLS is made to see the extra calculation required to produce multi-signatures under the same conditions, rather than comparing, since VT-BLS is not a multi-signature.

**Organization.** The rest of the paper is organized as follows: In Sect. 2, we provide the algorithms and protocols used in our construction. In Sect. 3, we explain our proposed designs to be used in real-world applications. In Sect. 4, we discuss the computational complexity to be able to evaluate the performance. Finally, in Sect. 5, we provide the conclusion and possible future work opportunities.

# 2 Preliminaries

## 2.1 Accountable Subgroup Multi-signatures (ASM)

An accountable subgroup multi-signature scheme is a type of multi-signature in which a message $m$ can be signed by any subgroup $S$ of a group $G$, and the signatories from the subgroup $S$ are responsible for the signature. ASM was defined first time in 2001 [2]. One of the most important improvements in ASM schemes is the ASM scheme constructed by Boneh et al. [1]. The objective of developing this "short" ASM scheme was to reduce its size which makes it efficient and easily applicable in the blockchain applications. In this algorithm, "short" means the signature size is $O(\lambda)$-bits, where $\lambda$ is the security constant. This ASM scheme showed that it is very practical and applicable to blockchain cryptosystems.

**ASM by Boneh et al.** Boneh et al.'s ASM scheme [1] consists of 5 tuples: KeyGen, Group Setup, SignatureGen, Signature Aggregation (Signature Aggr), and Verification. These steps are explained below. $PK$ is defined as the collection of public keys belonging to the members of group $G$, denoted by $pk_1, \ldots, pk_n$.

- **KeyGen:** Every user $i \in G$ gets a random secret key $sk_i \leftarrow \mathbb{Z}_q$ and calculates public key $pk_i \leftarrow g_2^{sk_i}$ where $g_2$ is the generator of the group $\mathbb{G}_2$
- **Group Setup:** Every user performs group setup using one round interactive protocol.
    - He/she is responsible for computing the group's aggregated public key $apk$ as: $apk = \prod_{i=1}^{n} pk_i^{a_i}$ where $a_i = H_1(pk_i, PK)$.
    - He/she sends

    $$\mu_{ji} := H_2(apk, j)^{a_i sk_i} \tag{1}$$

    to the $j$-th member within $n$ users. Note that, $j \neq i$.
    - $i$-th user receives $\mu_{ij}$, he calculates $\mu_{ii} = H_2(apk, i)^{a_i sk_i}$.
    - For a user $i$, the membership key is $mk_i = \prod_{j=1}^{n} \mu_{ij}$.
- **SignatureGen:** A signer calculates his/her individual signature as

    $$s_i = H_0(apk, m)^{sk_i} \cdot mk_i$$

    and delivers $s_i$ to the combiner.
- **Signature Aggr:** Initially, the combiner establishes the set of signers denoted as $S \subseteq G$. Subsequently, she calculates the aggregated subgroup multi-signature $\sigma = (s, pk)$ where $s = \prod_{i \in S} s_i$, $pk = \prod_{i \in S} pk_i$.
- **Verification:** The signature $\sigma = (s, pk)$ can be verified by anyone in possession of $par, apk, S, m, \sigma$ by checking if:

$$e(s, g_2) = e(H_0(apk, m), pk) . e(\prod_{j \in S} H_2(apk, j), apk)$$

## 2.2  Verifiable Timed Commitments (VTC)

The pairing-based verifiable timed version of a signature algorithm is given as VT-BLS in [3]. The authors also presented different designs for committing a value in a time-dependent manner. For example, verifiable timed commitment (VTC) or verifiable timed dlog (VTD) [4] is used to generate a timed commitment for a secret value $x \in \mathbb{Z}_q^*$ satisfying $h = g^x$ where $h$ is a publicly known value and $g$ is a generator of $G$, which is a group of order $q$. This structure of VTC is similar to VTS in terms of steps followed. In this study, we plan to use VTC to construct our timed version of the multi-signature.

- **Setup phase:** Run ZKSetup($1^\lambda$) to generate $crs_{range}$, generate public parameters
$$pp \leftarrow \text{LHTLP.PuzzleSetup}(1^\lambda, T)$$
and output
$$crs := (crs_{range}, pp).$$

- **Commit and prove phase:** For a given $(crs, wit)$, follow the steps:

  - $wit := x$, $crs := (crs_{range}, pp)$, $h := g^x$.

  - $\forall i \in [t-1]$, sample $x_i \leftarrow Z_q$ and fix $h_i = g^{x_i}$.

  - For all $i \in t, \ldots, n$ compute

$$x_i = \left( x - \sum_{j \in [t]} x_j.l_j(0) \right).l_i(0)^{-1} \tag{2}$$

and

$$h_i = \left( \frac{h}{\prod_{j \in [t]} h_j^{l_j(0)}} \right)^{l_i(0)^{-1}}, \tag{3}$$

where $l_i$ is the $i$-th Lagrange polynomial basis.

  - For $i \in [n]$:

$$r_i \leftarrow \{0,1\}^\lambda, Z_i \leftarrow \text{LHTLP.PuzzleGeneration}(pp, x_i; r_i)$$

and

$$\pi_{range,i} \leftarrow \text{ZKProve}(crs_{range}, (Z_i, a, b, T), (x_i, r_i)).$$

  - Calculate

$$I \leftarrow H'(pk, (h_1, Z_1, \pi_{range,1}), \ldots, (h_n, Z_n, \pi_{range,n})).$$

  - Output the commitment $C := (Z_1, \ldots, Z_n, T)$ and corresponding range proof
$$\pi := (\{h_i, \pi_{range,i}\}_{i \in [n]}, I, \{x_i, r_i\}_{i \in I}).$$

  - Final output is $(h, C, \pi)$.

- **Verification phase:** Given $(crs, h, C, \pi)$, the Vrfy works as follows:

  - Let $C := (Z_1, \ldots, Z_n, T)$ , $crs := (crs_{range}, pp)$ and

  $$\pi := (\{h_i, \pi_{range,i}\}_{i \in [n]}, I, \{x_i, r_i\}_{i \in I}).$$

  - If any of the below conditions are correct, the Vrfy algorithm outputs 0. Therefore, it is expected that these conditions are wrong.
    1. There is $j \notin I$ satisfying

    $$\prod_{i \in I} h_i^{l_i(0)} . h_j^{l_j(0)} \neq h.$$

    2. There is $i \in [n]$ satisfying

    $$\text{ZKVerify}(crs_{range}, (Z_i, a, b, T), \pi_{range,i}) \neq 1.$$

    3. There is $i \in I$ satisfying $Z_i \neq \text{LHTLP.PuzzleGeneration}(pp, x_i; r_i)$ or $h_i = g^{x_i}$.
    4. $I \neq H'(pk, (h_1, Z_1, \pi_{range,1}), \ldots, (h_n, Z_n, \pi_{range,n}))$.
- **Open phase:** The result of the open phase is opening the commitment and receiving $(x, \{r_i\}_{i \in [n]})$. The committer is expected to open at least the puzzles for the challenge set $I$ chosen by the verifier.
- **ForceOp (forced open) phase:** This phase takes $C := (Z_1, \ldots, Z_n, T)$ and:

  - Calculates $x_i \leftarrow \text{LHTLP.PuzzleSolve}(pp, Z_i)$ for $i \in [n]$ to retrieve all key shares. It should be observed that, given the committer has revealed $t - 1$ puzzles, the ForceOp step will only involve solving $(n - t + 1)$ puzzles.

  - Output $x := \sum_{j \in [t]} (x_j) . l_j(0)$ by considering the first $t$ signature shares are the expected ones.

## 2.3 Security Requirements

**Security Requirements for VTC.** The main security properties of the VTC [3] scheme are soundness and privacy. Soundness promises the user that the ForceOpen algorithm will reveal the committed value after T time, under the given commitment $C$. Privacy, on the other hand, means that all Parallel Random Access Machine (PRAM) algorithms with run-time less than $T$ can reveal the committed value using commitment and proof with only a negligible probability. The formal security definitions are explained in detail in article [3].

**Security Requirement for an ASM.** As an expected security property, the unforgeability of multi-signatures is important because it enhances security by preventing unauthorized parties from creating valid signatures. It ensures that transactions require the consensus and cooperation of multiple parties, reducing the risk of fraud, enabling distributed trust, and providing accountability in digital transactions.

**Definition 1 (Unforgeability).** *We define an opponent A as a $(\tau, q_S, q_H, \epsilon)$-forger for a multi-signature if it can successfully complete the following game within time $\tau$. They can make $q_S$-many signing queries, $q_H$-many random oracle queries, and they win with a probability of $\epsilon$ as a bare minimum. We say that a multi-signature is $(\tau, q_S, q_H, \epsilon)$-unforgeable if there is no such individual capable of forging.*

Although different security requirements to protect multi-signatures from attacks can be examined, only unforgeability is discussed in this paper.

# 3  Proposed Schemes

In this section, we construct a modified ASM, namely mASM, by slightly modifying Boneh *et al.*'s ASM scheme, which is useful for constructing VTC on membership keys. Thus, we made ASM compatible with VTC.

## 3.1  Modified Accountable Subgroup Multi-signature Scheme (mASM)

Boneh *et al.* showed that their ASM construction is efficient and applicable in blockchain cryptosystems. In this section, a modified version of ASM is introduced. The modified version of the ASM scheme, namely mASM, is similar to the ASM scheme until individual signature generation.

**mASM:** Individual signatures in the mASM scheme are calculated as follows:

- SignatureGen: Let $H_3$ be defined as an additional function that maps elements from $\mathbb{G}_1$ to $\mathbb{Z}_q$. A signer $i$ calculates his own signature as:

$$s_i = H_0(apk, m)^{sk_i \cdot H_3(mk_i)} \tag{4}$$

  and delivers $s_i$ and $pk_i^{H_3(mk_i)}$ to the combiner. Note that, the aim of this modification is creating a similar structure with VT-BLS to make it easily adaptable to the timed version.
- Signature Aggregation: The individual signatures let the combiner construct the set of signers $S \subseteq G$. After that, the combiner calculates the ASM $\sigma = (s, pk)$ where $s = \prod_{i \in S} s_i$ and $pk = \prod_{i \in S} pk_i^{H_3(mk_i)}$.
- Verification: With having $(par, apk, S, m, \sigma)$, anyone can check if:

$$e(H_0(apk, m), pk) = e(s, g_2)$$

- **Theorem 1 (Unforgeability).** mASM is an unforgeable multi-signature scheme under the computational co-Diffie-Hellman problem in the random-oracle model.

The proof Theorem 1 is similar to the proof of ASM [1].

## 3.2 VTC with mASM (VT-MASM)

VTC usage in mASM allows a user to send her membership key to the combiner so that the combiner can only receive individual membership keys after some predefined time $T$. In this way, membership keys will not be public at the beginning of the protocol but a combiner will be able to use them to construct a multi-signature on behalf of a group of $n$ people. The following steps show how a user sends her $mk$ with VTC. For simplicity, assume that a user has membership key $mk$ and membership key shares are defined as $mk_i$.

- **Setup phase:** Same as VTC Setup phase.
- **Commit:** For input $(crs, wit)$:

  - Parse $wit := sk \cdot H_3(mk)$, $crs := (crs_{range}, pp)$, $h := g^{sk \cdot H_3(mk)}$.

  - $\forall i \in [t-1]$, $sk_i' \xleftarrow{\$} Z_q$ and set $h_i' = g^{sk_i'}$.

  - $\forall i \in t, \ldots, n$, compute

  $$ sk_i' = \left( sk \cdot H_3(mk) - \sum_{j \in [t]} sk_j'.l_j(0) \right).l_i(0)^{-1} $$

  and

  $$ h_i' = \left( \frac{h}{\prod_{j \in [t]} h_j'^{l_j(0)}} \right)^{l_i(0)^{-1}}, $$

  where $l_i$ is the $i$-th Lagrange polynomial basis.

  - For $i \in [n]$, calculate puzzles and corresponding range proofs:

  $$ r_i \leftarrow \{0,1\}^\lambda, Z_i \leftarrow \text{LHTLP.PuzzleGeneration}(pp, sk_i'; r_i) $$

  and

  $$ \pi_{range,i} \leftarrow \text{ZKProve}(crs_{range}, (Z_i, a, b, T), (sk_i', r_i)). $$

  - Set
  $$ I \leftarrow H'(pk, (h_1', Z_1, \pi_{range,1}), \ldots, (h_n', Z_n, \pi_{range,n})). $$

  - Output the commitment $C := (Z_1, \ldots, Z_n, T)$ and corresponding range proof which is
  $$ \pi := (\{h_i', \pi_{range,i}\}_{i \in [n]}, I, \{sk_i', r_i\}_{i \in I}). $$

  - Final output is $(h, C, \pi)$.

– **Vrfy:** By using $(crs, h, C, \pi)$, the Vrfy algorithm works as follows:

- Let $C := (Z_1, \ldots, Z_n, T)$,
$crs := (crs_{range}, pp)$ and $\pi := (\{h'_i, \pi_{range,i}\}_{i \in [n]}, I, \{sk'_i, r_i\}_{i \in I})$.

- If any of the below conditions are correct, the Vrfy algorithm outputs 0. Therefore, the expectation is that these conditions are wrong.

1. There is $j \notin I$ satisfying

$$\prod_{i \in I} h_i'^{l_i(0)} \cdot h_j'^{l_j(0)} \neq h.$$

2. There is $i \in [n]$ satisfying

$$\text{ZKVerify}(crs_{range}, (Z_i, a, b, T), \pi_{range,i}) \neq 1.$$

3. There is $i \in I$ satisfying $Z_i \neq$ LHTLP.PuzzleGeneration$(pp, sk'_i; r_i)$ or $h_i = g^{sk'_i}$.
4. $I \neq H'(pk, (h'_1, Z_1, \pi_{range,1}), \ldots, (h'_n, Z_n, \pi_{range,n}))$.

– **Open:** The result of the open phase is opening the commitment and receiving $(sk \cdot H_3(mk), \{r_i\}_{i \in [n]})$. The combiner is expected to open at least the puzzles for the challenge set $I$ chosen by the verifier.

– **ForceOp:** This phase takes $C := (Z_1, \ldots, Z_n, T)$ and then performs the following steps.

- Calculates $sk'_i \leftarrow$ LHTLP.PuzzleSolve$(pp, Z_i)$ for $i \in [n]$ to retrieve all membership key shares. It should be observed that, given the committer has revealed $t - 1$ puzzles, the ForceOp step will only involve solving $(n - t + 1)$ puzzles.

- Publish $sk \cdot H_3(mk) := \sum_{j \in [t]} sk'_j . l_j(0)$ by considering that the initial $t$ shares are correct.

In this scenario, a combiner cannot change the membership keys as they are received within a verifiable commitment and are related to the user's secret keys. Also, a combiner cannot create an invalid multi-signature on behalf of a group of $n$ people, as verification of the multi-signature requires aggregated public keys of users which can be verified by any person. Note that, since the combiner needs to choose subgroup $S$ to create mASM, she does not have to calculate all individual signatures of users. She can only calculate the signatures of a subgroup which decreases computational load. Also, since multi-signature is defined as the multiplication of individual signatures in the subgroup, the combiner can first calculate the sum of membership keys of the chosen subgroup and use it to calculate multi-signature. This method can be considered a delegated multi-signature scheme. VT-mASM can also be reconstructed if the subgroup is known from the beginning of the protocol. Figure 1 shows the high-level construction of VT-mASM.

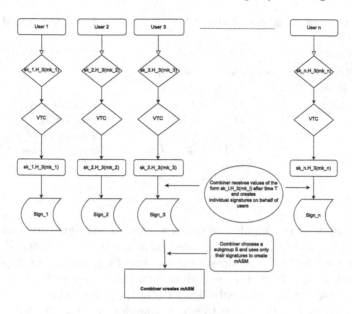

**Fig. 1.** VT-mASM

## Security of VT-MASM

- **Theorem 2 (Soundness).** If LHTLP is a time-lock puzzle with perfect correctness, then VT-mASM illustrated in Fig. 1 meets the soundness requirements set forth in Definition 1, assuming the random oracle model.
- **Theorem 3 (Privacy).** If LHTLP is a secure time-lock puzzle, then VT-mASM outlined in Fig. 1 meets the privacy requirements outlined in Definition 2.

Due to the strict page limitations, the complete proofs for all our theorems are in the full version of this paper.

## 4 Performance Evaluation

In this section, we calculate the time complexity of the VT-BLS algorithm [3] and our proposed VT-based accountable subgroup multi-signature scheme. The complexity of VT-BLS was calculated with our notation to understand how much more calculation would be needed to create a verifiable timed version of an accountable subgroup multi-signature using the method in a pairing-based setup. This comparison makes sense since our proposed VT-based scheme is also pairing-based and considering pairing is an expensive operation compared to other digital signature schemes (Schnorr, ECDSA, etc.) decreasing the pairing amount is an important improvement. Some operations are assumed to have relatively low computational complexity and are therefore ignored.

**Table 1.** Computational complexity of VT-BLS and proposed VT-mASM scheme

| Algorithm | Total Complexity | Additional Cost |
|---|---|---|
| VT-BLS (Thyagarajan et al., 2020) | $T_H.T_{Exp_1} + T_{pair} + T_{VTS_C} + T_{VTS_V}$ | N/A |
| VT-mASM | $T_H.max(T_{MExp_2} + 2T_{Exp_1}) + T_G.(n-1)T_{Exp_1} + T_S.(T_{MExp_2} + T_{Exp_1}) + T_{pair} + 3T_{MExp_1} + n.(T_{VTC_C} + T_{VTC_V})$ | $T_H.max(T_{MExp_2} + 2T_{Exp_1}) + T_G.(n-1)T_{Exp_1} + T_S.(T_{MExp_2} + T_{Exp_1}) + 3T_{MExp_1} + (n-1).(T_{VTC_C} + T_{VTC_V})$ |

Note that, $n$ is the number of users to join multi-signature and $s$ is the subgroup size for ASM. $T_H$ is the total hash queries for $H_0, H_1, H_2, H_3$. $T_G$ is the time complexity for group set-up queries. $T_S$ is the time complexity for signing queries. $T_{pair}$ is the time complexity for pairing operation for $e$. $T_{Exp_1}$ is the time complexity for exponentiation in $G_1$. $T_{Exp_2}$ is the time complexity for exponentiation in $G_2$. $T_{MExp_1}$ is the time complexity for multi-exponentiation in $G_1$. $T_{MExp_2}$ is the time complexity for multi-exponentiation in $G_2$. $T_{VTC_C}$ is the time complexity for VTC Commit and Prove phase. $T_{VTC_V}$ is the time complexity for the VTC Verification phase. Table 1 illustrates the extent to which our construction introduces additional costs to convert a VT-based signature into a VT-based multi-signature.

## 5   Conclusion and Future Work

Timed signature algorithms benefit many current applications especially when they are easily verifiable. In this study, we aim to construct the first timed version of an ASM scheme. We propose a modified version of an existing ASM scheme so that it provides relevant input for VTC construction. Regarding future work, our objective is to explore and examine the proposed scheme for known attacks like the Rogue key attack. In addition, implementing our VT-based scheme to see applicability is in our roadmap. Analysis of the efficiency of timed multi-signatures for blockchain-based payment channels would be interesting future work as well.

## References

1. Boneh, D., Drijvers, M., Neven, G.: Compact multi-signatures for smaller blockchains. In: Peyrin, T., Galbraith, S. (eds.) ASIACRYPT 2018. LNCS, vol. 11273, pp. 435–464. Springer, Cham (2018). https://doi.org/10.1007/978-3-030-03329-3_15
2. Micali, S., Ohta, K., Reyzin, L.: Accountable-subgroup multisignatures. In: Proceedings of the 8th ACM Conference on Computer and Communications Security, pp. 245–254 (2001)

3. Thyagarajan, S.A.K., Bhat, A., Malavolta, G., Döttling, N., Kate, A., Schröder, D.: Verifiable timed signatures made practical. In: Proceedings of the 2020 ACM SIGSAC Conference on Computer and Communications Security, pp. 1733–1750 (2020)
4. Thyagarajan, S.A., Malavolta, G., Moreno-Sanchez, P.: Universal atomic swaps: secure exchange of coins across all blockchains. In: 2022 IEEE Symposium on Security and Privacy (SP), pp. 1299–1316. IEEE (2022)

# Escrow and Pairing Free CP-ABE Scheme with Forward and Backward Secrecy for Healthcare Internet of Things

Sourabh Bhaskar$^{(\boxtimes)}$, Keyur Parmar, and Devesh C. Jinwala

Department of Computer Science and Engineering, S. V. National Institute
of Technology, Surat 395007, Gujarat, India
sourabhb440@gmail.com, keyur@coed.svnit.ac.in, dcj@svnit.ac.in

**Abstract.** Healthcare Internet of Things (HIoT) systems are a step forward in improving the efficiency and quality of patients' vital information. The HIoT system collects, encrypts, and outsources the patients' sensitive data over the cloud server for storage and sharing purposes. Pairing-free ciphertext-policy attribute-based encryption (PF-CPABE) is the prominent solution to provide lightweight and fine-grained access control over shared encrypted healthcare data. However, the existing PF-CPABE constructions suffer from one or more limitations, including a key escrow problem and inefficient user revocation while achieving backward and forward secrecy. In this paper, we propose an Escrow and Pairing Free CP-ABE Scheme (EPFCS) with forward and backward secrecy for HIoT. The proposed EPFCS ensures a key escrow-free HIoT system, facilitates the secure distribution of users' secret keys without using the secure channel in PF-CPABE, and enables efficient user revocation while achieving forward and backward secrecy even in dynamic healthcare scenarios. The security analysis confirms that the proposed EPFCS ensures confidentiality, key escrow freeness, forward and backward secrecy, and resistance against key collusion attacks. Furthermore, the performance analysis demonstrates that the proposed EPFCS is more effective and efficient in aspects of communication and computation costs than the existing schemes.

**Keywords:** Attribute-based encryption · Pairing-free · Elliptic curve cryptography · Key escrow · Access control · Data security · Healthcare IoT

## 1 Introduction

Healthcare Internet of Things (HIoT) comprises smart devices equipped with medical sensors, such as heart rate, SpO2, and blood pressure, aiding health monitoring and resolving medical queries [6]. Medical devices in HIoT record patient vital signs into the healthcare data, while a gateway encrypts and stores the data on cloud servers. The encrypted healthcare data is accessible to medical professionals, workers, relatives, and family members via a third-party cloud server [6].

V. Muthukkumarasamy et al. (Eds.): ICISS 2023, LNCS 14424, pp. 306–316, 2023.
https://doi.org/10.1007/978-3-031-49099-6_19

In the context of the HIoT system, several data security and privacy challenges need to be considered, such as confidentiality, integrity, and fine-grained access control (FGAC) [3,6]. The lack of addressing these concerns can result in the disclosure of healthcare data to unauthorized third parties. Therefore, attribute-based encryption (ABE) comes with the intrinsic capability of enforcing FGAC, while traditional encryption focuses on basic requirements of security and privacy [3]. Due to costly bilinear pairing operations in the pairing-based ABE scheme [3], researchers have proposed pairing-free ABE schemes [6,12,13,15], using Elliptic Curve Cryptography (ECC) and Rivest-Shamir-Adleman (RSA) to overcome ABE's less feasibility challenges in resource-constrained environments. However, these schemes are vulnerable to the key escrow problem and inefficient user revocation to manage forward and backward secrecy in dynamic healthcare scenarios. Authors proposed multi-authority and collaboration-based PF-CPABE schemes [6,13] to address the key escrow problem. However, these schemes rely on secure channels for key distribution and can be vulnerable to key generation authority collusion. Thus, the key escrow issue remains partially addressed. Existing schemes for forward and backward secrecy (FBS) [1,5,7,9] in dynamic healthcare scenarios incur high computational costs. To address these challenges, we propose an EPFCS, Escrow and Pairing Free CP-ABE Scheme with forward and backward secrecy for HIoT.

## 2    Related Work

This section discusses the existing literature on the key escrow problem and FBS.

**A. Eliminating Key Escrow**

Hur [8] proposed an escrow-free key generation protocol that provides the FGAC and executes between the cloud storage center and the KGC. However, two semi-trusted parties executing key generation protocol can collude. Therefore, the system [8] partially solves the key escrow problem. Authors [4,6] proposed the multi-authority-based CP-ABE scheme that provides the FGAC over the shared data and resists the key escrow problem. However, the security of multi-authority schemes relies on the trustworthiness of multiple authorities. If a certain number of authorities are compromised, the entire system can be compromised as well. The mentioned scheme's [4,8] construction is based on pairing-based cryptography that uses expensive bilinear pairing operations. Thus, these schemes are not applicable to resource-constrained environments for practical implementation. Therefore, researchers [12,15] proposed the PF-CPABE schemes that provide efficient computation cost compared to pairing-based CP-ABE schemes. Odelu et al. [12] proposed the RSA-based PF-CPABE scheme that provides ciphertext of constant size. However, the exponentiation operation of RSA are slightly higher than the scalar multiplication of ECC and encounter the issue of key escrow. The ECC-based schemes [6,13,15] were proposed to make the system lightweight and use a fully trusted entity to generate all the secret keys. However, schemes were vulnerable to key escrow problem and used secure channel for key distribution. Sowjanya et al. [13] proposed a key management scheme based on ECC to address the key escrow problem. However, scheme [13] makes the assumption that semi-trusted entities that are part of the key generation process cannot collude, and keys distribute through a secure channel. Thus, the key escrow is partially solved in scheme [13].

### B. Forward and Backward Secrecy

The FBS addressed in state-of-the-art literature uses well-known schemes, such as proxy re-encryption (PRE) [9], public key update [7], broadcast encryption [1], and proxy assisted decryption [5]. Broadcast encryption and public key updates do not support the backward secrecy of a revoked user. The PRE and proxy-assisted decryption techniques facilitate forward and backward secrecy. The PRE requires high computation cost for re-encrypting the number of ciphertexts (that belong to a revoked user's group) and the re-distribution and updation of secret keys [9]. The proxy-assisted decryption depends on third-party proxy servers, which can be malicious intentions that can lead to the failure of user revocation [5].

## 3   The Proposed EPFCS System and Threat Model

This section presents the system architecture of the proposed EPFCS. In addition, we discuss all aspects of the threat model.

### A. System Architecture

The subsection introduces the system architecture depicted in Fig. 1. The architecture comprises five entities, namely, the hospital infrastructure provider (HIP), the cloud server (CS), the data owner (DO), the data user (DU), and the key generation center (KGC).

**Data Owner:** The patient acts as the data owner in the HIoT system, defining FGAC policies to protect healthcare data. The DOs receive medical assistance from the HIP. HIoT monitors and collects the patient's sensitive healthcare data, including vital signs, which the gateway device aggregates, encrypts according to the access policy, and uploads to the CS via the public channel. In cases where the DO, such as an elderly patient, lacks the knowledge to define their healthcare data access policy, they can seek the help of their doctor within the HIP.

**Data User:** DUs, such as doctors, nurses, medical staff in the HIP, or family members, register with the HIP to acquire the users' system identity ($UID$) with a certificate ($Cert$). DUs can request access to encrypted healthcare data from the CS and decrypt it if the DUs' attribute secret keys meet access policy requirements.

**Cloud Server:** The CS provides computing capabilities and extensive storage for ciphertext data belonging to DOs. CS grants access to authorized DUs and performs ciphertext re-encryption upon HIP's request, sending the re-key to HIP.

**Hospital Infrastructure Provider:** The HIPs are the clinical foundations or hospitals that provide the HIoT infrastructure to the data owners (i.e., patients).

The HIP is responsible for user revocation, serve as a registration authority, and issue certificates and UIDs to authorized DUs. When a DU leaves, HIP updates re-encryption keys for the remaining users in the same attribute group. A group defines the DUs possessing a similar kind of attribute set. HIP assigns attributes to DUs based on their roles.

**Key Generation Center:** The KGC validates DUs via certificates and follows the key distribution protocol. The KGC generates public parameters and the master secret key (MSK) and uses a secure key distribution protocol to compute the user's secret keys. A KGC can generate partial secret keys. However, KGC is unable to generate complete secret keys for DUs.

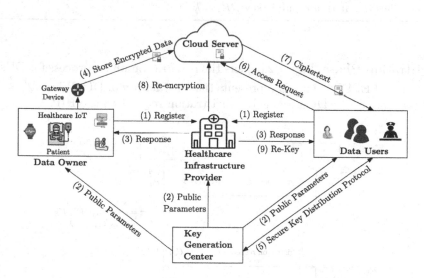

**Fig. 1.** System architecture of the proposed EPFCS.

## B. Threat Model

In our threat model, HIP is a trusted entity that registers the DUs and provides the certificate. The HIP manages all the DUs' groups. The KGC is a semi-trusted entity characterized by being honest but curious that generates all public parameters and a MSK that keeps itself confidential. The DUs are semi-trusted entities. DUs always try to gain access to data beyond their authorized access rights. The DOs are considered trusted entities as they generate healthcare data and define the access policies.

## 4  The Proposed EPFCS

This section presents the concrete construction algorithms for EPFCS. The proposed EPFCS comprises a registration phase and five algorithms: setup, encryption, re-encryption, key generation, and decryption.

**Setup Algorithm.** The KGC executes the setup Algorithm 1. Here, the elliptic curve E is defined over $F_p$, and G is a base point in E with a large prime order q, generating a cyclic subgroup of E. The $\lambda$ is the security parameter.

---

**Algorithm 1.** Setup

---

**Input:** $(1^\lambda)$
**Output:** $(PK, PK_i)$ and $(MSK)$

1. KGC picks a random integer $n \in Z_q$ as the MSK and generates $PK = n.G$ as public key of KGC.
2. KGC selects a random integer $k_i \in Z_q$ for each attribute $i$ in the system and publishes the attribute public key $PK_i = k_i.n.G$.

---

**Registration Phase.** Figure 2 depicts the registration phase process for DUs in the proposed EPFCS. The ID represents the real identity of DU. When $Q'_u \stackrel{?}{=} Q_u$ does not match, the DU resends the registration request to the HIP.

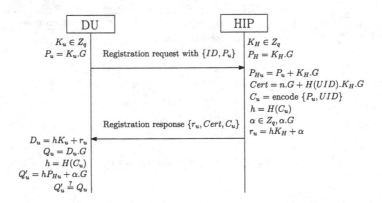

**Fig. 2.** Process of registration phase.

**Key Generation Algorithm.** The DU initiates the key generation process by sending their $UID'$ and $Cert$ to the KGC. The KGC then authenticates the user's identity by validating their certificate and $UID'$.

$$Cert' = PK + H(UID')P_H$$
$$Cert' = n.G + H(UID')K_H.G$$

KGC checks if $Cert' \stackrel{?}{=} Cert$ for DU authentication. Unauthorized DUs cannot proceed with the secure key distribution protocol. HIP pseudonymizes DU IDs

**Algorithm 2.** Secure key distribution

**Input:** $KeyGen_{user}(U_t) \longleftrightarrow KeyGen_{KGC}(K_i, n)$
**Output:** $SK_{i,UID}$

1. KGC first authenticate data user $u_j$.
2. KGC and DU participate in a secure key distribution protocol, utilizing the KGC's secret input $(K_i, n)$ and the DU's secret input $(U_t)$ for the computation.
3. The secure key distribution protocol uses a secure two-party protocol that yields a confidential output $x = (\frac{U_t}{n} + K_i)^{\frac{1}{n}}$ to DU.
4. DU picks $\sigma \in Z_q$ then computes $A = \frac{x}{\sigma}$ and sends $A$ to the KGC.
5. KGC computes $B = A.n^2/d$ and sends $B$ to DU.
6. DU computes a personalized key component $k' = B.\sigma$.

to create irreversible pseudonyms known as $UID$, ensuring user identity confidentiality and preventing direct re-identification in the EPFCS system. KGC and CS interact with DUs using $UID$.

Let $u_t \in Z_q$ be the private value of DU and $k_i$, $n$ be the private value of KGC. Then, the DU computes $U_t = u_t.d^2$ and the KGC computes $K_i = k_i.d$, where $d = H(UID)$. The $KeyGen_{user}(U_t) \longleftrightarrow KeyGen_{KGC}(K_i, n)$ are two interactive algorithms [8] that execute a secure key distribution protocol between each DU $(u_j)$ such that $j = \{1, 2, \ldots, t\}$ and the KGC. The notation $\longleftrightarrow$ represents the interaction between two algorithms. The DU outputs $k'$ as given in Algorithm 2. We simplify $k'$ as follows: $k' = B.\sigma = A.n^2\sigma/d = \frac{x}{\sigma}.n^2\sigma/d = (\frac{U_t}{n} + K_i)^{\frac{1}{n}}.n^2\frac{1}{d} = (u_t.d + k_i.n)$. Therefore, the final user's secret key is $SK_{i,UID} = (u_t.d + k_i.n)$.

**Encryption Algorithm.** The DO executes the encryption Algorithm 3 and encrypts the message M based on the access policy $(A, \rho)$ [2].

**Algorithm 3.** Encryption

**Input:** $M, (A, \rho), PK_{\rho(x)}$
**Output:** $CT = [C_a, C_{b,x}, C_{c,x}]$

1. Plaintext data maps into point M on $E(F_q)$.
2. DO chooses the random integer $s \in Z_q$ and computes $C_a = M + s.G$.
3. The encryption algorithm employs the access policy established by the DO and produces matrix A of dimensions $n \times l$ with mapping function $\rho$ to map the rows to attributes.
4. DO selects a random vector $v \in Z_q^l$, with $s$ as its first entry. Assume $\lambda_x$ denote the result of multiplying row $x$ of matrix $A$ with vector $v$, denoted as $A_x.v$.
5. DO selects a random vector $u \in Z_q^l$, with 0 as its first entry. Assume $w_x$ denote the result of multiplying row $x$ of matrix $A$ with vector $w$, denoted as $A_x.u$.
6. Then, the Do computes the ciphertext $C_{b,x} = \lambda_x.G + w_x PK_{\rho(x)}, C_{c,x} = w_x.G, \forall x$.

**Re-encryption Algorithm.** The CS executes the re-encryption algorithm at the request of HIP. The CS uses a random integer $cs$ to re-encrypt the ciphertext

$CT$ as outputs $CT'$ and then provides cs to the HIP as the re-key. The HIP sends the re-key to the group of DUs who have not been revoked from the system.

**Decryption Algorithm.** The DU executes the Algorithm 4 to decrypt the ciphertext data. The DUs with a sufficient attribute set to meet the access policy requirements can decrypt and access the plaintext data.

---

**Algorithm 4.** Decryption

---

**Input:** $CT', cs, SK_{i,UID}$
**Output:** $M$

1. The DU uses re-key $cs$ for obtaining $CT$ from $CT'$.
2. The DU computes $(C_{c,x}, \rho(x))$ as:
   $$\sum C_{c,x} SK_{\rho(x),UID} = \sum (w_x.G.(u_t.H(UID) + k_{\rho(x)}.n))$$
   $$\sum C_{c,x} SK_{\rho(x)} = \sum (w_x.u_t.H(UID).G + w_x.k_{\rho(x)}.n.G)$$
3. Then DU computes $\sum C_b, x - \sum C_{c,x} SK_{\rho(x)}$
   $$= \sum (\lambda_x.G + w_x PK_{\rho(x)}) - \sum (w_x.u_t.H(UID).G + w_x.k_{\rho(x)}.n.G)$$
   $$= \sum (\lambda_x.G + w_x.k_i.n.G) - \sum (w_x.u_t.H(UID).G + w_x.k_i.n.G)$$
   $$= \sum (\lambda_x.G) - \sum (w_x.H(UID).u_t.G).$$
4. DU chooses the constants $k_x \in Z_q$ such as $\sum k_x.A_x = (1,0,...,0)$ and computes:
   $$\sum k_x(\lambda_x.G - w_x.H(UID).u_t.G) = s.G.$$
5. Given vectors $v$ and $u$, as v.(1,0,...,0)=s and u.(1,0,...,0)=0.
6. Ultimately, $C_a - s.G = M$.

---

## 5    Security and Performance Analysis

This section provides a comprehensive analysis of the security and performance analysis of the proposed EPFCS.

### 5.1    Security Analysis

In this subsection, we discuss a security analysis of the proposed EPFCS.

**Key Escrow-Free.** To ensure user key security, the DU generates their secret key through a secure key distribution protocol involving the KGC and the DU. In this protocol, both parties engage in secure 2PC with their private inputs, preserving their underlying secrets. KGC's private input is $(k_i, n)$, and DU's is $u_t$. The KGC generates a partial key, and DU then forms the complete secret key, preventing anyone from generating it alone, ensuring key escrow freeness.

**Forward Secrecy.** To achieve forward secrecy, the proposed EPFCS re-encrypts the subsequent ciphertext and assigns the re-encryption key to group users whose access has not been revoked.

**Backward Secrecy.** To achieve backward secrecy, we use an additional numeric attribute that denotes as a timestamp (TS). The timestamp attribute is assigned to each data user as $TS_u t$ when he or she joins the system. The ciphertext timestamp $TS_c n$ is assigned when the ciphertext is generated. If $TS_c n < TS_u t$

(for the numeric attribute comparison refer [14]), then grant the access; otherwise, the error symbol is for not satisfying the access policy. Here, $TS_c n = \{TS_c 1, ..., TS_c n\}$ and $TS_u t = \{TS_u 1, ..., TS_u t\}$.

**Collusion Resistance.** We associate the $(UID)$ with their secret keys to prevent a collusion attack. Charlie and Katie cannot collude because $H(UID_{Charlie}) \neq H(UID_{Katie})$, and they cannot find $k_x \in Z_q$ such that $\sum_x k_x . A_x = (1, 0, ..., 0)$ workable. In this manner, the proposed EPFCS achieves collusion resistance.

## 5.2 Performance Analysis

In this subsection, we analyze and compare the efficiency of the proposed EPFCS with existing key escrow-free schemes [6,8,11,13] in terms of communication and computation costs.

**A. Communication Cost.** The parameters used for comparison include ciphertext (CT) size, public key (PK) size, and secret key (SK) size in Table 1. We assume that all schemes compare at an equivalent level of security and under the same set of attributes. We consider the standard 160 bit ECC to provide an equivalent level of security strength as RSA's 1024 bit [15]. The RSA is taken into consideration in bilinear pairing-based cryptographic schemes due to its use of similar exponentiation operations. According to the comparison strategy, the ECC point, represented as $2\mu$, comprises (160+160) bits corresponding to its x and y coordinates. ECC secret key consists of 160 bits, represented as $\mu$. Similarly, the sizes of the access tree and attribute set are considered as $\mu$. For bilinear pairing-based schemes, the PK and SK have a size of 1024 bits, which is equivalent to $6.4\,\mu$. The sizes of elements in groups $G_1$ and $G_2$ are 1024 bits $(6.4\,\mu)$ and 2048 bits $(12.8\,\mu)$, respectively. We consider the same for EPFCS as the study [13] sets the parameter values as number of leaf nodes in the access tree $l = 10$, the size of users' attribute set $u = 5$, and the total number of attributes in the system $n = 30$.

We can conclude from Table 1 that the CT size of the EPFCS is smaller than schemes [8,11,13] and equal to scheme [6]. Similarly, the EPFCS has a smaller PK size than schemes [6,8,11,13]. In addition, the SK size of our EPFCS is smaller than schemes [8,11,13] and equal to scheme [6]. Therefore, the proposed EPFCS has lower communication costs than existing key escrow-free schemes [6,8,11,13].

**B. Computation Cost.** The computation time for operations involved in computation costs is considered to be similar to the study [10]. The platform of the work [10] comprises a PIV 3-GHz processor, 512 MB of memory, and a Windows operating system. As the work [10], the execution time of pairing operation $P_b$ takes 20.04 ms, the execution time of exponentiation operation $E$ takes 5.31 ms, and the execution time of scalar multiplication operation $S_m$ takes 2.21 ms. We can infer from Table 2 and Fig. 3 that the proposed EPFCS has the lowest computational costs compared to existing schemes [6,8,11,13].

**Table 1.** Communication costs comparison.

| Scheme | CT size (in bits) | PK size (in bits) | SK size (in bits) |
|---|---|---|---|
| Hur [8] | $(2l+1)6.4\,\mu + 12.8\,\mu + \mu \approx 148.2\,\mu$ | $38.4\,\mu$ | $(2u+2)6.4\,\mu \approx 76.8\,\mu$ |
| Lin et al. [11] | $(l+1)6.4\,\mu + 12.8\,\mu + \mu \approx 84.2\,\mu$ | $(l+1)6.4\,\mu + 12.8\,\mu \approx 83.2\,\mu$ | $\mu + (u+2)6.4\,\mu \approx 45.8\,\mu$ |
| Sowjanya et al. [13] | $(6+2l)\mu \approx 26\,\mu$ | $(4+n)\mu \approx 34\,\mu$ | $(2u+4)\mu \approx 14\,\mu$ |
| Das and Namasudra [6] | $(2l+1)\mu \approx 21\,\mu$ | $(2n+2)\mu \approx 62\,\mu$ | $(u)\mu \approx 5\,\mu$ |
| Proposed EPFCS | $(2l+1)\mu \approx 21\,\mu$ | $(n+2)\mu \approx 32\,\mu$ | $(u)\mu \approx 5\,\mu$ |

**Table 2.** Computation costs comparison.

| Scheme | Setup | Encryption | Decryption |
|---|---|---|---|
| Hur [8] | $(P_b + 3E)$ | $P_b + (3+l)E$ | $3P_b$ |
| Lin et al. [11] | $(P_b + 2E)$ | $P_b + (3+l)E$ | $3P_b$ |
| Sowjanya et al. [13] | $2S_m$ | $(4l+1)S_m$ | $(u+2)S_m$ |
| Das and Namasudra [6] | $(2n+1)S_m$ | $(4l+1)S_m$ | $(u+1)S_m$ |
| Proposed EPFCS | $(n+1)S_m$ | $(3l+1)S_m$ | $(u+1)S_m$ |

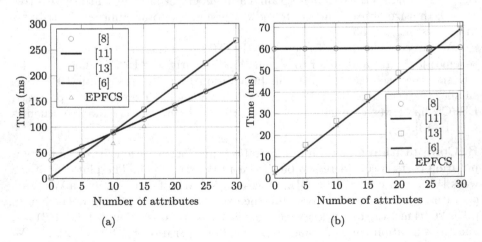

**Fig. 3.** Execution time (in milliseconds) for (a) Encryption (b) Decryption.

# 6    Conclusions and Future Works

In this paper, we proposed an EPFCS, escrow and pairing free CP-ABE scheme with FBS for HIoT. The proposed EPFCS facilitates FGAC over shared encrypted healthcare data, key escrow freeness, and secure key distribution without using a secure channel through our secure key distribution protocol. The proposed EPFCS achieves user revocation while ensuring FBS in dynamic healthcare scenarios. The security analysis confirms that the proposed EPFCS is resilient against compromising confidentiality, the key escrow problem, and key collusion attacks while ensuring efficient FBS. In addition, the performance analysis indicates that the proposed EPFCS is efficient and suitable for deployment in resource-limited environments. In the future, researchers can focus on developing formal security models and proofs for PF-CPABE schemes.

**Acknowledgements.** This research was a part of the project "Design and Analysis of Secure and Efficient Smart Contracts Using Blockchain Technology". It was partially supported by the SEED Money/Research Grant of the author, Dr. Keyur Parmar, Department of Computer Science and Engineering, S. V. National Institute of Technology (NIT), Surat, India.

# References

1. Attrapadung, N., Imai, H.: Conjunctive broadcast and attribute-based encryption. In: Shacham, H., Waters, B. (eds.) Pairing 2009. LNCS, vol. 5671, pp. 248–265. Springer, Heidelberg (2009). https://doi.org/10.1007/978-3-642-03298-1_16
2. Beimel, A.: Secure schemes for secret sharing and key distribution. Ph.D. dissertation, Technion-Israel Institute of technology (1996)
3. Bethencourt, J., Sahai, A., Waters, B.: Ciphertext-policy attribute-based encryption. In: Symposium on Security and Privacy, SP 2007, pp. 321–334. IEEE (2007). https://doi.org/10.1109/SP.2007.11
4. Chaudhary, C.K., Sarma, R., Barbhuiya, F.A.: RMA-CPABE: a multi-authority CPABE scheme with reduced ciphertext size for IoT devices. Futur. Gener. Comput. Syst. **138**, 226–242 (2023). https://doi.org/10.1016/j.future.2022.08.017
5. Cui, H., Deng, R.H., Li, Y., Qin, B.: Server-aided revocable attribute-based encryption. In: Askoxylakis, I., Ioannidis, S., Katsikas, S., Meadows, C. (eds.) ESORICS 2016. LNCS, vol. 9879, pp. 570–587. Springer, Cham (2016). https://doi.org/10.1007/978-3-319-45741-3_29
6. Das, S., Namasudra, S.: Multiauthority CP-ABE based access control model for IoT-enabled healthcare infrastructure. Trans. Ind. Inform. **19**(1), 821–829 (2023). https://doi.org/10.1109/TII.2022.3167842
7. Fan, C.I., Huang, V.S.M., Ruan, H.M.: Arbitrary-state attribute-based encryption with dynamic membership. Trans. Comput. **63**(8), 1951–1961 (2014). https://doi.org/10.1109/TC.2013.83
8. Hur, J.: Improving security and efficiency in attribute-based data sharing. Trans. Knowl. Data Eng. **25**(10), 2271–2282 (2013). https://doi.org/10.1109/TKDE.2011.78
9. Hur, J., Noh, D.K.: Attribute-based access control with efficient revocation in data outsourcing systems. Trans. Parallel Distrib. Syst. **22**(7), 1214–1221 (2011). https://doi.org/10.1109/TPDS.2010.203

10. Karati, A., Amin, R., Biswas, G.P.: Provably secure threshold-based ABE scheme without bilinear map. Arab. J. Sci. Eng. **41**, 3201–3213 (2016). https://doi.org/10.1007/s13369-016-2156-9

11. Lin, G., Hong, H., Sun, Z.: A collaborative key management protocol in ciphertext policy attribute-based encryption for cloud data sharing. Access **5**, 9464–9475 (2017). https://doi.org/10.1109/ACCESS.2017.2707126

12. Odelu, V., Das, A.K., Khurram Khan, M., Choo, K.K.R., Jo, M.: Expressive CP-ABE scheme for mobile devices in IoT satisfying constant-size keys and ciphertexts. Access **5**, 3273–3283 (2017). https://doi.org/10.1109/ACCESS.2017.2669940

13. Sowjanya, K., Dasgupta, M., Ray, S.: A lightweight key management scheme for key-escrow-free ECC-based CP-ABE for IoT healthcare systems. J. Syst. Architect. **117**, 102–108 (2021). https://doi.org/10.1016/j.sysarc.2021.102108

14. Xue, K., Hong, J., Xue, Y., Wei, D.S., Yu, N., Hong, P.: CABE: a new comparable attribute-based encryption construction with 0-encoding and 1-encoding. Trans. Comput. **66**(9), 1491–1503 (2017). https://doi.org/10.1109/TC.2017.2693265

15. Yao, X., Chen, Z., Tian, Y.: A lightweight attribute-based encryption scheme for the internet of things. Futur. Gener. Comput. Syst. **49**, 104–112 (2015). https://doi.org/10.1016/j.future.2014.10.010

# Blockchains

# Ensuring Data Security in the Context of IoT Forensics Evidence Preservation with Blockchain and Self-Sovereign Identities

Cristian Alves dos Santos[✉], Leandro Loffi, and Carla Merkle Westphall

Computer Science, Federal University of Santa Catarina (UFSC), PO Box 476,
Florianopolis, SC 88040-970, Brazil
{cristian.alves,leandro.loffi}@posgrad.ufsc.br,
carla.merkle.westphall@ufsc.br

**Abstract.** As Internet of Things (IoT) networks expand, significant challenges related to the secure management of data generated by these devices emerge. The integrity and reliability of this data are critical in sensitive sectors, such as forensic evidence preservation. In this context, we present an innovative architecture based on Self-Sovereign Identity (SSI) tailored for resource-constrained IoT devices.

Our proposal addresses the intrinsic limitations of current systems, which often fail to ensure the integrity, reliability, and traceability of data originating from IoT devices. To tackle this issue, we propose using decentralized identifiers (DIDs) to establish unique identities for IoT devices, accompanied by verifiable credentials (VCs) that attest to data ownership. To implement this solution, we have developed an application that serves as a gateway for resource-constrained devices, typically certified and connected to a broker. Our application utilizes Hyperledger Aries and Indy libraries, providing essential resources to address these challenges. Furthermore, we conducted comprehensive simulations and a performance analysis to validate the effectiveness of our approach. Integrating these technologies enables the certification of data collected by IoT devices, offering a robust framework for the data custody chain. Consequently, this substantially contributes to preserving this data's integrity, reliability, and traceability in critical environments.

**Keywords:** Internet of Things · Self-sovereign identity · Decentralized identifiers · Verifiable credentials

## 1 Introduction

With the rapid growth and continuous evolution of intelligent devices and systems, also known as the Internet of Things (IoT), new services drive complex interactions among these devices, services, and people. However, this growth and the exponential increase in the number of connected IoT devices generating and

V. Muthukkumarasamy et al. (Eds.): ICISS 2023, LNCS 14424, pp. 319–338, 2023.
https://doi.org/10.1007/978-3-031-49099-6_20

processing massive volumes of data raise significant concerns about the security of this information [1, 2].

In this context, the traceability and verification of data generated by these devices play a crucial role in managing the data custody chain to preserve forensic evidence. Digital forensic investigation plays a pivotal role in virtually all criminal investigations, given the abundance of available information and the opportunities presented by electronic data to investigate and substantiate crimes. However, during legal proceedings, these electronic pieces of evidence are often met with extreme suspicion and uncertainty, although in some situations, they are justified. The use of scientifically unproven forensic techniques is widely criticized in current legal procedures. Furthermore, electronic data's highly distinct and dynamic characteristics, combined with existing legislation and privacy laws, continue to pose significant challenges to the systematic presentation of evidence in a court of law [3].

Throughout all phases of forensic investigation, digital evidence is susceptible to external influences and contact with various factors. The legal admissibility of digital evidence is the capacity for this evidence to be accepted as proof in a court of law. The probative value of digital evidence can only be preserved if it is possible to establish that the records are accurate, meaning who created them, when they were created, and that no alterations have occurred [4].

Therefore, it is imperative to establish unequivocal device identification and ensure the integrity and authenticity of the generated data. These objectives can be achieved by adopting technologies based on decentralized identifiers (DIDs) [5] for identification and using verifiable credentials to certify the authenticity of measurements sent by IoT devices. This approach is essential in instilling trust and integrity in communications and transactions, bridging a significant gap in existing systems, and providing an additional layer of security and reliability in interactions between IoT devices and the systems to which they are connected.

By adopting Self-Sovereign Identity (SSI), IoT devices can be securely and reliably identified, establishing a unique identity and ensuring that transactions and communications are conducted authentically and immutably. This approach is particularly relevant in the face of significant challenges related to the sharing and preserving of forensic data in technological, legal, and operational terms. Demonstrating data integrity is crucial to ensure its validity and admissibility in legal proceedings.

However, IoT devices often have limited resources in terms of low processing power, storage, memory, and limited battery life [1]. This imposes a limitation on the use of DIDs and renders them incapable of storing digital wallets, running an agent, or maintaining the necessary protocol stack to enable SSI capabilities. Furthermore, IoT devices require cryptographic solutions to meet security, privacy, and trust requirements, which are crucial for enabling the use of DIDs and Verifiable Credentials (VCs) [6].

This limitation can pose a challenge in adopting these advanced technologies on resource-constrained devices, necessitating alternative approaches to ensure the security and integrity of communications and transactions in this specific context. One practical solution is to securely outsource processing to a more powerful external device to reduce the computational cost of cryptographic calculations and maintain data confidentiality.

To address these issues, we propose an SSI Gateway for IoT to identify and certify data emitted by these devices. Our approach seeks to establish means for managing the custody chain of data issued in the context of forensic evidence preservation. This architecture utilizes a blockchain-based SSI model [7] to safeguard the privacy of data collected from IoT devices.

This approach allows an IoT device, whether an emitter or connected to an emitter in a certified manner, to sign the data at its source when transmitting it, making it tamper-proof and verifiable, potentially rendering it trustworthy as long as the emitter is reliable. Consequently, the involved parties can preserve ownership of the collected information, enabling the sharing of verifiable credentials certifying the integrity and origin of data collection.

In summary, our main contributions are as follows:

1. We implemented an SSI Gateway architecture designed for IoT networks.
2. We developed a system for issuing verifiable credentials to ensure the integrity and traceability of data from IoT devices.
3. We implemented decentralized identifiers to strengthen the identification of devices within the architecture, thereby enhancing data custody chain security.

In our experiments, we utilized the Hyperledger Indy Software Development Kit (SDK) [8] to generate DIDs for device identification. We utilized Hyperledger Aries Cloud Agent Python (ACA-Py) [9] as a cloud agent for issuing VCs and establishing connections with other parties. The Von Network [10] was adopted as a permissioned blockchain to anchor DIDs, credential metadata, and verification keys. To assess the performance of the proposed architecture, we conducted simulations and, through performance testing during the DIDs registration and VCs issuance process, analyzed the results and identified potential areas for optimization.

The remaining part of the article is organized as follows: In Sect. 2, we provide the essential background. Next, Sect. 3 discusses related works and the techniques they address. In Sect. 4, we present an overview of the proposed architecture. Subsequently, Sect. 5 delves into the detailed performance test results and analyzes these findings. Finally, in Sect. 6, we discuss the conclusions drawn from this study and explore potential future research directions.

## 2   Background

### 2.1   Self-Sovereign Identities

Self-sovereign identity is a concept that describes an individual's ability to control and manage their digital identity in a decentralized manner. [11] first proposed the idea of self-sovereign identity and has been referenced by various authors in the literature. While there still needs to be a consensus on SSI, the widely accepted concept is described as a system where individuals can claim and manage their identity without needing a centralized trusted party [12].

SSI allows users to choose which identity information to share and with whom, as well as granting them access to their identity information at any time. Instead of relying on third parties, such as companies or governments, to manage and store their identity information, users can create, store, and control their digital identities through decentralized technologies like blockchain.

**Decentralized Identifiers.** Decentralized Identifiers are globally unique identifiers that enable an entity's verifiable and persistent identification for as long as the DID controller desires without relying on a centralized registry [13]. Just as there are various types of URIs complying with the URI standard, there is also a variety of DID methods, all of which must adhere to the DID standard [5]. Each DID method specification should define the name of the DID method, which should appear between the first and second colons (e.g., did:method:unique-identifier), the structure of the unique identifier following the second colon, and the technical specifications outlining how a DID resolver can implement operations to create, read, update, and deactivate a DID document using that method.

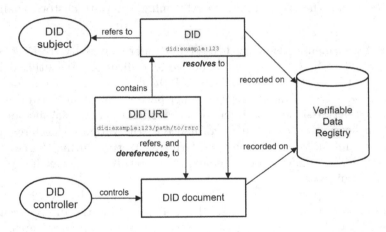

**Fig. 1.** Overview of DID architecture and the relationship of the essential components.

Figure 1 depicts a conceptual diagram of the W3C-proposed [5] DID architecture. A DID is linked to a DID document containing relevant DID-related information. This DID document can be accessed by resolving the DID itself. Within this document, essential elements for authentication and verification, including the DID itself and associated public key information, can be found. Hence, the DID document is pivotal in conducting secure authentication and verification processes using DID.

A DID points to a DID document, a JavaScript Object Notation (JSON) file with a format defined explicitly in the DID specification, and a set of information describing the DID subject. This document includes cryptographic public keys that the DID subject and a DID delegate can use to authenticate and verify their connection to the DID.

Each entity possesses one or more DIDs, which can be resolved through a DID Resolver, much like the Domain Name System (DNS) functioning in the context of SSI. When a valid DID is provided to a DID Resolver software, it operates as a browser, receiving a Uniform Resource Locator (URL), resolving the DID, and providing a DID document in response [14].

**Verifiable Credentials.** A verifiable credential is a digital representation of information typically found in physical credentials but with enhanced security and reliability, thanks to digital signatures. A credential comprises claims made by an entity, a person, an institution, or a machine, and metadata such as issuer, expiration date, representative image, and public key for verification [6].

A verifiable credential is founded upon a "triangle of trust," wherein the issuer trusts the subject, the subject trusts the verifier, and the verifier trusts the issuer. Depending on the context, this trust relationship can be established concerning individuals, institutions, or machines. The process of a verifiable credential consists of essential steps:

1. Recording the DID and Public Key on the Blockchain: The issuer or entity issuing credentials writes the DID along with its public key onto a blockchain or another trusted public service. This establishes a connection between the issuer and their DID.
2. Issuance of Verifiable Credentials: The issuer uses their private key to sign a verifiable credential digitally. This credential is then issued to a qualified subject, who stores it in their digital wallet.
3. Request for Proof by the Verifier: A verifier seeking to confirm the identity or specific information of the subject requests digital proof of the credentials from the subject. If the subject agrees, they generate and send the proofs to the verifier from their digital wallet.
4. Verification of Proofs by the Verifier: The proofs contain the issuer's DID. The verifier uses this DID to retrieve the issuer's public key and other cryptographic data from the blockchain. Subsequently, the verifier utilizes the issuer's public key to ascertain the validity of the proofs and whether the digital credential has been tampered with.

In the context of verifiable credentials, the blockchain serves as a registry where issuers publish cryptographic keys and credential metadata. This enables credential holders to generate presentations that verifiers can cryptographically verify. However, it is crucial to emphasize that, to ensure data privacy and security, storing the credentials themselves on the blockchain is not recommended. Instead, the standard practice is to store only the public keys of the issuer and the holder on the blockchain linked to their respective DIDs. Credentials containing personal information are securely kept in a private digital wallet. The availability of these keys is sufficient to verify the credentials, eliminating the need to store them on the blockchain [14].

**Zero Knowledge Proof.** Zero-knowledge proof (ZKP) is a cryptographic technique that allows one to prove possession of certain information without revealing its content, ensuring data privacy and transaction security. The Verifiable Credentials model combines the implementations of zero-knowledge proofs and verifiable credentials to reduce data and increase privacy. With this combination, provers can present proofs without disclosing sensitive and personal data to verifiers. In order to enhance privacy and security, the claims present in a verifiable credential can be exposed as a predicate or selective disclosure of zero-knowledge proof [15].

### 2.2 Relationship with Blockchain Technology

Blockchain exhibits characteristics that align with the desired properties of SSI. For instance, blockchain provides a decentralized domain that is not controlled by any single entity. Data stored on any blockchain is readily available to any authorized entity. The owner of specific data has complete control over it and determines how it can be shared with other users within the blockchain domain, thus satisfying the principle of ownership and disclosure.

In this context, Hyperledger Indy is one of the most advanced technologies concerning self-sovereign identity. This platform provides robust and innovative solutions for secure and decentralized digital identity management. In Hyperledger Indy, private content is not stored on the blockchain, ensuring enhanced privacy preservation in solutions utilizing this distributed ledger technology. The blockchain maintains only the public DIDs, schemas, credential definitions, and revocation records. This approach ensures that sensitive information is not exposed to the network, making the architecture more resistant to potential attacks or future vulnerabilities [15].

### 2.3 Use of Agents

Agents can represent individuals, organizations, or devices in SSI ecosystems. They are software responsible for securely managing and using DIDs and VCs stored in digital identity wallets. These software entities require access to the wallet to perform cryptographic operations on behalf of the represented entity. Their responsibilities encompass various essential tasks such as message sending and receiving, information encryption and decryption, digital signature on behalf of the entity, wallet management, and backup/restoration of information. Additionally, some agents can interact with the ledger, enabling the adoption of verifiable data models [15,16]. Among the existing agents, Hyperledger Aries [17] stands out as an advanced and comprehensive solution. It implements the Hyperledger Ursa [18] cryptographic library, ensuring a high level of security in cryptographic operations.

## 3    Related Work

From a research perspective, only a few studies have proposed the application of the SSI paradigm to IoT. Following a search for relevant keywords such as

"Internet of Things," "Self-Sovereign Identity," "Decentralized Identifiers," "Verifiable Credentials," and "Distributed Ledger Technology" in prominent research sources, several works were identified that briefly mentioned the intersection of SSI and IoT. While these studies provide an overview, they do not delve into credential exchange protocols or technical details. However, there are standout studies known for their specific proposals:

Initially, authors [19] explored the SSI paradigm for IoT, introducing DIDs and VCs for IoT. They also analyzed SSI's application in IoT ecosystems, convincingly demonstrating that this approach surpasses traditional certificates such as Pretty Good Privacy (PGP) and X.509 regarding privacy and effectiveness.

SSI can leverage a decentralized registry to store information such as DIDs, DID documents, and verifiable credential metadata. This registry can be implemented using Distributed Ledger Technology (DLT), enhancing the system's overall security while ensuring the integrity and availability of stored information. In this regard, several studies have conducted research.

For instance, authors [20] introduced an SSI scheme based on IOTA as a DLT to implement decentralized identity. They underscored its permissionless nature, absence of transaction costs, and scalability advantages. However, a significant limitation of this proposal lies in IOTA's need for complete decentralization, as it still relies on a coordinator, a centralizing element in the consensus process.

Some authors introduced concepts related to SSI and illustrated specific use cases for industrial IoT (IIoT). [21] proposed a protocol for device identity management based on Hyperledger Indy but did not provide implementation details. [22] suggested a digital identity framework for devices using a combination of Hyperledger Indy and Ethereum. However, the authors should have comprehensively addressed scalability issues, as the Ethereum platform entails costs that could pose significant challenges when dealing with increasing demand.

Other studies delve into the SSI paradigm for Medical Internet of Things (MIoT) devices. The authors [23] conducted a study on authentication mechanisms for medical devices. However, the proposal must discuss results and address performance and scalability issues. Some studies have addressed IoT as a service. For instance, the authors [24] introduced an SSI-based identity management system for the IoT-as-a-Service (IoTaaS) business model. However, the tests were conducted on specific devices with memory and processing capacity without considering the limitations of resource-constrained devices.

Table 1 compares our proposal, and various related works in the field of SSI applied to IoT. Each row represents a different study, identifying the authors, the application domain of the work, and the addressed problem. The first four criteria are vital indicators for analyzing the solution's suitability for constrained IoT devices and data integrity. It also considers scalability and performance evaluation. Our proposal stands out comprehensively and successfully addresses all these essential aspects.

Regarding devices with limited resources, the authors [25] proposed using DIDs as identifiers for IoT devices and conducted a precise examination of the requirements for IoT devices to implement an SSI-based identity management

**Table 1.** Comparison between related works and our proposal.

| Authors | Application Domain | Issue Addressed | Constrained IoT devices | Data Integrity Verification | Scalability | Performance Evaluation |
|---|---|---|---|---|---|---|
| [19] | IoT devices | Digital Identity | × | × | × | × |
| [20] | IoT devices | Data accessing | – | × | ✓ | ✓ |
| [21] | IoT Industrial | Data accessing | × | ✓ | × | × |
| [22] | IoT Industrial | Efficiency of data sharing | × | × | × | ✓ |
| [23] | IoT Medical | Access control | × | ✓ | × | × |
| [24] | IoT Services | Secure transactions | × | ✓ | × | ✓ |
| [25] | IoT devices | Digital Identity | ✓ | ✓ | – | × |
| [26] | IoT devices | Digital Identity | ✓ | × | – | × |
| [27] | IoT vehicles | Data integrity | × | ✓ | – | × |
| [28] | IoT vehicles | Data security | × | ✓ | – | × |
| This work | IoT Data | Data integrity verification | ✓ | ✓ | ✓ | ✓ |

system. They also put forward a proxy-based approach. Other authors [26] have also proposed proxy-based approaches, such as IoT Exchange, to establish the connection between IoT devices and users. However, it is worth noting that this proposal does not provide a concrete specification for implementing VCs for IoT, primarily focusing on analyzing DIDs as suitable identifiers for this specific environment.

In the study by [27], a framework was introduced to verify the authenticity of vehicle emission values through a decentralized authentication and authorization system utilizing blockchain technologies (Hyperledger Fabric and Indy). However, it is essential to consider the presence of central entities, including Registration Authorities (RAs), which raise questions about the actual degree of decentralization and control within the ecosystem. On the other hand, [28] presented a model for secure software updates in the ecosystem of embedded devices in vehicles, using a decentralized architecture with Hyperledger Indy. Nevertheless, the study needs more in-depth technical implementation details.

In this regard, it is essential to note that none of these studies addresses the specific nuances related to the data custody chain, which are crucial to ensuring data integrity, validity, and traceability, especially in resource-constrained devices. Furthermore, few research efforts have been dedicated to performance evaluation in similar contexts, making it challenging to draw comparisons to enhance this critical aspect within the IoT context.

## 4  System Overview

The proposal we present has as its primary objective the issuance of verifiable credentials to present and substantiate claims regarding data emitted by IoT devices. Furthermore, we propose identifying IoT devices and the traceability of the data they generate using Decentralized Identifiers anchored in a blockchain infrastructure. Both features aim to strengthen the integrity and validity of data from its source, thus contributing to a more robust and reliable chain of custody.

## 4.1 Definition of Tools and Technologies

We have used the Sovrin method [29] for DIDs, identifying each device and registering each data emission. Furthermore, we employ VCs in the AnonCreds [30] format to establish a robust foundation of verifiable evidence based on the data collected by IoT devices.

To implement these features, we used Hyperledger Indy and Aries. When evaluating platforms for SSI, we considered fundamental criteria such as the scalability of the permissioned blockchain and coverage of concepts grounded in SSI.

In Hyperledger Indy, unlike other DLTs, incentives are not required. As a result, all transactions encompassing various operations, such as the creation of DIDs, key rotation, credential schema creation, credential definition, and other functionalities, can exhibit improved performance [31]. Regarding the consensus algorithm, Indy employs Practical Byzantine Fault Tolerance (PBFT), enabling a high transaction rate [32]. The performance results presented in [33] demonstrate that Indy meets the criteria for global scalability in terms of record query speed.

We employ Hyperledger Aries as the agent for our Gateway, which provides capabilities such as interacting with other agents and the blockchain, supplying libraries for cryptographic wallet implementation, sending event notifications, and receiving instructions from the controller.

To facilitate communication with constrained devices, we utilize the Message Queuing Telemetry Transport (MQTT) protocol, designed for resource-limited devices [34]. For these devices, typically connected to a broker, we use Mosquitto. Both the devices and our application establish secure and certified connections to interact with messages transmitted by the broker.

These platforms and tools stand out as suitable choices for our architecture, aiming to meet the demands of the data custody chain in forensic scenarios.

## 4.2 Gateway-Based Approach for Constrained IoT Devices

Our approach is built upon an architecture structured into three interconnected and collaborative layers: Edge, Fog, and Cloud Computing. Figure 2 illustrates these layers along with their respective entities.

The Edge layer encompasses a variety of IoT devices, such as sensors, medical devices, surveillance cameras, and other manually embedded devices. In this context, the broker is crucial in receiving and transmitting data from these constrained devices.

The Gateway acts as an intermediary between the Edge and Cloud layers in the Fog Computing layer. At the core of the Gateway, the controller provides

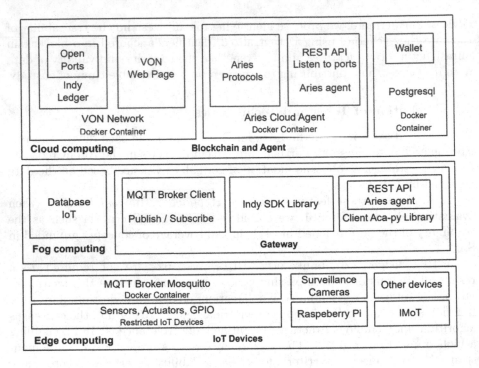

**Fig. 2.** Layered overview of the proposed architecture.

essential resources such as storage, processing capacity, and sources of entropy for cryptographic key generation through the functionalities of the Indy library, which also enables the implementation of DIDs and access to blockchains. Additionally, the Gateway performs the functions of a cloud agent controller, establishing secure connections with other agents and implementing features related to VCs.

In the Cloud Computing layer, ACA-Py is responsible for registering on the blockchain the schemas and credential definitions previously established in the previous layer. Registering DIDs previously set on the blockchain makes it possible to verify credentials using public keys. This enables decentralized verification of digital identities associated with devices and the data they emit in our architecture.

### 4.3    Use Case in Evidence Preservation

In the context of a use case scenario, our proposed architecture aims to establish a chain of custody for data originating from restricted devices. This approach seeks to create an environment that ensures forensic evidence's effective and reliable preservation.

Generally, the identification of devices connected to the broker is carried out at the Gateway. A unique DID is generated using the "did: sov" method when a new device is added to the system. This DID is subsequently registered on the blockchain with its alias: a serial number, UUID (Universally Unique Identifier), or MAC address (Media Access Control). This association establishes an immutable relationship between the device and its identification.

Optionally, when the broker receives data, the Gateway captures this data and creates a DID using the same method, which is then registered on the blockchain. This enables the identification and tracking of the collected evidence.

Subsequently, a verifiable credential is generated for the stakeholder, which can be a regulatory authority, regulatory entity, or a court. Another use case scenario involves on-demand credential issuance, with the data securely stored in a database and the credential issued upon request.

With this framework, it becomes possible to generate verifiable credentials containing information derived from IoT devices, where each attribute is given a signature. This approach ensures that the credential provides a tamper-proof and secure representation of the collected data. Interested parties can verify the authenticity and integrity of the data through a distributed ledger using the issuer's public key, enhancing trust in IoT applications and data sharing.

In the usage scenario depicted in Fig. 3, the intention is to present an architecture in which an application serves as a proxy between resource-constrained IoT devices and the cloud agent ACA-Py, which has communication capabilities with stakeholders and credential issuance abilities.

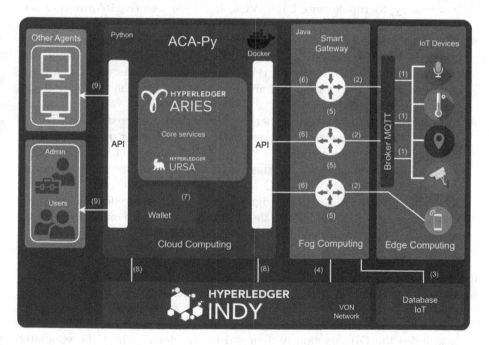

**Fig. 3.** Overview of the Proposed Architecture.

The following steps describe the sequence of the proposed architecture:

1. In the Edge Computing layer, devices establish secure connections using certificates and transmit data to the broker using the MQTT protocol.
2. In our application in the Fog Computing layer, we establish a secure connection with the broker using certificates and perform a prior subscription to the broker's message topic to receive data.
3. The received data is stored in an internal database to facilitate queries.
4. In the same layer, devices are registered. The DID and the device's serial number are registered once on the blockchain for identification and tracking. Additionally, another registration is conducted on the blockchain to identify each data collection associated with the corresponding device's DID.
5. After the device emits the data, a package is assembled, incorporating this information, the timestamp, device type, location, issuing entity, and collected data. In the data flow context, a generated file that cannot be directly included in the credential can be identified through a hash, verifying its integrity. Additionally, both the hash and the link to the corresponding storage location are recorded in the credential.
6. The Gateway, acting as a controller, uses Application Programming Interfaces (APIs) to access the cloud agent's resources and issue the credentials. The credential is issued to the stakeholder and stored in their wallet.
7. In this context, the Indy wallet is implemented using a PostgreSQL database. It stores cryptographic keys, DIDs, VCs, and other sensitive information necessary for interaction with the network.
8. The agent interacts with the blockchain to record the necessary transactions, known as NYM, which enable the creation of DIDs, ATTRIB, schema, and credential definitions. This interaction ensures the consistency and security of transactions within the proposed architecture, enabling the verification and validation of issued credentials.
9. Authorized users linked to the issuer can query the issued credentials. Holders can store these credentials and present them to the verifier or generate zero-knowledge proofs when compiling verifiable presentations before transmission. Interested entities can verify authenticity whenever necessary by querying the blockchain through the public key to which the credential was signed and verify integrity through the signature hash of each credential attribute. Furthermore, tracing the DID of the collection and device on the blockchain is possible, providing an additional layer of security to ensure data custody.

Thus, the Gateway enables secure and efficient communication between IoT devices and other domains. The utilization of VC resources in this context can be employed to preserve the integrity and authenticity of information.

In Fig. 4, we present a small portion of the JSON structure that comprises the issued credential based on telemetry data collected from IoT devices. This data includes the DID previously assigned to the device, the DID associated with each transmission, timestamps, device location, and the transmitted sensor readings.

```
"credential_proposal": {
  "@type": "https://didcomm.org/issue-credential/1.0/credential-preview",
  "attributes": [
    {
      "name": "Operator",
      "value": "LRG UFSC"
    },
    {
      "name": "device_did",
      "value": "did:sov:7jfceWZRA7jYdb866iFHRR"
    },
    {
      "name": "collection_did",
      "value": "did:sov:L5DknuZMuzchXyXLvmfAuX"
    },
    {
      "name": "data",
      "value": "50.5F"
    },
    {
      "name": "device_type",
      "value": "TemperatureSensor"
    },
    {
      "name": "location",
      "value": "living_room"
    },
    {
      "name": "timestamp",
      "value": "2023-10-02 00:31:03.669"
    }
  ]
},
"schema_id": "B3qPp5s37rQNYpWSUs9bXC:2:lrg:1.0",
"cred_def_id": "B3qPp5s37rQNYpWSUs9bXC:3:CL:82542:lgr"
```

**Fig. 4.** JSON Format Credential Proposal.

In the sequence diagram of the proposed architecture, depicted in Fig. 5, it is possible to observe the interactions among different parts of the architecture, highlighting the interactions between entities across all phases.

In this context, a mutual authentication process is conducted to establish secure communication with other agents, where both parties need to demonstrate possession of the signature keys corresponding to the paired DIDs. Following the successful completion of mutual authentication, credentials are signed using the verification keys and sent to other agents, ensuring the confidentiality of transmitted information.

### 4.4 Security Considerations

It is crucial to consider critical aspects related to the security and privacy of the proposed architecture.

Protecting cryptographic keys in the wallet is essential in the signing processes and data custody management. This protection can be strengthened through the use of Secure Enclaves [35].

To ensure the privacy of device attributes and collected data, one can utilize the Zero-Knowledge Proof technique when compiling verifiable presenta-

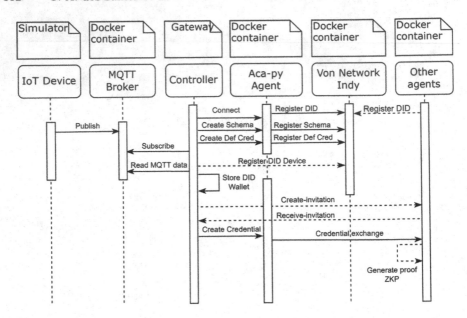

**Fig. 5.** Sequence diagram of the proposed architecture.

tions before sharing them with stakeholders. Another crucial aspect is aggregation, which occurs when stakeholders gather information from the same device, requesting various verifiable presentations. This can pose privacy challenges, but ZKPs can address this by concealing unnecessary data.

Moreover, when dealing with data custody involving IoT devices and the creation of VCs, it is crucial to consider security risks. Various types of side-channel attacks can be employed to obtain information about VCs. For instance, mechanisms on the Internet may track IoT devices and the data they generate, such as cookies, device fingerprints, or location information. The proposed scheme cannot prevent the use of these tracking technologies if they have been installed on the devices or the broker.

Another risk arises when links are embedded in VCs. While the credential itself is protected against tampering, its external content is not, making the links vulnerable to modifications by attackers. One way to mitigate this risk is by generating a hash of the external data and incorporating it into the credential. Another option to explore is using a private blockchain to store the data.

## 5    Experiments, Results, and Analysis

In this section, we present the results of the simulation tests and performance analysis conducted to assess the efficiency of our architecture.

## 5.1 Implementation

We utilized Java libraries for the implementation of our application. For the entities interacting with our application, we employed containers using Docker and Docker Compose [36] and Python scripts to generate telemetry data simulations. Below, we present the list of technologies employed.

1. Libraries to implement our application:
   - ACA-Py Java client [37] for instantiating cloud agent resources.
   - Indy SDK for creating DIDs and registering them on the blockchain.
   - Bouncy Castle [38] for secure connections with the broker using certificates.
   - Java Paho MQTT client [39] for subscribing to MQTT topics/messages.
2. Docker and Docker Compose for creating and running containers for entities:
   - The issuer agent, holder, and wallet in a PostgreSQL [40] database created using the ACA-Py library.
   - Von Network is like an Indy blockchain with four nodes and the ledger browser.
   - MongoDB [41] for storing data from IoT devices.
   - MQTT broker using Mosquitto [42].
3. Python scripts to simulate devices sending messages to the Mosquitto broker.

Through the developed application, it is possible to collect data via the broker while automatically issuing credentials. Additionally, we can store these collection-related pieces of information in a database, create DIDs that identify devices and collected data, and register them on the blockchain. Furthermore, the application enables connections with other agents and creates and lists schemas and credential models. We have implemented an API encompassing all these functionalities to streamline performance measurement tests. The application was developed using the Java programming language, and its source code is available on GitHub [43].

## 5.2 Results and Analysis

To conduct the tests, we utilized a single computer system equipped with an Intel Core i7-11700 processor, 16 GB of RAM, and running the Windows 11 Pro operating system. In this configuration, we measure the time required to register the DIDs of data collection on the Von network's blockchain. The registration of DIDs for devices follows a similar process, but it occurs only once for each device, unlike data registration, which can be resource-intensive. For this reason, we include this process in our tests. Subsequently, we record the time spent on credential issuance.

We conducted two independent tests, each involving the collection of 1000 samples. We calculated the means and standard deviations for each case. In the first test, we recorded DIDs on the blockchain for evidence identification, while the second test focused exclusively on credential issuance to another agent, excluding the registration of DIDs from the first scenario. Our objective was to analyze the impact of blockchain registration on the architecture and how credentials behave without this additional process. Our evaluations encompassed measuring the time required for each process and monitoring RAM and CPU usage in both tests.

The results obtained are summarized in Table 2 below.

**Table 2.** Experimental Results

| Test | Measure | Value |
|------|---------|-------|
| DID registration | Average Response Time | 1503.059 ms |
| | Standard deviation | 868.355 ms |
| | Average CPU usage | 0,3% |
| | Average RAM usage | 131 MB |
| VCs exchange | Average Response Time | 18.891 ms |
| | Standard deviation | 9.494 ms |
| | Average CPU usage | 0.4 % |
| | Average RAM usage | 171 MB |

The CPU utilization percentages were measured using the Netbeans Profiler [44]. The request simulation was conducted using JMeter [45]. The first scenario took approximately 50 min and 7 s, while the second required 36 s. CPU and RAM usage monitoring was carried out during these periods. To establish a baseline, the application startup, which loads the libraries mentioned in Subsect. 5.1 and establishes connections with the agent, broker, and blockchain, took approximately 3 s, consumed 121 MB of RAM, and utilized 8% of CPU capacity.

Based on these results, we can highlight the following conclusions:

- Considerably longer times were observed in the DID registration processes, indicating a significant overhead on the ledger nodes when handling multiple requests.
- Regarding RAM and CPU usage, we observed that it is not resource-intensive. Therefore, even with an increase in the number of devices sending data, the application should be able to perform these operations without significant issues.
- Based on our experiments, we found that the maximum RAM required was approximately 180 MB. Furthermore, tests conducted with multiple credential exchanges in parallel do not significantly impact CPU and RAM usage.

In conclusion, the credential exchange process in the Gateway proved to be significantly faster when the DIDs registration in the data collection blockchain was not performed. This is because, in the credential issuance process, once the schema and credential definition are created and registered on the blockchain, this procedure does not need to be repeated. It can be executed only once to generate numerous credentials, which will be signed with the public key stored in the wallet.

It is essential to note that our assessment does not address network latency since the tests are conducted on the same computer. Furthermore, outcomes may vary depending on the individual resources of each computer.

As a result, we conclude that the blockchain registration overhead will be the primary factor affecting performance. If evidence registration on the blockchain is necessary to compose the credential, this may pose a scalability challenge. Therefore, it is essential to evaluate the necessity of this step or consider alternative proposals aimed at reducing the overhead on the distributed ledger. However, the presented results are promising and suggest that issuing credentials on a large scale for IoT devices is feasible.

# 6  Conclusion

This study proposed an innovative Gateway architecture to integrate IoT devices with limited resources in Self-Sovereign Identity (SSI) technologies. The architecture enables data certification by facilitating the issuance of verifiable credentials (VCs) based on data collected from IoT environments and utilizing a distributed verifiable registry to identify devices. These attributes position it as a relevant solution with significant potential for applications requiring data ownership assurance in these environments. As a result, the proposed architecture ensures reliability, integrity, and traceability of information, crucial factors for data custody, especially in scenarios involving forensic areas and IoT devices.

Compared to the vast array of related works presented, our study stands out as a comprehensive solution for verifying data integrity in IoT devices, explicitly focusing on applying SSI to address these challenges. While numerous studies have tackled specific issues related to IoT, such as security, access control, and communication efficiency in various scenarios [19–28], our approach is unique in its exclusive concentration on the challenges related to resource-constrained IoT devices and data custody in these environments. This enables us to provide a reliable solution to enhance IoT applications and facilitate secure data sharing.

The robustness of the results and insights obtained from the performance metrics analysis validates the effectiveness and reliability of our architecture, as well as provides guidelines for future optimizations. In addition, future studies in this field will focus on implementing a client for our application running directly on IoT devices, exploring ways to optimize energy consumption and network utilization. Additionally, we consider the possibility of comparing our proposals with solutions in other domains and conducting scalability and application analyses in real-world scenarios.

# References

1. Algarni, S., et al.: Blockchain-based secured access control in an IoT system. Appl. Sci. (Switzerland) **11**(4), 1–16 (2021). https://doi.org/10.3390/app11041772

2. Gubbi, J., Buyya, R., Marusic, S., Palaniswami, M.: Internet of Things (IoT): a vision, architectural elements, and future directions. Futur. Gener. Comput. Syst. **29**(7), 1645–1660 (2013). https://doi.org/10.1016/j.future.2013.01.010
3. Arshad, H., Jantan, bin, A., Abiodun, O.I.: Digital forensics: review of issues in scientific validation of digital evidence. J. Inf. Process. Syst. **14**(2), 346–376 (2018). https://doi.org/10.3745/JIPS.03.0095
4. Shah, M., Saleem, S., Zulqarnain, R.: Protecting digital evidence integrity and preserving chain of custody. J. Digit. Forensics Secur. Law (2017). https://doi.org/10.15394/jdfsl.2017.1478
5. Sporny, M., Longley, D., Allen, C., Sabadello, M., Reed, D.: Decentralized identifiers (DIDs) v1.0. W3C, W3C Working Draft (2019). https://www.w3.org/TR/did-core/. Accessed 29 Sept 2023
6. Sporny, M., Noble, G., Burnett, D., Zundel, B., Longley, D.: Verifiable credentials data model 1.0. W3C, W3C Recommendation. https://www.w3.org/TR/vc-data-model. Accessed 29 Sept 2023
7. Hyperledger Indy. Hyperledger Foundation Projects INDY. https://www.hyperledger.org/projects/hyperledger-indy. Accessed 26 Sept 2023
8. Indy SDK. Hyperledger Foundation Projects INDY. https://github.com/hyperledger/indy-sdk. Accessed 20 Sept 2023
9. Hyperledger Aries. Hyperledger Aries Cloud Agent Python. https://github.com/hyperledger/aries-cloudagent-python. Accessed 29 July 2023
10. Verifiable Organizations Network (VON). https://github.com/bcgov/von-network. Accessed 02 Oct 2023
11. Allen, C.: The Path to Self-Sovereign Identity. [S.l.] (2016). http://www.lifewithalacrity.com/2016/04/the-path-to-self-sovereign-identity.html. Accessed 29 June 2023
12. Brunner, C., Gallersdörfer, U., Knirsch, F., Engel, D., Matthes, F.: DID and VC: Untangling Decentralized Identifiers and Verifiable Credentials for the Web of Trust (2021). https://doi.org/10.1145/3446983.3446992
13. Peer Did Method Specification. W3C. https://identity.foundation/peer-did-method-spec/index.html. Accessed 26 Sept 2023
14. Curran, S., Howard, C.: Becoming a Hyperledger Aries Developer. [S.l.] (2021). https://learning.edx.org/course/course-v1:LinuxFoundationX+LFS173x+3T2021/. Accessed 4 Dec 2022
15. Curran, S., Howard, C.: Introduction to Hyperledger Sovereign Identity Blockchain Solutions: Indy, Aries and Ursa. [S.l.] (2021). https://learning.edx.org/course/course-v1:LinuxFoundationX+LFS172x+2T2021. Accessed 1 Nov 2022
16. SOVRIN Foundation. Self-Sovereign Identity and IoT. [S.l.] (2020). https://sovrin.org/wp-content/uploads/SSI-and-IoT-whitepaper.pdf. Accessed 1 Oct 2022
17. Hyperledger Aries Explainer. Hyperledger Aries. https://github.com/hyperledger/aries. Accessed 29 Sept 2023
18. Hyperledger Ursa Explainer. Hyperledger Ursa. https://github.com/hyperledger/ursa. Accessed 23 July 2023
19. Fedrecheski, G., Rabaey, J.M., Costa, L.C.P., Calcina Ccori, P.C., Pereira, W.T., Zuffo, M.K.: Self-sovereign identity for iot environments: a perspective. In: Proceedings of the Global Internet of Things Summit, GIoTS 2020 (2020). https://doi.org/10.1109/GIOTS49054.2020.9119664
20. Luecking, M., Fries, C., Lamberti, R., Stork, W.: Decentralized identity and trust management framework for Internet of Things. In: IEEE International Conference on Blockchain and Cryptocurrency, ICBC 2020 (2020). https://doi.org/10.1109/ICBC48266.2020.9169411

21. Regueiro, C., Gutierrez-Agüero, I., Agüero, A., Anguita, S., de Diego, S., Lage, O.: Protocol for identity management in industrial IoT based on hyperledger Indy. Int. J. Comput. Digit. Syst. **12**(1), 2210142 (2022). https://doi.org/10.12785/ijcds/120153
22. Dixit, A., Smith-Creasey, M., Rajarajan, M.: A decentralized IIoT identity framework based on self-sovereign identity using blockchain. In: Proceedings of Conference on Local Computer Networks, LCN, pp. 335–338 (2022). https://doi.org/10.1109/LCN53696.2022.9843700
23. De Diego, S., Regueiro, C., Macia-Fernandez, G.: Enabling identity for the IoT-as-a-service business model. IEEE Access **9**, 159965–159975 (2021). https://doi.org/10.1109/ACCESS.2021.3131012
24. Kortesniemi, Y., Lagutin, D., Elo, T., Fotiou, N.: Improving the privacy of IoT with decentralised identifiers (DIDs). J. Comput. Netw. Commun. **2019** (2019). https://doi.org/10.1155/2019/8706760
25. Berzin, O., Ansay, R., Kempf, J., Sheikh, I., Hendel, D.: A troca de IoT. arXiv:2103.12131 (2021)
26. Terzi, S., Savvaidis, C., Votis, K., Tzovaras, D., Stamelos, I.: Securing emission data of smart vehicles with blockchain and self-sovereign identities. In: Proceedings of 2020 IEEE International Conference on Blockchain, Blockchain 2020, pp. 462–469 (2020). https://doi.org/10.1109/BLOCKCHAIN50366.2020.00067
27. Theodouli, A., Moschou, K., Votis, K., Tzovaras, D., Lauinger, J., Steinhorst, S.: Towards a blockchain-based identity and trust management framework for the IoV ecosystem. In: Proceedings of the Global Internet of Things Summit, GIoTS 2020 (2020). https://doi.org/10.1109/GIOTS49054.2020.9119623
28. Fotopoulos, F., Malamas, V., Dasaklis, T.K., Kotzanikolaou, P., Douligeris, C.: A blockchain-enabled architecture for IoMT device authentication. In: 2nd IEEE Eurasia Conference on IOT, Communication and Engineering 2020, ECICE 2020, pp. 89–92 (2020). https://doi.org/10.1109/ECICE50847.2020.9301913
29. Sovrin DID Method Specification. https://sovrin-foundation.github.io/sovrin/spec/did-method-spec-template.html. Accessed 27 Sept 2023
30. AnonCreds Specification. https://hyperledger.github.io/anoncreds-spec/. Accessed 29 Sept 2023
31. Official Documentation for the Indy SDK. Hyperledger Foundation Projects INDY. https://hyperledger-indy.readthedocs.io/projects/sdk/en/latest/docs/. Accessed 01 Oct 2023
32. Masood, F., Faridi, A.R.: Distributed ledger technology for closed environment. In: 2019 6th International Conference on Computing for Sustainable Global Development (INDIACom), New Delhi, India, pp. 1151–1156 (2019)
33. Lux, Z.A., Beierle, F., Zickau, S., Göndör, S.: Full-text search for verifiable credential metadata on distributed ledgers. In: 2019 Sixth International Conference on Internet of Things: Systems, Management and Security (IOTSMS), Granada, Spain, pp. 519–528 (2019). https://doi.org/10.1109/IOTSMS48152.2019.8939249
34. Light, R.A.: Mosquitto: server and client implementation of the MQTT protocol. J. Open Source Softw. **2**(13), 265 (2017). https://doi.org/10.21105/joss.00265
35. Aries RFC 0050: Wallets. https://github.com/hyperledger/aries-rfcs/blob/main/concepts/0050-wallets/README.md. Accessed 25 Sept 2023
36. Docker Community. https://www.docker.com/community/. Accessed 25 July 2023
37. ACA-Py Java Client Library. https://github.com/hyperledger-labs/acapy-java-client. Accessed 20 Sept 2023
38. The Bouncy Castle Crypto APIs. The Legion of the Bouncy Castle. https://www.bouncycastle.org/. Accessed 15 Sept 2023

39. Java Paho MQTT Client. Eclipse Paho Project. https://www.eclipse.org/paho/. Accessed 02 June 2023
40. PostgreSQL. PostgreSQL Global Development Group. https://www.postgresql.org/. Accessed 2 Ago 2023
41. MongoDB. https://www.mongodb.com/. Accessed 4 Ago 2023
42. Eclipse Mosquitto. https://mosquitto.org/. Accessed 2 June 2023
43. Self-Sovereign Identity Gateway for the Internet of Things. https://github.com/cristiandossantos/iot-ssi-gateway. Accessed 03 Oct 2023
44. Apache Software Foundation. Apache NetBeans. https://netbeans.org/. Accessed 02 July 2023
45. Apache Software Foundation. JMeter. https://jmeter.apache.org/. Accessed 06 July 2023

# Analysis of Optimal Number of Shards Using ShardEval, A Simulator for Sharded Blockchains

Vishisht Priyadarshi[(✉)], Sourav Goel, and Kalpesh Kapoor

Department of Mathematics, Indian Institute of Technology Guwahati, Guwahati,
Assam, India
{vishisht,sourav18a}@alumni.iitg.ac.in, kalpesh@iitg.ac.in

**Abstract.** Blockchain-based networks have found increasing usage in
various fields due to their distributed nature, immutability, public verifiability, and zero trust requirement. Monolithic blockchain systems such
as Bitcoin and Ethereum are not scalable. Sharding is a promising approach among the various solutions that have been proposed in the literature to improve the scalability of such monolithic systems. However,
designing, testing, and identifying critical parameters of sharding-based
protocols for blockchain networks is challenging. We present *ShardEval*, a
simulator to evaluate sharding-based protocols for blockchain networks.
We have used ShardEval to identify critical parameters of a sharded
blockchain network. In particular, we determine the optimal number of
shards in a network with a fixed percentage of cross-shard transactions.
The simulation results are validated against the rigorous theoretical analysis, confirming the correctness under reasonable assumptions. Using the
insights gained from simulation and theoretical analysis, we introduce
Lookup Table to improve the transaction throughput further. The theoretical framework and simulator bridge the gap between designing and
testing sharding-based protocols.

**Keywords:** Blockchain · Sharding · Throughput · Simulation

## 1 Introduction

Blockchain is a distributed ledger technology. It is a peer-to-peer network that
utilizes techniques, such as Proof-of-Work [4], to record transactions that can
be publicly verified and are difficult to forge. Bitcoin [13], the first practical
blockchain network, significantly impacted the adoption of blockchains, and they
have found numerous applications in different fields, especially Decentralized
Finance (DeFi) [5]. It has also led to the development of numerous cryptocurrencies and altcoins.

Sharding is a well-known technique for scaling databases [21]. In blockchains,
sharding is introduced by partitioning the network into smaller parts, or *shards*,
and allowing each shard to take on an independent set of tasks. Designing

© The Author(s), under exclusive license to Springer Nature Switzerland AG 2023
V. Muthukkumarasamy et al. (Eds.): ICISS 2023, LNCS 14424, pp. 339–359, 2023.
https://doi.org/10.1007/978-3-031-49099-6_21

sharding-based protocols and networks for blockchain is a challenging task. It requires several key parameters to be identified and managed to keep the system running. One such parameter is the optimal number of shards. There is minimal discussion in the literature [9] regarding this parameter and how to adjust it to gain maximum performance in terms of throughput.

Another aspect of the sharding-based protocol is to observe its behavior, usually done using a test deployment. Such methodology is used in protocols like ELASTICO [12] and OmniLedger [10], where nodes have been deployed on cloud and actual machines. As expected, this approach is not only expensive but also requires a significant amount of effort and time. Also, it becomes exceedingly difficult to ascertain the performance of protocols when deployed in an actual environment instead of a test network due to considerable differences between their size.

An alternative approach to observing the behavior of protocols is to use a simulator. Apart from solving the problems mentioned earlier, the simulator also brings in test-driven development to verify and establish the correctness of the protocol. However, a generic simulator that can be used with different sharding-based protocols has not been sought out in the literature. There are a few simulators, such as Shargri-La [15], for sharding that are still under development and have limited use cases. There is very little progress in creating a generalized sharding-based blockchain simulator. So far, none of them has used their simulator to provide an optimal shard number along with the theoretical agreement.

In this paper, we introduce a generic simulator for sharded blockchains and identify the optimal number of shards using this simulator. We find that the established theoretical results are per the empirical observations obtained after the simulations. In summary, this paper makes the following contributions:

(i) A simulator tool and modular simulation framework for sharded blockchain networks to execute operations at the transaction level.
(ii) Theoretical setup and analysis to evaluate the optimal number of shards for a given protocol/architecture.
(iii) Evaluation of the optimal number of shards for a fixed percentage of cross-shard transactions.

The remainder of the paper is organized as follows: Sect. 2 offers a review of the background and prior work. Section 3 introduces our simulator, ShardEval, detailing its architecture. Section 4 outlines the simulator workflow, while Sect. 5 conducts a theoretical study on the optimal number of shards. Empirical analysis, including simulations and insights, is presented in Sect. 6. Building upon the insights from both simulation and theoretical analysis, Sect. 7 introduces a method to optimize network throughput. Lastly, Sect. 8 provides the paper's conclusions.

# 2 Background and Related Work

Blockchain is a distributed database that sequentially stores a chain of data packaged into blocks, in a secure and tamper-proof way [1]. The data is a transaction, the atomic unit of a blockchain. The transaction represents the transfer or creation of an entity [7]. New blocks are added to the blockchain after they get validated by the network using some distributed consensus protocol. Widely used consensus algorithms include Proof-of-Work [4] and Proof-of-Stake [14]. They are sometimes collectively referred to as Proof-of-X protocols.

There are various approaches to improve the scalability of monolithic blockchain networks [2], such as sharding, Directed Acyclic Graph (DAG), payment channels, and sidechains. DAG is a blockchain structure that is a network of individual transactions linked to multiple other transactions [8]. Some protocols which utilize DAG are IOTA [16], Spectre [19] and PHANTOM [20]. The payment channel is a temporary off-chain trading channel, which transfers some transactions to this channel. This reduces the main chain's transaction volume while improving the entire system's transaction throughput [27]. Sidechain [8] proposes the concept of having another blockchain beside the main blockchain, that is, a sidechain beside the mainchain, for parallel processing.

In a sharded blockchain system, the nodes in the network are dynamically partitioned into subsets known as shards, where each shard performs storage, communication, and computation tasks without fine-grained synchronization with each other [11]. Sharding achieves scalability since adding newer nodes and creating more shards will lead to more task processing and better parallelism. In monolithic blockchain networks, every node stores the complete state, and each block is shared with every node before reaching a consensus. As a result, as the number of nodes in the network increases, the overhead increases, thereby decreasing the throughput. Sharding improves upon this overhead by dividing the network into smaller shards, resulting in efficient computation, storage, and data transmission [6]. Sharding was first introduced for blockchains by ELASTICO [12] to scale the transaction rates. Since ELASTICO, many sharding-based protocols such as OmniLedger [10], CycLedger [26], RapidChain [25] and Monoxide [23] have been proposed in the literature.

We now discuss the simulators related to our work. BlockEval [7] is a modular blockchain simulator to test the performance of non-sharding blockchain networks. It proposes a novel validation method and has been tested with Bitcoin statistics. Shargri-La [15] is a transaction-level sharded blockchain simulator that simulates Ethereum transfer. It analyzes users' behaviors and their effect on transaction fees.

Shyam et al. [9] proposed a sharding scheme for the OptiShard, a hierarchical blockchain architecture. The technique utilized the parameters such as performance and correctness of transaction validation to determine an optimal shard size for their architecture.

## 3   Architecture of ShardEval

First, we present the underlying details of ShardEval. In the following subsections, we will discuss the architecture, design structures, and various components of ShardEval. The source code of the simulator is made available in a public repository on GitHub [17].

### 3.1   Framework

For the simulation framework, Python is selected as the programming language. In particular, the discrete-event simulation is performed using the *SimPy* [18] library. The choice of programming language and simulation framework is primarily made following BlockEval [7] since ShardEval is built on top of BlockEval and utilizes several of its basic key components.

### 3.2   Network Components

The entire network of the simulator is modeled with the help of a *Network object*, consisting of Transaction Factory, Network Pipes, and Full Nodes (Principal Committee, Shard Nodes, and Shard Leaders). Each of these components represents real-world objects.

**Transaction Factory:** The Transaction factory is implemented as a generator function [18], which gets called when the network is initialized. Every node of the network participates in the transaction generation, and the transactions are broadcast to its neighbors. Each transaction generation event is followed by a random cooldown period, calculated using a probability distribution based on user-specified parameters.

**Transaction Pool:** Every node has a transaction pool in which the transactions received from its neighbors are kept with some priority. The priority defined here is the reward associated with each transaction. It implies that transactions with higher rewards are preferred over transactions with lower rewards. So, the transaction pool behaves as a priority queue of transactions, and acts as a storage medium for the propagation of transactions across the network (representation of *mempools*).

**Network Pipes:** Pipes model the propagation channels among nodes. Each Pipe object consists of a source and a destination location representing the connecting nodes. It also has a propagation delay based on the real-world locations of the associated nodes. As a result, the destination node receives the object (block or transaction) sent from the source node, using pipe, after a timeout value. A Pipe object is implemented using SimPy *Store* resource.

**Full Nodes:** The nodes taking part in the network are generated at different geographical locations (per user-defined parameters in the JSON configuration file). These nodes are termed as *Participating Nodes*. The participating nodes undergo a filtering process via *Sybil Resistance Mechanism* (see Sect. 3.3) to become a *Full Node*. Full Nodes are divided into principal committee nodes and shard nodes.

**Principal Committee:** *Principal Committee* consists a set of full nodes chosen to ensure that the shards do not behave in a byzantine manner. It collects information regarding the transactions from all the shards, undergoes a consensus process to determine their validity, and takes part in the final block generation process.

**Transaction Block:** *Transaction Block (Tx-block)* is a data structure containing the transactions generated by the shard nodes. The shard leader publishes a transaction block (object) depending upon the nature of transactions - *Intra-shard Tx-block* containing intra-shard transactions and *Cross-shard Tx-block* containing cross-shard transactions. The Intra-shard Tx-block is received by the current shard nodes, while the leaders of the other shards receive the Cross-shard Tx-block.

**Mini Block:** *Mini Block* contains all the validated transactions agreed upon by the shards. In particular, it is generated by the shard leader and has all the consensed upon transactions from that shard. Each shard produces its Mini Block, which is sent to the Principal Committee for final consensus.

### 3.3   Functional Components

ShardEval contains the following major functional components, which act in conjunction with the network components:

**Sybil Resistance Mechanism:** It is utilized in the ShardEval to simulate techniques to prevent a *Sybil Attack* and keep the system running. Sybil attack is a type of attack on a computer network service in which an attacker subverts the service's reputation system by creating a large number of pseudonymous identities and uses them to gain a disproportionately large influence [3].

ShardEval allows the flexibility to add suitable mechanisms and layers to prevent the Sybil attacks, such as Proof-of-X (where X can be anything). Currently, for the sake of simplicity, the nodes are filtered probabilistically by making suitable changes to the parameters specified in the configuration file.

**Streaming Leader Selection:** "Streaming" stands for continuous flow of some process/event. In our context, *Streaming Leader Selection* implies that the leaders of the shards are continuously being selected at every *slot* of an epoch. Currently, at the beginning of a slot, the leader of a shard is assigned probabilistically from the shard nodes. Provisions have been made to employ a better leader selection algorithm using techniques like stake or other Proof-of-X mechanisms. The leaders need to be streamingly selected to simulate the scenario when the shard leader can disrupt the process by behaving in a byzantine manner.

**Transactions Pre-processing:** The leader of the shards collects the transactions generated by the shard nodes and performs a pre-processing step on top of it. The pre-processing step is required to determine whether the transactions are intra-shard or cross-shard. Also, the pre-processing step coupled with the *Proof-of-History* [24] can be used for faster execution of the consensus process.

**Voting-based Consensus Algorithm:** ShardEval uses voting-based algorithm for achieving consensus on the validation of transactions. Since Sybil resistance mechanisms are in place, identities of the nodes remain preserved, and no Sybil identities get created. As a result, voting can be used as a consensus mechanism.

The consensus on the transactions is required at two different levels - shards and the principal committee. The shard leader leads the voting in each shard and finalizes the voting process (on the Intra-shard Tx-block). At the level of the principal committee, there also exists a leader responsible for handling the voting process and generating the final block (as per the achieved consensus) containing validated transactions.

## 4    Simulator Workflow

A generic sharding-based protocol is implemented on ShardEval for our study. The general protocol is motivated by the work on sharding blockchain systems by Yizhong et al. [11]. The implemented protocol takes various pieces and components from the protocols such as ELASTICO [12], OmniLedger [10], CycLedger [26], and Elrond [22] to make it as generic as possible. Note that each step in the protocol can be changed in the simulator as per user requirements to create and test different sharding-based protocols.

The simulation for the protocol begins by instantiating an object of the *Network* class, using the input parameters specified in a configuration file. Table 1 contains details of those parameters. The diagrammatic flow has been depicted in Fig. 1.

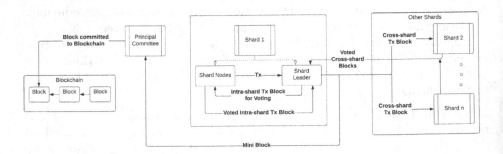

**Fig. 1.** Workflow of the simulator

### 4.1    Network Configuration

The simulator proceeds in *epochs* and *slots*. An epoch is the fixed time interval between the events of network reconfiguration in which nodes get allotted to different shards, and the principal committee is formed. Each epoch consists of multiple slots. Selection of a new shard leader (handled by *Streaming Leader Selection*) marks the beginning of a new slot.

At the beginning of every epoch, network configuration takes place. The participating nodes are instantiated and added to the network. Then they undergo a Sybil resistance mechanism to confirm their identities and get converted to the full nodes. After the full nodes are established, the principal committee is formed, followed by the formation of shards and leaders. Currently, the nodes are randomly selected to become principal committee nodes, but a suitable mechanism such as Proof-of-Stake or a reputation-based system can be easily utilized.

On completion of these events, the network connections are established through the Pipe instances. The principal committee forms a completely connected graph, that is, each node of the committee is connected to every other committee node. Next, the shard leaders connect with the principal committee nodes. But this time, the degree of every shard leader is fixed at $\lceil n/2 \rceil$, where n is the total number of principal committee nodes. Here, the degree is only considered for connecting shard leader nodes and principal committee nodes. The constraint, degree $\geq n/2$, guarantees a connected graph.

Following this, the connections are established between each shard leader. Same as the previous one, here also the (local) degree for a leader node is fixed at $\lceil n/2 \rceil$ (here, n = total number of shard leaders). Now for every shard, the connections are established among the shard nodes. A spanning tree is constructed among the shard nodes to facilitate the guided movement of messages between them and their leader.

## 4.2 Transactions and Tx-Blocks Generation

After the network configuration, the shard nodes initiate the generation of transactions. The shard nodes send the generated transactions to the shard leader for pre-processing and generation of the Tx-block. The transactions propagate through the network (see Fig. 2) and reach the transaction pool of the shard leader which is handled by the transaction factory.

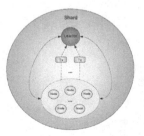

**Fig. 2.** Propagation of Transactions in a shard

The shard leaders collect these transactions and filter them on the basis of them being cross-shard or intra-shard. When sufficient number of transactions (a user-defined parameter) have reached the leader, the leader performs a pre-processing step on them and create an Intra-shard Tx-block or Cross-shard Tx-block. These tx-blocks are then sent out in the same shard (Fig. 3) or other shard leaders (Fig. 4), respectively, for reaching a consensus on them through voting.

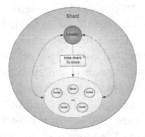

**Fig. 3.** Propagation of Intra-shard Tx-block in a shard

### 4.3   Voting on Tx-Blocks

First, we will discuss the voting on the Intra-shard Tx-blocks. Shard leader propagates the Tx-block to its nodes. Upon receiving the Tx-block, the node checks whether the voting process is completed or not. If it isn't complete, it implies that the node has not cast a vote due to the nature of the spanning tree route. The node will then verify the transactions and cast the votes as *Accept/Reject* for each of the transactions present in the block. After doing so, it will propagate the Tx-block further in the network (away from the leader) for other nodes to do the same. If the node observes that the voting has been completed, it will send the voted Tx-block towards the leader (using spanning tree route). In this manner, the voting takes place, and the Tx-block returns to the leader after voting.

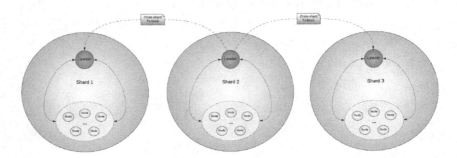

**Fig. 4.** Propagation of Cross-shard Tx-block across shards

Next, we will look at the voting on the Cross-shard Tx-block. The transactions in such blocks need verification from the nodes of other shards. The leader of the originating shard propagates the Tx-block to other neighboring shard leaders. When another shard leader receives such a block, it will propagate the Tx-block for voting in its shard. If the transactions present in the Tx-block are not relevant for this shard, the nodes will vote *Unknown*; otherwise, *Accept/Reject* vote is cast. After the voting is complete, the shard leader, upon receiving the voted Cross-shard Tx-block, will send the block to the originating shard for the final processing.

## 4.4 Mini-Blocks Generation

Upon receiving the voted Tx-blocks (Intra-shard and Cross-shard), the shard leaders verify the votes cast on the transactions by the shard nodes and filter the transactions which are voted a majority. These transactions are packed into a Mini-block while the rest of the transactions are rejected. Then the Mini-block is sent to the Principal Committee for the final consensus.

## 4.5 Consensus by Principal Committee

The Principal Committee receives the *Mini Blocks* generated by the shard leaders. On receiving the Mini Blocks, the consensus process is initiated by the leader of the principal committee. The consensus process is similar to the already discussed voting-based consensus algorithm. On achieving consensus, the leader begins the block generation step.

## 4.6 Blocks Generation

After the final consensus, the Principal Committee includes all the agreed-upon transactions in a single block and publishes the block across the network through the shard leaders. Upon receiving the block, the shard nodes update their blockchain and pass on the block further in the network.

# 5  Analysis on Optimal Number of Shards

As discussed earlier, we assume the generic sharding-based protocol to do a theoretical analysis and implement the same protocol in our simulator ShardEval. The results are then compared as a part of the empirical analysis in Sect. 6. The simulation proceeds in rounds, or *epochs*, in which shard nodes start transaction generation and all events occur. The analysis has been restricted to a single epoch, without leader re-election and shard reconfiguration.

We start our analysis assuming all the connections are made, and all nodes are ready to generate transactions. Throughout the study, we will consider the nodes to be active. The main aim of our analysis is to find the network's throughput change as the number of shards increases. We keep our focus limited to necessary variables and will not dive deeper into the low-level delays. Also, we are not considering the temporary/permanent unresponsiveness or byzantine behavior by network nodes.

Table 1 lists various variables representing the network parameters considered in this study. Note that there are only two types of transactions, viz. cross-shard and intra-shard, $r_{cs} + r_{is} = 1$. Therefore, the total number of cross-shard and intra-shard transactions generated by all the full nodes are $r_{cs} \cdot n_{tx}$ and $(1 - r_{cs}) \cdot n_{tx}$, respectively.

**Table 1.** Parameters for the study

| Parameter | Variable | Condition |
|---|---|---|
| Total number of nodes in the network | $n$ | |
| Number of Shards in the network | $n_{sh}$ | |
| Total number of transactions generated by the network | $n_{tx}$ | |
| Cross-shard transaction ratio | $r_{cs}$ | $0 \leq r_{cs} \leq 1$ |
| Intra-shard transaction ratio | $r_{is}$ | $0 \leq r_{is} \leq 1$ |
| Count of intra-shard transactions included in an intra-shard Tx-block | $f_{is}$ | |
| Network Delay | $\delta_{net}$ | |
| Delay incurred by all the Intra-shard Tx-blocks | $\delta_{is}$ | |
| Delay incurred by all the Cross-shard Tx-blocks | $\delta_{cs}$ | |
| Delay for a single Intra-shard Tx-block | $d_{is}$ | |
| Delay for a single Cross-shard Tx-block | $d_{cs}$ | |
| Network Throughput | $T$ | |

## 5.1 Computation of Delay and Throughput

**Intra-shard Transactions.** We will assume that the intra-shard transactions are uniformly distributed among the shard nodes (this is because all the shard nodes, including the shard leader, are alike in terms of transaction generation). Therefore, the number of intra-shard transactions per shard is $\frac{r_{is} \cdot n_{tx}}{n_{sh}}$. This implies that the number of intra-shard blocks published by a shard (leader) is $\frac{r_{is} \cdot n_{tx}}{n_{sh} \cdot f_{is}}$.

For a single Intra-shard Tx-block published by a shard, the shard leader must first broadcast it to all the shard nodes for verification and voting. Let $F_{IS}(sh)$ be a deterministic function, which takes the number of shards as a parameter and returns the overall delay incurred by a single Intra-shard Tx-block, published by some shard A. Since the function $F_{IS}$ is fixed for a particular value of $n_{sh}$; let us denote it by $d_{is}$. Here $d_{is}$ is the delay for a single Intra-shard Tx-block and includes the broadcast delay by a shard leader and the voting/verification delay by the nodes in Shard A. Now the intra-shard Tx-block delay incurred by all the Intra-shard Tx-blocks published by a particular shard A is $\frac{r_{is} \cdot n_{tx}}{n_{sh} \cdot f_{is}} \cdot d_{is}$.

Hence, the Intra-shard Tx-block delay by all the Intra-shard blocks published by all shards in the network is given by the Eq. (1).

$$\delta_{is} = \frac{r_{is} \cdot n_{tx}}{f_{is}} \cdot d_{is} \tag{1}$$

**Cross-Shard Transactions.** Again, we will be assuming that the cross-shard transactions are uniformly distributed among shards and also uniformly distributed among shard nodes (this is because shard formation is a uniform random function). Therefore, the number of Cross-shard transactions per shard is $\frac{r_{cs} \cdot n_{tx}}{n_{sh}}$.

This, in turn, implies that the number of Cross-shard Tx-blocks published by a shard (shard-leader) is $\frac{r_{cs} \cdot n_{tx}}{n_{sh} \cdot f_{cs}}$.

For a single Cross-shard Block published by a shard, the shard leader has to broadcast it to all the other shards for verification and voting. Let $F_{CS}(sh)$ be a deterministic function, which takes the number of shards as a parameter and returns the overall delay incurred by a single Cross-shard Tx-block, published by some shard A, in a single shard B. Since the function $F_{cs}$ is fixed for a particular value of $n_{sh}$ let us denote it by $d_{cs}$. Here the delay $d_{cs}$ is for a single Cross-shard Tx-block and includes the broadcast delay by a shard leader (say of shard A) to some other shard (say B), block receive latency by shard B and the voting/verification delay by the nodes in shard B.

Now for a single Cross-shard Block published by a single shard A, the overall delay incurred before it comes back to A is $d_{cs} \cdot (n_{sh} - 1)$.

This implies, Cross-shard block delay by all the Cross-shard Tx-blocks published a particular shard A is $\frac{r_{cs} \cdot n_{tx}}{n_{sh}} \cdot d_{cs} \cdot (n_{sh} - 1)$.

We conclude that the Cross-shard Tx-block delay by all Cross-shard Tx-blocks as published by the shards in the network is $\frac{r_{cs} \cdot n_{tx}}{n_{sh}} \cdot d_{cs} \cdot (n_{sh} - 1) \cdot n_{sh}$.

$$\delta_{cs} = \frac{r_{cs} \cdot n_{tx}}{f_{cs}} \cdot d_{cs} \cdot (n_{sh} - 1) \tag{2}$$

The total network delay ($\delta_{net}$) incurred by $n_{tx}$ transactions when the number of shards is $n_{sh}$ is the sum of individual delays, $\delta_{is}$ and $\delta_{cs}$.

$$\delta_{net} = n_{tx} \cdot \left( \frac{r_{is}}{f_{is}} \cdot d_{is} + \frac{r_{cs}}{f_{cs}} \cdot d_{cs} \cdot (n_{sh} - 1) \right) \tag{3}$$

The throughput ($T$) for $n_{sh}$ number of shards is defined as the ratio between $n_{tx}$ and $\delta_{net}$.

$$T = \frac{f_{is} \cdot f_{cs}}{r_{is} \cdot f_{cs} \cdot d_{is} + r_{cs} \cdot f_{is} \cdot d_{cs} \cdot (n_{sh} - 1)} \tag{4}$$

## 5.2   Variation with Change in Number of Shards

We now change the number of shards from $n_{sh}$ to $n'_{sh}$ where $n'_{sh} = n_{sh} + c$, and $c$ is a positive integer. The total number of transactions $n_{tx}$, the cross-shard transaction ratio $r_{cs}$ and the values $f_{cs}, f_{is}$ remain invariant as they are independent of the number of shards (since all the full nodes generate transactions). The delay variables ($d_{is}$ and $d_{cs}$) change (recall that we renamed $F_{CS}$ as $d_{cs}$ and $F_{IS}$ as $d_{is}$ where both $F_{CS}$ and $F_{IS}$ are functions of the number of shards).

We know that $d_{cs}$ is a function of the number of shards in the network. Earlier in our definition of $d_{cs}$, we said that it includes various delays and latencies incurred by a single Cross-shard Tx-block published by some shard. It is evident that out of all the latencies/delays, the dominating delay is the voting delay by the shard nodes. For simplifying the calculations, we assume that $\delta_{voting} \gg \delta_{others}$ (where $\delta_{others}$ refers to the smaller delays such as block receive latency). This gives us $d_{cs} \sim \delta_{voting}$, that is, Cross-shard block voting delay.

The $\delta_{voting}$ is directly dependent on the number of nodes in a shard. $\delta_{voting} \sim \frac{1}{n_{sh}}$, and $\therefore d_{cs} \sim \frac{1}{n_{sh}}$.

Using the above relations, we get $d'_{cs} \cdot n'_{sh} = d_{cs} \cdot n_{sh}$ implying that $d'_{cs} = d_{cs} \cdot \frac{n_{sh}}{n'_{sh}}$. Similarly we get, $d'_{is} = d_{is} \cdot \frac{n_{sh}}{n'_{sh}}$.

The delay and the throughput are given by Eqs. (5) and (6), respectively.

$$\delta'_{net} = \frac{n_{sh} \cdot n_{tx}}{n'_{sh}} \left( \frac{r_{is}}{f_{is}} \cdot d_{is} + \frac{r_{cs}}{f_{cs}} \cdot d_{cs} \cdot (n'_{sh} - 1) \right) \tag{5}$$

$$T' = \frac{n'_{sh} \cdot f_{is} \cdot f_{cs}}{n_{sh}(r_{is} \cdot d_{is} \cdot f_{cs} + r_{cs} \cdot d_{cs} \cdot f_{is} \cdot (n'_{sh} - 1))} \tag{6}$$

Using the previous results, we find the ratio, $R$, between throughput $T'$ and $T$. Putting $r_{cs} = r$, $r_{is} = 1 - r$, we get:

$$R = \frac{n'_{sh}}{n_{sh}} \left( \frac{(1-r) \cdot f_{cs} \cdot d_{is} + r \cdot f_{is} \cdot d_{cs} \cdot (n_{sh} - 1)}{(1-r) \cdot f_{cs} \cdot d_{is} + r \cdot f_{is} \cdot d_{cs} \cdot (n'_{sh} - 1)} \right) \tag{7}$$

The above ratio $R$ is the fractional change in the throughput observed when the number of shards is changed, keeping the number of nodes constant.

We analyse the ratio R for $c = 1$, which means we find the change in throughput by increasing the shard count by one, that is, $n'_{sh} = n_{sh} + 1$. Also we assume that $f_{is} = f_{cs}$. This is a fair assumption, keeping in mind that the transaction block architecture is not specific to the type of transaction.

However, first, for simplicity in calculations, we try to establish relation between $d_{cs}$ and $d_{is}$. Since $d_{is}$ is Intra-shard delay, it does not directly concern with the number of shards present in the system, while $d_{cs}$ directly depends on the number of shards in the network. So we can safely assume $d_{cs} = d_{is} \cdot G(n_{sh})$, where $G(n_{sh})$ is a real function which takes the number of shards as a parameter and returns a positive real number. Also, $G$ follows the inequality $G(n_{sh}) > 1$; this is taking into consideration the real-life situations where Intra-shard delay will always be lesser than Cross-shard delay. So we can rewrite $G(n_{sh})$ as $1 + H(n_{sh})$ where $H(n_{sh}) > 0$. For simplicity in calculations, we take $H(n_{sh}) = \alpha \cdot n_{sh}$. Using the above assumptions, we get the simplified final value of R as:

$$R = \frac{n_{sh}+1}{n_{sh}} \left( \frac{(1-r)+r \cdot G(n_{sh}) \cdot (n_{sh}-1)}{(1-r)+r \cdot G(n_{sh}+1) \cdot n_{sh}} \right) \tag{8}$$

## 5.3  Optimal Shard Value for a Fixed Cross-Shard Transaction Ratio

We will find an optimal value of the number of shards using the throughput ratio $R$. For a given cross-shard transaction ratio $r$, such that after that optimal value, an increase in the number of shards leads to a decrease in the throughput. We check this by comparing the value of $R$, for a fixed value of $r$, against $n_{sh}$. If the value of $R > 1$ for some fixed value of $r$ will mean that an increase in the number of shards increases the throughput and vice-versa.

We plot the graph of $R$ against $n_{sh}$, while fixing $r$, along with the plot $y = 1$. The points where the graph of $R$ is below $y = 1$ represent the region of decreasing throughput, and the points where the graph of $R$ exceeds $y = 1$ represent the region of increasing throughput.

In order to plot the graph of $R$, we take $G(x) = 1 + H(x)$, where $H(x) = \alpha \cdot x$, this definition for $G(x)$ ensures that $G > 1$, and the function $H$ ensures that there is an implicit dependence on the number of shards. We will keep $\alpha$ very small so that g is nearly constant. We do not want $d_{cs}$ to be very high than $d_{is}$ when the number of shards is high as that would be impractical.

Therefore the graphical equation for $R$ against $n_{sh}$ can be expressed as:

$$y = \frac{x+1}{x} \left( \frac{(1-r)+r \cdot G(x) \cdot (x-1)}{(1-r)+r \cdot G(x+1) \cdot (x)} \right) \tag{9}$$

and $G(x) = 1 + H(x)$ with $H(x) = \alpha \cdot x$.

Now we show the plot for the above graphical equation.

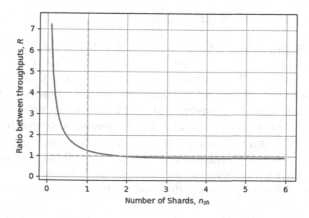

**Fig. 5.** Theoretical plot for the ration, $R$, against the number of shards, $n_{sh}$, for $r = 0.25$ and $\alpha = 0.4$

The graph in Fig. 5 represents the ratio of throughput on increasing a single shard against the number of shards. The line $y = 1$ is kept as a reference point to observe the behaviour of the ratio $R$. It is noteworthy that to the left of abscissa $x = 2$, the graph is strictly greater than 1; this signifies that the ratio $R > 1$, which means that throughput increases and in the right neighbourhood of abscissa $x = 2$, the graph goes below the co-ordinate $y = 1$. $R < 1$ signifies that the throughput decreases as we increase the number of shards. Therefore we can conclude that the point where the graph of $R$ cuts line $y = 1$ is the point of optimal shard number; let us call this point $OPT$. After the point $OPT$, the throughput will decrease monotonically with an increase in the number of shards, but as the graph suggests, the decrease would be gradual as the shards increase and the throughput would almost become constant after a certain large number of shards and would not decrease much.

# 6   Simulations and Observations

Simulations were run for varying input parameters on an Ubuntu 18.04 machine with 4 cores and 8 GB RAM. The simulated data are presented for the scenario when the number of nodes in the network is 100. ShardEval generates a log of all the events in the simulation and produces several key output parameters such as Transactions Per Second (TPS), length of blockchain, and the total number of transactions generated and processed, including intra-shard and cross-shard transactions.

TPS is the primary metric of our interest. It reflects the throughput of the network and is a representation of the efficiency of the sharded system. The key point to be noted here is that the TPS metric is different from the TPS in a real-life scenario. This is because a single time unit simulated in the Simpy environment is not equivalent to the unit of wall-clock time.

## 6.1   TPS Versus Number of Shards

In this section, we will analyze the plots for TPS vs the Number of Shards for the different ratios of cross-shard and intra-shard transactions. First, we will look into the plot where $r = 0$, implying that there are no cross-shard transactions generated by the network and all the transactions are intra-shard transactions. In the ideal scenario, the throughput should increase monotonically with the number of shards. This is because the more the number of shards in the network, the more the parallelism will be and the lesser the delay. It implies the fact that $d_{is}$ is directly dependent on the number of nodes in a shard, and as we increase the number of shards, keeping the number of nodes the same, the number of nodes per shard decrease, thereby decreasing the voting delay and increasing the throughput.

Figure 6 represents the observed behaviour for this scenario. As we can see, there is an increase in the throughput as we increase the number of shards. This is in line with our theoretical analysis, wherein if we put $r = 0$, we get

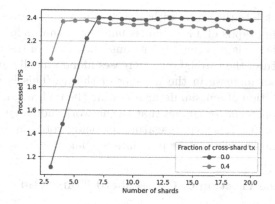

**Fig. 6.** TPS vs. Number of shards for *num_nodes* = 100 with cross-shard transactions ration $r = 0$ and 0.4

$y = \frac{x+1}{x}$; this indicates that the throughput will be higher for a higher number of shards, as observed in the figure. For a higher number of shards, the graph becomes almost constant. This is because the number of transactions generated remains fixed (the time for which we run the simulation is fixed). On increasing the number of shards, the transactions processed gradually catch up with the total number of transactions generated.

We now compare the plot for $r = 0.4$ alongside the plot with $r = 0$. In Fig. 6, in the graph with $r = 0.4$, we see a peak somewhere at around shard value 6, after which the TPS decreases with an increase in the number of shards. This behavior implies the existence of an optimal value for the number of shards in the network for a fixed value of $r$. The throughput of the network is maximum at this optimal shard value and decreases in the vicinity of this value.

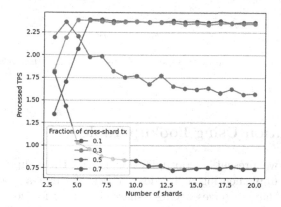

**Fig. 7.** TPS vs Number of shards for *num_nodes* = 100

Let us now look into the graph with higher values of $r$. Figure 7 is a combined comparison among graphs of TPS against number of shards for different values of $r$. Note that when $r$ is very high, 0.7 means when 70 % of the transactions are cross-shard in nature, the throughput decreases monotonically and converges to a constant with an increase in the number of shards. This is where we see a realistic representation of our simulator following the real world. A higher cross-shard transaction percentage implies that the network should get congested with cross-shard transaction blocks propagating for being voted upon and choke the intra-shard transactions since their population is large.

## 6.2  TPS Versus Fraction of Cross-Shard Transactions

Figure 8 presents the plot for TPS against the cross-shard transaction fraction $r$, for different number of shards. It shows that if the percentage of Cross-shard transactions in the network increases for a fixed number of shards, a decrease in throughput is observed. This is within our expectations because the intra-shard transactions get choked, and since cross-shard transactions incur more delay, their higher percentage leads to a decrease in the throughput.

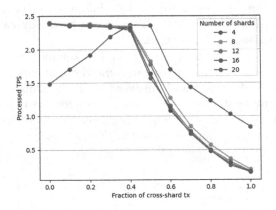

**Fig. 8.** TPS vs Fraction of cross-shard transactions for $num\_nodes = 100$

## 7  Optimization Using Lookup Table

In this section, we present an optimization in the throughput of cross-shard transactions by implementing a first-level check through a Lookup Table. As we know, every shard receives a Cross-shard Tx-block for voting and verification purposes, but this block may not contain any shard node as the receiver of any of the transactions present in the Cross-shard block. In this case, if the Cross-shard Tx-block enters into the shard for voting, it would lead to unnecessary overhead in the network. So we introduce the idea of having a lookup table in the receiver shard node (the shard leader in our case) to check the relevancy of the Cross-shard Tx-block and broadcast to shard nodes or mark it as non-applicable accordingly. The theoretical analysis follows the same notation and architecture as in Sect. 5. However, it involves a probabilistic approach to compute the relevance of a Cross-shard Tx-block for a particular shard. As a result, the deterministic delay, $\delta_{cs}$, changes to a probabilistic delay. An empirical analysis follows the theoretical analysis of the same architecture analyzed using ShardEval by changing its implementation to accommodate the lookup table optimization.

## 7.1    Probabilistic Modeling of Lookup Table

We first calculate the relevancy of a Cross-shard block to a particular shard. Note that we assume all the distributions and generations are uniformly randomly distributed and all the nodes are healthy and generate transactions.

Let $P_{cs} = P$(Cross-shard Tx-block relevant to a shard B for voting).

So, $P_{cs} = 1 - P$(Cross-shard Tx-block rejected by a shard B for voting).

This implies $P_{cs} = 1 - P_{rejection}$.

Now, we will calculate $P_{rejection}$. Since the transaction generation is a uniform random process, the receiver of a cross-shard transaction can be from any of the $n_{sh} - 1$ shards present in the network. Note that in real-life situations, the receiver of a transaction may follow a specific distribution. In that case, we can consider that distribution in the probability calculation. This analysis is based on the uniform distribution of cross-shard transactions.

So, $P$(A transaction does not belong to some Shard B) $= 1 - \dfrac{1}{n_{sh} - 1}$.

Now, a Cross-shard Tx-block contains $f_{cs}$ transactions. So,

$P_{rejection} = P$(No transaction of a cross-shard Tx-block belongs to Shard B).

This implies, $P_{rejection} = \left(1 - \dfrac{1}{n_{sh} - 1}\right)^{f_{cs}}$, and

$$P_{cs} = 1 - P_{rejection} = 1 - \left(1 - \dfrac{1}{n_{sh} - 1}\right)^{f_{cs}} \tag{10}$$

Since this is the probability of a Cross-shard Tx-block incurring a delay in some shard, the corresponding delay is given by the Eq. (11).

$$\delta_{cs} = \frac{r_{cs} \cdot n_{tx}}{f_{cs}} \cdot P_{cs} \cdot d_{cs} \cdot (n_{sh} - 1) \tag{11}$$

Note that the probabilistic model changes only the Cross-shard delay, while the Intra-shard delay remains the same. The total network delay and the throughput of the lookup table model are given by Eqs. (12) and (13), respectively.

$$\delta_{net} = n_{tx} \cdot \left(\frac{r_{is}}{f_{is}} \cdot d_{is} + \frac{r_{cs}}{f_{cs}} \cdot P_{cs} \cdot d_{cs} \cdot (n_{sh} - 1)\right) \tag{12}$$

$$T = \frac{f_{is} \cdot f_{cs}}{r_{is} \cdot f_{cs} \cdot d_{is} + r_{cs} \cdot f_{is} \cdot P_{cs} \cdot d_{cs} \cdot (n_{sh} - 1)} \tag{13}$$

The relation between $d_{cs}$ and $d_{is}$ is the same as discussed in Sect. 5.2, that is, $d_{cs} = d_{is} \cdot G(n_{sh})$. We choose the function $d_{is}(n_{sh}) = \frac{\beta}{n_{sh}}$ for this case (since the delay is inversely proportional to the number of shards in the network; this is reasonable assumption). So, the throughput now takes the form as shown in Eq. (14).

$$T = \frac{n_{sh} \cdot f_{is} \cdot f_{cs}}{\beta \cdot (r_{is} \cdot f_{cs} + r_{cs} \cdot f_{is} \cdot P_{cs} \cdot G(n_{sh}) \cdot (n_{sh} - 1))} \tag{14}$$

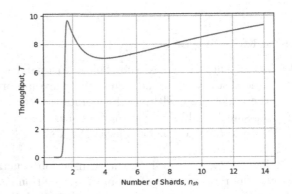

**Fig. 9.** Theoretical plot for throughput, $T$, against number of shards, $n_{sh}$, with LUT $(r = 0.7, \alpha = 0.1, f_{is} = f_{cs} = 5, \beta = 1)$

We plot the curve for throughput against the number of shards in Fig. 9. From the plot, we can conclude that given the values and under reasonable assumptions of our currently implemented protocol with LUT, the throughput initially decreases and then increases when 70% of the transactions are Cross-shard.

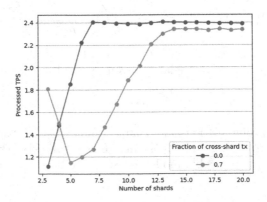

**Fig. 10.** Experimental plot for throughput, $T$, against number of shards, $n_{sh}$, with LUT for $r = 0$ and 0.7

## 7.2    Observations

Let us now check the empirical results of the same protocol implemented on ShardEval by changing the code of the simulator to accumulate the LUT change. The orange plot in Fig. 10 represents the experimental result obtained from ShardEval. It can be observed that the TPS decreases initially and then increases with the number of shards. This happens because an increase in the number of shards decreases $d_{is}$, it does increase $d_{cs}$, but the decrease in $P_{cs}$ balances, thereby increasing the overall throughput.

Therefore we conclude that ShardEval behaves correctly (in accordance with the developed theory), and we have established that lookup table is a significant improvement in the overall TPS of sharded-blockchain systems. Further, we emphasize the generic nature of our simulator, to include practically any protocol/algorithm (lookup table, for example) with minimal code changes and giving correct results to analyze and test several sharding-based protocols before their deployment.

## 8    Conclusions

Sharding is one of the promising solutions to the scalability problem faced by blockchain networks. A generic simulator to evaluate those protocols becomes necessary to analyze the sharding-based protocols. In this direction, a novel simulator, ShardEval, is presented for the sharded blockchain systems. The simulator offers a unified approach to comparing and benchmarking various sharding-based protocols.

Along with this, the theoretical study regarding the behavior of the sharding-based protocols in the presence of cross-shard transactions is carried out. The simulation results, backed by the theory, suggest that for a fixed percentage of cross-shard transactions, there exists an optimal value for the number of shards, and on deviating from this value, the performance of the sharded blockchain systems begins to degrade. With properly tuned parameters, the simulator can be used to determine this optimal number of shards.

## References

1. Andrian, H.R., Kurniawan, N.B., Suhardi: Blockchain technology and implementation: a systematic literature review. In: 2018 International Conference on Information Technology Systems and Innovation (ICITSI), pp. 370–374 (2018)
2. bitsCrunch: Monolithic to modular - solving the scalability trilemma (2022). https://www.bitscrunch.com/blogs/modular-vs-monolithic-blockchain
3. Douceur, J.R.: The Sybil attack. In: Druschel, P., Kaashoek, F., Rowstron, A. (eds.) IPTPS 2002. LNCS, vol. 2429, pp. 251–260. Springer, Heidelberg (2002). https://doi.org/10.1007/3-540-45748-8_24
4. Dwork, C., Naor, M.: Pricing via processing or combatting junk mail. In: Brickell, E.F. (ed.) CRYPTO 1992. LNCS, vol. 740, pp. 139–147. Springer, Heidelberg (1993). https://doi.org/10.1007/3-540-48071-4_10

5. Ethereum: Decentralized finance (DeFi) (2014). https://ethereum.org/en/defi/
6. Multivac Foundation: Multivac: a high-throughput flexible public blockchain based on trusted sharding computation (2018). https://www.mtv.ac/assets/file/MultiVAC_Tech_Whitepaper.pdf
7. Gouda, D.K., Jolly, S., Kapoor, K.: Design and validation of BlockEval, a blockchain simulator. In: International Conference on COMmunication Systems NETworkS (COMSNETS), pp. 281–289. IEEE (2021)
8. Hafid, A., Hafid, A.S., Samih, M.: Scaling blockchains: a comprehensive survey. IEEE Access **8**, 125244–125262 (2020)
9. Kantesariya, S., Goswami, D.: OptiShard: an optimized and secured hierarchical blockchain architecture. In: Arai, K., Kapoor, S., Bhatia, R. (eds.) FTC 2020. AISC, vol. 1289, pp. 393–411. Springer, Cham (2021). https://doi.org/10.1007/978-3-030-63089-8_26
10. Kokoris-Kogias, E., Jovanovic, P., Gasser, L., Gailly, N., Syta, E., Ford, B.: OmniLedger: a secure, scale-out, decentralized ledger via sharding. In: Symposium on Security and Privacy (SP), pp. 583–598. IEEE (2018)
11. Liu, Y., et al.: Building blocks of sharding blockchain systems: concepts, approaches, and open problems (2021). https://arxiv.org/abs/2102.13364
12. Luu, L., Narayanan, V., Zheng, C., Baweja, K., Gilbert, S., Saxena, P.: A secure sharding protocol for open blockchains. In: Proceedings of the 2016 ACM SIGSAC Conference on Computer and Communications Security, CCS 2016, pp. 17–30. Association for Computing Machinery, New York (2016)
13. Nakamoto, S.: Bitcoin: a peer-to-peer electronic cash system (2009). https://bitcoin.org/bitcoin.pdf
14. Nguyen, C.T., Hoang, D.T., Nguyen, D.N., Niyato, D., Nguyen, H.T., Dutkiewicz, E.: Proof-of-stake consensus mechanisms for future blockchain networks: fundamentals, applications and opportunities. IEEE Access **7**, 85727–85745 (2019)
15. Okanami, N., Nakamura, R.: Shargri-la: a transaction-level sharded blockchain simulator (2020). https://ethresear.ch/t/shargri-la-a-transaction-level-sharded-blockchain-simulator/7936
16. Popov, S.: The tangle (2018). http://www.descryptions.com/Iota.pdf
17. Priyadarshi, V., Goel, S., Kapoor, K.: ShardEval: Sharding-based Blockchain Simulator (2022). https://github.com/vishishtpriyadarshi/ShardEval
18. SimPy: "SimPy Documentation" (2022). https://simpy.readthedocs.io/en/latest/
19. Sompolinsky, Y., Lewenberg, Y., Zohar, A.: Spectre: a fast and scalable cryptocurrency protocol. Cryptology ePrint Archive, Paper 2016/1159 (2016). https://eprint.iacr.org/2016/1159
20. Sompolinsky, Y., Wyborski, S., Zohar, A.: Phantom and GhostDAG: a scalable generalization of Nakamoto consensus. Cryptology ePrint Archive, Paper 2018/104 (2018). https://eprint.iacr.org/2018/104
21. Stonebraker, M.: The case for shared nothing. IEEE Database Eng. Bull. **9**(1), 4–9 (1986)
22. TE Team: Elrond: a highly scalable public blockchain via adaptive state sharding and secure proof of stake (2019). https://elrond.com/assets/files/elrond-whitepaper.pdf/
23. Wang, J., Wang, H.: Monoxide: scale out blockchain with asynchronous consensus zones. Cryptology ePrint Archive, Paper 2019/263 (2019). https://eprint.iacr.org/2019/263
24. Yakovenko, A.: Solana: a new architecture for a high performance blockchain v0.8.13 (2017). https://solana.com/solana-whitepaper.pdf

25. Zamani, M., Movahedi, M., Raykova, M.: RapidChain: scaling blockchain via full sharding. In: Proceedings of the 2018 ACM SIGSAC Conference on Computer and Communications Security, CCS 2018, pp. 931–948. Association for Computing Machinery, New York (2018). https://doi.org/10.1145/3243734.3243853
26. Zhang, M., Li, J., Chen, Z., Chen, H., Deng, X.: CycLedger: a scalable and secure parallel protocol for distributed ledger via sharding (2020). https://arxiv.org/abs/2001.06778
27. Zhou, Q., Huang, H., Zheng, Z., Bian, J.: Solutions to scalability of blockchain: a survey. IEEE Access 8, 16440–16455 (2020)

# SoK: Digital Signatures and Taproot Transactions in Bitcoin

Anubha Jain[✉] and Emmanuel S. Pilli[iD]

Malaviya National Institute of Technology, Jaipur 302017, India
{2018rcp9114,espilli.cse}@mnit.ac.in

**Abstract.** Bitcoin has emerged as one of the most disruptive innovations since the advent of the internet. Its core principle of decentralization has not only revolutionized the way transactions are made but also paved the way for development of an entirely new blockchain industry. Its security is achieved through the implementation of cryptographic constructs based on elliptic curve cryptography. In this paper, we delve into use of digital signatures in Bitcoin. We provide an overview of Elliptic Curve Digital Signature Algorithm (ECDSA) and the recently adopted Schnorr signatures. Furthermore, we discuss Taproot, a soft fork introduced in Bitcoin, which enhances Bitcoin's versatility for complex applications. With Taproot, multiparty transactions can be designed with greater privacy for all parties involved, as well as for the underlying contracts. This paper offers a comprehensive review of both the ECDSA and Schnorr signature schemes, shedding light on their scripting capabilities within the Bitcoin ecosystem.

**Keywords:** Bitcoin · Digital signature · ECDSA · Schnorr signature · Taproot

## 1 Introduction

Bitcoin is one of the widely adopted cryptocurrency, with its ever-increasing transaction volume and user base per day. It is a decentralized ledger used to facilitate the transfer of funds between entities without any intermediaries. Users can identify themselves in the system using cryptographic keys which can be used to receive or spend bitcoins. As there is no centralized authority, the verification of transfer of funds is performed by the users. This is done by using cryptographic tools such as digital signatures to verify any claim to spend bitcoins. Two or more parties can enter a contract to mention or claim the spendability of their funds using the scripting capabilities of Bitcoin. The strong security assumptions of Bitcoin are based on the security of its underlying elliptic curve.

Other than the standard exchange of bitcoins between users, it can also be used to create escrows, hashed time lock contracts (HTLCs) [24], betting contracts, DeFi contracts, payment agreement from a multiparty wallet [1], etc. A recent upgrade in Bitcoin scripting capabilities, called Taproot [27,28], has

V. Muthukkumarasamy et al. (Eds.): ICISS 2023, LNCS 14424, pp. 360–379, 2023.
https://doi.org/10.1007/978-3-031-49099-6_22

included Schnorr digital signature [28]. This enhances the security of the system and the privacy of user agreements. The bitcoins can now be more privately locked for a combination of public keys and multiple conditions in a transaction. Spending these bitcoins have also become more secure and private with the use of new signature and transaction capabilities.

When two parties communicate over a network that is not reliable and the parties do not trust one another, we require certain mechanisms in place to ensure the security of the communication. Digital signatures are used in communication systems to ensure this requirement. Suppose that Alice wants to send a message to Bob, and when Bob receives the message he wants to be certain that the message is indeed from Alice. To ensure this, Alice can use a secure hash function, such as SHA256, to generate a hash value for the message. The hash value, signed by Alice's private key serves as a digital signature. Alice sends the message attached with the signature. On receiving the message from Alice, Bob calculates the hash value for the message and ensures that it is indeed same as the message hash signed by Alice. Using Alice's public key, Bob can also check if the signature is valid, as no one else has Alice's private key. So using a digital signature, the message is authenticated both in terms of its sender and its integrity.

While many studies on blockchains focus on their potential applications, others emphasize their security and scalability. However, only a handful delve into the cryptographic security underpinning blockchains. Ullah et al. [25] discuss elliptic curve cryptography's advancements and challenges. One of the focus of their work is the analysis of ECDSA in cryptosystems. Raikar et al. [21] presents a SoK of the existing and upcoming cryptographic concepts used in blockchains. None of these works delve in the details of application of digital signatures in Bitcoin. An analysis of the use of ECDSA and Schnorr in different type of transactions to build simpler to complex contracts is not provided. In this work, we have systematically reviewed the scripting capabilities of Bitcoin. We have presented the requirement of digital signatures and how these are used with various conditions on which funds are transferred. We've analyzed both ECDSA and Schnorr signatures in Bitcoin transactions. Additionally, we've delved into the Taproot upgrade, highlighting its components and Schnorr's role within Taproot. To the best of our knowledge, this is the first systematization of knowledge that gives a complete picture of the existing digital signatures used in Bitcoin.

The paper is divided into six sections: Sect. 2 is an introduction to the digital signature and its requirements. It explores the elliptic curve cryptography used in Bitcoin. Section 3 covers the usage of ECDSA in Bitcoin transactions. It also mentions the limitations and challenges of ECDSA on security and privacy when used in Bitcoin. Section 4 is an introduction to Schnorr signatures and its features that overcomes the limitations of ECDSA. In Sect. 5, details of Taproot upgrade are covered. It explains how Bitcoin transactions uses Taproot and Schnorr for complex multi-signature contracts. We have presented the security and privacy enhancements as well as the limitations of using Schnorr. Section 6 summarizes the key findings, emphasizing the use of Schnorr in Bitcoin transactions.

# 2   Digital Signatures Used in Bitcoin

Techniques such as digital signature, identity authentication, and time stamping are applied in Bitcoin transactions to provide integrity of the message. So if Alice has sent some bitcoins to Bob, he cannot create a different transaction and claim that it came from Alice. Neither can he update any information like the amount of Bitcoins transferred to him. Digital signatures also provide non-repudiation which means that participants cannot deny sending transactions. So Alice cannot deny sending a message to Bob as her private key is used to sign the transaction. Similarly, Bob cannot claim that he did not receive the transaction. In such situations when the sender and receiver do not trust the other party, digital signatures are required to resolve such disputes.

## 2.1   ECC in Bitcoin

Digital signatures in Bitcoin are based on Elliptic Curve Cryptography (ECC) [9]. It makes use of an elliptic curve whose variables and coefficients are all restricted to elements of a finite field. The elliptic curve chosen by Satoshi Nakamoto, denoted by secp256k1 over a finite field $F_p$ is specified in Eq. 1:

$$y^2 = x^3 + 7 \bmod p \tag{1}$$

where $p = 2^{256} - 2^{32} - 977 = 115792089237316195423570985008687907853269$ 98466564056403945758400790883467166

This defines an elliptic curve of order $q = 115792089237316195423570985000868$ 7908528375642790749043826051631415181614943337

The coordinates of generator point G for this curve are: ($x_0 = 550662630222773$ 4366957871889516853432625060345377759417550018736038911672924ة0, $y_0 = $ 32670510020758816978083085130507043184471273380659243275938904335757337 482424).

In bitcoin, the key pairs to receive and send bitcoins are generated with the help of this elliptic curve. The key pair (sk, pk) is made of a secret key, sk and a corresponding public key, pk. Here, Public key is a point on the curve, derived from the secret key using Eq. 2:

$$Pk = sk * G \tag{2}$$

To receive Bitcoins, public keys are provided in transactions, and to spend bitcoins the private key is used to digitally sign these transactions. Interested readers can refer to [9] for more details on ECC.

## 2.2   ECDLP and ECDSA

The Elliptic Curve Discrete Logarithm Problem (ECDLP) forms the basic assumption for the security of ECC. Given an elliptic curve E and points P and Q on the curve, the ECDLP is defined as finding an integer n such that

$n * P = Q$. This is the point addition $(P + P + P .... + unto\ n\ times)$, which is easy to solve. However, the inverse of the problem (point division to calculate P given n and Q) is not known to be easy. Despite knowing P, Q and curve E, there is no known method to calculate n efficiently for large numbers. This means that for sufficiently large inputs it is computationally infeasible to solve the problem. This one way nature of ECDLP makes ECC secure. An attacker who knows P and Q would not be able to compute n which is the private key corresponding to point Q on the curve.

---

**Algorithm 1:** ECDSA - Message Signing Algorithm

---

**Input**: m(message), $n_A$(Alice's private key), k(random integer), G(Generator Point), q (order of the elliptic curve group)
**Output**: s, r
1 Compute the point (R, Y) = k * G on the elliptic curve;
2 Compute r = R mod q;
3 Compute $s = k^{-1} (hash(m) + n_A * r)\ mod\ q$;
4 If s or r is 0, return to step 1;
5 Alice sends the signature (r, s) along with the message m to Bob;

---

So far, to prove ownership of funds, Bitcoin has relied on the Elliptic Curve Digital Signature Algorithm (ECDSA). As ECDLP is hard to solve, bitcoin can only be spent by using the secret key. This proves the ownership of bitcoins and the ability to spend them.

---

**Algorithm 2:** ECDSA - Signature Verification Algorithm

---

**Input**: $m_0$(received message), $s_0$(received signature component), $r_0$(received signature component), G(generator point), q(order of the elliptic curve group), $K_A$(Alice's public key)
**Output**: Valid or Invalid
1 Bob verifies that $r_0$ and $w_0$ are integers in the interval [1, q-1]. If not, the signature is Invalid;
2 Bob calculates the hash of the received message, $h = hash(m_0)$;
3 Calculate the modular inverse of the signature proof: $s_1 = s_0^{-1}\ (mod)\ n$;
4 Computer $u_1 = (h * w)\ (mod)\ q$, $u_2 = (r_0 * w)\ (mod)\ q$;
5 Calculate the point $(x_1, y_1) = u_1 * G + u_2 * K_A$ on the elliptic curve;
6 If $(x_1, y_1)$ is the point at infinity, then the signature is Invalid;
7 Signature is valid if $x_1\ (mod)\ q$ is equal to $r_0$ Otherwise, it is Invalid;

---

When a bitcoin transaction is created, it requires a valid signature, which can only be generated with valid digital keys, therefore anyone with a copy of both public and private keys has control of those bitcoins. So when Alice sends bitcoins to Bob she would sign the input in the transaction before transmitting it in the network. On receiving the transaction, miners in the network can verify and accept the transaction as valid and ensure that the bitcoins are indeed owned by Alice at the time of transfer. In Bitcoin, when Alice signs a transaction m, the public key $K_A$ is created using her private key $n_A$. Alice uses Algorithm 1 to digitally sign the message, using her key pair. Here q is the order of the elliptic curve. On receiving $(m_0, s_0, r_0)$, Bob uses Algorithm 2 to validate the signature.

## 3  Implementation of ECDSA in Bitcoin

### 3.1  Encoding of Keys and Signature

In ECC, public keys correspond to a point on the elliptic curve. The secp256k1 curve used by Bitcoin uses 32-byte numbers to represent x and y coordinates of a point. In ECDSA, these coordinates are encoded as per a standard defined in the SEC [4]. An uncompressed SEC format for representing a public key includes a one-byte prefix to indicate the uncompressed format, followed by the public key's 32 bytes x-coordinate and 32 bytes y-coordinate. It requires 65 bytes for a public key. Meanwhile, the more common representation, the compressed SEC format, reduces the size of encoding significantly by only including public key's x-coordinate. The corresponding y-coordinate can be derived using the curve equation from its x-coordinate. Each x-coordinate can have a positive and a negative y-coordinate. To resolve the ambiguity concerning the y-coordinate, its sign is also included in the encoding. So the compressed SEC format encodes public keys with only 33 bytes.

ECDSA signatures for the secp256k1 curve consist of two 32-byte numbers, r, and s. It follows the Distinguished Encoding Rules (DER) [15] for signature encoding. As per DER, each of the numbers, r, and s, is prefixed by two bytes: one to indicate the signed integer; the other to indicate the size of the following data which is 32 bytes for the values r and s. This makes for a total overhead of four bytes. There are two bytes at the beginning of each DER signature: one to indicate that the signature consists of two objects (r and s), and another to indicate the total size of the encoding. Finally, an additional byte at the end of the signature indicates the signature hash type, which is used by Bitcoin to determine which parts of a transaction to use when creating a signature.

Overall, this results in seven extra bytes to encode the two 32-byte values r and s [15]. This should result in a total signature size of 71 bytes. But sometimes for r or s values with their most significant bit (MSB) set, their encodings require an additional one-byte zero padding so they are not interpreted as negative numbers. So the ECDSA signature size can go up to 73 bytes.

### 3.2  Transactions Using ECDSA

In most bitcoin transactions, the sender needs to provide a digital signature in order to spend a transaction output. This condition is specified when the bitcoins are locked to the receivers' address in the form of locking script also known as scriptPubKey. Each transaction input is a Unspent Transaction output (UTXO) that had been created in a previous transaction. To spend these bitcoins, digital signature of the spending party is required. This is provided in the unlocking script of the transaction input, also known as the scriptSig. In SegWit transactions, the signature is provided in the witness section of the transaction [6]. In Fig. 1, the structure of each of these transaction constructs are mentioned.

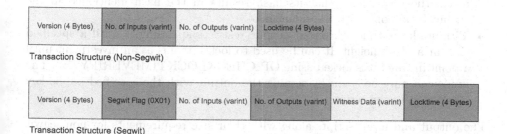

**Fig. 1.** Transaction Structure

Following are the types of non-segwit bitcoin outputs and inputs which require ECDSA signatures in order to be spent along with their locking and unlocking scripts:

- **Pay-to-Public-Key (P2PK):** A P2PK output is used to lock Bitcoins with the public key of the recipient. It is the most basic transaction type. P2PK input can be unlocked using a signature corresponding to the public key mentioned in the locking script.
- **Pay-to-Public-Key-Hash    (P2PKH):**    A    Pay-to-Public-Key-Hash (P2PKH) output locks the bitcoins using the hash of the recipient's public key. P2PKH output consists of both signature and public key.
- **Multisignature:** Before the Taproot upgrade, in order to create multi-signature transactions, OP_CHECKMULTISIG script instruction was available. Various m-of-n or n-of-n variants could be created in order to capture threshold and full multi-party contracts respectively [3]. The unlocking script provided with each multisig input when spending it has OP_0, a dummy Bitcoin Script instruction to address a bug in the implementation of OP_CHECKMULTISIG; sizes and encodings of signatures along with m signatures.
- **Pay-to-Script-Hash (P2SH):** Locking script of a Pay-to-Script-Hash (P2SH) output consists of the hash of redeem script [3]. If a multi-signature transaction is built using P2SH, its input script will have the data corresponding to the signatures required to satisfy the redeem script; the size of the redeem script; and the redeem script. Here data is the unlocking script for a multi-signature transaction and the redeem script is the multi-signature locking script.

- **Hashlock:** A Hashlock is a condition that can be mentioned in the output which locks it until a specified data is revealed [14]. It is used in applications like atomic swaps where both parties cannot swap their funds until a secret is exchanged between them. It can also be used in situations where multiple outputs are locked by the same Hashlock. By relieving the secret, all such outputs become spendable at the same time. A Hashlock is generally applied along with a public key hash. To spend the transaction the sender has to reveal the secret such that its hash results in the hash mentioned in the output lock along with the signature.

- **Timelock:** A timelock on an output restricts spending it until a specified time or a block height. It can be used to lock bitcoins as an investment until a point in time. It is locked using OP_CHECKLOCKTIMEVERIFY [19]. The funds can only be spent by signing the output with the specified public key mentioned in the script.

The output and input scripts along with their size requirements for non-segwit transactions are presented in Table 1. We take the average signature size to be 72 Bytes and the use of compressed public keys which are 33 Bytes in size.

**Table 1.** Input and Output Scripts for non-SegWit transactions

| Transaction Type | Locking Script | Unlocking Script | Locking Script Size | Unlocking Script Size |
|---|---|---|---|---|
| Pay-to-PubKey | <length of public key> <public key> OP_CHECKSIG | <size of signature> <signature> | 35 Bytes | 73 Bytes |
| Pay-to-PubKey-Hash | OP_DUP OP_HASH160 <length of hash> <hash> OP_EQUALVERIFY OP_CHECKSIG | <Size of signature> <Signature> <Size of public key> <Public key> | 25 Bytes | 107 Bytes |
| MultiSig (m-of-n scheme) | OP_m <length of $1^{st}$ pubkey> <$1^{st}$ pubkey> <length of $2^{nd}$ pubkey> <$2^{nd}$ pubkey>...<length of $n^{th}$ pubkey> < $n^{th}$ pubkey> OP_n OP_CHECKMULTISIG | OP_0 <Size of $1^{st}$ signature> <$1^{st}$ signature> <Size of $2^{nd}$ signature> <$2^{nd}$ signature> ... <Size of $n^{th}$ signature> < $n^{th}$ signature> | $34n + 3$ Bytes | $73m + 1$ Bytes |
| Pay-to-ScriptHash (m-of-n multisig) | OP_HASH160 <length of redeem script hash> <redeem script hash> OP_EQUAL | OP_0 <Size of $1^{st}$ signature> <$1^{st}$ signature> <Size of $2^{nd}$ signature> <$2^{nd}$ signature> ... <Size of $n^{th}$ signature> < $n^{th}$ signature> <Size of the redeem script> OP_m <length of $1^{st}$ pubkey> <$1^{st}$ pubkey> <length of $2^{nd}$ pubkey> <$2^{nd}$ pubkey> ... <length of $n^{th}$ pubkey> < $n^{th}$ pubkey> Op_n OP_CHECKMULTISIG | 23 Bytes | $73m + 34n + 5$ Bytes |
| HashLock | OP_HASH160 <Hash value> OP_EQUALVERIFY OP_DUP OP_HASH160 <hash of public key> OP_EQUALVERIFY OP_CHECKSIG | <Size of signature> <Signature> <Public key> <secret> | 45 Bytes | $106 + x$ Bytes where $size(secret) = x$ Bytes |
| TimeLock (Locking funds in a escrow) | <expiry time> OP_CHECKLOCKTIMEVERIFY OP_DROP OP_DUP OP_HASH160 <pubKeyHash> OP_EQUALVERIFY OP_CHECKSIG | <signature> <pubKey> | 30 Bytes | 105 Bytes |

Different types of segwit transactions [12] that can be built using ECDSA are:

- **Pay-to-Witness-Public-Key-Hash (P2WPKH):** A Pay-to-Witness-Public-Key-Hash (P2WPKH) output locking script has a witness version 0 along with hash of the public key of the receiver [18]. For P2WPKH, the data to satisfy the locking script resides in the witness, leaving the unlocking script empty. A P2WPKH witness contains the data used for unlocking the inputs: Public key hash and its corresponding signature.
- **Pay-to-Witness-Script-Hash (P2WSH):** The Pay-to-Witness-Script-Hash (P2WSH) is a segwit compatible transaction of type P2SH [18]. Its locking script consists of OP_0 to indicate a version zero witness program and SHA256 hash of the script to lock the output. Its unlocking script is empty. In case the transaction is to unlock a multisig P2WSH transaction, then the witness will have data and witness script. Data contains the signatures corresponding to the multisig public keys. The witness script will be the actual script whose hash was used to lock the outputs.

The output and witness scripts along with their size requirements for segwit transactions are presented in Table 2.

**Table 2.** Output Scripts and Witness for SegWit transactions

| Transaction Type | Locking Script | Witness | Locking Script Size | Witness Size |
|---|---|---|---|---|
| Pay-to-witness-publickeyhash | OP_0 OP_HASH160 <length of public key hash> <public key hash> | <No. of items> <length of signature> <Signature> <length of the pub key> | 22 Bytes | 108 Bytes |
| Pay-to-Witness-Script-Hash (multisig) | OP_0 OP_HASH160 <length of redeem script hash> <redeem script hash> OP_EQUAL | <No. of witness items> OP_0 <Size of $1^{st}$ signature> <$1^{st}$ signature> ... <Size of $m^{th}$ signature> < $m^{th}$ signature> OP_m <length of $1^{st}$ public key> <$1^{st}$ public key> ... <length of $n^{th}$ public key> < $n^{th}$ public key> OP_n OP_CHECKMULTISIG | 23 Bytes | $73m + 34n + 6$ Bytes |

## 3.3 Issues in ECDSA

The usage of ECDSA signatures in Bitcoin is very fragile and its vulnerabilities have been exploited previously as well. Following are a few of the challenges with the use of ECDSA in Bitcoin transactions:

- **Nonce Reuse Vulnerability:** One of the biggest challenges with ECDSA is the vulnerability associated with the reuse of random numbers, or nonces. If the same nonce is used for different messages for the same key, it can lead to the exposure of private key [2].
- **Signature Malleability:** ECDSA signatures are malleable, meaning that given a valid signature for a message, it is possible to generate another valid signature for the same message [5].
- **Lack of Formal Security Proof:** Security of ECDSA is not as formally established, which can be a concern in certain applications [10].

- **Single-Bit Nonce Bias Attacks:** It is vulnerable to attacks that exploit a bias in the least significant bit of the nonce [2]. If the nonce is not perfectly random, an attacker can potentially recover the private key.
- **Lack of Support for Aggregation:** It does not support key aggregation. Aggregation allows multiple signatures to be combined into one, reducing the size of the transaction data on chain and improving efficiency.
- **Lack of Full Privacy for Multi-Signature Use Cases:** ECDSA does not provide full privacy for multi-signature use cases. It's easy to identify multi-signature transactions because they have multiple distinct keys and signatures on chain, which could be a concern for users who desire privacy.
- **Lack of Batch Verification:** ECDSA does not support batch verification, a feature that allows multiple signatures to be verified at once for efficiency. Each signature in ECDSA must be verified individually.

## 4    Schnorr Signatures

Taproot upgrade [26] has built-in the use of Schnorr signature [28] when spending an output for a Pay-to-Taproot (P2TR) transaction. Schnorr signature [23] also uses the elliptic curve, secp256k1 as used in ECDSA. The security assumptions for the elliptic curve remain the same in Schnorr. Users can choose their secret keys and generate their public keys and addresses just like earlier.

In order to sign a message m using private key k, public key P, Schnorr digital signature mechanism requires the signer to choose a random integer, r. The corresponding point R on the elliptic curve is created as $R = r * G$, where G is the generator point for the curve. To compute the signature, message m is added to the random point on the curve as shown in Eq. 3.

$$e = hash(R \parallel m) \tag{3}$$

The signer calculates the signature s using Eq. 4. The sender then sends the signature (s,R) along with the message m. For verification, anyone having information about the public key and generator point can verify the signature if the Eq. 5 holds.

$$s = r + e * k \tag{4}$$

$$s * G = R + hash(R \parallel m) * P \tag{5}$$

In order to be employed as a secure signing mechanism for Bitcoin transactions, a few adjustments have been made in the signing process. One of these is to protect against the *related-key attack* [16]. The public key is prefixed along with the message and nonce commitment, R in $e = hash(R \parallel P \parallel m)$. If e is calculated using Eq. 3, then the signature (R,s) valid for public key P can be converted in signature $(R, s + x * e)$ for public key $(P + x * G)$ for the same message m and a random number x. This random number x can be an additive tweak to the signing key. It results in insecure signatures when keys are generated by tweaking the keys in taproot transactions.

To mitigate the related-key attack, the public key is prefixed to the message in the challenge hash input so that an additive tweak x to the public key and not the challenge hash by an attacker will result in an invalid signature. The signature is calculated using Eq. 6.

$$s = r + hash(R \parallel P \parallel m) * k \tag{6}$$

The signature can be verified using Eq. 7.

$$s * G = R + hash(R \parallel P \parallel m) * P \tag{7}$$

## 4.1   Comparison Between ECDSA and Schnorr Signature

The limitations of ECDSA are addressed by the Schnorr scheme which makes it a preferable choice for signing messages. While ECDSA signatures are non-linear, Schnorr signatures have a linearity property that allows for the creation of multisignatures, threshold signatures, and adaptor signatures. ECDSAs are less computationally efficient, particularly during the signature verification process due to multiple point multiplication operations. However, the Schnorr signature verification requires fewer computational steps compared to ECDSA, which makes it faster and less resource-intensive. In ECDSA, if a transaction requires signatures from multiple parties, each party must add their signature separately. This increases the size of the transaction data and can make the verification process slow and complex. Schnorr signatures natively support multisignature operations [13,17]. This means that multiple parties can collectively produce a single signature that validates the transaction. This single signature is indistinguishable from a single-signer signature, which enhances the privacy for involved parties. Table 3 lists the advantages of Schnorr over the limitations of ECDSA.

The nonce reuse vulnerability exists in Schnorr signatures as well, but the nonce in Schnorr signature is generated by hashing a concatenation of random number, message and the secret key. This makes the nonce deterministic and is less likely to be reused. A deterministic nonce use is also proposed in RFC 6979 [20] for ECDSA which is being used by some bitcoin wallet implementations. But the solution is vulnerable to lattice-based attacks to recover secret key [22].

## 4.2   Features of Schnorr Signature

### Linearity
Schnorr signatures are linear which allows easy aggregation of multiple signatures into one signature. This makes it usable to create multisignature contracts as the size of more complex transactions can be reduced when multiple parties are involved in a contract. Schnorr signature follows the linearity of the elliptic curve points. It allows key aggregation of public keys using musig [13] from multiple parties as follows:

Let A and B be two parties with their respective private keys as $d_a$ and $d_b$. Their corresponding public keys are points on the curve, $P_a$ and $P_b$. They both

**Table 3.** Differences between ECDSA and Schnorr Signatures

| Feature | ECDSA Signature | Schnorr Signature |
|---|---|---|
| Security | Vulnerable when random nonces are reused | Nonces are deterministically derived from the private key and message being signed |
| Security Proof | Lacks formal security proof | Existing security proof in the random oracle model [8] |
| Non-malleability | Malleable | Non-malleable |
| Linearity | Non-linear | Linear |
| Efficiency | Less computationally efficient | Faster and less resource-intensive |

sign a message using their private keys and respective nonce values $k_a$ and $k_b$,

$$s_a = k_a + e * d_a \qquad\qquad s_b = k_b + e * d_b$$

If we add these signatures as shown in Eq. 8, we get

$$s_a + s_b = k_a + k_b + e * (d_a + d_b) \tag{8}$$

Let $k' = k_a + k_b$ and $d' = d_a + d_b$, we get the combined signature mentioned in Eq. 9:

$$s' = k' + e * d' \tag{9}$$

S' is itself a valid Schnorr signature created using a public key which is the addition of A and B's public keys and addition of their individual nonce points. Thus parties can together sign transactions by aggregating their public keys in multiparty contracts. Using the linearity of Schnorr signatures, more transactions can be included in the same block size as transaction signatures can be aggregated.

For multisignature scheme, an adjustment is made in the key aggregation algorithm by adding a coefficient to each public key. This is done to mitigate the Key Cancellation Attack, also know as *Rouge Key Attack* [7], where a user can choose its key based on the other user's key in order to be able to sign a multisig transaction without the involvement of other party. For example, if Alice has key pair $(x_A, X_A)$ and Bob has $(x_B, X_B)$, then Bob can claim his public key to be $X'_B = X_B - X_A$. The aggregate key in this case will be $X_A + X'_B$, which only requires Bob's private key for spending. To mitigate this from happening, in musig, the aggregate key is calculated as a sum of multiples of participant keys, where the multiplication factor depends on a hash of all participating keys.

**Tagged Hashes:** Schnorr signature uses the same hash function as ECDSA. When creating and verifying Schnorr signatures, different tagged versions of hash functions are used in different contexts. This greatly reduces the possibility of hash collisions across these contexts. Tagged hashes prefix the data to be hashed with $SHA256(tag)\|SHA256(tag)$ [26]. Now the Schnorr signature should satisfy the Eq. 10.

$$s * G = R + tagged\ hash\ (R \| P \| m) * P \qquad (10)$$

**Non-malleability:** Traditional Bitcoin transactions are malleable. When a transaction is broadcasted in the network, a malicious recipient can alter the signature included in the transaction without the need of a private key as ECDSA signature can be modified. This changes the transaction id as it is a function of the signatures included in it. This way the recipient can make a claim to the sender of not receiving any fund. The sender when searches the blockchain with the original transaction id does not find it there as it has been changed without the sender noticing it. The sender can be tricked this way to send the funds again to the malicious receiver. The funds once sent are not revertible. This effectively means the sender effectively pays twice to the receiver.

SegWit introduced in BIP141 [12], addressed this transaction malleability by separating the signature from the transaction. The witnesses of all transactions' inputs are placed in a separate witness structure. In a segwit transaction, if a recipient modifies the signature, it does not alter the transaction id.

Schnorr signatures are inherently non-malleable as it is not possible to alter an existing signature into another valid signature on the same key and same message. Schnorr signature is secure against the chosen message attack (SUF-CMA). This ensures that the Schnorr signature cannot be modified and still be valid without knowledge of the secret key.

### 4.3   Encoding of Keys and Signature

Public keys in Schnorr signature correspond to a point on the underlying elliptic curve. Encoding of public keys in ECDSA follows the SEC standards in which a point in compressed format is stored as a 33-byte value. In Schnorr, a custom encoding is used [28], which includes only a point's x-coordinate. As per the elliptic curve, each x coordinate can have two corresponding y coordinates. So to resolve the ambiguity concerning the y-coordinate, its parity is defaulted to the even y value. The encoding of Schnorr public keys thus has a size of 32 bytes.

Schnorr signature consists of a curve point and a 32-byte value. To save space, the signature only contains P's 32-byte x-coordinate from which the corresponding y-coordinate can be derived (the y-coordinate can only be even). Unlike ECDSA signatures which follow DER encoding, in Schnorr, the two 32-byte values, r, and s, are encoded back to back with a total size requirement of 64 bytes.

In the transaction output incorporating Schnorr signature, only x-coordinate of the public key is included. The corresponding even y-coordinate is chosen as a valid point. This results in a 32-byte representation of the public key with a signature size of 64 Bytes.

## 5    Taproot

At block height 709632 (midnight 11 August 2021 UTC), Bitcoin rolled out a major upgrade called Taproot. The traditional Bitcoin transaction outputs can be distinguished based on their spending conditions as pay to a public key or pay to a script hash. Taproot represents these separate transaction outputs in the same way so that they are indistinguishable from each other. An output can have multiple script paths and a key path available to spend it. If it is unlocked using the key-based spending path, the possibility of spending through a script path is not even revealed. In case a particular script path is used to unlock an output, the other scripts are not revealed. This saves space and fee on the unused conditions in the transaction. This also increases the privacy of a contract between parties. Following are the features introduced in Taproot upgrade:

- Indistinguishable locking and unlocking using key or script path: When used properly, an observer will not be able to distinguish between a public key and a script-type transaction spending as they are detectable in P2PKH or P2SH transaction.
- Alternative signature scheme: Taproot upgrade introduces Schnorr signature scheme to create Bitcoin transactions. Using this, multiple public keys can be combined into one, making it indistinguishable from a single-party signing. This considerably reduces the signature size and verification time.
- Specifying spending paths in Merkelized Abstract Syntax Tree(MAST) [11]: The conditions tied to spending bitcoins can be hidden at the time of locking. When unlocking, only the condition which is used to spend the bitcoin is revealed, while others are not specified.

In the Taproot upgrade, a new transaction type is introduced, called Pay-to-Taproot (P2TR). This includes an output with a segregated witness version 1 and a 32-byte witness program. Its locking and unlocking conditions use modi-fied opcodes, OP_CHECKSIG and OP_CHECKSIGVERIFY to allow Schnorr signatures [27]. A new opcode, OP_CHECKSIGADD is introduced to allow multiple keys in an output. To create multisig transactions, traditionally used OP_CHECKMULTISIG and OP_CHECKMULTISIGVERIFY opcodes are dis-abled. Taproot also introduces a new hashtype called SIGHASH_DEFAULT to sign over all transaction inputs. It is implicitly applied in a taproot transaction unless any other hashtype is specified. Including SIGHASH_DEFAULT commits to all of the usual things committed to by SIGHASH_ALL in current Bitcoin transactions, but additionally commits to all of the transaction outputs being spent by the transaction being signed.

### 5.1    Transactions Using Schnorr Signature

In the following section, we will look at different steps when signing a transaction using Schnorr. We will begin with the construction of a taproot output. It is locked with scriptPubKey as mentioned in format 11.

$$<witness\ version\ 1><32Byte\ encoding\ of\ point\ Q> \tag{11}$$

Point Q, called Taproot output key, is computed using both the key path and script path conditions using Eq. 12.

$$Q = P + hash(P \parallel M) * G \qquad (12)$$

Here,

P = Taproot internal key corresponding to key path spending.

M = Root of Merkle tree whose leaves represent possible ways to unlock the locked bitcoins.

Each leaf of the script tree is represented as <leaf version> <script>. To spend this output, a signature for Q has to be provided, along with revealing:

- Taproot internal key, P.
- Leaf version of the script and the script which is spent.
- Inputs for the script which satisfies when it is executed.
- Merkle path from the script leaf to the merkle tree root so that presence of Q in the merkle tree can be confirmed.

In order to construct Q from P, to construct inner nodes of the script tree, and for the Schnorr signature, tagged hashes are used. The same public key generation mechanism for ECDSA is used in Schnorr signatures. The previous private keys can be used directly. The usual 33-byte compressed public keys can be used in Schnorr scheme by dropping their first byte.

When a user wants to lock funds in a taproot output, she will send the bitcoins to a taproot address which is formed from tweaking the internal public key with zero or more conditional statements written as Bitcoin scripts and each script arranged as a merkle tree leaf. Depending on the locking conditions, different locking mechanisms can be created as described in the following sections.

**Key Path Locking:** If the funds can be locked by only the public key P of the recipient, it is kept as the taproot internal key. If no script path is specified, then it becomes evident from the locking script that this output can be spent only with a public key. It can be either a single key or multiple keys aggregated as a single key and specified as taproot key. So it is advised to specify a script path even if it does not exist as an unspendable script as shown in Eq. 13.

$$Final\ taproot\ output\ key\ point,\ Q = P + (hash_{TapTweak}(P)) * G \qquad (13)$$

Here, P is the internal public key and G is curve generator point.

**Script Path Locking:** If funds can be locked with more than one condition, they can be split into multiple scripts (if-else conditional statements). Each script corresponds to one possible execution path specified as a merkle tree leaf. If all the conditions are equally likely to appear, they can be arranged in a balanced tree. In case the conditions are not equally probable, then they can be arranged as per their probability in a Huffman tree.

## 5.2   Script Tree

Script paths for a Taproot output are specified in a merkle tree [11]. Consider four possible scripts to spend an output, with equal probability to be used for spending the funds. Each condition is a script that is stored as a leaf in the merkle tree as shown in Eq. 14:

$$Leaf\ node\ of\ script\ tree = hash_{TapLeaf}(leaf\ version,\ size\ of\ script,\ script)$$
$$(14)$$

Here 'TapLeaf' is used as the tag for leaf nodes. Other than leaves, nodes of the merkle tree are created by hashing the child nodes. These nodes are computed as a tagged hash of their children in lexicographical order. In Fig. 2, a merkle tree arrangement for the script path A, B, C, and D are shown. Here A, B, C, and D are represented at level 0 as a tagged hash of version no, the size of the script, and the spending condition specified as a script. The leaf version serves as a versioning mechanism for the scripting language used in Bitcoin. Having a version bit associated with a leaf would allow nodes to distinguish between the old Script and the new ones There are a total of 41 possible leaf versions including (0xc0) for future upgrades. As per BIP 342, currently, the leaf version used is 0xc0.

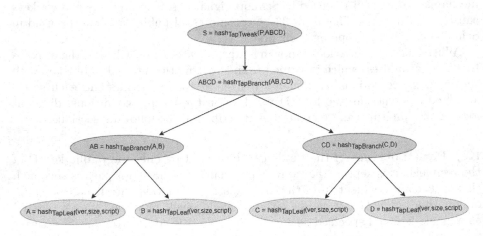

**Fig. 2.** Script Tree for four equally likely scripts

At level 1, the parent nodes AB and CD are calculated as a tagged hash of their respective children. Here 'TapBranch' is used as the tag for calculating hash as these are internal nodes. Note that at each level when creating a tap branch, its child nodes are hashed in lexicographical order.

The root node of the script merkle tree, ABCD is hashed with the internal public key, P to get the Taproot output key. Here, 'TapTweak' is used as the tag for hashing. This is called tweaking the internal public key with the merkle tree root hash. The scriptPubKey used to lock the taproot output is specified as

$$0X51\ 0X20\ <output\ public\ key>$$

Here 0X51 represents the segwit version 1. 0X20 represents the size of the public key (32 bytes) and the output public key is the x-coordinate of the taproot output key created using taproot internal key and the script tree.

## 5.3   Spending Taproot Input

In order to spend a taproot input, the secret key corresponding to the internal public key used in taproot output is also tweaked with the factor corresponding to the script tree mentioned in the taproot output. Only a secret key corresponding to an even y-coordinate is used, if not, the secret key corresponding to the internal public key is negated before applying the tweak.

**Schnorr Signature.** When singing a Taproot input, Schnorr signature algorithm, Sign(sk, m) is applied as follows:

1. Calculate the tweaked secret key. If the public key point P for the private key doesn't have an even y-coordinate, negate the secret key
2. Compute the random nonce r as a tagged hash of the Public key, message, and private key
3. Compute the Elliptic curve point R corresponding to this random nonce. If R doesn't have an even y-coordinate, negate it
4. Compute e as int(hashBIP0340/challenge(R || P || m)
5. Calculate Schnorr signature, s = r + e * sk

The signature sig = (R || s) is attached with the message m.

**Signature Verification.** The algorithm Verify(pk, m, sig) is defined as:

1. From sig, extract r and s.
2. Compute e as hashBIP0340/challenge(r || P || m)
3. Calculate R as s * G - e * P
4. Verify if the y-coordinate of R is even
5. Confirm if R is the same as the one received in sig

**Witness Validation Rules.** Now in order to verify the witness associated when spending a taproot input is correct, the following steps are followed:

1. Fail if 0 elements in witness stack
2. **Key path spending:** If the witness stack has only one entry, it is considered as a signature corresponding to taproot public key q. It is verified as per Schnorr signature verification algorithm.
3. **Script path spending:** If the witness stack has more than one element.

The components of witness stack are as shown in format 15 and 16

$$Witness\,stack: \; <script> <control\,block> \tag{15}$$

Control block = <leaf version><taproot internal key, p><Tap branches to calculate merkle tree root>                    (16)

From the control block's contents, it is verified whether the script mentioned in the script tree is satisfied or not. It follows the process mentioned:

1. Tagged hash of tapleaf is calculated as $hash_{TapLeaf}$(leaf version || size of script || script).
2. Calculate merkle tree root using tap branches and tap leaf spent. Tap branches included in the control block along with the tap leaf calculated above are used to calculate the merkle tree root hash.
3. Taproot output key is calculated as the 'TapTweak' tagged hash of taproot internal key and the merkle tree root hash calculated above.
4. Taproot output key calculated here is checked with the output key as mentioned in the locking script of the input. If they are the same then proceed.
5. Execute the script mentioned in the witness stack using the witness stack elements.

### 5.4   Use of Schnorr Signature in Multisignature Transactions

If the output requires signatures from multiple parties when spending, the key aggregation technique aggregates the multiple public keys in one key used for locking [13,17]. The aggregated key is specified as the internal key. The following possibilities can occur when combining keys:

- If a n-of-n signature scheme has to be built then only the key path spending which requires signatures from all involved n parties is mentioned.
- If a m-of-n signature scheme has to be built then both the key path and script path exist. Taking a scenario where a user uses a multiparty wallet provided by a cryptocurrency exchange. There are 3 keys, key 1 held by the user, key 2 by the crypto exchange, and key 3 is a backup key held by a key recovery service. Backup keys are generally stored in an offline system and only be used when one of the other keys is lost or not available to sign the transaction. There can be the following scenarios for spending the funds locked by this arrangement:
    - Key path spending: Key 1 + Key 2
    - Script path spending:

Script1:   Key1 + Key3          Script2:   Key2 + Key3

Taproot output key is built using the scenario as shown in the Fig. 3. The scripts used to lock funds are as follows:

ScriptSig of MuSig Key, $K_m = OP\_1\ K_m\ OP\_CHECKSIG$

Script 1: <Key1> OP_CHECKSIGVERIFY <Key3> OP_CHECKSIG

Script 2: <Key2> OP_CHECKSIGVERIFY <Key3> OP_CHECKSIG

Now depending upon the situation, in an m-of-n multisig contract, there can be (m choose n) spending paths in the script tree. The scripts can also involve complicated conditions like time locks, hashlocks, etc.

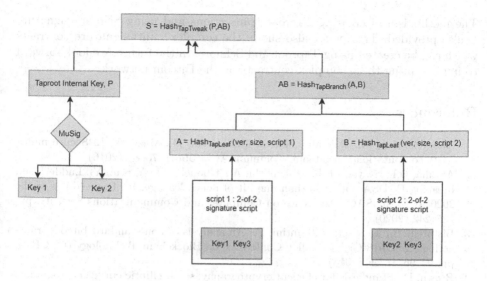

**Fig. 3.** Script Tree for a Multisig Transaction

## 5.5 Security and Privacy in Schnorr Signature

In non-taproot transactions, it's immediately revealed during the locking phase whether the transaction is spendable by a public key or a script. While in taproot, even if there is a script, the locking is done by the final taproot output key. So when spending a taproot output, it happens through the taproot output key. This obfuscates the observers from realizing if internally a key path or a script path is used as the spending condition. Within taproot, a key path can be payment to a single user or a multi-signature wallet, or any multi-party or multi-conditional contract. Taproot provides more privacy than earlier transaction types, as when it is spent, all possible conditions for spending an output are not mentioned. Instead, only the condition which is used for spending the output is published. Hash of the rest of the conditions is provided as the merkle tree path.

But when using a script path, it leaks the information that for unlocking, the key path is not used, instead the script path is being used. It also provides an estimate for the minimum depth of the tree giving an idea about the number of alternate spending conditions.

## 6 Conclusion and Future Work

Bitcoin provides multiple scripting options to create transactions involving simple money transfers as well as complicated contracts which can involve multiple entities. Both ECDSA and Schnorr digital signature schemes employed in these transactions are studied and analyzed for their usage, security, and enhancements they bring to the cryptosystem. The different types of transactions created in Bitcoin along with their locking and unlocking conditions are covered.

The mechanism of creating Taproot transactions and using Schnorr signature is also provided. This paper also shows the complex multi-signature contracts which can be created using Taproot and Schnorr. In the future, we look forward to implementing these complex contracts on the Bitcoin network.

# References

1. Andrychowicz, M., Dziembowski, S., Malinowski, D., Mazurek, L: Secure multiparty computations on bitcoin. Commun. ACM **59**(4), 76–84 (2016)
2. Aranha, D.F., Novaes, F.R., Takahashi, A., Tibouchi, M., Yarom, Y.: LadderLeak: breaking ECDSA with less than one bit of nonce leakage. In: Proceedings of the 2020 ACM SIGSAC Conference on Computer and Communications Security, pp. 225–242 (2020)
3. Bistarelli, S., Mercanti, I., Santini, F.: An analysis of non-standard bitcoin transactions. In: 2018 Crypto Valley Conference on Blockchain Technology (CVCBT), pp. 93–96. IEEE (2018)
4. Brown, D.: Standards for efficient cryptography, sec 1: elliptic curve cryptography. Released Standard Version 1 (2009)
5. Decker, C., Wattenhofer, R.: Bitcoin transaction malleability and MtGox. In: Kutyłowski, M., Vaidya, J. (eds.) ESORICS 2014. LNCS, vol. 8713, pp. 313–326. Springer, Cham (2014). https://doi.org/10.1007/978-3-319-11212-1_18
6. Delgado-Segura, S., Pérez-Solà, C., Navarro-Arribas, G., Herrera-Joancomartí, J.: Analysis of the bitcoin UTXO set. In: Zohar, A., et al. (eds.) FC 2018. LNCS, vol. 10958, pp. 78–91. Springer, Heidelberg (2019). https://doi.org/10.1007/978-3-662-58820-8_6
7. Drijvers, M., et al.: On the security of two-round multi-signatures. In: 2019 IEEE Symposium on Security and Privacy (SP), pp. 1084–1101. IEEE (2019)
8. Fleischhacker, N., Jager, T., Schröder, D.: On tight security proofs for Schnorr signatures. In: Sarkar, P., Iwata, T. (eds.) ASIACRYPT 2014. LNCS, vol. 8873, pp. 512–531. Springer, Heidelberg (2014). https://doi.org/10.1007/978-3-662-45611-8_27
9. Hankerson, D., Menezes, A.: Elliptic curve cryptography. In: Jajodia, S., Samarati, P., Yung, M. (eds.) Encyclopedia of Cryptography, Security and Privacy, pp. 1–2. Springer, Heidelberg (2021). https://doi.org/10.1007/978-3-642-27739-9_245-2
10. Hartmann, D., Kiltz, E.: Limits in the provable security of ECDSA signatures. Cryptology ePrint Archive (2023)
11. Lau, J.: BIP 114: Merkelized abstract syntax tree (2016). https://github.com/bitcoin/bips/blob/master/bip-0114.mediawiki
12. Lombrozo, E., Lau, J., Wuille, P.: BIP 141: segregated witness (2015). https://github.com/bitcoin/bips/blob/master/bip-0141.mediawiki
13. Maxwell, G., Poelstra, A., Seurin, Y., Wuille, P.: Simple Schnorr multi-signatures with applications to bitcoin. Des. Codes Crypt. **87**(9), 2139–2164 (2019)
14. McCorry, P., Möser, M., Shahandasti, S.F., Hao, F.: Towards bitcoin payment networks. In: Liu, J.K., Steinfeld, R. (eds.) ACISP 2016. LNCS, vol. 9722, pp. 57–76. Springer, Cham (2016). https://doi.org/10.1007/978-3-319-40253-6_4
15. Mitra, N.: Efficient encoding rules for ASN. 1-based protocols. AT&T Tech. J. **73**(3), 80–93 (1994)

16. Morita, H., Schuldt, J.C.N., Matsuda, T., Hanaoka, G., Iwata, T.: On the security of the Schnorr signature scheme and DSA against related-key attacks. In: Kwon, S., Yun, A. (eds.) ICISC 2015. LNCS, vol. 9558, pp. 20–35. Springer, Cham (2016). https://doi.org/10.1007/978-3-319-30840-1_2
17. Nick, J., Ruffing, T., Seurin, Y.: MuSig2: simple two-round Schnorr multi-signatures. In: Malkin, T., Peikert, C. (eds.) CRYPTO 2021. LNCS, vol. 12825, pp. 189–221. Springer, Cham (2021). https://doi.org/10.1007/978-3-030-84242-0_8
18. Pérez-Solà, C., Delgado-Segura, S., Herrera-Joancomartı, J., Navarro-Arribas, G.: Analysis of the SegWit adoption in bitcoin (2019). https://deic-web.uab.cat/guille/publications/papers/2018.recsi.segwit.pdf
19. Pieter, A.: Bip65: Op_checklocktimeverify (2014). https://github.com/bitcoin/bips/blob/master/bip-0065.mediawiki
20. Pornin, T.: Deterministic usage of the digital signature algorithm (DSA) and elliptic curve digital signature algorithm (ECDSA). Technical report (2013)
21. Raikwar, M., Gligoroski, D., Kralevska, K.: SoK of used cryptography in blockchain. IEEE Access **7**, 148550–148575 (2019)
22. Rowe, D., Breitner, J., Heninger, N.: The curious case of the half-half bitcoin ECDSA nonces. Cryptology ePrint Archive (2023)
23. Schnorr, C.P.: Efficient signature generation by smart cards. J. Cryptol. **4**, 161–174 (1991)
24. Thyagarajan, S.A., Malavolta, G., Moreno-Sanchez, P.: Universal atomic swaps: secure exchange of coins across all blockchains. In: 2022 IEEE Symposium on Security and Privacy (SP), pp. 1299–1316. IEEE (2022)
25. Ullah, S., Zheng, J., Din, N., Hussain, M.T., Ullah, F., Yousaf, M.: Elliptic curve cryptography; applications, challenges, recent advances, and future trends: a comprehensive survey. Comput. Sci. Rev. **47**, 100530 (2023)
26. Wuille, A.P., Nick, J., Towns, A.: BIP341: taproot: SegWit version 1 spending rules (2020). https://github.com/bitcoin/bips/blob/master/bip-0341.mediawiki
27. Wuille, Nick, J., Towns, A.: BIP342: validation of taproot scripts (2020). https://github.com/bitcoin/bips/blob/master/bip-0342.mediawiki
28. Wuille, P., Nick, J., Ruffing, T.: BIP 340: Schnorr signatures for sec256k1 (2020). https://github.com/bitcoin/bips/blob/master/bip-0340.mediawiki

# BCTPV-NIZK: Publicly-Verifiable Non-interactive Zero-Knowledge Proof System from Minimal Blockchain Assumptions

Nimish Mishra$^{(\boxtimes)}$ (iD) and S. K. Hafizul Islam (iD)

Department of Computer Science and Engineering, Indian Institute of Information Technology Kalyani, Kalyani 741235, West Bengal, India
neelam.nimish@gmail.com

**Abstract.** Non-interactive publicly-verifiable zero-knowledge proofs (PV-NIZKs) are essential to modern cryptography. However, historically, literature has used dependencies like the need for absolute trust in a third party or the existence of a truly random oracle to construct such proofs. Recently, the focus has shifted to exploiting the decentralized trust foundation of a generic Proof-of-Stake (PoS) blockchain to build such proofs. However, such proposals make unrealistic assumptions on the blockchain itself: static adversaries, assumptions on the future behavior of the players, and the existence of *first-time* miners in any given sequence of $n$ honestly mined blocks. While aiding good proofs, such assumptions undermine the practical adaption of such proof systems. This paper introduces a blockchain-based PV-NIZK (BCTPV-NIZK) system from standard blockchain assumptions. It assumes the existence of a publicly-verifiable, secret randomness generation scheme (widely studied in literature and requires no further assumptions on trust).

**Keywords:** Blockchain · Cryptography · Proof-of-Stake · Trust · Zero-knowledge proof

## 1 Introduction

Generally, publicly-verifiable zero-knowledge proof in a non-interactive setting (PV-NIZK) needs some intermediary that helps to establish to commonly shared string. The literature used heuristic assumptions (e.g., random oracle model) or a trusted third party to develop the Common Random String (CRS). However, very recently, Goyel and Goyel [9] merged the concepts of NIZK and blockchain, wherein the blockchain and its public-verifiability and immutability properties were used to establish a CRS. They made assumptions on the *future* behavior of both honest and adversarial parties in the blockchain. Blockchain is very dynamic, and assuming static adversaries is far-fetched. This shortcoming was discussed in [12] and [13], where Scafuro et al. [13] presented new construction of

© The Author(s), under exclusive license to Springer Nature Switzerland AG 2023
V. Muthukkumarasamy et al. (Eds.): ICISS 2023, LNCS 14424, pp. 380–395, 2023.
https://doi.org/10.1007/978-3-031-49099-6_23

a NIZK over a Proof-of-Stake (PoS) blockchain using components from existing literature and [12]. Scafuro et al. [13] offer the latest advancement in developing a NIZK over the blockchain. They do not shy away from restricting generalized assumptions on the blockchain. We formally treat these restrictions later and informally state them here. It is expected that out of any $n$ length of blocks in a blockchain, at least $\alpha$ are from honest parties. This is an informal statement of the standard chain quality assumption. Scafuro et al. restrict this assumption by assuming the existence of a blockchain wherein any sequence of $d$ blocks has at least $n$ blocks which first-time miners have mined, and the majority of those first-time miners are honest. We relax this restriction and propose a PV-NIZK over blockchain without amending the standard chain quality assumption.

## 1.1  Motivations

We start with the assumption that we have a generic PoS blockchain wherein we make no amendments to the standard chain quality and chain consistency properties. We assume an adaptive adversary and make no assumption on the *future* behavior of either the adversary or the honest player. Under these informal assumptions, we summarize our contributions. First, we give a general, informal idea regarding the constructions of PV-NIZK, why certain design decisions were made, and how we approached constructing the PV-NIZK over a generic PoS blockchain.

The way *zero-knowledge proofs (ZKP)* are treated in literature involves using a *simulator*. Suppose a polynomial-time verifier cannot distinguish proofs generated from an honest prover or a simulator. In that case, it is said the proof has leaked *no knowledge* of its origin, thereby branding it *zero-knowledge*. Another component used widely is *witness-indistinguishable proofs (WIP)*. In such proof, there exists a statement to be proved ($x \in \mathcal{L}$ where $\mathcal{L}$ is some language to which the statement belongs, and $w_1$, $w_2$ are *witnesses* that are, quite literally, *witness* to the truth of the statement $x$. Under a WIP, a verifier cannot discern whether $w_1$ or $w_2$ was used as the witness to create the proof.

Like [13], we follow the FLS paradigm (Feige - Lapidot - Shamir) [2,7]. FLS paradigm looks to convert a WIP to a ZKP by providing a *fake* witness to the black-box simulator such that the verifier cannot discern whether it interacted with the actual honest prover or the simulator. The key point that will be useful in analyzing and designing NIZKs over the blockchain is that *a polynomial-time prover does not access the simulator's witness*. Concretely, the FLS approach proves the OR of two statements: *either* $x \in \mathcal{L}$ *OR an intractable problem's solution is verifiably proved*. The *intractable problem* can only be proved with a fake witness available to the simulator and not to the prover. In the case of [13], this *intractable problem* was to predict the majority of honest blocks beforehand for the next $d$-blocks. In the case of [9], this *intractable problem* was to generate a *long* fork of the PoS blockchain. Informally, in our case, this *intractable problem* is to reliably predict the output of high-entropy pseudo-random generators and find collisions in secure hash functions.

A natural question at this point is to ask: what gives the simulator the witness to an *intractable problem*. The answer lies in [5]. The core idea is the simulator has *privileged* access to the blockchain, which it uses as a trapdoor theorem to generate a witness to the intractable problem in the proof. In Goyel ad Goyel [9], and Scafuro et al. [13], the simulator is allowed to control all honest parties of the blockchain, thereby knowing the information private to each honest player and using this knowledge to generate the proof. Evidently, any dishonest prover will not have access to the simulator's *fake witness* since the prover can't control *all* the honest parties in a generic PoS blockchain.

## 1.2   Contributions

Since we have all components discussed, we are discussing our contribution now. In [13], a special high-entropy string is attached to each block in the chain, and *pristine* blocks are defined as the blocks whose high-entropy string is unseen before in the chain. Since the simulator controlled all the honest parties, it could predict, in advance, the majority of *pristine* blocks added to the blockchain. The simulator extracted the high entropy string of most *pristine* blocks and generated the proof. Verification succeeded if (1) the commitments to predictions were published on the blockchain, (2) a majority of blocks in a given length of the chain after the publication of the predictions were *pristine*, and (3) the proof was honestly generated. A question in progression naturally arises: *Why the assumption that $\alpha \geq 0.5$ (wherein $\alpha$ is the fraction of honest blocks in a given length of the chain)?* For a generic PoS blockchain, we assume an adversary cannot control most of the nodes. In that scenario, if $\alpha$ is set to anything greater than or equal to 0.5, standard blockchain assumptions force the correctness of the proofs. However, suppose $\alpha$ was arbitrary. In that case, it may be possible that an adversary's control of the network (let's call it $\beta$) is such that $\beta > \alpha$, in which case, the adversary would be able to predict $> \alpha$ number of *pristine* blocks thereby fooling an honest verifier. Moreover, the restriction that every sequence of $d$ blocks must observe a sequence of $n$ *pristine* blocks out of which at least $\lceil \frac{n}{2} \rceil + 1$ blocks should be mined by first-time, honest miners is not valid in modern practical blockchains. This is because the number of miners in a network is limited, and by the given assumption in [13], a single miner can take part in generating a NIZK only *once*, thereby greatly limiting the flexibility as well as the number of proofs that can be generated in a given chain. We remove this amendment by requiring a one-time, publicly-verifiable, secret randomness. As long as the standard chain quality assumption holds (i.e., arbitrary $\alpha$ number of blocks in a given portion of the chain are honest), we reason that the problem of predicting *all* the secret randomness is intractable to an adversary and tractable to a simulator controlling all honest parties. A verifier verifies if *all* randomness is correctly predicted; if not, verification fails.

# 2  Background

The reason for separate $state_B$ and $state_P$ is that we assume a general execution of a blockchain wherein different parties will have different recent forks (or the tail of the local copies shall differ). Stability is achieved as time passes and the parties synchronize on the tail post, in which new blocks are added, thereby extending the tail and desynchronizing it once again. The cycle repeats itself. We list all the notations used in this study in Table 1.

**Table 1.** Notations used

| Notation | Meaning |
|---|---|
| $\lambda$ | Security parameter |
| $\mathcal{O}$ | Big-Oh notation |
| $state_B$ | General state of the ledger |
| $state_P$ | State of a party $P$ |
| $\mathcal{P}$ | Prover in the ZKP system |
| $\mathcal{V}$ | Verifier in the ZKP system |
| $\mathcal{P}_{pvWI}$ | Prover in the WIP system |
| $\mathcal{V}_{pvWI}$ | Verifier in the WIP system |
| **RA** | Randomness authority |
| $s$ | Transient secret of miner |
| $d$ | Number of blocks after which $s$ is made public |
| $n$ | Number of blocks to observe after posting commitments |
| $u$ | Scalar such that $u \times n$ is the number of commitments to make |
| $rand$ | Randomness generated by **RA** for each miner |
| $rand'$ | Randomness used as block identifier |

**Definition 1 (Negligible Function).** *A function $\epsilon(\lambda) : \mathbb{N} \to \mathbb{R}$ is said to be negligible if, for every integer $v > 0$, there exists an integer $u$ such that $\epsilon(k) \leq \frac{1}{\lambda^v}$ holds $\forall \lambda \geq u$*

## 2.1  Blockchain Protocols

We follow the same formalism of a blockchain as done in [9,12,13].

**Definition 2 (Validity Predicate).** *Validity predicate is defined as semantic check $\mathcal{V}(\mathbf{B})$ that outputs a binary decision $b \in \{0,1\}$, where $\mathbf{B}$ represents a sequence of blocks whose validity needs to be determined.*

Validity predicate as defined in Definition 2 is used to abstract semantics of the blockchain including, but not limited to, checking honest mining, preventing double-spending, dishonest behavior, and so on. A validity parameterizes a blockchain protocol predict $\mathcal{V}$ and consists of the following polynomial-time algorithms:

- **GetRecords**($state_B$, $1^\lambda$): Upon inputting the security parameter $\lambda$, and the state $state_B$ of the ledger **B** to this algorithm, it outputs the sequence of valid blocks in **B**.
- **GenerateBlock**($1^\lambda$, $x$, $state_P$, $state_B$): Upon inputting the transaction $x$, $state_P$ of the player $P$, and $state_B$ of **B** to this algorithm, it invokes **GetRecords**($state_B$, $\lambda$), and outputs a latest addition to **B** that satisfies the validity of $\mathcal{V}$.
- **Broadcast**($1^\lambda$, $m$): Input to this algorithm are $\lambda$, and a message $m$, it broadcasts $m$ to the network. This step is equivalent to synchronizing $state_{P'}$, for all players $P'$ in the network, with $state_P$ for player $P$ who generated a new block.
- **UpdateState**($1^\lambda$, $state_P$): Upon inputting $\lambda$, and $state_P$ of $P$, it updates $state_P$. This corresponds to listening to the broadcast for incoming messages and updating the local state accordingly.

**Definition 3 (Blockchain Compromise).** *We define compromising of the blockchain as the situation wherein an adversary $\mathcal{A}$ has generated a local state $state_\mathcal{A}$ that:*

- *violates $\mathcal{V}(\mathbf{B})$*
- *is able to influence $state_B$*

We now define standard tools used to evaluate security of a generic blockchain.

**Definition 4 (Chain Consistency).** *We define a chain consistency predicate $\mathcal{CC}(n)$ such that for any two distinct $state_P$ and $state_{P'}$ (where $P$ and $P'$ are honest parties), with overwhelming probability, the local copies of the ledger with $P$ and $P'$ differ in at most $n$ recent blocks at the tail of the blockchain.*

**Definition 5 (Chain Quality).** *We define a chain quality predicate $\mathcal{CQ}(n, \alpha)$ such that for every sequence of $n$ consecutive blocks in the blockchain **B** and for every $state_P$ (where $P$ is an honest player), at least $\alpha \times n$ blocks are mined by honest players with overwhelming probability.*

To relieve the restrictive assumption described in [13], we require an addition to the algorithm **GenerateBlock**($\cdot$). Concretely, we need an acquisition of a high-entropy publicly-verifiable short-lived random string to be appended to each block. This string is generated by the party running the algorithm **GenerateBlock**($\cdot$). Although we dwell on the details later, it is immediately clear how we relax the assumption on the chain quality suggested in [13]. As long as a minimal $\alpha$ fraction of blocks in a suitable chain of length, $n$ is honest, no adversary or dishonest prover can reliably guess random strings of $\alpha \times n$ blocks, thereby providing us with the trapdoor theorem to formulate the proposed PV-NIZK protocol. The details follow in later Sections. In the proposed construction, we assume a generic PoS blockchain wherein participants can execute arbitrary smart contracts, and the consensus protocol is both sound and correct.

## 2.2   Publicly-Verifiable Randomness

An essential ingredient in our construction is the notion of publicly-verifiable randomness that we borrow from [8]. Briefly, it's a blockchain-based randomness generator wherein the randomness generator authority (**RA**) is not required to be honest. We mold it to our requirements.

**Assumption 1.** *For every honest execution of* **GenerateBlock**$(\cdot)$, *we use a high-entropy, private random string as the block identifier, which is made publicly-verifiable post d blocks in the future after generation of the current block. In other words, every user intending to generate a block needs to repeat this procedure for every block they generate.*

Assumption 1 enforces the use of publicly-verifiable randomness in the block generation procedure and also provides a core component in our construction. Note that this assumption can be easily materialized through minor changes in how modern practical blockchains generate blocks: the miner appends this randomness to the block they have mined, and $d$ blocks later reveal the randomness such that it is publicly-verifiable. Considering $\ell \in \mathbb{N}$ and a publicly known post-quantum hash-function $H : \{0,1\}^* \rightarrow \{0,1\}^\ell$, the procedure is enumerated as follows for a miner $\mathcal{M}$:

- $\mathcal{M}$ chooses a secret $s \in \{0,1\}^k$ for $k > \ell$.
- $\mathcal{M}$ sends a *signed* request tuple $(\mathcal{M}_{ID}, \text{usage info}, H(s))$ to **RA**, where $\mathcal{M}_{ID}$ is the unique identifier identifying this user in the context of the blockchain, *usage info* is a commitment to a description of the usage of the randomness (for instance, appending to the newly generated block from **GenerateBlock**$(\cdot)$.
- **RA** posts the request on a public platform where anyone can verify the digital signature of $\mathcal{M}$ using its public key.
- **RA** submits a transaction $Tx = [\mathcal{M}_{ID}, H(\text{usage   info}), H(s)]$ to **B**.
- Suppose $b$ is the verified block where $Tx$ appears and $b'$ is the verified block following $b$. **RA** sends back to $m$ the following randomness: $rand = H(Tx \parallel H(b'))$.
- $\mathcal{M}$ uses the randomness $rand' = rand \oplus H(s \parallel \mathcal{M}_{id})$.
- $d$ blocks post **GenerateBlock**$(\cdot)$, $\mathcal{M}$ runs **Broadcast**$(1^\lambda, s)$ and becomes eligible to mine/generate another block in the future. Now everyone can use this $s$ to verify if $rand'$ and the block identifier of the block from **GenerateBlock**$(\cdot)$ are the same.

## 2.3   Publicly-Verifiable WIP (PV-WIP)

Another essential ingredient in our construction is the use of PV-WIP. We define $\Pi_{pvWI} = (\mathcal{P}_{pvWI}, \mathcal{V}_{pvWI})$ as the tuple of algorithms for the prover and the verifier exchanging a PV-WIP.

**Definition 6 (Witness).** *The proof for $x \in \mathcal{L}$ proceeds by finding a witness $w$ such that $(x, w) \in R$ for some relation $R$. We note:*

- $\| x \| \in \mathcal{O}(1^\lambda)$ and $\| w \| \in \mathcal{O}(1^\lambda)$
- *Given a published witness w, verification can be done in polynomial-time*
- $L = \{x \mid \exists w : (x, w) \in R\}$ *is a NP language*

**Definition 7 (PV-WIP).** *Given $\lambda$, a string $x \in \mathcal{L}$, and two witnesses $w_1$ and $w_2$ such that $(x, w_i) \in \mathcal{R}$ for $i \in \{1, 2\}$ as inputs, a PV-WIP is given over the execution of $\mathcal{P}_{pvWI}(x, \lambda, w_i)$ for $i \in \{1, 2\}$ such that a polynomial-time verifier $\mathcal{V}_{pvWI}$ is unable to computationally distinguish whether $w_1$ or $w_2$ was used in the proof.*

The $_{pvWI}$ proof system used as a component here is a *delayed input* system, which means the inputs $x$ and $w$ are used to compute the last message of the proof, directly implying that the all-except-last messages can be computed *offline* (before any knowledge of $x$ and $w$). Note how this property greatly reduces the amount of computation required to compute each proof. We rely on the $pvWI$ proofs discussed in [12] in our construction and thus directly inherit their properties, discussions, and formal proofs regarding the $pvWI$ component of our construction. The extra *assumption* because of this inheritance is: for any given sequence of $t$ consecutive blocks, there is at least a triple that is generated by honest execution of **GenerateBlock**($\cdot$). This is a natural extension of the chain quality assumption; the chain quality assumption with arbitrary $\alpha$ guarantees that $\alpha \times t$ number of blocks shall be from honest players; thus, this assumption is very valid for a careful value set for $t$. Another property of $pvWI$ construction from [12] (and corresponding proofs in [13]) is that the proof holds in the presence of blockchain failure.

## 2.4 NIZK System

The main goal of any zero-knowledge proof (ZK) system is to systematically prove that a string $x$ belongs to a language $\mathcal{L}$. In the case of a non-interactive zero-knowledge proof (NIZK) system, the prover, and verifier share a common random string (CRS). The probabilistic polynomial-time (PPT) prover publishes a proof for $x \in \mathcal{L}$, and the PPT verifier verifies its validity against the CRS. The existence of the CRS is what makes such proofs non-interactive. However, the process of establishing a CRS can be interactive or semi-interactive (which we support here). We now formalize our discussion.

**Definition 8 (ZK Argument).** *A zero-knowledge argument, on input security parameter $\lambda$, a string $x \in \mathcal{L}$, and a witness $w$ (refer Sect. 7 for details) to the prover such that*

- *The prover and verifier engage in an exchange that enables them to share a common random string $\sigma$.*
- *Using a witness indistinguishable argument of knowledge, the prover proves the knowledge of a witness $w$ such that $(x, w) \in \mathcal{R}$ (refer Definition 6 for $\mathcal{R}$) OR knowledge of a witness $w'$ such that $(\sigma, w') \in \mathcal{S}$, where $\mathcal{S} \in NP$ or higher complexity.*

The design of ZKP system as given in Definition 8 is such that if the verifier is honest, then $(\sigma, w') \notin \mathcal{S}$. If the verifier is dishonest, then the simulator shall be able to prove $(\sigma, w') \notin \mathcal{S}$. Any ZKP system exhibits two main properties: *completeness* and *soundness*. Informally, completeness implies the proof system can prove any true statement with overwhelming probability. Soundness implies that whatever the system proves is true (an untrue statement can't be proved with the proof system, with overwhelming probability). We demonstrate both of these properties for our proof system later.

## 3    Proposed BCTPV-NIZK System

In this section, we proposed a publicly-verifiable non-interactive zero-knowledge proof system from minimal blockchain assumptions (BCTPV-NIZK). We now present the proposed BCTPV-NIZK system $\Pi = (\mathcal{P}, \mathcal{V})$. Note that the assumption of the simulator controlling all the honest parties in the network does not extend to the simulator predicting which fork will remain in the blockchain when the chain stabilizes. Hence, the simulator can't provide tight predictions of the next $n$ blocks; the simulator thus provides predictions of the next $u \times n\,(u > 1)$ blocks, where $u$ is experimentally defined. The entire workflow is schematically depicted in Fig. 1.

- **Prover setup**
    - Compute $(commitment_i, decommitment_i) \leftarrow Com(0^\ell)$ for $i \in \{1, 2, \cdots, u \times n\}$ where $\ell$ is the length of $rand'$ as defined in Sect. 2.2.

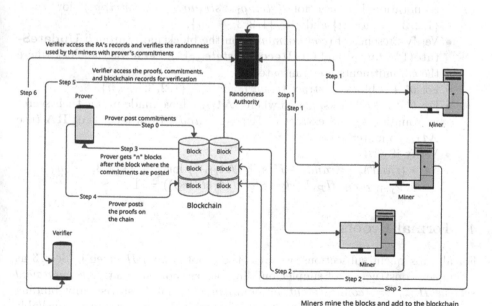

**Fig. 1.** Workflow of BCTPV-NIZK System.

- Delete all *decommitment* for $i \in \{1, 2, \cdots, u \times n\}$.
- Run $state_{\mathcal{P}} = \textbf{UpdateState}(1^\lambda, state_{\mathcal{P}})$ to get the latest state of the ledger.
- Run     $\textbf{Broadcast}(1^\lambda,$     $(commitment_1,$     $commitment_2,$     $\cdots,$ $commitment_{u \times n}))$ to update the network with the $u \times n$ commitments.
- Run $\textbf{GetRecords}(state_{\textbf{B}}, 1^\lambda)$ and receive $n$ additional blocks to the chain.

- **Prover procedure** $\mathcal{P}(x, w)$ *s.t.* $(x, w) \subset \mathcal{R}$
  - Let $rand_i' \in \{1, 2, \cdots, n\}$ be the publicly verifiable, secret randomness used in $\textbf{GenerateBlock}(\cdot)$ procedures to generate the $n$ blocks following publication of the commitments and let $\mathcal{M}_{ID_j}$ be the identity as defined in Sect. 2.2. Then input $x_\Pi$ to the prover procedure becomes $(x, (commitment_1, commitment_2, \cdots, commitment_{u \cdot n}), (rand_1', rand_2', \cdots, rand_n'), (\mathcal{M}_{ID_1}, \mathcal{M}_{ID_2}, \mathcal{M}_{ID_3}, \cdots, \mathcal{M}_{ID_n}))$
  - The $k$ messages of $\Pi$ are computed as follows:
    * $\pi_1 = \mathcal{P}_{pvWI}(1^\lambda, l)$
    * $\pi_2 = \mathcal{P}_{pvWI}(\pi_1)$
    * $\pi_3 = \mathcal{P}_{pvWI}(\pi_2)$

    $\vdots$

    * $\pi_k = \mathcal{P}_{pvWI}(\pi_{k-1}, x_\Pi, w)$
  - Output the proof $\Pi_{\mathcal{P}} = \{(\pi_1, \pi_2, \pi_3, \cdots, \pi_k), x_\Pi\}$
- **Verifier procedure** $\mathcal{V}(\Pi_{\mathcal{P}})$
  - Parse $\Pi_{\mathcal{P}}$ as $(\pi_1, \pi_2, \pi_3, \cdots, \pi_k)$ and $x_\Pi$.
  - Parse $x_\Pi$ as $(x, (commitment)_i, (rand')_j, (\mathcal{M}_{ID})_j)$ where $(string)_{i/j}$ is notational abuse for $(string_1, string_2, \cdots, string_j)$ for $i \in \{1, 2, 3, \cdots, u \times n\}$ and $j \in \{1, 2, 3, \cdots, n\}$.
  - Verify presence of $(commitment)_i$ on the blockchain through $\textbf{UpdateState}(1^\lambda, state_{\mathcal{V}})$ and $\textbf{GetRecords}(state_{\textbf{B}}, 1^\lambda)$. Let $b^*$ be the block where the commitments are transacted.
  - For $b^* + n$ blocks, extract $(rand')_j$ for $j \in \{1, 2, 3, \cdots, n\}$.
  - For $b^* + n + d$ blocks, match where $(\mathcal{M}_{ID})_j$ have made public their secret information $s_j$ and extract it. Extract $(rand)_j$ from records of $\textbf{RA}$ (use $\mathcal{M}_{ID}$ to match records).
  - Verify if
    * * $(rand')_j = rand_j \oplus H(s_j \parallel (\mathcal{M}_{ID})_j)$ for $j \in \{1, 2, 3, \cdots, n\}$
    * * $\mathcal{V}_{pvWI}(x_\Pi, \Pi_{\mathcal{P}}, UpdateState(1^\lambda, state_{\mathcal{V}})) = 1$

## 4   Formal Proofs

For all subsequent subsections, we treat the proof system $\Pi$ given in Sect. 3 as a complex construction of simpler building blocks: non-interactive *commitment scheme* $\Pi_{com} = (commitment, decommitment)$ that is statistically binding and a non-interactive, delayed input publicly verifiable witness indistinguishable proof system $\Pi_{pvWI}$.

## 4.1    Completeness

**Theorem 1 (Completeness).** *The BCTPV-NIZK system $\Pi$ from minimal blockchain assumptions described in Sect. 3 is complete.*

*Proof.* Completeness of $\Pi$ follows directly from the completeness of $\Pi_{com}$ and the completeness of $\Pi_{pvWI}$. We defer the proof of the latter to [13].

## 4.2    Soundness

**Theorem 2 (Soundness).** *The BCTPV-NIZK system $\Pi$ from minimal blockchain assumptions is sound, i.e., the bound on the probability of an adversary fooling a verifier is bounded by a negligible function.*

*Proof.* Assume an adversary $\mathcal{A}$ can prove an false statement. Then the challenger $\mathcal{C}$ inherits a subset of the simulator's powers: mainly $\mathcal{C}$ has access to all $rand'$ of all the parties in the ledger. We define a game between $\mathcal{A}$ and $\mathcal{C}$ as follows:

- $\mathcal{C}$ stores all $rand'$ of the players in **B**.
- $\mathcal{C}$ maintains a set of $k \cdot l$ private coins, where $l$ is the length of $rand'$, and $k$ is the maximum number of queries submitted to $\mathcal{C}$, and $\mathcal{A}$ have agreed upon before playing the game. Note that $k$ is polynomially related to $u$.
- For each request made by $\mathcal{A}$, $\mathcal{C}$ tosses $l$ coins and returns the bit-string generated
- After $\mathcal{A}$ has made at most $k$ requests to $\mathcal{C}$, $\mathcal{A}$ outputs it's guess of the $n$ number of randomness $rand'$, say $(rand'_{\mathcal{A}})_1, (rand'_{\mathcal{A}})_2, \cdots, (rand'_{\mathcal{A}})_n$.

Recall from our discussion in Sect. 1.1, the general structure of the proof is *either $x \in \mathcal{L}$ OR the solution of an intractable problem is verifiably proved.* Since the objective of $\mathcal{A}$ is to fool a verifier into accepting a proof for $x \notin \mathcal{L}$, the only choice $\mathcal{A}$ has is to prove the latter part of the statement. Recall again from Sect. 1.1 that the *intractable problem* in our case was to predict the output of high-entropy pseudo-random generators (concretely, predict the values of secret $rand'$ used *even* before the blocks are added to the blockchain and the secret is made public according to the procedure described in Sect. 2.2).

$\mathcal{A}$ wins the game **iff** $\mathcal{A}$ correctly predicts $rand'$ for the next $n$ blocks following the block where the commitments are posted. Recall that $\Pi_{com}$ is a perfectly binding commitment scheme, implying the commitments map back to just the original message; this implies once the commitments are posted, the scheme prohibits any induced confusion about the original message used to create those commitments. Therefore, $\mathcal{A}$ has no choice but to tightly predict *all* $u \times d$ commitments that an honest prover would have generated.

From the standard chain quality assumption, $\alpha \times u \times d$ blocks in a consecutive sequence of $u \times d$ blocks are from honest execution of **GenerateBlock**$(\cdot)$. $\mathcal{A}$ has no choice but to predict tightly $\alpha \times u \times d$ high-entropy pseudo-random strings. From the game described above, $\mathcal{A}$ receives the *correct* value of one $rand'$ among $\alpha \times u \times d$ high-entropy pseudo-random strings with probability $\frac{1}{2^l}$. Since all $rand'$

are mutually independent, the probability of $\mathcal{A}$ winning the game is $(\frac{1}{2^\ell})^{\alpha \times u \times d}$. It is straightforward to see how this is bounded by some negligible function $\epsilon$. Moreover, as shown in [13], this negligible probability directly contradicts the soundness property of $\Pi_{pvWI}$ defined in [13] (which is also used verbatim in our construction) thereby contradicting the assumption that $\mathcal{A}$ is successful.

### 4.3   Zero Knowledge

**Theorem 3 (Zero knowledge).** *The delayed input BCTPV-NIZK system $\Pi$ is zero-knowledge assuming:*

- *validity of chain consistency and chain quality predicates,*
- *$\Pi_{com}$ is statistically binding,*
- *$\Pi_{pvWI}$ is delayed input witness indistinguishable proof that is complete and sound, and*
- *Assumption 1 holds.*

*Proof.* We introduce three entities: verifier $\mathcal{V}$, simulator $\mathcal{S}$, and prover $\mathcal{P}$. We define the view of $\mathcal{V}$ as follows:

**Definition 9 ($V_{\mathcal{V}}^t(\mathcal{X})$).** $V_{\mathcal{V}}^t$ *is defined as the view of $\mathcal{V}$ at any given instant $t$. $V_{\mathcal{V}}^t$ comprises of:*

- *$state_B$,*
- *$state_{\mathcal{V}} = UpdateState(1^\lambda, state_{\mathcal{V}})$, and*
- *$\Pi_{\mathcal{X}}$, where $\mathcal{X}$ is the party that created the proof, i.e. $\mathcal{X} \in \{\mathcal{P}, \mathcal{S}\}$.*

The proof system $\Pi$ can be said to be *zero-knowledge* **iff** the *view* of $\mathcal{V}$ is statistically indistinguishable for either value of $\mathcal{X}$. For notational convenience, let $V_{\mathcal{V}}^t(\mathcal{X}) = 1$ imply that $\mathcal{X}$ has indeed generated the proof $\Pi_{\mathcal{X}}$. Concretely, the following relations holds:

$$\Pr[(\mathcal{V}_{pvWI}(x_\Pi, \Pi_{\mathcal{P}}, UpdateState(1^\lambda, state_{\mathcal{V}})) = 1, \textbf{and}, V_{\mathcal{P}}^t = 1) -$$

$$\mathcal{V}_{pvWI}(x_\Pi, \Pi_{\mathcal{S}}, UpdateState(1^\lambda, state_{\mathcal{V}})) = 1, \textbf{and}, V_{\mathcal{S}}^t = 1)] \leq \epsilon(k)$$

where $\epsilon(k)$ is some negligible function and $\Pr$ denotes probability. Informally, we mean that if a verifier $\mathcal{V}$ cannot distinguish *who* generated the proof with non-negligible probability, the proof system is zero-knowledge. To show this is indeed true, we first note the steps $\mathcal{S}$ follows that is different from $\mathcal{P}$ and then reason how the two distributions are statistically indistinguishable. $\mathcal{S}$ follows the following steps to generate the proofs:

- **Simulator setup**
  - For all $i = \{1, 2, \cdots, n\}$, $\mathcal{S}$ samples secret $s_i$ and the identity $m_{ID_i}$ of the miner $\mathcal{M}$ uniformly at random from $\{0,1\}^*$
  - Compute $(commitment_i, decommitment_i) \leftarrow Com(0^\ell)$ for $i \in \{1, 2, \cdots, u \times n\}$, where $\ell$ is the length of $rand'$ as defined in Sect. 2.2
  - Delete all $decommitment$ for $i \in \{1, 2, \cdots, u \times n\}$

- Get the latest state of the ledger $state_{\mathcal{P}} = \textbf{UpdateState}(1^{\lambda}, state_{\mathcal{P}})$
- Update the network with the $u \times n$ commitments $\textbf{Broadcast}(1^{\lambda},$ $(commitment_1, commitment_2, \cdots, commitment_{un}))$
- Get $n$ additional blocks of the chain $\textbf{GetRecords}(state_{\text{B}}, 1^{\lambda})$
- **Simulator prover procedure** $\mathcal{P}(x, w)$, s.t. $(x, w) \in \mathcal{R}$
  - Let $rand'_i \in \{1, 2, \cdots, n\}$ be the randomness computed by $\mathcal{S}$ using $s_i$ sampled earlier and $rand_i$ received from **RA** as usual. $\mathcal{S}$ runs $\textbf{GenerateBlock}(\cdot)$ on the behalf of each honest player in the network using corresponding values of $rand'$s computed. Then input $x_\Pi$ to the prover procedure becomes $(x, (commitment_1, commitment_2, \cdots, commitment_{un}), (rand'_1, rand'_2, \cdots, rand'_n), (\mathcal{M}_{ID_1}, \mathcal{M}_{ID_2}, \mathcal{M}_{ID_3}, \cdots, \mathcal{M}_{ID_n}))$
  - The $k$ messages of $\Pi$ are computed as follows:
    * $\pi_1 = \mathcal{P}_{pvWI}(1^{\lambda}, \ell)$
    * $\pi_2 = \mathcal{P}_{pvWI}(\pi_1)$
    * $\pi_3 = \mathcal{P}_{pvWI}(\pi_2)$
    
    $\vdots$
    
    * $\pi_k = \mathcal{P}_{pvWI}(\pi_{k-1}, x_\Pi, w)$
  - Output the proof $\Pi_{\mathcal{S}} = \{(\pi_1, \pi_2, \pi_3, \cdots, \pi_k), x_\Pi\}$

Informally, the difference between $\mathcal{S}$ and $\mathcal{P}$ lies in the way $rand'$s are generated. $\mathcal{S}$ has access to $rand'$ of all honest parties and thus has the witness to the second part of the FLS (Feige - Lapidot - Shamir) [2]- [7]: *either $x \in \mathcal{L}$ OR the solution of an intractable problem is verifiably proved* where the *intractable problem* in our case was to predict the output of a high-entropy pseudo-random generator and find collisions in collision-resistant hash functions.

How? Ideally, the *intractable problem* in our case is to know a witness to knowledge of all $rand'$ in the upcoming $n$ blocks after publication of the commitments. Through $rand' = rand \oplus H(s \parallel \mathcal{M}_{ID})$, there are two ways to know $rand'$, either

- Predict $rand'$ directly, which means predict the output of a high-entropy pseudo-random generator, **OR**
- With $rand$ being public information, find collisions in the collision-resistant hash function $H(\cdot)$ such that $\mathcal{A}$ knows $s'$ for which the following holds for each $i \in \{1, 2, \cdots, n\}$:

$$rand'_i = rand_i \oplus H(s'_i)$$
$$= rand_i \oplus H(s_i \parallel (\mathcal{M}_{ID})_i)$$

Since both these paths have been shown to be computationally hard and are common knowledge (based on the choice of the hash function and the randomness generator), the hardness argument is valid. Moreover, there is no statistical difference between $\mathcal{S}$'s and $\mathcal{P}$'s generation of $rand'$ since both use **RA**'s aid to generate $rand$ and use same distribution to generate $s_i$. We thus have that there is no statistical difference in the way $\mathcal{S}$ and $\mathcal{P}$ generate $\Pi_{\mathcal{S}}$ and $\Pi_{\mathcal{P}}$ respectively, which directly implies the indistinguishability of these two from $V_{\mathcal{X}}^t$ for $\mathcal{X} \in \{\mathcal{P}, \mathcal{S}\}$.

## 5　A Note on Blockchain Collapse

Since we assumed an adaptive adversary that can corrupt anyone anytime, some adjustments need to be made. However, since the corruption portion of the proof system is similar to the one elaborated in [13], namely, removing the *decommitment information* to keep the *view* of the adversary same in case of *corrupted* and *non-corrupted* simulator/prover. The idea is that *after* the proof has been published, the *decommitment* information is no longer available with the player who generated the proof. This directly implies that even if the adversary, in the future, corrupts the player, the *commitments* can not be *decommited*. This is the core idea of *secure erasure* mentioned in [13], which we avoid going into detail here for brevity.

## 6　Experiments

We used NoKnow protocol [1] as the core of the sigma protocol. NoKnow protocol is based on [4], and [10] as $\Pi_{com}$. However, since both sigma protocols and $\Pi_{com}$ used are external modules to our construction and not internal design, one could easily replace these with any other construction, and they would also work. We experimented with Rinkeby, Ethereum's test network for blockchain. Our results are briefed in Table 2. We parameterized $n = 20$, $u = 5$, and $d = 10$. All experiments were run on MacBook Air running macOS High Sierra v10.13.6 with 1.8 GHz Intel Core i5 processor, 8 GB 1600 MHz DDR3 memory, and Intel HD Graphics 6000 1536 MB graphics.

**Table 2.** Experimental results

| Operation | Projected time | Execution time (second) |
|---|---|---|
| Ethereum mining (1 block) | $T_B$ | 14.57 |
| Block retrieval | $T_R$ | 2 |
| Commitment generation (10 KB) | $(\Pi_{com})_{com}$ | 5.247635841369629 |
| Commitment verification (10 KB) | $(\Pi_{com})_{ver}$ | 6.466604709625244 |
| Prover setup | $(\Pi_{com})_{com} + (\Pi_{com})_{ver} + T_B + nT_R$ | 70.34 |
| Prover procedure | $2\tau(\Pi_{com})_{com} + 2T_B + dT_R + \mathcal{O}(1)$ | 1307.60 |
| Verifier procedure | $(n+d)T_R + \mathcal{O}(1) + (\Pi_{com})_{ver}$ | 776.79 |

In Table 2, $T_B$ denotes the average time elapsed between submitting a transaction and it appearing on the blockchain. $T_R$ is the time to retrieve a block from the blockchain, assuming that the block already exists. In the prover procedure, we set $\tau = \frac{10!}{3!(10-3)!}$. $\mathcal{O}(1)$ denotes the upper bound on the cumulation of constant-time operations like parsing, hashing, string concatenation, and so on, for which we do separately denote projected time. In Table 3, a sample *Rinkeby* block is tabulated to illustrate the information posted in each transaction.

**Table 3.** This is a sample *Rinkeby* transaction added to the chain.

| Key | Value |
|---|---|
| Transaction Hash | 0x9c77ee08356b526671af6e846ab80fb2dd$\cdots$ |
| | 6a79e3e00d0bc270a36071b07aee6a |
| Status | Success |
| Block | 9198392 |
| Timestamp | 1 min ago (Aug-29-2021 06:18:05 AM +UTC) |
| From | 0xa500b2427458d12ef70dd7b1e031ef99d1cc09f7 |
| To | Contract 0xc0fa6c4377cea5bde5bdc57cac9f8380d2d97f7a |
| Value | 0.01 Ether ($ 0.00) |
| Transaction fee | 0.810559 Ether |
| Gas Price | 0.000000001 Ether (1 Gwei) |
| Gas Limit | 21,000 |
| Gas Used by Transaction | 21,000 (100%) |
| Base Fee per gas | 8 wei (0.000000008 Gwei) |
| Burnt fees | 0.000000000000168 Ether |
| Nonce | 49703 |
| Input Data | 0x (message call or contract creation) |

# 7  Conclusion

Practical BCTPV-NIZK systems are becoming increasingly crucial as use-cases arise wherein the prover-verifier interaction is not feasible. It becomes essential thus to make advances in this field. However, due to stringent constraints on NIKZ, like the existence of a true random oracle or trusted third party, the research community has moved to consider decentralized sources of trust: blockchains. The community is advancing to improve the security of such constructions while reducing the extra assumptions on generic blockchains. This work *loosens* such stringent assumptions like requiring a certain number of *new* miners in every sub-chain of a certain length, requiring static adversaries, or requiring fixed behavior from blockchain players in the foreseeable future. We provide a delayed-input, BCTPB-NIZK system that uses the concept of publicly verifiable, secret randomness as block identifiers. By also tying the source of this publicly verifiable randomness to blockchain, we also prevent the scope of any direct attack onto this randomness, thereby guaranteeing its security, and transitively, the security of our NIZK system. We provide proofs of various desirable properties from the proof systems and experimentally validate the same.

Future works can add to this idea and develop homomorphic proof systems that combine proof from two sources and generate a piece of combined evidence. Doing so in the setting we used in this paper is still an open problem.

Finally, we conclude by highlighting practical use-cases of NIZK, where works like ours can pave way to better privacy-preserving constructions. For instance, NIZKs have been used to develop privacy-preserving authentication schemes in the context of Internet of Things [6,11], wherein user identity is not revealed. Likewise, NIZKs have also been used for digital signatures as well [3]. In such use cases, by extending NIZKs to PoS blockchains, the use case also leverages the security guarantees of a blockchain.

# References

1. Archer, A.: noknow PyPI. https://pypi.org/project/noknow/. Accessed 20 Aug 2021
2. Barak, B.: How to go beyond the black-box simulation barrier. In: Proceedings 42nd IEEE Symposium on Foundations of Computer Science, pp. 106–115. IEEE (2001)
3. Bellare, M., Goldwasser, S.: New paradigms for digital signatures and message authentication based on non-interactive zero knowledge proofs. In: Brassard, G. (ed.) CRYPTO 1989. LNCS, vol. 435, pp. 194–211. Springer, New York (1990). https://doi.org/10.1007/0-387-34805-0_19
4. Chatzigiannakis, I., Pyrgelis, A., Spirakis, P.G., Stamatiou, Y.C.: Elliptic curve based zero knowledge proofs and their applicability on resource constrained devices. In: 2011 IEEE Eighth International Conference on Mobile Ad-Hoc and Sensor Systems, pp. 715–720. IEEE (2011)
5. Choudhuri, A.R., Goyal, V., Jain, A.: Founding secure computation on blockchains. In: Ishai, Y., Rijmen, V. (eds.) EUROCRYPT 2019. LNCS, vol. 11477, pp. 351–380. Springer, Cham (2019). https://doi.org/10.1007/978-3-030-17656-3_13
6. Dwivedi, A.D., Singh, R., Ghosh, U., Mukkamala, R.R., Tolba, A., Said, O.: Privacy preserving authentication system based on non-interactive zero knowledge proof suitable for internet of things. J. Ambient Intell. Humaniz. Comput. 1–11 (2021)
7. Feige, U., Lapidot, D., Shamir, A.: Multiple non-interactive zero knowledge proofs based on a single random string. In: Proceedings [1990] 31st Annual Symposium on Foundations of Computer Science, pp. 308–317. IEEE (1990)
8. Goldwasser, S., Klein, S., Mossel, E., Tamuz, O.: Publicly verifiable randomness (2018)
9. Goyal, R., Goyal, V.: Overcoming cryptographic impossibility results using blockchains. In: Kalai, Y., Reyzin, L. (eds.) TCC 2017. LNCS, vol. 10677, pp. 529–561. Springer, Cham (2017). https://doi.org/10.1007/978-3-319-70500-2_18
10. Kelkboom, E.J., Breebaart, J., Kevenaar, T.A., Buhan, I., Veldhuis, R.N.: Preventing the decodability attack based cross-matching in a fuzzy commitment scheme. IEEE Trans. Inf. Forensics Secur. 6(1), 107–121 (2010)

11. Martín-Fernández, F., Caballero-Gil, P., Caballero-Gil, C.: Authentication based on non-interactive zero-knowledge proofs for the internet of things. Sensors **16**(1), 75 (2016)
12. Scafuro, A., Siniscalchi, L., Visconti, I.: Publicly verifiable proofs from blockchains. In: Lin, D., Sako, K. (eds.) PKC 2019. LNCS, vol. 11442, pp. 374–401. Springer, Cham (2019). https://doi.org/10.1007/978-3-030-17253-4_13
13. Scafuro, A., Siniscalchi, L., Visconti, I.: Publicly verifiable zero knowledge from (collapsing) blockchains. IACR Cryptology ePrint Archive 2020/1435 (2020)

# Proof-of-Variable-Authority: A Blockchain Consensus Mechanism for Securing IoT Networks

Lenoah Chacko, Pavithra Rajan$^{(\boxtimes)}$, Varun Anilkumar, and Vinod Pathari

National Institute of Technology, Calicut, Kozhikode 673601, India
lenoahchacko@gmail.com, pavithra.rajan01@gmail.com,
varunca2001@gmail.com, pathari@nitc.ac.in

**Abstract.** In today's world, Internet of Things (IoT) has become an integral part of our daily lives. As IoT networks continue to gain importance, the need for efficient network management mechanisms becomes crucial. Currently, the prevalent approach involves utilizing a centralized server as the core management device, along with interfaces provided by major corporations. In this paper, we explore blockchain technology for IoT network management, aiming to empower individuals to retain control over their data and eliminate the risks associated with a single point of failure. However, implementing a consensus mechanism for IoT devices in distributed systems is challenging due to the high computational demands of existing options. This poses a significant challenge in securing IoT networks, especially when most devices are low-powered. To overcome this challenge, we propose modification to the Proof-of-Authority (PoA) consensus mechanism by introducing a decentralized approach to the original solution.

**Keywords:** Blockchain · Internet of Things · Consensus Mechanism

## 1 Introduction

The emergence of IoT devices has led to the creation of interconnected networks, revolutionizing various domains such as education, health care, economy and many more. By sharing information with each other, IoT systems are capable of performing numerous tasks, highlighting its importance in our society. However, this exponential growth of IoT devices has led to significant communication challenges amongst the vast array of inter-connected devices. Consequently, the need for a robust dynamic identity management solution has become important [2].

Effective IoT device management is essential to ensure the reliability, security, and performance of IoT networks. It enables organizations to ensure that devices are properly configured, patched, and updated to prevent security vulnerabilities. It can also help organizations to scale their IoT networks more efficiently. Additionally, verifying the authenticity of device state changes initiated by IoT devices is essential for maintaining the integrity and reliability of IoT networks, as any unauthorized modifications or transaction errors could result in significant financial and operational risks [2].

This paper aims to provide a comprehensive overview of our approach to secure IoT networks using blockchain. Section 2 describes the motivation for our work, highlighting the challenges and needs in this domain. Section 3 provides a detailed background of the existing literature, focusing on current modes of securing IoT systems. Section 4 presents the design of our proposed system, including its architecture, components, process flow and functionalities. Section 5 explores the potential scenarios within an IoT network and outlines the expected outcomes with our proposed work, assessing theoretical applicability and resilience. Section 6 describes how our proposed design has been implemented. Finally, in Sect. 7, we analyse the performance of the proposed work in contrast to existing ones and detail the factors to be considered while scaling.

## 2  Motivation

At present, numerous instances exist where centralized IoT device management platforms are deployed. The introduction of smart city infrastructure paved the way for significant advancements in citizen services, guaranteeing modern amenities for safety and efficient coordination of events [1]. In such an infrastructure, a centralized platform can manage devices such as traffic sensors, streetlights, and waste management systems. The platform can monitor the devices' performances and detect issues, such as a malfunctioning traffic sensor or a filled waste bin. This information can be used to schedule maintenance and repairs, reducing downtime and improving the system's overall efficiency. Furthermore, the platform can provide remote access to the devices, enabling administrators to control the devices' settings and configurations from a single interface, such as adjusting the brightness of streetlights, changing traffic signal timings, or altering waste collection schedules.

However, the utilization of such centralized servers raises conventional security issues. Some of the potential risks include [1]:

- **Single Point of Failure:** In a centralized network, all the data is stored on a central server, making it vulnerable to a single point of failure. Any breach in the server can compromise the entire network.
- **Message Forgery and Tampering:** The central entity that manages data is susceptible to being compromised by an attacker. Passive monitoring of the network communication enable malicious actors to tamper with or forge messages and re-transmit them.
- **Access Control:** A smart city is monitored by numerous IoT devices. Maintaining individual privacy and security becomes challenging when dealing with publicly used IoT devices. Furthermore, in a smart city, it is extremely challenging to manage access for different users, especially when dealing with diverse needs and multiple services.

To mitigate these risks, it is essential that applications of IoT device management systems, for instance, smart city systems, are designed with privacy and security in mind. The following section discusses the design of one such centralized platform for IoT device management and outlines methods to mitigate the risks mentioned earlier. This section also focuses on different consensus mechanisms for distributed systems.

# 3  Background

The introduction of the **IoT Central Hub Project** [11] proved to be pathbreaking for home automation. Though there were similar centralized device management platforms in existence earlier, this project solved the issues of high installation requirements and usability complexity. This yielded more flexibility to home users. As a primary requirement, this prototype mandated an initial connection and authentication of data to be performed by a local network. Wireless technology connectivity facilitated the identification of these devices. Once the devices were paired, communication was carried out by parameters sent from one gateway to another. The application served as the server and permitted users to change or modify the functionality of applications. All the data flowed through the central hub, allowing it to record it for the purpose of surveillance [11].

By adopting standard protocols for structuring data models, the IoT Central Hub Project enabled seamless integration and extensibility with various systems. Its notable achievement was in simplifying the configuration processes and eliminating the necessity for technical specialists to operate it effectively. Furthermore, the installation of the platform was straightforward and direct, without extraneous configuration steps. This offered home users the convenience of installing the application seamlessly. Ultimately, the development focus of this prototype was to ensure full functionality and ease of testing. However, this opened up a few security concerns. Having a single point of failure allowed an unauthorized actor to potentially tamper with the recorded data. Additionally, rogue devices could be connected to the network, and their prevention solely depended on the security conventions of the network. In addition to this, the ability of users to make changes to functionalities without adequate validation was a concern.

The advent of blockchain technologies has provided a method to enhance data-sharing while preserving trust. Blockchain preserves data trustworthiness through its principles and mechanisms that is inherent to its design. Each block in a blockchain is a cryptographic hash of the previous block. It is impossible to alter a block's content without changing the subsequent blocks. The immutability of blockchain ensures that once data is recorded, it cannot be tampered with [9].

The flaws mentioned in the previous section for centralized IoT device management platforms can be solved by incorporating the immutable, auditable, transparent features of blockchain.

- **Immutable and Tamper-proof Ledger:** In a blockchain-based IoT network, all the devices are registered and verified on the network. The registration process ensures that only authorized devices can participate in the network. When a device sends data to the network, the transaction is verified and recorded on the blockchain. This ensures that the data shared on the network is authentic and trustworthy. Moreover, as the blockchain is an immutable and tamper-proof ledger, it becomes impossible for any rogue device to modify the data without being detected [9].

- **No Central Point of Failure:** The decentralized nature of blockchain ensures that there is no central point of failure. All the devices in the network store a copy of the blockchain, making it almost impossible for any hacker to compromise the entire network [9].

- **Transparent Access Control:** In a blockchain-based IoT network, no single company or device has complete control over the network, making it fair for all the devices in the network. This is because blockchain technology ensures that all devices have equal access to the network's resources, and the information on the network is transparent to everyone. This is vital in IoT networks like Smart Cities for safeguarding individual privacy and security. In Smart Cities, a multitude of IoT devices are distributed in public areas. Efficient access control measures deter unauthorized users from tampering with these devices, ensuring their proper functioning and reducing the potential for misuse or harm. Given the interconnected nature of Smart Cities, effective access control becomes imperative to safeguard critical infrastructures like power grids, transportation systems, and healthcare facilities.

Additionally, the use of a Certificate Authority (CA) ensures the integrity of the devices that can communicate in the IoT network [4].

When dealing with an IoT system where there may be network failures and latency issues, we must have an algorithm which takes these problems into account when reaching a consensus in the blockchain. In [7], the Byzantine Generals Problem is introduced, which demonstrates how reaching a consensus is difficult in a distributed system. Algorithms that are able to address this problem, with some assumptions and constraints, are known as Byzantine Fault Tolerant (BFT) algorithms.

Among the BFT algorithms, **Proof-of-Work (PoW)** is the most used algorithm in blockchain with proven reliability. However, PoW algorithms have faced immense criticism as they consume a lot of power [15]. Considering that we have devices which could be power constrained, we have to be conservative about using its resources. Hence, PoW is a poor match for an IoT system.

**Proof-of-Authority (PoA)** is an algorithm that is energy efficient and resistant to Sybil attacks [12,14]. Sybil attacks involve creating multiple fake identities to control or manipulate a network, which can be used maliciously. However, critics point out that PoA is not a truly decentralized algorithm. This is because everyone is aware of the identities of the Deciding Agents (DA). This makes it vulnerable to third-party manipulation. Additionally, these DAs are pre-defined. Hence, it is a form of decentralized delegated centralization [8]. The next section discusses how the PoA algorithm can be modified to be more decentralized, making it more suitable for an IoT system, which is the crux of our work.

## 4  Design

We begin the design with a few assumptions regarding the system. First, we define the entities in this system:

- **Device:** This can be any IoT device that seeks to be part of the network containing the verified IoT devices. We are assuming that these devices can generate their own private-key public-key pair.
- **Node:** This is a logical entity which is an IoT device that has been verified and added to the network. Each node possesses an identifier called "Digital Profile".
- **Digital Profile:** This is a unique global identifier used to issue device certificates. To generate the Digital Profile, a minimal set of its attributes is concatenated and hashed using Keccak hashing function to yield a 160-bit Digital Profile ID. The minimal set of attributes contains the device serial number, manufacturer name, MAC address and product name [10].
- **Certificate Authority (CA):** CA is a trusted entity that issues certificates to devices to confirm their validity. Devices are valid only if they possess a certificate from the valid root CA.
- **Blockchain:** Blockchain is a shared, immutable ledger that facilitates the process of recording state changes and nodes in a network. From here on, the term blockchain refers to a private blockchain.
- **Smart Contracts:** These are programs that are executed when specific conditions are met. These are usually used to automate the implementation of an agreement. Smart Contracts are stored on a blockchain.

We primarily use two methods to keep rogue devices out of our information channels.

- A digital certificate issued by the CA is used to prove that a device is from the chain of trust.
- The private key of the device can be used to sign the Digital Profile so that the nodes on the network can verify whether the device broadcasting the state is a rogue device or not.

While certificates are distributed in a centralized fashion, their verification is done in a distributed way to prevent single-point attacks. The addition of devices to the network and the recording of state changes are decentralized.

There are two main types of transactions that we discuss in this paper:

- Registration of a device in the network
- Broadcasting a sender's state to other listeners on the network

The sender, a device in the network, has a message it wants to share with the other devices on the network. This message can be a state change. The listener refers to all the devices listening for a state change in the network. Figure 1 depicts the architecture diagram of the various components of our proposed design.

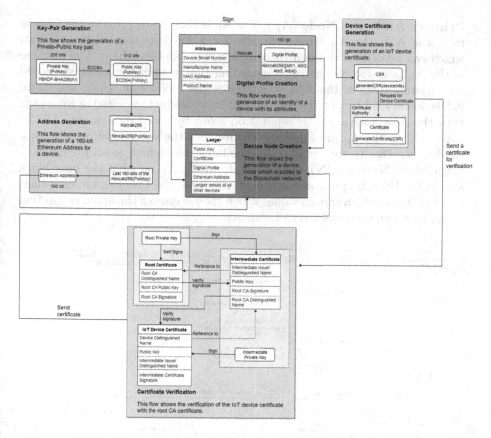

**Fig. 1.** Architecture diagram of various components of PoVA

PoA consensus algorithm exhibits energy efficiency and facilitates low-latency transactions, making it well-suited for IoT systems that are operating with constrained resources. Given these advantages, our research endeavours to enhance PoA's decentralization by building upon its foundation. To address this, we introduce **Proof-of-Variable-Authority (PoVA)**, where each node in the network receives a **reputation score**, enabling it to get promoted as an authority node. This creates a system to demote inactive authority nodes and promote candidate nodes that vote in consensus with the authority nodes. The details pertaining to the three different types of nodes that we referenced here are as follows:

- **Follower Nodes (FN)**: Any node that does not take part in the consensus is marked as FNs. They receive a copy of the updated ledger after consensus is attained.
- **Authority Nodes (AN)**: When a node has a reputation score greater than a certain threshold, it becomes an AN. These nodes take part in the voting process, and they seal and propagate new blocks. All ANs must vote often in order to keep their status.

- **Primary Authority Node ($A_P$):** The $A_P$ is chosen in a round-robin fashion from the ANs. An $A_P$ retains its role for a fixed number of transactions which can be defined through the properties of the blockchain. The purpose of the $A_P$ is to receive the votes regarding the incoming transaction. Based on majority votes of the ANs, it validates the blockchain. Upon successful validation of the block by the $A_P$, the candidate nodes that voted in consensus with the ANs, increase their reputation score by a certain amount. All the votes sent to the $A_P$ are signed to ensure that the votes have come from a valid node. The $A_P$ then propagates the latest blockchain to all the nodes.
- **Candidate Nodes (CN):** CNs can vote to the $A_P$ on what the next block should be. By voting in consensus with the ANs, the CNs can increase their reputation score by a certain value. When they acquire a threshold reputation score, they can be promoted to be an AN.

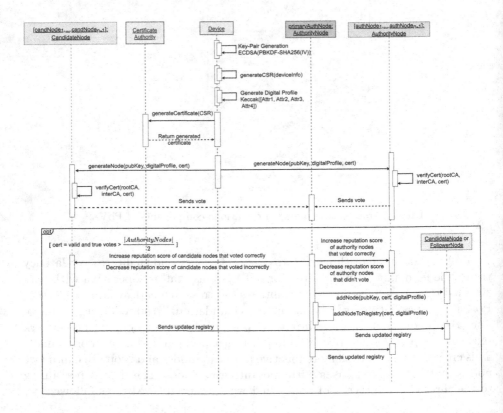

**Fig. 2.** Sequence diagram of device registration

### 4.1 Registration

If an IoT device wants to join a network, it must first generate its own private/public key pair using ECDSA. Then it generates a Certificate Signing

Request (CSR), using the public key and the device serial number to send to the CA for requesting a certificate. This certificate is used to prove that the device is valid. Once it receives the certificate from the CA, it sends a registration request to all the nodes in the network.

A smart contract is executed once the request reaches all the nodes. If the majority of the ANs decide that the device's certificate is valid, then the device's public details are added to the registry of $A_P$. The $A_P$ then sends the updated registry to all the nodes in the network. The device may register as an FN or CN. It holds a copy of the registry too. Figure 2 shows the sequence diagram for registration of an IoT device in a network. Apart from the sequence flow shown above, these are a few additional flows:

- The updated registry is sent to the FNs as well.
- The CNs that voted in consensus with the ANs receive an increase in their reputation. The CNs that voted contrary to the consensus of the ANs will be penalized. However, the CNs that could not vote will not be penalized. This is because CNs may experience intermittent periods of inactivity and have the ability to commence operations at any given moment.
- The ANs that voted in consensus also receive an increase in reputation. ANs that did not vote at all receive a decrease in reputation. However, ANs that voted contrary to the consensus will not be penalised. This is due to the fact that ANs significantly influence the consensus which necessitates continuous

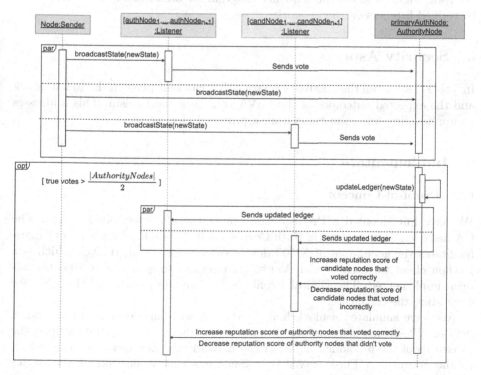

**Fig. 3.** Sequence diagram of broadcasting and verification

activity to uphold the integrity of the consensus mechanism. It is possible that an AN votes differently from the majority. This is not considered unexpected behaviour and may be the result of a number of factors such as physical distance and network latency spikes.

- A CN may be promoted to an AN only a limited number of times, beyond which it is prevented from being promoted.
- During validation, if an $A_P$ is found to disobey the consensus and add another block of its choice to the ledger, it is permanently blacklisted from the network. This validation is performed by the remaining ANs. This is to enhance the resilience of the system as it will eradicate the risk of a node getting the privilege of adding multiple erroneous blocks to the blockchain as an $A_P$.

### 4.2   Broadcasting and Verification

From here on, a node that wishes to update its state in the blockchain is referred to as a sender. There are listeners on the network waiting for a state update. Initially, the sender broadcasts its state change signed with its private key to all the listeners on the network. The listeners can then verify the identity of the sender. An AN votes in favour of the first incoming state change. If a state change receives votes from more than half of the ANs, then it is added to the ledger by the $A_P$. The $A_P$ then sends the updated ledger to all the nodes in the network. Figure 3 shows the sequence diagram for broadcasting a sender's state to verified listeners on the network.

## 5   Security Aspects

In Table 1, we detail the possible scenarios that can take place in the IoT network and the expected outcomes of the PoVA consensus mechanism. This addresses its applicability and robustness from a practical view point.

## 6   Implementation

### 6.1   Proof-of-Concept

We have implemented a Proof-of-Concept of the aforementioned design. The CA has been developed using HashiCorp's Vault [6]. Vault's PKI Secrets Engine facilitates the generation of X.509 device certificates. Using HVAC, which is a Python client to interact with Vault, an interface to generate certificates has been implemented. The Digital Profile is used in the payload of the CSR for generating the certificate.

We have simulated a blockchain in Python with the consensus mechanism devised. This blockchain can accept a device certificate, and depending upon the consensus of the pre-added nodes in the network, the new device can be added to the network. A Flask server that facilitates the verification of the device certificate with the CA chain has been deployed. A request is made by each

**Table 1.** Analysis of potential scenarios and their outcomes

| SL. No | Scenario | Expected Outcome |
| --- | --- | --- |
| 1 | A single $A_P$ controlled by a malicious actor attempts to defy the consensus and add an erroneous block to the blockchain | After the block is signed by the $A_P$, the ANs validate the block to ensure its integrity. If the added block is found to be erroneous, the block is ignored and the $A_P$ is blacklisted from the network |
| 2 | A single or a few ANs are taken over by a malicious actor. The actor attempts to make the consensus arrive at an invalid state | Arriving at a consensus requires a majority of the ANs to vote similarly. A few ANs cannot force the consensus to an invalid state |
| 3 | Majority of the ANs are taken over by a malicious actor. The actor attempts to make the consensus arrive at an invalid result | As consensus is determined by the majority of the ANs, it is possible for an actor controlling a majority of the ANs to control the blockchain. However, the distributed nature of the blockchain makes this a difficult task |
| 4 | A single or a few ANs fail at once | Arriving at a consensus requires a majority of the ANs to vote similarly. A few ANs not voting will not halt the consensus |
| 5 | Majority of the ANs fail at once | If the majority of the ANs fail at once, the blockchain halts as consensus cannot be reached as the majority of the ANs do not vote in favour of anything |
| 6 | Majority of the ANs fail gradually | A failed AN is not able to vote for the consensus and receives a penalty (a deduction in reputation score) for not voting. Over a defined period, varying in duration based on the penalty size, ANs are gradually demoted to CNs. Each node has a limited number of opportunities to be elevated to an AN, after which it will no longer receive such promotions. This enables the network to avoid the situation where majority of the ANs are in a failed state, making it impossible to reach a consensus |
| 7 | A malicious actor without access to the Certificate Authority attempts to spoof another node using its digital profile and issue a transaction | Every broadcasted transaction requires a verification of identity as a preliminary step. Hence, the malicious transaction will be invalid |

voting node with the X.509 device certificate and CA chain as data. Table 2 indicates the input-output specification for the registration of a device to the network.

As specified in the design, the nodes can fetch a state change broadcast through the network. The $A_P$ adds it to the blockchain depending on the result of the consensus. To simulate real-world conditions, we have introduced network noise that affects the propagation of the state to different nodes and their voting. Subsequently, the nodes are rewarded based on the specifications detailed in the design. Table 3 depicts the input-output specification of the broadcasting and verification scheme.

**Table 2.** I/O specification for the registration of a device to the network

| Utility | Actors | Input | Output |
|---|---|---|---|
| Key Pair Generation | Devices | Initialization Vector | Private Key, Public Key |
| Digital Profile Creation | Devices | MAC Address, Manufacturer Name, Device Name | Unique ID for the device |
| Generate CSR | Devices | Device ID, TTL, Root Domain Name | Certificate request protocol sent to CA |
| Certificate Generator | Root CA, Intermediate CAs | Device ID, TTL, Root Domain Name | Generated Certificate, Private Key |
| Node Registration Request | Devices | Public Key, Digital Profile, Certificate, Ethereum Address | Joint registration protocol |
| Certificate Verification | Nodes | Certificate, Chain of trusted certificates | Bool (T or F) |
| Registration (Consensus) | Nodes | Joint registration protocol | Approved/Rejected consensus |
| Add Transaction to Blockchain | $A_P$ | Transaction Vote | Merkle tree with new transaction block |
| Increment Reputation | $A_P$ | Node, Reputation to increase | Node reputation increased |
| Decrement Reputation | $A_P$ | Node, Reputation to decrease | Node reputation decreased |
| Test Trustworthiness | $A_P$ | Votes of the CNs, Next transaction (already selected) | If CN voted correctly, increase reputation. If CN voted incorrectly, decrease reputation |
| Updated Ledger Propagation | $A_P$ | FNs, CNs, ANs, New Device, Updated Ledger | Nodes receive updated ledger |

## 6.2    Geth Implementation

We have utilized Go-Ethereum (Geth) [5], which is an Ethereum execution client, to handle transactions and deploy smart contracts. Geth utilizes Clique [13] which is an implementation of PoA. When using Clique, the genesis block is configured via the `genesis.json` file consisting of various attributes that have been modified for Clique from the primary PoW consensus implementation.

**Table 3.** I/O specification of the broadcast and verification scheme

| Utility | Actors | Input | Output |
|---|---|---|---|
| Decide Order of Transactions (ANs) | ANs | Transaction | Transaction vote (consensus) |
| Add Transaction to Blockchain | $A_P$ | Transaction Vote | Merkle tree with new transaction block |
| Verify Blockchain | ANs | New Merkle tree, Old Merkle tree | Reputation decreased if invalid. Reputation increased if valid |
| Decide Order of Transactions (CNs) | CNs | Broadcasted transaction | Vote of the transaction (candidate vote protocol) |
| Increment Reputation | $A_P$ | Node, Reputation to increase | Node reputation increased |
| Decrement Reputation | $A_P$ | Node, Reputation to decrease | Node reputation decreased |
| Test Trustworthiness | $A_P$ | Votes of the CNs, Next transaction (already selected) | If CN votes correctly, increase reputation. If CN votes incorrectly, decrease reputation |

Similarly, we have tailored each of these attributes for our design to use Geth for the consensus devised. The template for the important values in the genesis block is given below.

```
{
  "config": {
    "chainId": <Unique Chain identifier>,
    "clique": {
      "period": <Block Period>,
      "epoch": <Number of blocks in Epoch>
    }
  },
  "difficulty": "1",
  "extradata": "<Extra Vanity> <Signer Addresses> <Extra Seal>",
  "alloc": {
    <account addresss 1>: { "balance": <Initial balance 1> },
    <account addresss 2>: { "balance": <Initial balance 2> },
    ...
    <account addresss n>: { "balance": <Initial balance n> },
    "0000000000000000000000000000000000000001": {
      "balance": "10000000000000000000",
      "data": <Contract Bytecode>
    }
  }
}
```

The votes of the nodes are recorded by a smart contract. This can be compiled using Truffle [3] or any alternative Solidity compilers. When a block is sealed, the A$_P$ facilitates rewarding all the nodes that have voted to match the consensus. Once the reputation has been updated, the votes are reset. If a signer is below a certain threshold reputation, it is removed from the list of signers. Consequently, if CNs have a reputation greater than the threshold, they are added to the list of signers. However, only a limited number of transitions are permitted for each node. Additionally, we have extended the web3 library to include methods to query the blockchain from a JavaScript client for the PoVA consensus mechanism. The code demonstrating the proposed design as a Proof-of-Concept along with the Geth implementation can be found at https://github.com/PoVA-Consensus.

## 7   Performance Analysis

In Table 4, we compare PoW and PoA with PoVA on the basis of energy efficiency, susceptibility to Sybil attacks, level of decentralization and scalability.

**Table 4.** Comparison of PoVA with PoW and PoA

| Algorithm | Energy efficiency | Susceptibility to Sybil attacks | Decentralization | Scalability |
|---|---|---|---|---|
| PoW | Energy intensive due to high computational requirements | Susceptible | High level of decentralization | Not highly scalable as computational requirements increase as more nodes become a part of the network |
| PoA | Energy efficient with low block creation times | Resistant | Low level of decentralization as validators are predetermined | Scalable until the hardware of the validators cannot handle more requests |
| PoVA | Energy efficient | Resistant | High level of decentralization as any of the nodes can become validators provided they have the computational capacity to do so | Highly scalable as more nodes can become validators dynamically |

In the attempt to attain higher levels of decentralization, PoVA introduces additional steps which leads to increased overhead when compared with conventional centralized systems. When implementing this design on a larger scale, various factors come into play that impact the overall latency of the blockchain system.

Network speed and congestion, physical distance between devices, block size, block time, and smart contract execution time for maintaining the reputation system increase the latency of the system. Congested or slower networks can increase confirmation times, thereby increasing latency. Subsequently, the geographic distribution of nodes can introduce delays due to longer information propagation times. Optimal block size and block time trade-offs are necessary to minimize latency. Execution of smart contracts can cause delays in transaction confirmation and contribute to overall latency. These factors should be considered for implementing PoVA at scale.

# 8    Conclusion

This paper demonstrates the use of blockchain technology for mitigating security vulnerabilities in IoT networks. The objective to modify the PoA algorithm to be more decentralized while being suitable for an IoT system is achieved through the proposed PoVA consensus algorithm. PoVA introduces a reputation-based system where each node is capable of validating blocks to become Authority Nodes. The reward mechanism for honest nodes results in a more dynamic and resilient system. Additionally, the use of device certificates issued by a trusted Certificate Authority ensures the validation of new devices, thus preventing malicious activities. The implementation of this system maintains a distributed ledger among blockchain network nodes, recording and validating the state changes while preventing unauthorized access and tampering.

# References

1. Biswas, S., et al.: Interoperability benefits and challenges in smart city services: blockchain as a solution. Electronics **12**(4), 1036 (2023)
2. Bouras, M.A., Lu, Q., Dhelim, S., Ning, H.: A lightweight blockchain-based IoT identity management approach. Future Internet **13**(2), 24 (2021)
3. ConsenSys Software Inc.: Truffle suite: The most comprehensive suite of tools for smart contract development. https://trufflesuite.com/. Accessed Jan 2023
4. Cooper, D., Santesson, S., Farrell, S., Boeyen, S., Housley, R., Polk, W.: RFC 5280: Internet X. 509 public key infrastructure certificate and certificate revocation list (CRL) profile (2008). Accessed Nov 2022
5. Ethereum Foundation: Go ethereum (2017). https://github.com/ethereum/go-ethereum. Accessed Jan 2023
6. HashiCorp: Build your own certificate authority (ca): Vault: Hashicorp developer. https://developer.hashicorp.com/vault/tutorials/secrets-management/pki-engine. Accessed Oct 2022
7. Shostak, R., Pease, M., Lamport, L.: The byzantine generals problem. ACM Trans. Program. Lang. Syst. (TOPLAS) **4**(3), 382–401 (1982)
8. Manolache, M.A., Manolache, S., Tapus, N.: Decision making using the blockchain proof of authority consensus. Procedia Comput. Sci. **199**, 580–588 (2022)
9. Nakamoto, S.: Bitcoin: a peer-to-peer electronic cash system. Decentralized Bus. Rev. 21260 (2008)

10. Omar, A.S., Basir, O.: Identity management in IoT networks using blockchain and smart contracts. In: 2018 IEEE International Conference on Internet of Things (iThings) and IEEE Green Computing and Communications (GreenCom) and IEEE Cyber, Physical and Social Computing (CPSCom) and IEEE Smart Data (SmartData), pp. 994–1000. IEEE (2018)
11. Rodrigues, A.: Centralized management IoT platform. In: Rocha, Á., Fajardo-Toro, C.H., Riola, J.M. (eds.) Developments and Advances in Defense and Security, pp. 65–75. Springer, Cham (2023). https://doi.org/10.1007/978-981-19-7689-6_6
12. Sheikh, S., Azmathullah, R.M., Rizwan, F.: Proof-of-work vs proof-of-stake: a comparative analysis and an approach to blockchain consensus mechanism. Int. J. Res. Appl. Sci. Eng. Technol. **6**(12), 786–791 (2018)
13. Szilágyi, P.: EIP-225: clique proof-of-authority consensus protocol. Ethereum Improvement Proposals (2017)
14. Wood, G., et al.: Ethereum: a secure decentralised generalised transaction ledger. Ethereum Project Yellow Paper **151**(2014), 1–32 (2014)
15. Yadav, A.K., Singh, K.: Comparative analysis of consensus algorithms and issues in integration of blockchain with IoT. In: Tiwari, S., Trivedi, M.C., Mishra, K.K., Misra, A.K., Kumar, K.K., Suryani, E. (eds.) Smart Innovations in Communication and Computational Sciences. AISC, vol. 1168, pp. 25–46. Springer, Singapore (2021). https://doi.org/10.1007/978-981-15-5345-5_3

# An Efficient Two-Party ECDSA Scheme for Cryptocurrencies

Habeeb Syed[✉], Arinjita Paul, Meena Singh, and MA Rajan

TCS Research and Innovation, Tata Consultancy Services, Chennai, India
{habeeb.syed,arinjita.paul,meena.s1,rajan.ma}@tcs.com

**Abstract.** Threshold signatures have emerged as a promising solution to secure cryptocurrencies. While some signature algorithms like Schnorr, BLS, EdDSA are threshold-friendly, the structure of ECDSA makes it challenging to construct such schemes. As such the known threshold ECDSA schemes use complex zero-knowledge proofs. However, these impact their performance negatively. Further, these schemes have attempted to achieve efficiency in signature computation part while accepting complexity in the key generation. To be more specific, in the known 2-of-2 schemes the two parties need to perform key generation together to be able to run signature computation. In this work, we propose an efficient two-party ECDSA protocol that enables two parties to "aggregate" their ECDSA signature (on a single message) without participating in any kind of key generation process. Our protocol is based on additive sharing of (ECDSA) private keys and homomorphic properties of Paillier encryption. All the zero-knowledge proof we use are non-interactive. As a result, our key generation is 7x faster than state-of-the-art. In terms of overall time complexity, our scheme is comparable with state of the art 2-of-2 ECDSA scheme.

**Keywords:** Pailler · ECDSA · Cryptocurrency · Two Party Protocol · Threshold Signature

## 1 Introduction

The current popularity and widespread acceptance of cryptocurrencies have led to frequent cryptocurrency thefts. As per recent survey reports [6], a total of 14 billion dollars equivalent of cryptocurrencies have been stolen as of 2021. Private (aka secret) keys are critical components for securing cryptocurrencies and users must be able to protect the keys from unauthorized access. Typically, a digital signature requires only one signatory (one private key) per transaction. However, such a technique is vulnerable to single point of failure such as loss or compromise of device. As a solution to the problem, multi-signatures [17] were introduced, which require multiple parties to authorize a single transaction. A multi-signature scheme allows $n$ different signers with distinct public keys $pk_1, \cdots, pk_n$ to collectively sign a message $m$, yielding a multi-signature $\sigma$ that certifies $m$ under all public keys $pk_1, \cdots, pk_n$ simultaneously. The downside of multi-signatures is that they require multiple signatures from each party

V. Muthukkumarasamy et al. (Eds.): ICISS 2023, LNCS 14424, pp. 411–430, 2023.
https://doi.org/10.1007/978-3-031-49099-6_25

involved for every transaction. Consequently, these signatures take more space and require public keys of all cosigners to verify signatures. It is desirable to have schemes that give advantages of multisignatures without any of their downsides. Threshold signatures seem to be best fit in this scenario. These schemes also require multiple parties to sign a transaction. However, the parties share a single signing key, instead of each one having a separate key. The output of a threshold signature is same as the one generated by standard signature algorithm and hence verification algorithm remains the same. Thus threshold schemes have all the advantages of multi-signatures without any of its downsides.

A $(t, n)$−threshold signature scheme enables $n$ parties to share a private key such that any subset of $t + 1$ players can sign, but any smaller subset cannot. The main advantage of threshold schemes is that an adversary needs to compromise at least the threshold number of parties to forge a signature, which is hard compared to one party case. Threshold signature schemes have emerged as an important component in cryptocurrency security toolkit. Elliptic Curve Digital Signature Algorithm (ECDSA) [18] is part of a wide range of applications. Compared to other versions of digital signature algorithms, it has the advantage of being efficient (requires much shorter key lengths), making it a better candidate for several applications such as TLS [16], DNSSec [16], and cryptocurrencies like Ethereum [22]. Despite its popularity, few attempts have been made at designing an efficient threshold signature scheme for ECDSA, unlike other schemes such as Schnorr and RSA signatures. This can be attributed to the difficulty involved in designing a threshold signature protocol for ECDSA. To give some details, the scheme requires the distributed computation of (a random) $k, k^{-1}$ modulo a prime by multiple parties without any party knowing the value of $k$ [see Sect. 6]. On the top of this any threshold protocol must be secure against malicious parties. At the least it must ensure that if a (threshold number of) parties are malicious then they cannot obtain correct output from the protocol. For such checks and balances, existing threshold ECDSA schemes rely on tools like interactive zero-knowledge proofs and large-modulus exponentiation computations, adding considerable overheads. In this work we consider the problem of designing 2-of-2 threshold ECDSA signature scheme. Our aim is to enable two parties to perform signature computation without first participating in key generation. This will enable two parties who already have their ECDSA keys to produce a valid signature together [see Sect. 5.1].

### Related Work and Contribution

**Threshold Signatures Schemes for ECDSA.** Though threshold signature schemes have been around for a long time [21] there has been a resurgence of interest in the last few years mainly due to their use in cryptocurrencies. Unlike other popular signature algorithms such as Schnorr, the design of the ECDSA signatures poses a unique challenge to the construction of an efficient threshold scheme. In the last few years, several threshold ECDSA schemes have been proposed. Some of these solutions are aimed at solving general $(t, n)$-case [3,5,8,11–13,20] while others are focused on 2-of-2 cases. Each of these schemes has its own pros and cons. For instance the scheme proposed by Gennaro et al. [13] uses threshold Paillier. It is a known fact that distributed key generation for Paillier is very costly and impractical. In [11] Gennaro and Goldfeder constructed a general $(t, n)$ threshold ECDSA using an efficient technique that converts multiplicative shares of a key into additive shares. A distinct feature of their scheme is the way they address the problem of malicious parties. Instead of using any zero-knowledge proofs [as is usually done] the authors instead conjecture that even if some of the parties behave maliciously private information of honest parties is not leaked. For a comprehensive survey on the state-of-the-art threshold ECDSA schemes we refer to [1].

From a practical application perspective, 2-of-2 schemes seem to be more attractive [4,9,19,21,23]. Of these, Lindell's scheme [19] has an efficient signature generation protocol with reported throughput of 100 signatures per second. However, their key generation protocol is computationally complex. In the protocol one of the parties encrypts its key-share (with Paillier) and shares the ciphertext with the other party along with a *range-proof* that proves in zero-knowledge that the ciphertext is encryption of a random number $\leq q/3$. This range proof is "expensive", mainly because it is interactive. Authors claim that since key generation happens only once this does not matter. However, in practice, we must refresh the key shares[1] frequently to maintain the security level. And, whenever this happens the parties have to run the interactive range proof. Thus, the key generation protocol impacts the overall complexity of the scheme. Furthermore, in [2] Aumasson and Shlomovits present an attack on the key refresh protocol as implemented in one of the commercial deployments of [13]. The attack allows one of the parties (participating in signature) to recover private key bits of another party. Another efficient scheme is due to Doerner et al. [9] in the two-party setting secure under the hardness of the Computational Diffie Hellman assumption. Their protocol employs a novel two-party multiplication method to generate the signatures, based upon semi-honest Oblivious Transfer (OT). Although the scheme demonstrate very high efficiency, given the fast operations for generating the threshold signature, its dependence on OT leads to multiple rounds of interaction between the parties during the key generation and signature generation phases, which may not be desirable in applications with communication constraints.

**Our Contribution.** In this work, we propose a new efficient two-party threshold scheme for ECDSA. The main features of our scheme are

- We use a mix of key sharing methods: The private keys are shared additively while session keys are shared multiplicatively.
- All the zero-knowledge proofs are non-interactive, which makes our scheme highly efficient.
- Each of the parties locally compute partial signature then use homomorphic properties of Paillier to aggregate and obtain the final output.

---

[1] Replace key shares with new random ones such that the public key remains the same.

- Our scheme is particularly useful in the scenario where two parties want to use their existing ECDSA keys to jointly sign a document or a transaction (see Sect. 5.1).
- Our construction is secure against malicious adversaries in the hybrid model.
- Key generation is 7 times faster as compared to the best known scheme 5. This is an important factor in cryptocurrency scenario where reusing keys is considered to be a bad practice and hence new keys are required for every transaction.

## 2    Preliminaries

A digital signature scheme $\pi$ is a triple of algorithms $(KeyGen, Sig, Ver)$. These algorithms are assumed to be efficient, in the sense that their running is bounded by polynomials in terms of parameters. $KeyGen$ is the key generator algorithm: on input the security parameter $\kappa$, it outputs a pair $(y, x)$, such that $y$ is the public key and $x$ is the secret key of the signature scheme. $Sig$ is the signing algorithm: on input a message $m$ and the secret key $x$, it outputs $\sigma$, a signature of the message $m$. Since $Sig$ can be a randomized algorithm, there might be several valid signatures $\sigma$ of a message $m$ under the key $x$; let $Sig(m, x)$ denote the set of such signatures. $Ver$ is the verification algorithm. On input a message $m$, the public key $y$, and a string $\sigma$, it checks whether $\sigma$ is a proper signature of $m$, i.e. if $\sigma \in Sig(m, x)$. The strongest notion of security for signature schemes is captured by the following definition of existential unforgeability against adaptively chosen message attack.

**Definition 1.** *We say that a signature scheme* $\pi = (KeyGen, Sig, Ver)$ *is unforgeable if no PPT adversary $\mathcal{A}$ who is given the public key $y$ generated by $KeyGen$, and the signatures of $k$ messages $m_1, \cdots, m_k$ adaptively chosen, can produce the signature on a new message $m$ (i.e., $m \notin \{m_1, \cdots, m_k\}$) with non-negligible (in $\kappa$) probability.*

We define an experiment $Exp\text{-}Sign_{A,\pi}(\kappa)$ to present a game-based definition for the security of a digital signature scheme $\pi = (KeyGen, Sig, Ver)$, which we shall use while proving the security of our protocol, presented for the sake of completeness:

1. $(vk, sk) \leftarrow KeyGen(\kappa)$
2. $(m^*, \sigma^*) \leftarrow \mathcal{A}^{Sign_{sk}(\cdot)}(\kappa, vk)$
3. Let $\mathcal{Q}$ be the set of all messages $m$ queried by $\mathcal{A}$ to its oracle. Then, the output of the experiment equals 1 IFF $m^* \notin \mathcal{Q}$ and $Verify_{vk}(m^*, \sigma^*) = 1$

### 2.1    Threshold Signature

Let $\pi = (KeyGen, Sig, Ver)$ be a signature scheme. A $(t, n)$-threshold signature scheme $\Pi$ for $\pi$ is a pair of protocols $(ThreshKeyGen, ThreshSig)$ for a set of players $P_1, \cdots, P_n$. $ThreshKeyGen$ is a distributed key generation protocol used by the parties to jointly generate a pair $(y, x)$ of public/private keys on input a security parameter $\kappa$. At the end of the protocol, the private output of player $P_i$ is a value $x_i$ such that the values $(x_1, ..., x_n)$ form a $(t, n)$-threshold secret sharing of private key $x$. The public output of the protocol contains the public key $y$. Public/private key pairs $(y, x)$ are produced by $ThreshKeyGen$ algorithm with the same probability distribution as if they were generated by the $KeyGen$ protocol of the regular signature scheme $\pi$. $ThreshSig$ is the distributed signature protocol. The private input of $P_i$ is the value $x_i$. The public inputs consist of a message $m$ and the public key $y$. The output of the protocol is a value $\sigma \in Sig(m, x)$. The security model for threshold signature schemes is analogous to the notion of existential unforgeability under chosen message attack as defined by Goldwasser, Micali and Rivest [14] and is defined as below.

**Definition 2.** *We say that a $(t, n)$-threshold signature scheme given by $\Pi = (ThreshKeyGen, ThreshSig, Ver)$ is unforgeable, if no malicious adversary who corrupts at most $t$ players can produce, with non-negligible probability (in $\kappa$), the signature on any new (i.e., previously unsigned) message $m$, given the view of the protocols $ThreshKeyGen$ and $ThreshSig$ on input messages $m_1, \cdots, m_k$ chosen adaptively by the adversary.*

## 2.2 Security Model

Given our contribution in the two-party threshold signature setting, we define the security for a distributed signing protocol in the context of two parties by an experiment $Exp\text{-}DistSig_{A,\Pi}^b(\kappa)$, which captures the concurrent signing executions under the assumption that if an abort occurs, all executions abort immediately, termed as **concurrent executions with instantaneous global abort** [19].

The experiment $Exp\text{-}DistSig_{A,\Pi}^b(\kappa)$ considers that the adversary $\mathcal{A}$ controls party $P_b$ in the protocol $\Pi$ for the two-party distributed signature generation, where $b \in \{1, 2\}$. $\Pi_b(\cdot, \cdot)$ is a stateful oracle that executes the instructions of honest party $P_{3-b}$ in our protocol $\Pi$. The adversary $\mathcal{A}$ can choose which messages are to be signed and can concurrently interact with multiple instances of party $P_{3-b}$ to generate signatures. The oracle is defined such that the distributed key generation phase is first run once, followed by multiple signing protocols executing concurrently between two parties. $\mathcal{A}$ can query the oracle with two inputs: the first input is a session identifier ($sid$) and the second is either an input or a next incoming message. The oracle works as follows:

- Upon receiving a query $(0, 0)$ for the first time, $P_{3-b}$ instructs the oracle to initialise a machine $M$. If party $P_{3-b}$ sends the first message in the distributed key generation protocol, then the oracle replies with this message.
- Upon receiving a query $(0, m)$, if the key generation phase has not been executed, then the oracle hands the machine $M$ with the message $m$ as the next incoming message and returns the output of $M$. If the key generation phase has been executed, the oracle returns $\bot$.

- If a query $(sid, m)$ is received such that $sid \neq 0$, and the key generation phase with $M$ has not been executed, then the oracle returns $\bot$.
- If a query $(sid, m)$ is received and the key generation phase has been executed and this is the first oracle query with the given identifier $sid$, then $P_{3-b}$ instructs the oracle to invoke a new machine $M_{sid}$ with identifier $sid$ and input message $m$ to be signed. $M_{sid}$ is initialised with the key share and any state that is stored by $M$ at the end of the key generation phase. If party $P_{3-b}$ sends the first message in the signing protocol, then this message is the oracle reply.
- Upon receiving a query $(sid, m)$, if the key generation phase has been executed and this is not the first oracle query with the identifier $sid$, the oracle hands $M_{sid}$ with the incoming message $m$ and returns the next output sent by $M_{sid}$. If $M_{sid}$ completes, the output obtained by $M_{sid}$ is returned.
- If any query $(sid, m)$ results in $M_{sid}$ sending **abort**, then the oracle returns **abort** and halts all executions.

The security experiment is formalized by providing $\mathcal{A}$ who controls party $P_b$ with an oracle access to $\Pi_b$. If the adversary $\mathcal{A}$ can forge a signature on a message that has not been queried in the oracle queries, then $\mathcal{A}$ wins. Note that $\mathcal{A}$ can concurrently run multiple executions of the signing protocol.

**Definition 3.** *A protocol $\Pi$ is a secure two-party distributed signature generation protocol if for every probabilistic polynomial-time adversary $\mathcal{A}$ and every $b \in \{0, 1\}$, there exists a negligible function $\epsilon$ such that for every $\kappa$,*

$$\Pr[Exp\text{-}DistSign_{\mathcal{A},\Pi}^{b}(\kappa) = 1] \leq \epsilon(\kappa)$$

## 3    Our Proposed Scheme

### 3.1    Technical Overview of Construction

In this section we give a technical overview of our protocols and give a proof of correctness. For simplicity we consider two users Alice and Bob as the two parties involved in the protocols, viz., distributed key generation protocol and the 2 party signature computation protocol. For the sake of completeness we have included description of standard ECDSA algorithm in Appendix 1.

**Pailler Key Generation.** Note that Paillier modulus is given by $\mathsf{N}$ which is product two primes generated using standard RSA assumptions. However, if we want to use additive homomorphic properties of Paillier then we must ensure that $GCD(\mathsf{N}, \phi(\mathsf{N})) = 1$. To generate such primes one can use the proof techniques described in [15].

**System Parameters.** Based on security parameter $\lambda$ Alice and Bob choose system parameters $(p^r, E, \mathsf{G}, q)$ where

- $\mathbb{F}_{p^r}$ is the finite field
- $E$ is the elliptic curve defined over $\mathbb{F}_{p^r}$
- $\mathsf{G}$ is a fixed point on $E$ that generates a cyclic group of prime order $q$.

An example of parameter set are the Bitcoin curve.

**Distributed Key Generation.** The distributed key generation algorithm *ThreshKeyGen* consists of the following steps:

1. Alice generates private key share $a_1 \xleftarrow{\$} \mathbb{Z}_q$ and computes $A_1 = a_1 G$
2. Alice shares $A_1$ with Bob
3. Bob generates $a_2 \xleftarrow{\$} \mathbb{Z}_q$ and computes $A_2 = a_2 G$
4. Bob shares $A_2$ with Alice
5. Each party locally computes public key $A = A_1 + A_2 = (a_1 + a_2) G$ and share their output with other.
6. If all the locally computed values of public key are same then parties output the public key otherwise they abort and restart the process.

**Distributed Signature Generation.** The distributed signatures computation algorithm *ThreshSig* is explained in detail here. Recall that a signature on message $m$ is given by a tuple $\sigma_m = (r, \mathbf{s})$. In this tuple $r$ is referred to as session key and $\mathbf{s}$ as signature part. In the following first we explain computation of $r$ and then move to $\mathbf{s}$ part.

1. Alice generates $k_1 \xleftarrow{\$} \mathbb{Z}_q$, computes $R_1 = k_1 G$ and shares it with Bob
2. Bob generates $k_2 \xleftarrow{\$} \mathbb{Z}_q$ computes $R_2 = k_2 G$ and shares it with Alice
3. Alice and Bob locally (and independently) compute $R$ as follows:

$$\text{Alice} : R = k_1 R_2 = k G \quad \text{and} \quad \text{Bob} : R = k_2 R_1 = k G$$

where $k = k_1 k_2 \pmod{q}$
4. Alice and Bob exchange respective values of $R$ and compare it with locally computed value. if there are not same then they abort and restart.
5. Alice and Bob set $r = x_R = x-$coordinate of the point $R$.

Next task is to compute intermediate value $\mathbf{s} = k^{-1}[m + (a_1 + a_2) r] \pmod{q}$ without leaking information about shares of $k$ and $a$. Our proposed method works as follows:

Alice performs the following steps:

6. Generates $\tilde{k} \xleftarrow{\$} \mathbb{Z}_q$ and computes $\tilde{R} = \tilde{k} R_1$
7. compute the following:

$$\mathbf{s}_1 = \tilde{k}^{-1} k_1^{-1}(m + a_1 r) \pmod{q} \text{ and}$$
$$X = -\tilde{k}^{-1} k_1^{-1} a_1 \pmod{q} \tag{1}$$

8. Obtains ciphertext $\text{Enc}^2$ $C = \text{Enc}(X, \text{pk}_A)$
9. Alice sends $\mathbf{s}_1, \tilde{R}, C$ to Bob.
10. Bob keeps $\mathbf{s}_2, \alpha$ ready, where

$$\mathbf{s}_2 = k_2^{-1}(m + a_2 r) \pmod{q} \text{ and}$$
$$\alpha = k_2^{-1} a_2 r^2 \pmod{q}. \tag{2}$$

---

[2] Partially Homomorphic Encryption using Alice Paillier keys.

11. Bob computes

$$Y_1 = \text{Enc}(s_1 s_2, \text{pk}_A) \quad \text{and} \quad Y_2 = C^\alpha \mod N^2 \tag{3}$$

and then multiplies $Y_1, Y_2$ modulo the Paillier modulus $N^2$

$$Z = [Y_1 * Y_2] \mod N^2 \tag{4}$$

Finally Bob sends $Z$ back to Alice.

Before proceeding further, we explain connection between $Z$ and final output value of $s$. Using the homomorphic properties of Pailler it is easy to see that the values of $Y_1, Y_2$ are encryptions of

$$Y_1 = \text{Enc}[\tilde{k}^{-1} k_1^{-1} (m + a_1 r) \cdot k_2^{-1} (m + a_2 r) \pmod N)]$$
$$Y_2 = \text{Enc}[(-\tilde{k}^{-1} k^{-1} a_1 a_2 r^2) \pmod N)]$$

Recall that all the encryptions are under the Paillier public key of Alice so we skip adding $\text{pk}_A$ here. Thus the value of $Z$ (again using the Homomorphic property of Paillier) is given by

$$Z = \text{Enc}(\tilde{k} \, k^{-1} (m + a_1 r) \cdot (m + a_2 r) - \underbrace{\tilde{k}^{-1} k^{-1} \, a_1 \, a_2 r^2}_{T} \pmod N)). \tag{5}$$

It is easy to see that upon simplification this becomes

$$Z = \text{Enc}[(m \cdot \tilde{k}^{-1} s + T) \pmod N - T \pmod N)] \tag{6}$$

The values of $m, s \in \mathbb{Z}_q$ and hence their values satisfy $0 < m, s < q$. We need to choose Paillier modulus $N$ such that $N > q^2$ to ensure that the value of $s$ does not wrap around it. However, the values of $m \cdot s + T$ (and $T$) can be larger than $N$ and may wrap around $N$ during decryption. We need to choose correct decryption of $Z$. Suppose $s' = \text{Dec}(Z, \text{sk}_A) \cdot \tilde{k} \, m^{-1} \pmod q$. Then the value of $s$ is given by

$$s = \begin{cases} s' & \text{if} \quad m \cdot s + T \pmod N > T \pmod N \\ N - s' & \text{otherwise} \end{cases} \tag{7}$$

However, Alice does not know which one of the values is the correct one. So, she needs to test the validity of signature $(r, s)$ by considering both values for $s$ as in (7) and choose the correct one. With this explanation we go back to next step in signature computation.

12. Alice computes $s' = [\text{Dec}(Z, \text{sk}_A)] \cdot m^{-1} \pmod q$
13. Alice verifies signature given by $(r, (N - s') \pmod q)$. If it is valid then she outputs $\sigma = (r, s)$ as signature on the message $m$ and ends protocol.
14. Alice verifies signature given by $(r, s')$. If it is valid then she outputs $\sigma = (r, s)$ as signature on the message $m$ and ends protocol.
15. Alice outputs the message "Signature computation failed" and aborts.

## 3.2   Proof of Correctness

Let us assume that Alice and Bob have private keys $a_1, a_2$ (respectively) such that the full private key is $a_1 + a_2$. While computing signature each party holds one of the partial session keys $k_1, k_2$ and also know the session key $r$ as described in steps 3 and 4 in the previous section. If the Paillier modulus $\mathsf{N}$ satisfies $\mathsf{N} > q^2$ and both parties follow the protocol then it follows from the previous section that Alice and Bob obtain correct signature output $(r, \mathsf{s})$ on any message $m$. For example if we are using NIST P-256 curves then size of $q$ is 256 bits. In this case if we choose a 2048 bit RSA modulus then our protocol generates valid signature values.

## 3.3   Construction

We prove our threshold protocol secure in a hybrid model with ideal functionalities $F_{zk}, F_{com-zk}$ that securely compute the zero-knowledge and non-interactive zero-knowledge functionalities for a relation $S$ respectively as shown below:

- $F_{zk}$ : On an input (prove, $sid, x, y$) from a user $P_i$, where $i \in \{1, 2\}$: if $(x, y) \notin S$, or session key $sid$ has been utilized previously, ignore the message. Otherwise, send (proof, $sid, x$) to user $P_{3-i}$.
- $F_{com-zk}$ : On an input (com-prove, $sid, x, y$) from a user $P_i$, where $i \in \{1, 2\}$: if $(x, y) \notin S$, or session key $sid$ has been utilized previously, ignore the message. Otherwise, store $(sid, i, x)$ and send (proof-receipt, $sid$) to user $P_{3-i}$. On receipt of (decom-prove, $sid$) from a user $P_i$, where $i \in \{1, 2\}$, if $(sid, i, x)$ has been stored, then send (decom-proof, $sid, x$) to user $P_{3-i}$.

Commitments are required in the following two scenarios:

- Distributed Key Generation: During this step, Alice must provide a commitment of its partial public key share $A_1$ and provide a zero-knowledge proof of knowledge of $a_1$ (discrete logarithm of $A_1$). Same applies for user Bob.
- Distributed Signature Generation: During this step, Alice and Bob may provide commitment of the partial intermediate signing values and provide a zero-knowledge proof of the discrete log values as well.

We present our two proposed protocols: Protocol 1 **ThreshKeyGen** and Protocol 2 **ThreshSig** in the following pages.

## 3.4   Security Proof

Our scheme is secure against malicious adversaries based on the assumption that ECDSA is secure. For the sake of simplicity in proofs we use $P_1, P_2$ (instead of Alice and Bob) to denote the two parties.

**Theorem 1.** *Given that the Paillier encryption scheme is indistinguishable under chosen-plaintext attacks and ECDSA scheme is existentially-unforgeable under chosen-message attacks, then our distributed two-party signature generation protocol for ECDSA is secure in the $(\mathcal{F}_{com-zk}, \mathcal{F}_{zk})$ hybrid model.*

*Proof Sketch..* We prove the security of our protocol in the $(\mathcal{F}_{com-zk}, \mathcal{F}_{zk})$ hybrid model for the discrete logarithm relation S, for the setting of concurrent executions with instantaneous global support. In our distributed protocol, if the adversary $\mathcal{A}$ can break the protocol in hybrid model with probability $\epsilon(\kappa)$, then it can break the real protocol with probability at most $\epsilon'(\kappa)$ for some negligible function $\epsilon'$ under concurrent executions. We prove security for the case of a corrupted party $P_1$ and a corrupted $P_2$ separately for our two-party signing protocol.

---

**Protocol 1 ThreshKeyGen:** The distributed key generation protocol

---

*Inputs.* Elliptic curve parameters, finite field size $p$ base point G, group size $q$.

*Goal.* The two parties Alice and Bob generate their (private) key share and together compute public key.

*The protocol:*

1. Alice generates $a_1 \xleftarrow{\$} \mathbb{Z}_q$ and computes $A_1 = a_1 \, \mathsf{G}$.
2. Alice sends commitment and proof of knowledge as (com-prove, $1, A_1, a_1$) to $\mathcal{F}_{com-zk}^S$.
3. Bob receives (proof-receipt,1) from $\mathcal{F}_{com-zk}^S$.
4. Bob generates $a_2 \xleftarrow{\$} \mathbb{Z}_q$ and computes $A_2 = a_2 \, \mathsf{G}$.
5. Bob sends (prove, $2, A_2, a_2$) to $\mathcal{F}_{zk}^S$.
6. Alice receives (proof, $2, A_2$) from $\mathcal{F}_{zk}^S$. It sends (decom-proof, 1) to $\mathcal{F}_{com-zk}^S$.
7. Each party locally computes $A = A_1 + A_2 = (a_1 + a_2) \, \mathsf{G}$ and send the other party.
8. Each party compares the value of public key it received (from the other party) with the public key it has computed. If they are not same, it "aborts" the protocol and both parties go back to step 1.
9. Both parties broadcast A as the public key.

---

In the above Algorithm the point $T$ is given by $T = (m + a_1 r) \, \mathsf{G}$. If Alice has computed the value of $s_1$ as per protocol then $tmp = s_1^{-1} = k_1(m + a_1 r)^{-1}$. Thus $tmp \cdot T = k_1 \, (m + a_1 \, r) \, (m + a_1 \, r)^{-1} \mathsf{G} = k_1 \, \mathsf{G}$ and in Step 4 the comparison $R_1 == T$ should return TRUE. For any adversary $\mathcal{A}$ attacking the protocol, we can construct an adversary $\mathcal{S}$ who can forge the ECDSA signature as per experiment $Exp\text{-}Sign_{S,\pi}(\kappa)$ (See Sect. 2.1, Definition 1) with probability negligibly close to the probability with which $\mathcal{A}$ can forge a signature as per experiment $Exp\text{-}DistSign_{A,\Pi}^b(\kappa)$ (See Sect. 3.1, Definition 3). Formally, we prove that, if the Paillier encryption system is secure against chosen-plaintext attacks, then for all PPT adversaries $\mathcal{A}$ and every $b \in \{1, 2\}$, there exists a PPT algorithm $\mathcal{S}$ and a negligible function $\epsilon'$ such that $\forall \kappa$:

$$|\Pr[Exp\text{-}Sign_{S,\pi}(\kappa)] - \Pr[Exp\text{-}DistSign_{A,\Pi}^b(\kappa)]| \leq \epsilon'(\kappa), \qquad (8)$$

where $\Pi$ denotes our threshold signature protocol and $\pi$ denotes the ECDSA signature scheme.

**Proof Given $P_1$ is Corrupted ($b=1$).** Let $\mathcal{A}$ be a probabilistic polynomial time adversary in $Exp\text{-}DistSign^1_{\mathcal{A},\Pi}(\kappa)$ who can forge a signature using our threshold signing protocol; we construct a probabilistic polynomial time adversary denoted by $\mathcal{S}$ for experiment $Exp\text{-}Sign_{\mathcal{S},\pi}(\kappa)$ who can forge an ECDSA signature. The adversary $\mathcal{S}$ simulates the execution of the adversary $\mathcal{A}$ as formally shown below:

- In $Exp\text{-}Sign$, the adversary $\mathcal{S}$ receives public parameters $(\kappa, A)$, where $A$ denotes the public verification key of ECDSA scheme.
- $\mathcal{S}$ invokes $\mathcal{A}$ on input $\kappa$ and simulates oracle $\Pi$ for $\mathcal{A}$ in $Exp\text{-}DistSign$, by responding as described below:
    1. $\mathcal{S}$ replies with a $\perp$ to all queries of $\mathcal{A}$ of the form $(sid, \cdot)$ to $\Pi$ by $\mathcal{A}$ before the key-generation phase is executed. $\mathcal{S}$ replies with a $\perp$ to all queries from $\mathcal{A}$ before it queries $(0,0)$.
    2. Once $\mathcal{A}$ sends query $(0,0)$ to $\Pi$, the adversary $\mathcal{S}$ receives $(0, m_1)$ as $P_1$'s first message in the distributed key generation phase. $\mathcal{S}$ computes the oracle reply as follows:
        (a) $\mathcal{S}$ parses $m_1$ into the form $(\text{com-prove}, 1, A_1, a_1)$ that $P_1$ sends to $\mathcal{F}^S_{com-zk}$ in the hybrid model.
        (b) $\mathcal{S}$ verifies that $A_1 = a_1 \cdot G$. If it holds, it computes $A_2 = (a_1)^{-1} \cdot A$; else, $\mathcal{S}$ just chooses a random $A_2$.
        (c) $\mathcal{S}$ sets the oracle response of $\Pi$ as $(proof, 2, A_2)$ and sends it to $\mathcal{A}$.
    3. $\mathcal{S}$ receives the next message of the form $(0, m_2)$, which it processes as follows:
        (a) $\mathcal{S}$ parses $m_2$ into the form $(\text{decom-proof}, sid\|1)$ which is the message that $\mathcal{A}$ would send to $\mathcal{F}^S_{com-zk}$.
        (b) If $A_1 \neq a_1 \cdot G$, then $\mathcal{S}$ simulates an abort and the experiment concludes. If $\mathcal{S}$ does not abort, the distributed key generation phase is completed.
    4. Once $\mathcal{S}$ receives a query of the form $(sid, m)$, where $sid$ is a new session identifier never queried before, $\mathcal{S}$ queries the signing oracle in experiment $Exp\text{-}Sign$ with message $m$ and receives back signature $(r, s)$ from the signing oracle. Next, using the ECDSA verification algorithm, $\mathcal{S}$ computes the Elliptic curve point $R$. Once $\mathcal{S}$ receives queries from $\mathcal{A}$ with identifier $sid$, they are processed as follows:
        (a) The first message $(sid, m_1)$ is processed by parsing the message $m_1$ as $(\text{com-prove}, sid\|1, R_1, k_1, \tilde{R}, \tilde{k})$. If $R_1 = k_1 \cdot G$ and $\tilde{R} = \tilde{k} \cdot R_1$, then $\mathcal{S}$ sets $R_2 = k_1^{-1} \cdot R$, otherwise it chooses $R_2$ at random. $\mathcal{S}$ sets the oracle reply to $\mathcal{A}$ with message $(proof, sid\|2, R_2)$ which $\mathcal{A}$ expects in return.
        (b) The second message $(sid, m_2)$ is processed by first parsing $m_2 = (\text{decom-proof}, sid\|1)$ from $\mathcal{A}$. If $R_1 \neq k_1 \cdot G$, then $\mathcal{S}$ simulates $P_2$ aborting and the experiment ends.
        (c) The third message $(sid, m_3)$ is processed by first parsing $m_3 = (\text{com-prove}, sid\|3, C, \tilde{k}^{-1}k_1^{-1}(-a_1))$ from $\mathcal{A}$. If $C \neq Enc(\tilde{k}^{-1}(k_1)^{-1}(-a_1), pk_1)$, by means of ZKP verification

using $(C, pk_1)$ then $\mathcal{S}$ simulates $P_2$ to abort and the experiment concludes.

(d) The fourth message $(sid, m_4)$ is processed by first parsing $m_4 =$ (com-prove, $sid\|3, S_1, \tilde{k}^{-1}k_1^{-1}(m + a_1 r))$ from $\mathcal{A}$. Now $\mathcal{S}$ verifies $(S_1, \tilde{R}))$ is valid ECDSA signature, incase it is invalid then $\mathcal{S}$ simulates $P_2$ to abort and the experiment concludes. Else, $\mathcal{S}$ computes cipher-text $Z \leftarrow Enc(s \cdot m, pk)$, wherein $s$ is calculated using $(k_2, m, a_2, S_1)$ and sets the oracle reply to $\mathcal{A}$ as $Z$.

- Whenever $\mathcal{A}$ halts and outputs a pair $(m^*, \sigma^*)$, the adversary $S$ outputs $(m^*, \sigma^*)$ and halts.

Next, we proceed to prove that Eq. 8 holds. In the distributed key generation phase, the only difference between the simulation and real execution lies in the generation of $A_2$. During the simulation with $\mathcal{A}$, $\mathcal{S}$ generates the public key equal to the public key $A$ received from experiment $Exp - Sign$. Note that, $\mathcal{S}$ defines $A_2 = (a_1)^{-1} \cdot A$, and $\mathcal{A}$ is committed to $A_1 = a_1 \cdot G$. Therefore, the public key is defined as $a_1 \cdot A_2 = a_1 \cdot (a_1)^{-1} \cdot A = A$ as required. Therefore, the view between the real execution and simulation of $\mathcal{A}$ is identical, and the public verification key is $A$.

Next, we show that the view of $\mathcal{A}$ in the simulation above is statistically close to the view in the real execution of our protocol in the distributed sig-nature generation phase. The only difference between the real execution and simulation of $\mathcal{A}$ is the generation of ciphertext $Z$. $R$ is generated from ECDSA, and hence the distribution of $k_1^{-1} \cdot R$ and $k_2 \cdot G$ is identical. Similarly, the zero-knowledge proofs and verifications are also identically distributed in the $\mathcal{F}_z k, \mathcal{F}_{com-zk}$ hybrid model. In the ECDSA signature, $s = k^{-1} \cdot (m + ar)$ mod $q = (k^{-1}(m + a_1 r) \cdot (m + a_2 r) - k^{-1} a_1 a_2 r^2) \cdot m^{-1}$. Therefore, there exists some $l \in \mathbb{Z}_q$ such that $(k^{-1}(m + a_1 r) \cdot (m + a_2 r) - k^{-1} a_1 a_2 r^2) \cdot m^{-1} = s \cdot m + l \cdot q$.

Thus, the distribution of $Z$ in the real execution and simulation is statisti-cally close. The pair $(m^*, \sigma^*)$ output by $\mathcal{A}$ is a valid signature with negligible probability in the simulation and experiment $Exp\text{-}DistSign$. Since the public key in the simulation is the same public key that $\mathcal{S}$ receives in $Exp\text{-}Sign$, a valid forgery by $\mathcal{A}$ in $Exp\text{-}Sign$ implies a valid forgery by $\mathcal{S}$ in $Exp\text{-}Sign$. Thus, Eq. 8 follows.

**Proof Given $P_2$ is Corrupted ($b=2$).** We follow the same proof technique as for the case where $P_1$ is corrupted, by constructing a simulator $\mathcal{S}$ that simulates the view of $\mathcal{A}$ while interaction as per experiment $Exp\text{-}Sign_{S,\pi}(\kappa)$. The only difference in the simulation is the case where the last message from $P_2$ to $P_1$ is an encryption $Z$, which may be maliciously constructed by $\mathcal{A}$ and the simulator fails to detect it. In order to solve this, we construct $\mathcal{S}$ such that $\mathcal{S}$ simulates $P_1$ aborting at some random point. Let $\mathcal{S}$ choose $i \in \{1, 2, \cdots, p(\kappa) + 1\}$ randomly, where $p(\kappa)$ is the upper bound of the number of queries made by $\mathcal{A}$.

**Protocol 2 ThreshSig**: The distributed signature generation protocol

*Inputs.*

- A hash value $m = \texttt{HASH}(\texttt{M})$, where M is a message string.
- Paillier modulus N.
- Unique session id sid that has not been used before.

*Goal.* The two parties Alice and Bob compute a valid signature $(r, \mathbf{s})$ on $m$ or output abort.

*The protocol:*

1. Alice generates $k_1 \xleftarrow{\$} \mathbb{Z}_q$, computes $R_1 = k_1 \, \mathsf{G}$.
2. Alice sends commitment and proof of knowledge as (com-prove, $sid \, \|1, R_1, k_1$) to $\mathcal{F}^{S}_{com-zk}$.
3. Bob receives (proof-receipt, $sid \, \|1$) from $\mathcal{F}^{S}_{com-zk}$.
4. Bob generates $k_2 \xleftarrow{\$} \mathbb{Z}_q$, computes $R_2 = k_1 \, \mathsf{G}$.
5. Bob sends (prove, $sid \, \|2, R_2, k_2$) to $\mathcal{F}^{S}_{zk}$.
6. Alice receives (proof, $sid \, \|2, R_2$) from $\mathcal{F}^{S}_{zk}$. If not, it aborts.
7. Alice sends (decom-proof, $sid \, \|1$) to $\mathcal{F}^{S}_{com-zk}$.
8. Bob receives (decom-proof, $sid \, \|1, R_1$) to $\mathcal{F}^{S}_{com-zk}$.
9. Alice computes $R = k_1 R_2$ and Bob computes $R = k_2 R_1$.
10. Alice and Bob locally compute $r = x_R \pmod q$.
11. Alice generates $\tilde{k} \xleftarrow{\$} \mathbb{Z}_q$, computes $\tilde{R} = \tilde{k} R_1$.
12. Alice computes $\mathbf{s_1} = \tilde{k}^{-1} k_1^{-1} (m + a_1 \, r) \pmod q$
13. Alice computes and $\mathsf{C} = \texttt{Enc}(\tilde{k}^{-1} k_1^{-1}(-a_1), \, \mathsf{pk_A})$
14. Alice computes NIZK-proof $\Pi_5$ (See Appendix A) which states the following:
    - That C is a valid encryption of under the public key of Alice.
15. Alice sends $(\mathbf{s_1}, \tilde{R}, \mathsf{C}, \Pi_5)$ to Bob.
16. Bob verifies that the value of $\mathbf{s_1}$ is computed using valid keys and agreed value of $m$. For this he verifies that $\sigma_1(\mathbf{s_1}, \tilde{R})$ is a valid signature (with Alice private keys ) on $m$.
17. Bob verifies $\Pi_5$ and aborts if not valid.
18. Bob computes $\mathbf{s_2} = k_2^{-1} \cdot (m + a_2 \cdot r) \pmod q$
19. Bob computes $\alpha = k_2^{-1} a_2 \, r^2 \pmod q$
20. Bob computes

$$Y_1 = \texttt{Enc}(\mathbf{s_1} \cdot \mathbf{s_2}, \, \mathsf{pk_A}) \qquad Y_2 = \mathsf{C}^\alpha \mod \mathsf{N}^2 \tag{9}$$

and then multiplies them

$$Z = (Y_1 * Y_2) \mod \mathsf{N}^2 \tag{10}$$

which is sent back to Alice.
21. Alice computes $\mathbf{s'} = [\texttt{Dec}(Z, \mathsf{sk_A}) \cdot \tilde{k} m^{-1}] \pmod q$
22. Exactly one of the two values $(r, \mathbf{s'})$ or $(r, (\mathsf{N} - \mathbf{s'}) \pmod q)$ is valid signature. Alice verifies both values and chooses $\mathbf{s}$ accordingly.
23. Alice outputs $\sigma = (r, \mathbf{s})$ as signature on the message $m$.

Since $\mathcal{S}$'s choice of $i$ is correct with a probability $\frac{1}{p(\kappa)+1}$, therefore $\mathcal{S}$ can simulate $\mathcal{A}$'s view with a probability $\frac{1}{p(\kappa)+1}$. This means that, $\mathcal{S}$ can forge a signature in $Exp\text{-}Sign_{\mathcal{S},\pi}(\kappa)$ with probability at least $\frac{1}{p(\kappa)+1}$ times the probability with which $\mathcal{A}$ can forge a signature in $Exp\text{-}DistSign^2_{\mathcal{A},\Pi}(\kappa)$. Let $\mathcal{A}$ be a PPT adversary. $\mathcal{S}$ proceeds to simulate the query response of $\mathcal{A}$ as follows:

- In $Exp\text{-}Sign$, adversary $\mathcal{S}$ receives public parameter $(\kappa, A)$, where $A$ is the public key for ECDSA.
- Let $p(\cdot)$ be an upper bound on the number of queries made by $\mathcal{A}$ to $\Pi$. $\mathcal{S}$ chooses a random $i \in \{1, \cdots, p(n)+1\}$.
- $\mathcal{S}$ invokes $\mathcal{A}$ on input $\kappa$ and simulates oracle $\Pi$ for $\mathcal{A}$ in experiment $Exp\text{-}DistSign$ by responding to the queries as shown below:
  1. $\mathcal{S}$ replies with a $\perp$ to all queries of the form $(sid, \cdot)$ to $\Pi$ by $\mathcal{A}$ before the key-generation phase has completed. Before a query sent of the form $(0,0)$, $\mathcal{S}$ replies with a $\perp$ to all queries from $\mathcal{A}$.
  2. Once $\mathcal{A}$ sends a query $(0,0)$, adversary $\mathcal{S}$ responds with $(proof - receipt, 1)$ as expected by $\mathcal{A}$.
  3. $\mathcal{S}$ processes the next message $(0, m_1)$ as follows:
     (a) $\mathcal{S}$ parses $m_1$ into the form $(prove, 2, A_2, a_2)$ that $P_2$ sends to $\mathcal{F}^S_{com-zk}$ in the hybrid model.
     (b) $\mathcal{S}$ verifies if $A_2$ is a non-zero point on the curve and $A_2 = a_2 \cdot G$. If the verification fails, $\mathcal{S}$ simulates $P_1$ aborting and halts.
     (c) $\mathcal{S}$ sets the oracle response to $\mathcal{A}$ to be $(decom\text{-}proof, 1, A_1)$ where $A_1 = (a_2)^{-1} \cdot A$. $\mathcal{S}$ stores $(a_2, A)$ and the key distribution phase is concluded.
  4. Upon receipt of a query $(sid, m)$ where $sid$ is a new session identifier never queried before, $\mathcal{S}$ computes the oracle reply as $(proof\text{-}receipt, sid\|1)$ as expected by $\mathcal{A}$ and sends to $\mathcal{A}$.
     Next, $\mathcal{S}$ queries the signing oracle in experiment $Exp - Sign$ with message $m$ and receives signature $(r, s)$. $\mathcal{S}$ uses the ECDSA verification algorithm to compute the Elliptic curve point $R$, and responds to the queries from $\mathcal{A}$ with identifier $sid$ as shown below:
     - $\mathcal{S}$ parses the first message $(sid, m_1)$ as $(prove, sid\|2, R_2, k_2)$ that $\mathcal{A}$ sends to $\mathcal{F}^S_{zk}$. $\mathcal{S}$ verifies that $R_2 = k_2 \cdot G$ and $R_2$ is a non-zero point on the curve. If not, it simulates $P_1$ and aborts the protocol. $\mathcal{S}$ computes $R_1 = k_2^{-1} \cdot R$ and sets the oracle reply as $(decom - proof, sid\|1, R_1)$ as expected from $\mathcal{F}^S_{com-zk}$.
     - The second message $(sid, m_2)$ is processed by $\mathcal{S}$ by parsing $m_2$ as $Z$. If this is the $i$th call to the oracle by $\mathcal{A}$, then $\mathcal{S}$ simulates $P_1$ aborting, else it continues.
- Whenever $\mathcal{A}$ halts and outputs a pair $(m^*, \sigma^*)$, the adversary $\mathcal{S}$ also outputs $(m^*, \sigma^*)$ and halts.

Let $j$ be the first query to oracle $\Pi$ of the form $(sid, m_2)$, and $P_1$ does not obtain a valid signature $\sigma = (r, s)$ corresponding to the public key $A$. If

$j = i$, then the difference between the distribution of the simulation and the real execution lies in the ciphertext $C$. Therefore, we can show that,

$$| \Pr[Exp\text{-}Sign_{S,\pi}(\kappa) = 1|i = j] - \Pr[Exp\text{-}DistSign_{A,\Pi}^2(\kappa) = 1]| \leq \epsilon'(\kappa).$$

Therefore,

$$\Pr[Exp\text{-}DistSign_{A,\Pi}^2(\kappa) = 1] \leq \frac{\Pr[Exp\text{-}Sign_{S,\pi}(\kappa) = 1]}{1/(p(\kappa) + 1)} + \epsilon'(\kappa)$$

That is,

$$\Pr[Exp\text{-}Sign_{S,\pi}(\kappa) = 1] \geq \frac{Exp\text{-}DistSign_{A,\Pi}^2(\kappa) = 1}{1/(p(\kappa) + 1)} - \epsilon'(\kappa)$$

The above implies that if $\mathcal{A}$ forges a signature using our threshold signing algorithm in $Exp\text{-}DistSign_{A,\Pi}^2$ with a non-negligible probability, then $\mathcal{S}$ forges a general ECDSA signature in $Exp\text{-}Sign_{S,\pi}$ with non-negligible probability, which contradicts the assumed security of ECDSA. This completes the proof of the theorem.

## 4   Experiments

We have simulated our protocols and measured their performance (in terms of) time taken for key generation and signature generation. The experimental setup includes two parties viz. Alice and Bob on two different machines connected over WAN. They follow steps and jointly compute the shared secret key and signature in the key generation and signature generation protocols respectively. We have used the 2048 bits Paillier modulus and ECDSA defined on the standard Bitcoin curve (SECP256k1). The entire code base is built in C using the openssl based ECC library for the elliptic curve operations and MPZ library for all the number theoretic operations. The ECDSA signature generated by our two party scheme can be verified by any ECDSA verification algorithm. The experiments were run on nodes running on Intel I5 pro processor with 8 cores each with processor speed of 1.7 Ghz. The Random Access Memory (RAM) of the machine is 16 GB with Ubuntu 18.0 operating system. Our implementation was optimized with multithreads. Of all the known 2-of-2 schemes our scheme has the most efficient key generation protocol. In case of cryptocurrencies where key generation happens for every transaction our method seems to be suitable. If we consider the overall performance, our scheme is comparable with the state of the art.

Some other two party ECDSA schemes include a scheme by Castgnoes et al. [4] which generalizes Lindell's approach. In terms of timings, this scheme (on P256 curve) takes about 5521 ms, 101 ms for key gen and signing respectively. More recent two party ECDSA is by Haiyang et al. [23] which proposed a scheme based on online-offline techniques. Main idea in the scheme is to delegate most of the computations to offline phase while minimising computations and communications during signing phase. Their scheme has two varieties, one using Paillier and another using OT based techniques. In Paillier based technique their scheme takes about 141 ms in offline phase while 0.2 ms in online phase (cf. Table 1).

**Table 1.** Comparison of Timings

|  | Key Generation | Signature Computation |
|---|---|---|
|  | Time in Milliseconds | |
| Lindell [19] | 2435 | 36.8 |
| Doerner et al. [9] | 44.32 | 2.27 |
| Our Scheme | 5.1 | 39 |

## 5  Efficiency Comparison

In the known two party ECDSA schemes the most efficient one are by Lindell [19] and Doerner *et al.* [9]. The protocol by Lindell requires the following number of operations. The key generation protocol in [19] appears to be very expensive with approximately 350 numbers of Paillier encryptions/exponentiations by each party. The cost is primarily dominated by Paillier exponentiations and range proofs for Paillier encryptions. For the signing protocol in [19], party $P_1$ computes 7 Elliptic curve multiplications and 1 Paillier decryption, while party $P_2$ computes 5 Elliptic curve multiplications, 1 Paillier encryption, 1 homomorphic scalar multiplication and 1 Paillier homomorphic addition. The protocol by Doerner *et al.* requires the following number of operations. The key generation protocol requires 10 exponentiations. In their signing protocol, both the parties compute 17 modular exponentiations.

Our protocol remarkably improves the efficiency of the key generation algorithm with each party computing only 4 Elliptic curve multiplications inclusive of the zero-knowledge proofs. For our signing algorithm, party $P_1$ computes 11 Elliptic curve multiplications (including the computations in the zero-knowledge proofs), 1 Paillier encryption and 1 Paillier decryption, while party $P_2$ performs 5 Elliptic curve multiplications, 1 Paillier encryption and 2 Paillier scalar multiplication. Table 1 shows a comparison analysis of our scheme against the two existing efficient threshold signature scheme. From the table we see that our key generation protocol is very efficient as compared to the existing two schemes and overall, is as efficient as the state-of-the-art efficient scheme due to Doerner *et al.* [9].

### 5.1  Efficient ECDSA Semi-aggregation Property

Signature aggregation means combining two or more (independent) signatures into a single one that can be verified using a single (aggregated) public key. It is well known that such aggregation can be very useful. Our proposed two party ECDSA scheme has "semi-aggregation" property that comes very close to aggregation. Suppose there are two parties $P_1, P_2$ who already have their ECDSA keys $(a_1, A_1), (a_1, A_2)$ (respectively). Using these keys the parties can sign on any message (hash) $m$ by running Protocol 2 [Signature Computation protocol]. The output signature can be verified using the public key given by

$A_1 + A_2$. In contrast the known protocols like [9,19] require that the parties first run key generation protocol and then compute signature. This is a useful tool, especially in cryptocurrencies. Example use case scenarios where our proposed two party scheme is useful are as follows:

- In blockchain scenario usually digital assets [like cryptocurrencies] are bound to public keys. If two different users are pooling their currencies from two different addresses then the transaction will include two signatures along with two public keys. Considering the fact that the size of block is fixed, this overhead affects the number of transactions processed per each block. By our signature aggregation the user can append only one signature (and corresponding public key). In such scenario the two party ECDSA scheme proposed in this paper is most suitable.

## 5.2 Extension to General $(t, n)$ Threshold Scheme

A 2-of-$n$ threshold signature scheme is one in which the private key is distributed among $n$ parties such that any two of them can compute signature. It is a known fact that any 2-of-n threshold scheme can be extended to a 2-of-n scheme. The only modification needed to achieve this is to let each party distribute its private key using a $(2, n)$ threshold (verifiable) secret sharing scheme. Note that verifiable secret sharing schemes (as against simple secret sharing ones) can be used in a trustless set up. A more challenging task is to extend our two party ECDSA scheme to a general $(t, n)$ threshold scheme. Currently this work is in progress.

## 6   Conclusion

The design of ECDSA algorithm makes it particularly challenging and unsuitable for threshold schemes. Consequently, most of the known solutions involve complex cryptographic tools, making them inefficient for practice. This work presents a novel threshold ECDSA scheme in the two-party setting, based on the hardness of the ECDSA scheme in the random oracle model. Our scheme uses additive sharing of ECDSA keys with multiplicative sharing of session keys and this combination gives very efficient key generation protocol. Empirical analysis shows that our scheme is as efficient as the state-of-the-art design by Doerner *et al.*. An additional advantage of our scheme is that it enables two parties to aggregate their signature easily without requiring any key generation [or exchange] protocol. Our scheme can be easily extended to a $(2, n)$ threshold scheme. However, extending it to a general $(t, n)$ scheme seems to be more challenging. This work is currently in progress.

## Appendix 1. Elliptic Curve Digital Signature Algorithm

The ECDSA algorithm is parameterized by a group $\mathcal{G}$ of order $q$ generated by a point $\mathsf{G}$ on an elliptic curve over the finite field $\mathbb{Z}_q$ of integers modulo a prime $q$.

The curve coordinates and scalars are represented in $\kappa = |q|$ bits, which is also the security parameter. The algorithm makes use of a hash function which we denote by HASH. The ECDSA scheme consists of the following algorithms:

- **KeyGen:** The key generation algorithm consists of the following steps:
    - Select private-key: $a \xleftarrow{\$} \mathbb{Z}_q$
    - Compute public-key as the point (on $\mathcal{G}$) given by $A = a \cdot \mathsf{G}$.
- **Sig:** The signature generation algorithm takes as input a message M and computes the signature as below:
    - Hash M onto $\mathbb{Z}_q$: $m \longleftarrow$ HASH(M).
    - Generate nonce: $k \xleftarrow{\$} \mathbb{Z}_q$.
    - Compute $k \cdot \mathsf{G} = R = (x_R, y_R, 1)$ and set $r = x_R \pmod q$.
    - Set: $\mathsf{s} = k^{-1} \cdot (m + a \cdot r) \in \mathbb{Z}_q$.
    - Output $\sigma = (r, \mathsf{s})$ as a signature on M
- **Ver:** The signature verification algorithm takes as input a message M and signature $\sigma = (r, \mathsf{s})$ and verifies it as below:
    - Compute $\mathsf{s}^{-1} \pmod q \, [= k \, (m + ar)^{-1}]$
    - Obtain hash of M: $m \longleftarrow$ HASH(M).
    - Set $R' \longleftarrow \mathsf{s}^{-1} m \cdot \mathsf{G} + \mathsf{s}^{-1} r a \cdot \mathsf{G}$ (which simplifies to $k\mathsf{G}$)
    - If $x_{R'} = r$ then return 'signature valid' else return 'signature not valid'.

## Appendix 2. NIZK Proof of Knowledge of Plaintext using Paillier Encryption

We use a NIZK protocol from [7] to prove knowledge of plaintexts $X_1$ and $X_2$ in zero knowledge, in Sect. 3.3, under *ThreshSig* algorithm. The following $\sum$-protocol provides a non-interactive ZKP that the prover has knowledge of the plaintext without revealing the plaintext to the approver. Let the input encryption be $C_1 = X_1 \cdot G + N \cdot r \mod N^2$, where $X_1$ is encrypted using randomness $r$. The proof proceeds as below:

1. Prover $P$ chooses $x \in \mathbb{Z}_N$, $u \in \mathbb{Z}_{N^2}^*$ at random and *computesthe*following and sends to the verifier:

$$A = x \cdot G + N \cdot u \mod N^2$$

2. The verifier picks a random challenge $e$ and sends to the prover $P$.
3. The prover $P$ computes the following and sends to the verifier:

$$w = x + eX_1 \mod N, \; z = u + e \cdot r \mod N^2$$

4. The verifier checks the following:

$$w \cdot G + N \cdot z \stackrel{?}{=} A + e \cdot C_1 \mod N^2$$

The verifier accepts the proof if and only if the above check passes.

The above $\sum$ protocol proves knowledge of $X_1, r$ such that $C_1 = X_1 \cdot G + N \cdot r$. A similar protocol is run to prove the knowledge of the plaintext $X_2$ for ciphertext $C_2$ with zero knowledge.

# Appendix 3. Schnorr's ZKP for Discrete Log

We give a zero-knowledge proof of discrete logarithm [10] given as input the description of a prime-order group $\mathbb{G}$ of order $q$ and a generator $G$, and a group element $h$. The prover has a witness a value $x \in \mathbb{Z}_q$ such that $x \cdot G = h$. The proof of discrete log without revealing the logarithm value proceeds as below:

1. Prover $P$ picks $r \in \mathbb{Z}_q$, computes the value $\rho = r \cdot G$ and $e = \mathtt{HASH}(\rho, G, h)$.
2. Next, it computes $d = e \cdot x + r \mod q$ and sends $(d, \rho, h)$ to the verifier.
3. The verifier computes $f = \mathtt{HASH}(\rho, G, h)$ and accepts the proof if and only if the following check is satisfied:

$$d \cdot P \overset{?}{=} f \cdot h + \rho$$

The protocol proves the verifier that the prover knows the discrete log of $h$ in zero knowledge.

# References

1. Aumasson, J.-P., Hamelink, A., Shlomovits, O.: A survey of ECDSA threshold signing. IACR Cryptol. ePrint Arch. **2020**, 1390 (2020)
2. Aumasson, J.P., Shlomovits, O.: Attacking threshold wallets. Cryptology ePrint Archive, Report 2020/1052 (2020). https://ia.cr/2020/1052
3. Canetti, R., Gennaro, R., Goldfeder, S., Makriyannis, N., Peled, U.: UC non-interactive, proactive, threshold ECDSA with identifiable aborts. Cryptology ePrint Archive, Paper 2021/060 (2021). https://eprint.iacr.org/2021/060
4. Castagnos, G., Catalano, D., Laguillaumie, F., Savasta, F., Tucker, I.: Two-party ECDSA from hash proof systems and efficient instantiations. Cryptology ePrint Archive, Paper 2019/503 (2019). https://eprint.iacr.org/2019/503
5. Castagnos, G., Catalano, D., Laguillaumie, F., Savasta, F., Tucker, I.: Bandwidth-efficient threshold EC-DSA revisited: Online/offline extensions, identifiable aborts, proactivity and adaptive security. Cryptology ePrint Archive, Paper 2021/291 (2021). https://eprint.iacr.org/2021/291
6. Chainalysis.     https://blog.chainalysis.com/reports/2022-crypto-crime-report-introduction/. Accessed 9 Feb 2022
7. Cramer, R., Damgård, I., Nielsen, J.B.: Multiparty computation from threshold homomorphic encryption. In: Pfitzmann, B. (ed.) EUROCRYPT 2001. LNCS, vol. 2045, pp. 280–300. Springer, Heidelberg (2001). https://doi.org/10.1007/3-540-44987-6_18
8. Damgård, I., Jakobsen, T.P., Nielsen, J.B., Pagter, J.I., Østergaard, M.B.: Fast threshold ECDSA with honest majority. In: Galdi, C., Kolesnikov, V. (eds.) SCN 2020. LNCS, vol. 12238, pp. 382–400. Springer, Cham (2020). https://doi.org/10.1007/978-3-030-57990-6_19
9. Doerner, J., Kondi, Y., Lee, E., Shelat, A.: Secure two-party threshold ECDSA from ECDSA assumptions. In: 2018 IEEE Symposium on Security and Privacy (SP), pp. 980–997 (2018)
10. Fiat, A., Shamir, A.: How to prove yourself: practical solutions to identification and signature problems. In: Odlyzko, A.M. (ed.) CRYPTO 1986. LNCS, vol. 263, pp. 186–194. Springer, Heidelberg (1987). https://doi.org/10.1007/3-540-47721-7_12

11. Gennaro, R., Goldfeder, S.: Fast multiparty threshold ECDSA with fast trustless setup. In: Proceedings of the 2018 ACM SIGSAC Conference on Computer and Communications Security, pp. 1179–1194 (2018)

12. Gennaro, R., Goldfeder, S.: One round threshold ECDSA with identifiable abort. IACR Cryptol. ePrint Arch. **2020**, 540 (2020)

13. Gennaro, R., Goldfeder, S., Narayanan, A.: Threshold-optimal DSA/ECDSA signatures and an application to bitcoin wallet security. In: Manulis, M., Sadeghi, A.-R., Schneider, S. (eds.) ACNS 2016. LNCS, vol. 9696, pp. 156–174. Springer, Cham (2016). https://doi.org/10.1007/978-3-319-39555-5_9

14. Goldwasser, S., Micali, S., Rivest, R.L.: A digital signature scheme secure against adaptive chosen-message attacks. SIAM J. Comput. **17**(2), 281–308 (1988)

15. Hazay, C., Mikkelsen, G.L., Rabin, T., Toft, T.: Efficient RSA key generation and threshold Paillier in the two-party setting. In: Dunkelman, O. (ed.) CT-RSA 2012. LNCS, vol. 7178, pp. 313–331. Springer, Heidelberg (2012). https://doi.org/10.1007/978-3-642-27954-6_20

16. Hoffman, P., Wijngaards, W.C.: Elliptic curve digital signature algorithm (DSA) for DNSSEC. RFC **6605**, 1–8 (2012)

17. Itakura, K., Nakamura, K.: A public-key cryptosystem suitable for digital multisignatures. NEC Res. Dev. **71**, 1–8 (1983)

18. Johnson, D., Menezes, A., Vanstone, S.A.: The elliptic curve digital signature algorithm (ECDSA). Int. J. Inf. Sec. **1**(1), 36–63 (2001)

19. Lindell, Y.: Fast secure two-party ECDSA signing. In: Katz, J., Shacham, H. (eds.) CRYPTO 2017. LNCS, vol. 10402, pp. 613–644. Springer, Cham (2017). https://doi.org/10.1007/978-3-319-63715-0_21

20. Lindell, Y., Nof, A.: Fast secure multiparty ECDSA with practical distributed key generation and applications to cryptocurrency custody. In: Proceedings of the 2018 ACM SIGSAC Conference on Computer and Communications Security (2018)

21. MacKenzie, P., Reiter, M.K.: Two-party generation of DSA signatures. In: Kilian, J. (ed.) CRYPTO 2001. LNCS, vol. 2139, pp. 137–154. Springer, Heidelberg (2001). https://doi.org/10.1007/3-540-44647-8_8

22. Wood, G., et al.: Ethereum: a secure decentralised generalised transaction ledger. Ethereum Proj. Yellow Pap. **151**(2014), 1–32 (2014)

23. Xue, H., Au, M.H., Xie, X., Yuen, T.H., Cui, H.: Efficient online-friendly two-party ECDSA signature. In: Proceedings of the 2021 ACM SIGSAC Conference on Computer and Communications Security, pp. 558–573 (2021)

# Secure Smart Grid Data Aggregation Based on Fog Computing and Blockchain Technology

Kamalakanta Sethi[1]($\boxtimes$), Aniket Agrawal[2], and Padmalochan Bera[2]

[1] Indian Institute of Information Technology, Sri City, Chittoor, India
kamalakanta.s@iiits.in
[2] Indian Institute of Technology, Bhubaneswar, Bhubaneswar, India
aa22@iitbbs.ac.in, plb@iitbbs.ac.in

**Abstract.** As part of the fourth industrial revolution, it is projected that a huge number of Internet of Things (IoT) devices would be supplied and employed. However, the preexisting Internet may not appropriately address concerns about information security in an unfamiliar setting. Therefore, for the smart grid application, we propose a privacy-preserving data aggregation scheme under a permissioned blockchain based fog system architecture. First, the user data is acquired with a specific frequency through the IoT meters deployed at the industrial, commercial and residential locations. Second, the users leverage the modified ElGamal homomorphic cryptosystem to enable the additive computability and secrecy of their extracted energy information. Here, the encryption is performed using the public key of the district aggregator fog node as well as the user secret share. Fog nodes employ a private enterprise blockchain framework called Hyperledger Fabric to facilitate the user transaction record consistency, validation and traceability for their respective districts. Then, the resulting electricity consumption ciphertext is progressively aggregated throughout the day as it journeys from the end-user grid edge device to the power supply company (PS) in the cloud via the fog layer. We ensure robustness towards major cyberattacks and integrity of the data while in transit through pairing-based modified Boneh-Lynn-Shacham short signature, time-stamping and hashing function (SHA-256). Lastly, demand response is vital to maximize the benefits of diverse parties by promoting a shift of the energy consumption from higher-priced peak hours of the day with maximum power demand to leaner demand periods when power supplies can be relatively inexpensive. It is essential on a broad scale to minimize the blackout risk when demand threatens to surpass supply and trip the power lines. Therefore, our advocated fog cryptosystem premised on a modular blockchain ensures secure and tamperproof data processing from multiple participants in a decentralized setup.

**Keywords:** Smart grid · IoT meter · Fog computing · Blockchain · Hyperledger Fabric · ElGamal homomorphic encryption · Shamir secret sharing · Demand response · Price elasticity · Clustering

© The Author(s), under exclusive license to Springer Nature Switzerland AG 2023
V. Muthukkumarasamy et al. (Eds.): ICISS 2023, LNCS 14424, pp. 431–448, 2023.
https://doi.org/10.1007/978-3-031-49099-6_26

# 1   Introduction

In the 21$^{st}$ century, the Fourth Industrial Revolution (Industry 4.0, 4IR) aims to define a forthcoming factory ecosystem featuring smart automation through interconnectedness of the industrial system components. Internet of Things (IoT) can play a vital role in this revolution for the energy consumption data collection and analysis under the advanced metering infrastructure (AMI). The created IoT framework can be used to provide "smart" communication and computation functionalities at all meter nodes by installing resources fewer than a standard computer [1]. Nevertheless, the application of IoT in industrial settings is still in its infancy. Therefore, Industrial IoT (IIoT) emphasizes more on the real time integration of computational and the physical elements also referred to as cyber physical system (CPS).

IIoT will act as one of the core elements of Industry 4.0 which anticipates significant changes in technology employed by CPS [2]. One such critical CPS, smart grid AMI employs networked digital meters and communication architecture that are technologically more superior and advanced than their traditional predecessors. This next-generation electrical grid enables the power utility firm to significantly improve their electricity generation and dissemination, digital consumption information collection and analysis, and power system management [3]. But, the energy consumption data collected through the AMI network can be used by power supply companies for prediction related to the usage pattern and, as a direct consequence, reception of information related to the behaviour of various types of consumers by tracking their equipment power use throughout the day [4]. Conversely, it may also be used to investigate burglary or other criminal activity, as well as to conduct demand response programs to guarantee grid stability.

In nutshell, such data driven insights are indeed a fundamental benefit of the smart grid and a major risk in terms of user privacy breach [5]. Furthermore, false data injection (FDI) and cyber tampering might well be detrimental, potentially as a result of malicious users and cyber-terrorists forging massive volumes of energy consumption statistics for their illegitimate benefits [6]. Also, utilities may delegate information management to a third party, resulting in some loss of control over the sensitive user data. Undoubtedly, the privacy-enhanced technologies resilient to typical grid attacks [1,7] are essential for reconciling the aforementioned goals associated with the data sensitivity prior to aggregation [8].

For the smart grid CPS, Industry 4.0 as a double-edged sword, has a potential to introduce some unknown and unprecedented cybersecurity challenges, because of which the users and power supply companies may have to incur massive financial losses. Therefore, the privacy-preserving smart grid data aggregation (PPSGDA) technique is needed for the energy consumption ciphertext at various geographical levels and frequencies.

## 1.1    Contributing Features

The majority of PPSGDA works do not support the integration of fog computing, blockchain and other essential functionalities. The primary design goal of our novel scheme is to architect a robust and practical mechanism equipped with combination of the following characteristics:

1) **Platform and Software as a service (PaaS + SaaS) Cloud Computing model:** Under the fog computing architecture, it is essential to securely connect, manage and aggregate the power data of a plethora of IoT devices as part of the AMI network. In Indian context, the number of such gadgets might be in the order of millions or crores. It is also crucial to store, maintain and analyze massive volumes of data fast and securely via parallellization. Therefore, to achieve scalability, we have leveraged the data storage services, computational capabilities, and other products of Google Cloud Platform (GCP), which is one of the largest and popular cloud service providers worldwide. In the performance analysis section, we have explained the services used and the obtained results in great detail.

2) **Enhanced Security and Performance:** To accomplish this, exponential ElGamal homomorphic cryptosystem and modified BLS short digital signature with timestamps are employed. This allows the energy supplier and intermediate district fog nodes to perform additive operations on, verify the integrity and authenticate the source of the ciphertext. The random share generated via Shamir secret sharing along with their efficient updates offer an additional layer of security to remedy the individual data privacy issue. The costly overall aggregation is parallellized and optimized via treatment of each fog node as a thread.

3) **Decentralized Architecture:** We have integrated the fog computing and Hyperledger Fabric blockchain technologies in order to decentralize, expedite and make our PPSGDA cryptosystem more practical. In the proposed configuration, a subscriber is expected to submit a data transaction record to the AMI network nodes belonging to his/her district. Then, this is verified by the mining fog node who further reports the endorsement results. The obtained transactions are written into the ledger and a newly generated block is broadcasted in the concerned channel. In this way, each fog node aggregates the user data upon incremental database updates for the district participants under its control.

4) **Demand Response:** Power supply company determines the consumer electricity price by how much and when electricity is to be used to maintain the grid stability. For this, it mathematically quantifies the user response using the concepts of microeconomics. Specifically, we emphasize more on the demand elasticity with regard to the changes in the electricity price rather than the user income. We use a renowned and unsupervised machine learning (ML) algorithm called k-means++ clustering in order to recognize and filter out the right participants for the specific time frame.

## 2   Related Work

In literature, several schemes [9–14,39] achieved PPSGDA through fog devices [15] which can be utilised for reduction and redistribution of the computational and storage overhead of its cloud-based equivalent designs [16] to the edge of the devices at the end-point. The fogging functionality assists in making the cloud computing services accessible to the end users through their extension to the network edge. But, when a huge volume of grid data is transferred to the parent node, queuing delay due to network congestion impacts the prerequisites for a real-time response. Homomorphic cryptography is extensively used in this regard to enhance the secure data aggregation technology across various channels by minimizing communication cost and conserve bandwidth [17]. However, its malleability allows an attacker and consumers to counterfeit data by generating new ciphertext which decrypts to another pertinent plaintext through computational operations in the considered encrypted domain. Also, encryption when used solely may ensure data security but not privacy. Therefore, it is important to prevent the internal/external adversary from jeopardizing individual data privacy through a differential attack all across the data aggregation procedure [18]. A few schemes achieved differential privacy to remedy the mentioned issue [12–14]. The majority of the mentioned PPSGDA cryptosystems were centered on the additive homomorphic nature of Paillier encryption [19,20] while some needing one extra multiplication as well (mostly, for computing the encrypted dot product) have employed Boneh-Goh-Nissim (BGN) scheme [21,22]. A few works have used ElGamal encryption also [23,24] which is reported to be more efficient than its Paillier counterpart. But, additive ElGamal also necessitates a computable discrete logarithm, which culminates in a far more time-consuming decryption. [25]. Fortunately, several square root-related methods coupled with a decent computation capability make this calculation eminently practicable.

Ciphertext aggregation techniques require optimization as homomorphic encryption is slow by design. Numerous works have leveraged a well-known number theorem called Chinese remainder theorem (CRT) for speeding up encryption and decryption procedures [24,26,27]. For additive ElGamal, using CRT can be beneficial for reducing the time required to find the discrete logarithm. But, millions of users have to transmit multiple ciphertexts taking into consideration the modulus w.r.t. divisors of the original number. This significantly raises the total communication overhead and the required encryption time for millions of users merely to optimize single decryption by fog node in a specific time period. Therefore, we focus more on parallellization and inclusion of other essential features rather than exploiting the properties of the known mathematical techniques for optimization. A few works employed different versions of map-reduce techniques [28,29] to decomposed a large problem into smaller sub-problems that can be addresses concurrently. Some schemes facilitated functionalities such as anonymous authentication through blind and short randomizable signature techniques [11]. Data unforgeability, source authentication and non-repudiation were ensured in some PPSGDA schemes by adopting bilinear pairing based signature [7,30]. Several schemes also leveraged blockchain technology in order to deal with fairness and trust issues while performing secure multi-party computation (SMPC). For SMPC, blockchain [38,40] has been extensively utilised to ensure tamperproof records in a decentralized architecture in finance, IoT, healthcare and so on without necessitating the involvement of a trusted central authority. In paper [31], authors segregated the users into different groups, each with their own private blockchain. In paper [32], authors advocated a PPSGDA scheme for multidimensional data collection in the consortium blockchain. To overcome the limitations associated with public and permissionless blockchain lacking modularity, a few works relied on Hyperledger Fabric to enable involvement of peers, partial transparency of the user data and spatial collaboration [33]. In addition to the security concepts outlined above, maintaining the stability of the electric grid is also critical for its successful operation.

Partial power outages (brownouts) for temporary period and complete electricity shutdown (blackouts) occur for a variety of causes. For example, the world's first large-scale blackout, Ukraine power grid hack, occurred in 2015 due to a cyberattack whereas for the 2012 India blackout, which affected nearly 63 crore people of northern and eastern parts of India, it was speculated that a few north Indian states drawing power beyond the permissible limits was a major cause. In the former scenario, most of the system vulnerabilities can be mitigated by using advanced cryptographic protocols outlined earlier. We examine the latter case, wherein the excess consumption induces a demand-supply imbalance tripping the transmission lines with a cascading effect. One of the potential solutions, demand response (DR) has emerged as a viable research area for maintaining stability while billing in the smart grid AMI network. It targets the intended adjustments in energy consumption pattern to better match the user temporal electricity demand with the supply profile [14,19]. Offering suitable incentive methods for electricity grid businesses and customers is critical to maximise the benefits of various players. Here, the households are encouraged to reduce their total peak period consumption by shifting some loads from peak hours to off-peak hours. This is achieved through imposition and distribution of relatively higher and lower electricity prices when their demand should be decreased and increased throughout the day, respectively [34,35]. However, considering the large diversity in the industrial, residential, commercial and other consumers to be served in India, a variety of DR modules need to be prepared to cater to their diverse needs. Large scale industries can be the most important participants as they can alter their consumption to a great extent. But, a section of industrial users may have slow demand-response characteristics and less influenceable demand depending upon the nature of their business or industrial activity. For eg, power demand for a solar plant needing daytime sunlight for its operation must be high during day time. On the other hand, some residential households' demand profile may be influenced easily as they can use their appliances according to their needs at any time which is not fixed by any constraints. So, both kinds of the users can together help in achieving the desired total demand as flexibility shown by one kind of users by adjusting their consumption can be used to over compensate other's rigid and flat demand profile.

Therefore, when different types of subscribers are incentivized to utilise energy in coordination with the distributor needs, it may create a win-win situation for all sides.

## 3 Proposed Scheme Methodology

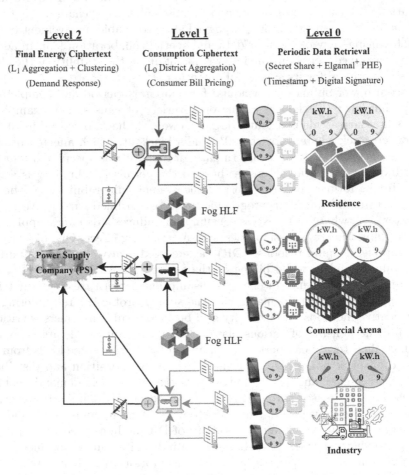

**Level 2**
**Final Energy Ciphertext**
($L_1$ Aggregation + Clustering)
(Demand Response)

**Level 1**
**Consumption Ciphertext**
($L_0$ District Aggregation)
(Consumer Bill Pricing)

**Level 0**
**Periodic Data Retrieval**
(Secret Share + Elgamal$^+$ PHE)
(Timestamp + Digital Signature)

**Fig. 1.** Our Proposed PPSGDA System Model.

The smart grid cryptosystem is organized and shown pictorially in Fig. 1. The participating entities are the different types of consumers (U), share distributors (SD) and district fogging aggregators (DA) defining the fog layer at level 1 (L1), Hyperledger Fabric (HLF) for DAs, and the cloud power supplier (PS) at the final level (L2). It is assumed that there are $n$ districts in total with district $i$ having $t_i$ users. $\{SD_i\}_{0 \leq i < n}$ generates secret shares for the users residing in district $i$ $\{U_{i,j}\}_{0 \leq j < t_i}$ whose data is aggregated and verified by $\{DA_i\}_{0 \leq i < n}$. The step-wise system architecture is depicted pictorially in Fig. 1 from right to

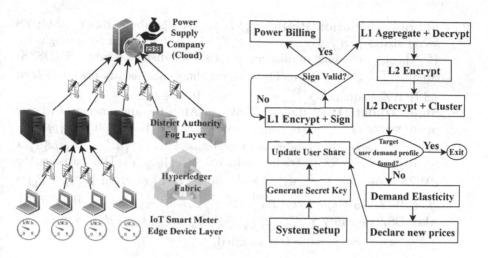

**Fig. 2.** Operational System Flow Diagram.

left, beginning with periodic data retrieval from various level 0 smart meters on an hourly basis. This is followed by aggregation of the encrypted data and decryption by DA fog mining nodes at L1. The aggregate is re-encrypted and block is create corresponding to it. Lastly, PS at L2 reads the chain for final decryption, processing, and analysis. This is followed by a elasticity and clustering based demand response (DR) program conducted in iterative manner. For better understanding, operational system and flow diagrams are shown in Fig. 2. Implementation of the majority of algorithms such as share distribution, key generation, data processing such as encryption, re-encryption and decryption is in off-chain mode, whereas data validation and aggregate block write and read by DA and PS, respectively, are secure on-chain computational transactions. The timing of the processes is shown through a sequence diagram in Fig. 3. The following detailed algorithms present the methodology chronologically through theoretical and mathematical formulation:

1) **System Setup($1^\kappa$) → GPP**: $PS$ generates the system parameters with input as a security parameter $1^\kappa$. It selects a 512-bit cyclic group $G$ having a prime number $q$ as its order and a generator $g$ $(\mathbb{G}, q, g, g)$ and a collision-resistant hash function $H : \{0,1\}^* \to \mathbb{Z}_q^*$. It initializes the price vector $P = \{p_k\}_{k \in [24]}$ describing the electricity cost for 24 h. Global public parameters $GPP = \{G, H, q, g, P\}$ are published.

2) **Secret Creation(GPP)**: All the participating cryptosystem entities are involved in either secret key generation or share distribution and updation.

   2.1) **Key Generation(GPP)**: $PS$ with identifier $ID_{PS}$ chooses $x_{PS}$ randomly from $Z_q^*$ and computes its secret key as $H(ID_{PS})^{x_{PS}}$ and public key $h_{PS} := g^{x_{PS}}$. $DA_i$ chooses its private key $x_{DA_i}$ from $Z_q^*$ randomly and computes its public key $h_{DA_i} := g^{x_{DA_i}}$. Each user of every district $\{U_{i,j}\}_{0 \le i < n, 0 \le j < t_i}$ chooses a random $x_{i,j} \in Z_q^*$ and generate their own public key $h_{i,j} := g^{x_{i,j}}$.

2.2) **Share Distribution(P):** Here, $\{SD_i\}_{0 \leq i < n}$ distributes $24 * t_i$ 10-bit ZS secret shares $\{uz_{i,j,k}\}_{0 \leq i < t_i, k \in [24]} \in Z_q^*$ via $(k_i, t_i)$-Shamir S3 among users $\{U_{i,j}\}_{0 \leq j < t_i}$ residing in district $i$ satisfying district share ZS (DSZS) equality $\sum_{j=0}^{k_i-1} uz_{i,j,k} = 0$. These secret shares also satisfy price weighted ZS (PWZS) equality $\sum_{k=0}^{23} uz_{i,j,k} * p_k = 0 \ \forall i \in [t_i]$.

2.3) **Share Update(P, P′, uz$_{i,j,k}$)** $\rightarrow$ **uz$'_{i,j,k}$:** After the announcement of new price vector $P' = \{p'_k\}_{k \in [24]}$ by $PS$, $\{SD_i\}_{0 \leq i < n}$ finds $\{pp_k = p_k * p'^{-1}_k\}_{k \in [24]}$. It updates zero secret shares as $\{uz'_{i,j,k} = uz'_{i,j,k} * pp_k\}_{k \in [24], 0 \leq i < t_i}$ for district $i$ residents $\{U_{i,j}\}_{0 \leq j < t_i}$. This satisfies the PWZS constraint $\sum_{k=0}^{23} uz'_{i,j,k} * p'_k = 0 \ \forall i \in [t_i]$ as given $\sum_{k=0}^{23} uz_{i,j,k} * p_k = 0$, $\sum_{k=0}^{23} uz_{i,j,k} * p_k * p'^{-1}_k * p'_k = \sum_{k=0}^{23} uz'_{i,j,k} * p'_k = 0 \ \forall i \in [t_i]$. Also, DSZS equality $\sum_{j=0}^{k_i-1} uz'_{i,j,k} = \sum_{j=0}^{k_i-1} uz_{i,j,k} * p_k * p'^{-1}_k = p_k * p'^{-1}_k * \sum_{j=0}^{k_i-1} uz_{i,j,k} = pp_k * 0 = 0$ is satisfied.

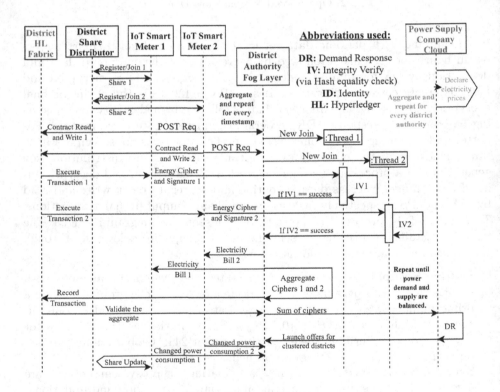

**Fig. 3.** Sequence Diagram.

3) **Encrypt(L1)(GPP, m$_{i,j,k}$, uz$_{i,j,k}$)** $\rightarrow$ **CP$_{i,j,k}$** : Consider district $i$, where each consumer $\{U_{i,j}\}_{j \in [t_i]}$ encrypts its reading $m_{i,j,k}$ at timestamp $TS_k$. This is repeated on an hourly basis throughout the day. For this, it chooses

24 random constants $uz_{i,j,k} \in Z_q^*$ such that the price dot product vanishes $\sum_{k=0}^{23} uz_{i,j,k} * p_k = 0$. Then, it also selects $y_{i,j,k} \in Z_q^*$ at random and computes $C_{i,j,k} = Enc(m_{i,j,k}) = c_{1\{i,j,k\}}||c'_{2\{i,j,k\}} = g^{y_{i,j,k}}||g^{m_{i,j,k}+uz_{i,j,k}} \cdot h_{DA_i}{}^{y_{i,j,k}}$ using the public key of $DA_i$.

4) **Signature for ciphertext integrity check:** The mining node is responsible for validating the data transaction records. Here, $DA_i$ enables data non-repudiation and source authentication via an aggregable digital signature.

4.1) **BLS Signature($GPP, x_{i,j}, C_{i,j,k}, TS_k$)** $\rightarrow \sigma_{i,j,k}$: At $TS_k$ timestamp, $U_{i,j}$ creates $\sigma_{i,j,k} = (H(C_{i,j,k}||TS_k))^{x_{i,j}}$ as per the modified BLS short signature algorithm.

4.2) **Verify ($GPP, TS_k, \{C_{i,j,k}, \sigma_{i,j,k}\}$)** $\rightarrow$ **(True/False)**: Now, $DA_i$ validates the source and integrity of the collected ciphertexts $\{C_{i,j,k}\}_{j \in [t_i]}$ at timestamp $TS_k$. It is achieved via batch verification of the signatures $\{\sigma_{i,j,k}\}_{j \in [t_i]}$ for all the users $\{U_{i,j}\}_{j \in [t_i]}$. An equality check is performed whether $e(\prod_{j=0}^{t_i-1} \sigma_{i,j,k}^{\rho_j}, g) == (\prod_{j=0}^{t_i-1} e(H(C_{i,j,k}||TS_k), h_{i,j}^{\rho_j}))$. Its validity ensures the accuracy of the concatenated ciphertext. It indicates that rogue public key, FDI and replay attacks are not launched on $C_{i,j,k}$ with high probability.

$$Equality: LHS = e(\prod_{j=0}^{t_i-1} \sigma_{i,j,k}^{\rho_j}, g) = \prod_{j=0}^{t_i-1}(e(\sigma_{i,j,k}^{\rho_j}, g) =$$

$$e(H(C_{i,j,k}||TS_k)^{x_{i,j}*\rho_j}, g) = e(H(C_{i,j,k}||TS_k), g^{x_{i,j}*\rho_j}))$$

$$= \prod_{j=0}^{t_i-1} e(H(C_{i,j,k}||TS_k), h_{i,j}^{\rho_j}) = RHS$$

**Note:** If this temporal district batch verification equality does not hold, it implies that the value of at least one of the ciphertexts or timestamps was fabricated, assuming that the operation is carried out correctly and legitimately. In this situation, all signatures must be verified independently or using a divide and conquer approach by redoing the same technique for various subsets to ascertain the origin of the faulty data.

5) **Power Billing:** $DA_i$ receives data from every user $U_{i,j}$ 24 times per day. Daily price vector $P$ is used to bill the electricity consumption of $U_{i,j}$. Temporal electricity consumption throughout the day is processed for billing.

5.1) **Day Cost($P, \{C_{i,j,k}\}_{k \in [24]}$)** $\rightarrow PD_{i,j}$: For a user $U_{i,j}$ from the district $i$, $DA_i$ segregates the ciphertext $C_{i,j,k}$ collected for $TS_k = \{TS_k\}_{k \in [24]}$ to extract two parts $c_{1\{i,j,k\}}$ and $c_{2\{i,j,k\}}$. It aggregates all the user ciphers $CT_{i,j} = \prod_{k=0}^{23} (c_{2\{i,j,k\}}/c_{1\{i,j,k\}}^{x_{DA_i}})^{p'_k}$.

5.2) **Final Calculation($CT_{i,j}$)** $\rightarrow DC_{i,j}$: $DA_i$ decrypts $CT_{i,j}$ to get $U_{i,j}$'s daily bill $PD_{i,j} = Dec(CT_{i,j}) = \sum_{k=0}^{23} m_{i,j,k} * p'_k + \sum_{k=0}^{23} uz_{i,j,k} * p_k = \sum_{k=0}^{23} m_{i,j,k} * p'_k$.

$$\text{Correctness}: CT_{i,j} = \prod_{k=0}^{23} (c_{2\,\{i,j,k\}}/c_{1\,\{i,j,k\}}^{x_{DA_i}})^{p_k'}$$

$$= \prod_{k=0}^{23} (g^{m_{i,j,k}+uz_{i,j,k}} \cdot h_{DA_i}{}^{y_{i,j}} / g^{y_{i,j}*x_{DA_i}})^{p_k'}$$

$$= \prod_{k=0}^{23} (g^{m_{i,j,k}+uz_{i,j,k}} \cdot g^{y_{i,j}*x_{DA_i}} / g^{y_{i,j}*x_{DA_i}})^{p_k'} = \prod_{k=0}^{23} (g^{m_{i,j,k}+uz_{i,j,k}})^{p_k'}$$

$$= \prod_{k=0}^{23} (g^{m_{i,j,k}\cdot p_k' + uz_{i,j,k}\cdot p_k'}) = g^{\sum_{k=0}^{23}(m_{i,j,k}\cdot p_k' + uz_{i,j,k}\cdot p_k')} =$$

$$g^{(\sum_{k=0}^{23} m_{i,j,k}*p_k' + \sum_{k=0}^{23} uz_{i,j,k}*p_k)} = g^{\sum_{k=0}^{23} m_{i,j,k}*p_k'} \ (Take\ DL)$$

6) **District level aggregation**: Each $DA_i$ decrypts and re-encrypts the data not using the same homomorphic method. This is because the total message is not allowed to exceed $2^{30}$ or have more than 30 bits as additive variant of Elgamal encryption requires a calculable discrete log forcing a certain bound on the message. The fog $DA_i$ mining node creates a block for the re-encrypted aggregate for its district. $PS$ reads the chain for further computation and analysis for demand response.

6.1) **User data aggregation** $(\mathbf{L1})(\{\mathbf{C_{i,j,k}}\}_{\mathbf{j\in[k_i]}}) \rightarrow \mathbf{M_{i,k,0}}$ : Power ciphertext is aggregated for some users of a specific district at the same timestamp for demand response. For a user $U_{i,j}$ from the district $i$, $DA_i$ segregates the ciphertext $C_{i,j,k}$ to extract the two parts $c_{1\,\{i,j,k\}}$ and $c_{2\,\{i,j,k\}}$. It aggregates all the user ciphers $CP_{i,k,0} = \prod_{j=0}^{k_i-1} c_{2\,\{i,j,k\}} / = (\prod_{j=0}^{k_i-1} c_{1\,\{i,j,k\}})^{x_{DA_i}}$ on day 0. Then, it decrypts the district aggregate energy consumption using its secret key $x_{DA_i}$, $Dec(CP_{i,k}) = M_{i,k,0}$. This day 0 plaintext is utilised to commence the analysis and initiate the granular demand response program.

$$\text{Correctness}: Dec(CP_{i,k,0}) = \prod_{j=0}^{k_i-1} (c_{2\,\{i,j,k\}}/c_{1\,\{i,j,k\}}^{x_{DA_i}})$$

$$= \prod_{j=0}^{k_i-1} (g^{m_{i,j,k}+uz_{i,j,k}} \cdot g^{y_{i,j}*x_{DA_i}} / g^{y_{i,j}x_{DA_i}}) = \prod_{j=0}^{k_i-1} (g^{m_{i,j,k}+uz_{i,j,k}})$$

$$= g^{\sum_{j=0}^{k_i-1}(m_{i,j,k}+uz_{i,j,k})} = g^{(\sum_{j=0}^{k_i-1} m_{i,j,k} + \sum_{j=0}^{k_i-1} uz_{i,j,k})}$$

$$= g^{\sum_{j=0}^{k_i-1} m_{i,j,k}} = g^{M_{i,k,0}}$$

6.2) **Re − encrypt(L2)($g^{M_{i,k,0}}$) → $EM_{i,k,0}, H_{i,k,0}$:** For day 0, $DA_i$ computes $K_i = e((g^{x_{PS}})^{x_{DA_i}}, H(ID_{PS}))$ and a hash $H_{i,k,0} = H(g^{M_{i,k,0}}||TS_{k,0})$. Here, $TS_{k,0}$ refers to the $k^{th}$ timestamp of day 0. Then, it re-encrypts $M_{i,k,0}$ as $EM_{i,k,0} = g^{M_{i,k,0}}.K_i^{TS_{k,0}}$. For day 0, $DA_i$ computes a hash $H_{i,k,0} = H(g^{M_{i,k,0}}||TS_{k,0})$. Here, $TS_{k,0}$ refers to the $k^{th}$ timestamp of day 0. $DA_i$ creates a block for $\{EM_{i,k,0}, H_{i,k,0}\}$ as shown in Fig. 4.

6.3) **Decrypt($EM_{i,k,0}, H_{i,k,0}$) → $M_{i,k,0}$:** $PS$ reads the chain as shown in Fig. 4. Power data is analyzed and aggregated for all the districts at the same timestamp for demand response. For block corresponding to $DA_i$, $PS$ computes $K_i = e(g^{x_{DA_i}}, H(ID_{PS})^{x_{PS}})^{TS_{k,0}}$ and decrypts $g^{M_{i,k,0}} = EM_{i,k}.K_i^{-1}$. It verifies message integrity via an equality check $H_{i,k,0} = H(g^{M_{i,k,0}}||TS_{k,0})$. It computes the discrete logarithm $M_{i,k,0} = DL(g^{M_{i,k,0}})$.

6.4) **District data aggregate (L2)($\{M_{i,k,0}\}_{i\in[n]}$) → $FM_{k,0}$:** Power plaintext is aggregated for all districts at timestamp $TS_{k\{k\in[23]\}}$ for demand response on day 0, $\sum_{i=0}^{n-1}\{M_{i,k,0}\} = FM_{k,0}$.

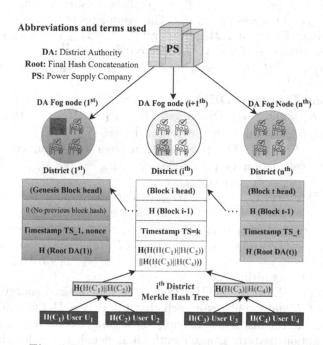

**Fig. 4.** District Blockchain for PPSGDA System.

**Note:** Here, taking DL is even more time consuming as the aggregate data $FM_{k,0}$ is allowed to have at the most 30 bits. Therefore, from the next day onwards, only the data difference between two consecutive days is taken into account which is allowed to have at the most 25 bits. This concept is similar to differential pulse code modulation (DPCM) which is used to save bits in data compression in multimedia systems.

7) **Demand Response**: For this, $PS$ analyzes the individual data to perform clustering to filter the right participants for a particular time frame. It uses the aggregate data for the districts $i \in [n]$ wherein $k_i$ clients are assumed to participate in the demand response program. A vector $SP_d$ is declared where $sp_{k,d}$ represents the daily power supply differential desired between timestamps $TS_{k-1}$ and $TS_k$ on day $d$. The optional correction factors $\alpha_k$ are declared which come into action from the second iteration onwards if required. These are meant to tune the expression aggressively for price declaration next day so that desired district demand profile is achieved more quickly. If negative $\epsilon_P$ and constant $Y$ are assumed, negative/positive $sp_{k,d}$ value should mandate proportionate increase/decrease in day 0 price $p_{k,0}$ at timestamp $TS_k$ wrt desired decrease/increase in $FM_{k,0}$, respectively.

7.1) **Price Publish ($\mathbf{P_0}, \mathbf{SP_0}, \mathbf{FM_0}$) → $\mathbf{P_1}$**: Inputs taken on day 0 are 24 element vectors $P$, $SP$ and $FM$. Intuitively, the consumer $U_{i,j}$ with constant income $Y_{i,j}$ will like to keep his/her daily cost $DC_{i,j}$ almost same. So, the new prices for day 1 are published using a simple formula as $p_{k,1} = p_{k,0} * (1 - SP_{k,0}/FM_{k,0})$. This completes $0^{th}$ iteration.

7.2) **Difference Encrypt(L2)($\mathbf{g^{M_{i,k,0}}, g^{M_{i,k,1}}}$) → $\mathbf{H_{i,k,1}, DM_{i,k,1}}$**: For day 1, $DA_i$ computes $DM_{i,k,1} = Dec(Enc(g^{M_{i,k,1}}))/g^{M_{i,k,0}} = g^{M_{i,k,1}-M_{i,k,0}}$ It computes $DEM_{i,k,0} = g^{M_{i,k,1}-M_{i,k,0}}.K_i{}^{TS_{k,0}}$ and a hash $H_{i,k,1} = H(g^{M_{i,k,1}-M_{i,k,0}}||TS_{k,1})$.

7.3) **Demand Elasticity($\mathbf{DEM_{i,k,0}}$ → $\mathbf{\epsilon_{k,e}}$)**: PS computes $g^{M_{i,k,1}-M_{i,k,0}} = EM_{i,k}.K_i^{-1}$ and takes DL to get $Diff_{i,k,1} = M_{i,k,1} - M_{i,k,0}$. For day $e$, it aggregates all such differences to get $\sum_{i=0}^{n-1} M_{i,k,e} - M_{i,k,e-1} = FM_{k,e} - FM_{k,e-1}$. The temporal consumer behaviour can be quantified via calculation of price elasticity $\epsilon_{k,e} = ((FM_{k,e} - FM_{k,e-1}) * p_{k,e-1})/((p_{k,e} - p_{k,e-1}) * Q_{k,e-1})$.

7.4) **Price Declare($\mathbf{\alpha_{k,e}, \epsilon_{k,e}}$) → $\mathbf{p_{k,e+1}}$**: For calculating new price $p_{k,e+1}$ using old elasticity $\epsilon_{k,e}$, correction factor $\alpha_{k,e}$ can be used as $(1 + \alpha_{k,e}) * sp_{k,1} = \epsilon_{k,1} * FM_{k,1} * (p_{k,2} - p_{k,1})/p_{k,1}$. Now, publish prices $p_{k,2}$ such that $p_{k,2} = (1 + \alpha_k) * sp_{k,1} * p_{k,1}/(\epsilon_{k,1} * FM_{k,1}) + p_{k,1}$. So, prices for $e^{th}$ iteration is $p_{k,e} = (1 + \alpha_k) * sp_{k,e-1} * p_{k,e-1}/(\epsilon_{k,e-1} * FM_{k,e-1}) + p_{k,e-1}$. Go back to algorithm 7.2.

7.5) **Clustering($\mathbf{Diff_{i,j,1}}$) → $\mathbf{CL}$**: PS creates a 24*n sized energy differential matrix $CL$ and populates it such that $CL[i][j] = Diff_{i,j,1}$. Clusters are created and the districts belonging to the same cluster have similar power consumption pattern. Consequently, it is decided that for the next day (here, day 2), which districts should be focused upon for a particular subset of 24 hourly time frames.

## 4 Performance Analysis

In the proposed scheme, we have used additive ElGamal PHC which mandates efficient discrete logarithm calculation. For this, we assume that the maximum length of the user bill and aggregate district energy consumption are 20 and 30 bits, respectively. If the power measurements are transmitted on an hourly basis, we assume that the transmitted consumption falls in the [0-1] kWh range for an average Indian household and commercial arena smart meter. For small to large-scale industries, the average hourly range can be assumed to be [0-4] kWh. In $Z_n^*$, representing such ranges needs 10 bits for residential and commercial smart meters. The requirement rises to 12 bits for industrial smart meters. We have already assumed that the hourly energy consumption of a district does not exceed $2^{30}$ kWh. So, a bound needs to be placed on the number of participants in the demand response program or $k$ as in Shamir (k,n) S3. The districts primarily consisting of residential and commercial sites are assumed to have roughly $k = 2^{20} \approx 10^6$ (1 million = 10 lakhs) participating meters at the most. However, for their industrial counterparts, the maximum allowable number is $k = 2^{18} \approx 2.5 * 10^5$ or 2.5 lakh participants. These participants, though, low in number are capable of changing their demand profile, significantly. We need to also ensure that bits required for user's daily bill which is computed by DA does not exceed 20. It is given that the maximum hourly consumption for a residential/commercial user does not require more than 10 bits. We also know that in the worst case, the 10-bit power needs to be taken 24 times in consideration for price aggregation on daily basis. Now, the maximum number bits allowed for price is $\lceil log_2(2^{10}/24) \rceil = 5$. So, a bijective mapping can be established between $2^5$ points of domain $\{0, 1, ...., 31\}$ and hourly price range $\{0₹, 0.25₹, 0.5₹, \cdots, 7.75₹\}$ in rupees (₹). The final obtained price simply needs to be divided by four in order to get the final user bill.

## 4.1    System Configuration, Tools and Platform

For the proposed PPSGDA scheme, experiments are conducted on a Ubuntu 20:04:2 LTS WSL system having an Intel Core(TM) i3-5005U CPU @ 2.00 GHz x64-based processor, 4.00 GB RAM. For bilinear map operations (pairing based cryptography) specifically, we used the Charm crypto platform which is an extensible Python language-based framework for rapid prototyping advanced cryptosystems [37]. We employ a symmetric curve with a 512-bit base 'SS512'. Group (G) used is a 512-bit multiplicative cyclic prime order group. We used Google Colab Notebook to perform all the non-pairing based cryptographic operations. For inverse and power modulus operations, 'gmpy2' module is used as it supports fast multiple-precision arithmetic. A few simulation experiments are run on Google Cloud Platform (GCP) as well to manage and automate the created scalable architecture. For deployment of Hyperledger Fabric on GCP, Python software development kit (SDK) for HLF is used.

## 4.2    Theoretical Implementation Analysis

We assume our cryptosystem to have $n$ districts, $|DA_i|$ district users and $k_i$ DR program participants. For daily billing of district $i$ members, the total transmitted data size between all the district users and the $DA_i$ fog node per day is

$$= 24*|DA_i|*(|C_{i,j,k}|+|s_{i,j,k}|) = 24*|DA_i|*(|c_{1\{i,j,k\}}|+|c'_{2\{i,j,k\}}|+|s_{\{i,j,k\}}|) =$$
$$24 * |DA_i| * (512 + 512 + 512) = 24 * |DA_i| * 1536\, bits = 4608.|DA_i|\, bytes.$$ For demand response, the hourly transmitted data size between all the district users and the $DA_i$ fog node is $= |k_i| * (|C_{i,j,k}| + |s_{i,j,k}|) = |k_i| * (512 + 512 + 512) = |k_i| * 1536\, bits = 192.|k_i|\, bytes.$ The size of hourly re-encrypted data transmitted by the $DA_i$ fog node to $PS$ is the sum of sizes of the pairing and the message hash $|EM_{i,k,0}| + |H_{i,k,0}| = (512 + 512)bits = 128\, bytes.$

### 4.3  Practical Implementation Analysis

We have conducted 50 trials and the results shown graphically reflect the average. The semi-log line graph (left) shown in Fig. 5, exhibits the time complexity for inverse operation for decryption, table creation and discrete logarithm computation using BSGS technique w.r.t. the maximum length of the underlying message in bits. The line graph towards right in the same figure shows the time complexities for the average encryption, re-encryption through bilinear pairing and aggregation procedures w.r.t. the number of district users.

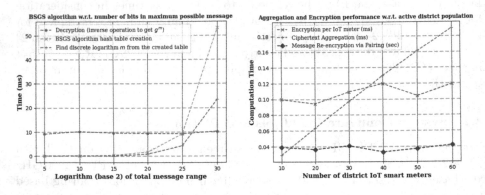

**Fig. 5.** Performance of various algorithms w.r.t. various parameters.

**Observation and Inference:** In the left plot, the decryption performed by district IoT smart meter via an inverse operation is not dependent on the message length as the group size is fixed at 512 bits beforehand. It can be easily seen that the table creation and discrete logarithm search processes of BSGS are time-consuming and the computation time varies exponentially as the message range is squared for both procedures. In the right plot, the encryption and re-encryption performed by district IoT smart meter and DA fog node, respectively, are not dependent on the number of district nodes. Therefore, their time complexities vary, abruptly. It is intuitive that the aggregation time required rises in a linear manner with linear increase in the number of district smart meters, i.e., $\approx 0.033.(|DA_i| - 1)\, ms.$

### 4.4  Experimental Execution

As already mentioned, IIoT has real-time CPS monitoring and maintenance as one of its major agendas. As components of the technology stack employed for simulation, following are the GCP products used for their specified purposes.

1) **GCP IoT core and Cloud Pub/Sub:** Several organizations have or are planning to employ it for a multitude of their smart applications including prevention of unplanned downtime for globally dispersed smart grid meters [36]. Here, it is just used for a basic simulation where the DA fog nodes manage the registration, authentication, and authorization of IoT smart meters of their concerned districts. The meters use a standard data-centric lightweight communication protocol called MQTT (Message Queuing Telemetry Transport) to establish two-way device connection with their respective DAs. The product also allows creation of gateways to enable offline operation capabilities and device registry to group the similar devices.

2) **GCP BigTable:** It is a fully managed and mutable NoSQL database service for large scale data analytics. Traditional row-based relational databases are designed and optimized to handle and process the data in form of rows. But, for our purpose, the primary focus is the column storing user meter reading data which can be zipped together with sensor IDs to create a columnar family for aggregation. Therefore, we use BigTable as a wide columnar and sparsely populated data storage because not all of the sensors are assumed to transmit their readings each hour. To integrate it with our IoT framework, we connect Pub/Sub to BigTable via Dataflow template. This is used by DA to store the ElGamal PHC encrypted data streamed from lakhs of IoT meters corresponding to their unique sensor IDs and the 24 hourly timestamps. When the table gets fully populated, this data is used for billing purposes for each sensor on a daily basis. The created table is also used for L1 aggregation and analysis to obtain the values which are passed to PS for the demand response (DR) program. The columnar configuration renders the SQL queries more challenging but the concerned subcolumns can be exposed as subfields. For example, a sample query to compute the count of active residential participants at a specific timestamp from a district taking into account consumer column family will be like SELECT COUNT(1) FROM 'dataset.table' WHERE consumer.type.cell.value= "residential" AND consumer.time.cell.value= "01-04-22 14:00".

3) **GCP BigQuery ML:** BigQuery is a serverless, highly scalable, flexible and persistent SQL data warehouse which facilitates efficient querying of voluminous and complex datasets. When PS reads the data blocks uploaded by the DAs for all the timestamps from the Fog HLF (blockchain) deployed using python SDK, it stores them in a table for performing district level clustering. For this, k-means++ initialization and Euclidean distance are chosen as parameters in the query CREATE MODEL 'dataset.model' OPTIONS (MODEL_TYPE='KMEANS', NUM_CLUSTERS=6,KMEANS_INIT_METHOD='KMEANS++',DISTANCE_TYPE ='EUCLIDEAN') AS SELECT * FROM 'dataset.table'.

446    K. Sethi et al.

# 5  Outlook and Conclusion

In this paper, we proposed a PPSGDA cryptosystem which features a decentralized fogging architecture premised on a private and permissioned blockchain (Hyperledger Fabric). We maintain the confidentiality of the user power reading data prior to aggregation by fog node through use of additive ElGamal PHC. We enable the data privacy on an individual basis in a flexible manner via the provision of secret shares which can be updated efficiently. In addition, our scheme achieves ciphertext integrity, non-repudiation and resilience in face of major cyberattacks through timestamps, hashing and digital signature. Along with security, ensuring grid stability is also crucial for which we propounded a simple distributed demand response mechanism. The Western world has reaped benefits from the adoption of innovative technology in the form of enhanced grid CPS stability and security. India, however, has smart grid AMI network in its nascent stages and may emulate the aforementioned merits in the coming decades. It is known that the restoration of human hands and brains into the industrial framework is expected to be the emphasis of Industry 5.0. For this, the proposed scheme may have laid the foundation for a smart grid CPS where man and machine harmonize and identify effective strategies to collaborate under the IIoT ecosystem.

## References

1. Saleem, A., et al.: FESDA: fog-enabled secure data aggregation in smart grid IoT network. IEEE Internet Things J. **7**(7), 6132–6142 (2020)
2. Hermann, M., Pentek, T., Otto, B.: Design principles for industrie 4.0 scenarios. In: Proceedings of the 49th Annual Hawaii International Conference on System Sciences, HICSS 2016, pp. 3928–3937 (2016)
3. Serizawa, Y., Ohba, E., Kurono, M.: Present and future ICT infrastructures for a smarter grid in Japan. In: Innovative Smart Grid Technologies, pp. 1–5 (2010)
4. Yu, L., Li, H., Feng, X., Duan, J.: Non-intrusive appliance load monitoring for smart homes: recent advances and future issues. IEEE Instrum. Meas. Mag. **19**, 56–62 (2016)
5. Prasad, V.K., Bhavsar, M., Tanwar, S.: Influence of montoring: fog and edge computing. Scalable Comput. Pract. Exp. **20**(2), 365–376 (2019)
6. Guo, Y., Ten, C.-W., Jirutitijaroen, P.: Online data validation for distribution operations against cybertampering. IEEE Trans. Power Syst. **29**(2), 550–560 (2014)
7. Fan, H., Liu, Y., Zeng, Z.: Decentralized privacy-preserving data aggregation scheme for smart grid based on blockchain. Sensors **20**(18), 5282 (2020)
8. Zhang, Y., Wu, A., Zheng, D.: Efficient and privacy-aware attribute-based data sharing in mobile cloud computing. J. Ambient Intell. Hum. Comput. **9**, 1039–1048 (2018)
9. Li, F., Luo, B., Liu, P.: Secure information aggregation for smart grids using homomorphic encryption. In: 2010 First IEEE International Conference on Smart Grid Communications (SmartGridComm), pp. 327–332. IEEE (2010)
10. Ni, J., Zhang, K., Alharbi, K., Lin, X., Zhang, N., Shen, X.S.: Differentially private smart metering with fault tolerance and range based filtering. IEEE Trans. Smart Grid **8**(5), 2483–2493 (2017)

11. Zhu, L., et al.: Privacy-preserving authentication and data aggregation for fog-based smart grid. IEEE Commun. Mag. **57**, 80–85 (2019)

12. Bao, H., Lu, R.: DDPFT: secure data aggregation scheme with differential privacy and fault tolerance. In: IEEE International Conference on Communications (ICC), pp. 7240–7245 (2015)

13. Guan, Z., Si, G., Du, X., Liu, P., Zhang, Z., Zhou, Z.: Protecting user privacy based on secret sharing with fault tolerance for big data in smart grid. In: 2017 IEEE International Conference on Communications (ICC), pp. 1–6 (2017). https://doi.org/10.1109/ICC.2017.7997371

14. Knirsch, F., Eibl, G., Engel, D.: Multi-resolution privacy-enhancing technologies for smart metering. EURASIP J. Inf. Secur. **2017**, 6 (2017)

15. Gao, C.Z., Cheng, Q., He, P., Susilo, W., Li, J.: Privacy-preserving Naive Bayes classifiers secure against the substitution-then-comparison attack. Inf. Sci. **444**, 72–88 (2018)

16. Wang, H., Wang, Z., Domingo-Ferrer, J.: Anonymous and secure aggregation scheme in fog-based public cloud computing. Futur. Gener. Comput. Syst. **78**, 712–719 (2018)

17. Zhang, Y., Lang, P., Zheng, D., Yang, M., Guo, R.: A secure and privacy-aware smart health system with secret key leakage resilience. Secur. Commun. Netw. **2018**, 7202598 (2018)

18. Dwork, C.: Differential privacy. In: Bugliesi, M., Preneel, B., Sassone, V., Wegener, I. (eds.) ICALP 2006. LNCS, vol. 4052, pp. 1–12. Springer, Heidelberg (2006). https://doi.org/10.1007/11787006_1

19. Xue, K., et al.: PPSO: a privacy-preserving service outsourcing scheme for real-time pricing demand response in smart grid. IEEE Internet Things J. **6**(2), 2486–2496 (2019). https://doi.org/10.1109/JIOT.2018.2870873

20. Agrawal, A., Sethi, K., Bera, P.: IoT-based aggregate smart grid energy data extraction using image recognition and partial homomorphic encryption. In: IEEE International Conference on Advanced Networks and Telecommunications Systems, pp. 322–327 (2021)

21. Liu, H., Gu, T., Liu, Y., Song, J., Zeng, Z.: Fault-tolerant privacy-preserving data aggregation for smart grid. Wirel. Commun. Mob. Comput. **2020**, Article ID 8810393, 10 p (2020)

22. Khan, H., Khan, A., Jabeen, F., Rahman, A.: Privacy preserving data aggregation with fault tolerance in fog-enabled smart grids. Sustain. Urban Areas **64**, 102522 (2021)

23. Cui, J., Shao, L., Zhong, H., et al.: Data aggregation with end-to-end confidentiality and integrity for large-scale wireless sensor networks. Peer-to-Peer Netw. Appl. **11**, 1022–1037 (2018). https://doi.org/10.1007/s12083-017-0581-5

24. Ziad, M.T.I., Alanwar, A., Alkabani, Y., El-Kharashi, M.W., Bedour, H.: Homomorphic data isolation for hardware trojan protection. In: 2015 IEEE Computer Society Annual Symposium on VLSI, pp. 131–136 (2015)

25. Knirsch, F., Unterweger, A., Unterrainer, M., Engel, D.: Comparison of the Paillier and ElGamal cryptosystems for smart grid aggregation protocols. In: ICISSP (2020)

26. Hu, Y., et al.: Enhanced Flexibility for Homomorphic Encryption Schemes via CRT (2012)

27. Shafagh, H., Hithnawi, A., Burkhalter, L., Fischli, P., Duquennoy, S.: Secure sharing of partially homomorphic encrypted IoT data. In: Proceedings of the 15th ACM Conference on Embedded Network Sensor Systems (SenSys 2017), Article 29, pp.

1–14. Association for Computing Machinery, New York (2017). https://doi.org/10.1145/3131672.3131697

28. Dong, Y., Milanova, A., Dolby, J.: SecureMR: secure mapreduce using homomorphic encryption and program partitioning. SIGPLAN Not. **53**(1), 389–390 (2018). https://doi.org/10.1145/3200691.3178520

29. http://hdl.handle.net/123456789/32016

30. Guan, Z., et al.: APPA: an anonymous and privacy preserving data aggregation scheme for fog enhanced IoT. J. Netw. Comput. Appl. **125**, 82–92 (2019)

31. Guan, Z., et al.: Privacy-preserving and efficient aggregation based on blockchain for power grid communications in smart communities. IEEE Commun. Mag. **56**, 82–88 (2018)

32. Fan, M., Zhang, X.: Consortium blockchain based data aggregation and regulation mechanism for smart grid. IEEE Access **7**, 35929–35940 (2019)

33. Yao, S., Tian, X., Chen, J., Xiong, Y.: Privacy preserving distributed smart grid system based on Hyperledger Fabric and Wireguard. Int. J. Netw. Manag. **33**, e2193 (2021)

34. Gellings, C.W.: The Smart Grid: Enabling Energy Efficiency and Demand Response. The Fairmont Press Inc., Atlanta (2009)

35. Palensky, P., Dietrich, D.: Demand side management: demand response, intelligent energy systems, and smart loads. IEEE Trans. Industr. Inf. **7**(3), 381–388 (2011)

36. https://cloud.google.com/customers/kiwigrid

37. Akinyele, J.A., et al.: Charm: a framework for rapidly prototyping cryptosystems. J. Cryptogr. Eng. **3**, 111–128 (2013)

38. Mengelkamp, E., et al.: A blockchain-based smart grid: towards sustainable local energy markets. Comput. Sci.-Res. Dev. **33**, 207–214 (2018)

39. Caprolu, M., et al.: Increasing renewable generation feed-in capacity leveraging smart meters. In: 2020 IEEE Green Energy and Smart Systems Conference (IGESSC). IEEE (2020)

40. Agung, A.A.G., Handayani, R.: Blockchain for smart grid. J. King Saud Univ.-Comput. Inf. Sci. **34**(3), 666–675 (2022)

# Crypto-Ransomware Detection: A Honey-File Based Approach Using Chi-Square Test

Ajith Arakkal, Shehzad Pazheri Sharafudheen, and A. R. Vasudevan[✉]

Hardware and Security Group, Department of Computer Science and Engineering,
National Institute of Technology, Calicut, Kozhikode, Kerala, India
ajith1202@gmail.com, shehzadps@gmail.com, vasudevanar@nitc.ac.in

**Abstract.** Ransomware is a type of malware that restricts access to
the data or computing device and threatens to sell the data or keep
it inaccessible unless the victim pays the attacker a ransom. Crypto-
ransomware is a type of ransomware that encrypts the files of the victim and demands a ransom to decrypt the files. Existing techniques
for addressing crypto-ransomware attacks include detection using honeypots, monitoring kernel-level system routines, techniques using machine
learning, monitoring network activities, system resources and system
usage among others. Such detection techniques are unable to distinguish
between the genuine process and a ransomware process, and requires
frequent user intervention in killing a ransomware process. Also, high
false alarms render such techniques ineffective. In this paper we propose
a solution for crypto-ransomwares by incorporating the chi-square test
on the entropy of user files in a honeypot environment. The proposed
design also automates the solution in the kernel/user level. The empirical results of chi-square test on common file types are computed resulting
in reduced false alarms.

**Keywords:** Crypto-Ransomware · Honeypots · File-analysis

## 1 Introduction

Ransomware, a malicious software, intrudes a system through phishing techniques or malicious links. It then encrypts the user files using cryptographic
techniques (crypto-ransomware) or just locks the system (locker ransomware).
A ransom note is displayed to the user on the user's desktop. It demands payment in crypto-currency from the user, with the promise of giving them the
decryption key. This key is used to decrypt the encrypted files and recover the
system back to normal.

Among the existing anti-ransomware solutions, honeypot-based solution
caters to a wide range of ransomwares because it just relies on the basic functionality of crypto-ransomware which is to encrypt files and folders, unlike the
network-based, that relies on the ransomware establishing a connection with the

© The Author(s), under exclusive license to Springer Nature Switzerland AG 2023
V. Muthukkumarasamy et al. (Eds.): ICISS 2023, LNCS 14424, pp. 449–458, 2023.
https://doi.org/10.1007/978-3-031-49099-6_27

C&C server. However, the current honeypot approaches are not fully practical in normal user systems owing to false detections and hence we aim to make the whole process automated and more accurate.

## 2 Problem Statement

Honeypot-based solutions for ransomware detection are efficient in preventing zero-day ransomware attacks. However, the existing approaches lack practicality, owing to their high false positive rates. Such techniques fail to distinguish between user processes and ransomware processes. In this paper we aim to address these issues by incorporating the chi-square test for file encryption analysis and propose a full-fledged honeypot-based anti-ransomware solution.

## 3 Literature Survey

Based on the study done on various detection and recovery techniques for crypto-ransomwares, it can be broadly categorized into three categories.

### 3.1 Detection Using Honeypots

Honeypots are a set of dummy/decoy files placed in the file-system of the user so as to detect the action of ransomware on those files. This comes from the notion that no other user program may attempt to access these "honeyfiles". A few different approaches for detection have been proposed on the basis of specific use-cases.

**R-Locker:** R-Locker [1] not only detects crypto-ransomware, but also halts the execution. It uses named pipes to implement honey-files that act as a regular file and establishes a communication channel between the reading and writing processes; causing a ransomware process to be blocked by the kernel once it starts to read the contents of the file. R-Locker reduces the overhead by using a single trap/honey-file and populates all the user directories with symbolic links (soft links) of the same.

### 3.2 Network Analysis

Most ransomware variants communicate with a Command and Control (C&C) server for obtaining asymmetric encryption keys used for the encryption process. Cabaj and Mazurczyk [2] proposed an SDN based approach on the basis of a study on CryptoWall, a popular ransomware. The technique is based on dynamic blacklisting of C&C servers and their proxies. Once a packet has been found to travel to and from a malicious domain name, the connection is blocked, thereby preventing encryption of the user files.

### 3.3    File Analysis

Crypto-ransomwares usually overwrite a large number of the user's files during the process of encryption. These changes can be monitored in order to detect a possible ransomware attack. Some prominent metrics used to detect file system changes are described below:

**File Entropy:** Scaife et al. [3] employed file entropy and other metrics to detect ransomware. Shannon's Entropy, a popular entropy calculation technique, when calculated, takes values from 0 - no randomness, to 8 - totally random. If a file is encrypted, it would have a considerably higher entropy than that which is not encrypted. Even though Shannon's entropy is used widely in literature, its inability to differentiate between the encrypted and non-encrypted counterparts of even the popular file types like PDFs, JPGs, DOCs and so on, makes it a non-viable metric for normal user file-systems.

**File Type:** Ransomwares usually tend to change the type/extension of the files it encrypts. Huge changes in file extensions in a short time can be used as a method to detect ransomware. Menen [4] applied this concept to monitor large number of files with the same extension. Scaife et al. [3] describes magic number as a way to get information about file type and says that the *file* utility program can compare and track the change in file types using the magic database, which contains hundreds of type signatures. However, file type changes alone cannot be used to detect ransomwares as software updates could also change the file formats of many files.

## 4    Proposed Design

For ransomware detection, we propose a honeypot based approach combined with file entropy analysis. Usual honeypot approaches incur high false positive rates, because honey files, even though hidden, may not be accessed only by ransomwares; it can be accessed by benign user programs such as, copying a folder or folder compression techniques. So, the proposed method not only detects ransomwares using honeyfiles, but also ensures lower false positive rates by clearly distinguishing the access of honey files by ransomwares and user processes using chi-square test on files. The detailed flowchart of the proposed design is shown in Fig. 1

### 4.1    Honeypot

Initially for monitoring the honey-files, we setup the auditd daemon in the root directory of the user file-system. Then the honeypot executable creates the root honey-file, after which symbolic links to the root file are populated recursively to all sub-directories in the user file-system.

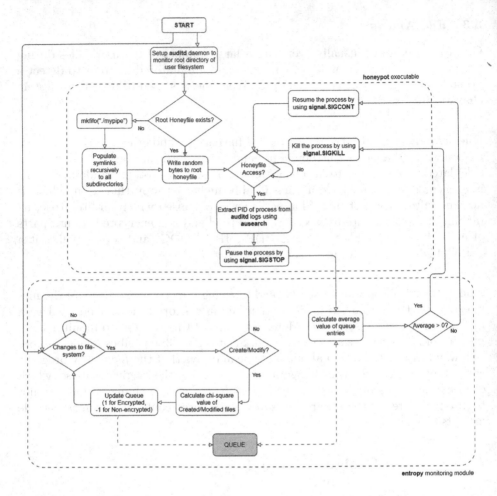

**Fig. 1.** Low-level design of the proposed solution.

The next step is to write some random bytes to the root honey-file. This acts as a writing process for the named pipe, which essentially gets blocked by the kernel until a corresponding reading process tries to access the file.

Once a suspicious process or a benign user process accesses the honey-file or any of its symlinks populated across the file-system, we extract the PID of the corresponding process. Once the PID is obtained, we pause the process by sending a **SIGSTOP** signal to the process using the *kill* command. This is to avoid any suspicious/harmful activity by the process while we check for its genuiness.

Once the checks are completed and the results are sent over by the Entropy monitoring module, we kill the process using a **SIGKILL** signal, or continue execution of the process using a **SIGCONT** signal depending on whether the process is malicious or not.

## 4.2   Entropy Montoring

The Entropy monitoring module checks for the genuineness of the process under consideration by the honeypot executable. It aims to achieve this by maintaining a FIFO queue of size k, which contains details of the last k file writes in the user's file-system.

The queue entries only include the numbers 1 and -1, signifying encryption and non-encryption operations respectively. The module checks for any changes to the file-system using the **watchdog** module in python based on the **inotify** utility. Once a change is detected, two handlers are present - one for handling deletions, the other for handling creations, modifications, renaming and moving of files and folders.

If the change detected is a create/modify event, the chi-square values are calculated for the corresponding files. This is followed by the enqueueing of a specific value into the queue, depending on whether the file was encrypted or not.

The chi-square goodness of fit test is done by comparing the chi-square value of each file with the critical chi-square value. This critical value is calculated by taking 255 degrees of freedom (corresponding to 256 possible byte values), and a significance level of 0.01 (1%), which gives the value as 310.46. If the chi-square value of a file is less than this critical chi-square value of 310.46, it is considered encrypted, and if its greater, non-encrypted. This is done on the basis that encrypted files are similar to a file with equal frequencies of all byte values.

If the chi-square value of a file turns out to be greater than the critical value of 310.46, the value **-1** is added to the queue, corresponding to a non-encrypted content write in file. On the other hand, if it turns out to be less that 310.46, the value **1** is added to the queue, signifying an encryption operation.

## 4.3   Integration

Once the honeypot executable pauses the process using the SIGSTOP signal, it transfers control over to the entropy monitoring module. The module with the help of the FIFO queue which is constantly updated, calculates the average value of the queue entries.

If the queue average turns out to be greater than zero, it signifies that more than half of the last k file writes have resulted in encryption. Consequently, a notification is sent to the honeypot executable to kill the corresponding process. Whereas if the queue average turns out to be less than or equal to zero, it signifies that the process accessing the honey-file is a benign user process. As a result, a similar notification is sent to the honeypot executable to continue the execution of the process. The communication between honeypot executable and entropy monitoring module is done through socket programming.

## 4.4  Optimisations

Design and implementation level optimisations have been incorporated so as to improve the detection of ransomwares and reduce false positives in terms of multiple symlinks and inclusion of timestamp.

**Multiple Honey-Files per Folder:** To improve the chances of honey-file access by ransomware, multiple symlinks to the root honey-file are created in each folder. This increases the likelihood of the ransomware accessing the honey-file and speeds up detection compared to having only one symlink per folder.

**Timestamp:** Timestamp variable is introduced to mitigate false positive case when a user downloads or copies encrypted files (or generally, files with chi-square value less than the critical value). If the number of such files is more than half the size of our FIFO queue, this means more than half of the queue entries are flagged with 1s and if by chance a honeypot is accessed (maybe by a user or any process), the process will be killed, falsely assuming its a ransomware.

To mitigate this problem, we rely on the fact that most ransomwares encrypt files consecutively within a short span of time. So, the honey-file access by ransomware happens within very short time from it's previous encryptions. Users do not tend to access the honey-file this way, and we leverage on that. So, what we did is, anytime a honey-file is accessed, the entropy monitoring module checks the time difference between the last encryption operation (which is stored in a timestamp variable) and the honey-file access time. If it is greater than a threshold, the process is deemed a user process and let go. Else, the process is sent to further countermeasure checking like queue average, as described in the Integration section before.

## 5  Experimental Results

### 5.1  Chi-Square Analysis

We have performed a detailed analysis of chi-square as a metric. This was mainly done to check the suitability of using chi-square calculation on files to distinguish encrypted files from non-encrypted files. Since this chi-sqaure concept was vital in our whole solution to detect ransomware encryption using encrypted file writes, we performed a thorough analysis using more than 40,000 files of commonly used file types.

The data was obtained from the NapierOne [5] mixed file data set. It consisted of 16 most common file-types. For each file type, we also encrypted it to get their encrypted counterparts. For instance, 1000 pdf files obtained from the data set were all encrypted to get the total count of encrypted and non-encrypted versions of pdf files to be 2000.

**Table 1.** Analysis on common file-types using Chi-square (CS) Test.

| File Type | No. of files analysed | Median CS | | Avg CS for Enc | Max CS for Enc | % of wrongly detected Enc files | % of wrongly detected Non-Enc files | % of wrongly detected files |
|---|---|---|---|---|---|---|---|---|
| | | Enc | Non-Enc | | | | | |
| pdf | 2000 | 257.02 | 43115.18 | 258.43 | 415.16 | 1.50 | 0.00 | 0.75 |
| mp3 | 2000 | 256.99 | 62021.32 | 257.27 | 326.58 | 1.50 | 0.00 | 0.75 |
| rar | 2000 | 268.42 | 2810.98 | 270.51 | 460.46 | 9.10 | 3.00 | 6.05 |
| tar | 2000 | 265.12 | 1165758.19 | 268.68 | 434.86 | 8.10 | 0.00 | 4.05 |
| zip | 2000 | 254.10 | 3193.47 | 255.02 | 324.49 | 0.80 | 0.00 | 0.40 |
| pptx | 2000 | 253.69 | 147929.42 | 255.19 | 329.85 | 0.80 | 0.00 | 0.40 |
| txt | 2000 | 254.86 | 25727.58 | 258.98 | 630.19 | 2.50 | 1.70 | 2.10 |
| xlsx | 2000 | 255.41 | 57994.32 | 255.65 | 339.40 | 1.79 | 0.00 | 0.89 |
| docx | 2000 | 256.32 | 73122.94 | 256.36 | 322.03 | 0.80 | 0.00 | 0.40 |
| exe | 2000 | 255.33 | 1311368.26 | 259.66 | 1121.71 | 3.60 | 0.00 | 1.80 |
| webp | 1600 | 257.10 | 2204.32 | 257.76 | 336.52 | 2.00 | 30.50 | 16.25 |
| jpg | 12000 | 254.31 | 8429.79 | 255.15 | 342.13 | 1.00 | 0.00 | 0.50 |
| png | 12000 | 259.56 | 20121.44 | 260.16 | 355.22 | 2.12 | 0.00 | 1.06 |
| mp4 | 2000 | 260.70 | 104376.94 | 261.80 | 337.70 | 2.00 | 0.00 | 1.00 |
| mkv | 2000 | 260.83 | 81404.24 | 261.31 | 337.03 | 1.80 | 0.00 | 0.90 |
| gzip | 2000 | 252.63 | 3396.65 | 253.90 | 333.81 | 1.20 | 1.60 | 1.40 |

Table 1 shows the detailed analysis of chi-square values for each file type, along with the percentage of misclassifications. The misclassifications and correct classifications are what is more important to us from the table. The following bar graphs will visualize the False Positive Rates (FPR) and False Negative Rates (FNR) for all 16 file types.

The bar graph in Fig. 2 shows that the file-type **webp** has the highest false positive rate (30.5%). This may be due to the high compressibility feature of webp that gives good quality images with small size. The paper [8] also mentions this high FPR of chi-square test on webp files as an issue. However, this FPR is not flagged as a serious issue in the proposed design because the normal download/write of webp files by a user will not be flagged as a ransomware activity even though it is misclassified as encrypted file writes. This is handled by the timestamp variable as explained in the Optimisation section of the proposed design.

Figure 2 also shows the false negative rates (classification of encrypted files as non-encrypted), almost all the types give satisfiable results except for **rar** and **tar**. For these types, using *Serial Byte Correlation Coefficient* method [6] can be advantageous to reduce misclassification.

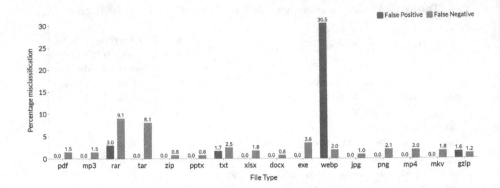

**Fig. 2.** False Positive and False Negative Rates for various File-types.

# 6    Design-Based Comparison with Existing Solutions

## 6.1    R-Locker

R-locker also deploys honeypot to detect ransomware activity. However, once the honeypot is accessed in R-locker, the user receives a prompt and has to manually provide the command to kill or continue the process. In contrast, in our proposed solution, once the honeypot is accessed, the Entropy Monitoring Module automatically decides whether to kill or continue the process based on the chi-square analysis of the last few file writes. This automatic check enhances the practicality of the proposed solution.

Another feature of the proposed design is the incorporation of multiple symlinks per folder that increases the probability of honeypot access when the files are randomly accessed by the ransomware. Also, these multiple symlinks to the honeypot are provided with different names, in case the ransomware accesses the files in alphabetical order. However, the R-Locker installs one symlink per folder thereby resulting in an increase in the encryption of user files.

## 6.2    Data Aware Defence

Data Aware Defence (DaD) [7] is one of the anti-ransomware solutions that incorporates chi-square test on files as a metric. Application of chi-square test on files to distinguish encrypted files and non-encrypted file writes is the common factor between DaD and the proposed solution. DaD is implemented as a mini-filter driver that installs between the user area and the kernel and all system calls for file write operations are diverted through that driver. DaD constantly keeps track of a sliding window of chi-square values for the last 50 file writes and maintains a sliding median. Once the sliding median is lesser than the critical chi-square value, the process states are dumped and then the malicious process is killed.

Table 2. Design comparison between the proposed solution and existing solutions.

| Feature Comparison | R-Locker | DaD | Proposed Design |
|---|---|---|---|
| Operating System | Linux | Windows | Linux |
| Human Intervention | Yes | No | No |
| Operation mode | Kernel mode | Driver mode | Kernel mode |
| Type of solution | Honeypot based | File analysis based | Honeypot and File analysis based |
| Symlinks per folder | Single | Not Applicable | Multiple |
| Statistical metric | NIL | Chi-square | Chi-square |
| Significance level | Not Applicable | 0.05 | 0.01 |

## 6.3 Design Comparison

The proposed design is compared with the existing solutions, R-Locker and DaD, based on the design features incorporated in building the system. Table 2 shows the design comparison between the anti-ransomware solutions discussed.

The proposed solution monitors the queue and finds the queue average only when the honeypot is accessed, thereby reducing the overhead in communication between the honeypot and the entropy monitoring module. The difference between our solution and DaD is that in the proposed solution the significance level for chi-square test is 0.01 while in DaD it is 0.05. A chi-square test was conducted with both the significance levels and it was noticed that changing the significance level to 0.01 reduced the misclassification rate of chi-square test on files.

## 7 Conclusion

This paper proposed a solution for detecting ransomware attacks and improved upon the existing detection techniques. The proposed design was implemented in a Unix-based system. The main contribution in the proposed solution is the incorporation of chi-square test of files in a honeypot environment. The proposed design relied on the automated detection of changes to the files and folders in the system the crypto-ransomware initiates rather than solely relying on the communication with the C&C server or specific functional calls to the cryptographic modules the traditional anti-ransomware solutions provide. Keeping honeypots (or honeytraps) throughout the user file-system enabled the detection of the ransomware at the instance of the encryption operation. Our solution automated and improved upon the existing honeypot-based techniques with the help of chi-square test on files.

For future work, the implementation of the proposed design can be extended to Windows-based systems. The scope of other prominent statistical measures can also be studied for reducing false-positive rates for certain file types.

# References

1. Gómez-Hernández, J., Álvarez González, L., García-Teodoro, P.: R-locker: thwarting ransomware action through a honeyfile-based approach. Comput. Secur. **73**, 389–398 (2018)
2. Cabaj, K., Mazurczyk, W.: Using software-defined networking for ransomware mitigation: the case of cryptowall. IEEE Netw. **30**(6), 14–20 (2016)
3. Scaife, N., Carter, H., Traynor, P., Butler, K.R.: Cryptolock (and drop it): stopping ransomware attacks on user data. In: IEEE 36th International Conference on Distributed Computing Systems (ICDCS), pp. 303–312. IEEE 2016 (2016)
4. Ramesh, G., Menen, A.: Automated dynamic approach for detecting ransomware using finite-state machine. Decis. Support Syst. **138**, 113400 (2020)
5. NapierOne: a modern mixed file data set alternative to Govdocs1. Forensic Sci. Int. Digit. Invest. **40**, 301330 (2022)
6. Davies, S.R., Macfarlane, R., Buchanan, W.J.: Comparison of entropy calculation methods for ransomware encrypted file identification. Entropy **24**(10), 1503 (2022)
7. Palisse, A., Durand, A., Le Bouder, H., Le Guernic, C., Lanet, J.-L.: Data aware defense (DaD): towards a generic and practical ransomware countermeasure. In: Lipmaa, H., Mitrokotsa, A., Matulevičius, R. (eds.) NordSec 2017. LNCS, vol. 10674, pp. 192–208. Springer, Cham (2017). https://doi.org/10.1007/978-3-319-70290-2_12
8. Pont, J., Arief, B., Hernandez-Castro, J.: Why current statistical approaches to ransomware detection fail. In: Susilo, W., Deng, R.H., Guo, F., Li, Y., Intan, R. (eds.) ISC 2020. LNCS, vol. 12472, pp. 199–216. Springer, Cham (2020). https://doi.org/10.1007/978-3-030-62974-8_12

# PSDP: Blockchain-Based Computationally Efficient Provably Secure Data Possession

Jayaprakash Kar[✉]

Centre for Cryptology, Cybersecurity and Digital Forensics,
Department of Computer Science and Engineering, The LNM Institute
of Information Technology, Jaipur, Rajasthan, India
jayaprakashkar@lnmiit.ac.in

**Abstract.** Provable Data Possession is a protocol that helps the client
to verify the integrity of the data that has been stored in cloud or a
remote server. It allows the client to verify that the data possessed by the
server is not modified, damaged or lost i.e. the data is original in all forms
without retrieving it. Probabilistic proof of possession are constructed
by the model by performing random sampling to choose random blocks
of data from the remote server. To verify this, client maintains a data
of fixed volume. This reduces the input and output costs drastically.
We have constructed an efficient and lightweight provably secure Data
Possession (**PSDP**) using Elliptic Curve Digital Signature Algorithm
(ECDSA) in the signing process in this paper.

**Keywords:** Data possession · Provable security · Cloud server ·
ECDSA · Blockchain

## 1 Introduction

Now a day with the increasing development of advanced network technology and
requirement of computer resources, the enterprises would like the outsourcing
their storage and computing needs. In order to decrease the load of maintaining the data and saving cost of purchase, increasing the number of people and
enterprises prefer to store their data on the remote cloud. This makes the user's
compatibility for accessing and sharing files. Due to rapid growth of business, a
numerous of could service provider (CSP) such as Dropbox, SkyDrive, OneDrive,
ZipCloud etc. have emerged to provide data outsourcing. With respect to security, reliability, speed and price, the user can select a CSP. The stored data of
the users might be confidential and have the expensive value. The data stored
on remote serve is not under the control of the corporate or enterprise. If some
information stored in the server is modified or lost, these enterprises will have to
bear great loss. The malicious cloud server will hide their mistake to save itself
from compensating the damaged enterprises. So authenticity and integrity of
remote data is a very serious issues in storing data on untrusted remote server.

V. Muthukkumarasamy et al. (Eds.): ICISS 2023, LNCS 14424, pp. 459–468, 2023.
https://doi.org/10.1007/978-3-031-49099-6_28

PDP performs random sampling on a set of file blocks stored in the server and executes the a probabilistic proof of possession. This allows the verifier to ensure the integrity of the remote data that is present with a remote server without downloading or retrieving the data. Therefore the cost of input and output reduces drastically by this method. To check for the authenticity and the integrity of data, the client submits the queries in the form of challenges, the remote server performs the verification of the output generating the responses against the query (challenges). The protocol comprises four actions namely pre-process, inquiry, confirmation and verification. During the pre-processing, the client splits the file $F$ into a number of blocks say $n$ and forms a metadata considered as auxiliary data. This is used to ensure that the data in a remote server or cloud is the original data and the that it's integrity is maintained. The auxiliary data represents block tags and shows the properties of files and blocks. To reduce the space taken up by the data, before uploading on the server, client may alter the file say $F'$ and delete the original file from his local PC. The server stores the altered file $F'$ so that storage space would be $\Omega(n)$ for all blocks while the storage space at the client is $\mathcal{O}(1)$. To verify the ownership of a file, the client sends a random challenge $\gamma$ to the remote server, then the server designs a proof of data possession and transfers it to the client as a response. Upon receiving the response, client compares it with the stored auxiliary data in his local PC. To confirm the successful storage of the file by the server, client performs the data possession challenge before the process of deletion the file's local copy stored in it. Encryption of the file can be done by the clients before out-sourcing for security reasons [4]. The basic structure is depicted in the following Fig. 1.

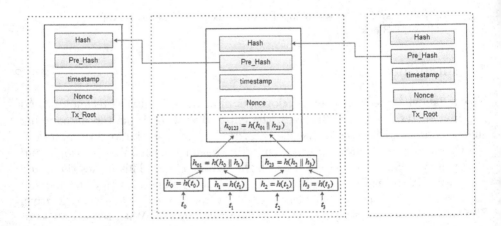

**Fig. 1.** A generic structure of blockchain

## 1.1   Related Work

The paradigm of PDP (Provable data possession) was introduced by Atenies et al. in 2007 [1], The goal of PDP scheme is used for integrity of the remote data of the client that is stored in a remote server. It is a probabilistic approach. They constructed two PDP schemes which are provably secure. Subsequently Ateniese et al. introduced a dynamic PDP scheme where operation of insertion cannot be performed [2]. In 2009, Erway et al [5] designed a full-dynamic PDP scheme using authenticated flip table which support insert operation. A numerous of authors [7,9] have proposed various PDP schemes. Hao et al. [7] gave a PDP scheme to ensure public verifiability and data dynamic which means that it preserved the privacy of the data. A mechanism to verify the stored file using RSA based hash function for remote server [3] was designed by Deswarte et al. Subsequently similar kind of technique was provided by Filho et al. [6]. These schemes allow the client to use the same metadata to perform different challenges on it. In this case the storage and communication complexities are $\mathcal{O}(1)$. The algorithm's drawback is the complexity on the computational level at the server, which grows exponentially according to the file size because we need to access all file blocks. Recently, Yannan et al. [8] proposed an blockchain-based PDP in the name "IntegrityChain" for decentralized storage. The files to peers are stored in a blockchain network by the system model and is formalized as the data owner. The integrity is to be checked periodically by paying bitcoins and the remote server can earn the money if it provides the storage serves honestly. However the scheme does not provide reliability and a stable decentralized outsourcing storage.

## 1.2   Contribution

Data privacy and integrity is very crucial and challenging for outsourcing storage. In order to preserve these security goals, we have developed a very efficient PDP namely **PSDP** with provable security. The proposed scheme uses blockchain which stores the metadata for client. The data irreversibility of blockchain helps the client to check the integrity of the remote data. Listed below are our contributions:

1. We introduce an efficient and provably secure data possession **PSDP** using blockchain technology which contains the metadata and signature. The metadata is to be queried and verified by the client.
2. We perform formalization of the two models- 1. system model and 2. the security/adversary model for **PSDP**, where we include blockchain as one entity so as to check the integrity of remote data.
3. The construction of **PSDP** uses the signing algorithm ECDSA, an cyclic group (additive in nature) of a large prime order $\mu$ and blockchain for checking of remote data integrity (Table 1).

**Table 1.** Nomenclature

| Nomenclature | Description |
|---|---|
| $n$ | A large prime number($\geq 2^{160}$-bits) |
| $p$ | Odd prime $\geq 3$ |
| $\mathbb{Z}_p$ | $\{0, 1, 2 \ldots p - 1\}$ |
| $\mathbb{Z}_p^*$ | $\{0, 1, 2 \ldots p - 1\}/\{0\}$ |
| $E$ | Elliptic curve defined over $\mathbb{Z}_p$ |
| $G$ | Additive cyclic group $n$ |
| $H$ | Collision resistant hash function |
| $P$ | A generator of group $G$ of order $n$ |
| $R$ | Any arbitrary element of $G$ |
| $R_x$ | $x$-coordinate of point $R \in G$ |
| $(d, Q)$ | Private and public key pair, where $Q = d \cdot P$ |
| $\mathcal{O}$ | Point at infinity |

## 2  System and Protocol Model

The proposed protocol works with a system model which is made up of four participating entities **Client**: $C$, **Cloud Server**: $S$, **Blockchain** and **System Administrator**. The communications between these entities are illustrated in Fig. 2. It is discussed as bellows:

1. **Client**: An entity regarded as data owner which has massive data would like to store on cloud for maintenance and computation. The file is divided and metadata is created along with the signature. Then **Client** uploads the file on the **Cloud server**. The metadata and signature are being sent to the **Blockchain** at the same moment. The challenge is generated by the entity who might be individual consumer or corporate and sends it to both the **Cloud Server** and the **Blockchain**. Upon receiving the responses, these are verified by the **Client**. Verification is considered successful if the remote data is considered as integer and unsuccessful if it is considered as non-integer.
2. **Cloud Server**: The cloud service provider maintains a cloud server with high computational capability and storage space. This stores the **Client**'s data. So **Cloud Server** is one of the entity in the system model.
3. **Blockchain**: It is the entity which stores the client metadata that is later used to ensure the integrity of the data stored in a remote server. When **Blockchain** receives the **Client**'s challenge, it performs some computation using the metadata present with it and then sends it to the **Client**. Due to the data i properties of blockchain, the remote data integrity is checked.
4. **System Administrator**: An entity which is a trusted third party (TTP) which creates or generates both public and private system parameters of the **Client** and **Cloud Server**. The public parameters are being published where as the secret parameters are kept secret. The secret parameters are sent to corresponding entities through a secure channel using TLS protocol.

All the above steps are depicted in the following Fig. 2.

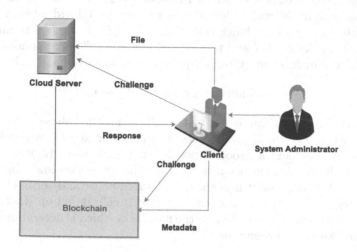

**Fig. 2.** System model

## 3 Provable Data Possession Based on Blockchain

This section presents a generic framework of blockchain-based PDP which comprises six polynomial-time algorithms namely KeyGen, SignBlock, Challenge, GenProof, VerProof and Compensation. These are described as follows:

1. KeyGen: This algorithms execute in a probabilistic polynomial time. A value $k$ is taken as an input and matching public and private keys are generated using it forming a pair of keys. This is performed by the client to setup and does the setting. Formally we can represent as

$$\text{KeyGen}(1^k) \rightarrow (pk, sk).$$

2. SignBlock: The client runs this algorithm in a probabilistic polynomial time. This takes the public parameters *i.e* the public key $pk$ and secret (private) key $sk$ as input and the file blocks are uploaded. This generates the metadata corresponding to the uploaded file. The file is then uploaded to the **Cloud Server** and the metadata to the **Blockchain** via a secure channel using TLS protocol. Formally we can represent as

$$\text{SignBlock}(pk, sk, F_1, F_2 \ldots F_n) \rightarrow \sigma_F.$$

Where the file $F$ has been divided into $n$ blocks $F_1, F_2 \ldots F_n$ of equal sizes.
3. Challenge: It is a random nonce generated by the **Client** to make sure the integrity in the data is maintained and is sent to the **Cloud Server** and **Blockchain**.

4. GenProof: When the **Cloud Server** receives challenge, it computes a values from the data stored as a **Proof of Possession** and send this value to **Client** as response. The following algorithm is run by the **Cloud Server**. It takes the public key $pk$, a file block collection $F = \{F_1, F_2 \ldots F_n\}$ in an ordered fashion, a challenge $chal$ and the ordered metadata $\Psi$ corresponding to each of the blocks in $F$ as input and outputs a proof of possession $\eta$. Formally

$$\texttt{GenProof}(pk, F, chal, \Psi) \to \eta.$$

5. VerProof: This algorithm is run by the **Client** for the validation of the proof of possession. The input parameters are the public key $pk$, a secret key $sk$, a challenge $chal$ and a proof of possession $\eta$. Additionally, it submits the query to the blockchain, then it executes the algorithm and obtains some metadata. Finally, **Client** uses the metadata, response and verifies the remote data integrity. It returns "**success**" or "**failure**", based on whether $\eta$ is a appropriate proof of possession for the file blocks which is determined by $chal$. Formally, we can represent as

$$\texttt{VerProof}(pk, sk, chal, \eta) \to \text{"1"}/\text{"0"}.$$

Where "**success**" or "**failure**" are denoted by 1 and 0 respectively.

6. Compensation: In case some data is improper or broken then the **Client** communicates with the **Cloud Server** and can ask for a compensation from **Cloud Server**.

**Definition 1. Unforgeability**: In random oracle model, there exist an probabilistic polynomial time adversary $\mathscr{A}$ i.e dishonest **Cloud Server** which has negligible probability to go safely through the verification process if the data that is challenged to the server is either altered or lost.

The game takes place between the adversary $\mathscr{A}$ and the challenger $\mathscr{C}$ with following phases:

- **Setup**: Secret value $k$ is taken as input and the **KeyGen** algorithm is run on it by the challenger. The challenger also computes the public and private key pairs $(pk, sk)$. The public key $pk$ is sent to $\mathscr{A}$ and private key $sk$ is kept by the challenger secretly.
- **Phase-I Queries**: The adversary submits the signing and hash queries to the challenger $\mathscr{C}$ in an adaptive manner. $\mathscr{C}$ answers each queries. Here a random oracle is how the hash function has been modelled. It chooses a block $F_1$ and sends it to $\mathscr{C}$. Similarly $\mathscr{A}$ continues to submit the queries to the challenger $\mathscr{C}$ for verification of metadata $\sigma_i$, for all $i = 2 \ldots n$ for other files $F_2 \ldots F_n$ respectively. $\mathscr{C}$ runs the SignBlock algorithms and computes $\sigma_{F_i}$ i.e. $\texttt{SignBlock}(pk, sk, F_i) \to \sigma_{F_1}$. Then $\mathscr{A}$ stores the block files as an order of collection $F = (F_1, F_2 \ldots F_n)$, along with the corresponding metadata $\sigma_{F_1}, \sigma_{F_2} \ldots \sigma_{F_n}$ for verification.

- **Challenge:** A challenge *chal* is generated by $\mathscr{C}$ and $\mathscr{C}$ then constructs challenged blog-tag pairs. Then requests for a proof of possession to $\mathscr{A}$ for the blocks $F_{i_1}, F_{i_2} \ldots F_{i_c}$ determined by *chal*, for all $1 \le i_j \le n$, $1 \le j \le c$, $1 \le c \le n$.
- **Phase-II Queries:** This is similar to phase-I queries. Here there exist a minimum of one challenge-block pair which hasn't been queried by $\mathscr{A}$.
- **Forge:** $\mathscr{A}$ gives the proof of possession or response $\eta$ for the file blocks that are shown by *chal*, returns $\eta$ and send it to $\mathscr{C}$.

$\mathscr{A}$ is considered as the winner if the verification equation holds for the proof of possession $\eta$ in the data possession game. Formally

$$\texttt{CheckProof}(pk, sk, chal, \eta) \to \text{"1"}$$

Where "1" indicates for success.

$\mathscr{A}$ obtains a bit $\delta'$ and wins the DPG when $\delta' = \delta$. The $\mathscr{A}$'s advantages is given as

$$\text{Adv}_{\text{PSDP}}^{\text{UF}}(\mathscr{A}) = |2\Pr[\delta' = \delta] - 1|,$$

where $\Pr[\delta' = \delta]$ denotes the probability that $\delta' = \delta$.

## 4 Construction of Data Possession Scheme

The scheme consists of six polynomial solvable algorithms namely KeyGen, SignBlock, Challenge, GenProof, VerProof and SignVer. Let the stored file is denoted by $F$. The file may be either plaintext or ciphertext. If it needs the privacy, the file can be stored in the form of ciphertext otherwise, it is in plaintext. Let without lost of generality, the file $F$ is divided into multiple blocks of the same size i.e. $n$ number of blocks as $\{F_1, F_2 \ldots F_n\}$. The algorithms are described below:

- KeyGen: This algorithm constructs the signing and verification keys. The system sets the following parameters
  - $E$ be the elliptic curve defined over prime field $\mathbb{Z}_p$. The total number of points in $E(\mathbb{Z}_p)$ should be divisible a prime $\mu$.
  - Select $P \in E(\mathbb{Z}_p)$ of order $\mu$ i.e $\mathcal{O}(P) = \mu$.
  - Select $d \in [1, \mu-1]$ at random which is statistically unbiased and unique.
  - Signer's public key is $(E, P, \mu, Q)$, where $Q = d \cdot P$.
  In addition, it chooses pseudo random function $\phi$ and pseudo-random permutation $\psi$ to generate of proof which are defined as:
  $$\phi : \mathbb{Z}_p^* \times \{1, 2 \ldots n\} \to \mathbb{Z}_p^*.$$
  $$\psi : \mathbb{Z}_p^* \times \{1, 2 \ldots n\} \to \{1, 2 \ldots n\}.$$
- SignBlock: The client runs this algorithm on the given blocks $\{F_1, F_2 \ldots F_n\}$ using his own private key $d$. The signing process follows the Algorithm 1.

**Algorithm 1**

**Input:** $\{F_1, F_2 \ldots F_n, d, P\}$
**Output:** $\sigma = (r, s)$
1: **for** $i = 1$ to $n$ **do**
2:     Compute $f_i = F_i \bmod n$ and $Q_i = f_i \cdot P$.
3: **end for**
4: Select $k \in [1, n-1]$ randomly.
5: Compute $R = k \cdot P$.
6: $r \leftarrow R_x \bmod n$.
7: Computes $(H(Q_1, Q_2 \ldots Q_n), f_h)$ and convert it to integer $e$.
8: Compute $s = k^{-1}\{e + dr\} \bmod n$.
9: **if** $s = 0$ **then**
10:     **goto** 5
11: **end if**
12: **return** $\sigma = (r, s)$.

After obtaining the signature, the protocol performs the following steps

1. Upload $\{Q_1, Q_2 \ldots Q_n\}$, hashed value $h_f = H(F)$ and the signature $\sigma$ to **Blockchain**. At the same time upload the $n$ blocks $\{F_1, F_2 \ldots F_n\}$ and the hashed value $h_f$ to **Cloud Server**.
2. Upon receiving $\{F_1, F_2 \ldots F_n\}$ and $h_f$, **Cloud Server** verifies whether $h_f = H(F)$ holds.
3. **Cloud Server** also verifies whether $h_f$ has been uploaded to **Blockchain**. The $n$ blocks and the $\{F_1, F_2 \ldots F_n\}$ and the hashed value $f_h$ are accepted by the **Cloud Server** if both the conditions hold true.

- **Challenge: Client** chooses the tuples $(c, t_1, t_2)$ as his challenge, where $c \in [1, n]$ and $t_1, t_2 \in \mathbb{Z}_p^*$. Let it is denoted by $\gamma$. The challenge $\gamma$ is then sent to the **Cloud Server**.
- **GenProof:** The **Cloud Server** performs the following steps after it receives the challenge $\gamma$ from the **Client**, and then it computes $F^*$.
  1. $\alpha_i = \psi_{t_1}(i)$ and $\beta_i = \phi_{t_2}(i)$, for all $i \in [1, c]$.
  2. Computes $F^* = \sum_{i=1}^{c} \beta_i F_{\alpha_i}$.
  3. Forwards $F^*$ to **Client**.
- **VerProof: Client** performs the following steps, after receiving $F^*$.
  1. For the received challenge $\gamma$, computes $\alpha_i = \psi_{t_1}(i)$ and $\beta_i = \phi_{t_2}(i)$, for all $i \in [1, c]$.
  2. Computes $\bar{f} = F^* \bmod \mu$.
  3. Submits query to **Blockchain** and obtains $\{Q_{\alpha_1}, Q_{\alpha_2} \ldots Q_{\alpha_n}\}$.
  4. In the given group $G$, check the following equation holds:

$$\sum_{i=1}^{c} \beta_i \cdot Q_{\alpha i} = \bar{f} \cdot P \tag{1}$$

and it returns "Success", or "failure" accordingly.

- SignVer: When the data stored in the server is altered, then the **Cloud Server** verifies or compensates for **Client**. Hence for the verification that the data present in the server belongs to **Client**, the **Cloud Server** runs the Algorithm 2 and check the signature $\sigma = (r, s)$.

---

**Algorithm 2**

---

**Input:** $\sigma = (r, s)$.
**Output:** " 1" or "0"
1: **if** $r, s \in [1, \mu - 1]$ **then**
2:     return "1"
3: **end if**
4: Compute $\omega = s^{-1} \bmod \mu$
5: Compute $u_1 = e\omega \bmod \mu$ and $u_2 = r\omega \bmod \mu$
6: Compute $R = u_1 P + u_2 Q$
7: **if** $R = \mathcal{O}$ **then**
8:     **return** ''0''
9: **else**
10:     Convert $R_x$ to $\bar{R}_x$ as integer
11:     $v = \bar{R}_x \bmod \mu$.
12: **end if**
13: **return** "1" or "0" $\iff v = r$

---

### 4.1 Proof of Correctness

$$\sum_{i=1}^{c} \beta_i \cdot Q_{\alpha i}$$
$$\sum_{i=1}^{c} \beta_i \cdot (f_{\alpha i} P)$$
$$\sum_{i=1}^{c} \beta_i \cdot (F_{\alpha i} P)$$
$$= F^* \cdot P$$
$$= \bar{f} \cdot P$$

The proof of correctness of verification/compensation is presented below:
$s = k^{-1}\{e + dr\} \bmod \mu$
Taking inverse both sides, we obtain
$s^{-1} = k\{e + dr\}^{-1} \bmod \mu$.
So $\omega = k\{(e + dr)^{-1} \bmod \mu$.
$\implies \omega\{(e + dr\} \bmod \mu = k$
$\implies (\omega e + \omega dr)P = kP$
Hence $u_1 P + u_2 Q = kP = R$.

## 5   Conclusion

Confidentiality and data integrity is very essential and challenging for cloud storage. We have constructed an blockchain-based PDP using ECDSA which requires smaller keys to provide equivalent security. Our scheme **PSDP** is based on blockchain technology. Due to i of blockchain, the scheme ensures the remote data integrity. The proposed scheme **PSDP** also protect the **Client**'s anonymity. Since the schemes proposed by Huaqun et al. [10], Ateniese's scheme [1] works on RSA-1024 bit whereas our scheme works on ECC-160 bit achieving same level of security not Analysing the performance of our technique, we observe that our scheme is more efficient in term of computation cost and have the security properties confidentiality, unforgeable, public and batch audible. Further, for improving the efficiency with respect to key escrow and certificate management, the scheme that we have proposed can be designed by using certificate-less public key cryptography (CL-PKC).

# References

1. Ateniese, G., et al.: Provable data possession at untrusted stores. In: Proceedings of the 14th ACM Conference on Computer and Communications Security, pp. 598–609 (2007)
2. Ateniese, G., Di Pietro, R., Mancini, L.V., Tsudik, G.: Scalable and efficient provable data possession. In: Proceedings of the 4th International Conference on Security and Privacy in Communication Networks, pp. 1–10 (2008)
3. Deswarte, Y., Quisquater, J.-J., Saïdane, A.: Remote integrity checking. In: Jajodia, S., Strous, L. (eds.) Integrity and Internal Control in Information Systems VI. IIFIP, vol. 140, pp. 1–11. Springer, Boston (2004). https://doi.org/10.1007/1-4020-7901-X_1
4. Dhakad, N., Kar, J.: EPPDP: an efficient privacy-preserving data possession with provable security in cloud storage. IEEE Syst. J. **16**(4), 6658–6668 (2022)
5. Erway, C.C., Küpçü, A., Papamanthou, C., Tamassia, R.: Dynamic provable data possession. ACM Trans. Inf. Syst. Secur. (TISSEC) **17**(4), 1–29 (2015)
6. Gazzoni Filho, D.L., Barreto, P.S.L.M.: Demonstrating data possession and uncheatable data transfer. IACR Cryptology ePrint Archive 2006, 150 (2006)
7. Hao, Z., Zhong, S., Yu, N.: A privacy-preserving remote data integrity checking protocol with data dynamics and public verifiability. IEEE Trans. Knowl. Data Eng. **23**(9), 1432–1437 (2011)
8. Li, Y., Yu, Y., Chen, R., Du, X., Guizani, M.: Integritychain: provable data possession for decentralized storage. IEEE J. Sel. Areas Commun. **38**(6), 1205–1217 (2020)
9. Sebé, F., Domingo-Ferrer, J., Martinez-Balleste, A., Deswarte, Y., Quisquater, J.J.: Efficient remote data possession checking in critical information infrastructures. IEEE Trans. Knowl. Data Eng. **20**(8), 1034–1038 (2008)
10. Wang, H., He, D., Fu, A., Li, Q., Wang, Q.: Provable data possession with outsourced data transfer. IEEE Trans. Serv. Comput. **14**, 1929–1939 (2019)

# Private and Verifiable Inter-bank Transactions and Settlements on Blockchain

Harika Narumanchi[1]([✉]), Lakshmi Padmaja Maddali[1], and Nitesh Emmadi[2]

[1] Tata Consultancy Services, Hyderabad, India
{h.narumanchi,lakshmipadmaja.maddali}@tcs.com
[2] Hyderabad, India
niteshemmadi@gmail.com

**Abstract.** Blockchain based inter-bank payments enhance accountability, transparency and ensure faster payments by recording transactions on a shared ledger, eliminating reconciliation needs. However, a blockchain network can only validate that a bank (or a user) transacts with another bank (or another user). It records only a portion of transactions and cannot verify debits/credits between sender/receiver bank as balances are private to the banks. In this paper, we propose a solution based on permissioned blockchain to address privacy concern of customer financial information such as balances, while providing cryptographic guarantees for transaction debits and credits without revealing customer balances and transaction amounts. Our solution offers fully auditable inter-bank payments as well as faster end-of-cycle settlements using cryptographic primitives such as bilinear pairings for enhancing customer privacy. Bilinear pairings such as BLS are used to create verifiable proofs, called the authenticators, for transaction amounts and customer balances, striking a balance between user privacy and transaction auditability. These BLS signatures (authenticators) are stored on blockchain act as global proof for enabling verifiable audits. Furthermore, blockchain ensures data transparency among banking entities and enables automation of settlement process through smart contracts. We demonstrate practical performance and security guarantees through evaluation.

**Keywords:** Blockchain · Private Auditable Transactions · Private Auditable Inter-Bank Settlements · BLS Signature

## 1 Introduction

Traditional inter-banking systems maintain confidential transactions between relevant parties but often share sensitive customer data with third-party service providers, such as marketing firms or data brokers, raising privacy concerns. For example, customer information is shared with credit bureaus to compute credit scores, and in such systems, customer balances and transaction amounts are accessible to bank employees, increasing the risk of data breaches. Moreover,

© The Author(s), under exclusive license to Springer Nature Switzerland AG 2023
V. Muthukkumarasamy et al. (Eds.): ICISS 2023, LNCS 14424, pp. 469–479, 2023.
https://doi.org/10.1007/978-3-031-49099-6_29

banks store vast amounts of customer sensitive data, making them attractive targets for attackers who could gain unauthorized access and potentially manipulate it. For instance, in 2018, a data breach at HSBC exposed sensitive customer information [4], leading to severe financial consequences and extensive monitoring of financial transactions, potentially infringing on customer privacy [1]. Traditional banking systems lack transparency in financial and customer information, requiring explicit reconciliation. The banking and financial sector is among the industries most affected by data breaches [1], emphasizing the critical importance of safeguarding customer data. The potential applications of blockchain extend far beyond cryptocurrencies. Industries such as finance, supply chain, healthcare, and more are exploring and adopting blockchain to enhance security, privacy, efficiency, and accountability in their operations [14,17].

Blockchain-based inter-bank payment systems [16], address privacy concerns in traditional banking by storing customer information on an immutable global ledger accessible only to authorized entities like banks and regulators. This tamper evident system reduces the risk of unauthorized data disclosure. Blockchain also enables the use of smart contracts, eliminating the need for correspondent banking relationships and associated settlement delays. Furthermore, the transparency provided by blockchain allows auditing authorities to easily validate transactions and detect anomalies or fraud, eliminating the need for explicit reconciliation, enhancing process efficiency and enabling faster near real-time settlements. These systems offer several advantages but have limitations. They mainly validate transactions between banks, without verifying the actual debit/credit at the sender/receiver. Essentially, blockchain only records a part of the transaction. Figure 1a depicts blockchain network and Fig. 1b illustrates the transaction process involving two customers, $C_A$ and $C_B$, from different banks, Bank A and Bank B. For instance, when $C_A$ from Bank A initiates a transfer to $C_B$ from Bank B, the blockchain records the transaction but can't ensure Bank A debited $C_A$ and Bank B credited $C_B$ correctly since balances $U_A$ and $U_B$ are private. Furthermore, regulatory authorities like RBI can access customer data, and there is a lack of privacy during audits. Also, current settlements are long and require access to all transactions.

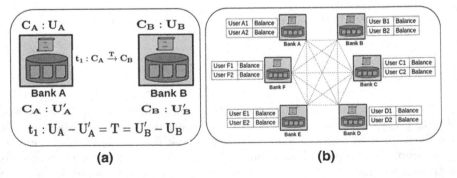

(a)     (b)

**Fig. 1.** a) The Problem: Transaction Completeness b) Blockchain Network

In this paper, we propose a blockchain-based system called "Private and Verifiable Inter-bank Transactions and Settlements" that enables banks to verify transactions while preserving privacy. Our protocol offers cryptographic guarantees for transaction debits and credits without revealing customer information (balances). The proposed protocol is based on Hyperledger Fabric (HLF) [5,10] permissioned blockchain and bilinear pairing cryptographic primitives [6], that enhance transaction privacy and auditability while ensuring transparency and transaction integrity using blockchain. We use bilinear pairings to authenticate and verify individual transactions and end-of-cycle settlements while preserving customers' and banks' privacy. Blockchain secures customer information against tampering and allows trusted public verification. We provide simulation results demonstrating practical performance while enabling strong privacy guarantees.

The paper is organized as follows: Sect. 2 reviews existing inter-bank blockchain-based protocols. Section 3 briefly covers the Boneh-Lynn-Shacham (BLS) signature scheme, a key component of our protocol. Section 4 presents our main contributions, and Sect. 5 evaluates the protocol's performance.

## 2  Related Work

With the increased awareness of privacy and stringent data privacy regulations across the globe such as GDPR, maintaining privacy of customer information in any application is crucial for all business firms to run successfully. The impact of privacy breach is even more crucial in sectors such as banking and financial services and plays a crucial role in maintaining trusted relationship with the financial institutions. In banking sector, one of the most fundamental operation is performing inter-bank transactions and settlement systems. The problem of protecting privacy of customer information while performing audits, in the context of banking and finances is well studied in literature and is addressed by several research works such as [7,8,11–13]. Hereafter, we review state-of-the-art protocols that mention privacy preserving auditable and verifiable transactions. Jeong et al. [11] proposed a system that enables verifiable and auditable transactions while preserving transaction privacy in blockchain based systems by leveraging Zero-Knowledge Proofs (ZKP). This is achieved through generation of proofs using ZKP protocols and verifier verifying these proofs to ensure the auditability without learning anything about transaction details. Androulaki et al. [7] designed a system that proves validity of token payments in a privacy preserving manner without revealing details such as transaction amount or the recipient. Authors use ZKP to generate verifiable proofs for the token payments which can be used while auditing to successfully audit the transaction. Kang et al. [12] proposed a system Fabzk that ensures data privacy while executing the smart contracts while enabling auditor to verify the transaction validity. Fabzk also uses ZKP to enable auditability of transactions. Banerjee et al. [8] build an auditablity solution in the context of outsourcing large files to cloud servers. Here, the authors prevent adversaries from cheating and colluding in case of disputes and implement a practical auditing solution using bilinear pairings in case of file audits. Narula *et al.* [13] proposed a system based on non-interactive ZKP to protect privacy of participants and to efficiently reconcile inter-organization transactions. This protocol does not require a trusted third party, rely on widely used cryptography building blocks for their construction.

While there have been significant advancements in privacy-preserving auditable transactions and settlements using blockchain, there are still notable research gaps. Many existing solutions rely on computationally intensive ZKP, that demands enormous computing resources. Additionally, the current end-of-cycle settlement process could potentially expose sensitive financial data, like customer account balances, to regulatory authorities like the RBI (Reserve Bank Of India). The banks may either share complete transaction histories for a particular cycle with RBI, compromising financial data privacy, or handle settlements themselves in turn hampering the overseeing authority of governing body. Our approach solves these problems as discussed in the following sections.

## 3   Preliminaries: BLS Signature

$KeyGen(1^\lambda)$: Key generation algorithm takes security parameter $\lambda$ as input, outputs public and private key pair $(pk, sk)$. Let $e : G \times G \to G_T$ be a bilinear map, where $G$, $G_T$ are groups of prime order $r_p$. Let $g$ be the generator of $G$ and $H : \{0,1\}^* \to G$ is a BLS hash function. The algorithm randomly selects private key, $\alpha \xleftarrow{R} \mathbb{Z}_p$, such that $0 < \alpha < r_p$. Public key $v$ is calculated as $v = g^\alpha$ [9,15]. We use type A pairing with group order 160-bits and order of base field is 512-bits and pairings are constructed on the curve $y^2 = x^3 + x$ over the field $F_q$ for some prime $q = 3\ mod\ 4$. Public and private key pair is $(pk, sk) = (v, \alpha)$.

$Sign(sk, \mathbf{Cred})$: Sign algorithm takes secret key and set of inputs to generate set of signatures. Given a secret key $\alpha$ and inputs $c_1 \ldots c_n$ where each input is an element of $\mathbb{Z}_p$ where $p$ is a $\lambda$-bit prime, signatures $\sigma_1 \ldots \sigma_n$ are created as follows: $\forall x \in n, \sigma_x = (H(c_x).u^{c_x})^\alpha$ *where* $u \xleftarrow{R} G$

$GenProof(\mathcal{P}, \mathcal{V})$: $GenProof$ is an interactive proof between prover and verifier. Verifier sends challenges $\{i, r_i\}$ where $i$ is index of input to be verified and $r_i$ is a challenge corresponding to the input $i$. These challenges are sent to prover to prove some claim. Prover authenticates the challenges and performs selective disclosure of inputs represented by $c_j$ and signatures represented $\sigma_j$, where $j \in J$ which are a subset of claims and signatures respectively, received from the verifier. Prover creates a proof using signatures of inputs as below and sends proof $c_j$ and $\mu, \sigma$ to verifier for verification.

$$\mu = \sum_{j \in J} r_j c_j \qquad \sigma = \prod_{j \in J} \sigma_j^{r_j}$$

$VerifyProof(pk, \{c_j\}, \mu, \sigma, u)$: $VerifyProof$ takes public key $v$, $u$, generator $g$ and inputs $c_j$, proof $\mu, \sigma$ from prover. From this, verifier computes hash of desired claims and runs verification algorithm. Verification algorithm outputs the verification result. Verification is carried out as follows:

$$e(\sigma, g) \overset{?}{=} e(\prod_{j \in J} H(c_j)^{r_j}.u^\mu, v)$$

# 4   Proposed Protocol

Our proposed permissioned blockchain protocol ensures fully auditable inter-bank payments and faster end-of-cycle settlements while protecting customer privacy. Our protocol leverages Hyperledger Fabric platform and primitive such as bilinear pairings (such as BLS) to create verifiable auditable proofs safeguarding sensitive customer information. BLS signatures enable privacy-preserving data signing, allowing verifiers to authenticate data without accessing sensitive information. Verifiers receive proofs on sensitive data will verify signatures using BLS public key and data hashes, ensuring data integrity. We choose HLF as it offers practical setup with modular architecture without the additional overhead of maintaining cryptocurrency assets or tracking the gas consumption as opposed to other blockchain platforms yet get the benefits of blockchain required for inter-bank settlements. In our protocol, BLS signatures preserves privacy while verifying transaction correctness without revealing transfer amounts and customer balances. It also enables the verification of financial information under the oversight of regulatory bodies.

Key features of our proposed solution are as follows:

- Auditable transactions with customer's information (balances) privacy.
- Verifiable cryptographic guarantees for debits and credits.
- Data transparency among banking entities using Blockchain.
- Automation of settlement process through smart contracts.
- Faster privacy enabled inter-bank settlements.
- Controlled access to transaction data by governing authority
- Reusable cryptographic proofs for audits

## 4.1   Solution Setup

This section outlines the entities, the network topology, and the onboarding process for entities, in our proposed system.

**Entities:** In our system, we have distinct entities, including financial institutions (banks), customers, regulators, and auditors/verifiers. *Banks* handle transaction validations, securely store customer balances on private data collection (PDC). *Customers* use the blockchain for financial operations. *Regulators* oversee compliance and regulatory aspects, while *auditors/verifiers* independently verify and audit transactions and records on the blockchain(BC).

**Network Topology:** In our system, banks form a consortium and establish a unified permissioned blockchain network for conducting transactions collectively and seamlessly perform audits. We choose HLF, a permissioned blockchain platform, with all network entities having verified identities. Our network topology uses HLF's channel [2] and PDC [3] features. We bootstrap a BC network with single channel and multiple PDCs to efficiently handle customer information privately and share it as needed among counter-party banks, authorized verifiers, and customers. Maintaining PDCs in a single channel reduces administrative complexity and improves practicality. Each counter-party banks maintain their $PDC_A$ for bankA and $PDC_B$ for bankB containing customer balance data and there's a common $PDC_{AB}$ shared between bankA and bankB to store transaction amounts (individual credits and debits) for inter-bank settlements. Additionally, $PDC_{ABR}$ involves counter-party banks and the governing authority (e.g., RBI) to store settlement amounts, consolidating total credits and debits over a predefined time interval. Through PDCs, our solution adds an additional layer of data protection, ensuring that sensitive customer information is only accessible to authorized banks and regulatory authorities as needed.

**Onboarding Entities:** The onboarding process involves registering entities to the BC network, enabling them to engage in transactions and interact with other network entities. Each entity within the BC network generates a random BLS signing key pair, consisting of a public key ($spk$) and a private key ($ssk$). These key pairs are registered on the BC and each entity selects a random $\alpha \xleftarrow{R} \mathbb{Z}_p$, computes $v = g^\alpha$, and maintains $\alpha$ as a secret. The secret key $sk$ is represented as ($\alpha, ssk$), while the public key $pk$ is represented as ($v, spk$). The entity's public key ($pk$) is stored on the blockchain and used for generating signatures.

## 4.2   Inter Bank Fund Transfer Transaction Flow

In the scenario of transferring funds between two customers ($C_A$ and $C_B$) from different banks (Bank A and Bank B), as depicted in Fig. 1a, the inter-bank fund transfer process includes the following steps:

1. **Transaction Initiation**: The customer of Bank A ($C_A$) initiates a transaction ($t_1$) to transfer funds ($T$) to the customer of Bank B ($C_B$). This transaction proposal may include sender and receiver information, the transfer amount, and other transaction-specific details. The proposal is sent to relevant blockchain nodes for endorsements. $t_1 : C_A \xrightarrow{T} C_B$
2. **Transaction Validation**: The transaction ($t_1$) is validated by nodes of Bank A, deducts $T$ from current balance $U_A$ of $C_A$ and stores the new balance $U'_A$ in bankA's private data collection $PDC_A$: $U_A - T = U'_A$. Similarly, $t_1$ proposal is also validated by BankB, adds $T$ to the current balance $U_B$ of customer of Bank B, $C_B$ and stores the new balance $U'_B$ in bank B's $PDC_B$: $U_B + T = U'_B$. Figure 2 depicts authenticator creation.
   **Authenticator Generation:** Each of the banks A and B generate authenticators separately at their end. Bank A and Bank B choose a random element $u_A$ and $u_B$ respectively from $G$ and stores $u_A$ and $u_B$ privately. The nodes of each bank computes authenticators for their customers ($C_A$, $C_B$) and new balances($U'_A$ and $U'_B$) with timestamps $ts$ as follows:

$$\sigma(U_A) = (H(U_A||ts).u_A^{(U_A||ts)})^{\alpha_A} \quad \sigma(-U'_A) = (H(-U'_A||ts).u_A^{(-U'_A||ts)})^{\alpha_A}$$

$$\sigma(U'_B) = (H(U'_B||ts).u_B^{(U'_B||ts)})^{\alpha_B} \quad \sigma(-U_B) = (H(-U_B||ts).u_B^{(-U_B||ts)})^{\alpha_B}$$

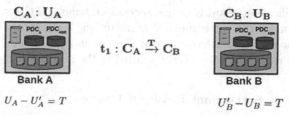

$$U_A - U'_A = T \qquad\qquad U'_B - U_B = T$$

**Authenticator Generated by Bank A**   **Authenticator Generated by Bank B**

$$\sigma(U_A) = (H(U_A\|ts).u_A^{(U_A\|ts)})^{\alpha_A} \qquad \sigma(U'_B) = (H(U'_B\|ts).u_B^{(U'_B\|ts)})^{\alpha_B}$$

$$\sigma(-U'_A) = (H(-U'_A\|ts).u_A^{(-U'_A\|ts)})^{\alpha_A} \qquad \sigma(-U_B) = (H(-U_B\|ts).u_B^{(-U_B\|ts)})^{\alpha_B}$$

$$H(U_A\|ts),\ H(-U'_A\|ts) \qquad\qquad H(-U_B\|ts),\ H(U'_B\|ts)$$

**Bank A creates a proof for transaction**    **Bank B creates a proof for transaction**

$$\mu_A = (U_A\|ts) - (U'_A\|ts) \qquad\qquad \mu_B = (U'_B\|ts) - (U_B\|ts)$$

**Regulatory authority receives verifiable proofs from Bank A and Bank B to audit the correctness of transaction**

$$e(\sigma_A, g_A) \overset{?}{=} e(H(U_A\|ts).H(-U'_A\|ts).u_A^{\mu_A}, v_A)$$

$$e(\sigma_B, g_B) \overset{?}{=} e(H(U'_B\|ts).H(-U_B\|ts).u_B^{\mu_B}, v_B)$$

**Fig. 2.** Authenticator Generation, Proof Generation and Verification

These signatures $\sigma(U_A)$, $\sigma(-U'_A)$, $\sigma(-U_B)$, $\sigma(U'_B)$ and hashes $H(U_A\|ts)$, $H(-U'_A\|ts)$, $H(-U_B\|ts)$, $H(U'_B\|ts)$ are stored on blockchain. Timestamp $ts$ is stored on banks PDCs ($PDC_A$ and $PDC_B$).

3. **Proof Generation**: Bank A and Bank B creates a proof for transaction $t_1$ i.e. $U_A - U'_A = T$ for customer $C_A$, and $U'_B - U_B = T$, for customer $C_B$ respectively as follows:

$$\mu_A = (U_A\|ts) - (U'_A\|ts) \qquad \mu_B = (U'_B\|ts) - (U_B\|ts)$$

During audit, bank A and bank B shares $u_A^{\mu_A}$ and $u_B^{\mu_B}$ respectively to the regulatory authority or verifiers.

4. **Proof Verification**: The verifier, such as RBI verifies the correctness of transaction histories by challenging banks. After receiving the proofs ($u_A^{\mu_A}$, $u_B^{\mu_B}$) from Bank A and Bank B, correctness of the transaction is verified by the verifier as follows:

$$e(\sigma_A, g_A) \overset{?}{=} e(H(U_A\|ts).H(-U'_A\|ts).u_A^{\mu_A}, v_A)$$

$$e(\sigma_B, g_B) \overset{?}{=} e(H(U'_B\|ts).H(-U_B\|ts).u_B^{\mu_B}, v_B)$$

Here, $\sigma_A$ and $\sigma_B$ in LHS are computed from $\sigma(U_A)$, $\sigma(-U'_A)$, $\sigma(-U_B)$, $\sigma(U'_B)$ retrieved from blockchain acts as global immutable proof as follows:

$$\sigma_A = \sigma(U_A).\sigma(-U'_A) \qquad \sigma_B = \sigma(U'_B).\sigma(-U_B)$$

The verification result is either *success* or *failure*. If the verification is *success* it guarantees the correctness of transaction. If the verification is *failure*, disputes have to be settled between the counter-party banks. This verification result is reused by other verifiers during the audit.

## 4.3   Private Settlement Between Banks

Inter-bank settlement involves banks reconciling their transactions and balances with each other at the end of a specific period (end of month/year). This reconciliation process checks transaction history and compares balances to identify discrepancies. In this context, we focus on private settlement, where each bank maintains its transactions and customer balances privately throughout the settlement period. The process begins with one bank initiating the settlement proposal, and counter-party banks independently consolidate their credits and debits. In this process, $T_{AD}$ and $T_{AC}$ represent the sum of debits and sum of credits respectively at BankA, while $T_{BD}$ and $T_{BC}$ represent the same for BankB.

**Settlement Proof Generation:** Banks A create authenticator for the settlement amount and shares with Bank B and vice versa.

$$\sigma_{T_{AD}-T_{AC}} = (H(T_{AD}).u_A^{T_{AD}}.H(-T_{AC}).u_A^{-T_{AC}})^{\alpha_A}$$

$$\sigma_{T_{BD}-T_{BC}} = (H(T_{BD}).u_B^{T_{BD}}.H(-T_{BC}).u_B^{-T_{BC}})^{\alpha_B}$$

**Settlement Proof Verification:** Bank B verifies the settlement using their debits and credits against the proof received from Bank A and vice versa.

$$e(\sigma_{T_{AD}-T_{AC}}, g) \overset{?}{=} e(H(T_{BC}).u_A^{T_{BC}} * H(-T_{BD}).u_A^{-T_{BD}}, v_A)$$

$$e(\sigma_{T_{BD}-T_{BC}}, g) \overset{?}{=} e(H(T_{AC}).u_B^{T_{AC}} * H(-T_{AD}).u_B^{-T_{AD}}, v_B)$$

LHS of the above equations are proofs $(\sigma_{T_{AD}-T_{AC}}, \sigma_{T_{BD}-T_{BC}})$ received from Bank A and Bank B respectively, which are verified against the consolidated debits and consolidated credits of Bank B $(T_{BC}, T_{BD})$ and Bank A $(T_{AC}, T_{AD})$ on RHS. After the settlement transactions are executed, the settlement along with the proofs are stored on $PDC_{ABR}$ shared with governing authority, while the transaction details are stored on blockchain network.

## 5   Results

**System Setup:** We implemented our protocol as a proof-of-concept on Hyperledger Fabric version 2.3. Our test setup ran on a system with an Intel Core i7-8565U CPU @ 1.80 GHz, 8 GB RAM, and Ubuntu 20.04.4 LTS. Our network architecture uses a single channel to facilitate seamless communication between multiple banks, authorized verifiers, and customers. The network consists of 2 organizations, represented as banks (*Bank A* and *Bank B*), each maintaining two peer nodes and a Certificate Authority (CA). We employed *CouchDB* as state database and raft consensus for transaction ordering. To ensure customer privacy, each bank has its designated PDCs ($PDC_A$, $PDC_B$) for storing customer balances. In our test setup, bank nodes, the orderer, CouchDB, CAs, and the chaincode ran on separate docker containers on the same host machine. End-users interacted with the BC ledger through chaincode, implemented in the golang. We integrated a pairing-based library from Stanford University [6] to leverage cryptographic properties, specifically using the BLS signature scheme for authenticators, proof generation, and verification. To streamline integration between the chaincode and the external library, we developed a dedicated service called *pbc_ service*, running on each node. This service allowed the chaincode to perform required cryptographic operations via socket connections.

## 5.1 Performances

In this section, we provide detailed timings for authenticator generation, proof generation and proof verification processes. These timings help us to evaluate the efficiency and practicality of the proposed protocol. The compressed signature size for creating authenticator for one customer balance using bi-linear pairing primitive leveraging the pairing-based cryptography library is 128 bits, achieved within a time-frame of 13 s.

**Table 1.** Timings: Authenticator, Proof Generation & Verification

| Function | Time (ms) |
|---|---|
| Authenticator Creation | 26 |
| Proof Generation | 7.17 |
| Proof Verification | 18.83 |

In Table 1, authenticator functionality involves the process of signature creation for updated balances of bank A and bank B customer's ($C_A$ and $C_B$). These authenticators are further used in proof generation and verification process to validate on the transaction correctness (debits and credits of Bank A and Bank B customers) and settlements (consolidated debits and credits of Bank A and Bank B). On average, the authenticator creation process takes approximately 26 ms, while the proof generation process is completed in around 7.17 ms. And the proof verification step, takes an average time of approximately 18.83 ms. These values were obtained by conducting multiple trials and calculating the average time for each of the mentioned functionalities. The timings obtained here indicate the performance without using blockchain. When these functionalities are executed by integrating with blockchain, we observed an average overhead of 570–600 ms. These performance metrics provides a detailed insight into the efficiency and feasibility of our protocol. By analyzing the timings associated with authenticator creation, proof generation, and proof verification, our solution offers practical performance metrics making it suitable for real-world inter-bank settlements and enables transaction auditability. Its efficiency and reliability ensures fast and seamless transactions between banks enhancing the overall inter-bank transaction and settlement process.

# 6   Conclusion and Future Works

In this paper, our main contribution is the design of protocol for privacy preserving, auditable, and verifiable inter-bank transactions and settlements. Our protocol enables third-party auditors to verify the authenticity of credits and debits in inter-bank transactions without accessing sensitive customer information, such as balances. We achieve this by leveraging two key cryptographic primitives: bilinear pairings and the blockchain. Bilinear pairings enable verifiable proofs without revealing the actual data, while the blockchain ensures transparency and maintains an immutable global record of proof for verifiers to access as needed. We believe that the use of bilinear pairings for generating verifiable proofs is of significant interest to the research community for designing efficient protocols. Additionally, bilinear pairings simplify the system compared to existing state-of-the-art that use zero-knowledge proofs, making it more efficient.

As a part of future work, we aim to enhance the protocol's resource utilization efficiency by exploring alternative ways to store customer data. We also plan to investigate computationally lighter primitives that maintain practical performance while preserving privacy.

# References

1. Banking and finance data breaches: costs, risks and more to know. https://securityintelligence.com/articles/banking-finance-data-breach-costs-risks/
2. HLF channels. https://hyperledger-fabric.readthedocs.io/en/latest/channels.html
3. HLF Collections. https://hyperledger-fabric.readthedocs.io/en/latest/private-data/private-data.html
4. HSBC bank USA admits breach exposing account numbers and transaction history. https://www.forbes.com/sites/daveywinder/2018/11/06/hsbc-bank-usa-admits-breach-exposing-account-numbers-and-transaction-history/?sh=3ebaa0885af3
5. Hyperlegder fabric. https://www.hyperledger.org/use/fabric
6. Pairing based cryptography. https://crypto.stanford.edu/pbc/
7. Androulaki, et al.: Privacy-preserving auditable token payments in a permissioned blockchain system. In: Proceedings of the 2nd ACM Conference on Advances in Financial Technologies, pp. 255–267 (2020)
8. Banerjee, et al.: Blockchain enabled privacy preserving data audit. arXiv preprint arXiv:1904.12362 (2019)
9. Boneh, D., Lynn, B., Shacham, H.: Short signatures from the Weil pairing. In: Boyd, C. (ed.) ASIACRYPT 2001. LNCS, vol. 2248, pp. 514–532. Springer, Heidelberg (2001). https://doi.org/10.1007/3-540-45682-1_30

10. Androulaki, E., et al.: Hyperledger fabric: a distributed operating system for permissioned blockchains. In: Proceedings of the Thirteenth EuroSys, pp. 1–15. EuroSys (2018)
11. Jeong, et al.: Azeroth: auditable zero-knowledge transactions in smart contracts. IEEE Access (2023)
12. Kang, et al.: FabZK: supporting privacy-preserving, auditable smart contracts in hyperledger fabric. In: 2019 49th Annual IEEE/IFIP International Conference on Dependable Systems and Networks (DSN), pp. 543–555. IEEE (2019)
13. Narula, et al.: zkLedger: privacy preserving auditing for distributed ledgers. In: 15th USENIX Symposium on Networked Systems Design and Implementation (NSDI 2018), pp. 65–80 (2018)
14. Emmadi, N., et al.: Practical deployability of permissioned blockchains. In: International Conference on Business Information Systems conference, pp. 229–243. BIS (2018)
15. Barreto, P.S.L.M., Kim, H.Y., Lynn, B., Scott, M.: Efficient algorithms for pairing-based cryptosystems. In: Yung, M. (ed.) CRYPTO 2002. LNCS, vol. 2442, pp. 354–369. Springer, Heidelberg (2002). https://doi.org/10.1007/3-540-45708-9_23
16. Nakamoto, S.: Bitcoin: a peer-to-peer electronic cash system. Decentralized Business Review (2008)
17. Wust, K., Gervais, A.: Do you need a blockchain? IACR Cryptology ePrint Archive, pp. 229–243 (2017)

# Author Index

Printed in the United States
by Baker & Taylor Publisher Services